# INSIGHT GUIDE

# United States On The Road

AMIGO'S CAFE

W9-BIP-321

Discovery CHANNEL

**APA** PUBLICATIONS

Part of the Langenscheidt Publishing Group

L

# ABOUT THIS BOOK

## INSIGHT GUIDE
### UNITED STATES On The Road

### Editorial
**Editor**
Martha Ellen Zenfell
**Editorial Director**
Brian Bell

### Distribution
**UK & Ireland**
**GeoCenter International Ltd**
The Viables Centre, Harrow Way
Basingstoke, Hants RG22 4BJ
Fax: (44) 1256-817988
**United States**
**Langenscheidt Publishers, Inc.**
46-35 54th Road, Maspeth, NY 11378
Fax: (1) 718 784-0640
**Canada**
**Thomas Allen & Son Ltd**
390 Steelcase Road East
Markham, Ontario L34 1G2
Fax: (1) 905 475 6747
**Australia**
**Universal Press**
1 Waterloo Road
Macquarie Park, NSW 2113
Fax: (61) 2 9888 9074
**New Zealand**
**Hema Maps New Zealand Ltd (HNZ)**
Unit D, 24 Ra ORA Drive
East Tamaki, Auckland
Fax: (64) 9 273 6479
**Worldwide**
**Apa Publications GmbH & Co.**
**Verlag KG (Singapore branch)**
38 Joo Koon Road, Singapore 628990
Tel: (65) 865-1600. Fax: (65) 861-6438

### Printing
**Insight Print Services (Pte) Ltd**
38 Joo Koon Road, Singapore 628990
Tel: (65) 865-1600. Fax: (65) 861-6438

©2001 Apa Publications GmbH & Co.
Verlag KG (Singapore branch)
*All Rights Reserved*

*First Edition 2001*

**CONTACTING THE EDITORS**
We would appreciate it if readers
would alert us to errors or out-
dated information by writing to:
**Insight Guides, P.O. Box 7910,
London SE1 1WE, England.
Fax: (44 20) 7403-0290.**
insight@apaguide.demon.co.uk

This guidebook combines the interests and enthusiasms of two of the world's best-known information providers: Insight Guides, whose titles have set the standard for visual travel guides since 1970, and Discovery Channel, the world's premier source of nonfiction television programming.

The editors of Insight Guides provide both practical advice and general understanding about a destination's history, culture, and people. Discovery Channel and its web site, www.discovery.com, help millions of viewers explore their world from the comfort of their own home and also encourage them to explore it first-hand.

This book is carefully structured to convey an understanding of the United States and its unique, on-the-road culture, as well as to guide readers through the country's variety of sights and activities:

◆ The **History and Features** section, indicated by a yellow bar at the top of each page, covers the history and travel culture of the country in a series of informative essays.

◆ The main **Routes** section, indicated by a blue bar, is a complete guide to all the sights and areas worth visiting. We sent out four writers to travel five east-west or north-south routes, which together cover the very best of the USA. Each route begins, and some end, in a major "hub" city, as we believe most visitors start a journey from a large city, and then hit the road in earnest after that.

MERMAID XING

Because this book is a celebration of rural areas and small-town life, we have given both the hub cities and the major towns along the routes special treatment, condensing the information into easy-to-assimilate, bite-size features. This leaves the body of the book to stand as free-wheeling, on-the-road narrative text, fun to read but even more rewarding to follow on a cross-country trip of your own.

◆ The **Travel Tips** listings section, with an orange bar, provides a handy point of reference for practical information. The section begins with general travel, hotel and cultural tips on the country as a whole, then follows the same geographical breakdown as the Routes section, giving suggestions, first in the hub city, then town-by-town, on where to stay, where to eat, and where to shop.

## The contributors

The guiding hand behind this book was that of **Martha Ellen Zenfell**, a London-based American who has been the project editor of most of Insight Guides' North American titles; she was also responsible for selecting the pictures for the book.

The first of our highwaymen to be commissioned were ace writers and photo snappers **Greg Ward** (Southern Route) and **Paul Kerr** (Atlantic and Northern Routes). The Central Route was undertaken by Insight Guides stalwart **John Wilcock**, together with **Teresa Machan**, who did not know each other until meeting up in Washington, DC, the hub city for that 3,000-mile (4,800-km) journey; we await with interest the *real* story of what it is like to travel across the country with a perfect stranger. Wilcock also tackled the Pacific Route, with help from Zenfell, who drew on a trip through Big Sur on a Harley-Davidson to supply that bugs-in-the-teeth realism.

**Paul Taylor** was our first and only choice to write the feature on Route 66; as publisher of *Route 66 Magazine* he *has* to be the favored son of the Mother Road. All copy was processed through **Jason Mitchell** in London, then sent to Arizona to **Barbara Balletto** who refined the narrative flow; Balletto has also produced her own Insight Guides to Italy. Texan **Alyse Williams** compiled the massive Travel Tips section.

**Catherine Karnow** was only one of the many photographers whose images helped to shape this book, which is based on the 1980s original *Insight Guide: Crossing America*. Particular thanks to **Adam Liptak**, **Robert Seidenberg** and **Rich Taskin** for producing such a timeless title.

## Map Legend

| | |
|---|---|
| — ·· — | International Boundary |
| — — — | State Boundary |
| ⊖ | Border Crossing |
| — ● — | National Park/Reserve |
| ═══ | Highway |
| ══ | Other Multi-lane Highway |
| ── | Principal Highway |
| ── | Through Highway |
| ── | Other Road |
| (5) | Interstate Highway |
| (1)(29) | US Highway |
| (50)(239) | Other Highway |
| —→ | On the Road Routes |
| ✈ ✦ | Airport: International/ Regional |
| ★ | Place of Interest |

The main places of interest in the guide section of the book are coordinated by number with a full-color map (e.g. ❶). A symbol at the top of every right-hand page tells you where to find the map.

# INSIGHT GUIDE
# United States On The Road

# CONTENTS

## Maps

New York to
South Carolina **56**

South Carolina
to Key West **82**

Boston to Buffalo **104**

Buffalo to Badlands **124**

Badlands to
the Olympic Peninsula **144**

Washington, DC to
Oklahoma City **184**

Oklahoma City to
Los Angeles **204**

Atlanta to San Antonio **248**

San Antonio to
San Diego **282**

San Diego to
San Francisco **326**

San Francisco
to Seattle **354**

Inside front cover:
Routes across America
Inside back cover:
Road Signs of America

## Introduction

We're on the Road to
    Somewhere ......................**15**

## History and Features

Decisive Dates..........................**20**
The Transportation
    Revolution ........................**23**
Artists and the Road ..............**29**
Route 66 ..............................**35**
Burma Shave ..........................**38**

## Places

THE ATLANTIC ROUTE.................. **51**
    New York to Virginia ............**55**
    Baltimore..............................**60**
    North Carolina to
        Savannah ......................**69**
    Savannah ..........................**78**
    Georgia to the Florida Keys ..**81**
    Orlando ............................**85**
THE NORTHERN ROUTE..................**99**
    Boston to Buffalo ..............**103**
    Buffalo to the Badlands ....**123**

The
beginning
and the end
of the road,
Florida Keys

## Travel Tips

Getting Acquainted .. 386

Planning the Trip .... 386

Practical Tips ...... 387

Getting Around ..... 389

Where to Stay ...... 391

The Atlantic Route ... 392

The Northern Route .. 405

The Central Route ... 426

The Southern Route .. 439

The Pacific Route .... 450

Further Reading ..... 460

◆ **Full Travel Tips index
is on page 385**

## Hub Cities

New York City ........................52

Miami....................................92

Boston................................ 100

Seattle .............................. 172

Washington, DC ................. 180

Los Angeles .......................236

Atlanta ..............................244

San Diego...........................322

Chicago ........................... 130

Badlands to Yellowstone ....143

Yellowstone to the
    Olympic Peninsula ........157

THE CENTRAL ROUTE.................179

DC to Arkansas ...............183

Memphis ..........................196

Oklahoma to New Mexico ..203

Arizona to Los Angeles ......221

THE SOUTHERN ROUTE................243

Atlanta to New Orleans ......247

New Orleans ........................262

New Orleans to
    San Antonio ...............265

Houston............................274

San Antonio to
    Southern New Mexico ..281

Southern Arizona
    to San Diego...............299

Phoenix ............................308

THE PACIFIC ROUTE...................321

San Diego to Los Angeles ..325

LA to San Francisco .......... 339

San Francisco ..................350

San Francisco to Oregon ....353

Oregon to Washington ......367

Portland ...........................376

# WE'RE ON THE ROAD TO SOMEWHERE

*Americans are always on the move. A French explorer in the 1800s identified this unique trait and called it "restlessness amidst prosperity"*

The most basic images of American life – the heavy wagon train rumbling across the prairie, a railroad car speeding through the night, the arrival of immigrants at Ellis Island – are powerful symbols of the United States' timeless obsession with movement. In fact, in a nation where change is the only constant, movement and travel have established the ever quickening tempo of American history, from Lewis and Clark's exploration of the territories west of the Mississippi River, to Neil Armstrong's historic walk on the moon.

If the exploration and colonization of America is an example of travel, is there any real connection with the day-trip into the countryside? Is it possible to seriously suggest that the 17th-century Puritan seeking refuge in Boston has anything in common with the 22-year-old computer whiz who moves from Lexington, Massachusetts, to Seattle, Washington, in search of a higher paying job? Do Lewis and Clark have any common bond with vacationers of the 1950s rolling down Route 66?

## Epic adventure

Every one of these travelers believed that movement might bring prosperity, discovery, and renewal. The difference lies in the purpose of the journey. Travel in pre-modern America was a very serious affair: an essential part of discovering and populating the continent. While a few wealthy Americans embarked on European *wanderjahrs*, and some even traveled for pleasure to Newport and Saratoga Springs, we do not associate such ease and comfort with the days of old. Rather, we recall Daniel Boone leading pioneers through the Cumberland Gap; young men heeding Horace Greeley's advice

**PRECEDING PAGES:** vintage surf car, southern California; friends on good form, the Southwest; biker with "rat bike," Florida; taking a call, northern California.
**LEFT:** on the road up in the hills.
**RIGHT:** hitching a ride on Route 66.

and going West to grow up with the country; the Mormons' perilous flight across the Great Plains; or the stagecoach company that warned its riders not to "point out where murders have been committed, especially if there are women

passengers." Given the harsh landscape, we think of travel in early America as a dangerous and epic adventure.

In the early 21th century, when we take a trip there is little heroic about it , nor much physical discomfort. Yet, Americans still migrate for economic reasons, particularly to the Sunbelt states in the South, or to the Pacific Northwest. But this anonymous and isolated movement of people lacks the drama of the pioneers, or the great "Dust Bowl" migration of the 1930s, immortalized in the ballads of Woody Guthrie and John Steinbeck's novel *The Grapes of Wrath*. Still, it is very likely that an American historian in the next century will judge this movement to be as significant a force during these millennium years as it was in past times.

The sheer number of automobiles in America today suggest that the experience of travel is now available to almost everyone. Travel has been democratized, and plays no small role in contributing to the American tendency to view cars, boats, and planes as symbols of equality, if not distinction. For better or worse, to be an American is to believe that personal liberty and the freedom to travel, be it on an errand or in search of Utopia, are inseparable.

Is there any truth in this belief? Is there a vital link between the uniquely democratic culture

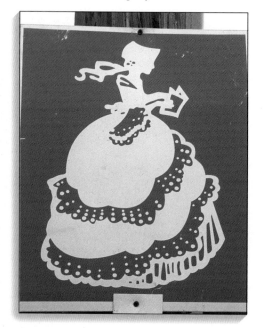

of the United States and the transportation revolution of the past two centuries? Michael Chevalier thought so. Chevalier, a French aristocrat sent to the United States in the 1830s to study its public works, and author of a report on its political and social machinery, believed that improved means of travel would hasten the collapse of the old order and play an important role in the emergence of "modern society." During his tour, he was amazed by the readiness with which Americans embraced new means of travel: first (after initial disinterest), roads had been constructed with passionate intensity, then canal building had become a national mania. And Chevalier bore witness to

the birth of the age of the railroad, for which he rightly forecast a glorious future.

Riding a steamboat into New Orleans, Chevalier noted that "formerly it was possible only for a patrician to travel, and the great bulk of mankind were then attached to the globe, chained to the soil by the difficulty of locomotion." But as avenues of economic exchange opened to increasing numbers of people, both ideas and populations were transmitted hither and yon along with pelts, peppers, and teas. Travel became, in Chevalier's words, a catalyst "to equality and liberty," and he was convinced that modern transportation would "increase the rights and privileges of the greatest number as truly and as amply as could be done by electoral laws."

## Restless spirits

Chevalier wrote at the beginning of the Industrial Revolution in America, and believed deeply in the 19th-century maxim of progress through science. We now know all too well the mixed blessing of living in a world of rapid transit and rapid deployment systems; but also how those technological achievements have routinized experience while eliminating labor and opening up new paths to the multitudes. And even though the pursuit of freedom and adventure at the end of the road is now much easier, the allure of crossing America has lost little of its appeal to restless spirits.

For, as Alexis de Tocqueville – author of the quote about "restlessness amidst prosperity" – observed two centuries ago: "An American will build a house in which to pass his old age and sell it before the roof is on; he will plant a garden and rent it just as the trees are coming into bearing; he will clear a field and leave others to reap the harvest; he will take up a profession and leave it, settle in one place and soon go off elsewhere with his changing desires. If his private business allows him a moment's relaxation, he will plunge at once into the whirlpool of politics. Then, if at the end of a year crammed with work he has a little spare leisure, his restless curiosity goes with him traveling up and down the vast territories of the United States. Thus he will travel 500 miles in a few days as a distraction from his happiness." ❑

**LEFT:** modern roadsign in the antebellum South.
**RIGHT:** a man, his best friend, and his dog.

# Decisive Dates in American History

**1492** Tierra! Tierra! Explorer Christopher Columbus reaches America, landing at San Salvador.
**1585** Sir Walter Raleigh founds the soon-to-be-lost colony of Roanoke, in Virginia.
**1607** Jamestown, Virginia settled by the British.
**1619** First African slaves sold in Jamestown.
**1620** The Plymouth Company finances 66 Puritans to establish a permanent settlement in North America. They found Plymouth Colony, on Cape Cod Bay.

**1773** In the "Boston Tea Party," 60 men in disguise dump tea crates over the railings of three ships in the harbor in protest against taxes.
**1774** On September 5, the First Continental Congress convenes at Philadelphia.
**1775** Paul Revere rides from Boston warning Minutemen of the impending arrival of British troops. The following day the "shot heard 'round the world" begins a battle leaving eight Minutemen dead, and the American Revolution commences.
**1776** On July 4, the Continental Congress, meeting in Philadelphia, adopts the Declaration of Independence, penned by Thomas Jefferson.
**1787** Philadelphia's Constitutional Convention convenes for the first time.

**1787-88** All states but North Carolina and Rhode Island ratify the Constitution.
**1789** George Washington takes the first presidential oath at New York's Federal Hall.
**1792** An open-air money market is founded beneath a tree on New York's Wall Street.
**1804** Lewis and Clark set out on their 8,000-mile (13,000-km) expedition to the Pacific Coast.
**1814** Francis Scott Key pens the national anthem, "The Star Spangled Banner."
**1825** The Erie Canal, known as the "Big Ditch," connects the Hudson River with the Great Lakes.
**1836** Siege of the Alamo in San Antonio, Texas, results in the death of all 189 American defenders.
**1838** New Orleans' first Mardi Gras parade takes place on Fat Tuesday.
**1848** Gold is discovered at Sutter's Fort, California, bringing over 200,000 prospectors within the next three years. The Chicago Board of Trade, the world's oldest and largest futures exchange, is established.
**1858** After a 25-day journey, John Butterfield's Overland Stage delivers its first sack of mail to the West Coast.
**1860** South Carolina secedes from the Union, and the Confederate states are born.
**1862** Confederates open fire on Fort Sumter, in the first shots of the Civil War. Abraham Lincoln legally frees all slaves by issuing the Emancipation Proclamation.
**1864** The transcontinental telegraph connects Seattle, Washington, with the rest of the US.
**1865** With the surrender of Robert E. Lee to Ulysses S. Grant in Virginia, the Civil War ends. President Abraham Lincoln is assassinated in Washington, DC.
**1869** The Central Pacific and Union Pacific railroads meet in Ogden, Utah, completing the first transcontinental railroad. Major John Wesley Powell leads an expedition through the Grand Canyon.
**1871** The Great Chicago Fire kills 300 people and destroys 18,000 buildings.
**1876** General George A. Custer leads his 264 men into battle at LIttle Bighorn Creek. All are wiped out in "Custer's Last Stand."
**1881** Wyatt Earp and Doc Holiday kill cattle rustlers at the "Gunfight at the OK Corral" in Arizona.
**1886** In a ceremony on Ellis Island, Grover Cleveland presents France's gift to honor America: the Statue of Liberty.
**1890** A US Army regiment attacks a camp near Wounded Knee Creek in South Dakota's Pine Ridge Reservation, killing 300 Indians.

**1906** A massive earthquake measuring 8.2 on the Richter Scale, followed by a devastating fire, flattens San Francisco.

**1907** Neiman-Marcus store opens in Dallas, Texas.

**1908** Henry Ford begins mass production of the Model T car. Filmmaker William Selig completes *The Count of Monte Cristo*, California's first commercial movie.

**1915** Thomas Watson, a resident of San Francisco, receives the first transcontinental phone call from Alexander Graham Bell. New Orleans music is introduced to Chicago. It is called "jazz."

**1919** Eighteenth Amendment to the Constitution outlaws alcoholic beverages.

**1920** Nineteenth Amendment to the Constitution guarantees women's right to vote.

**1921** Margaret Sanger founds the American Birth Control League.

**1925** The Grand Ole Opry opens its doors in Nashville, Tennessee.

**1927** 60-year-old sculptor Gutzon Burgham begins work on South Dakota's Mount Rushmore.

**1929** Wall Street crashes, and with it comes the beginnings of the Great Depression.

**1930** An oil find outside Dallas initiates the East Texas Oil Field, the largest petroleum deposit known to the world at that time.

**1930s** Because of misuse of land and years of water shortages, the "Dust Bowl" forces thousands from farmlands around Oklahoma on a migrant trek west to California in search of work.

**1931** The Empire State Building opens.

**1934** Depression-era bank robbers Bonnie Parker and Clyde Barrow meet a hail of bullets, ending a 102-day manhunt by Texas Rangers.

**1937** Golden Gate Bridge opens in San Francisco.

**1941** Japan attacks Pearl Harbor, and the United States enters World War II.

**1945** First atomic bomb detonates in New Mexico; bombs dropped on Hiroshima and Nagasaki. United Nations charter drafted in San Francisco.

**1955** Rev. Martin Luther King, Jr leads the Montgomery (Alabama) Bus Boycott.

**1963** President John F. Kennedy is assassinated while touring Dallas, Texas.

**1967** Hippies, leftists, and idealists, drawn to San Francisco's Haight-Ashbury district, celebrate the Summer of Love.

**1968** Division over the Vietnam War bursts into street violence, culminating with a "police riot" against demonstrators at Chicago's Democratic National Convention. James Earl Ray kills Martin Luther King, Jr in Memphis, and Robert F. Kennedy is assassinated in Los Angeles.

**1969** *Apollo 11* commander Neil Armstrong communicates with Houston from the moon.

**1974** Richard M. Nixon, 37th president, resigns after facing impeachment proceedings due to a 1972 break-in and cover-up at the Watergate Hotel.

**1980** Mount St Helens in Washington erupts, dev-

astating the surrounding region and blanketing the Pacific Northwest with ash.

**1986** Seattle's Bill Gates takes Microsoft public, and becomes one of the richest men in the world.

**1989** An earthquake (7.1 on the Richter Scale) collapses a freeway and causes chaos and destruction in the San Francisco area.

**1993** Agents storm a cult compound near Waco, Texas, resulting in more than 80 deaths. A bomb explodes below New York's World Trade Center.

**1998–99** Revelations about the sexual conduct of President Bill Clinton keeps Americans glued to TV sets; Clinton narrowly escapes impeachment.

**2000** Record forest fires rage through the West as America gears up for a presidential election. ❑

**PRECEDING PAGES:** the joining of the Central and Pacific railroads in 1869 linked the East and West coasts.

**LEFT:** President Thomas Jefferson paid $15 million in 1803 for the land between the Mississippi River and the Rocky Mountains, doubling the size of the US.

**RIGHT:** Neil Armstrong, astronaut and moon walker.

# THE TRANSPORTATION REVOLUTION

*From wagon trains to the iron horse to today's superhighways,
travel is at the heart of America's history*

During the 17th and 18th centuries, white settlers in early America followed the network of paths that Native Americans had carved out for themselves, and travel conditions were notoriously wretched. During the time of colonization with Great Britian, it cost less to transport goods across the Atlantic Ocean from London to Philadelphia than to carry those same goods 100 miles to Lancaster, Pennsylvania. In 1776, news of the Declaration of Independence took 29 days to reach the people of Charleston, South Carolina. No wonder New England delegates at the Constitutional Convention in 1787 had more things in common with their brethren in Britain than with their fellow countrymen down South in the Carolinas and Georgia.

Fifty years later, when Alexis de Tocqueville, Michael Chevalier, and a host of European travelers (*see page 16*) examined the American experiment of self-government, conditions on dry land were little improved. Whereas the Roman Empire made the construction of great roads an important function of its central government, in 19th-century America *laissez-faire* attitudes predominated, leaving the construction of highways a state and local responsibility. Often, farmers and laborers who were unable to meet their tax obligations ended up doing the little road work that was done.

## Tolerance of mud

As a direct consequence of the American belief in "the less government the better," roads suffered from neglect and disrepair. Pioneers, such as Abraham Lincoln's father Thomas, had to possess courage, physical strength, and an incredible tolerance of mud. William Herndon, Lincoln's law partner and biographer, described the Lincoln family's move from Indiana to Illinois in March of 1830 as one which "suited the roving and migratory spirit of Thomas Lincoln." With the "obscure and penniless" 21-

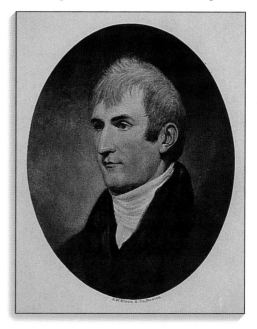

year-old Abe commanding a wagon drawn by two oxen, "the journey was a long and tedious one." Basing his literary account of the trip on Lincoln's recollections, Herndon memorably evokes the experience of thousands of similar travelers. "The rude, heavy wagon," he wrote, "with its primitive wheels, creaked and groaned as it crawled through the woods and now and then stalled in the mud. Many were the delays."

In antebellum America, geography created a formidable barrier to migration. Even as late as the 1830s, approximately 80 percent of the American population still continued to reside east of the Allegheny Mountains. One might have been inclined to agree with Thomas Jefferson's earlier prediction that it would take close to 1,000 years to settle the entire vastness of the North American continent.

As it turned out, Jefferson was wrong by about 910 years. Indeed, his decision to send those two intrepid travelers, Captain Meriwether Lewis and Lieutenant William Clark, to

---

**LEFT:** pioneers on wagon trains faced harsh conditions.
**RIGHT:** explorer Meriwether Lewis.

explore the territories west of the Mississippi River charted the way for settlement of the vast, important region. President Jefferson dispatched Lewis and Clark shortly after the Louisiana Purchase in 1803. His motives for asking for a $2,500 appropriation from Congress to finance the expedition were mixed. Even at this late date it appears Jefferson had not abandoned all hope that a passage to Asia might be found. He was also confident that the explorers would discover trade routes to benefit fur traders. Nor was Jefferson without hope of further expanding what he liked to call the "empire of liberty." But this is not to say that the president was prevaricating

when he explained to the Spanish Minister that the purpose of the mission was the "advancement of science." Jefferson, a child of the Enlightenment Era, saw the active study of the physical universe as an important chapter in the life of the mind.

Lewis and Clark did not disappoint Jefferson. Their voluminous journals provided detailed descriptions of what eventually became the Oregon Trail. Perhaps what is remembered most from sampling their writings are the descriptions of the geology, fauna and wildlife of the West. Their wide range of learning, courage displayed in the face of physical

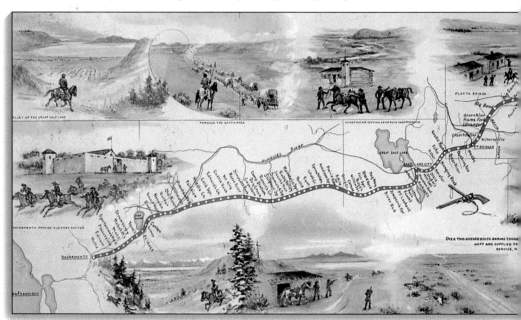

## THE PONY EXPRESS

One of the 19th century's most romantic enterprises, the Pony Express, galloped across the western landscape and into the history books in just over 18 months. From April 1860 through October 1861, Express horsemen formed a record-setting, trans-Mississippi relay team that won over the hearts of Americans, if not the pocketbooks of the US Congress. The daring young mail carriers braved rain, snow, sleet, dead of night, and Indian attacks between St Joseph, Missouri and Sacramento, California, to deliver 35,000 letters, telegrams, and newspapers. The riders tallied up 650,000 miles (1 milllion km) on the 1,966-mile-long (3,164-km) Pony Express Trail. And they lost only one mailbag.

Newspaper ads for Express riders did not mince words: "WANTED – Young, skinny, wiry fellows not over 18. Must be expert riders willing to risk death daily. Orphans preferred." Eighty riders, almost all weighing less than 125 pounds (57 kg), were hired initially, including a fatherless 15-year-old named William F. Cody, later known as Buffalo Bill. The pay was attractive, at least $50 a month, plus free lodging and food. Each rider took an oath, agreeing not to use profane language, not to get drunk, and not to fight with other employees. Each horseman also received a copy of the Bible, plus two Colt revolvers, a knife, and a carbine. The journey took 10 days each way.

deprivation, and eloquence are inspiring. Lewis and Clark prepared the way for the invasion of the West that is still in progress today.

By the mid-19th century, poets and orators matched hyperboles in an effort to describe what one person called the "untransacted destiny of the United States." One orator even forecast that the American lamp of liberty would be visible from Tierra del Fuego to the Aurora Borealis.

In the 1840s, the journalist John O'Sullivan popularized the phrase "manifest destiny" to

### A PRESIDENT PREDICTS

Thomas Jefferson thought it would take close to a thousand years to settle the lands west of the Mississippi River; he was mistaken by more than 900 years.

## Age of the iron horse

Before the Union could be linked by rail, the United States was plunged into the Civil War. It took four weeks for the news of the opening volley at Fort Sumter to reach San Francisco, but by the end of the war the nation was forging the bonds of union. The age of the turnpike, steamboat, and canal had been overtaken by the iron horse; it is widely conceded that the North's superior transportation system played a crucial role in crushing the Southern rebels. In 1863, the

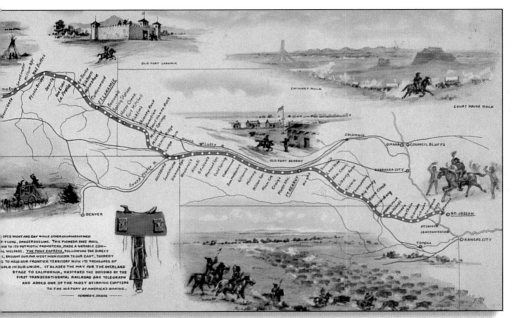

describe this widespread expansionist ideology.

Western politicians such as Stephen Douglas based their political fortunes on promoting the future greatness of the West as the ultimate destination and demanded the construction of a transcontinental railroad in order to link the nation's rapidly expanding economy. Douglas repeatedly argued during the 1840s and '50s that the West was not only the stage for the nation's future, but that it would also be an effective alternative to the increasingly nasty bickering between the North and the South.

**LEFT AND ABOVE:** the Pony Express lasted only 18 months, but inspired countless stories.

North was able to transport 25,000 troops by rail from Washington, DC, to Chatanooga, Tennessee to turn the tide in a major battle.

Mark Twain and Charles Dudley Warner dubbed the final third of the 19th century "the Gilded Age," an era of conspicuous consumption and corruption. Perhaps the age might better be thought of as being the age of the railroad. The railroad barons – the Goulds, Huntingtons, and Vanderbilts – all understood that the railroad was the lubricant of both a booming economy and sleazy politics.

The railroad also made long-distance travel for pleasure a realistic possibility for middle-class Americans. The creation of the Pullman

Palace Car Company in 1868 reflected the growing number of Americans interested in taking vacations. Although a period of rest and relaxation did not sit well with those devoted to work ("the sum of wisdom" according to Emerson, is that "the time is never lost that is devoted to work"), so publicists for the new leisure ethic stressed that Americans were growing unhealthy – both physically and spiritually – as a result of their obsession with success. Regeneration through contact with the great outdoors and the vigorous life was a stock promise from popularizers of the West.

In 1893, the year of the Chicago World's Fair,

two bicycle mechanics, Charles and J. Frank Duryea, successfully tested the first automobile on the streets of Springfield, Massachusetts, and a new age began.

## Car crazy

Public roads were among the initial benefactors of the age of the automobile. The movement to upgrade the quality of American highways had begun during the 1880s when bicycling organizations like the League of American Wheelmen led the call for improved roads. When automobiles began to appear in the streets and villages in greater numbers after 1900, the drive for surfaced roads attracted increasing support. The instinctive American distrust of Federal intrusion into the lives of its citizens was overcome by the politically popular demand that the US Mail ought to be delivered directly to rural Americans over improved roads. In 1916, President Woodrow Wilson signed a Federal Aid Road Act which was the first of a series of occasions when Federal intrusion into the nation's transportation system met with widespread public approval.

The constituency for such governmental action grew larger with each passing decade. And the person who probably deserves the greatest share of credit for democratizing the automobile and travel is Henry Ford, who introduced to the industry the assembly line which revolutionized the production and sale of cars; by 1922 he was selling an astonishing 1.3 million Model Ts. And while their uniformity would soon render them obsolete, the Tin Lizzie had made the automobile a badge of social distinction as well as a necessity.

The impact of the widespread ownership of cars upon travel cannot be overstated. It was probably the single most important factor in the opening of American life not only to travelers seeking remote scenes, but also to 20th-century movers and migrants.

What would the 1930s have been like, after all, if John Steinbeck's literary Tom Joad and his fellow wandering poor could not have climbed into a car and headed for California where, as a Jimmie Rodgers song promised, the "water tastes like cherry wine?" The increased mobility the automobile offered underscores the judgement of George F. Pierson, who in his book *The Moving American* describes this freedom as "the great American permit to be both more free and more equal than our contemporaries could manage to become in the more static societies of Europe."

In the early years of the new millennium, people are traveling faster and farther than ever before in ever-increasing numbers. The Frenchman de Tocqueville's American of the 1800s who traveled "500 miles in a few days as a distraction from his happiness" has been replaced by a far-reaching, highly mobile globe-trotter pursuing equally elusive dreams. ❑

**LEFT:** cycling the steps of the Capitol, Washington, DC. Cyclists were responsible for improving highways.
**RIGHT:** the West is seen as the ultimate destination.

# AMERICAN ARTISTS AND THE ROAD

*Novelists, poets, musicians, film-makers – the*
*romance of the open road seduces them all*

merican artists are perpetually on the run. Their work epitomizes the wanderlust of the American people: the belief in movement for movement's sake. "The sound of a jet," John Steinbeck wrote in 1961, "an engine warming up, even the clopping of shod hooves on pavement brings an ancient shudder, the dry mouth and vacant eye, the hot palms and the churn of stomach high up under the rib cage."

A century before Steinbeck, Herman Melville depicted travel as a balm to a depressed soul. "Whenever I find myself growing grim about the mouth," he mused in the famous first paragraph of *Moby Dick*, "whenever it is a damp, drizzly, November in my soul; …whenever my hypos get such an upper hand of me, that it requires a strong moral principle to prevent me from deliberately stepping into the street, and methodically knocking people's hats off – then, I account it high time to get to sea as soon as I can." In the classic American fiction of Melville, Edgar Allan Poe, James Fenimore Cooper, and Mark Twain, we encounter characters fleeing the inertia of polite society for a jaunt into the wild.

## A change of place

"I wish for a change of place," J. Hector St John de Crevecoeur wrote in *Letters from an American Farmer.* "The hour is come at last, that I must fly from my home and abandon my farm!" Crevecoeur's threat to flee into the Indian territory "and revert into a state approaching nearer to that of nature, unencumbered either with voluminous laws, or contradictory codes" was pure fiction.

As unlikely to occur as Mark Twain hooking up with Huck Finn a century later when Huck threatened to "light out for the territory." Still, Crevecoeur is only one of many

writers who celebrated the movement away from complex modern life.

Indeed, the great writers of 19th-century America viewed travel as a "stay against confusion" in a society committed to material gain. Melville, Nathaniel Hawthorne, and Cooper felt alienated from the climate of the times and

sought refuge in foreign travel.

Their despair with the democratic masses stands in marked contrast to one of the greatest American poets of the open road, Walt Whitman. A journey along the open highway suited his desire to comprehend the whole of life: the casual meeting, the encounter between the eye of the seer and the landscape and the timelessness of nature. Whitman saw the open road as the passage to wisdom and fraternity.

The act of traveling itself is a democratic gesture to the poet, a source of inspiration and a symbol of his personal liberty. Not only were the "American people the greatest poem," but the American environment itself was an incu-

**LEFT:** Marlon Brando as *The Wild One*, one of the first anti-heroes of the silver screen.
**RIGHT:** Tom Hanks as *Forrest Gump*, who runs across America and participates in much of its recent history.

bator of freedom and unity. As he wrote in his acclaimed "Song of the Open Road:"

*I think all heroic deeds were all conceiv'd in the open air, and all free poems also,*
*I think I could stop here myself and do miracles,*
*I think whatever I shall meet on the road I shall like, and whoever beholds me shall like me.*
*I think whoever I see must be happy.*

Mark Twain used the voyage as a metaphor for change. In his greatest novel, *The Adven-*

> ### LONESOME ROAD BLUES
>
> I'm going down that long, lonesome road
> And I ain't gonna be treated this a-way.
> —Going Down the Road Feelin' Bad.

loneliness, and the traveler as a solitary figure.

Since World War II, the accelerated pace of travel has produced a literature equally frenetic. The most famous road book of the age has been Jack Kerouac's *On the Road*, the definitive statement of Beat culture and the cultural radicals of the 1960s and '70s. Kerouac's prose may impress less now, but his celebration of the possibilities of finding spiritual truths while racing across the continent makes the work compelling in ways that transcend conventional literary canons.

*tures of Huckleberry Finn*, he made it clear that the voyage was a learning experience and a rebellion against conventional morality. Some of the book's most moving passages are Huck's accounts of life on the river. Each time Huck and the escaped slave Jim touch base with people on shore, trouble, trickery, and cruelty predominate. The book ends with Huck's famous vow to flee civilization and its hypocrisy. But, of course, the old-fashioned frontier was disappearing when Twain was writing in the 1880s, so Huck's dream of flight belonged to a vanishing world. Still, Huck's words at the close of *Huckleberry Finn* bring to mind another characteristic of American literature:

Kerouac's work continued the tradition of artist as pathfinder and spiritual voyager; William Least Heat Moon's *Blue Highways* picked up that tradition and carried it into the 21st century. Moon traversed the nation in his van "ghost dancing" after being laid off from his job at a small college in the Midwest. His report is both a rumination on travel literature in general, and a revealing study of the state of the nation in particular.

Whereas Kerouac filtered all experience through his ahistorical frame of mind, Moon, by letting people speak for themselves, captures the diversity of the landscape that often overwhelms the trans-American traveler.

## Music to their ears

It is not just literary artists who have sung of the loneliness and vagaries of the open road. Country music in particular often focuses on that "lonesome guy" Hank Williams sang about on "the lost highway." Cowboys, singing at night to fight off despair and keep cattle from stampeding, often reworked old Irish and English ballads about murder and betrayal. Much of the music produced under such circumstances was often grim and filled with resignation. In the 1940s and

> ### BORN TO RUN
>
> *Baby, this town rips the bones from your back/It's a death trap, it's a suicide rap/We gotta get out while we're young/ 'Cause tramps like us, we were born to run.*

cops, and anything that might get in the way.

The theme of the open road extends to rock music and blues as well. Is it any wonder that one of the rock anthems of the 1970s was Bruce Springsteen's "Born to Run"?

Or that avant garde New York performance artist and musician Laurie Anderson chose Melville's travel-as-balm *Moby Dick* to reinterprete and take on a world tour in the year 2000?

Ace bluesman Robert Johnson evoked the road as a haunting meeting place. In his highly

'50s, cowboy singers such as Roy Rogers evoked the nostalgia of the open range for listeners confined by harsh economic circumstances to lives of poverty and loneliness.

Not all country music is downbeat, however. A whole genre of music has arisen devoted to the lives of the modern riders of the open range: truckdrivers. These contemporary folk figures form a loyal audience for country music, and songs like the admired and much-recorded "Six Days on the Road" are pure Walt Whitmanesque whoops of triumph over the law, the

influential song "Crossroads" (recorded by Eric Clapton and others), it is hard to say exactly why "he got down on his knees and prayed" – perhaps because the crossroad is where suicides are buried? Or because Johnson sold his soul to the devil in exchange for playing the guitar? Whatever the reason, what is most clear is the musician's anguish and fear.

If Walt Whitman is the most boyant celebrator of the open road and Robert Johnson the most serious habituate of the dark side of the street, surely Woody Guthrie is the "bard of the open road." Even a simple listing of some of his songs – "Dust Bowl Refugees," "I Ain't Got No Home," "Walkin' Down the Railroad Line"

**LEFT:** Jack Kerouac and Woody Guthrie.
**ABOVE:** John Steinbeck and Walt Whitman.

– suggests the prominence he assigned to "walkin' down the line." Like Whitman, he attempted to capture the whole of America in the verses of "This Land is Your Land." In songs like "The Great Historical Bum," he even laughed at his persona as the roustabout poet:

> *I'm just a lonesome traveler, the great*
> *    historical bum.*
> *Highly educated from history I have come,*
> *I built the Rock of Ages, it was in the*
> *    year of one*
> *And that's about the biggest thing that*
> *    man has ever done.*

Guthrie lived the life he wrote about after his family was wrecked by tragedy and disease. His best work is timeless – not surprisingly, many of his tunes borrow heavily from hymns and ballads – and will live as long as there are roads to walk and people to sing.

## Sagas of the silver screen

The great road films of Hollywood are the best visual sagas of the open plains. People all over the world think of the United States as a land of wide open spaces, thanks to the images they receive from the films of directors John Ford and other Western movie-makers. Again we encounter solitary figures in an uncomfortable

### ON THE ROAD MOVIES

*American Graffiti* (George Lucas, 1973)
*Badlands* (Terrence Malick, 1973)
*Down by Law* (Jim Jarmusch, 1986)
*Duel* (Steven Spielberg, 1971)
*Electra Glide in Blue* (James William Guercio, 1973)
*Five Easy Pieces* (Bob Rafelson, 1970)
*The Grapes of Wrath* (John Ford, 1939)
*It Happened One Night* (Frank Capra, 1934)
*Leningrad Cowboys Go America* (Aki Kaurismaki, 1989)
*My Own Private Idaho* (Gus Van Sant, 1991)
*Natural Born Killers* (Oliver Stone, 1994)
*The Outlaw Josey Wales* (Clint Eastwood, 1986)

*North by Northwest* (Alfred Hitchcock, 1959)
*Paris, Texas* (Wim Wenders, 1984)
*Pee-Wee's Big Adventure* (Tim Burton, 1985)
*Rain Man* (Barry Levinson, 1988)
*The Sugarland Express* (Steven Spielberg, 1974)
*The Searchers* (John Ford, 1956)
*Something Wild* (Jonathan Demme, 1986)
*The Sure Thing* (Rob Reiner, 1985)
*Two Lane Blacktop* (Monte Hellman, 1971)
*Vanishing Point* (Richard C. Sarafian, 1971)
*Wild at Heart* (David Lynch, 1990)
*The Wizard of Oz* (Victor Fleming, 1939)

relationship with polite society. Ready to right wrong wherever they find it, the cowboy must move along in the last reel.

## Anti-heroes

Clint Eastwood's *Pale Rider* attempted to revive this formula in the 1980s, but since the '60s motor-driven outlaws have replaced the cowboy as the stars of mythic road films. From Marlon Brando in the *The Wild One* to Mel Gibson in *The Road Warrior*, films set on the road have focused on wandering anti-social, anti-heroes alienated from society. Robert Zemeckis's *Forrest Gump* (1994) added a twist:

make their getaway to the sound of rebellious country music.

*Bonnie and Clyde* brought the road film skidding into the tumultuous 1960s, but few films of the recent past inspired more real-life voyages than *Easy Rider* (Dennis Hopper, 1969). Those who see the film as a period piece and high camp have no idea how its original viewers saw it. *Rider* was probably the most powerful advertisement for the counter-culture to appear in movie houses throughout the heartland of the nation. To this day, there are middle-aged workers who dream of throwing away their beepers, mounting a Harley motorcycle,

the main character is too simple to know if he is hero or anti-hero, or to realize the significance of the events he witnesses.

*Bonnie and Clyde* (Arthur Penn, 1967) is an example of the perfect tragi-comic road picture. Viewed through the counter-cultural lens of the 1960s, the story of Clyde Barrow and Bonnie Parker seems like a folk tale of the Depression-era '30s. Bonnie and Clyde rob banks that rob the poor of their dreams and

**LEFT:** Dennis Hopper and Peter Fonda hit the open road in *Easy Rider*.
**ABOVE:** Warren Beatty and Faye Dunaway as runaway bank robbers in *Bonnie and Clyde*.

and setting off for Mardi Gras in New Orleans.

*Thelma and Louise* (Ridley Scott, 1991) updated this story, using cars and women to illustrate the hi-jinks and low life of on-the-road escapism. The final scene, when the women decided to end it all, is in the tradition of the best Westerns of the 1950s.

The swoop of history follows us down every highway, and the traveler has many teachers to choose from before embarking on an adventure. For William Moon, Walt Whitman served as the model. For Ridley Scott, John Ford was the inspiration. As you head out on the highway, listen to these voices, but be aware that there is no experience like an original one. ❑

# ROUTE 66: AMERICA'S MAIN STREET

*Quirky motels, mom 'n' pop diners, drive-in movie theaters:*
*in its heyday, many thought this was the most magical road in the world*

In 1926, US Highway 66 put down its roots near Lake Michigan at the corner of Michigan Avenue and Jackson Boulevard in Chicago, Illinois. With its catchy double-six road markers, it stretched its 2,448 miles (3,900 km) of asphalt and concrete westward through three time zones, across eight states – Illinois, Missouri, Kansas, Oklahoma, Texas, New Mexico, Arizona, and California – to the shores of the Pacific Ocean at Santa Monica. Route 66 was one of the country's first continuous spans of paved highway, linking the eastern part of America with the west.

## A stroll on wheels

US Highway 66, with undisputed certainty, reigns as the most storied highway in the United States. A recurring theme in American literature, Route 66 has been the star of more stories, books, songs, movies, and television shows than any other. The road is more popular than Route 1 from Maine to Key West. From the mid-1920s to the mid-1970s, it was more traveled than Highway 101 on the Pacific Coast, and better known than the Pennsylvania Turnpike or the Alcan Highway. And before the advent of the interstate systems, US 66 came closer than any other highway to becoming the National Road. Route 66 was soon known as "the most magical road in all the world." A legend was in the making.

And what a legend it would be. During its glory days, authors, songwriters, and movie moguls all seemed to be headed west on Route 66. Nobody could possibly know how many Americans – from the Dust Bowl famine victims in Oklahoma to the flower children headed for California's Haight Ashbury – would consider Route 66 to be first, and foremost, an invitation for an extended stroll on four wheels.

The nation first became aware of US Highway 66 when the 1928 International Transcontinental Foot Marathon (affectionately known as the Bunion Derby) followed Route 66 from

Los Angeles to Chicago, then on to Madison Square Garden in New York, a distance of 3,448 miles (5,500 km). The winner was handed $25,000. Andy Payne, a part-Cherokee Indian from Oklahoma, won the purse.

Three decades later, for a fee of $1,500, Peter McDonald walked on stilts from New York City to Los Angeles, a distance of 3,200 miles (5,150 km). From Chicago to Los Angeles, his way out west was Route 66. Pete was neither the first nor the last to place the road in the public eye – wild, weird, and wondrous celebrants were to follow. Two such celebrities were Happy Lou Phillips and his friend Lucky Jimmy Parker. The pair of intrepid travelers

---

**LEFT:** family outings along Route 66 were common in the 1940s and '50s.

**RIGHT:** Happy Lou Phillips made headlines by roller-skating from Washington, DC to San Francisco.

strapped on skates and rolled their way along America's Main Street, as it was called, during their cross-country journey from Washington, DC to San Francisco. Through the state of Arizona, a newspaper reported, "They walked a great deal, since at that time (1929) Route 66 was only paved through towns."

"Hobo" Dick Zimmerman routinely walked Route 66 from California to Michigan, pushing a wheelbarrow, to visit his 101-year-old mother. Dick was 78.

Another student of perambulating the old

National magazines called Route 66 "America's worst speed trap," naming the tiny hamlets where cops and judges had their palms outstretched for bribes. The American Automobile Association reported on towns that should be avoided, unless drivers were prepared to sweeten the police treasury. Route 66 was a highway of flat tires, overheated radiators, motor courts, cars with no air conditioning, tourist traps, treacherous curves, narrow lanes, and detour signs.

In the Roaring Twenties, desperadoes and

### SING IT LOUD

*If you ever plan to motor west;*
*travel my way, take the highway*
*that's the best.*
*Get your kicks on Route Sixty-six!*

highway was "Shopping Cart" Doughtery, who, sporting a white beard and turban, traveled 9 to 16 miles (14 to 25 km) a day on Route 66 with all his worldly possessions in a shopping cart. History doesn't tell us the final destination of Doughtery.

## Joggers and baton twirlers

In 1972, John Ball, a 45-year-old South African, jogged from California to Chicago on Route 66, and then became a hero on the East Coast. The journey took 54 days.

The Mother Road has also seen its share of high school baton twirlers, who have marched along Old 66 setting dubious records.

bootleggers – the likes of John Dillinger, Al Capone, Bugs Moran, Bonnie and Clyde, and Ma Barker and her god-fearing boys – lurched down Old 66, using it as an escape route. Occasionally the Associated Press warned travelers of the dangers of "the criminally few who mix with the tourist throng."

Route 66 was Burma Shave signs, neon signs, full-service gas stations, mom 'n' pop diners, blue-plate specials, homemade pies, and waitresses who called everybody "honey," winked at the kids, and yelled at the cook. Hitchhiking was safe, and billboards along the highway were legal. People guzzled Grape Nehi, and summer lasted longer because of drive-in movies, and miniature golf, and slow-pitch softball under the lights. Motels didn't take reservations. And doctors didn't mind making house calls.

Through good times and hard times, the highway became a symbol of faith for the future. Novelist John Steinbeck set the tone of the highway in his Pulitzer Prize-winning book *The Grapes of Wrath*, when he found a nurturing quality in Route 66 and called her "The Mother Road." It was the "Road of Second Chance." To some, like the immigrants of the

## SING IT LOUD

*It winds from Chicago to L.A.*
*More than two thousand miles*
*all the way.*
*Get your kicks on Route Sixty-six!*

Trail, Wire Road, Postal Highway, Grand Canyon Route, National Old Trails Highway, Ozark Trail, Will Rogers Highway, and because it went through the center of so many towns, the Main Street of America.

### All-night radio

Route 66 was hundreds of locally improved and maintained lanes going from one town to the next. In Vega, Texas, a story – probably sprinkled with a little local folklore – is told of the town's baseball team. They wanted to play the team in

Dust Bowl, it was the "Glory Road." To architect Frank Lloyd Wright, it was the chute of a tilting continent, on which everything loose seemed to be sliding into southern California. And to travel agencies it was the chosen thoroughfare of the growing numbers of discriminating American tourists.

Route 66 was to carry a sundry of names at different locations throughout her history – names like the Pontiac Trail, Osage Indian

**LEFT:** whimsical motels like the Iceburg in Albuquerque, New Mexico, have been demolished. **ABOVE:** DJ Wolfman Jack was the voice on the radio accompanying most long-distance drives.

a nearby community but there was no connecting road. So the ambitious folks in this small Texas down built one. Today, that former deep-rutted path is said to be Route 66.

Route 66 was all-night radio out of Del Rio Texas, Continental Trailways and Greyhound buses, lemonade stands, family reunions, 25¢ haircuts, and a 5¢ cup of coffee. Kids counted telephone poles on the road, waved at engineers on trains, slept in a wigwam in Holbrook, Arizona, and signs in New Mexico promised "Tucumcari Tonight."

"Route 66," Bobby Troup's hit song of 1946, became a highway national anthem. Originally crooned by Nat "King" Cole, the simple tune

# Burma Shave

The Burma Shave company was founded by an imaginative insurance salesman to provide a speedy, brushless shave for the businessman on the go. Clinton Odell, father of the company's present CEO, collaborated with pharmacist Carl Noren to produce an item that became one of the most famous in America by virtue of being seen along every highway.

"By the start of the year we were getting the first repeat orders in the history of the company – all from druggists serving people who traveled these

roads," Odell told Frank Rowsome, Jr., who wrote the history of the company.

*Does Your Husband/Misbehave/Grunt and Grumble/Rant and Rave/Shoot the Brute Some/ Burma Shave* was one of the earliest signs, its lines spaced 100 paces apart – like most of the thousands that followed. In his book, *The Verse by the Side of the Road*, Rowsome explained that, traveling at 35 mph, the sequence took 18 seconds to read – "far more time and attention than a newspaper or magazine advertiser could reasonably expect from the casual viewer." Alexander Woollcott maintained that it was as difficult to read a single sign as it was to eat one salted peanut.

In those early days, rival advertisers soon became jealous. Many of them had been spending thousands on marketing their product, only to see a perky upstart impress its name on the consumer in a way that was remembered long after the signs ceased to exist. Sensing their annoyance, the signs cheekily responded by rubbing it in: *Let's Give the/Clerk a Hand/ Who Never/ Palms Off/Another Brand.* Burma Shave also knew how to needle the latest electric competition: *A Silky Cheek/Shaved Smooth/And Clean/Is Not Obtained/With a Mowing Machine.*

There were once 35,000 Burma Shave signs, but by 1963 they were removed. By this time they were costing the company almost a quarter of a million dollars a year and clearly were having a diminishing effect on sales. *Our Fortune/Is Your/Shaven Face/It's our Best/Advertising Space,* the company had once boasted.

"The commercial fortunes of the Burma-Vita Company can be read like tea leaves in the jingles themselves," wrote Rowsome. There were many reasons for the downturn in sales: people were driving too fast, superhighway rights of way frequently banned commercial signs, and possibly the fact that people were becoming too sophisticated to regard them as anything more than corny relics.

Most people were sad to see the Burma Shave signs disappear, as their growing insignificance proved to be just one more nail in the coffin of the vibrant Mother Road. As early as 1930, the company had been spending $65,000 a year (prompting $3 million in annual sales), but it was not only passing drivers that enjoyed them: friendly relations had been established with hundreds of farmers on whose land the red-and-white signs appeared. Although rentals rarely topped $25 per year, many farmers were so proud of the signs that they made their own repairs when necessary. Incidentally, horses found them to be perfect backscratchers – until the company got wise and raised the height of the signs.

There was never a chance that Burma Shave would run out of slogans. An annual contest offering $100 for each jingle used drew more than 50,000 entries. These would be whittled down to the best 1,000 stanzas. Of course, there were thousands of entries that were not considered "appropriate" and hence were never used: *Listen, Birds/These Signs Cost Money/So Roost a While/But Don't Get Funny.* ❑

---

**LEFT:** once upon a time there were 35,000 Burma Shave signs marching down American highways.

went on to be immortalized by Bing Crosby, Chuck Berry, The Rolling Stones, and a host of other recording artists – at last count over 100 of them. Nothing captured America's love affair with the road more than this song.

It celebrated the end of World War II, and the end of gas and food rationing. The lyrics invited Americans to get their kicks on Route 66, and millions of motoring adventurers, addicted to the smell of gasoline and the drone of rubber on the pavement, took Bobby's suggestion to heart.

> ### NAME GAME
>
> Route 66 has had many names over the years. Three of them are the Mother Road, the Glory Road, and the Road of Second Chance.

Mom wrote "Wish you were here" messages on picture postcards. The kids bought rich, gooey Pecan Logs at Stuckeys mini-mart while Dad filled the gas tank at 17¢ a gallon and bought the entire family sticky, orange-flavored popsicles out of the freezer.

The toll fare at the Chain of Rocks Bridge over the mighty Mississippi River was 35¢ a automobile, and brightly colored signs on the outskirts of St Louis, Missouri advertised "the Greatest Show under the Earth" at the nearby Merimac Caverns.

## Itchy Feet

Americans with itchy feet were ready to hit the road. They removed the musty canvas that had covered and protected the Plymouth ragtop and the Oldsmobile Woody since the outbreak of the war. And although the cars had been stored on blocks, folks replaced the pre-war tires with a set of six-ply Allstate clinchers at a total cost of $43.80. Vacationers shined up their new postwar sedans and thumbed through state maps and plotted a course on the road to adventure – Route 66.

**ABOVE:** the 1960s weekly series sold more Corvette sports cars than any TV commercial.

*Now you go thru Saint Looey and*
   *Joplin, Missouri*
*And Oklahoma City is mighty pretty.*

The 1950s saw Route 66 reach genuine celebrity status. Families could leave their homes in the East and Midwest and drive to the Painted Desert or Grand Canyon. They could drive all the way to the Pacific Ocean on a highway that passed through towns where the young outlaw Jesse James robbed banks, where Abraham Lincoln practiced law, and cross the great river Mark Twain wrote about. Tourists could see snake pits and caged wild critters and mysterious caverns and real live cowboys and

Indians, and visit Mickey's Magic Kingdom in Disneyland, California.

*Won't you get hip to this timely tip,*
*When you make that California trip.*
*Get your kicks on Route Sixty-six!*

Route 66 reached even greater popularity when a nomadic pot-boiler of a book by the same name as the highway became a hit TV show during 1960–64. *route 66* (yes, the 'r' was not capitalized in the show title) was the story of two young adventurers, Buz (George Maharis) and Tod (Martin Milner), getting their

kicks on Route 66 in a Corvette. Among its 116 episodes, few were actually filmed on Route 66. Sponsored in part by Chevrolet, it is probably the only show that sold more Corvettes than any TV commercial, and established the Vette as an American icon.

When the Federal Highway Act of 1956 called for the construction of interstate systems throughout the United States, it looked as if the bright lights of fame and fortune that had shined on Route 66 for so many years was beginning to dim.

Little by little, here and there, pieces of Route 66 were replaced by the interstate. Bypassing of the towns that the fabled highway served was a

task that took five different super highways to achieve – Interstate 55 from Chicago to St Louis, Interstate 44 from St Louis to Oklahoma City, Interstate 40 from Oklahoma City to Barstow, Interstate 15 from Barstow to San Bernardino, and Interstate 10 from San Bernardino to Santa Monica.

The last stretch of Route 66 was bypassed in 1984 at Williams, Arizona when the old highway was replaced by Interstate 40. There was a ceremony, almost a wake. The late Bobby Troup was there to give a speech. As tears streamed from his eyes, he called the occasion "a very sad day."

## Wurlitzer jukeboxes

In 1985, US Highway 66 was decertified, giving way to superhighways of diesel fumes and fast-food chains. Because the road is no longer classified as a federal highway, some folks will tell you the road is no longer there.

But progress does not necessarily conquer all. Beyond the endless, blandness of the interstates, there is a powerful rhythm in an old two-lane highway that still rises and twists and turns across rolling hills, the mountains, and the deserts. Slowing through quiet towns, then rushing on and up again to the next ridge, you'll find the road waiting to be discovered in each of the eight Route 66 states.

Cafés and roadside attractions have been revived, restored, and reopened. Vintage Wurlitzer jukeboxes blare out old road songs. Folks in classic cars cruise into a drive-in for a hamburger and shake. Service station attendants offer to check under the hood and wash the windshield. Family-owned restaurants serve homemade pie, and a waitress in a starched pink uniform still calls you "Hon!" and yells at the cook. The old road still beckons pilgrims not only from across the US, but from nearly every compass point of the world.

With the car open to the wind, and an AM station riddled with static from a thunderstorm on the horizon, memories flicker in the sweetness of the moment. The miles themselves dissolve every question except the one that matters. What lies waiting, there, just over the next rise of Route 66? ❏

**LEFT AND RIGHT:** bypassing the towns that Route 66 served was a task that took five different super-highways to achieve.

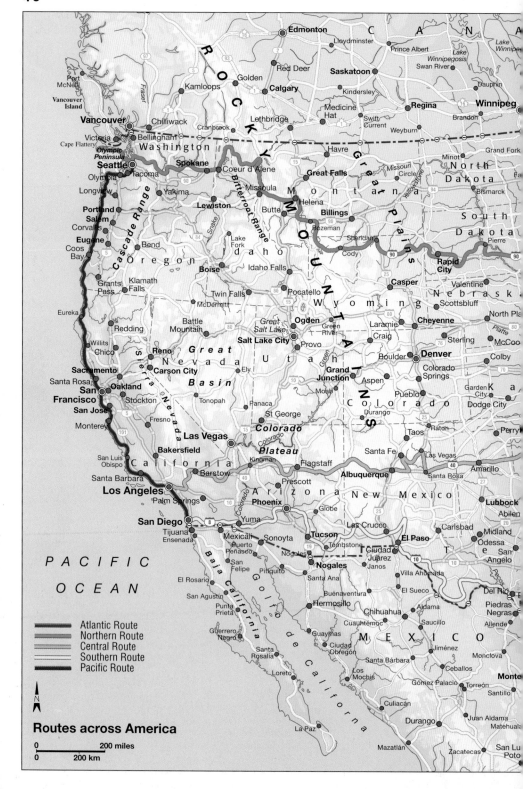

**Routes across America**

Atlantic Route
Northern Route
Central Route
Southern Route
Pacific Route

0          200 miles
0          200 km

PACIFIC

OCEAN

# THE ATLANTIC ROUTE

*A detailed guide to the attractions of the eastern seaboard,
with principal sites cross-referenced by number to the maps*

The systematic colonization by the British of America's East Coast was only accomplished once settlers had learned to use its waterways: the Atlantic coastline's bays, the long rivers running out of the Appalachian Mountains, and the languid tidal inlets so vital to inland transport in the flat but densely foliated southern states. It was at the mouths of rivers and ports that virtually every important eastern city sprang up.

Appropriately, then, our route south will rarely stray very far from water. Beginning in New York City, undisputed king of America's cities, we will then pass through a close succession of two more important cities, each with its own distinct personality: Philadelphia, cradle of American independence, and Baltimore, originally a fishing town and one still largely dependent on port activities.

From there, we will move inland to make two exceptionally scenic drives in Virginia, passing at last into North Carolina and examining one of the South's most pleasant states. We will cut east through tobacco fields to the coastline and ride along water once again through South Carolina and Georgia, each time stopping to linger over a beautiful old city or a small half-forgotten town.

Once in Florida, the weather – and the temperature of the water – will turn steadily warmer as we zigzag south from the nation's oldest settlement, St Augustine on the Atlantic Ocean, to Orlando's lakes, Tampa's mild Gulf of Mexico waters, and past the edge of south Florida to the vast (and moist) natural area known as the Everglades. At long last we will emerge at the Atlantic coast once more, skimming past Miami and its attached beaches – in order to come back later – to continue on to the Florida Keys, a place where water is more influential and obvious than it is anywhere else, probably, in North America. ❏

**PRECEDING PAGES:** Highway 1, Big Sur, California; winding through the Badlands, South Dakota; heat haze on the highway, Nevada.
**LEFT:** Kawasaki fan, Florida.

# A SHORT STAY IN NEW YORK CITY

*New York is the city that never sleeps; it has energy and confusion, culture, and great charm. Here's a list of the not-to-be-missed attractions:*

◆ Dubbed the Crossroads of the World, Times Square used to be dirty and dangerous, but clean-up campaigns have made it the icon of New York. You can buy Broadway tickets here, too.

◆ The Statue of Liberty, a gift from France and once the symbol of America for immigrants, still draws the crowds. Catch a boat to Staten Island from downtown Manhattan.

◆ The Ellis Island Immigration Museum provides a visual history of the port that 40 percent of all Americans can trace their roots to, and documents the migration from the world to the United States from the 1850s to the mid-20th century.

◆ New York's Museum of Modern Art (MoMA) houses the greatest collection of modern art in the US, which makes sense in the city than made Andy Warhol famous for more than 15 minutes.

◆ Famous for the Rockettes, Radio City Music Hall hosts spectacular music and theater shows. Tours are also available during the day of this Art Deco institution.

◆ The hub of much of New York City's night life, Greenwich Village is still a center for musicians, artists, the eccentric and the shoppers.

◆ SoHo and Tribeca, with their art galleries and watering holes, are perfect for Saturday strolling. Chinatown is just a walk away if you're hungry.

◆ More than just the center of global capitalism, Wall Street in historic downtown New York is lined with beautiful architecture; tours of the trading floor can be taken, too.

 For visitors interested in staying longer in the Big Apple, pick up a copy of *Insight Guide: New York City*. A companion to the present volume, it is packed with insightful text and stunning pictures.

△ **CENTRAL PARK**
Ice-skating in the wintertime, outdoor concerts in the summertime – the tree-filled park in the center of the city keeps New Yorkers sane.

◁ **CHRYSLER BUILDING**
The shimmering, Art Deco Chrysler Building was the tallest building in the world in 1930, until it was surpassed by the Empire State Building one year later.

◁ **SKYLINE OF THE CITY**
Star of stage, screen and countless photographs, the skyine (*left*, showing the Twin Towers of the World Trade Center), never fails to impress.

△ **GUGGENHEIM MUSEUM**
Designed by Frank Lloyd Wright and opened in 1959, the spiral ramp inside allows for constant viewing of the priceless art collection.

▷ **EMPIRE STATE BUILDING**
The platform on the 102nd floor offers the best city view in the US, particularly at dusk.

## THE BIG APPLE

There is a mix of freedom and foreignness in New York that is unsurpassed anywhere. You want to have a cocktail on a level with the clouds? Go dancing when the moon is high and the mood overtakes you? Want to go in-line skating, ice skating, or take in that Broadway show? You've come to the right town. New York's skyline is instantly recognizable; its attractions the best in the world. Its cultural life is matched only by its culinary awareness; there are over 15,000 eating places. If there are more ways of making it here, there are also more ways of spending it, so bring a fat wallet and lots of stamina.

▽ Red arrows on the map indicate routes from the city detailed in this book

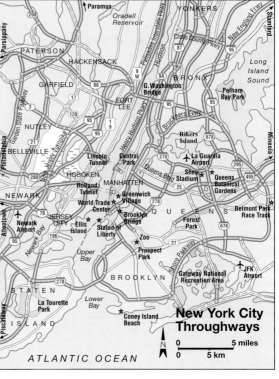

**New York City Throughways**

## Important Information

**Population:**
7.5 million
**Dialing codes:**
212, 646, 347, 718
**Website:**
www.nycvisit.com

**Tourist information:**
810 Seventh Avenue,
NY 10019
Tel: 212-484-1222;
freephone 1800-
NYCVISIT

# NEW YORK TO VIRGINIA

*Just beyond the frenzy of New York City lie*
*national historic sites and cities of colonial interest,*
*as well as the green, green hills of Virginia*

This first leg of the Atlantic route takes in some of the most historic sites in the United States – places where the Revolutionary and Civil Wars were fought, and where the brash, new nation was conceived. But in order to take this cruise through history, a bit of contemporary, behind-the-wheel negotiation is required first. There are three ways to leave **New York City ❶** *(see page 52)* and cross the Hudson River into the neighboring state of New Jersey. Although all – depending on the time of day – can be unnervingly congested (and all charge a toll), the northernmost of these "escapes" from Manhattan is probably also the least unpleasant: across the **George Washington Bridge**. The simplest way to find it, from wherever you are in Manhattan, is to head towards the mighty Hudson until you hit SR 9A (the Henry Hudson Parkway), and head north until it intersects with I-95 and the bridge. If you don't feel like driving north to eventually go south in New Jersey, then your only option is to go *under* the river via the extremely tedious **Lincoln** or **Holland tunnels**, both located more at the southern end of Manhattan.

Whichever way you choose, eventually you'll be steered onto the New Jersey Turnpike (I-95). New Jersey's nickname, the Garden State, seems a cruel joke at first: the early miles reveal nothing more than bleak industrial landscape. Past the factories, warehouses, and landfills, however, you pass into a more diverse region of some natural beauty and historical significance.

**LEFT:** hanging out over the green fields of Virginia.
**BELOW:** the Blue Ridge Parkway.

## Slower pace

If you've taken the Lincoln Tunnel out of Manhattan, head south on the New Jersey Turnpike. If you've opted for the Holland Tunnel, then head north for a short stretch: your aim is to cut west on I-280 toward the Oranges. Here, the harsh landscape begins to soften. Luxurious greenery replaces the drab scrub along the turnpike, and the smoke-belching factories give way to white churches and comfortable middle-class homes.

Only 15 minutes out of the Big Apple, small-town life already begins to take the place of the urban crush, and the pace of day-to-day life slows considerably. Get off the freeway at either exit 9 or 10 and head east to connect with Main Street, heading north through the town of **West Orange** past the town hall. You will arrive at the **Edison National Historic Site** (tel: 973-736-0550).

This lab complex, sometimes described as "the cradle of American industry," is maintained by the National Park Service, which offers an excellent tour by well-informed guides.

The tour begins in a chemistry lab filled with antique burettes and beakers, then continues through

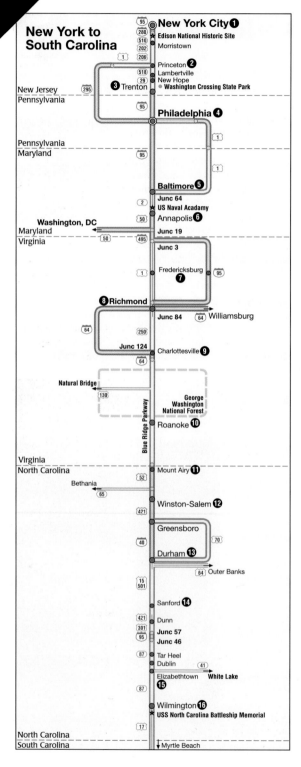

**New York to South Carolina**

New York City ❶
Edison National Historic Site
Morristown
Princeton ❷
Lambertville
New Hope
Washington Crossing State Park
❸ Trenton
Philadelphia ❹
Baltimore ❺
Junc 64
US Naval Acadamy
Annapolis ❻
Junc 19
Junc 3
Fredericksburg ❼
❽ Richmond
Junc 84    Williamsburg
Junc 124
Charlottesville ❾
Natural Bridge
George Washington National Forest
Blue Ridge Parkway
Roanoke ❿
Mount Airy ⓫
Bethania
Winston-Salem ⓬
Greensboro
Durham ⓭
Outer Banks
Sanford ⓮
Dunn
Junc 57
Junc 46
Tar Heel
Dublin
Elizabethtown    White Lake ⓯
Wilmington ⓰
USS North Carolina Battleship Memorial
Myrtle Beach

New Jersey
Pennsylvania

Pennsylvania
Maryland

Washington, DC
Maryland
Virginia

Virginia
North Carolina

North Carolina
South Carolina

the experimental machine shop in which Thomas Edison and his associates fabricated the parts necessary for the construction of products that have altered irrevocably the course of modern life: the light bulb, the phonograph, and the motion picture camera, to name only three important inventions. A gorgeous library is on display in the building, lined with thousands of leather-bound volumes in numerous languages.

On the walls hang portraits of Edison, as well as various placards inscribed with sayings of which he was fond: "There is no expedient to which a man will not resort in order to avoid the real labor of thinking" (Sir Joshua Reynolds), and Edison's own famous description of genius as "1 percent inspiration and 99 percent perspiration." Edison supposedly claimed that Reynolds' quotation served as his 1 percent inspiration.

### First film studio

Included on the tour is a walk by a reconstructed version of Black Maria, the world's first film studio, preceded by a screening of *The Great Train Robbery*, the first feature film to be produced at Edison Studios. You may well leave the complex filled with a powerful sense of wonder at Edison's artistic vision and technical prowess.

Before leaving West Orange, don't forget to visit **Glenmont** (tel: 973-736-0550), Edison's beautiful Victorian residence, located a half mile from the Laboratory Complex in the private residential community of Llewellyn Park.

Jog south a bit, then turn west onto State 510 through enclaves of great wealth to reach **Morristown**, home to a constellation of Revolutionary War sites. At 230 Morris Street stands the lovely **Jacob Ford Mansion**, the colonial house that General George Washington used as headquarters during the bitter winters of 1777 and 1780.

It is part of the **Morristown National Historical Park**, as are – 6 miles (10 km) southwest of Morristown proper in the Fort Nonsense unit of the park – **Jockey Hollow**, where the Revolutionary army encamped under Washington, and **Wick House**, a 18th-century farmhouse rich with the smell of firewood. On weekends women and children dressed in colonial garb cook in the kitchen.

## Cloistered wealth

Head south on US 202 to get more of the country flavor of the Garden State; the road here is verdant and calming. Just after Bridgewater US 202 continues with a sharp turn to the southwest, but you want to continue due south on US 206. You soon arrive at **Princeton ❷**, home to elegant **Princeton University** – which possesses one of the most beautiful campuses in the Northeast. A Gothic architectural style dominates, although there are a few modern structures thrown in for good measure as well – and you'll also find a fine collection of outdoor sculpture scattered about the grounds. **Nassau Hall**, the oldest building on campus, played host to the Continental Congress in 1783 when mutinous soldiers forced Congress to leave Philadelphia.

Princeton remains a bastion of cloistered wealth, with preppie college kids browsing in the rich boutiques of Nassau Street as they have always done, but it is also one of the nation's finest educational institutions. Author F. Scott Fitzgerald was one famous alumnus who walked its halls, typifying a mixture of privilege and skill that still characterizes its students today.

From Princeton, you've got several options. You can shoot straight down busy US 1 or I-295 to Philadelphia, or – with time on your hands – sidetrack through the lovely **Delaware River Valley**.

To do that, backtrack north up US 206 to State 518, then head west. At the river, you'll pass through quiet **Lambertville** with old inns, antique shops, and

Map on page 56

*Princeton has one of the most beautiful campuses in the East.*

**BELOW:** Cleveland Tower, Princeton University.

a narrow bridge connecting it to **New Hope**, Pennsylvania. Both **Washington Crossing State Park**, where General George Washington landed on Christmas Eve, 1776, and the state capital of **Trenton ❸**, where Washington's army captured Hessian soldiers in battle that night, sit directly downriver and can be reached via twisting Route 29. It's a fitting colonial and historical introduction to what awaits in the "City of Brotherly Love," Philadelphia, just beyond (Route 29 will connect with I-95 just as you get into Trenton; take that south).

## Philadelphia

At the time of the American Revolution, **Philadelphia ❹** was the economic and political center of the fledgling United States. During the early years of the Republic, however, the nation's economic heart was transplanted north to New York City while governmental power traveled south to the new city of Washington, DC. This left the city with a bit of an identity crisis. An interesting ethnic mix has sustained the place ever since, however, making it today one of America's most vibrant – and low-profile– large cities.

The nation's fifth most populous city, this is for tourists and historians – along with Boston – an American city *par excellence.* Film buffs cannot help but feel a swell of emotion, either, when viewing the Public Library stairs Sylvester Stallone ran up to Bill Conti's soaring score in the film *Rocky.* Stallone wasn't a local, but his choice of Philly for the *Rocky* screenplay – which sent him to stardom – was apt: this is a gritty, lively, and fascinating place, despite the derogatory jokes made by American music hall comedians.

Situated at the conjunction of the Schuylkill (pronounced *skoo-kill*) and Delaware rivers, the city was founded in 1682 by the English Quaker William Penn. Penn envisioned a colony in which the right to freedom of religious expression would not be quashed, so it's not surprising that when representatives of the 13 colonies convened to sign the Declaration of Independence, they did so here on July 4, 1776, thereby giving birth to the United States of America.

**BELOW:**
architectural detail
in Philadelphia's
Elfreth's Alley, the
oldest continuously
occupied street in
America.

### A nation is born

At **Independence National Historic Park** (tel: 215-597-8974; open daily), which extends from Second to Sixth streets between Walnut and Chestnut, the extraordinary sequence of events that led to the founding and empowering of the United States becomes palpable. The Declaration of Independence and the Constitution were signed in elegant **Independence Hall**, where the Liberty Bell, the best known emblem of Philadelphia, once stood. The **Assembly Room**, which contains the inkstand used by the signers of the Declaration as well as the chair in which George Washington supposedly sat during the drafting of the Constitution, should not be missed. Not far away is **Congress Hall**, where the US Congress convened between 1790 and 1800 when Philadelphia was briefly the nation's capital.

A block up from Independence Hall stands the curious Liberty Bell Pavilion, a glass structure that has been home to the famous cracked **Liberty Bell** since its 1976 removal from the exterior of Independence

Hall. It is invariably packed with tourists. Continuing down Market Street toward the Delaware River, you'll find **Franklin Court**, site of Ben Franklin's residence. His home no longer exists but is commemorated by an evocative outline of painted white steel beams. Beneath the courtyard, a museum features multimedia displays and a film about Franklin's rich life as an author, traveler, scientist, gastronome, and colonial mover and shaker.

Map on page 56

    **Christ Church**, at Second Street just above Market, was built in 1695 and was the preferred house of worship for the men of the Continental Congress. Plaques mark pews once occupied by George Washington, Ben Franklin, and Betsy Ross. Nearby, **Betsy Ross House** was the place where Ross stitched the new nation's first flag.

## High Society

From Independence Hall, wend your way toward South Street via the cobblestone streets and garden paths of **Society Hill**, Philly's original residential district and a place of elegant 300-year-old Federalist-style homes.

*The Liberty Bell, cast in England in 1752, is the emblem of Philadelphia.*

    During the late 1970s, Philadelphia's waterfront – like that of many eastern seaboard cities – underwent considerable rehabilitation. **Penn's Landing**, between Market and Lombard streets along the Delaware River, is where William Penn came ashore in 1682. Today the area features the **Port of History Museum** – several historic ships moored in the harbor – and views of **Camden**, New Jersey (home to the monumental American poet Walt Whitman) across the river. Also stroll down one block below Lombard to **South Street**, where you will find a stimulating array of punk haberdashers as well as chic boutiques.

    **City Hall**, at the intersection of Broad and Market streets, is the largest munic-

**BELOW:** reenacting the American Revolution in Trenton, NJ.

# BALTIMORE: CHARM CITY

*Baltimore is a big city with a small-town feel – the home of good food, great baseball, and "The Star Spangled Banner"*

**B**altimore's favorite food is the local Maryland blue crab, found in abundance in the many seafood restaurants of the town's Inner Harbor. The sports equivalent of the blue crab, in popularity at least, is the city's beloved baseball team, the Orioles. Baseball addicts will enjoy visiting the Babe Ruth Birthplace/Baltimore Orioles Museum (tel: 410-727-1539; open daily) on Emory Street. Babe Ruth, a native of the city, still casts a huge shadow over the game even in death; his mighty home-run swats at Yankee Stadium changed the way the game was played forever.

Afterward, get a look at the bigger picture

of the town from the Top of the World observation deck, located on the 27th floor of the pentagonal World Trade Center.

Not far away at Pratt Street is the fine National Aquarium (tel: 410-576-3800; open daily), one of the nation's best, complete with a simulated Amazon rainforest, coral reef display, and 220,000-gallon (830,000-liter) open ocean tank.

Fell's Point, Baltimore's first ship-building and maritime center, still has the charm of an old port town. Among the cobbled streets stand more than 350 original Colonial homes, many in perfect condition. Interspersed are old pubs, antique shops, and, of course, great places to eat. You can also take a stroll through the original wooden Broadway Market.

The best-known attraction on the waterfront is Fort McHenry (tel: 410-962-4290; open daily). During the war of 1812 this fort withstood a 25-hour bombardment from the British fleet, later prompting Francis Scott Key to pen the lyrics that were to eventually become America's national anthem, "The Star Spangled Banner."

Mount Vernon Place, designated a National Historic Landmark, features many of Baltimore's oldest and most elegant townhouses, churches, and cultural institutions. At the center of the district stands the Washington Monument, the first formal monument to George Washington. Climb the 228 stairs of this 178-foot (54-meter) white marble column for another unobstructed view of the city.

Head up Charles Street to Johns Hopkins University, which since the late 19th century has been a major force in medical research. Right next door stands the respected Baltimore Museum of Art (tel: 410-396-7100; closed Mon–Tues), which contains works by Picasso and Matisse, art from Africa, and a beautiful modern sculpture garden. ❑

---

**LEFT:** National Aquarium; Federal Hill area.
**ABOVE:** ships and entertainment complexes are common around Baltimore's Inner Harbor.

Map on page 56

ipal building in the US. It was patterned loosely after the Louvre, though it more resembles Paris's Hôtel de Ville (city hall). The 37-foot (11-meter) high rooftop statue of William Penn is the tallest sitting atop any building in the world. Until recent years, in fact, the Philadelphia skyline was capped by an ordinance declaring no structure could exceed the height of Penn's hat.

The **Benjamin Franklin Parkway**, built in the 1920s, was modeled after the Champs-Elysées in Paris. This broad road cuts diagonally through Philly's square grid from City Hall to Fairmount Park. On the parkway at 20th Street, visit the **Franklin Institute** (tel: 215-448-1200; open daily), a science museum that is also a memorial to Franklin containing many of his personal possessions. Four floors of science exhibits are sure to amuse and educate all ages. In addition, the **Fels Planetarium** offers several shows daily.

## Art in the city

Two blocks away is the **Rodin Museum**, with an excellent collection of casts and originals by the great French sculptor. Among them is *The Thinker*, one of the most beloved statues in the world. At the end of the parkway stands the Rodin Museum's "parent", the **Philadelphia Museum of Art** (for both museums, tel: 215-763-8100; closed Mon), one of the great American art museums. Among the works in its collection are Breughel's *Village Wedding* and Picasso's *Three Musicians*, as well as an extraordinary collection of art and artifacts from the Middle Ages.

After hours spent walking the streets of Philly's historic districts and visiting its museums, the greenery of **Fairmount Park** – the country's largest municipal park – rejuvenates even the most exhausted traveler. In addition to grassy meadows and acres of woodland, the park features a horticultural center, zoo, Japanese house, tea garden, and several historic homes along the banks of the Schuylkill. If you're road-weary, bring a picnic lunch and spend a full day taking in the pleasures of this gorgeous park before taking to the road again toward **Baltimore ❺** *(see page 60)*. From Philadelphia, it's no more than an hour's drive down either I-95 or the somewhat quieter US 1 to Maryland: a journey that travels across the Mason-Dixon line which separates, many say, the North from the South.

**BELOW:** Calder sculpture and the Philadelphia Art Museum.

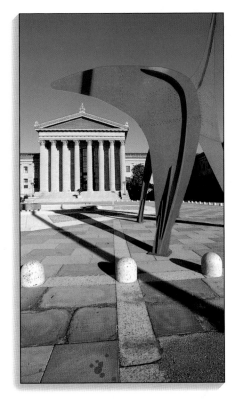

## ON TOWARD VIRGINIA

Leaving Baltimore, take State Route 2 south to Annapolis. As you cross the Severn River, you might well get a view of sailboats crisscrossing a sparkling expanse of water.

**Annapolis ❻** sparkles, too, in a way particular to towns built on and sustained by the sea. At dusk, its elegant Georgian houses and winding narrow streets shimmer in the dying light of day. Walking is an easy way to see the town, starting at the top where the **Maryland State House** sits. It was here that the Continental Congress ratified the Treaty of Paris, which officially ended the War of Independence.

Wend your way toward the beautifully preserved 18th-century waterfront to the **US Naval Academy** and its museum at **Preble Hall** (tel: 410-293-2108;

*During four Civil War battles in the Fredericksburg area, 110,00 people died – the site is called the "bloodiest ground" in North America.*

open daily), with exhibits on maritime life and the history of this venerable institution. You'll be feeling suitably red, white, and blue by the time you climb back into your car and drive the short 30 miles (48 km) west along US 50 towards America's capital, **Washington, DC** *(see "Central Route," page 181).* For our purposes on this route, we'll bypass the city using the I-495 loop; take the highway south to connect up with I-95 (or the slower, but more interesting, highway US 1 that runs parallel to it). You're on your way to the heart of the Confederate South.

## Confederate South

Only 52 miles (84 km) outside of Washington, DC, and midway between it and the once-opposing capital of Richmond *(see page 63),* it is not surprising that **Fredericksburg ❼** was a major battleground during the Civil War. In fact, with 110,000 casualties occurring during the four major battles fought in the vicinity of the city, it has been said that it is the "bloodiest ground" on the North American continent.

In recognition of the men who died during those battles, in 1927 the US Congress established the 9,000-acre (3,660-hectare) **Fredericksburg and Spotsylvania County Memorial National Military Park**, the largest military park in the world. The park lies just west of the city on either side of Route 3. Both the Fredericksburg Battlefield and the Chancellorsville Battlefield have visitor centers that are open daily and feature exhibits and slide programs; historians are also on hand to answer questions. The park includes several important historic structures, including **Chatham Manor** (tel: 540-373-4461; open daily), which served as Union headquarters during the battle of Fredericksburg and where

Clara Barton and Walt Whitman joined in the efforts to treat hundreds of wounded soldiers. Fredericksburg was also the home of George Washington. **Ferry Farm** (tel: 540-373-3381, ext. 28; open daily), where he grew up, is just across the Rappahannock River on Route 3 – it was here that young George allegedly uttered that line, "I cannot tell a lie," and came clean about chopping down a certain cherry tree. The nation's fifth president, James Monroe, also hailed from here; the **James Monroe Museum and Memorial Library** (tel: 540-654-1043; open daily) on Charles Street contains a collection of the personal possessions, furnishings, and papers of Monroe and his wife, Elizabeth.

## 18th-century tavern life

Today's Fredericksburg still remains very much rooted in the past, helped along considerably by its large (40-block) **National Register Historic District** containing not only historic attractions and restored private homes, but antique shops, restaurants, art galleries, and craft boutiques. Some buildings, like the elegant **Kenmore Plantation and Gardens** (tel: 540-373-3381; open daily Mar–Dec and weekends Jan–Feb) on Washington Avenue, give a taste of how the city's elite lived in bygone days. But everyday life is also represented at places like the **Hugh Mercer Apothecary Shop** (tel: 540-373-3362; open daily) – where visitors can hear about how to treat a lady's hysteria and other Colonial medical concerns – and the **Rising Sun Tavern** (tel: 540-371-1494; open daily), which provides a lively interpretation of 18th-century tavern life. Both are on Charles Street.

Head back down I-95 (or US 1) for another 55 miles (88 km) to what locals consider to be the "birthplace of America," **Richmond ❸**. It was here – at St

Map on page 56

**BELOW:** patriots set the pace in colonial Williamsburg.

# DETOUR: WILLIAMSBURG

A 54-mile (87-km) drive from Richmond along SR 60 ends at colonial Williamsburg, which does more than just revive buildings, streets and gardens: it recreates the everyday life of the nation's infancy. Established in 1633, Williamsburg grew into an outpost of culture, fashion, and festive living. After the state government moved to Richmond in 1780, the city languished until the Rev. W.A.R. Goodwin approached John D. Rockefeller, Jr in 1926 for funds to save those historic buildings still standing and rebuild others. Using original blueprints and materials, Goodwin resurrected the entire town, from the Congress – where George Mason's Declaration of Rights to the House of Burgesses laid the foundation for the Constitution – to the Raleigh Tavern, where George Washington plotted military strategy in the revolt against Great Britain. Nearly 2,000 "residents" recreate the original Williamsburg community. The blacksmith pounds away at glowing iron as visitors look on; the cabinetmaker carves chair legs while clad in knee breeches and powdered wig; a maid in bonnet and hooped skirt weaves linen at a 200-year-old loom. The baker, the printer, and the glass-blower are all represented, too. For tour information, tel: 757-220-7645.

**John's Church** on Broad Street – where the 2nd Virginia Convention was held in 1775, a stirring event that culminated in Patrick Henry's famous "Give Me Liberty, or Give Me Death" speech. Discovered by British explorers in 1607 and named after a borough of London, the city of Richmond wasn't founded until 1737. Laid out on the fall line of the James River, its location made it a natural center for commerce. By 1779, this more centrally located city had replaced colonial Williamsburg as the capital of Virginia.

Thomas Jefferson designed the striking neoclassical **State Capitol**, which is home to Jean-Antoine Houdon's full-size statue of George Washington, one of America's most valuable pieces of sculpture. During the Civil War, Richmond became the capital of the Confederacy, and about two blocks away from the State Capitol – at 12th and Clay streets in the city's historic **Court End** neighborhood – is the **Museum of the Confederacy** (tel: 804-649-1861; open daily), consisting of a modern museum and the restored White House of the Confederacy. If it's Civil War artifacts you're interested in, this is the place: it has the world's largest and most comprehensive collection.

Civil War buffs can also fuel their interest in this ever-interesting subject by visiting the **Hollywood Cemetery** on Cherry Street (final resting place of Confederate president Jefferson Davis, US presidents James Monroe and John Tyler, and more than 18,000 Confederate soldiers); **Monument Avenue** (home to – surprise! – a wealth of monuments to various key Civil War figures); and strings of battlefield parks and trails in the area.

Despite its huge historic neighborhoods and attractions, Richmond remains surprisingly untouristy, and also has a pleasant dash of modernity in its skyline and its cosmopolitan atmosphere. The city is renowned for its symphony, opera, and ballet, as well as for the highly regarded **Virginia Museum of Fine Arts** (tel: 804-340-1400; closed Mon) on Grove Avenue.

**BELOW:**
Virginia license
plates all in a row.

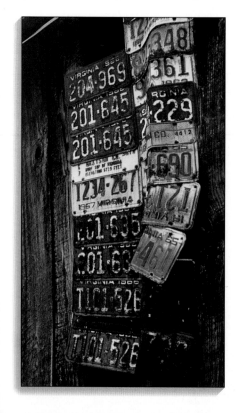

## Land of Jefferson

From Richmond take I-64 or US 250 east for 74 miles (119 km) to **Charlottesville ❾**, site of the University of Virginia and the home of Thomas Jefferson. Although the city now has its fair share of chain restaurants and hotels, it has still managed to retain something of a countrified splendor.

Jefferson designed the original buildings and campus of the **University of Virginia** in the 1820s and claimed, late in life, that it was of this achievement that he was most proud. His architecture is based on European classical style, adapted to local materials such as red brick and painted wood. Daily tours of the university leave from the **Rotunda**, which is modeled after the Roman Pantheon. Looking out from the elevated walkway of the Rotunda, you will see the splendid swath of grass known as "**The Lawn,**" bordered by columned pavilions. Originally these were the residences of all the students and professors of Jefferson's "academic villages" – now they are inhabited by school officials and honor-grade students. **West Range** is on McCormack Road, where Edgar Allan Poe lived during his unsuccessful undergraduate tenure here. His former room is open to visitors.

Continue down University Avenue to "**The Corner**," a collection of restaurants and shops catering to students, tourists, and local residents, if you want to see the modern-day beneficiaries of Jefferson's dream – a university consistently ranked near the top in lists of public universities in the United States.

Map on page 56

## Colonial gadgetry

Even before you arrive at **Monticello** (tel: 804-984-9800; open daily), the "little mountain" estate of Thomas Jefferson, you will be familiar with its shape; its image adorns the tail side of the US nickel. This elegant, dome shape is particularly Jeffersonian, for not only does it appear on the Rotunda at the University of Virginia, but also as the roof of the Jefferson Memorial building in Washington, DC. Jefferson designed every aspect of Monticello, and the imprint of his active mind is everywhere apparent.

*Every aspect of Thomas Jefferson's home, Monticello, was designed by the inventive president.*

Try to arrive early, as the wait for the mandatory tour is known to extend up to two hours at midday. The walk takes you through the ground floor of the residence; afterward you're free to wander about the lovely grounds of the mansion. The house's gadgetry is particularly endearing, especially the seven-day clock by the entrance, the double writing machine in Jefferson's study, and the dumbwaiter in the dining room. Be sure and ask about the home's extraordinary toilet system. Library walls are lined with leather-bound books, many written by the philosophers of the French Enlightenment who so strongly influenced Jefferson. The former president's grave is visible as you leave the grounds to return to the parking lot.

**BELOW:**
Jefferson's Rotunda at the University of Virginia.

Jefferson's good friend James Monroe, fifth president of the United States, lived nearby at **Ash Lawn-Highland** (tel: 804-293-9539; open daily). Though

Map on page 56

not nearly as stately as Monticello, Monroe's residence has a friendly charm of is own. As you drive back toward I-64 to continue south, you will pass by **Michie Tavern**, once a pre-Revolutionary watering hole but now a museum filled with colonial furniture and artifacts.

### The road to Natural Bridge

Take I-64 west to Rockfish Gap, where the breath-taking 459-mile (739-km) **Blue Ridge Parkway** begins. Cutting through the **George Washington National Forest**, the Parkway was – like its nearby counterpart, the Skyline Drive *(see page 184)* – cut into the side of the Blue Ridge Mountains. However, as this is not a national park, you'll note one big difference: this drive is filled not only with forest and flowers but also with working farms. Trees carpet the surrounding mountains, which seem bluer and bluer as they recede in the distance. If you're driving alone, don't allow the superb views to lure your eyes too far from the road or you'll end up tumbling over the edge of a cliff.

If you want to experience a questionable slice of Americana, get off the Parkway at Mile 61 (Km 98) via State 130 west to **Natural Bridge** – and prepare yourself for some of the crassest come-ons in the whole grand tour. Billboards blare "See the Natural Bridge!" and offer to throw a wax museum and cavern into the bargain. In order to get down to the Natural Bridge, which is an extraordinary 215-foot (66-meter) high rock formation, you are forced to pass through a knick-knack shop as big as a department store which is absolutely packed with junky tourist paraphernalia. Descend the stairs, walk past the electronic game room, and begin the short hike down to the main attraction.

The Monocan Indians called this "The Bridge of God," and no doubt the enormous limestone arch must have been a place of great wonder in the past. By the time you arrive there, however, you may be so queasy from the overload that it becomes difficult to conjure up the requisite awe; loudspeakers on high blare recordings of church bells. Things get even worse after dark, when the concern that owns Natural Bridge goes so far as to audaciously project a nightly religious film right onto the stone side of the bridge.

**BELOW:** Natural Bridge, Virginia. **RIGHT:** rocky mountain view in the Blue Ridge.

### End of the line

Back on the Parkway, gratefully continue south toward North Carolina. Below the pretty town of **Roanoke** ❿ *(see page 187)* the road continues to climb and dip, winding through attractive farmlands where the hay is gathered and neatly rolled into picturesque bales. Wooden fences turned silver-gray by time line the road, keeping the cows right where they are – grazing languidly in green pastures.

Just before the North Carolina border, the Blue Ridge Parkway ends and you begin to pass through a stretch of farmers' markets selling local produce and religious curios at bargain prices. The accent of the people is now very heavy, you will notice, almost incomprehensible to an ear accustomed to Northerners. If you are beginning to feel you are entering another country altogether, you are right. You are entering the Deep South. ❏

# NORTH CAROLINA TO SAVANNAH

*Pine-scented mountains, sandy beaches,
plantation homes, and antebellum cities –
the Deep South begins here*

Map on page 56

All that remains of the first-known settlement in present-day North Carolina is one word. That word – Croatan – has kept etymologists and philologists busy for centuries, ever since it was found scraped into a tree in the vanished colony of Fort Raleigh on Roanoke Island. Nothing else was left of the "lost colony," which was founded in 1587.

Today the state is experiencing rapid transformation from a country backwater to a manufacturing and educational power. Jobs and suburbs are sprouting up all along the Interstate 85 corridor, particularly in light industrial trades. Charlotte has become the banking power of the South. And the Raleigh-Durham area contains a very high concentration of quality universities. It's a measure of this success that you can now watch ice hockey in a state where it rarely snows, and professional football, too; both have recently arrived along with the new jobs. Strains of folk and bluegrass music can still be heard in the mountainous Appalachian third of the state, but you've got to hunt a bit for them now.

**LEFT:** Great Smoky Mountains and the bears.
**BELOW:** rustic living in North Carolina.

## Weeping willow trees

US 52 takes you over the border from Virginia's Blue Ridge Parkway through trim **Mount Airy** ⑪ – birthplace of Carolina hero Andy Griffith, and the model town for his wildly popular classic TV program *Mayberry RFD* – then on down to Winston-Salem *(see page 188)*. Take the "King and Tobaccoville" exit and follow the back roads to **Bethania**, a town founded by Moravians who came to the New World to escape religious persecution.

The road is lined with graceful weeping willow trees and leads past fields covered, as you'd expect, with tobacco plants; visit in summer, and they'll be high and big-leafed, but come back in autumn and they'll be a mess of tangled vines burned black.

State 67 east (continue on US 52 if you did not detour to Bethania) leads on to **Winston-Salem** ⑫, home of the R.J. Reynolds tobacco factory, which produces more than 450 million cigarettes daily. The odor of tobacco wafts throughout the town, a constant reminder of the second-largest industry in North Carolina (textiles are first). The Reynolds plant is located, naturally, on Reynolds Boulevard and it's open to visitors during the week. This is also stock-car racing country, an area where many NASCAR greats were reared and still live.

The Salem half of Winston-Salem was founded by Moravians in 1766. The name is derived from the Hebrew word "shalom," meaning peace. In 1913 it

*North Carolina is moving away from agriculture and into technology and big banking.*

**BELOW:**
tobacco drying in the sun.

was incorporated with its neighbor Winston, and when its old buildings fell into disrepair, a restoration project during the 1930s saved them. The success of this effort can be seen in **Salem Old Town**, which is entered from the Old Salem Road near the center of town. Particularly interesting are the **Mikisch Tobacco Shop**, thought to be the oldest tobacco shop still standing in America; the **Winkler Bakery**, a restored Moravian bakery that produces lovely bread Monday through Saturday; and the **Salem Tavern** with its **Barn and Farm Museum**. **God's Acre**, a Moravian graveyard nearby, possesses 4,000 graves, many graced with flat marble markers symbolizing the equality of the deceased. *(For more information on Winston-Salem, see page 188.)*

Busy four-lane US 421 leads east through undistinguished country toward growing **Greensboro**, once the home of short story master O. Henry (William Sydney Porter) and long a major producer of textiles; white-collar jobs are now springing up here as well. A Woolworth's store in the central downtown area, now closed, unfortunately, was the site of one of the very first civil rights actions in the South – a sit-in at a soda fountain by local black activists.

## The Research Triangle

Continue along either US 70 or Interstate 40 east to the town of **Durham** ⑬, home of **Duke University**. Along with **Chapel Hill** and **Raleigh**, Durham is part of the Research Triangle, a liberal oasis in the middle of North Carolina which claims to have more Ph.D.'s per capita than any other area in the nation. This is also the place to come for top-quality college basketball in winter: North Carolina is a hoops-crazy state, and its Duke Blue Devils, North Carolina Tar Heels, and North Carolina State Wolfpack – all playing in the Triangle – do

## DETOUR: OUTER BANKS

A leisurely 193-mile (311-km) drive along SR 64 from Raleigh leads to the Outer Banks, which emerge like the head of a whale breaching into the Atlantic. Two national seashores, Cape Hatteras and Cape Lookout, preserve 120 miles (190 km) of these beaches on Bodie, Hatteras and Ocracoke islands, and Core and Shackleford banks. While most coastal islands lie within 10 miles (16 km) of shore, the Outer Banks belong to the realm of the sea; in places, 30 miles (48 km) of water separate Hatteras Island from the mainland. The National Seashores of the Outer Banks have personalities unique to the rest of North Carolina. The islands have wide, water-thrashed beaches, while scattered patches of sea oats and beach grasses bind low dunes behind them. Here and there, clumps of shrubby marsh elder and bayberry dot the swales. The mainland side of each island hosts extensive tidal marshes of swaying cordgrass. Distinctly patterned lighthouses mark the shores for passing ships, in particular the spiral-painted Cape Hatteras lighthouse. The lighthouse now stands less than 200 feet (61 meters) from the shore, although it was built 1500 feet (450 meters) away. The Outer Banks Chamber of Commerce, tel: 252-441-8144.

the state proud. Duke's campus is among the most beautiful in the South, filled with Gothic and Georgian buildings filling neat quadrangles and plenty of nice botanical gardens and lawns for picnicking. Figure out a legal place to park, then head for the Duke University Chapel to see the **Benjamin N. Duke Memorial Flentrop Organ**, a 5,000-pipe extravaganza. The **Duke Woods**, nearby, provides a short walk through the pines if you're wanting to get outside.

Map on page 56

## Southern summer evenings

The city is also interesting for its lively mixture of tobacco warehouses and chic restaurants, working-class mill hands and college professors, old Southerners and new Yankee up-starts. **Ninth Street** is the place to go for youth, with plenty of good record shops, bookstores, coffee shops, and eateries.

Also make a point of finding the Durham Bulls' minor-league ballpark, one of the nation's finest and the perfect spot to spend a warm summer evening watching future stars play baseball the way it was meant to be played. Note the outfield bull, which snorts steam when a home run is hit. The Bulls' former ballpark, El Toro Field, was even more authentic – one side consisted of tobacco warehouses, and the steam-snorting bull made its debut here during the filming of the baseball film *Bull Durham* – though the place has lately fallen into disuse; you can still take a look, though, as it is easily walkable from Downtown.

Just to the southwest of Durham, smaller **Chapel Hill** is the home of the pleasant **University of North Carolina** campus. UNC is said to have been the first state university chartered in the US. Fans of astronomy will enjoy the **Morehead Planetarium**, while sports fans will take joy in the fact that the great, all around athlete Michael Jordan played college ball here.

**BELOW:**
Winston-Salem
was settled by
Moravians.

## Toward the coast

Continue along US 15-501 (also known as the Jefferson Davis Highway) south through residential Chapel Hill toward **Sanford** ⓮, where pottery is becoming a popular cottage industry. At Sanford, change onto US 421, a road lined with fast-food shops, and angle southeast. You are now on the way to Wilmington, principal deep-water port on the North Carolina coast and a refreshing change from this hot and dusty road, where roadside fields are again densely covered with tobacco plants and the occasional weeping willow or algae-covered pond does little to dispel the oppressive heat.

At **Dunn**, turn south on State 301 toward **Fayetteville**. This smaller road runs through farm country, through corn and tobacco fields extending for acres back from the highway. There are innumerable small churches along the road, the majority of which are Baptist; you are truly in the South now.

Use the I-95 to get around Fayetteville, exiting shortly to continue south on State 87, a scenic route to the coast taking you deep into the heart of southeast Carolina. Along the way, you'll pass through the tiny settlements of **Tar Heel** and **Dublin,** but little else of size.

By the time you reach **Elizabethtown** ⓯, you may be so tuckered out from driving that a swim will seem a tantalizing idea. Follow State 41 east to **White Lake**, an oasis in the middle of the Cape Fear region. On the eastern side of the lake is **Goldston's Beach**, a public beach with the requisite tourist shops. The water is warm and soothing, though, and the sandy beach might well prove a haven to muscles weary of driving. The small amusement park nearby has pinball machines from the 1960s and old skee-ball games, which lend an anachronistic air to the place, as though it had been bypassed by 40 years of history. Many of the small towns of the Deep South, you will find, have just this same feeling to them: frozen in another era.

**BELOW:**
North Carolina has both mountains and beaches.

## Cape Cod in Carolina

Continue on State 87 to **Wilmington** ⓰, NBA great Michael Jordan's hometown. It's interesting to note that the town's good looks and extremely savvy marketing camapign have created a recent film boom. A number of popular television programs and movies are filmed and produced here in a huge studio lot – with Wilmington standing in for the likes of Cape Cod, California, and so forth.

For sightseeing,why not think about visiting the *USS North Carolina* **Battleship Memorial** (tel: 910-251-5797; open daily)? Nicknamed "The Showboat," the ship was commissioned in 1941 and was considered at the time to be the greatest fighting vessel the United States had yet produced. In town, many historic houses are to be seen, among them the **Zebulon Latimer House** at 126 South Third Street and the **Burgwin-Wright House** at Third and Market streets. None appear affected by the high flooding from a recent spate of tropical storms and hurricanes.

The Southern grace of Wilmington's finer homes will pique your interest, and prepare you for the even more splendid homes of Charleston and Savannah that lie just to the south.

## SOUTH CAROLINA

On December 20, 1860, South Carolina became the first state to secede from the Union. John C. Calhoun's efforts to combat federal laws had not been enough to keep the South's economic and social order – built as it was on the institution of slavery – intact. Knowing its way of life was threatened, South Carolina insisted in 1860 on the right of states to disavow the Federal union. That one step plunged the nation into one of its bloodiest wars: a war with itself.

Even after the Civil War ended in defeat, South Carolina refused to grant the right to vote to its newly freed blacks – a situation that led to the imposition of martial law for a time. This refusal to change with the times kept the state mired in an economic backwater until after World War II, when the state's economy began to switch from an agricultural one to a newly developing industrial base. Textiles, furniture, and chemical industries began to flourish. (Agriculture remains strong, however: this is America's top peach producer and its only producer of tea.)

In succeeding years, the modern industry of tourism also began to gather steam here. Nowhere can this burgeoning industry be better seen – for better and worse – than along the Carolina coast, from Myrtle Beach and the Grand Strand down to Charleston and beyond.

Take US 17 south from Wilmington into South Carolina, and you will have entered the 55-mile (88-km) stretch of beach resort known as the **Grand Strand**. The first oddity you will encounter is the ubiquity of fireworks shops. This is the only East Coast state to have legalized the sale of fireworks, and throughout the area they are big business, hawked perhaps a little too enthusiastically at dozens of roadside stands.

**Map on page 56**

*Southerners are great storytellers. In Wilmington, ask about the unsolved murder of 1760, which involved a man, a snake ring, and a riderless horse on a rainy night.*

**BELOW:** an off-the-road alternative: the Intracoastal Waterway.

*Myrtle Beach's coastal position and leisure activities makes it one of the most popular resorts on the East Coast.*

**Myrtle Beach** ⓱ is the third most popular tourist resort on the East Coast, after Disney World and Atlantic City. The extraordinary commercialization of the area may well overwhelm you, as the grandly named King's Highway (US 17) consists of mile after mile of high-rise condominium developments, miniature golf courses, and honky-tonk shops dispensing the accessories that go with beach culture. The city's **Boardwalk**, with amusement parks, fast-food stands, and hordes of tourists, is a typical slice of American beach excess. If you must have excitement, try the Corkscrew, a harrowing roller coaster that turns you upside down at oblique angles and over death-defying humps.

For swimming, you're best advised to eschew the crowded strand at Myrtle Beach in favor of less spoiled beaches to the north or south. **Pawley's Island** ⓲ has one particularly beautiful beach where you can enjoy the warm waters and good body-surfing of the Carolina coast minus the throngs and relax in one of the hammocks for which the island is famous.

South of Myrtle Beach on US 17, across the Pee Dee River, lies quieter and more genteel **Georgetown** ⓳. An early failed attempt by the Spanish to settle this coast, it today consists mostly of museums, churches, old homes, and plantations. The **Rice Museum** (tel: 843-546-7423; closed Sun) gives a look at the crop that sustained this area for much of its early history.

## Historic Charleston

**BELOW:** by carriage is an appropriate way to view elegant Charleston.

South again along US 17, you pass over a steep and narrow double set of bridges over the Cooper River before touching down in **Charleston** ⓴. Located on the peninsula formed where the Cooper meets the Ashley River, this was the first permanent settlement in the Carolinas. The prosperity of the city's early days is

reflected in elegant 18th-century homes that fill the residential area south of Broad Street. In fact, this is one of America's top walking cities (more compact Savannah, just to the south, is another). Charleston suffered massive damage when Hurricane Hugo raged onto its shore in 1989, but fortunately the historic district was spared heavy damage. Amble about the cobbled streets at your leisure, taking in the many museums and monuments here.

Map on page 82

## Moss-draped walks

The palmetto-lined **Battery** faces Charleston Harbor and is a good place to begin a walking tour of town. In **White Point Gardens,** you can see gorgeous live oak trees with languid Spanish moss hanging from them. At Number 21 East Battery sits the **Edmondston-Alston House**, built around 1828 by a wealthy wharf owner and decorated in Greek Revival style; it offers an unobstructed view of the harbor. Be sure to sit on the "**joggling board**" located behind the house. This board is 16 feet (5 meters) long and works as a kind of rocking chair; once thought to have therapeutic properties in the cure of rheumatism, the joggling board is also said to prevent spinsterhood – though scientific studies have never been made to test this theory.

The **Nathaniel Russell House,** at 51 Meeting Street, is also worth a visit – quite elegant, with an impressive flying staircase spiraling unsupported to the top. Both these homes are maintained by the Historic Charleston Foundation, a non-profit restoration agency founded in 1947 to protect Downtown's architectural treasures. Informative tours given by the foundation explain the intricacies of design of each home, as well as the histories and customs of the families that have lived in them.

**BELOW:** the palmetto-lined Battery faces Charleston Harbor.

In addition, the Charleston Museum administers tours of the very handsome **Heyward-Washington House** at 87 Church Street and the **Joseph Manigault House** at 350 Meeting Street, both highly regarded as architectural attractions. Perhaps the best way to see Charleston's historic homes in one fell swoop is to visit the city during early spring, when the annual Festival of Houses opens many normally private homes to public walking tours. Watch for classic examples of the "Charleston single house" – long, narrow homes with side piazzas and a marked West Indian influence.

## Slave market

At the **Old Slave Mart Museum** on Chalmers Street you can see, among other items, facsimiles of bills of sale used in the slave trade. "A prime gang of 25 negroes accustomed to the culture of Sea Island Cotton and Rice," reads one placard advertising the upcoming sale of 25 human beings into bondage. It is a startling and sobering museum, especially so when one realizes this heinous practice was still in full swing just a century and a quarter ago. The self-contented opulence south of Broad suddenly appears quite different after a long, thoughtful visit to the slave market.

Charleston is chock-full of historic churches, as well as all its other cultural and social attractions. Two of the more interesting are the **Huguenot Church**, a Gothic structure built by French Protestants, and **St Michael's Episcopal Church** with its 186-foot (57-meter) high steeple. Nearby **Fort Sumter**, site of the Confederate attack on Union forces that touched off the Civil War, is accessible from Charleston Harbor: a 2½-hour tour leaves several times daily from the Municipal Marina.

**BELOW:**
18th-century slave cabins at Boone Hall Plantation.

## Plantations a'plenty

Three plantations in the vicinity of Charleston are also worth a visit if you have the time. **Magnolia Plantation and Gardens** (tel: 843-571-1266; open daily) on Ashley River Road (State Route 61) has beautiful gardens, a children's petting zoo, an 18th-century herb garden, and a 16th-century horticultural maze to lose yourself in. At **Middleton Place** (tel: 843-556-6020; open daily), farther up the road, you can see the oldest landscaped gardens in the country – the result of nearly 10 years' labor by 100 slaves. Just north of Charleston on US 17 is **Mount Pleasant**, and the achingly beautiful avenue of live oak trees featured in the movie version of *Gone With the Wind*. At the end of the drive lies **Boone Hall**, most people's idea of the perfect antebellum residence. In fact, the house was rebuilt only in 1935, but the nine slave cabins are authentic.

After Charleston, follow US 17 south through the so-called "Low Country" toward the Georgia border. Turn onto State 174 for a ride beneath a canopy of oaks, and in 24 miles (39 km) you arrive at **Edisto Island**, a resort community whose commercialism has not yet eliminated its rustic charm. Farther south, turning east onto US 21 from US 17 is **Beaufort** (pronounced *bew-ford*), the second oldest town in South Carolina and one that's still quite compact and attractive. Hollywood movie producers come calling to make use of the gorgeous antebellum waterfront homes as set pieces. Indigo and rice cultivation brought wealth during the 18th century, when most of these houses (some are inns) were constructed. The best way to experience this town is to wander about, enjoying the friendly talk of residents at any one of the seafood restaurants before moving on south again into Georgia and that beautiful "Southern belle" of a city, **Savannah ㉑** *(see page 78).*  ❑

Map on page 82

*The slave cabins at Boone Hall were built of bricks made on the premises; among several other industries the plantation had a working brick and tile yard.*

**BELOW:**
the gardens at Magnolia Plantation date from the 16th century.

# SAVANNAH: FIRST CITY OF GEORGIA

*The port of Savannah is a strange, seductive place – equal parts history, treachery, revelry, and oddity*

**B**est known for its gorgeous, moss-draped live oaks, cobblestone streets, and light, pastel-colored buildings, an air of mystique still hovers over Georgia's original settlement. Savannah is a strange, seductive place – equal parts history, treachery, revelry, and oddity.

The saucy, best-selling book *Midnight in the Garden of Good and Evil* made this city a household name, with a corresponding increase in the city's tourism. Today, a visit is likely to consist of a horse-drawn carriage ride through stately squares, lunch in an outdoor café – and a roaring evening in a gay bar where transvestites waltz across stage.

Founding father James Edward Oglethorpe must be turning in his grave.

In 1733, Oglethorpe received a royal charter to establish "the colony of Georgia in America" – and protect the coast from Spanish Florida while producing wine and silk for the Crown. Oglethorpe laid out a grid of broad thoroughfares, punctuated at regular intervals with two dozen spacious public squares. The 20 that remain have been refurbished, forming the nucleus of Savannah's Historic District – one of the largest urban national historic landmark districts in the United States, and probably the most beautiful. The district is bounded by the Savnnah River to the north and Forsyth Park to the south, covering a 2½-mile (4-km) radius in all.

Each square has a distinctive character; Bull Street, running the length of the district north to south, links some of the most beautiful squares to each other. These squares excel in Savannah's most characteristic details: fancy ironwork and atmospheric Spanish moss. They are also enlivened with daily activity – art vendors, hot dog stands, and street performers. Summer brings free jazz concerts to John Square near the river, but early spring is the best time to visit, when the city's azaleas are in full blossom.

The Historic Savannah Foundation has preserved many of the city's treasures. Anyone interested in history or architecture should see the Owens-Thomas House (124 Abercorn Street), the Hamilton-Turner Mansion at Lafayette Square, and the Cathedral of St John the Baptist, also by Lafayette Square. One of the nation's most beautiful synagogues is located here. Yet another notable structure is Juliette Gordon Low's birthplace at 142 Bull Street, a handsome home that is associated with the founder of the Girl Scouts of America.

Horticulturists should seek out Trustees' Garden on East Broad Street, planted in the 1700s as Georgia's first experimental garden; it is now filled with exotic plants from around the world. Afterward, join a jovial crowd upstairs at Hannah's East, where Emma Kelly, a real-life character from the *Midnight* novel, plays each evening.

Several historic buildings in the next few blocks were designed in Regency style by

English architect William Jay on his arrival in 1817, most notably the Alexander Telfair home (121 Barnard Street) – once the official residence of visiting state governors – and the William Scarbrough house (41 West Broad Street), which once hosted President James Monroe.

But the most talked-about residence in recent memory is Mercer House, located on Monterey Square and built by composer Johnny Mercer's grandfather. This was the home of the late antique dealer Jim Williams, an eccentric millionaire who shot his 22-year-old male companion in 1981. Convicted twice of murder, he was later acquitted; today his sister occupies the house, a magnificent antique-filled structure that is not open to the hordes of tourists drawn to it.

For lunch, stop by Mrs Wilkes' Boarding House on Jones Street. Tucked away between stately homes, her Southern-style restaurant serves up fried chicken, bowls overflowing with fresh vegetables, and bottomless cups of sweet iced tea. Mrs Wilkes' round tables comfortably seat 10 to 12 diners at a time; you'll sit elbow-to-elbow with locals and other Savannah fans.

The Historic District's procession of squares ends nicely in beautiful Forsyth Park, a 31-acre (13-hectare) setting of constant outdoor activity. At the center of the park stands an elaborate fountain.

Savannah's harborside of old brick warehouses and shipping offices have become tourist attractions, reached by a series of steep steps; these are now inns, pubs, restaurants, and gift shops that run the length of River Street.

Walking is the best way to see the city, unless the heat is oppressive, in which case, the Hyatt Regency Hotel and the Savannah Visitors' Center are your best bets for catching a tour bus. You can choose from a wide selection of transportation, from modern mini-buses to horse-drawn carriages.

Leave Downtown by heading east on Victory Drive in the direction of the coastal islands to visit Bonaventure Cemetery, a

luxurious final resting place for Savannah's most distinguished citizens. A former plantation, Bonaventure is wistfully beautiful, dripping with moss and overflowing with azaleas, jasmine, magnolias, and live oak trees. The images on several of the gravestones have become synonymous with both the *Midnight* book and the city itself.

Thunderbolt, 6 miles (10 km) east of Downtown on US 80, is a shrimping and fishing village on the banks of the Intracoastal Waterway. Continue east along US 80 over more bridges to Skidaway and Tybee islands, where the breeze is as fresh as the seafood in the restaurants alongside the water. ❑

LEFT: detail on River Street; one of Savannah's beautifully preserved buildings.
RIGHT: tomb statuary from the cover of *Midnight*; Oglethorpe monument; Mercer House.

# GEORGIA TO THE FLORIDA KEYS

Map on page 82

*Small-town ambiance, a tropical paradise, alligators in the Everglades and the southernmost point in the US highlight the end of the Atlantic Route*

The Georgia coast is one of the Southeast's most interesting natural regions, a string of marshes, largely undeveloped islands, and good beaches rarely sought out by the traveler focused solely on getting through the state via Interstate 95 as quickly as possible. No wonder this region is known locally as the Golden Isles. The inattentive traveler's loss, however, has been others' gain: a number of unusual birds live secreted along this coast, and there are also vestiges of African culture from the dark days when slaves were shipped across the Atlantic to work the plantations of the South.

From Savannah, take Victory Drive (US 17) west out of town, where it shortly becomes Ogeechee Road – and also becomes much more rural in character. About 25 miles (40 km) along, stop in **Midway** ㉒ for a look at the small, whitewashed village church, a copy of the original church erected here in the late 1700s by displaced New Englanders. Get its key from the gas station just beside and take a look around, noting the eerie presence inside of a section that was designated specifically for slaves and a gracefully kept cemetery outside. Adjacent to the church stands the small **Midway Museum** (tel: 912-884-5837; closed Mon), with a collection of period items.

**LEFT:** just in time for dinner.
**BELOW:** barbershop pole in a small Southern town.

## Small town life

Past Riceboro, home to an agricultural research station, the highway passes beneath I-95 again and crosses a bridge over a tidal inlet into McIntosh County. To learn more about the politics, poverty, and small-town intrigue of the county, look for the biting nonfiction book *Praying for Sheetrock*, which won awards for its clear-eyed portrait of local life.

If you make a left just after the bridge onto unnumbered Harris Neck Road, you can find **Harris Neck National Wildlife Refuge**, a pocket of wilderness that was saved from development because a former military airstrip occupied the land. Fishing is the most popular activity here, but you can also drive a one-way dirt loop road for a look at the waterfowl in their natural environs. Just offshore sits St Catherines Island, an off-limits island used as a breeding ground for rare birds and animals by the Brooklyn Zoo.

South again on US 17, make a brief detour onto Georgia 99, which reveals some truly old-fashioned towns and dwellings – shacks, mostly, many them occupied by the modern-day descendants of freed slaves. These small communities – Crescent, Valona, Meridian, Carnigan, and Ridgeville – are fishing and shellfishing communities now.

At **Darien**, rustic Georgia 99 rejoins US 17 again.

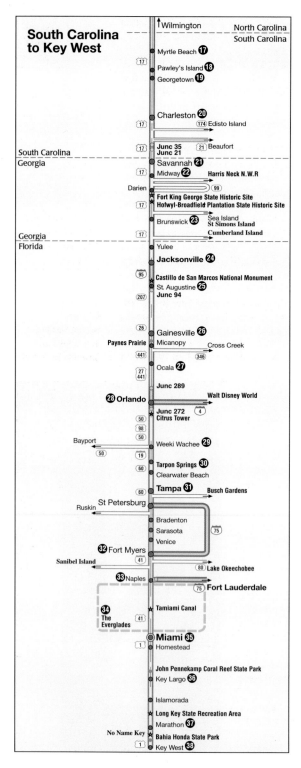

**South Carolina to Key West**

↑Wilmington

North Carolina
South Carolina

Myrtle Beach **17**
17
Pawley's Island **18**
Georgetown **19**

Charleston **20**
17
174 Edisto Island

South Carolina
Georgia
17
Junc 35
Junc 21
21 Beaufort
Savannah **21**
17
Midway **22**
Harris Neck N.W.R
Darien
99
★ Fort King George State Historic Site
17 Hofwyl-Broadfield Plantation State Historic Site
Brunswick **23**
Sea Island
St Simons Island
Cumberland Island

Georgia
Florida
17
Yulee
**Jacksonville 24**
95
Castillo de San Marcos National Monument
★ St Augustine **25**
207
Junc 94

26
Gainesville **26**
Paynes Prairie
Micanopy
Cross Creek
441
346
27
441
Ocala **27**
Junc 289

**28** Orlando
Walt Disney World
50
★ Junc 272
4
Citrus Tower
98
50
Bayport
Weeki Wachee **29**
50
19
60
Tarpon Springs **30**
Clearwater Beach
60
**Tampa 31**
Busch Gardens
Ruskin
St Petersburg
60

Bradenton
Sarasota
75
Venice

**32** Fort Myers
41
Sanibel Island
80 Lake Okeechobee
**33** Naples
75 Fort Lauderdale

**34**
★ Tamiami Canal
The Everglades
41

◎ **Miami 35**
1
Homestead

John Pennekamp Coral Reef State Park
Key Largo **36**

Islamorada

★ Long Key State Recreation Area
Marathon **37**
No Name Key ★ Bahia Honda State Park
1
Key West **38**

The **Fort King George State Historic Site** (tel: 912-437-4770) here recreates a Colonial-era blockhouse; this is where the British first settled Georgia and for a brief period administered to the area .

Five miles (8 km) south, at the mouth of the Altamaha River, sits the **Hofwyl-Broadfield Plantation** (tel: 912-264-7333) – prettifying the story of slavery somewhat as it demonstrates how the know-how of slaves imported from Africa was crucial to the successful cultivation of rice on these islands.

Hold your nose as you enter industrial **Brunswick 23**, a major center for paper and chemical production. Despite its industrial character, Brunswick's Downtown is surprisingly slow-paced and old-Southern, with an attractive grid of streets, homes, and moss-draped live oak trees. One such oak tree, the so-called Lover's Oak, is believed to have stood for hundreds – possibly even close to one thousand – years.

The city is also set on a wide, beautiful (if not exactly pure) marsh immortalized by poet Sidney Lanier as the **"Marshes of Glynn"** (for Glynn County). A turnout facing the marshes has information explaining their formation, which provides an opportunity to stretch your legs, take some snapshots, and pick up lots of tourist information.

## Lush islands

From the marshes, turn east and cross the toll bridge for a look at lush, though somewhat exclusive, **St Simons Island**. Palm fronds, live oak trees, and flowers cover both sides of the road in perpetual green as you drive through the road to the single attractive harborfront, and you might consider staying the night in these restful environs. A museum in the former lighthouse tells the history of coastal Georgia, and there's a good beach out beyond the main settlement. **Sea Island**, an even more exclusive resort reached via another series of roads on the island, possesses beautiful beaches and a world-class golf course.

South again on US 17, you cross more bridges and then pivot inland through tiny towns. At Kingsland, you can make a turnoff to catch the ferry for elegant **Cumberland Island**, one of the most attractive islands in the Georgia chain. Once the exclusive domain of wealthy families, it is now mostly owned by the US government as a "national seashore," meaning there are a small number of rudimentary campsites available to the public. Spirited jockeying for these few camping spots begins well in advance, however, so don't expect to just waltz in and secure one at the last moment.

Map on page 82

## FLORIDA

Crossing the St Marys River, really little more than a tidal inlet, you're greeted with a double row of palm trees and, possibly, the presence of police cars: you have reached Florida. The first town you reach is **Yulee**, named for legislator and entrepreneur David Yulee. Yulee built a railroad from coast to Florida coast, and it thrived for a short time, but politics and the Civil War soon did it in and town is of little consequence today. It isn't very long afterward that the rural roads give way to sprawl, announcing the outskirts of **Jacksonville ㉔**.

*"Tree spirit" on St Simons Island, Georgia.*

Once a crime-ridden backwater, Jacksonville is trying hard to remake itself over as a new urban destination, and corporate headquarters are relocating here to take advantage of the excellent weather and pristine beaches. And there are cultural attractions, too – the town is justly proud of its **Riverwalk** and the associated **Museum of Science and History** (tel: 904-396-6674), for example, while the **Cummer Museum of Art and Gardens** (tel: 904-356-6857; closed Mon) stands amid lush gardens right on the St Johns River.

Still, it's not a place to spend much time. Move on southward on I-95, instead, to the indisputable jewel of northern Florida, a town small enough to explore in

**BELOW:**
wild horses and
Dungeness ruin,
Cumberland Island.

Map on page 82

a day: **St Augustine ㉕**. This town, founded by Spanish explorers in 1565 and later occupied by the British, lays claim to being America's oldest continuously occupied city. Most of downtown's buildings aren't nearly so ancient, but a pleasantly Mediterranean atmosphere has been preserved with narrow alleys, flowers, shops, and Spanish architecture. A number of museums and attractions compete for the traveler's attention – some boasting rather dubious "oldest this" or "oldest that" claims – and there's also a good set of beaches and state parks just across the Lions Bridge, which can be crossed from the center of town.

Several attractions are of special note, including the star-shaped **Castillo de San Marcos** fort (tel: 904-829-6506; open daily), right on the water, which defended the Spanish town from invaders. **Spanish Quarter Village** interprets 18th-century Spanish life with blacksmiths, woodworkers, and the like. A series of buildings constructed by oil and railroad magnate Henry Flagler are notable, particularly the **Memorial Presbyterian Church** that Flagler built as a memorial to his daughter. Finally, note the huge round **zero milestone** across the road from the visitors' center: this stone marks the endpoint in a string of Spanish missions that once stretched to San Diego.

## Sweet potatoes and greens

From St Augustine, head southwest out of town on Florida 207, passing beneath the interstate and then through fields of sweet potatoes, cabbages, and greens – you are back in deep-southern farm country – across the broad St Johns River. The route passes Newnans Lake and comes directly into **Gainesville ㉖**, home to the University of Florida. As a result, there are a number of gardens and nature trails, not to mention a good choice of restaurants and cultural offerings, within city limits.

**BELOW:** Castillo de San Marcos, St Augustine, Florida.

US 441 exits the city south, shortly cutting right through the middle of **Paynes Prairie State Preserve**, a huge expanse of marsh and grassland bridged by the four-lane highway. The preserve is home to rare bison and cranes, among other creatures, and you can get a glimpse at some of them from a high wooden viewing tower. Or take one of the park-sponsored tours. Just south is tiny **Micanopy**, a town of dirt roads and simple buildings – an anomaly, something like what the old Florida must have looked.

For an even closer look at the state's recent past, take State Route 346 a few miles east, then follow signs south along Route 325 for a look at **Cross Creek** – a tiny town, not even a town, really, but rather a place strongly identified with Florida author Marjorie Kinnan Rawlings. You can tour Rawlings' former home, where she penned *The Yearling* and endured a tough life of farming and ranching, then dine, if you like, in a fine upscale restaurant on the premises. Highway 441 continues south through horse country to **Ocala ㉗**, a small Southern market town with a square and old-fashioned eateries. From Ocala, US 441 get busy and inches through quiet lake towns, lush citrus groves, and sharp-smelling juice-processing plants. Soon enough you enter the extensive suburbs announcing the most improbable Florida success story of all, **Orlando ㉘** *(see page 85)*.

# ORLANDO: THE WORLD'S BEST PLAYGROUND

*Not long ago, Orlando was just another agricultural town. Now it's Florida's best success story, a transformation made possible by a cartoon mouse*

The most obvious attraction at Orlando is just southwest of the city. Walt Disney World (tel: 407-934-7639; open daily), with its vast complex of entertainments divided into four sections, is thronged year-round by American and international tourists alike.

The Magic Kingdom, which is the amusement component, was Mickey Mouse's domain and the original facility. It still remains the most popular with visitors of all ages, and is divided into four distinctive theme areas – Tomorrowland, Adventureland, Fantasyland, and Frontierland.

Housed inside a glittering "geospherical" dome, the Future World exhibits at EPCOT Center, the second part of the Disney complex, provide an invigorating look at science past, present, and future. The other half of EPCOT is its World Showcase, where you can "travel the world" in less than a day through a variety of cultural (and culinary) attractions.

Rides and tours in the Disney-MGM Studios portion of the Disney World experience. give a closer look at "show business," with perspectives as seen from both sides of the cameras. Disney's Animal Kingdom, a recent addition to the Mickey Mouse empire, invites visitors to explore the world of animals on a safari, in a prehistoric world, and at special stage shows held throughout the day.

Not far from Disney World – but a completely separate entity – is Universal Studios Florida (tel: 407-363-8000; open daily). Opened the same year as Disney-MGM's facility, this attraction offers a similar experience: a chance to learn more about live television and film production, with a number of exciting movie-themed rides thrown in as well. Look for the spotlights just west of Interstate 4.

There are dozens of similar amusements scattered about the greater Orlando area. Water slides, weird museums, and amusement park rides are especially prevalent, and kids will go crazy with joy as parents just go crazy.

The most intriguing non-Disney or movie-related spot in the area, however, isn't within the city limits at all, but is definitely worth traveling the few extra miles to see.

About 40 miles (70 km) to the east, on a sandy stretch known as Cape Canaveral, the Kennedy Space Center (tel: 321-452-2121; open daily) provides a fascinating up-close look at the workings of America's space program. If you're lucky, your visit will coincide with a space shuttle or rocket launch, but even when it doesn't, you can still tour the same runways, training areas, assembly buildings, and launch pads that NASA uses to prepare the crafts – and their crews – for flight. ❑

**LEFT:** Mickey's Kingdom; NASA space exhibit.
**RIGHT:** EPCOT Center; Universal Studios, Florida.

*Marmalade from local oranges makes a great gift.*

**BELOW:**
locally caught sponges for sale, Tarpon Springs.

## SOUTH FLORIDA

The vast majority of those travelers heading out from Orlando use the interstates and toll roads, but for more of the real Florida take the state highways awhile longer. Florida 50 (also called West Colonial Drive) leaves Orlando's city center and cuts due west, shedding the suburbs. In about 15 miles (25 km) you come to Clermont, singular for its drab but undeniably tall **Citrus Tower** – a slightly odd testament to the oranges, grapefruits, lemons, and limes for which this state is so well known. You can pay to ride an elevator 23 stories to the top if you fancy a view of the surrounding lakes and hills.

Florida 50 now passes through the limestone spine of central Florida – a land of scrubby trees and prickly plants, sand dunes, citrus groves heavy with fruit in mid-winter, golf courses, even cowboys working cattle herds. Backroad stands sell everything from bovine medicine to boiled peanuts, a local specialty that makes a starchy, salty mess and is definitely an acquired taste.

The route continues west, brushing the edge of Withlacoochee State Forest before arriving at whimsically named **Weeki Wachee** ㉙, a town famous with tourists for its natural warm-water spring – and the water park, cruise facility, zoo, and other attractions that have "sprung" up around it. It all requires a certain sense of humor and tolerance for excess to enjoy properly.

If you're in a hurry to get a glimpse of the **Gulf of Mexico**, press west a few additional miles to tiny **Bayport** with its picnic area overlooking the water. Otherwise, turn south down US 19 and prepare for a spell of thick four-lane traffic and plenty of stoplights. During early spring, this area is home to the training grounds for a number of major league baseball teams.

It's 30 miles (50 km) down US 19 to the junction with Alt-19. Take Alt-19 to **Tarpon Springs** ㉚, a harbor community that is fascinating not for its physical appearance but its population: the town is largely Greek. Greeks originally settled this area to dive for the sponges that live abundantly in the warm surrounding seas, and today local shops and restaurants continue to reflect this heritage.

Past Dunedin, take Florida 60 west across the causeway to **Clearwater Beach**, a relaxed town of seafood restaurants and beach homes. It's a fine place to swim in warm water and lie on the beautiful – and public – white sand beaches.

Turn south down the beach road (which eventually becomes Florida 699), crossing several short toll bridges linking the various sandbars. You will pass through more waterfront towns, most with excellent sand but some too overdeveloped for their own good. The finest beach on the entire string is probably the southernmost one, **Passe-a-Grille Beach**, some 20 miles (30 km) of slow driving onward from Clearwater. Gawk at the huge and expensive pink **Don Cesar Hotel**, an Art Deco masterpiece right beside the blue Gulf waters, then hit the sand.

Downtown **St Petersburg** is strangely vacant for stretches, with long blocks of cheap package stores and adult dance clubs, but in the central downtown district on Third Street you will find the interesting **Salvador Dalí Museum** (tel: 727-823-3767; open daily), which displays hundreds of the artist's paintings – without

Map on page 82

question the central cultural attraction of the city. East across Tampa Bay via either I-275 or US 92, and set right on the water facing St Pete, is sprawling **Tampa ③**. This city's Cuban influence is nowhere clearer than in **Ybor City**, with its concentration of Cuban diners and cigar manufacturers. Ybor City was built on empty scrub by a local cigar maker in the late 1800s, and soon became not just a manufacturing center but also the city's most swashbuckling quarter; while yuppies have clearly discovered the place, converting many former factories into brewpubs and the like, Spanish is still the language of the streets.

Be a little bit careful here if you come after dark, but be sure to sample the extremely vibrant nightlife and good restaurants. Other city attractions include a full February slate of events, kicked off by a wild Mardi Gras-like parade, and Tampa Bay itself – best viewed during a stroll along the sidewalk arcing around upscale Bayshore Boulevard.

## Frolicking manatees

Most visitors to Tampa also make a visit to **Busch Gardens** (tel: 888-800-5447; open daily), a slightly strange amusement park with an African-exploration theme that seems contrived. The park does feature heart-dropping roller coasters, water slides, and simulated rapids, however, not to mention world-famous performances of water ballet, waterskiing skills, and the like.

Take US 41 south out of Tampa, stopping a moment outside **Ruskin** where the Little Manatee River empties into the bay. As you'd expect from the name, you can sometimes find manatees frolicking at this inlet in winter, when they swim here to enjoy the warm water.

US 41 plunges due south through strings of heavily built-up towns and cities, many catering to elderly retirees. A much faster route would take the parallel Interstate 75.

**Bradenton** and **Sarasota** are next, twin cities on the Gulf of Mexico, offering very favorable weather, spring baseball, and more good sandy beaches with warm ocean water. The beaches continue, in fact, through Siesta Key and Casey Key to **Venice** and beyond. The highway circles around Charlotte Harbor and crosses the Caloosahatchee River into well-known **Fort Myers ③**. The mild climate has made this a popular winter resort town for a very long time; Northerners Thomas Edison and Henry Ford were neighbors on the riverfront, for example, and you can tour both their adjacent winter homes on one combined ticket. The highlight is a museum collecting some of Edison's inventions. If you're in a mood to do some seashell collecting (known here as "shelling"), follow signs over the toll bridge to **Sanibel Island.**

Sanibel may offer the finest shell collecting in all of America. Devotees come out here so often that someone coined a phrase to describe the parade of hunched-over collectors inspecting the backwash of each wave for new finds: they call this posture the "Sanibel stoop". You can expect to find a number of brightly colored shells here in the balmy surf, not to mention fossilized shark's teeth as well.

The route continues south to exclusive **Naples ③**, haunt of the rich and the beautiful. Now you have a

**BELOW:** head over heels in Busch Gardens, Tampa.

choice of routes east between **Alligator Alley**, as the high-speed toll route of Interstate 75 is known, or else older US 41 farther south, cutting alongside the **Tamiami Canal** that connects the Atlantic Ocean with the Gulf of Mexico.

## The Everglades

US 41 goes on for miles and miles through the quiet heart of Florida, passing no towns at all save the occasional gas station. There are no towns because you are slowly penetrating the **Everglades** ㉞, a vast pocket of swampland partially protected by law and difficult, in any case, to build on.

This strange landscape is home to alligators, poisonous snakes, sinuous blackwater creeks overhung by lush vegetation, and probably a few desperado-like characters too; it also supplies the bulk of the drinking water to greater Miami. Authors, including Marjory Stoneman Douglas and Peter Matthiessen, have written about the unique people and creatures here in books like *River of Grass* and *Killer Mister Watson*, but the place to this day remains somewhat inscrutable. Bear in mind carefully all warnings about the sun, snakes, stinging insects, reptiles, navigation, and other potential troubles: it's a tricky place to spend a few days, but intensely rewarding, too.

Midway through the 'Glades you encounter a sliver of the **Miccosukee Indian Reservation**, a bit depressing for its hawking of cheap goods and casino gambling; there is no sign at all of heroic Seminole warriors like Osceola, who outfoxed Federal troops in these endless swamps for more than a year rather than surrender to a government that had broken treaties and promises and spilled his people's blood. Just a few miles east, the Parks Service has constructed a loop road at **Shark Valley** that can only be toured by bicycle or tram. The tour

**TIP**

The best way to explore the Everglades is to rent a canoe or boat, or get in touch with one of the licensed outfitters who also provide guides. Seeing this exotic place only from land does not do justice to its mystery.

**BELOW:**
fish, coral, and sponges taking over a ship's hull.

## LAKE OKEECHOBEE

A 58-mile (93-km) drive along SR 80 from Fort Myers brings you to Lake Okeechobee and its 750 sq miles (1,940 sq km) of crystal waters. Florida's largest lake is as beautiful as it is sad; the lake reflects the damage being done to the sensitive Everglades' environment by the booming population of Florida. The water from Lake Okeechobee once fed the wide shallow river of the Everglades, but dikes, pumping stations, and canals were constructed to tame this dramatic lake and its flooding waters. While this has made the surrounding area an agricultural paradise (the area produces enough sugar to supply 15 million Americans' sweet tooth for an entire year), the projects have brought ecological hardships to the surrounding environment. Both the Everglades and South Florida's cities have been threatened with drought by the dwindling water level of the lake. Excessive pumping of the Everglades' mother waters for the booming population along the Gold Coast is also sucking it dry. Still a popular destination for anglers, fish camps punctuate the lake's perimeter. Okeechobee, the largest town on the north shore of the lake, is the best base if you want to explore the area. Boat trips can be easily arranged.

terminates at an observation tower that allows unhindered views out over miles of the southern Everglades. Sitting here in the humid silence, it's a bit odd to consider how you're a mere half-hour's drive from the hustle, bustle, and danger of downtown; you somehow feel safer here, among the vines and snakes, than you will there.

**Map on page 82**

## FLORIDA KEYS

If you want to hold off diving into downtown **Miami** ㉟ *(see page 92)* – or are already there and want to make an escape to another type of landscape altogether – by all means get yourself down to the **Florida Keys**. This 100-mile (160-km) string of islands forms the end of the line for the north-to-south traveler, and they are one of the most distinctive places in the USA. The Keys' tropical climate and physical isolation mean you will find birds and fish here that live nowhere else in the land, plus a landscape in which water is never far away and a system of good state parks from which to enjoy it all. Even the light is different here, a mysterious, turquoise shade of blue that reflects off everything it touches. It is a wonder, really, that these disparate islands are connected to each other or the mainland at all. Yet a series of 42 highway bridges does indeed bridge the many gaps between land and water.

From Miami, US 1 proceeds south through **Homestead**, a quiet community that was demolished by the winds of Hurricane Andrew in August 1992 – one of the most powerful hurricanes to strike North America, although loss of life was low. A branch road here, Florida 9336, leads through a wild section of Everglades National Park that terminates on Florida Bay, but it's a long side trip down and back. Skip it if you're hurrying to see the Keys.

**BELOW:** the Overseas Highway, Florida Keys.

## Key information

US 1 enters the Keys as the Overseas Highway at **Key Largo** ㊱, immortalized in the Humphrey Bogart/Lauren Bacall film of the same name (which wasn't actually filmed here), and right away you get an opportunity to view the sea up-close. At **John Pennekamp Coral Reef State Park**, one of the most popular parks in Florida, you can gaze through glass-bottomed boats at the most incredible formations of coral reef beneath the surface of the sea, a living ecosystem that is easily harmed by contact with boats or humans. Equally compelling are the fish and shellfish swimming and living throughout the reef. Key Largo is also home to what is probably the world's only undersea lodge, Jules'.

If this reef is the best place to see the nature of the Keys, the next park, **Long Key State Recreation Area**, some 30-odd miles (50 km) farther along US 1, is your best bet for a swim or reclining in the sun before proceeding west. Stop midway between the two parks for a bite at **Manny and Isa's**, a longstanding, popular Cuban diner in **Islamadora** that is famous for its Key Lime pie.

For a lesson on what made the Keys into such a unique place, journey 20 more miles (30 km) beyond Long Key to the best museum in the region, the **Museum of Natural History of the Florida Keys** (tel: 305-743-9100) in the resort town of **Marathon** ㊲. Marathon itself is more like a big town than an island paradise, and is best used for stocking up on supplies.

The mangrove forests thicken beyond here, and the touristic accoutrements begin to slip away as nature begins reclaiming the westernmost islands. You'll get plenty of water views on both sides of the car now as you cross **Seven Mile Bridge**, landing briefly on beautiful **No Name Key** and its **Bahia Honda State Recreation Area** – yet another wonderful state-run park.

Please Do Not Feed the Crocodiles. THEY MIGHT BITE!

*Florida wildlife is not for feeding.*

**BELOW:** Jules' Undersea Lodge, Key Largo.

## Key West

You cross more bridges still, landing on **Big Pine Key**, **Sugarloaf Key**, and **Looe Key**, each with its own personality and laid-back seafood eateries. The pace, too, downshifts almost to a crawl as you meet former stockbrokers owning T-shirt shops and the like. Eventually the highway touches land for the final time, coming to rest upon balmy **Key West ⑱**, last island in the chain – and also the name of the town here that has been drawing interesting characters for a very long time. Today it's a mixture of fishermen, retirees, Cubans, and tourist tack, as well as a thriving gay and lesbian population.

The writer Ernest Hemingway lived here, and purveying "Papa's" image has become one of the town's hottest cottage industries. To get a taste of how he lived, visit the **Ernest Hemingway Home and Museum** (tel: 305-294-1575), where Hemingway wrote for a decade; notable are the gardens he personally tended and the cats that overrun the place. As tour guides will tell you, they are all descendants of the writer's own cats. The bars lining **Duval Street**, including several once frequented by Hemingway, are a lively refreshment spot, and the Hemingway look-alike contest held every year is a highlight of a noisy social season that is busy to begin with.

The two most popular sights in town, however, are both free. The first is **Mallory Square Dock**, where residents and tourists alike have been turning out every night for decades to cheer the beautiful sunsets over the water. The other free attraction is also a good one: the brightly colored buoy that marks the **southernmost point** in the continental 48 states. Locals claim that on a very clear night you can even faintly make out the lights of Cuba, lying less than 100 miles (160 km) away. ❑

Map on page 82

TURTLE XING

*Help a turtle cross the street by slowing down in your car.*

**BELOW:**
Key West
guest house.

# A SHORT STAY IN MIAMI

*Sensual and warm, spicy and seductive, Miami appeals to the visitor who is longing for escape. Here's a list of the not-to-be-missed attractions:*

◆ Coral Gables is an enchanting Mediterranean-style city, home to the glorious Biltmore Hotel (1926) and the Venetian Pool, sometimes called "the most beautiful swimming hole in the world."

◆ The largest tropical garden in the US, Coral Gables' Fairchild Tropical Garden maintains an outstanding collection of tropical flowering trees, and more than 5,000 ferns, plants, and orchids.

◆ Coconut Grove is a vibrant, eclectic neighborhood of funky houses, dense natural greenery, and good shopping at Coco Walk.

◆ I.M. Pei designed the futuristic International Place, a 47-story building in downtown Miami that changes color at the flick of a switch.

◆ Bayside Marketplace is a flashy outdoor arcade full of neon signs and impulse items.

◆ Lummus Park combines the oldest structures in Miami (the William English Slave Plantation House and the William Wagner House) with a white-sand beach stretching along the coastline.

◆ Little Haiti is home to immigrants from the Caribbean island of Haiti. The area offers great food and an encounter with a rich culture.

◆ Key Biscayne, an island paradise connected by bridge, offers many water-related recreations, like jet-skiing, windsurfing and, of course, lying on your back under the sun.

◆ Metrozoo has lots of tropical wildlife, with wild animals from Africa, Asia, and Australia. The zoo area is divided into little animal kingdom islands connected by bridges.

**For visitors interested in staying longer in the big city, pick up a copy of *Insight Guide: Miami*. This is a companion to the present volume, and is packed with insightful text and stunning pictures.**

▷ **ART DECO DISTRICT**
Stars, models and wannabes flock to the pastel-colored fantasy buildings in South Beach, which have now been converted into hotels, restaurants, bars and shops.

△ **DECO DETAIL**
In 1979, the 500 playful buildings with their colorful frills constructed in the 1930s became the youngest historic district in the United States.

△ **SEAQUARIUM**
Dolphins, porpoises, sea lions and a killer whale are among the mammals that perform at the Miami Seaquarium, a bay-front marine park dedicated to the preservation of sea life.

▷ **CUBAN CIGAR FACTORY**
Visit a cigar factory, brush up on your Spanish, eat spicy Caribbean food and stroll through Little Havana, the US's most highly concentrated neighborhood of Cubans.

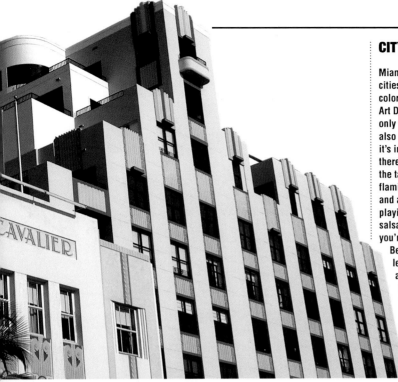

## CITY OF FANTASY

Miami is everything other cities are not – pastel colors, swaying palms and Art Deco balconies are not only easy on the eye, but also kind to the disposition: it's impossible to fret when there's a fizzy cocktail on the table, a pink plastic flamingo on the counter, and a three-piece band playing loud and sassy salsa in your eardrums. If you're staying in South Beach, you can also leave your car behind and stretch those weary legs before getting them tanned on the sandy beach across the street. Miami has a lot of things worth discovering. But don't forget the sunscreen.

▽ Red arrows on the map indicate routes from the city detailed in this book

△ VIZCAYA MUSEUM
It may look like an old Italian country villa, but Vizcaya and its fantastic gardens are only about 100 years old.

▷ MIAMI BEACH
The beaches and bronzed, beautiful people of Miami have been attracting tourists since the 1920s.

## Important Information

**Population:**
400,000
**Dialing code:**
305
**Website:**
miamiandbeaches.com

**Tourist information:**
Convention & Visitors
Bureau, 701 Bricknell
Avenue, Suite 2700,
FL 33131
Tel: 305-539-3000

# THE NORTHERN ROUTE

*A detailed guide from east to west, with principal sites
clearly cross-referenced by number to the maps*

This northern route across the US is framed on either side by one of the nation's most interesting cities and some of its most unspoiled lands. On the road between Boston and Washington state's Olympic Peninsula you will encounter a collage of farmlands, ranches, wilderness, port towns, declining industrial cities, reborn urban centers, and constant reminders of the nation's history.

The first half of the journey is largely marked and guided by water. From Boston, you follow the Atlantic coast through the best of New England up to Maine; later, from the Albany area, your route will swing west alongside the once-busy, now-dormant Erie Canal.

The Great Lakes dominate the next portion of the trip, including Chicago, the great midwestern crossroads, and a city of marvelous architecture at the southern tip of Lake Michigan. From here to the thriving twin cities of Minneapolis and St Paul the tour is never far from water, most significantly when it runs right beside the mighty Mississippi for a beautiful, scenic stretch.

Once you reach western Minnesota, however, the character of the land begins to change and water becomes scarce indeed. As you cut across South Dakota, the geography overwhelms: rising out of the prairie are the otherworldly Badlands, the Black Hills, and Wounded Knee, a reminder of the nation's brutal treatment of Native Americans. Along a legendary stagecoach route, come towns of the notorious Wild West that were once inhabited by the likes of Wild Bill Hickok, Calamity Jane, and Buffalo Bill Cody. The sky here is huge and the land seems vast, populated mainly by small buttes, sagebrush, cattle, and deer. The route through Wyoming and Montana passes the site of General Custer's last stand against the Indians.

From here the tour passes into the northern portion of the Rocky Mountains, where the main attractions are the gorgeous national parks. Crossing the Continental Divide on paths previously traveled by mountain tribes, gold prospectors, and homesteaders, the route cuts through the forests, lakes, and buffalo reserves of Montana, the Idaho panhandle, and into the state of Washington, where the land modulates between deserts, canyons, and irrigated farmland.

The final portion of the route runs westward toward the Pacific Ocean like a river, west to Seattle and the Olympic Peninsula. Suddenly water is abundant again, almost pervasive, as you enter America's only rainforest. This is among the nation's most remote and wildly beautiful spots, an ideal place to reflect upon your just-completed trans-American journey. ❑

**PRECEDING PAGES:** Grand Teton National Park, Wyoming; covered bridge and grazing cattle, Vermont.
**LEFT:** ready to hit the open range.

# A SHORT STAY IN BOSTON

*The many colleges in this historic and attractive city ensure it retains a youthful, vibrant outlook. Here's a list of the not-to-be-missed attractions:*

◆ A full-scale replica of the *Brig Beaver II* sits in the harbor at the Boston Tea Party Ship and Museum, commemorating the 1773 dunking of taxed tea from Britain, an incident that fueled the flames of the American Revolution.

◆ Built in 1676, the Paul Revere House is the oldest residence in downtown Boston; Revere lived here from 1770 to 1800. Exhibits include the saddlebags the patriot used on his famous midnight ride to warn of a British attack.

◆ On July 4, 1795, Massachusetts Governor Samuel Adams and Paul Revere laid the cornerstone for the "new" State House. The building overlooks Boston Common and can be explored on a (free) guided tour.

◆ The oldest botanical garden in America, the Public Garden is Boston's prettiest green space. The focus is the lagoon, surrounded by willow trees and crossed by a mock suspension bridge.

◆ Constructed in 1826, Quincy Market served for almost 150 years as a distribution center for meat and produce. Now restored, it houses foodstalls, restaurants, shops and a flower market.

◆ Opened in 1895, the Boston Public Library is designed in the Renaissance Revival style. The interior includes murals by John Singer Sargent; the courtyard is reminiscent of 16th-century Italy.

◆ The Isabella Stewart Gardner Museum has many architectural elements, from Venetian window frames to Roman mosaic floor tiles. The galleries hold paintings by Titian, Raphael, Degas and Rembrandt.

For visitors interested in staying longer in the big city, pick up a copy of *Insight Guide: Boston*. This is a companion to the present volume, and is packed with insightful text and stunning pictures.

▷ **CHARLES RIVER BASIN**
The Back Bay, with the Salt and Pepper Bridge, named for its four recognizable towers. The cleaning and greening of the basin changed the area.

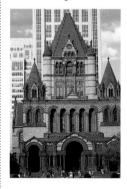

△ **TRINITY CHURCH**
Designed by H.H. Richardson in 1872, the church is one of the finest ecclesiastical buildings in the US. Stained-glass windows are by La Farge.

◁ **THE OLD STATE HOUSE**
The lion and unicorn on the facade, symbols of British royalty, recall the days when th first governors resided here.

▽ **USS CONSTITUTION**
Known as "Old Ironsides," the ship emerged victorious from all 40 of the battles she fought. She is now berthed in Charlestown Navy Yard.

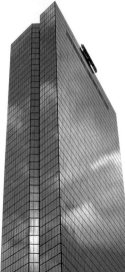

◁ **JOHN HANCOCK TOWER**
At 740 feet (222 meters), the tower is Boston's tallest building. There's a rooftop observatory and great views of the city from the top.

## THE BACK BAY CITY

"I have learned never to argue with a Bostonian," said poet Rudyard Kipling in the early 1900s, and that is still true now. By American standards, Boston is old. Cobbled streets lit by gas-lamps; National Historic Landmarks; individual buildings of great stature and charm. A couple of decades ago, Boston was in danger of becoming a museum of living history, forever trapped in its 1700s and 1800s heyday. Then a change took place: the basin was cleaned, the buildings washed and, due to the high-tech industries of nearby Cambridge, businesses began to flock back. Boston is booming again, so go check it out. And no arguing.

**MUSEUM OF FINE ARTS**
The permanent collection includes works from Asia and Egypt, along with American and European fine art.

**WITCHES CROSS HERE**
The nearby town of Salem is famous for its witch trials of 1692. Salem was also a busy port in the 1700s.

## Important Information

**Population:**
555,000
**Dialing code:**
617
**Website:**
www.bostonusa.com

**Tourist information:**
Greater Boston C&V
2 Copley Place, Suite
105, MA 02116
Tel: 617-536-4100
Fax: 617-424-7664

▽ Red arrows on the map indicate routes from the city detailed in this book

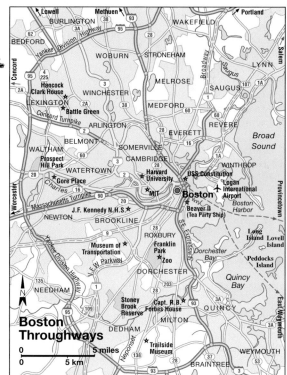

Boston Throughways

0   5 miles
0   5 km

# BOSTON TO BUFFALO

*Take a drive through the prettiest parts of New England
before beginning a coast-to-coast trek to the West,
starting with the old route of the Erie Canal*

Map
on page
104

**B**eginning in downtown **Boston ❶** *(see page 100)*, the Northern route across the United States starts out by visiting "suburban Boston." This is accomplished by crossing the Charles River into busy **Cambridge ❷**. Cambridge's combination of old-fashioned leafy streets, active squares, and buzzing student life make it one of Greater Boston's most interesting areas. The activity focuses around triangular **Harvard Square** and more rough-and-tumble but no less vibrant **Central Square**. While here, explore the quiet brick buildings and carefully manicured greens of **Harvard University**, the second-oldest educational institution in the land; it was chartered back in 1636 and remains one of the finest universities in America, with a number of good museums on the quiet campus.

The city's beautifully kept **Mount Auburn Cemetery** is worth seeing, as well; its peaceful grounds harbor the remains of such artistic luminaries as Henry Longfellow, Oliver Wendell Holmes, and Winslow Homer.

Keep following signs for 2A, a scenic route that leads out from Massachusetts Avenue into quieter towns. You soon come to **Arlington**, now suburban and high-tech but once a textile community where retreating British soldiers skirmished with local residents known as "Minutemen" – they were said to have been ready at a minute's notice to fight – in April of 1775 as the British backtracked along this road.

## Paul Revere's ride

At **Lexington**, about 10 miles (16 km) outside Boston proper, turn off 2A into the downtown area for a look at the town green, the main stage of the Battle of Lexington on that fateful April night. A number of statues and monuments commemorate this spirited American defense of their town, considered critical in turning the tide of the American Revolution; silversmith Paul Revere rode his horse here from Boston under cover of night to warn the residents of a British attack. There are also several old taverns in the area, one of which – Munroe Tavern – served as the makeshift British hospital and command center during the battle.

Continue west along 2A, where American Revolution events are further cataloged in the now-peaceful **Minute Man National Historical Park**, which occupies both sides of the highway in a green patch just northwest of the village green.

**Concord**, the next town, is another significant site. This town was a center of literature and philosophy during the 19th century, as evidenced by such prominent residents as Ralph Waldo Emerson, Henry David Thoreau, and Louisa May Alcott, among others. Alcott's former home, **Orchard House** (tel: 978-369-4118; open daily), where she wrote *Little Women*, is

**LEFT:** New England pumpkin patch dressed for Halloween.
**BELOW:** fall in Vermont.

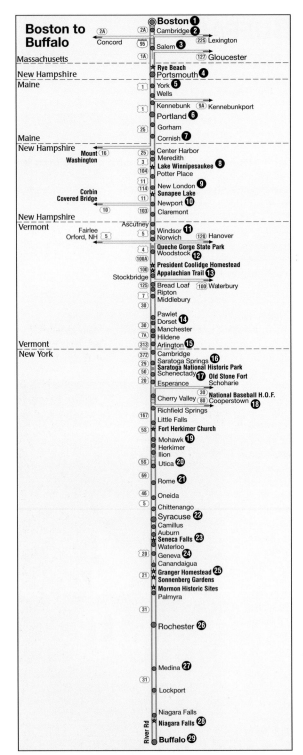

**Boston to Buffalo**

Massachusetts

New Hampshire

Maine

Maine
New Hampshire

New Hampshire
Vermont

Vermont
New York

Boston **1**
Cambridge **2**
Salem **3**
Gloucester
Rye Beach
Portsmouth **4**
York **5**
Wells
Kennebunk · Kennebunkport
Portland **6**
Gorham
Cornish **7**
Center Harbor
Meredith
Lake Winnipesaukee **8**
Potter Place
New London **9**
Sunapee Lake
Newport **10**
Claremont
Windsor **11**
Norwich · Hanover
Quechee Gorge State Park
Woodstock **12**
President Coolidge Homestead
Appalachian Trail **13**
Bread Loaf · Waterbury
Ripton
Middlebury
Pawlet
Dorset **14**
Manchester
Hildene
Arlington **15**
Cambridge
Saratoga Springs **16**
Saratoga National Historic Park
Schenectady · Old Stone Fort
Esperance · Schoharie
Cherry Valley · National Baseball H.O.F.
Cooperstown **18**
Richfield Springs
Little Falls
Fort Herkimer Church
Mohawk **19**
Herkimer
Ilion
Utica **20**
Rome **21**
Oneida
Chittenango
Syracuse **22**
Camillus
Auburn
Seneca Falls **23**
Waterloo
Geneva **24**
Canandaigua
Granger Homestead **25**
Sonnenberg Gardens
Mormon Historic Sites
Palmyra
Rochester **26**
Medina **27**
Lockport
Niagara Falls
Niagara Falls **28**
Buffalo **29**

first as you approach town, on the right. **Emerson House** (tel: 978-369-2236; closed in winter) comes next, less than half a mile beyond on the left, with items from the life and work of the influential Transcendentalist thinker.

From the center of town, take Walden Street south a short distance to visit **Walden Pond Reservation,** a testament to Henry Thoreau's life, work, and unique viewpoint. Thoreau built a simple cabin beside this pond in 1845 and lived there for a time, later writing *Walden* about the experience. "I went to the woods because I wished to live deliberately," he proclaimed, emerging with a view of nature as teacher – rather than slave – of man, and though the book sold poorly in his time it has since become one of the enduring classics of American literature. The pond isn't nearly as peaceful as it was in his time, but you can still get a sense of what Thoreau must have felt.

## ENTERING NEW ENGLAND

Before leaving Boston bound for the wild West, it's worth a short detour north first through the splendors of back-road New England, where America began and a delightful small-town neighborliness can still be felt today.

Begin, then, by heading north from downtown Boston on State Route 1A (North Street from Downtown) towards **Salem 3**. This sea town was one of the earliest capitals of the Massachusetts Bay Colony, and is filled with period captain's homes and the like. It's more famous, though, for the **Salem Witch Trials** that began in 1692, an attempt to root out suspected witchcraft among local women and children; nearly two dozen were killed during the height of the frenzy – a symbol, ever after, for misplaced persecution. (The term "witch hunt," broadly applied to political activities, remains in the American lexicon today.) The popular **Salem Witch Museum** (tel: 978-744-1692; open daily), beside the city's large central green, offers an explanation of the trials. Writer Nathaniel Hawthorne was born in one of the houses on the **House of the Seven Gables Historic Site** (tel: 978-

744-0991; open daily), on the city waterfront nearby; the famed gabled house about which he later penned the well-known novel is also there; its "official" name is the Turner-Ingersoll Mansion.

Route 1A heads due north from Salem and continues on a scenic track through salt marshes, small drawbridges, farmland, and little fishing and commuter towns such as Ipswich, Rowley, and Newbury. Along the way, you may wish to detour east to **Gloucester**, the entrance to lovely Cape Ann and home port to large numbers of fishing and whale-watching boats.

## NEW HAMPSHIRE AND MAINE

After entering **New Hampshire**, 1A frees itself from ticky-tacky beach development to reveal the Atlantic itself at **Rye Beach** – your first true glimpse of the open ocean on this tour. Continue a few miles to **Portsmouth ❹**, New Hampshire's most attractive city and one with a salty taste.

Originally known as Strawberry Banke for the wild fruits covering the ground, Portsmouth was ideally situated at the meeting place of a river mouth and the ocean; founded in 1630, it has been a fishing and shipping center ever since. Fine old seamen's homes still crowd the downtown area, and while designer coffeeshops and microbreweries are rapidly crowding out the old salts – this is only an hour's commute from Boston, remember – you can still find good clam chowder in the local diners.

North across the Piscataqua River and its bridges lies **Maine**, the "Pine Tree State." Pull off busy US 1 after 6 miles (10 km) to visit **York ❺**, Maine's first settlement, which possesses a clutch of old buildings (including an old jail) by the waterfront, all connected by a coastal walking track. Most visitors come,

Map on page 104

*The Massachusetts port of Gloucester was the setting for* The Perfect Storm, *the best-selling book and movie of the same name. The story was based on a real-life tragedy, when several local fishermen died at sea.*

**BELOW:** night-time in a small New England town.

however, for the long stretch of good beach known as **Long Sands**, framed at one end by a much-photographed lighthouse, the Cape Neddick Light Station, known locally as **Nubble Light**. Buy exceptional homemade ice cream in the summer months from a long-running family business just uphill of the famous beacon; choose between apple pie, checkerberry (a New England berry tasting of wintergreen), or Danish cream flavors if they're in stock.

North again on US 1, **Wells** is a fairly forgettable beach town, but just north lies the **Wells Estuarine Reserve** – a protected section of marshland on the sea. Its presence commemorates scientist Rachel Carson, whose books about the ocean, songbirds, and ecology changed the way Americans thought about the natural world.

## Upper crust

Farther north you hit the Kennebunks, two towns physically joined at the hip by a bridge but quite different in character. **Kennebunk** is more workaday, with an exclusive beach several miles east, while **Kennebunkport** is a slice of quaint, upper-crust New England – all gift shops, designer beers, and fish houses, a bit rich for the blood. Former president George Bush's family compound stands among dramatic shore rocks and crashing waves east of Downtown.

It's 20 more slow miles (38 km) north along US 1 (or you can pay to take Interstate 95) to **Portland ❻**, the state's largest city and cultural center, if rather a humdrum place. At least there's a good collection of beaches, parks, and restaurants to sample before moving along.

**Eastern Promenade Park** makes a good first stop, with its panoramic view of islands in the bay and part of the city's working waterfront. The **Old Port** dis-

*Lobsters 2 go.*

**BELOW:** Cape Neddick Light Station, also known as Nubble Light, in York, Maine.

Map on page 104

trict, once a maze of rough streets frequented by sailors, has now been entirely taken over by gift shops, overpriced restaurants, and cut-rate bars aimed at day-trippers; avoid it and go instead for the residential **West End**, where the **Morse-Libby Mansion** (also known as the Victoria Mansion; tel: 207-772-4841; open May–Oct; closed Mon) on Danforth Street stands as an excellent example of Victorian architecture. Or take a ferry to tranquil little **Peaks Island** for a closer look at the sea. Back in the center of town, the **Portland Museum of Art** (tel: 207-775-6148; closed Mon from Columbus Day to Memorial Day) sometimes hangs good exhibits. Just watch the time on your parking meter: ticketers around town are needlessly ruthless.

From Portland, quieter Route 25 cuts swiftly west through suburbs and then rolling farmland. The town of **Gorham** is little more than a four-way intersection and the rural main campus of the University of Southern Maine; stay on Route 25, proceeding through more small towns. At Limington, the bridge crosses the slow Saco River, a superb canoeing river that winds from deep in western Maine to the sea. A free park on the left-hand side of the road here provides a scenic little picnic and swimming spot; rocks make for good sunning, and a pathway leads downriver to a wider place in the river, out of the sometimes-swift current.

Farther west, the route passes through more countryside to **Cornish ❼**, one of western Maine's very handsome towns. The activity here is focused around a small triangular green space lined with small shops and a hardware store, most in typical whitewashed New England fashion. Each September, an annual apple festival showcases local pies, cider, and other apple products on the town common – and the winner gets a night for two at the venerable Cornish Inn that stands beside the green. The best part comes after the judging, when all pies – winners and losers – are auctioned off to lingering spectators.

**BELOW:** the Maine tools for local fishermen.

## Windy heights

Keep to Route 25 as it jogs west into New Hampshire, the "Granite State," then briefly north; if you kept going north on Route 16, you would soon pass **Mount Washington,** at 6,288 feet (1,900 meters) the tallest peak east of the Mississippi – and home to the highest recorded winds on the planet.

At West Ossipee, however, make a turn inland again and follow Route 25 through Moultonborough, **Center Harbor** – whose little general store features old-fashioned wooden iceboxes of cola – and finally **Meredith**, a resort town with a doll museum set on big **Lake Winnipesaukee ❽**, New Hampshire's largest body of water.

Head south a short while on Route 3 as the road passes right beside the lake. Going uphill as you leave the town, bear right to take state Route 104 through small, typically New Hampshire towns. At Danbury, cut south on US 4 a short distance to Route 11, and then turn west again just after **Potter Place**.

It's only 10 miles (16 km) more to the prim town of **New London ❾** (turn onto Route 114 just past Elkins), which has a fine central green and good views of the surrounding hills and mountains. This is known

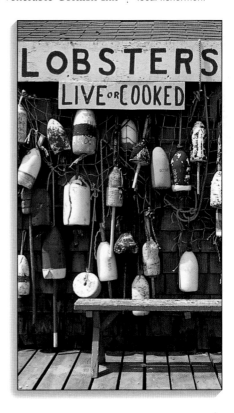

locally as a college town, with attractive Colby-Sawyer College located right next to the village green. This former women's college was long one of America's few remaining single-sex institutions of higher education, and became co-educational only in recent years. Connecting with Route 11 from Route 114, the road passes through the hamlets of Georges Mills (a general store, coves on either side of the road, and little more) and the lake town of Sunapee, with a pretty harbor on **Lake Sunapee** – reputedly one of the cleanest lakes in America, and one circled by hills of hardwoods.

Six more miles (10 km) east on Route 11, **Newport ⑩** spreads out in the Sugar River Valley, a small textile and arms manufacturing town with an old opera house, wooden covered bridge, and the handsome rectangular "town common" so typical of older New England towns. These green pastures once served as common grazing spaces for local livestock, but today serve mostly as the settings for soccer matches, carnivals, bake sales, and picnics.

Newport is perhaps best known for Sarah Josepha Buell Hale (1788-1879). Despite early tragedies including the loss of her mother, sister, and husband, Hale rose to prominence in Boston and Philadelphia as one of America's early feminists and female editors. She advocated education and equal opportunity for women, convinced President Abraham Lincoln to create Thanksgiving Day, and penned the popular children's nursery rhyme "Mary Had a Little Lamb." Her birth home is on Route 11 a few miles before you enter town, across the street from a once-famous woolen mill.

## Bridge to the past

For a look at the **Corbin Covered Bridge**, drive through Newport's main street and continue north on Route 10 for a mile or so, then turn left, passing the town airport and driving through a corridor of pine trees. The bridge at the edge was constructed as a copy to replace the original jewel, which was burned by a thoughtless arsonist during the 1990s. Such bridges are sprinkled throughout New England, their distinctive design both a shield from poor weather and, some say, a method of keeping horses drawing carriages from being spooked by rushing rivers below.

The craftsman who built this particular bridge was such a perfectionist for detail that he copied the original design and then hauled the bridge to its Sugar River home with an oxen team – both to transport it undamaged and to preserve a sense of history.

From central Newport, Route 103 proceeds west through **Claremont**, a fading mill city that nevertheless still possesses an impressive old block of central buildings known as Tremont Square and a fine Opera House with a good summer program of folk and orchestral concerts. Just west of the city, the highway crosses the broad and picturesque Connecticut River dividing New Hampshire from its similar-sized (but very different-thinking) cousin, Vermont.

At **Ascutney**, on the far side of the river, the antenna-topped peak of Mount Ascutney fills the eye; Vermont 5 keeps it to one side and the broad Connecticut River to the other as it heads due north.

*The distinctive roof of a New England covered bridge served two purposes: first, as a shield against poor weather; and also as a method of keeping horses that were pulling carriages from being spooked by the river waters rushing below.*

**BELOW:** covered bridges are found all over New England.

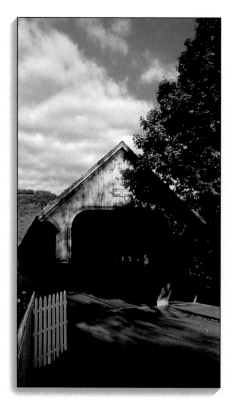

Shortly thereafter, the road arrives in **Windsor** ⓫ – a town that rightly claims itself the "Birthplace of Vermont." In Elijah West's tavern on Main Street, now known as **Old Constitution House** (open Wed–Sun May 27–Oct 8), Vermont's Constitution was drafted and signed in 1777, making it for a time an independent republic that was neither British nor American. This independent streak still marks Vermonters today – in the 1990s they elected and re-elected the only Socialist sitting in the US House of Representatives.

Map on page 104

The **Simon Pearce** glassblowing shop, also in Windsor, may be one of the nation's finest such shops. (The establishment also operates a restaurant in **Quechee**, serving meals on the glass. "Don't wash just *any* dishes" says a help-wanted advertisement.)

Still heading north on Vermont 5, you dip and curve riverside and soon enough come to **Norwich**, a tiny, typical Vermont town with its classic general store – the first of many you'll see on this drive. Near the interstate, the local **King Arthur Flour Baker's Store** sells the company's superior stone-milled flour, plus some top-grade cooking supplies and cookbooks, at a picturesque store on Vermont 5. Outside town, the **Montshire Museum of Science** (tel: 802-649-2200; open daily) provides children with a terrific hands-on look at ecology and nature amid riverside fields.

## Ivy-clad Dartmouth

Cross the Connecticut River into New Hampshire once more on Route 120 to **Hanover**, an attractive town largely thanks to the elegant, ivy-clad presence of **Dartmouth College**. Dartmouth was founded in 1769 by the Reverend Eleazer Wheelock to educate (and, of course, convert) local Indian children. Now it is one of America's finest private colleges, with especially strong programs in the sciences, humanities, and Native American studies. The pleasing Dartmouth Green is a center of town life, surrounded on all sides by college buildings, including the **Hopkins Center** performing arts space – designed by the same architect who later went on to plan New York's Metropolitan Opera House.

The downtown district also features the excellent Dartmouth Bookstore, as well as one of New England's most-beloved natural food cooperatives. It isn't unusual to see haggard, unshaven hikers lugging huge backpacks tramping through town, either, as the bridge from Norwich and downtown Hanover form one of the most civilized stretches of the entire Appalachian Trail.

For a little more of New England character before moving west, continue farther north on Route 5, which snuggles between the interstate and the river, mostly passing through dairy pastures and cornfields. Several of the small towns have interesting gathering spots, such as the Fairlee Diner in **Fairlee**, Vermont. Across a small bridge from Fairlee, in **Orford**, New Hampshire, beautiful white wooden and red brick homes from the 1900s – not to mention the Orford Social Library and a general store full of local characters – line the town's main street. It was from here that local car salesman Mel Thompson rose to become

**BELOW:**
Dartmouth College in Hanover, New Hampshire dates from 1769.

a multi-term governor of the state, never straying from his extremely Republican view of things. On summer weekends, the **Mount Cube Sugar House**, in the hills east of Orford down Route 25A, serves huge breakfasts with their own maple syrup: a delicious taste of the region that should not be missed if you are in the area. Locals swear by them.

From Hanover, cross back to Vermont and proceed a short distance south before turning west on US 4. You soon come to little Queechee, nondescript but for deep **Quechee Gorge**. This 165-foot (50-meter) cut in the rock, made by the Ottauquechee River, is accessible from several viewpoints; you can't hike down the steep, narrow walls, but you can hike the woods and camp in a state park across the street. Unfortunately, a small touristic complex has sprung up right beside the gorge.

## Leaf-peepers

Ten miles (16 km) beyond, compact **Woodstock** ⑫ sits prettily among trees, ridges, and river. On an autumn afternoon, the town is jammed tightly with leaf-peepers crowding the streets, but early October is the time to come – an annual chili cook-off and apple festival compete with the stunning foliage. From Downtown it is just a few paces to the handsome **Middle Bridge** covered bridge, which is located beside a row of exceptionally fine homes surrounding the village green.

The Woodstock Historical Society leads tours of some of these homes that encircle the central common, and two outstanding museums nearby – the **Billings Farm and Museum** (a look at 19th-century dairy farming; open daily May–Oct) and the **Vermont Institute of Natural Science** (tel: 802-457-2779;

**BELOW:** the Appalachian Trail stretches from Maine to Georgia.

## APPALACHIAN TRAIL

A scenic 19-mile (31-km) drive along SR 100 from the town of Bridgewater Corners, Vermont, leads to one of the longest marked footpaths in the world, winding a total of 2,135 miles (3,435 km) from Maine to Georgia. Benton MacKaye, who proposed the trail in 1921, wrote about his great project: "The ultimate purpose? There are three things: 1) to walk; 2) to see; 3) to *see* what you see... Some people like to record how speedily they can traverse the length of the trail, but I would give a prize for the ones who took the longest time." His idea was for a super-trail running the length of the industrialized East Coast. This would be a trail that was wild, yet within reach of major urban centers and the throngs of workers who were alienated from outdoor life. He felt the trail would grace all who spent time on it with the healing tonic of wilderness. Winding from north to south, it traverses the many distinct ranges that make up the Appalachian chain, touching the tops of many of the states it enters. Though not the first of its kind, the Appalachian Trail remains a favorite with outdoors people, enjoying celebrity status among the great hikes of the world. For more information, call the Appalachian Tourist Board on 304-535-6331.

open daily; closed Sun Nov–Apr), with its good record of nursing birds of prey back to health – provide additional diversion. Just 2 miles (3 km) west of town out US 4, the community of **West Woodstock** already has a slightly less manicured feel. The White Cottage Snack Bar serves up fried clams, ice cream, and similar summertime snacks, while the Woodstock Farmers' Market purveys gourmet foods and produce next door. You pass a llama farm, dipping with the steepening terrain, and go several more miles to **Bridgewater Corners**, home of the Long Trail Brewing Company and its locally popular Long Trail Ale.

Turn left onto Vermont 100A for beautiful little detour through some of the state's nicest scenery – past haybales and syrup signs, red barns, spotted cows, and grazing horses: pure Vermont. The stretch is particularly beautiful when leaves are changing color. About 6 miles (10 km) along, take a right onto the dirt drive for a look at the **President Calvin Coolidge Historic Site** (open daily from end of May to mid-Oct), the farm homestead where "silent Cal" was raised and periodically returned.

When President Warren G. Harding died in office in 1923, Coolidge was sworn into office on the spot here by his father, a notary public. He remains to this day a hero to Vermonters, symbol of a kind of taciturn, humanistic work ethic that still drives Vermont farmers and politicians alike.

## Famed footpaths

Continue on Route 100A until it ends at Vermont 100, making a right and driving north. You pass numerous B&Bs in the agreeable small towns; if you're in a hurry to get west, turn at **Killington** and cut through the scenic mountains to Rutland. With time to spare, however, you should continue north on Route 100 to the junction of routes 4 and 100. This is the spot where two of America's famous hiking trails – the **Appalachian Trail**  and Vermont's **Long Trail** – diverge. Making a right on 100 north, you can park and take a short stroll the trail on the left (through Gifford Woods State Park) or the right, around the shore of Kent Pond.

Stay on Vermont 100 through little **Stockbridge** until it connects with Route 125, then make a choice: food or nature? If you are hungry, continue north up 100 to **Waterbury** and take a tour of the Ben & Jerry's ice cream plant. We, however, suggest a left turn onto Vermont 125 to begin 13 gorgeous miles (21 km) of national forest land. You'll discover why it's been designated a state scenic route as you wind through **Green Mountain National Forest**. Partway along, just before **Ripton**, pull over for a peek at several Robert Frost-related sites.

Frost, one of America's best-loved poets, moved to this area and wrote his finest poetry in a farmhouse here. **Bread Loaf**, the complex of yellow buildings on the right, is a campus of Middlebury College that becomes an internationally famous school of writing each summer; the yellow Bread Loaf Inn offers lodging on-site. The **Robert Frost Interpretative Trail**, on the left, combines passages from his writing with the typical elements – stone walls, maple trees – that inspired it. There are also a number of impressive

Map on page 104

*Kids love the tour of Ben & Jerry's ice cream plant in Waterbury, Vermont.*

**BELOW:** ice cream for all.

hikes off the main road, clearly signposted, although to reach them requires driving some rough gravel and dirt roads.

The twisty final miles of Route 125 snake down the western slope of the Green Mountains beside the Middlebury River and must be driven carefully, but they are rewarded at last with a stunning view of the misty stacks of the Adirondacks as the route coasts down into the village of East Middlebury. At US 7, turn right and enter **Middlebury**, a college town with its own handsome buildings and microbrewery.

Now we head south on Vermont 30, which angles almost due south. It's delightful driving through classic Vermont scenes of grazing spotted cows, rivers, red barns, and the like. You pass several quiet lakes with good camping grounds, then through **Pawlet**, which possesses one of Vermont's best country stores, now called Mach's: among the wooden iceboxes of beer and stacks of rakes and rubbers, you can actually see the river running beneath the store through a grate. It was once a hotel, and there's a sepia 1900s photograph of dapper men with mustaches who once stayed at the place.

Next comes East Rupert, and then **Dorset ⓮**, an attractive town with a downtown golf course close beside classic New England homes, many of which are now characteristic bed-and-breakfast establishments.

## Rockwell country

Crowds begin appearing again in **Manchester**, a tourist-filled town nestled on the **Battenkill River**, itself one of the world's finest fly-fishing rivers. You can learn more at the **American Museum of Fly Fishing** (tel: 802-362-3300), which displays the rods and gear of famous fishermen like Hemingway and Eisenhower, among others. Not surprisingly, this is also home to the outdoor equipment and clothing manufacturer Orvis and loads of other shops – no longer the real Vermont, despite the presence of Norman Rockwell memorabilia everywhere.

Breeze right through town and continue south down Vermont 7A, here known as "Historic 7A," as it passes Robert Todd Lincoln's former home, **Hildene** (tel: 802-362-1788; open daily mid-May–Oct). This beautiful Georgian Revival mansion features a huge pipe organ, and just after Christmas tour guides lead walks through the home by candlelight; the rest of the year, you can tour it by day. The road then takes in the pleasing ridge of **Mount Equinox**, especially stunning in fall. A toll road rises to the top, if you wish to drive it. Apple orchards, meadows, and cows continue to be the prevailing themes along 7A.

At **Arlington ⓯** you can have a look at the famed **Norman Rockwell Exhibit** (tel: 888-781-8357; open daily; closed Jan), a collection of the artist's work. The artist lived in two homes in this area, and locals often served as models for his so-American portraits.

Turn west onto Vermont 313, and as you leave town and Vermont, there's one final treat: just before the New York border you pass by the covered **Arlington Bridge**, a small bridge over the Battenkill with a plain, typical New England church behind – a composition Rockwell himself was said to have especially

*The illustrator Norman Rockwell (1894–1978) was known for his realistic and humorous scenes of small-town life. His best work appeared as covers for the magazine* The Saturday Evening Post.

**BELOW:** shopping for arts and crafts.

loved. As these are a local specialty, this is the last one you'll see on this cross-country trip. Linger awhile contemplating the river – and the New England – you have seen.

## NEW YORK STATE

As you greet the sign welcoming you to **New York** state, you have not only crossed a line on a map separating one state from another. You have also crossed an imaginary, but no less real, boundary where yard sales at once become tag sales, tonic becomes soda, beef-on-*wick* replaces grinders for lunch, and where the clipped, shorthand speech of New Englanders becomes the louder, more persistent one of New Yorkers.

Entering on State Route 313, you arrive shortly to a pleasant picnic spot beside the Battenkill River. Then you pass through **Cambridge**, a small town with antiques and an attractive little general store, more form than function these days. You'll also pass the Cambridge Hotel, built in 1885, self-proclaimed "home of pie à la mode." Change to Route 372, join State 29, and continue driving west. Ten or 12 miles (20 km) on, the road crosses the **Hudson River** at Schuylerville, unimpressive here since it's split up into so many parts; in fact, the great river seems tame indeed – there is no hint yet of the power and beauty that will soon fill a great valley and inspire countless artists.

It was only a few miles downstream from these banks that the two Battles of Saratoga were fought in 1777, resulting in a crushing defeat of British troops by the Americans – a crucial momentum swing in the Revolution. A turnoff leads to the **Saratoga National Historical Park**, commemorating the battles, where you can drive or be guided through the fields.

Map on page 104

**BELOW:** Arlington, Vermont, is the home of the Norman Rockwell Exhibit. The artist often used local people for his rural portraits.

Continue to **Saratoga Springs** ⑯, long a resort town due to the mineral springs that bubble up from beneath it and more recently a popular weekend town. It is also home to Skidmore College students and faculty, and thus a fair number of coffeehouses, ice-cream shops, and bookstores speckle the downtown district. The Saratoga Performing Arts Center, within a green park on the southern edge of town, frequently hosts big-name concerts. Summertime also brings crowds to the harness track here, where horse racing is king – witness the presence here of the **National Museum of Racing and Hall of Fame** (tel: 518-584-0400; open daily). Finally, don't miss **Caffé Lena**, an upstairs joint on a central street which is said to have been the first American coffeehouse to host regular folk music performances. It still does.

*Oh, the Er-i-ee is arisin' / And the gin is agettin' low / And I scarcely think we'll get a drink / 'Til we get to Buffalo –*
OLD ERIE CANAL SONG

### Erie Canal

Route 50 brings you south through Ballston Spa, home of the eccentric **National Bottle Museum** (tel: 518-885-7589; open daily in summer; closed weekends in winter), to the Mohawk River and the Erie Canal. Tracing this great inland water route west to Buffalo is not the shortest way to get from here to there, but it is a route that runs rich with American history.

The idea of a canal connecting the port cities of Albany (on the Hudson River) and Buffalo (on Lake Erie) was greeted with skepticism and derision at first. Detractors called it "Clinton's Ditch" after DeWitt Clinton, champion of the project. Completed in 1825, and eventually bypassed in the early 20th century, the Erie Canal was responsible for the settling of the Midwest and the rise of the state of New York. The old canal towns, once the sites of boisterous activity, are quiet now, many down on their luck.

**BELOW:** father, son, and the family business.

Begin tracing the route in **Schenectady** ⑰. A plaque in this town sums up its early history: "Settled by Van Curler 1661. Burned by French and Indians Feb 8, 1690."

Because it was the farthest west of all Dutch settlements in the New World, the town's settlers built a stockade around the land, which was bounded by the Mohawk River and the Binne Kill. The stockade is now gone, dismantled during the American Revolution, but the area it protected is still known as the **Stockade** and is now a historic district containing an eclectic array of buildings that spans over three centuries of American life.

Schenectady's strategic riverfront location has historically made it an important center for commerce and transportation. The city supplied Revolutionary troops battling in the Mohawk Valley, and in the 19th century it was a major port. In 1931 it became the terminus of the nation's first passenger steam train, the "DeWitt Clinton," an innovation stimulated by the protracted process of traversing the 23 locks between Albany and Schenectady.

Schenectady has not been exempt from the exodus of industry out of the Northeast. In the 19th century it progressed from being a center for the manufacture of brooms, to "the city that lights and hauls the world." The Schenectady Locomotive Works (later the American Locomotive Company) opened in 1851, followed by Edison and his Machine Works – which later became General Electric. The Locomotive Company pulled out of town in 1970, but the lights are still switched on at GE.

Map on page 104

## Leatherstocking trails

New York's heartland is generally considered to begin west of the industrial triangle of Albany, Troy, and Schenectady. This essentially rural area north of the Catskill Mountains and south of the Adirondacks is also known as the **Leatherstocking District**, after the protective garb once worn by trailblazers. Native son James Fenimore Cooper immortalized the region in his *Leatherstocking Tales* and other works. And the numerous Revolutionary War battles that took place throughout the Mohawk River Valley are the subject of Walter D. Edmonds' historical novel, *Drums Along the Mohawk*.

Schenectady's Broadway leaves town in a southwesterly direction (State 7). It passes through Rotterdam and Duanesburg, where State 7, US 20, and I-88 converge. From there US 20 travels to **Esperance** on Schohairie Creek. This pleasant town features old houses, antique shops, and the obligatory country store. About 8 miles (13 km) south of here along State 30, which follows the creek, is the town of **Schohairie**, the third oldest village upstate. Its **Old Stone Fort Museum Complex** (tel: 518-295-7192) started as a church in 1722, became a fort during the Revolution, and has served as museum and library specializing in early Americana since 1889.

An interesting chapter out of Schohairie's past includes the Middleburg and Schohairie Railroad, built in the late 1860s. This short, 6-mile (9-km) run down the Schohairie Creek Valley transported hops and other local products. The railroad's president was fond of pointing out that although it wasn't as long as other railroads, it was just as wide. In its last days the line's single locomotive faltered physically and financially, and operation was finally stopped in 1936.

## Take me out to the ballgame

US 20 west of Sharon and Sharon Springs is one of the loveliest stretches of road in central New York, providing a panoramic view of **Cherry Valley**, the site of an infamous massacre in 1778, now crimson only in autumn.

It would be a mistake not to detour 10 miles (16 km) south down State 80 to visit **Cooperstown ⑱**, a charming town with several important attractions. James Fenimore Cooper's house and museum is one, but the main draw is the **National Baseball Hall of Fame** (tel: 607-547-7200; open daily) – a tremendous experience of the history of the sport, which has inspired countless novels, films, and even poems. Make time for a visit to the monuments, biographies, and collections here.

Past **Richfield Springs**, known for its sulfur springs and fossil-hunting grounds, State 167 travels north toward **Little Falls**. Not far up this road stands the **Russian Orthodox Holy Trinity Monastery**, startling to the eye in a land of colonial history, 19th-century buildings, and rustic farm houses. Little

**BELOW:** the National Baseball Hall of Fame is located in Cooperstown, New York.

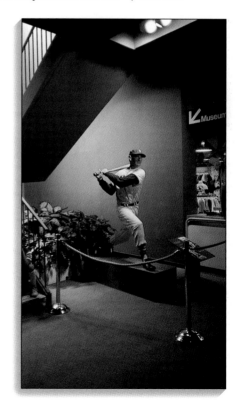

Falls' **Herkimer Home**, former residence of Revolutionary War hero Brigadier General Nicholas Herkimer, provides a glimpse of colonial life, with maple sugar gathering, sheep shearing, and other exhibitions. This canal town once had the world's highest lock, at 41 feet (12.5 meters).

West along State 5 is Herkimer, named after the general whose statue still commands attention. The **Herkimer County Courthouse** was the site of the Gillette murder trial, which inspired Theodore Dreiser to write *An American Tragedy*, depicting the dark side of the American dream. George Stevens' film version, *A Place in the Sun*, featured Montgomery Clift, Shelley Winters, and Elizabeth Taylor.

## Christmas all year-round

Between Herkimer and **Mohawk ⓭**, along State 5S, stands the **Fort Herkimer Church**, built in 1730. But Mohawk's most unusual attraction is **Dorothea's Christmas**, an estate overlooking the Mohawk Valley that harks back to 1790. The front parlor and ballroom of the 23-room house contain 20 Christmas trees decorated with European glass ornaments and antique miniatures. This fanciful indoor forest is open from May Day to Christmas Eve.

**Ilion**, a small industrial pocket, is located just beyond Mohawk. The **Remington Firearms Museum** (tel: 315-895-3200; open daily; closed Sun Nov–Apr) here is devoted to the great guns made by Remington Arms Company, past and present. Continuing west, the road terminates in **Utica ⓴**, the only city of any size you'll have seen since Schenectady.

Utica, once named Fort Schuyler, is rich in colonial and revolutionary history. But the biggest attraction here is the **Munson-Williams-Proctor Institute** (tel:

**BELOW:** boat rides on the Erie Canal are a good way to see the sights.

Map on page 104

315-797-0000; closed Mon), reputed to have one of the finest collections of 18th- through 20th-century American and European art in the northeast, housed in a building designed by Philip Johnson. On a much less cultural note, Utica's **Matt Brewery** serves its beer up in a Victorian-era tavern built in 1888. It's all part of a brewery tour that culminates in a trolley ride to the tavern.

State 69 leaves Utica for **Rome ㉑**, best known for its crucial role in the building of the Erie Canal. Beyond this point there were no continuous natural water routes westward. This is where excavation began. Commemorating this important chapter in its history is the **Erie Canal Village** (tel: 315-337-3999; open Wed, Thurs, Sun), a reconstructed 1840s village near a refurbished section of the old canal. The biggest tourist attraction here is the *Independence*, a packet boat towed down the canal by horses for a half-hour ride. When the snow flies in winter, the village also features sleigh rides, a pleasantly old-fashioned experience on a crisp, clear day.

The canal brought industry to Rome, some of which remains. There is also a military presence here – the Strategic Air Command's 416th Bombardment Wing at Griffiss Air Force Base. Tours of the base are available throughout the summer months. Rome has always been serious about America: this, after all, is where native son Francis Bellamy wrote the famous "Pledge of Allegiance" that every American school child learns by heart.

State 46 takes you from Rome to **Oneida**, still home to the Oneida Indians. The Oneida Community, associated with this town but actually just southeast in Sherrill, was established in the mid-19th century by John Humphrey Noyes and his followers. Calling themselves perfectionists, they adhered to a strict sexual code as part of a community-determined system of selective breeding. In their spare time they produced high quality silver-plated flatware. The community was dissolved in 1881, but the silver-plate business continues to thrive.

From Oneida, **Chittenango** is a short drive along State 5. (If you can't wait for Niagara Falls, head straight for **Chittenango Falls**.). Don't be surprised, in town, to see a yellow brick sidewalk, for this is "**Oztown, USA**." The sidewalk is a tribute to L. Frank Baum, author of the beloved *Wizard of Oz*. Stay on State 5 and it will lead right into Syracuse, the biggest city for miles around in these parts.

## Finger Lakes

Busy **Syracuse ㉒** is the urban gateway to the Finger Lakes. State 5 becomes Erie Boulevard as it cuts through the heart of the city along a path carved by the Erie Canal. The **Weughlock Building**, built in 1849 in Greek-Revival style, once weighed canal boats for the purpose of toll collection. At the turn of the 19th century it was converted into an office building, while in its most recent reincarnation it serves as the **Erie Canal Museum** (tel: 315-471-0593; open daily).

Thanks to the canal this was once a center for the salt trade, and some still refer to it as "Salt City." The town boomed during the 19th and early 20th centuries on the back of salt and other industries, and its well-preserved architecture testifies to former prosperity. The **Landmark Theatre**, an ornate "fantasy palace"

BIKE ROUTE

*Ride a bike along the Seneca Wine Trail that winds around Seneca Lake.*

**BELOW:** Finger Lakes vineyards produce wine for the East Coast.

**TIP**

In Auburn, New York, be sure to visit the Harriett Tubman home. Tubman was an escaped slave who coordinated a network called the Underground Railroad to spirit other slaves out of the South.

**BELOW:** the former mansion of George Eastman, who founded Kodak, now houses the International School of Photography.

built in the 1920s, has recently been renovated and functions now as a multi-dimensional entertainment center.

But the main draw here today is **Syracuse University**, elevated on a hill above the city, which brings crowds of students, sports fans, and other audiences to its huge **Carrier Dome**. Basketball games are especially well-attended, though football games and rock concerts follow a close second. For the more sedate, the campus also offers the **Joe and Emily Lowe Art Gallery**. Those same art lovers also should not miss the **Everson Museum of Art** (tel: 315-474-6064; closed Mon), designed by renowned architect I.M. Pei.

State 5 leaves Syracuse on its way to **Camillus**, where you can canoe to your heart's content along 7 miles (11 km) of navigable canal in the **Camillus-Erie Canal Town Park**. Farther along, State 5 merges with US 20, a route that strings together the northern tips of the largest **Finger Lakes**.

Following close on the heels of the Leatherstocking region, this series of 11 watery depressions was created by scraping glaciers. The region is characterized by vineyards, gracious inns, water pursuits, and hot-air ballooning. The area's vines look especially beautiful when their leaves begin to turn coppery red in late summer, and the colorful balloons are also an attractive sight. The small city of **Auburn**, on US 20/Route 5, isn't quite set on the lakes but does have one site to visit: the **home of Harriett Tubman** (tel: 315-252-2081) on South Street.

## Seneca Lake

After Auburn, US 20/Route 5 then passes Cayuga Lake and follows the Seneca River to **Seneca Falls** ㉓, where the First Women's Rights Convention was convened. The site has been developed into a National Historic Site and includes

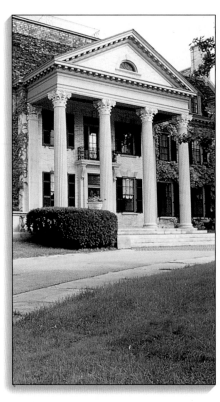

the **Women's Hall of Fame** (tel: 315-252-2081; closed Mon–Tue from Nov–Apr). **Waterloo**, also in between fingers, prides itself on being the birthplace of Memorial Day. The road through here passes by the old Scythe Tree, upon which local farm boys planted their scythes on their way to wars past.

**Seneca Lake** follows, the town of **Geneva** ㉔ its jewel, replete with elegant inns and mansions. This town is also the gateway to a circuit round the lake known as the Seneca Wine Trail; the drive takes in several dozen vintners, including two specializing in champagne and mead (honey wine). It is very pretty in fall, when the grape and maple leaves are changing color. Seneca Lake may seem small and thin, but it's actually one of the deepest freshwater lakes in the world – going down and down to a depth of more than 600 feet (180 meters). The US Navy used the lake to test depth charges during World War II.

Approximately 20 miles (32 km) west of Geneva on US 20/Route 20 is **Canandaigua**, at the northern tip of Canandaigua Lake. Of particular interest here is the Federal-style **Granger Homestead** ㉕ (tel: 716-394-1472; closed Mon) built in 1816, with its collection of 40 horse-drawn vehicles. North of town – take State 21 – are the **Sonnenberg Gardens** (tel: 716-394-4922; open daily May–Oct), acres of Victoriana with a mansion incorporating the Canandaigua Wine Tasting Room.

Remain on State 21 and you will pass through Shortsville on the way to **Palmyra**, a pilgrimage site for Mormons. This was the home of Joseph Smith who, according to Mormon belief, received and translated ancient records in the Book of Mormon, buried them here and subsequently founded the Church in the 1820s. Religious sites and Smith's restored farm homestead are open to the public, as is the **Martin Harris Landmark Cobblestone House**. Built in 1850, the house is typical of the farmers' homes that sprang up along the Erie Canal.

It's about 20 miles (30 km) from Palmyra to Rochester along State 31. The names of the towns along the way are perhaps more exotic than the towns: after Palmyra comes Macedon and then Egypt, where the New York State Barge Canal stands in for the Nile.

Map on page 104

### Pretty as a picture

Like other upstate cities, **Rochester** ㉖ thrived during the canal era and suffered economically with the advent of alternative modes of transportation. But it has adjusted to change better than its siblings and is on the upswing as a center for high-tech industries, while still preserving much of its 19th-century architectural ambiance. Eastman Kodak is the big name in Rochester, so big they still call it "Picture City." Kodak offers tours of its facilities.

The former mansion of George Eastman, who founded Kodak, now houses the **International Museum of Photography** (tel: 716-271-3361; closed Mon), devoted to the history of this art and science. The **Eastman School of Music** sponsors musical events, from jazz to rock to folk to symphonic works, while the **Eastman Theatre** is the home of the Rochester Philharmonic. For those who still enjoy childish things, the **Margaret Woodbury Strong Museum** (tel: 716-

**BELOW:** U-pick all U-like at this strawberry farm near Seneca Lake.

Map
on page
104

263-2700; open daily) has one of the most extensive collections of dolls in the western world, as well as many exhibits relating to life in early America.

Winters are severe in Rochester, thanks to its northern location on Lake Ontario, the easternmost Great Lake. But in late May, **Highland Park** is abloom during the annual Lilac Festival – featuring the world's largest display of these blossoms – when Rochester really is "pretty as a picture."

## On to the falls

State 31 continues along the path of the Erie Canal from Rochester to Niagara Falls. The names of the towns along this route, including Spencerport, Brockport, Middleport, and Gasport, continue to remind the traveler of the canal's former importance. But there are other reminders as well. **Medina** ㉗ has its cobblestone buildings and Culvert Road, which passes beneath the canal. **Lockport** also has its share of cobblestone houses, though it is best known for its magnificent flight of five locks.

From Lockport, State 31 (here called Saunders Setara Settlement Road) travels directly to **Niagara Falls** ㉘ . Once known as America's "Honeymoon Capital," the town is fond of referring to itself as an international tourist destination. And, indeed, this remains one of the top tourist draws in all of the United States despite its endless tackiness. Quite simply, the 700,000 gallons (3 million liters) of water plummeting from top to bottom each second here are a wondrous assault on the senses, something that must be experienced while in America. The magnetic draw of these falls has even inspired some visitors to attempt crossing them on a tightrope or riding them in a barrel, with sometimes-tragic results; both activities are now illegal, though daredevils still occasionally try.

**BELOW:** late
afternoon in the
summertime.
**RIGHT:** Niagara Falls
and the *Maid of the
Mist* boat tour:
weatherproof
gear is provided.

The natural beauty of the site might have been irreparably compromised had it not been for the efforts of landscape architect Frederick Law Olmsted, landscape painter Frederic Church and others. Their "Free Niagara" (from commercialism) campaign resulted in the establishment of the Niagara Reservation in 1875. One of the best ways to experience the falls today is by donning the provided foulweather gear and taking a boat ride on the *Maid of the Mist*. Alternatively, you might drive across the river to Canada and enjoy what many consider to be a superior view.

River Road hugs the eastern branch of the Niagara River, past the falls and through industrial lansdcape to **Buffalo** ㉙. Like other industrial giants past their prime, New York's second-largest city has acquired a somewhat bad reputation; and it certainly is not the classy destination it formerly was. As the 19th-century terminus of the Erie Canal, Buffalo once served as a funnel through which raw materials, cash, pioneers, and immigrant labor flowed into the midwestern states. Today it's a bit ragged. Still, there are reasons to stop for a visit. For one thing, you can eat well and cheaply here. A local specialty is spicy chicken wings, which anywhere else are called "Buffalo wings," but here are simply "wings." Available all over town, you might like to go to the source, the Anchor Bar, whose owner is said to have invented the dish.

# BUFFALO TO THE BADLANDS

*Follow the shores of Lake Erie though New York, Pennsylvania, and Ohio, then continue through the Midwest and the Great Lakes for the bleak, beautiful hills of the Badlands*

Map on page 124

**B**uffalo was an important point of departure for 19th-century settlers heading for the Midwest. From Buffalo they traveled to major ports of the Great Lakes in order to start their new life. Today, the road from Buffalo to the midwestern states follows the shore of Lake Erie through New York, Pennsylvania, and Ohio. Although known primarily as an industrial area, there are still some unspoiled stretches of coastline that are remarkable for their beauty. At Toledo the highway diverges from the shoreline on its way to big, busy, beautiful Chicago.

South of Buffalo along US 62 is the town of **Hamburg**, where the hamburger – perhaps America's greatest contribution to world cuisine – was purportedly invented in 1885. In celebration of the centennial of this event, J. Wellington Wimpy came to town and was honored as the undefeated hamburger-eating champion of the world. Essentially a rural town, Hamburg has been host to America's largest county fair since 1868. It's only about 5 miles (8 km) from here to Lake Erie, where you can pick up State 5, a lakeside road that takes you to Ohio.

**LEFT:** heading to the home of the urban blues: Chicago.
**BELOW:** buy homemade crafts to take home.

## Antique trail

Lake Erie has suffered more than its sister Great Lakes at the hands of industry, yet miles of its beautiful, sandy, ocean-like shoreline are still unspoiled. The stretch from Silver Creek, New York to the Pennsylvania border has been called an "antique trail" for the abundance of antique shops located just off the road. But more importantly, it cuts directly across a region devoted to the gentle art of viniculture.

State 5 takes you past terrain blanketed with grape vines and other fruit trees. In **Silver Creek**, go straight to the site of the **Skew Arch Railroad Bridge** on Jackson Street. Built on an angle in 1869, it is one of only two such bridges in the world.

Dunkirk and Fredonia follow, in the heart of the Concord Grape Belt (the world's largest) which extends into Pennsylvania. **Dunkirk**, with its natural harbor, is also a center for boating and the "Chautauqua (County) wine trail." **Fredonia**, to the south, is home of Grange Number One, America's first such farmers' organization.

Continuing along the lake, the road passes pretty **Lake Erie State Park** ➌ in **Brocton**, where campers will find a pleasant place to pitch their tents. **Westfield** follows, calling itself "The Grape Juice Capital of the World" and dominated by the various production facilities of a popular grape jelly. Combined with peanut butter and two pieces of bread, it vies with Hamburg's hamburgers as *the* American food.

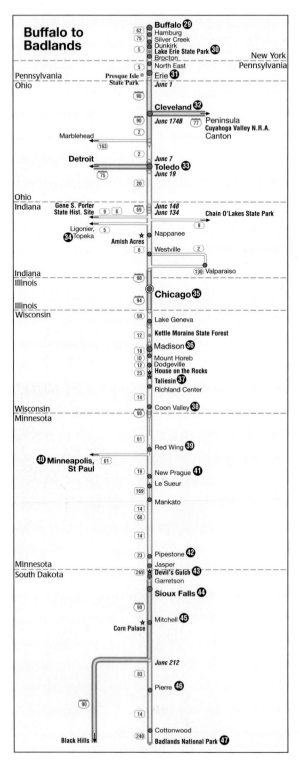

There is no obvious transition between New York and its westerly neighbor other than a town named State Line, Pennsylvania. The landscape remains the same – a sparkling lake on one side and lush vineyards on the other. In season, roadside stands sell the local grapes in every imaginable form. Only 63 miles (100 km) of Lake Erie shoreline prevents Pennsylvania from being a landlocked state (an econonic decision to do with lake access), and it knows just what to do with it. Past State Line is the town of **North East**, center of the state's tiny wine industry. Several wineries do fairly good business here and all offer tours and tastings.

About 15 miles (24 km) west of wine country on State 5 sits the city of **Erie** ③, off whose shores Commander Oliver Hazard Perry's fleet defeated the British in the Battle of Lake Erie during the War of 1812. Despite his motto – "Don't give up the ship!" – the flagship *Niagara* was left to sink in what later became known as **Misery Bay**. That bay is now a quiet fishing cove off Presque Isle, and the ship was rescued a century later. A reconstructed *Niagara* now sits high and dry along the Erie waterfront.

On the other side is Erie's finest physical feature, **Presque Isle**, a claw of land – almost an island, really – reaching out into the lake. You can drive its length, pass Presque Isle Lighthouse, and then loop around along the southern end going past Misery Bay. You'll find lovely sand beaches, wooded trails, fishing holes, and lazy lagoons.

## THE TOP OF OHIO

Before you can say "knee high by the Fourth of July," you're in Ohio. Interstate 90 cuts through the gently rolling farmland of this part of the state past Ashtabula, Geneva, and Euclid before reaching the **Cleveland** ② area. Despite popular notions to the contrary, Cleveland has its share of high culture, including the well-regarded Cleveland Orchestra and the **Cleveland Museum of Art** (tel: 216-421-7340; closed Mon), which is known for its extensive Chinese collection. And, as in other cities characterized by ethnic diversity, you can eat very well here; Hungarian food is a particular specialty.

It's well worth a short detour south from Cleveland to explore the green **Cuyahoga Valley**. The valley's ridges were settled during the late 18th century by the New Englanders who first surveyed its boundaries, and their influence remains today. The tiny town of **Peninsula**, reached by Interstates 77, 80, and 271, is a prime example – all Cape Cod-style whitewashed houses fronted by maple trees. A scenic small-gauge railroad line runs upriver to the even smaller nearby hamlet of Boston, and a cycling path has been constructed along the Ohio & Erie canal towpath that was built beside the river.

Map on page 124

## Football Hall of Fame

Sport fans will want to make a brief detour south down I-77, through the smoky industrial city of Akron – tire and rubber capital of America – to the city of **Canton**. Here the **Pro Football Hall of Fame** (tel: 330-456-8207; open daily) offers a look at the heroes of American football. Things peak in late August, when an annual game is played here to kick off each season.

State 2 leaves Cleveland on its way west, diverging from I-90 and running closer to Lake Erie. At Ceylon it comes right to the lake, loops around Sandusky, then bridges Sandusky Bay to arrive on the Marblehead Peninsula. State 163 takes you out to land's end and reveals the peninsula as a slightly rundown but refreshingly unpretentious place, full of lively harbors, the Prehistoric Forest, orchards, and fruit stands. At its rocky tip is **Marblehead Lighthouse**, which has been in continuous use since 1821, longer than any other beacon on the Great Lakes. It protects ships and boats from this, the most treacherous outcropping along Lake Erie. Looking back south across the bay, you'll see the

*Time for lunch: both hamburgers and peanut butter and jelly sandwiches have claims to this part of the US.*

**BELOW:** go slow whenever you see a school bus.

roller coasters and other thrill rides of **Cedar Point** (tel: 419-627-2350; open daily mid-May–Aug; weekends Sept–mid-Oct), a popular 364-acre (147-hectare) amusement park located on the tip of a peninsula accessible from Sandusky. Off the Marblehead Peninsula, State 2 proceeds toward Toledo. This region was once part of the **Black Swamp**, a refuge for wildlife which extended from Sandusky to Detroit. Small remnants of the swamp have managed to survive along this route.

## Famous hot dogs

The road emerges from the swamp and continues straight as an arrow to the town of **Toledo** ❸, past bait shops, drive-through liquor stores, and drive-in movie theaters. The "Toledo Strip" was once the subject of a border dispute between Ohio and Michigan. When Ohio got the Strip, Michigan got its Upper Peninsula from Wisconsin Territory as compensation – a swap in which Michigan probably made out like a bandit.

At first glance, Toledo seems like an industrial wasteland. Still, there are signs of rejuvenation and redevelopment in the downtown riverfront area along the Maumee. If you've got the time, drop into Tony Packo's Cafe – made famous by Corporal Max Klinger in the long-running TV series *M*A*S*H* – a fun restaurant known for its "Hungarian hot dogs" and quirky collection of hot dog buns autographed by celebrities.

Leaving Toledo and Lake Erie behind at last, US 20 heads due west, cutting straight through Ohio farm country to the Indiana border, a distance of about 60 miles (100 km). The road here parallels the Michigan border, which is just a few miles to the north.

**BELOW:**
Detroit, Michigan's Fox Theater was built in 1928; the style is described as "Siamese Byzantine."

## DETOUR – DETROIT

A 45-mile (72-km) drive beside Lake Erie on I-75 leads from Toledo, Ohio to Detroit, Michigan – the Motor City. Henry Ford was the single most influential American in motoring history, forming the Ford Motor Company in 1903. Six years later he had 10,000 orders for his newest car, the Model T, and by 1919, was selling close to a million cars. His innovations bolstered Detroit's economy, increased the automobile's popularity, and gave more people jobs; the city still revolves around his industry. The 260-acre (105-hectare) Henry Ford Museum and Greenfield Village complex in the nearby town of Dearborn is the world's largest indoor/outdoor museum, commemorating Ford's contribution to the city. The Ford Museum holds Henry's collection of wheeled technology and decorative arts, including early automobiles, while the Village houses recreations of famous businesses and residences, including Thomas Edison's Menlo Park laboratory. Detroit is also the home of Motown records,, created by former Ford assembly line worker Berry Gordy, Jr in 1958, which produced stars of the Detroit Sound such as Smokey Robinson and Diana Ross. The Motown Historical Museum charts the label's influence from the 1960s to the present. The Detroit Visitors Bureau is on 800-338-7648.

# INDIANA

They call **Indiana** the Hoosier state, and native Indianans Hoosiers. Some say the name comes from a common inquiry from the pioneer days, "who's yer?" Others say the nickname comes from a canal-builder named Samuel Hoosier, who liked to hire Indiana men over other workers; the workers became known as Hoosiers, and the name stuck. Other versions exist as well, and the question may never be properly settled. Whatever the case, this state has produced such high-profile celebrity residents as basketball star Larry Bird, singer John Mellencamp, and television personality David Letterman.

## Meanest man in the world

Ten miles (16 km) inside the state at Angola, leave US 20 for I-69 south; you'll immediately note a proliferation of stands selling fireworks, which are illegal in adjoining states but freely available here. Fifteen miles (25 km) later, cut over to US 6, which will carry you westward through northern Indiana to Illinois. Fields of golden grain (mostly corn) and silos announce it: you are solidly in the Midwest now. At Brimfield, detour a few miles north up Indiana 9 to the **Gene Stratton-Porter Limberlost Historical Site** (tel: 219-368-7428; closed Mon), a log cabin where the writer lived and wrote her well-loved books and essays about Midwestern nature. It's a peaceful spot among trees on a lake, perfect for a picnic.

On the other side of Brimfield, south on Indiana 9, sits another fine park – **Chain O'Lakes State Park**, a refreshing string of oases in the middle of Noble County. This county was once home of the "meanest man in the world," according to Indiana's contribution to the 1930s WPA American Guide Series. Legend

Map on page 124

*At the same time as fans the world over were hysterical with grief over the sudden death of James Dean, the 1950s Hollywood heartthrob was being laid to rest in his Indiana hometown of Fairmount.*

**BELOW:** sunset over golden grain, the Midwest.

has it that this man divorced his wife, after which she landed in the poorhouse. In order to get funds, the institution would farm people out to the highest bidders, and when his ex-wife was put on the auction block, the "meanest man" purchased her to do the housework that his second wife had refused to do.

Back on US 6, tiny towns punctuate a landscape of corn in this region, known for the productivity of its land and for its considerable Amish population. The Amish have been in this area for more than a century. These inventive, industrious, and deeply religious people go about their business while shunning worldly things such as buttons, zippers, electricity, and motor vehicles. Cut north up Indiana 5 for a look at their farms, homes, and horse-drawn buggies.

*The Amish splintered off from Swiss Anabaptists in 1693 and settled in Pennsylvania. Now nearly half the states in the US have communities, and the number of followers is growing.*

## Life in the past lane

First you pass through **Ligonier**, a real find of a small town complete with a single main street – which, for some reason, boasts a surprising number of Mexican eateries. The interesting town clock here was erected by John Cavin, son of local pioneer Isaac Cavin, in memory of the father who laid the town out in 1835. Also have a look at the **Indiana Historic Radio Museum**, with its collection of old radio memorabilia.

Continue north on State 5 and then turn right at a gas station to reach **Topeka ㉞**, a tiny town whose slogan is "Life in the Past Lane." It's the kind of place where Amish buggies line up in parking lots, and hardware and feed stores outnumber banks three-to-one. Amish ride cycles around town, work the counter at restaurants, and just generally blend into life in this farming community. For a more intimate experience, enquire locally about the Amish Bed and Breakfast network, or just drive one of the many other county roads in this area. White

**BELOW:**
the horse is the prime symbol of the Amish identity.

farmhouses with full clotheslines and empty driveways are usually Amish, though you should always check ahead with tourism offices before attempting to visit a private home.

Now retrace your steps back to US 6 and continue west. **Amish Acres** in **Nappanee** (tel: 800-800-4942; open daily; closed Jan–Feb), a historic farm homestead which interprets the Amish lifestyle for visitors, is fun though a bit over-commercialized. The round red barn hosts theater performances.

Beyond that, it's more lovely country driving through more fields of corn and occasional stands of maple trees. Drifting along US 6 like the "Windiana winds" through the last of rural Indiana before Chicago's industrial fringe, the route takes you over the Kankakee River (a good fishing stream) and on to **Westville**, home of an annual Pumpkin Festival that brings a carnival – and piles of orange pumpkins, of course – to town early each October.

## Old-fashioned atmosphere

If you're hungry, make a quick swing down to US 30, on Indiana 2, and the town of **Valparaiso**, where Al's Diner serves up old-fashioned atmosphere in the form of open-faced sandwiches, "Green River" sodas, and thick malts beneath walls decked out with pictures of James Dean, Marilyn, and Elvis. The town was also the home of bow-tied popcorn magnate Orville Redenbacher, and you'll still find occasional popcorn stands in these parts of northern Indiana. In fact, this is a region of America that sometimes appears permanently frozen in 1950 – you'll encounter plenty of classic cars, crew cuts, and friendly folks. Make the most of it before you reach the sensory assault – and very different pace – of **Chicago** ㉟ *(see page 130)*.

Map on page 124

*The Amish shun worldliness for small-scale values, with emphasis on the community.*

**BELOW:**
the Amish have been in Indiana for over 100 years.

# CHICAGO: THE WINDY CITY

*Broad-shouldered and big-hearted,*
*Chicago has a long a list of aliases:*
*Chitown and Second City are just two*

Although a few people might well dispute the authenticity of some of Chicago's various nicknames, one in particular will remain forever true: Crossroads of the Midwest. Chicago's railroad yards are the largest in the world. O'Hare claims to be the world's busiest airport. Even the Art Institute of Chicago straddles train tracks. Visitors get around by a light railway known as the El, for "elevated," because it usually is.

The site, at the confluence of the midwestern prairie, the Chicago River, and Lake Michigan, was an obvious place for a town to spring up. With the building of a canal in the 1840s – essentially linking the Great Lakes with the Mississippi River drainage system – followed by the advent of railroading, Chicago spread like the proverbial wildfire as commerce and masses of immigrants descended upon it.

Then, in 1871, wildfire became a reality. As the story goes, a certain Mrs O'Leary's cow knocked over a certain lantern, starting a disastrous blaze known as the "Great Chicago Fire." The fire signified the beginning of a new era in Chicago. The city became the workshop of architects like William LeBaron Jenny (the father of the skyscraper), Louis H. Sullivan, Frank Lloyd Wright, and later Ludwig Mies van der Rohe.

From the Chicago Water Tower and Pumping Station, the only public building to survive the Great Fire, to the Sears Tower, tallest building in America, the city's buildings and skyline are built to impress.

A few remnants of the 19th century have managed to survive, particularly in the Prairie Avenue Historic District. Once known as the "Avenue of Avenues," it experienced a mass exodus during the early part of the 20th century. However, those that remain are now being restored and lovingly protected.

Chicago has made the most of its magnificent lakeshore. A huge front yard encompasses 29 miles (46 km) of beaches, wonderful parks with distinct personalities, and some of the nation's finest cultural institutions: open daily are the Museum of Science and Industry (tel: 773-684-1414) on the South Side, and Field Museum of Natural History (tel: 312-922-9410), Shedd Aquarium (tel: 312-939-2438), and the Art Institute of Chicago (312-443-3600), all in Grant Park. The Art Institute is known for its collection of French Impressionists, and is also the home of that stoic couple staring out of Grant Wood's painting *American Gothic*.

Chicago is crazy about outdoor sculpture. All the big names are represented – including Oldenburg, Calder, Picasso, Miro, and Dubuffet. A more recent public art craze has also taken over the central city – a spreading network of fiberglass cows, artistically rendered to reflect their environs. It's almost become an inside joke by now, and any visitor must get the city's map to the cows and go figure out the meaning behind each one. Bring a camera, too.

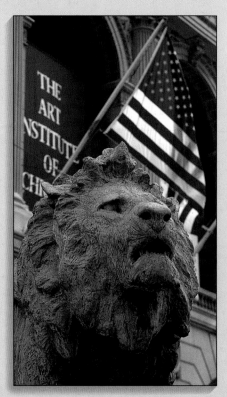

Chicago is the ultimate *film noir* set piece. Never has a place been so closely associated with gangsters and political corruption, the latter almost an institution. Eternally proud of those things that set it apart, the city has made little attempt to dispel these images even if they are quite unrealistic today. The real life of Chicago is a bit different. Politics are one face of it: black activist Jesse Jackson started his political career here and former mayor Richard J. Daley – gone but never forgotten – pulled the town's strings for so long that time is now measured in years AD ("After Daley").

This is also a writer's town, as articulate as it is brash. A steady stream of writers have interpreted their hometown for the rest of the world, everyone from James T. Farrell and Richard Wright to Saul Bellow, Studs Terkel, David Mamet, and the columnist Mike Royko.

Dark, smoky blues clubs have long been part of the Chicago scene, ever since players and singers from fields in the rural South relocated and invented "electric blues" here. You can hear all about it at B.L.U.E.S. on North Halsted or at the Checker Board Lounge on the city's rougher South Side, where generations of University of Chicago undergraduates have learned about the important things in life from bluesman Muddy Waters.

There's a new brightness to the hip North Side of Chicago, although some locals never wanted the lights to shine – the lights of ivy-walled Wrigley Field, that is. After a long and impassioned debate, the home of the Chicago Cubs was the last Major League baseball park to get lights, thereby facilitating night games. Cub fans are fanatics.

The communities flanking Chicago have become part of the silver screen in a number of films poking fun at suburbia. Glencoe, to the north, is familiar to many as the home of Joel, the fictional teenager played by Tom Cruise in the movie *Risky Business* who submerges his father's Porsche in Lake Michigan. Aurora was the setting for the wacky comedy *Wayne's World*. And Joliet's peniten-

tiary briefly housed John Belushi in *The Blues Brothers*.

Landlocked Oak Park is west of Chicago's Loop via I-290, on the other side of the city limits. Ernest Hemingway grew up here, and Frank Lloyd Wright lived and worked in Oak Park during the early part of his career before moving to Wisconsin. He left behind 25 buildings, making this the world's largest repository of his work. Wright's home and studio, built in 1889, is most revealing of his personality and genius: every touch, from the distinctive and renowned streamlined Prairie Style to the Scottish proverb that's carved over a fireplace, bears his characteristic imprint. ❏

**LEFT:** Marshall Field's department store clock; lions in front of the Art Institute of Chicago.
**RIGHT:** Chicago Theatre; sculpture by Miro; Chicago Bulls statue on North Michigan Avenue.

*Wisconsin's rural road sign is in the shape of the state.*

**BELOW:** scaring the crows away.

## THE WINDY CITY TO THE TWIN CITIES

Leaving Chicago, take Lake Shore Drive straight north out of the city and follow either US 41 or hop onto I-94 for a spell. Soon enough you're in **Wisconsin**, the unofficial Cheese Capital of America, a friendly place settled by blond Scandinavians still very much in evidence today.

A few miles inside the state, turn west on Wisconsin 50 to make a lovely country drive past orchards, fruit stands, and small lake towns – one of which is called **Lake Geneva**, attractive if not exactly a match for its counterpart in Switzerland. Turn north on US 12, passing plenty of maple trees, small cafés, burger joints, and rustic roads (so marked by state road signs).

You'll also come through **Kettle Moraine State Forest**, named for unusual features of the landscape – ridges of rock and silt, and circular ponds – produced here by the last great glaciation of North America. Rent a cycle to explore the area at your leisure.

At Whitewater, a small university town, you'll note a preponderance of custard stands serving burgers and frozen custard – a concoction invented in nearby Milwaukee. By state law, custard must contain a certain percentage of cream and a certain number of eggs. It's like ice cream, but sinfully richer; a spoon is barely adequate to pry it from the cup.

US 12 brings you to **Madison ❸**, Wisconsin's capital and one of the Midwest's most agreeable cities. The city boasts a splendid downtown grid of streets with a capital building at its center, a university district to match, and miles of lake frontage popular with joggers, boaters, skiers, and skaters – depending on the season. Snack on "brats" (short for bratwurst, local sausages of German origin) and beer, or enjoy the open-air market that takes over the university's main square in summer, a market purveying everything from Turkish food to African food to tofu dogs. There are also a number of museums here.

From Madison, take US 18 west through green pastures and roadcuts revealing the limestone underlying the countryside. This area is an anomaly in the normally flat Midwest, with numerous ridges popping up between you and the horizon; farms top distant hilltops like ships on sea swells. At the little town of **Mount Horeb**, exit onto County Road ID – in Wisconsin, unusually, minor roads are lettered instead of numbered – for a look at two attractions. The National Natural Landmark, **Cave of the Mounds**, provides a scenic look below ground; **Little Norway** (tel: 608-437-8211; open daily May–Oct) is a somewhat tacky attraction celebrating the Norwegian immigrants who largely settled this state.

Get back onto US 18 and continue to County Road BB, where a short detour south brings you to the **Folklore Village** (tel: 608-924-4000; closed Mon), a small complex of period buildings. The highlight is a one-room 1882 church, very simple but nicely restored; it was jacked up and moved from a nearby town. There is also a schoolhouse and working well pump on the property, which is often booked up by school groups.

**Dodgeville**, home to clothier Land's End, is just a few miles on. Take Wisconsin 23 north past the headquarters. On the way out of town you will pass the **Don Q Inn**, an eccentric lodging which comes with its very own Boeing jet airplane (free tours for guests) called, yes, the *Don Q*.

More dips and rises in the road lead to the **House on the Rock** (tel: 608-935-3639; open daily mid Mar–Oct), Wisconsin's quirkiest must-see attraction. This absolutely unique complex of buildings on top of an odd rock formation was built up over a period of decades by inveterate collector Alex Jordan Jr. Its many attractions include rooms and rooms of art, antiques and oddities, an "Infinity Point" glass bridge with views down a gorge, and a huge assemblage of dolls. It's well worth the expensive admission price, if only for a look at the fruits of a single man's manic obsession – you could easily spend the better part of a day roaming around this kitschy complex. If you don't have time for a long visit, there's an attractive  spot just north of the entrance to park, walk a spell and get a distant glimpse of the house.

## Frank Lloyd Wright's Wisconsin

Wisconsin 23 soon comes to the sandy banks of the Wisconsin River, where you'll be surprised to suddenly come upon Frank Lloyd Wright's **Taliesin ㉟**. The modern main building here, designed by the architect, contains research and exhibit facilities, but you must take a bus tour to get to Wright's actual former home. The setting is peaceful and lovely.

The route continues to the pretty little town of Spring Green, turns west onto US 14, and abruptly flattens before passing through **Richland Center**, the humdrum county seat renowned for being Wright's birth town. Then the road begins climbing and wrinkling again, indicating the approach of the Mississippi River.

Map on page 124

**BELOW:** farm stand in rural Wisconsin.

At **Coon Valley** ❸, neatly tucked within a surprisingly deep valley, you'll marvel at the surroundings and the town's solid Lutheran church. The **Norskedalen** (tel: 608-452-3424; open daily mid-Apr–Oct; closed Sun rest of year) complex outside town provides a pleasant look at Norwegian heritage in a quiet natural setting. Speed right through industrial La Crosse, hop onto I-90, and take the big bridge across the Mississippi; get off again on the other side at signs for Bob Dylan's Highway 61. You have entered **Minnesota** and are now following the **Great River Road** toward the river's source. The route north clings to the bluffs of the Mississippi, revealing spectacular colors in fall and outstanding river views at any time of the year. Patrons once rode steamboats all the way upriver from St Louis to gaze upon these high, beautiful bluffs.

US 61 is mostly grand views and plain towns from here to the Twin Cities, but there are a few worthy stops along the way. **Pepin**, back across the great river on the Wisconsin side, is famous for being the birthplace of Laura Ingalls Wilder of *Little House on the Prairie* fame. There's a copy of the cabin just north of town, and a small museum (open daily, mid-Apr–mid-Oct) as well.

North again, **Red Wing** ❸, with an especially good vista of the valley, makes a good place for a picnic and a photograph. There's an Indian reservation close by, as well, and it's good to have a look round before plunging into the suburban ring of towns and highways that have replaced what, until very recently, were cornfields but now serve as the suburban bases for legions of commuters into Minneapolis and St Paul.

## The Twin Cities

Because of their proximity, **Minneapolis** and **St Paul** ❹, on opposite sides of the Mississippi, will eternally be known as Minnesota's "Twin Cities." Fraternal rather than identical, they are like sides of the same coin: different, yet inseparable. St Paul, the more conservative, ethnic, and parochial of the two, presents an earthier and more weatherbeaten appearance. There's a more neighborly feel, and malt shops, health-food stores, and homes are more common here than the apartments, condos, and skyscrapers across the river. Minneapolis, more competitive and cosmopolitan, dresses for success while living and breathing the concept of quality time. Local radio humorist Garrison Keillor puts it this way: "The difference between St Paul and Minneapolis is the difference between pumpernickel and Wonder Bread."

Yet together they are responsible for an urban success story, the envy of every overcrowded and crime-ridden metropolis. Minnesota pioneers were forced by circumstances to cooperate with one another, and a genuine spirit of friendliness toward strangers prevails to this day.

People here put a lot of stock in politics and have developed a rather civic, populist bent: this state nourished the careers of Hubert Humphrey and Walter Mondale. More recently, Senator Paul Wellstone – and, outrageously, Governor Jesse "The Body" Ventura, a former professional wrestler – have continued this populist tradition, if in very different ways.

**SLOW!! BUSY STREET AHEAD**

*Highways have replaced cornfields in many parts of Minnesota.*

**BELOW:** Minneapolis.

## MINNESOTA: LAND OF 10,000 LAKES

It always comes back to the lakes. Without its waters, Minnesota wouldn't even be Minnesota; the name itself comes from the Sioux, meaning "sky-blue water." The shore of **Lake Superior** marks the border of its northeast corner and the **Mississippi River** courses down its eastern flank. State license plates affirm "Land of 10,000 Lakes," but there are even more than that in the state.

During the 18th century, French explorers stumbled onto this region and named it *L'Etoile du Nord*, the Star of the North. Over the next 150 years, the Sioux and Ojibwa Indians who originally occupied the territory were frequently set upon by hundreds of white settlers, and violent clashes between the two Indian groups escalated.

In order to protect the early settlers and establish a secure trading station, **Fort Snelling** was built in 1819, high on river bluffs at the site of what is now Minneapolis. As rampaging Indians crossed the plains, white farmers fled to the fort for refuge; thus was the city born. Today, Fort Snelling has been reconstructed and staffed with actors who give visitors a first-hand glimpse of frontier life, *circa* 1827.

An increase in commerce along the river gave birth to the towns of St Paul and Minneapolis. The former sprang up as a local center of navigation and was originally known as Pig's Eye, after "Pig's Eye" Parrent, proprietor of a river-front saloon. Seeking a better image, its residents renamed it St Paul.

Ever-industrious Minneapolis, "the city of water," evolved upstream around **St Anthony Falls**, source of power for sawmills and gristmills. Both towns were flooded with a wave of immigrants, mostly northern Europeans, on their way to harvest the bounty of the Great North Woods: lumber and iron ore. In the wake of the Homestead Act, more settlers then poured in to help cultivate a sea of wheat.

The Twin Cities' status in the world of agriculture, in fact, is never far from the minds of Minnesotans. Reports from the Minneapolis Grain Exchange, the nation's largest cash market, monopolize the local airwaves; General Mills and Pillsbury are headquartered here. Magnificent grain elevators, standing tall above the Mississippi, vie for attention with the likes of Minneapolis's **Investors Diversified Services** (IDS) building – the tallest one between Chicago and San Francisco – **St Paul's Cathedral**, and the handsome **Capitol Building**.

### Weather watchers

Characterized by stable neighborhoods and superbly planned public places and open spaces, the Twin Cities runs smoothly even in cold weather. They've given a lot of thought to the weather here, after all, and over the years have refined methods of dealing with a winter that is typically cruel and unrelenting. Glass-enclosed skywalks radiate from the Crystal Court of the IDS building, as they do in downtown St Paul, and the **Hubert H. Humphrey Metrodome** (enclosed) hosts sports events and concerts year-round – including two World Series titles for baseball's Minnesota Twins and success for the football team, the Vikings.

Map on page 124

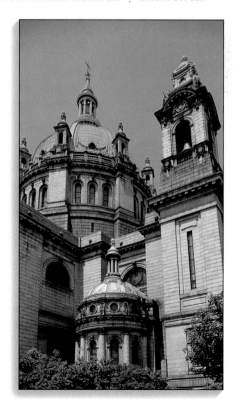

**BELOW:** St Paul.

Yet people here are also perversely proud of their ability to withstand record-cold temperatures, and they celebrate the ice and snow at the St Paul's Winter Carnival, an annual event since 1886.

Culture is well-endowed and thriving, particularly in Minneapolis. The **Walker Art Center** is a forum for contemporary visual and performing arts that *The New York Times* called "one of the best contemporary art exhibition facilities in the world." The Center incorporates the **Guthrie Theatre**, indisputably one of the premier repertory theaters. The **Northrup Dance Season** puts together one of the most impressive dance series. The **American Swedish Institute** archives and the European collections of the **Minneapolis Institute of Arts** (tel: 612-870-3131; closed Mon) are within a short distance of each other; both are terrific.

And there's still more to be found – avante-garde films, classical music, art galleries, jazz. At **Mendota**, a tiny riverfront community just west of the Mississippi, you'll find the **Hall Bros. Emporium of Jazz**, said to be the oldest jazz club in town.

## Famous state fair

The annual **Minnesota State Fair**, the nation's second-largest (behind New York's) should not be missed if you're coming through in late summer. Held at the State Fairgrounds, it's a week-long stream of fishing and farming demonstrations, folk and country music performances, and carnival rides – accompanied by every sort of meat or cheese one can imagine, placed onto a stick and fried. It's a huge dose of Midwestern popular culture, a little overwhelming but absolutely authentic.

**BELOW:**
the town of Blue Earth, in some of the most productive farmland in the US.

## THE MISSISSIPPPI TO THE BADLANDS

The region extending from the Mississippi River in Minnesota to the Missouri River in South Dakota marks the transition from the midwestern to the western states – geographically, culturally, and spiritually.

The transition can be subtle. If you listen to the car radio, up-to-the-minute reports from the floor of the Minneapolis Grain Exchange will be heard with progressively less frequency. Western idioms begin to turn up in small farm towns. The changes in geography are more abrupt, as the Missouri River serves as a sharp boundary between the Grain Belt and the true West.

### Sodbusters

The region of Minnesota southwest of "The Cities" is unmistakably farm country. This land was settled by European and Scandinavian immigrants during the latter half of the 19th century. Some called them "sodbusters" as they indiscriminately cleared land and penetrated virgin sod, exposing the rich soil of the midwestern prairie. Many of their grandchildren and great-grandchildren still farm the land here, an occupation known these days as agribusiness.

The founders of **New Prague ④**, a town dominated by **St Wenceslaus Church**, clearly had no desire to hide their Eastern European heritage. West of the town, along State 19, are peculiarly medieval-looking buildings with domed roofs, looking incongruous in the midst of all-American corn country.

Those who believe the Valley of the Jolly Green Giant to be a mythical place created by television advertising executives are mistaken. At **Le Sueur**, renowned for its peas, US 169 intersects the Minnesota River and passes through this lush, green valley, marked by the Green Giant himself sprouting from the top of a billboard.

Branching southwest toward **Mankato**, the road enters Blue Earth country across the **Blue Earth River**. This is some of the most productive farmland in the state, a green expanse interrupted only by lakes. Modern farming is still a family business here, and it isn't unusual to see an entire family out in the fields working various pieces of machinery.

From Mankato, take US 14 west as far as tiny Florence, passing many more farms along the way, and then turn south onto Minnesota 23 for a more scenic stretch. In **Pipestone ④**, near the South Dakota border, the strong suit is Sioux quartzite rather than agriculture. Buildings constructed from this local, pinkish stone appear up and down historic Main and Hiawatha streets; significant not only because they are lovely to look at, but because they are among the last of their kind. The use of Sioux quartzite is no longer considered cost-effective.

But for a period of less than 20 years before the turn of the 19th century, Pipestone went to town with it – the **County Courthouse**, the **Public Library**, the **Bank Building**, the **Calumet Hotel**, and, most impressively, **Moore Block** (*circa* 1896) are all made of this material. L.H. Moore embellished the block bearing his name with fanciful images of the sun, angels, gargoyles, a jester, and the devil.

Underlying and veining Sioux quartzite is a mater-

*Pipestone, Minnesota is only a few miles short of being halfway between the Atlantic and the Pacific oceans.*

**BELOW:** man on fire at the Minnesota State Fair: don't miss it.

ial called pipestone, which gave the town its name. Longfellow's *The Song of Hiawatha* tells of "the great Red Pipestone Quarry," and the quarries in Pipestone and the land which surrounds them are still sacred ground of the Sioux and other Native Americans today – a land of legend and tradition, and now also a national monument.

To see more, take the **Circle Trail**, a mile loop through the prairie surrounding the quarries. It goes past **Hiawatha Lake**, **Winnewisa Falls**, quartzite cliffs, and wind-carved formations known as **Old Stone Face** and the **Oracle**. A stone inscription along the trail documents the past presence of the Nicolet expedition, members of which traveled through here in 1836 while exploring the lands of the isolated Upper Mississippi region.

Continue south from Pipestone along Minnesota 23, passing through **Jasper** (which also has its share of quartzite buildings). Angle onto Route 269, and in a few miles you will have crossed another state line – and you will be poised exactly halfway between the Atlantic and the Pacific oceans.

## THE PINK ROAD TO SOUTH DAKOTA

The South Dakota Department of Highways chose to make use of the locally plentiful quartzite, and so a pink road unfolds at the border of their state. It takes you to **Garretson**, known for its **Devil's Gulch** ❹. The gulch is a sliver in the quartzite cliffs that loom above **Split Rock Creek**. According to one legend, the rocks were split by the Great Spirit's tomahawk. According to another, outlaw Jesse James jumped across the gap while being pursued by a posse. Fortunately for modern travelers they can now cross the gap over a short, nonthreatening bridge. Devil's Gulch lends Garretson an Old West image, but it is primarily a small farming community.

**BELOW:** the Corn Palace, Mitchell, South Dakota.

The prairies of eastern South Dakota and the pioneers who settled this land have been immortalized both on canvas and in popular literature. The paintings of Harvey Dunn, son of homesteaders and sodbusters, depict the reality and the dignity of these people. These same themes are mirrored in the work of Laura Ingalls Wilder, author of the beloved *Little House on the Prairie* and other books concerning life in the pioneer era before it was changed by modern times. (The books have now become an enormous industry, with over 50 million volumes having been sold. With the aid of some of Ingalls' descendants, ghostwriters have been employed to continue the series.)

To save time through this stretch of the Great Plains, get onto I-90, which cuts through eastern South Dakota in a nearly straight line through terrain that becomes a bit hillier and less green as rainfall becomes scarcer and the cultivation of hay and wheat mingles with that of corn.

These crops will eventually be taken to busy and industrious **Sioux Falls** ❹, the state's commercial center, a city of little interest although it can claim the headquarters of the Gateway computer company – a firm started by two Iowa brothers whose computers are now shipped in distinctive, cow-spotted black-and-white boxes.

Farther west, in **Mitchell** ❹, they have created a

monument to and with all the amber-colored grains: the **Corn Palace** (tel: 605-996-7311; closed weekends in winter). It's one good reason to stop in Mitchell – the other being to take a much-needed break from the interstate. The Corn Palace is most certainly the world's only Byzantine structure decorated with murals of corn and other grains; each year, the patterns change according to local whim. It is a slice of quintessential Americana.

As I-90 approaches the Missouri River, which divides South Dakota into "East River" and "West River," a very different type of terrain lies ahead.

## Where the West begins

Western South Dakota is unquestionably where the West begins. Visually, the Badlands and the Black Hills rise out of the prairie and hit you with a one-two punch; they are equally unexpected and stunning. But there is more to these regions than just their bleak beauty. They have been witnesses to some pretty tumultuous history.

If you're hurrying, stay on I-90 through to these twin wonders, but if you've got the time and inclination to explore rural South Dakota then meander west instead along US 14, which you can pick up at the rather ordinary state capital of **Pierre ⑳**, reached on US 83 north from Vivian. After crossing the banks of the Missouri River, set your watch back an hour and prepare to traverse mound after mound of prairie grass. This route also coincides with a section of the **Old Deadwood Trail**, a legendary wagon-train and stagecoach route.

The wagon-trains and stagecoaches were destined for uncivilized parts of the expanding nation; nevertheless, they had certain rules. "If you must drink, share the bottle," was one. Chewing tobacco was permitted, though it was requested the chewer spit "with the wind, not against it." And specified topics of conversation were forbidden: stagecoach robberies and Indian uprisings, to name but two.

US 14 cuts due south and then west again toward **Cottonwood**, foretold by grove after grove of cottonwood trees – the almost magical tree with the ability to find water in an arid landscape, and then reproduce in small communities. This tree was the single most useful tool the prairie settlers had: they could build a fence with it, sit under its shade, even cut into its bark to drink a bit of watery pulp in an emergency. Whenever you see the cottonwood's big-toothed leaves in a valley, you know there is water nearby, whether it be in the form of river, stream, or some other hidden source.

Continuing west, the motorist is besieged by a growing number of signs imploring him to stop at Wall Drug, located in Wall on the northern edge of the Badlands *(see page 143)*. Depending on your degree of thirst, hunger, illness or defiance, you can continue west and arrive at Wall in no time at all, or turn south at Cottonwood directly into the Badlands.

This area is also known as the Dakota by the Sioux Indians, which roughly translates as "land bad." French trappers in the early part of the 19th century described it as "a bad land to cross." Many contemporary travelers bypass the Badlands (rarely visible

Map on page 124

**TIP**

After crossing the Missouri River, set your watch back by one hour; Central time gives way to Mountain time here.

**BELOW:** these boots were made for walking; buy custom-made in South Dakota.

from the interstate) while rushing to the Black Hills and the stone faces of Mount Rushmore, but it is an absolutely unique landscape and one certainly worth seeing – even if it can be a brutally hot place in summer.

## Sand castles and canyon walls

This constantly eroding landscape has often served as a metaphor of youthful malaise and rootlessness: Terence Malick used it as a title for an acclaimed film (*Badlands*, 1973), and Bruce Springsteen later sang about "Badlands" on his 1978 album "Darkness at the Edge of Town." Despite all the discouraging words, there is a rare and striking beauty to be found here – it's well worth a detour off the interstate and the $10 per vehicle charge that it costs to enter the national park.

The region has been described as "Hell with the fires burned out," but fire has played no part in it; it has been shaped chiefly by wind and water. Spires, turrets, and ridges comprise a silent skyline, which changes with each gust of wind and torrential (though infrequent) downpour. **Badlands National Park** ⓭ is not a single piece of land, but rather several chunks of territory loosely strung together and carved out of **Buffalo Gap National Grassland** and the **Pine Ridge Indian Reservation**.

It is possible to be driving through rolling grasslands and suddenly be confronted without warning with Badlands terrain: huge sand castles and canyon walls. A 40-mile (64-km) loop road traverses the park and provides access to points of geological and paleontological interest, including a number of hikes through the strange terrain.

This was once the stomping ground of ancient camels, three-toed horses, and saber-toothed tigers, whose fossilized remains continue to be uncovered by the elements. Many of these fossils, dating back to the Oligocene Epoch, 25 to 35 million years ago, have been preserved by the **South Dakota School of Mines and Technology** and are exhibited at their **Museum of Geology** (tel: 800-544-8162; open daily) in Rapid City. The largest of the Oligocene mammals was the titanothere, known in Sioux mythology as the Thunderhorse. It was believed by the Sioux that this creature descended from the heavens during thunderstorms and killed buffalo.

Enthusiasts were well on their way toward cleaning out the Badlands of its fossil treasures before the government and Federal protection intervened, and the abundant wildlife that once roamed here was also largely gone by the 1890s – depleted by the throng of humanity *en route* to the Black Hills in search of "the devil's metal" – gold.

## Antelope and buffalo

Thanks to reintroduction and protection, however, the park is today a sanctuary for pronghorn antelope and buffalo. Prairie dogs also thrive here in their own metropolis. These peculiar rodents employ an elaborate system of tunnels, entry holes, and sentries; a shrill "barking" rings throughout the prairie if anyone ventures too closely.

These dogs are not especially well-liked by ranch-

**BELOW:** a Sioux artist paints a teepee, Badlands National Park.

ers, as cattle can be severely injured by stepping into their holes – nor is the weather, which here is as severe as it is unpredictable. Old-timers still talk about the blizzard of May 1905, when the weather progressed from balmy to icy. Thousands of head of cattle and horses drifted south with the wind and eventually fell to their death by pitching over the north wall of the Badlands.

Comparatively few people visit the Badlands, and those who do keep their visits short. Even fewer call this inhospitable landscape home. Two of those who do are Ansel Woodenknife and Lavanne Green, proprietors of the **Woodenknife Drive-Inn** in **Interior**. You can't miss the Woodenknife. Its neon signs beam across the barren landscape, addressing the most primal of needs: "EAT" and its companion, "FOOD."

## Life in the Badlands

Lavanne grew up in Interior and says she "couldn't wait to get out." Get out she did, roaming around for a while, seeing the world, having adventures, only to return in 1975, after many years. Now she and son-in-law Ansel fix delicious and authentic Indian tacos, fry bread, and buffalo burgers for weary travelers passing through the area who eventually find their colorfully painted little café. Once in a while they even make a special dish: *wojapi* (whoa-jah-pee), a seasonal fruit soup made with local chokecherries or wild plums. The soup is usually served at powwows, Ansel says, but can be whipped up on request if the fruits are ripe and available.

The café is not just a living but also a passport to meet people from across the United States and around the world – something the two clearly enjoy as much as they do the cooking. ❏

*Map on page 124*

*The Badlands have "a rare and striking beauty." For the visual evidence, see pages 44–45.*

**BELOW:** branding cattle.

# THE BADLANDS TO YELLOWSTONE

*Drive through the land of Buffalo Bill, Wild Bill Hickok, Calamity Jane and the Sundance Kid to see Mount Rushmore and the tragic sites of the Indian Wars*

Map on page 144

L eaving the **Badlands** ⓐ behind and heading west through South Dakota on Route 44, you'll come upon tiny **Scenic**, a ramshackle place named by someone with an extremely wry sense of humor; in exactly the same spirit, a sign along the main road ("Business District") signals your arrival. There's a tiny church here, a few abandoned shacks, several vintage mobile homes, a hole-in-the-wall US Post Office, a heap of junked cars, and, on the edge of town, the place people come here to see: the **Longhorn Saloon**.

The Longhorn was established in 1906, and the ankle-deep sawdust on the floor has been collecting ever since, as have the bullet holes and cattle brands on the ceiling. In its heyday it was always the site of a recent shootout, and even now discomfort pervades the atmosphere. Tractor seats mounted on metal barrels serve as bar stools. Its façade features longhorn skulls and a weatherbeaten sign that says "no Indians allowed." But, actually, this is an anachronism; the staff are often Oglala Sioux from the nearby Pine Ridge Reservation, and Native American customers are more than welcome. Route 44 will take you on to Rapid City.

**LEFT:** make friends with a llama at Custer State Park, South Dakota. **BELOW:** fresh eggs for breakfast.

## Wounded Knee

The **Pine Ridge Reservation** surrounds the southern tier of Badlands National Park and coincides with Shannon County, which has the lowest per capita income in the United States. On this bleak land, **Wounded Knee Creek** bleeds off from the White River to the site of the infamous massacre of December 29, 1890 – when 250 Sioux, mostly unarmed, were slaughtered by the army. Chief Sitting Bull was a casualty of this skirmish – the last tragic episode of the Indian Wars – and the name "Wounded Knee" has become an enduring symbol of unfathomable loss.

**Wall Drug**, in the town of Wall (located on Interstate 90), is a one-of-a-kind roadside stop – though it can't possibly live up to the miles of repeated advertising painted onto abandoned trucks and wooden signs as you come west. Never has there been a more elaborate drugstore: located on the northern wall of the Badlands alongside the interstate, it is difficult to pass through this part of South Dakota without dropping in.

Apothecary Ted Hustead began posting the ubiquitous signs along the highway in the early 1930s, inspired by the old Burma Shave signs. By the time drivers hit the Missouri River, even the most stoic of travelers perceives a need for a glass (or maybe even a jug) of Wall Drug's famous ice water – although it

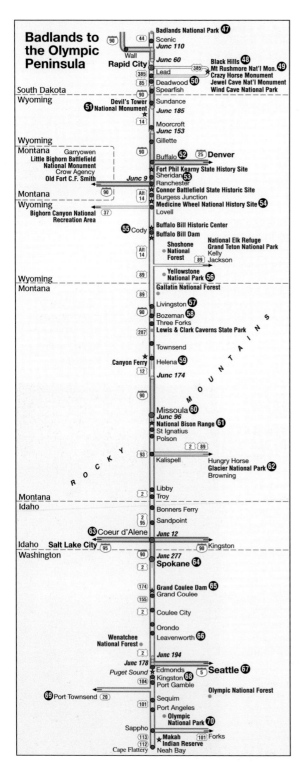

**Badlands to the Olympic Peninsula**

does sell other drinks as well. Hence, what began as the only drugstore in a small, dusty town became famous as the "Ice Water Store" and now takes up most of Main Street.

Wall Drug has, among other things, a chapel for those in need of solace; a clothing and boot shop for those in need of Western duds; a fine bookstore; a harness shop for serious riders; an art gallery; and a staggering assortment of Western "attractions," from a replica of Mount Rushmore (for those tired of driving) to a mythical 6-foot (2-meter) "jackalope," a mounted buffalo, and life-sized carvings of Butch Cassidy and the Sundance Kid. Donuts and coffee are free for hunters, skiers, honeymooners, missile crewmen, and drivers of 18-wheelers. Approximately 20,000 folks stop by Wall Drug on a good day. It's the archetypal American success story, and Ted Hustead defines the lesson of his success in this way: "there's absolutely no place on God's earth that's godforsaken."

The ride from Wall to **Rapid City** along I-90 is approximately 50 miles (80 km) of rolling, treeless prairie and wheat fields. You'll note black cattle dotting the grasslands, rolling hills slowly increasing in elevation, and occasional patches of sunflowers. Rapid City, settled by prospectors in 1876 and slowly becoming a sophisticated place, is the gateway to the Black Hills.

## The Black Hills

These words, taken together, summarize the course of late 19th-century history in the **Black Hills** ④⑧, indeed throughout the West. It was an era characterized by greed, deception, and bloodshed. The Sioux were "granted" eternal rights to this land that held little interest for the white man until the discovery of gold. After that, of course, it was a different story.

George Armstrong Custer led an army reconnaissance expedition through here in 1874. The presence of gold was barely confirmed before a deluge of humanity swept through the hills, leaving the treaty of 1868 shredded in its wake. Years of bloodshed followed, and the Sioux would never regain exclusive rights to their sacred *Paha Sapa*. A steady stream of travelers continue to flow through the Black Hills today – mostly past Mount Rushmore, the "shrine of democracy" that was never completed.

Going on past Rapid City and all the rampant commercialism of US 16, you'll encounter a road of another color, a 17-mile (27-km) corkscrew known as the **Iron Mountain Road**. It is one of the spectacular, specially engineered Black Hills highways built in the 1930s and intended for pleasure driving. The inspiration of Highway Commissioner Peter Norbeck, the roads are characterized by hairpin turns, switchbacks, granite tunnels (which are placed to provide remarkable vistas), and pigtail bridges using native pine columns in place of steel.

## Heads above the rest

Rather than sashaying around the mountain, Iron Mountain Road heads straight for the top. It passes by **Mount Rushmore National Memorial ㊾** (tel: 605-574-2523; open daily), which first appears framed at the end of a tunnel. This sight is akin to watching Hitchcock's *North by Northwest* (1959) on television from across the room. You may find yourself squinting to see if those specks up there are actually Cary Grant and Eva Marie Saint escaping across the six-story, granite faces.

Rushmore, the (uncarved) mountain, was purportedly named for Charles E. Rushmore, a New York attorney who visited here in 1885. When he asked a local about the name of the (then-nameless) peak, the fellow is said to have obligingly replied, "It is called Mount Rushmore." In the 1920s, Doane Robinson, the official historian of South Dakota, was considering various projects aimed at attracting visitors to the Black Hills. He decided on the concept of a

Map on page 144

*Twins and friends forever.*

**BELOW:** sculptor Gutzon Borglum began work on Mount Rushmore in 1927, at the age of 60.

colossal mountain carving, envisioning statues of legendary mountain men such as Jim Bridger, John Colter, and Kit Carson. But the more universally admired presidential subjects (George Washington, Thomas Jefferson, Abraham Lincoln, and later, Theodore Roosevelt) were finally chosen.

In 1927 sculptor Gutzon Borglum (then 60 years old) was commissioned to do the work. The enormous endeavor took him the remainder of his life, and work on the mountain came to a permanent halt following Borglum's death and then the Japanese attack on Pearl Harbor. It's interesting to note that Borglum had intended the figures to be carved to the waist, and had he begun from the bottom rather than the top, the US would have been left with a rather peculiar shrine of democracy.

The project was always plagued by controversy and a lack of funding, largely as a result of Borglum's artistic temperament and egotism. Some say he pushed for the inclusion of Roosevelt because he considered the president's spectacles to be a particular challenge to his skills, for instance. He also planned a 500-word chiseled inscription to be written by President Calvin Coolidge – an idea aborted following a ruthless and undiplomatic edit by Borglum. But the sculptor's ambition and talent were of the highest order, even if he was a difficult man to work with. The stone memorial is a testament to his own peculiar genius, and must be seen simply because it is unique to the United States.

**BELOW:** scale model of the Crazy Horse Memorial, with rock and the work-in-progress in the background.

## Crazy Horse

Mount Rushmore is not the only mountain carving in the Black Hills. There is also the **Crazy Horse Memorial** (tel: 605-673-4681; open daily), a work-in-progress by the late Korczak Ziolkowski. Whereas Mount Rushmore remains

Map on page 144

ncomplete, Crazy Horse, even more ambitious in scale, is still in its infancy. Ziolkowski left detailed plans and instructions behind, and the grounds – the own of Crazy Horse now – are literally abuzz with workers.

Ziolkowski was engaged to carve this depiction of the great Sioux warrior by Chief Henry Standing Bear so that the white man might know that "the red man had great heroes, too." Although some 8 million tons of rock have been blasted off the mountain since 1949, it is still difficult to visualize a figure on horseback without the aid of a 1/34th scale plaster model. Still, the figure is gradually taking shape. Come for a look at the mountain and also to visit the ever-expanding **Indian Museum of North America**, as well as Ziolkowski's studio. Learning about the sculptor, his life, and his ambitions for this place is time well spent. Ziolkowski was a fascinating giant of man, as a father, artist, and humanitarian. He liked to think of himself as a "storyteller in stone," and these are words he personally inscribed on the door of his tomb.

South of Mount Rushmore and Crazy Horse is **Wind Cave**, the first cave to be named a National Park. Wind Cave and **Jewel Cave** (its sister to the west) are the eighth- and fourth-largest caves in the world, respectively. They are characterized by calcite crystals and honeycomb formations known as "boxwork," found more extensively here than anywhere else in the world.

*The best driving experience in the Black Hills is to meander along Needles Highway through huge granite spires. Frank Lloyd Wright called the spires "an endless, supernatural world."*

## Supernatural highway

North of Wind Cave in the direction of Lead is **Needles Highway**, another Black Hills driving experience. The road was built to show off the Needles, granite spires which reach for the sky. Frank Lloyd Wright called it "an endless supernatural world more spiritual than Earth, but created out of it." The highway meanders and climbs several miles up into the firmament, at times through tiny granite tunnels. You must sound your horn before proceeding and don't let your attention stray too far.

Past Needles Highway, continuing north toward **Lead** on US 385, the aroma of pine pervades the atmosphere as the road passes through thick, dark stands of ponderosa pine. The appearance of these trees from afar gave the Black Hills its name. Lead, (pronounced *leed*), named for a lode or vein of ore, is the site of **Homestake Mine**, which today produces more gold than any other gold mine in the Western Hemisphere. It's still a company town of pickup truck-driving roughnecks, though tourists now mix curiously with them on the patchwork main street. Although all mining here now takes place underground, the town's main tourist attraction is the old "**Open Cut**" – a gash in the side of the mountain where gold was originally discovered in 1876. Locals are proud of their rough-hewn town, and like to point out that it's a mile high, a mile long, a mile wide – and a mile deep.

**Deadwood** ㊿, three miles (5 km) northeast of Lead on US 14A, is the other Black Hills town built by gold. In fact, this was the original center of local gold mining activity – immortalized in the Eric Taylor/Nanci Griffith song "Deadwood, South Dakota" – before Lead overtook it. During the 1870s, Deadwood gained

**BELOW:** Cathedral Spires – Needles Highway was built to show them off.

*Old-style saloon in Deadwood, the "town built by gold." Calamity Jane and Wild Bill Hickok are buried in a cemetery near here.*

**BELOW:** South Dakota is full of Indian reservations.

a reputation as the quintessential Wild West town thanks to local characters like "Wild Bill" Hickok, Calamity Jane, and others. Wild Bill and Calamity are buried beside each other in **Mount Moriah Cemetery** high above Deadwood, in accordance with Jane's last wishes, but today the place is rather tame and highly overdeveloped, its every nook devoted either to perpetuating a faux-"Wild West" image or to milking tourists out of their cash at one of the several gambling casinos.

If you must, visit **Saloon No. 10**, where Wild Bill was fatally shot by Jack McCall – but you have to find it first, as several bars claim the location. The real one is billed as "Home of the Deadman's Hand" and "The Only Museum in the World With a Bar," but the most interesting attractions of this area lie outside the town as you head further west. Descend from the hills via spectacular **Spearfish Canyon**, reached by driving north from Deadwood on US 385 for just a few miles. You can turn off onto a still rougher Forest Service road at the town of **Savoy** to glimpse the landscape where part of the movie *Dances With Wolves* was filmed.

## Last green oasis

Back on 14A the canyon, threaded by the highway, winds down and down right alongside the cool, shaded Spearfish River. You'll have plenty of motorcycles and recreational vehicles for company, but there are a number of pull-offs where you can park and hike up or down the canyon in some solitude, noting the striking high cliffs of sandy-colored rock topped with aspen and pine trees. As this is the last green oasis before some very long and open stretches of forlorn Western country, you'd be well advised to do so.

## WYOMING AND SOUTHERN MONTANA

Map on page 144

Quite simply, the West is not like the rest of the country. The professional sport of choice here is not football or baseball, but rodeo. The sky seems larger here than anywhere else, and you'll see frequent references to "Big Sky" country. This is a land of last stands, last chances, lost dreams; it is also a region of sparsely populated open spaces characterized by a wild natural beauty.

And Wyoming and Montana are the quintessential western states. They lead all others in statistical extremity – the most bars, drive-ins, gas stations, cars, and mobile homes per capita. The myths of the West live on here in the hearts and lives of the people who call this vast country home; theirs is not an easy life, they will tell you, but they would not trade it for anything.

Descending from the Black Hills of South Dakota by way of Spearfish Canyon brings you right to I-90, less than 10 miles (16 km) from the **Wyoming** border. The "Cowboy State," known locally as simply "Wyo," greets you with a sign proving you're in the West: while neighboring South Dakota has chosen somber presidential faces for its license plates, Wyoming has opted for a silhouette of a cowboy riding a bucking bronco. You'll notice this icon everywhere you go in the state.

Wyoming has a small piece of the **Black Hills National Forest**, located not far from the border outside of plain **Sundance** — the town "Where the Kid Got His Name." Indeed, Hardy Longabaugh, better known as the "Sundance Kid," was said to have shot a deputy sheriff near here and subsequently headed for his infamous **"Hole-in-the-Wall"** hideout about 150 miles (240 km) southwest. Once little known outside the West, his memory now lives on — and his name has become a household word — thanks to George Roy Hill and Robert Redford, director and star of the everlastingly popular movie *Butch Cassidy and the Sundance Kid.*

Past Sundance, US 14 loops up toward the Black Hills and **Devil's Tower ③**, the object of obsession in a very different but equally popular film, *Close Encounters of the Third Kind.* Visible from almost 100 miles (150 km) away, this 860-foot (260-meter) fluted, butte-like rock formation is the tallest of its kind in America. It stands on the other side of the Belle Fourche River, where the Black Hills meet the gullies and grasslands of the plains.

The first white men to explore this region, supposedly misinterpreting a benign name ascribed to it by Native Americans, called it Devil's Tower. It held a prominent place in the folklore and legends of the Sioux, and it later served as a landmark for those traveling west, just as it does today.

You can hike around the base of the tower, but beware of rattlesnakes. The majority of visitors simply stare at its almost supernatural shape and size — particularly luminous at sunrise or by the light of the moon. The sight of it so impressed Teddy Roosevelt that he designated it the nation's first national monument in 1906.

South of the monument, the road loops back onto I-90 at **Moorcroft**, an old cow town. The old Texas Trail made its way through here in the 19th century, trampled by cowboys driving cattle all the way to

*"There's gold in them thar hills"*
−US ARMY SCOUTS,
1874

**BELOW:** Devil's Tower is well known to fans of *Close Encounters of the Third Kind.*

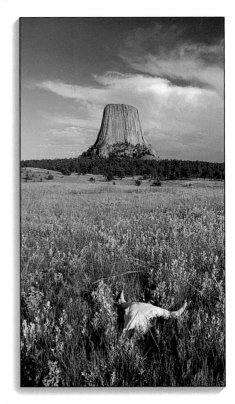

Montana. Farther west, through and beyond drab **Gillette**, the plains are vast and beautiful, marked only by cattle and the occasional river bottom of aspen and cottonwood trees. Even before crossing the Powder River and its tributary, Crazy Woman Creek, you can see the improbable pile of the Crazy Mountains looming, and then the snow-streaked peaks of the **Bighorn Mountains** in the distance: a tremendous relief for the traveler weary of the Great Plains.

## A town called Spotted Horse

If you're taking US 14, you'll go through towns with colorful names such as Spotted Horse and Ucross. Take I-90, though, and you must drive a sparse (if beautiful) 70-mile (112-km) stretch without so much as a town or gas pump to interrupt you, only miles of empty ranch lands. The lone break in this stretch is a forlorn rest area among trees at the crossing of the Powder River.

Traveling westward, the Bighorns gradually become closer. They were named for bighorn sheep, once prevalent here but now infrequently seen. As abrupt as they are majestic, the Bighorns foretell the Rocky Mountain ranges just beyond. These eastern foothills are today traversed by I-90 just as they once were by the Bozeman Trail, a bloody shortcut in the 19th-century push westward through Sioux, Crow, and Cheyenne Indian hunting grounds.

**Buffalo** ㊉, where the interstate highway bends north for Montana, was actually named after the town in New York and not for the formidable animals that once thundered across the plains. It was one of the earliest settlements in this corner of Wyoming, and the main street was formerly an old trail that negotiated Clear Creek. There's little here to see now besides a short main street, but it is a convenient stocking-up point for excursions into the mountains.

*Buffalo, Wyoming is named for the town of Buffalo, New York, not for the hairy bison that roamed the plains and which can still be seen near Yellowstone.*

**BELOW:**
rancher's wife
with rancher-to-be.

## DETOUR – DENVER

A drive of grand vistas along the base of the Rocky Mountains on I-25 from Buffalo, Wyoming, leads after 82 miles (132 km) to Denver, home of the first ice cream soda and the first bowl of shredded wheat. Celebrating the Gold Rush that built the city is the grand Capitol building, covered in 250 ounces (7 kg) of 28-carat gold leaf. In the mid-1800s weary, unlucky prospectors flocked to Denver for guns, booze, and women; the gambling halls never closed. Throughout the 1880s money from silver camps bolstered the economy, and the population increased nearly threefold, beginning the city's urbanization. Attractions like the Coors Brewery (free samples), the US Mint (no free samples), and the Denver Art Museum, specializing in Asian, pre-Columbian, and Native American art, give the area a metropolitan flavor, but for all its culture, the city's natural setting is an easy distraction. Not only do the Rocky Mountains lie less than an hour away, but Denver is in charge of the largest park system in the country. Even its ever-popular concert venue, Red Rocks Amphitheater, is a natural outdoor wonder, hollowed out of red sandstone on a site high above the city. The Denver Visitors' Bureau is on 303-892-1112.

The road from Buffalo to Sheridan passes near the remains – now a national landmark – of **Fort Phil Kearny**. This was the most hated army outpost of all along the Bozeman Trail, and when it was finally abandoned in 1868, it was immediately burned to the ground by local Native Americans.

About 20 miles (32 km) south of the Montana border lies the small historic city of **Sheridan** ㊳, where I-90 and US 14 meet and county seat in a region once inhabited by Crow Indians but now a major cattle-producing area. The railroad came to town in 1890 following the discovery of coal, and continued to play a major role in the development of the city. There are a number of historic homes, but the real pleasure is strolling Main Street among real-life saloons, cowboys, and western-wear stores. Have a drink at the Mint Bar, a most distinctive watering hole, then grab a hat at Dan's Western Wear.

## An important inn

Although cattle is of primary importance here, Sheridan is perhaps best known for its annual American Indian Days celebration each July and for its hotel, the **Sheridan Inn**. Across the street from the old railroad station in Sheridan, the inn was built in 1893 by the Burlington Railroad and Sheridan Land Company. A gracious structure with a long, inviting front porch, it fell into disuse and was scheduled for demolition during the mid-1960s. Fortunately, it was saved by a rancher and is once again open for business, not just a way-station for travelers to dine elegantly but also a living museum. After all, William F. "Buffalo Bill" Cody once owned part of this inn and made it his second home; it was customary for Cody to sit on the porch and audition acts for his Wild West Show.

Modeled after a Scottish inn, most of the materials used in its construction

Map on page 144

**BELOW:** bison (buffalo) in the Black Hills. No longer endangered, their numbers are now thought to be about 250,000.

were shipped from back East by rail. In its day, it was considered to be the finest hotel between Chicago and San Francisco; presidents and such celebrities as Ernest Hemingway, General Pershing, and Will Rogers all stayed the night here, and this was the first building in the area to feature bathtubs and electric lights. The lights were powered by an abandoned threshing machine and illuminated from dusk until midnight, when a whistle was blown to warn of impending darkness. Later came a telephone, first in the county, with a direct line to the drugstore. But the inn's pride and joy was its bar, constructed in England from oak and mahogany and hauled from Gillette by ox team. Still in use today, it's known as the "Buffalo Bill Bar."

Along I-90 north of Sheridan, as you approach the Montana border, sit two of the most infamous sites of the 1860s "Indian Wars." **Ranchester** is the location of **Connor Battlefield**, where General Patrick E. Connor led a division of more than 300 soldiers in an ambush of an Arapaho encampment. The Arapaho lost 64 of their people and their camp was virtually destroyed. Women and children were brutally massacred here, and as a result Connor lost his command.

Just north of Ranchester is the **Montana** line — also the beginning of the massive, empty-seeming **Crow Indian Reservation**. I-90 passes right through its heart, through the desolate-looking but neatly kept ranch lands of the reserve

*The Battle of Little Bighorn, also known as "Custer's Last Stand," took place on June 25, 1876. The battle lasted only one hour, during which time the 7th Cavalry lost over 200 soldiers, the Sioux and Cheyenne fewer than 100 men.*

**BELOW:** General G.A. Custer, RIP.

## Battle of Little Bighorn

The town of **Garryowen**, named after an Irish drinking song, leads you into the legendary **Little Bighorn Battlefield**. The Battle of Little Bighorn, better known as "Custer's Last Stand," took about as long as it takes for a white man to eat his dinner, according to one observer. But the Sioux and Cheyenne who fought

Map on page 144

that day were to lose the greater struggle. Two-hundred and sixty white marble stones now sanctify this place along with the words of Oglala Chief Black Elk, in Lakota and English: "Know the Power that is Peace."

Beyond the battle site is **Crow Agency**, headquarters of this 2.5 million-acre (1 million-hectare) reservation — far less than the lands outlined in the original treaty, which designated 38 million acres (15 million hectares) as Crow land. This area, bisected by the Bighorn River and characterized by rolling hills, was described by Crow Chief Rotten Belly in the 1830s as being "exactly in the right place. Everything good is to be found there. There is no country like the Crow Country." To get a glimpse of what modern Indian life is like out here today, pull off the interstate and drop into the gas station or grocery store.

Back on the highway, you'll begin to notice the first of many signs indicating "chain up areas" — turnouts where truckers wrap heavy chains around their tires in foul weather to obtain better traction through the treacherous mountain passes that await further inside Montana.

Make time at the northern edge of the Crow reservation, just south of Hardin, for a stop at the **Big Horn County Museum** (tel: 406-665-1671). This collection of architectural structures from around the huge, spare county — which is tops in agricultural production for this state — includes a train station, German church, and the original farmhouse and barn that occupied the site. The museum also serves as your first pickup point for Montana information, and its helpful staff can direct you to area attractions such as the superb fishing in **Bighorn Canyon**. Crow guides will take you up the canyon for a price, and if you'd like to stay on the reservation, lodges and motels are thick on the ground in **Fort Smith**.

From Crow Agency to Billings, I-90 skirts the northern boundary of the reservation through towns with names like Big Timber. It doesn't get interesting again, really, until you've reached Livingston and Bozeman. If you have the time and wish to see Yellowstone, you can also reach those towns via a scenic — if roundabout — method, by backtracking south a bit to Ranchester, Wyoming.

## Towards Yellowstone

Approaching the Bighorn Mountains via I-90 in clear weather, you can sometimes discern a road switch-backing its way up the snow-streaked slopes. Traveling west from Ranchester to Lovell allows you to experience it firsthand. US 14 out of Ranchester ascends Bighorn National Forest past bullet-ridden signposts to **Burgess Junction**. The road is treacherous beyond this point: several runaway truck ramps and brake-cooling turnouts help drivers negotiate the steep grades and sharp turns.

About 20 miles (30 km) beyond Burgess Junction is a 3-mile (5-km) bumpy gravel road leading to the Indian **Medicine Wheel ❸**. Although well paved, the road is extremely narrow and winding, at one point crossing a narrow ridge. But the views from these highest reaches of the Bighorns are stupendous, and the immediate countryside is sprinkled with wildflowers. Near its end, the road forks and presents you with a clear choice: the 20th-century radar facility to the left or the ancient medicine wheel to the right. Go right.

**BELOW:** tall in the saddle.

*Buffalo Bill rose to fame through a series of dime novels based on his character. His Wild West show hit the road in 1883 and by the 1890s was performing in Europe in front of royalty.*

**BELOW:** Buffalo Bill Historical Center, Cody, Wyoming.

This medicine wheel is the most elaborate of a series of stone circles found east of the Rocky Mountains, its 28 spokes forming an almost perfect circle 74 feet (22 meters) in diameter. It is thought to be about 600 years old, but its creators and its purpose still remain a mystery. According to Crow legend, the wheel was here when they arrived in the 1770s. Today it serves a ceremonial function for Native Americans. Perhaps a certain amount of visitors, looking over at the radar station, might wonder how *that* structure will be interpreted centuries from now.

Past the Medicine Wheel, US 14A plunges directly down the mountain into the **Big Horn Basin**. Protected by the mountains, this region enjoys a milder climate than the rest of Wyoming. It is a prime cattle-producing area that saw one of the last great range wars between cattlemen and sheepherders in the early part of the 20th century.

US 14A travels from Lovell to Cody through Shoshone River Valley. **Lovell**, a well-groomed town, was founded by ranchers in the 1870s and remains identified with cattle, though it is also known as the "Rose Town of Wyoming." Past Garland, the Rocky Mountains loom into view for the first time, with square-topped **Heart Mountain** in the foreground. A short drive from here is Cody, a town named after William F. "Buffalo Bill" Cody.

## Buffalo Bill's town

You can't pass through **Cody** ❺ without confronting the memory of Buffalo Bill, that one-time Pony Express rider, soldier, buffalo hunter, Army Chief of Scouts, rancher, frontiersman, actor, and showman. He has accurately been called a "kaleidoscope of white man's western experience." Through his Wild West Show, his own screen roles, and other films that dealt with his character (played by everyone from Roy Rogers to Charlton Heston and Paul Newman), he has, more than any single person, influenced the world view of the West – for better and worse. And he certainly left his mark on Cody.

The place is unquestionably tourist-crazy. When Yellowstone attained national park status, this town jumped in with both feet, billing itself as gateway to the park. (Note, however, that the eastern gate to Yellowstone — the one facing Cody — sometimes closes down for years at a stretch so that crews can repair park roads.) Today there are enough tour buses, tourist attractions, and hoopla in the town that the inclination is to step on the gas. If you can withstand souvenir shops and the phony façade, however, you will discover a bit of the Old West here.

Best is the **Buffalo Bill Historical Center** (tel: 307-587-4771; closed Mon Nov–Mar), which is actually four outstanding museums in one. The **Buffalo Bill Museum** is devoted to the man's vast collections of memorabilia. He was known for his flamboyance and excess, and the collection is all the better for it. The **Whitney Gallery of Western Art** spans the period from the 1800s to the present. All the greats are represented – Catlin, Bierstadt, Moran, Remington, Russell; Remington's studio has been recreated here, as well. The **Plains Indian Museum** displays perhaps the world's finest collections of Sioux, Cheyenne, Shoshone, Crow, Arapaho, and Blackfoot artifacts.

Extremely interesting is a series of precise pictographs executed by Chief Sitting Bull while imprisoned at Fort Randall in 1882. Drawn on Fort Randall stationery, they depict what he considered to be the important events in his life.

Map on page 144

## Rodeo capital of the world

Cody is also known for its **Night Rodeo**, a tradition which, along with the annual Fourth of July Cody Stampede, legitimizes the town's proud claim to be the "Rodeo Capital of the World." **Old Trail Town** (tel: 307-587-5302; open daily mid-May–mid-Sept), which includes the **Museum of the Old West**, is located west at the original town site. The beloved obsession of Bob and Terry Edgar, this is an impressive collection of authentic frontier buildings, horse-drawn vehicles, and other artifacts from Wyoming's past. The "**Hole-in-the-Wall Cabin**," used by Butch Cassidy and the Sundance Kid, is also here, marked by a rock with the oldest inscribed date in northern Wyoming (1811).

*Buffalo Bill, claimed by Cody, Wyoming, was actually born in Iowa. The modern artist Jackson Pollock was born in Cody, a fact that is virtually ignored.*

A number of legendary frontiersmen have been reburied here at the cemetery, among them John "Jeremiah Liver-eating" Johnson, portrayed by Robert Redford in the film *Jeremiah Johnson*. Johnson died in an old soldiers' home far from the mountains where he lived, and his reburial was marked by a moving ceremony featuring Robert Redford and the Utah Mountain Men, who served as pallbearers. The plaque on his grave simply reads "No More Trails."

US 14 west out of Cody follows the Shoshone River, winding through the formations of **Shoshone Canyon** and past the **Buffalo Bill Dam**, the world's first concrete arch dam. It tunnels through **Rattlesnake Mountain** and continues on through the **Shoshone National Forest** (the nation's first). As you take leave of it, you'll soon find yourself at the entrance to Yellowstone National Park. ❑

**BELOW:**
Old Town Trail,
Cody, Wyoming.

# YELLOWSTONE TO THE OLYMPIC PENINSULA

Map on page 144

*The Northern Route concludes its coast to coast journey
by traveling through several of the most glorious national parks
in the land to the far northwestern corner of the US*

The national parks of the northern Rockies – Yellowstone, Grand Teton, and Glacier – are regions of breathtaking natural beauty, vignettes from a more primitive North America. These mountain parks all share an abundance of wildlife, but each possesses a distinct personality. Yellowstone has its geysers; Grand Teton encompasses the incomparable Teton Range, rising above cattle country; and Glacier has its spectacular mountain passes.

The route between Yellowstone and Glacier passes through the westernmost **Great Plains**, the traditional hunting grounds of the Plains Indians. First described by Lewis and Clark in the early part of the 19th century, and later depicted by Charles Russell, the landscape is now dominated by cattle ranches and wide open fields of wheat.

## Symbol and sanctuary

**Yellowstone National Park ㊱** is both symbol and sanctuary. Located in the northwest corner of Wyoming, it was the world's first national park – and for many people still the most magnificent despite the damage done by widespread wildfires in 1988. This primitive landscape, forged by fire and water, has been called the "greatest concentration of wonders on the face of the earth," its shapes and colors "beyond the reach of human art." It is a hotbed of geothermal activity, with more than 10,000 thermal features, as well as being one of the last remaining habitats of the grizzly bear in the continental United States. All this, and enough canyons, cliffs, and cataracts to please the most jaded eye.

Though Native Americans hunted here for centuries, credit for the region's discovery goes to John Colter, the first white man to set foot in what is now Wyoming. Later in the 19th century, trappers and prospectors passed through, among them Jim Bridger, a celebrated mountain man and teller of tall tales. Impressed by the petrified trees of **Specimen Ridge**, he embellished his description a bit, raving of "petrified trees full of petrified birds singing petrified songs." In 1870, Henry Washburn, the Surveyor General of Montana Territory, headed up a more illustrious expedition endeavoring to set the record straight. They returned awe struck and committed to the creation of a "nation's park" – a dream realized in 1872.

Yellowstone encompasses an area of more than 2 million acres (800,000 hectares). Those who prefer being at one with nature can rest assured that 95 percent of this area is backcountry. For the less intrepid, there are nearly 300 miles (500 km) of roads. The

**LEFT:** Old Faithful, Yellowstone National Park.
**BELOW:** skiing near Yellowstone's Mammoth Hot Springs.

*Cowboy country around Yellowstone is also bison, elk, and grizzly bear country.*

**Grand Loop Road** provides access to most of the major attractions, from **Yellowstone Lake** and the **Grand Canyon of Yellowstone** to **Mammoth Hot Springs** and **Old Faithful**. They are simply magnificent.

Many visitors view Old Faithful's performance with a sense of obligation. Although not as faithful as it once was, the geyser pleases the crowd regularly – 21 to 23 times daily. This is also a prime location for people-watching; a chance to glimpse a real slice of American life frozen in anticipation.

## Don't pet the bears

Some come here primarily to view wildlife, and few depart disappointed. Stopped cars along the road generally indicate that some large mammal is grazing nearby. Unfortunately for both man and beast, visitors tend to forget their natural fear of and respect for these truly wild creatures. A park ranger relates that people who would ordinarily be reluctant to pet a neighbor's dog have no qualms about posing for a snapshot with a wild animal twice their size. Bison gorings are quite common and can be serious. Of ever greater concern to park officials are the bears – both black bears and grizzlies, but the latter are more dangerous and more endangered.

One way to avoid bears is to visit the park in winter, a time of hibernation and a season that comes early to Yellowstone. Snowmobiles and snowcoaches provide limited access, but probably the best way to explore this quintessential winter wonderland is on skis. Kick and glide your way to the thermal areas, good places to spot wildlife warming their hooves and paws.

With the coming of winter, the Yellowstone elk population leaves the high country and heads for the National Elk Refuge outside of Jackson, Wyoming.

Though not exactly following in their hoofprints, US 89 south nevertheless takes you from the southern boundary of Yellowstone Park, through magestic **Grand Teton National Park** and Jackson Hole, alongside the refuge, to Jackson, the perennial boomtown.

If the Rockies are the crown, then the **Teton Range** is its jewel. Exquisitely beautiful, amethyst-tinged, jagged, snowcapped, and hypnotic, they loom above the horizon west of the highway. The **Snake River**, running true to its name, intervenes. The Tetons and **Gros Ventre** ranges encircle the **Jackson Hole** valley. Trappers worked this territory in the early 19th century and it was named for David E. Jackson, a prominent member of the trade. Settlers came in the 1880s as outlaws, homesteaders, and ranchers. This is a gorgeous landscape, never more visually stunning than in the classic 1953 western movie *Shane*, filmed on location here.

It is still cattle country, but tourism has become the economic mainstay now. People flock from all over the country to ski here, especially the well-to-do. Nearby **Rendezvous Mountain**'s claim to fame is its vertical drop – the greatest of any US ski resort, which can be appreciated even in summer by taking a ride on the aerial tram with a sheer ascent of nearly 1 mile (1.6 km). The view from the summit is stupendous – to Grand Teton and far beyond.

## Million dollar cowboy bar

The Old West and the New West have converged in **Jackson**, land of condos and cowboys. This is a big-name resort with its share of local color; you just have to look for it. Look beyond the boutiques, the ski chalets, the nightly "shoot-outs," and the stagecoach rides. Bars are generally the best place for this sort of quest, so pull up a saddle (mounted on a bar stool) at the **Million Dollar Cowboy Bar** and hoist a few beers with the locals.

North of Jackson is the **National Elk Refuge**, established in 1912 and now the winter habitat of a herd some 8,000 strong. Once victims of starvation and disease, these elk are now protected by law. Regularly scheduled sleigh rides transport visitors briefly into the company of these graceful creatures. In spring the elk shed their antlers, which are expeditiously retrieved by area Boy Scouts and later auctioned off at a considerable profit.

Gardiner, Montana sits along US 89 just north of Yellowstone on the southern fringe of **Gallatin National Forest**. Out of Yellowstone, the road passes through barren plains, irrigated farms, and a land of many hot springs – mineral bath resorts are thick on the ground here – before reaching the forest, rich in minerals. The road plays hide-and-seek with the Yellowstone River awhile longer before intersecting with US 191 at Livingston.

**Livingston** 🕤 was put on the map by both the Northern Pacific Railroad and its proximity to Yellowstone, just 56 miles (89 km) to the south. Retaining some of its pure-West authenticity, it has also been the popular haunt of Western authors and painters such as Russell Chatham and Jim Harrison – not to mention modern movie stars and media types such as

Map on page 144

**BELOW:** around 8,000 elk spend the winter near Jackson, Wyoming.

Finger pickers should check out Bozeman, Montana. Highly desirable Gibson guitars are made at a factory just outside of town. For tour information, call 406-587-4117.

Andie MacDowell, Ted Turner, and Jane Fonda, among others. The town consists of a small grid of streets with bars and cafés; its proximity to Bozeman has also brought an increasing number of university students and professors.

A little west along I-90 sits **Bozeman** ⑬, nestled in the Gallatin Valley beneath 9,000-foot (2,700-meter) peaks that seem close enough to touch in the gin-clear air. This was known as the "Valley of Flowers" by the Blackfeet, Crow, Cheyenne, and Snakes who hunted here. William Clark passed through the area with their blessing in 1806 on the return trip of his path-finding expedition. John Bozeman and Jim Bridger later guided wagon trains through in direct violation of treaty, at considerable risk. The trail became Bonanza Trail, the Bridger Cut-Off, and the Bloody Bozeman – a treacherous shortcut for impatient pioneers.

Like so many other western cities, Bozeman has a historic main street. But it also has a state university – which has brought outdoor gear shops, health food stores, and the like – and is becoming another popular Montana spot for movie stars to buy ranch houses. The Gibson Guitar company manufactures quality guitars at a plant just outside town. You might also care to make a visit to the **Museum of the Rockies** (tel: 406-994-2251; open daily), an institution devoted to the physical and cultural heritage of the northern Rockies. Bozeman's own "boot hill" is **Sunset Hills Cemetery**, final resting place of journalist Chet Huntley, pioneer John Bozeman, and Nevada miner Henry T. P. Comstock.

## Lewis and Clark

**BELOW:** friends on that lonesome road.

Northwest of Bozeman, along Montana 2, sits Manhattan – which doesn't have much of a skyline at all – followed by the town of **Three Forks** across the Madison River. This town was named for the Missouri Headwaters – the Gallatin, Madison, and Jefferson rivers – all named by Lewis and Clark. Meriwether Lewis and William Clark led their historic expedition through here in July 1805, having accepted the challenge of exploring the recently acquired Louisiana Purchase by tracing the Missouri River and its tributaries to (they hoped) the Northwest Passage. By the time they reached the Three Forks area, however, they realized that the Missouri drainage system did not in fact lead to the Pacific. Nevertheless, the success of their expedition remains undisputed. They opened up the West for a generation and for all time; a deluge of exploration – and exploitation – soon followed.

Gone today is the abundant wildlife Lewis and Clark found at the headwaters, although a state park has been developed to commemorate and interpret its historical significance. Here you can have a picnic at the very spot where the expedition stopped to have breakfast on July 27, 1805 and then climb up to **"Lewis Rock,"** where Lewis sketched a map of the countryside. At the entrance to the park are the remains of a ghost town, **Second Gallatin City**.

The town moved here from across the headwaters so as to sit astride a main stagecoach route, having by that time been abandoned by the steamboat. But its existence was unfortunately short-lived, bypassed by

the next wave of transportation – the "iron horse" itself, the mighty railroad.

A few miles west of Three Forks on I-90, the color suddenly changes to the gold of wheat, and US 287 enters, going north toward Helena. Past **Townsend**, **Canyon Ferry Lake** appears to the east of the road like an oasis on the prairie. Behind it stand the **Big Belt Mountains**. US 287 continues north and merges with I-15, skirting **Helena ➒**, Montana's seat of government.

Map on page 144

## Last Chance Gulch

In Helena they continue to make Lewis and Clark bourbon, and you still hear talk of Last Chance Gulch – though now it's a pedestrian mall. Fans of cowboy-artist Charles Russell will want to stop by the **Montana Historical Society** (tel: 406-444-2694; closed Sun Sept–May), which houses a collection of his work. Acclaim for Russell runs high in Montana, and one of his masterpieces graces the chambers of the House of Representatives: an enormous, colorful mural with a name to match, "Lewis and Clark Meeting the Flathead Indians at Ross' Hole."

From Helena, US 12 runs up and over 6,300-foot (1,920-meter) MacDonald pass – don't try this if winter is approaching – and the **Continental Divide**. Spill a drop of water now, and it will (eventually) run into the Pacific instead of the Atlantic. To the west of the Divide, at Garrison, you must get back onto I-90 for another stretch of rugged mountains; you are solidly within the Rockies now, with minor ranges such as the Garnet Range to either side of the road. A rest area on the interstate provides a good chance for you (and your vehicle) to rest from all the mountain-climbing while gazing at the surrounding peaks.

Then it's down to **Missoula ➏**, the state's most liberal-leaning town thanks to the influence of the University of Montana. You'll note a giant "M" carved in the hills outside town, and that marks the university. The trail actually runs on campus property and makes for a popular hike. The town boasts the usual rough-and-tumble Western bars, certainly, but also good health food shops, bookstores, and music – not a bad place to spend the night.

From Missoula, take US 93 due north and begin climbing again, at least for a bit, as you begin to enter the **Flathead Indian Reservation**. Roadside stands and restaurants sell bison burgers and huckleberry shakes, the local twist on fast food. This area was once all Flathead Indian territory by decree of treaty, but the tribal lands were gradually settled by missionaries and sold piecemeal to speculators. Today a mixture of residents manage to co-exist amid lovely, wild scenery.

At the junction of Montana 200, turn west a short ways to tour the **National Bison Range ➌** (tel: 406-644 2211), where some 300 to 500 of these magnifent animals – as well as many other species of wildlife – roam over more than 19,000 acres (7,700 hectares) of beautiful grassland and park-like patches of timber. Again, however, remember not to get too close – technically, you are not even supposed to get out of your car while driving through.

A few miles north again on US 93, **St Ignatius** beckons as a turn-off beneath the splendid Mission Mountain range. The town's chief draw today is

**BELOW:** Helena is Montana's seat of government.

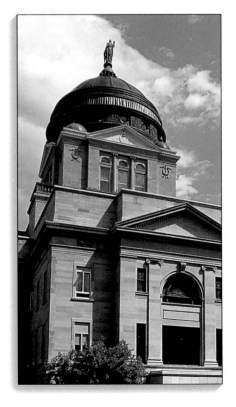

actually its impressive mission (tel: 406-745-2768; open daily), built in 1854 and possessing some interesting fresco work within. The surrounding mountains are still occupied by Flatheads, and you need tribal permits to fish, hunt, or visit. It's a beautiful and rugged country; bears and mountain lions are frequently seen.

North again, US 93 becomes ramrod-straight – one of the most accident-prone stretches of highway in the land, so look sharp. It continues north alongside the mountains to the folksy town of **Polson**, where huge **Flathead Lake** drains through a gorge; then the road bends to circle the lake's western shore. A giant Flathead-owned casino has somewhat marred what was once pristine scenery here, but the lake is still marvelous to contemplate as you climb around it to **Kalispell**, population center of the area and a base for excursions into Glacier National Park. Fittingly, its name means "prairie above the lake."

US 2 turns east to pass through Columbia Falls and then **Hungry Horse**, named for some freight horses that once escaped and nearly starved to death before being discovered and nursed back to health. The highway crosses the middle fork of the Flathead and meanders through the pristine, cathedral-like wilderness of **Flathead National Forest** before finally reaching the natural wonders of the park.

## Glacier National Park

**BELOW:** tour boat on Lake Josephine in beautiful Glacier National Park.

**Glacier National Park** ② is more remote and less crowded than Rocky Mountain Park or Yellowstone, yet traffic can still be heavy. Traveling here is therefore most satisfying at off-peak times – at sunrise or sunset or during early summer and autumn. It is generally plowed and fit for driving from mid-June to mid-October, when the Park Service closes it down for the winter.

Near the park's western edge is **McDonald Creek**, a final resting place for kokanee salmon who travel here in late autumn from Flathead Lake to spawn. This event attracts hundreds of bald eagles, which in turn attracts an increasing number of bird-watchers, who silently peer through binoculars to watch as nature takes its course.

The Continental Divide forms Glacier's backbone, crossed by spectacular **Going-to-the-Sun Road** at Logan Pass. Opened in 1933, this is the only road that crosses the park, bisecting it into two nearly equivalent sections. It has been called "the most beautiful stretch of road in the world," its twisting 50 miles (80 km) of two-lane pavement climbing from the settlement of West Glacier to the shore of Lake McDonald, to Garden Wall, and finally crossing Logan Pass and descending to St Mary.

Along the road, stop for spectacular vistas of the **Hanging Garden Trail**, which leads to vast alpine meadows. Columbian ground squirrels greet hikers at the trail head, which proceeds past deformed trees known as *Krummholz* (the German word for "elfin timber" or "crooked wood") and across the meadow. There is an ever-changing repertoire of glacier lilies, Indian paintbrush, red monkey flowers, and mountain heath. Mountain goats can sometimes be sighted from here, as well as grizzly bears, who feed on the meadow's plentiful bulbs and roots. **The Highline Trail**, across the road from the Hanging Garden, is a more challenging and potentially dangerous trail – not recommended for the faint-hearted. Opportunities for backcountry hiking abound inside the park. Its approximately 50 glaciers, 200 lakes, alpine meadows, and forests are a haven for fishermen, hikers, and wildlife alike. And two rustic stone chalets (called **Granite Park** and **Sperry**), reached only by foot or horseback, offer overnight accommodations; both were built around 1914 by the Great Northern Railroad.

At the eastern edge of the park – and Going-to-the-Sun Road – sits the small town of **St Mary**, which separates Lower St Mary Lake from St Mary Lake proper, and is best known for being at the eastern end of the spectacular road. It's a friendly town, attentive to the needs of visitors on their way in or out of the giant park.

Even the drive out of the park along US 89 is dramatically beautiful, descending rapidly from St Mary to Kiowa and winding sharply as it goes, then turning due east out of the mountains. From there, the enticing road goes to **Browning,** headquarters of the **Blackfeet Reservation** and also the home of the truly interesting **Museum of the Plains Indian** (tel: 406-338-2230; closed weekends Oct–May), which houses the most comprehensive collection of Blackfeet artifacts in existence.

Of particular note are the Assiniboine drums, some of which have been painted with wonderful visionary designs reminiscent of hallucinatory images; it is thought the hallucinations were caused by prolonged fasting. Browning's biggest event of the year occurs each July, when the town hosts the festival **North American Indian Days**, one of the largest gatherings of its kind.

Map on page 144

*A Plains Indian Assiniboine drum.*

**BELOW:**
Going-to-the-Sun Road, Montana, has been called "the most beautiful stretch of road in the world."

*In the summer of 2000, forest fires raged throughout the West, the worst in 50 years. The Bitterroot Valley, southwest of Libby near the Idaho border, was the worst affected. Check locally if you're thinking of visiting these areas, as the fires have burned thousands of acres of forest.*

## BEYOND THE GREAT DIVIDE

As waters flow west of the **Continental Divide** toward the Pacific, so too do paths of civilization. The Nez Percé, the Kootenai, the Pend d'Oreille, the Flathead, and other mountain tribes lived and hunted here in peace. Later the Blackfeet came from the plains across the Divide on horse-stealing raids, a journey many have since followed for different reasons.

The first white people to arrive were trappers and traders in the early part of the 19th century, followed by prospectors in search of gold and silver. Homesteaders heading west conquered the Rockies and moved on, some settling in eastern Washington. With the coming of the railroad, the lumber industry found a permanent home in the forests west of the Divide.

## Fire! Fire!

From Browning, take US 2 west over **Marias Pass** and skirt the southern edge of Glacier Park, passing through Hungry Horse and Kalispell once more. West of Kalispell, the **Kootenai National Forest** takes over where the Flathead leaves off. Along the highway toward **Libby**, evidence of the lumber industry's presence in this area becomes progressively more apparent. Timber has been big business here since 1892, when the Great Northern Railroad arrived. But as with all national forests, the Kootenai is a mixed-use area and within its boundaries (an area nearly three times the size of Rhode Island) lie many acres of wilderness: the habitat of elk, moose, deer, and Rocky Mountain bighorn sheep. There is one unique way for outsiders to grasp the beauty of this place – and the **Libby Ranger Station** (tel: 406-293-7773; open weekdays) holds the key. A system of observation towers, manned around the clock, were once the primary

**BELOW:** Mormon reenactment near Salt Lake City.

## SALT LAKE CITY

A long but beautiful 793-mile (1,276-km) journey from Coeur d'Alene, Idaho, on US 95 goes through five national forests on the way to the capital of the Mormon church: Salt Lake City, Utah. Founded in 1847 by Brigham Young, who led Mormons from the persecution in the East to the promised lands of the Utah basin, about 70 per cent of Salt Lake's current population belong to the church. The Mormon temple (one of over 100 in the world) is the town's focal point, and is a sacred place for members; the faith reserves the temple for its most special occasions, so it is not open to visitors. However, the immaculate grounds and visitor's center do allow a glimpse into this close and well-ordered religion. The Mormons live by a strict code shunning alcohol, tobacco, and even hot drinks like tea and coffee. Smoking is banned in most places in Salt Lake, and much of the state is dry, meaning the purchase of alcohol can be difficult. Like many cities in the Southwest, Salt Lake is blessed with a breath-taking setting: mountains in the background offset the desert in the foreground and the strikingly distinctive architecture of this rare religious capital. The Salt Lake City Visitors' Bureau can be reached on 801-538-1030.

method of forest fire surveillance. As fire detection methods became more sophisticated, these structures were gradually vacated. The Libby Ranger Station has opened its lookout atop **Big Creek Baldy Mountain** to the public, which is available on a reserve-ahead and pay-ahead basis. That being arranged, you drive into Libby and pick up directions and the key. State Highway 37 out of Libby leads to forestry service access roads, the last of which winds its way up to the foot of Big Creek Baldy Lookout. The last mile or so is extremely rough and steeply graded. However, the thrill of making it to the top, mingled with awe upon viewing the panorama that awaits, will take anyone's breath away. A tame mule deer has been known to greet visitors as they disembark. And it gets even better after climbing the steps of the 41-foot (12-meter) tower.

The 225-sq-foot (20-sq-meter) space with unobstructed windows and an observation deck on all sides contains items essential to survival and comfort and nothing more – save a fire-sighting device smack in the middle of the floor. Below, the tranquil beauty of the forest stretches for many miles in all directions; the wind becomes much more than a whistle, no longer muffled by the trees. This is a solitary, spiritual, romantic place to spend the night.

From Libby, where the **Cabinet Mountains** can be seen from downtown, it is a short drive west along US 2 to the Idaho border along the Kootenai River, passing near lovely and dramatic **Kootenai Falls** and through **Troy**, home of the largest silver mine in the United States. You are leaving a land of cowboy hats and rejoining a land of loggers and miners.

## INTO IDAHO

The road enters Boundary County – aptly named, as it borders not just Montana but also British Columbia and Washington – joining US 95 just north of **Bonners Ferry**. At **Sandpoint**, on the shores of the huge **Lake Pend d'Oreille**, US 2 splits off to the west, while US 95 bridges the lake on its way southwest toward Coeur d'Alene. From 1890 to 1910 three transcontinental railroad lines forged their way through this part of Idaho, creating a string of towns that dot the highway.

Before reaching **Coeur d'Alene** ㊸, US 95 greets the interstate. It is worth back-tracking east along Interstate 90 a little here, not only because the road hugs the banks of **Coeur d'Alene lake** for some 11 miles (17 km), but primarily because it leads to two vestiges of 19th-century Idaho, both unique in their way and completely dissimilar: the Old Mission and the Enaville Resort.

The **Coeur d'Alene Mission of the Sacred Heart** (also known as the Old Mission; tel: 208-682-3814) stands atop a hill overlooking the main road (I-90), as it has done since 1853. It is the oldest standing building in Idaho. Constructed of timber, mud, and wooden pegs by Father Anthony Ravalli and the Coeur d'Alene Indians, it is said to have risen "like a miracle in an almost total wilderness where even log houses were rare."

The Jesuits, Ravalli among them, came to this part of Idaho knowing they would be welcomed by the Coeur d'Alene Indians, who had been told by neigh-

Map on page 144

**BELOW:** buddies on a bench.

boring tribes of the great powers of the "Black Robes." Truly a Renaissance man, Ravalli's European training was reflected in the mission's design, perhaps best described as Native American-Italianate. The spacious, cathedral-like interior is decorated with chandeliers made from tin cans, whitewashed newspaper painted with floral motifs, carved pine crosses, a wooden altar painted to resemble marble, and many other precious artifacts.

In 1877 the Coeur d'Alene were forced to abandon their beloved mission for a reservation to the south, but they still consider it their mission today and return each August 15th to celebrate the Feast of the Assumption. Due to its location, the mission also became a rendezvous point for mountain men, fur traders, and "all sorts of riff-raff," in the words of the cavalrymen who were often called in to maintain peace and order. July brings an annual Historic Skills Fair – a modern-day rendezvous of crafts, mountain men, Coeur d'Alene, and tourists – back to the area.

The Old Mission had no confessional until the late 1800s when one was established, presumably to serve white settlers, some of whom may have sinned at an establishment now called the **Enaville Resort**, located in **Kingston,** east of the mission along I-90 and then north on Coeur d'Alene River Road. The resort was built in 1880 as an overnight stop *en route* to gold and silver country, gaining several nicknames over the years – the Snakepit, Josie's, the Clark Hotel. Located strategically across from a lumberyard, a rail crossroads, and a fork of the Coeur d'Alene River, it has served in its time as boomtown bar, hotel, and house of ill repute.

Today the Enaville is merely a relaxing place to stop for a drink, eat a bite, and meet the locals. Furnishings have piled up over the years and include many pieces hand-wrought by a mysterious man from Finland known only as Mr Egil. His materials were pine burls, antlers, horns, and animal hides; his only recompense was a room, board, and free beer.

**BELOW:** riding horseback in Washington state.

## WASHINGTON STATE

A short drive west on I-90 takes you out of Idaho and into eastern **Washington**, a land of deserts, canyons, coulees, wheat fields, and irrigated farmland – a sharp contrast to the densely forested terrain of northern Idaho. Historically, this region was home to numerous Native American peoples, most of whom lived along the banks of the Columbia River. Their descendants, members of the Colville Confederated Tribes, live today on a reservation bordered on two sides by the Columbia River. This was uninviting territory for early white explorers. The Grand Coulee itself presented a major obstacle, with few openings through which to pass. In the 1880s the first white settlers in the region faced enormous hardships. Their numbers remained relatively few until the completion of the Grand Coulee Dam. Built during the height of the Great Depression, the dam and the Columbia Basin irrigation and electrification project changed the face of this region for all time.

Outside **Spokane** ❻, US 2 travels through golden wheat fields toward the dam. Road signs become a little confusing as the road approaches not only the

Map on page 144

Grand Coulee Dam, but the towns of Electric City, Grand Coulee, Grand Coulee Dam, and Coulee City. At Wilbur, State 174 goes north to the town of Grand Coulee, where State 155 continues on to the dam. As they say, "You can't miss it." The impact of the **Grand Coulee Dam** ⑥ cannot be overestimated – economically or visually. Its aims, achievements, and sheer size are all on a grand scale. Although it is over 50 years old, the design of the dam is of such stylistic integrity that it still looks modern today.

The drive along State 155, from the dam to **Coulee City** and US 2, is surprisingly scenic. The road skirts the lake on one side and the algae-clad coulee walls on the other. West of Coulee City along US 2, gently sloping fields of wheat, dotted with the occasional farmhouse, give the appearance of a vast desert. Layers of blue mountains appear in the distance like a mirage – the first of the coastal chains.

At **Orondo**, the highway meets, follows, and crosses the **Columbia River** and then branches off, tracing its tributary the Wenatchee into foothills of the **Cascade Range**. This is orchard country: green patches of fertile land jut into the river and contrast with the golden hills; some of the local stands put out ripe apricots for sale.

Now US 2 climbs and enters a realm of tall timber, passing through the town of **Leavenworth** ⑥ – a self-styled, pseudo-Bavarian ski resort and gateway to the **Wenatchee National Forest**. Over the rushing south fork of the Skykomish River, and through the **Snoqualmie National Forest**, past several small towns with no-nonsense names like Gold Bar and Startup, US 2 continues west, bringing you just to the northeast of **Seattle** ⑥ *(see page 172)*, where you catch the expressway and (hopefully) breeze into one of America's most interesting and attractive cities.

*The Washington State Ferry system, the largest in the US, runs ferries to the Olympic Peninsula from Seattle.*

**BELOW:** Sol Duc Falls, Olympic Peninsula.

## THE OLYMPIC PENINSULA

Before you dig in your heels in Seattle, however, another nearby destination beckons. Washington's **Olympic Peninsula** is the northwesternmost corner of the contiguous 48 states – a remote, exotic and wildly beautiful region within easy reach of both Seattle and Victoria, British Columbia. It is set apart from these places not merely by Puget (pronounced *pyew-jet*) Sound and the Strait of Juan de Fuca, but by its climate, its geology, the mystery of its peaks and forests, and by the natural rhythms that guide the pace of life.

From **Edmonds**, due north of Seattle, a ferry crosses the short, scenic distance across the sound to **Kingston** ⑥ on the peninsula. From here it is a lovely drive west and north to the peninsula's northeastern tip at the entrance to Puget Sound.

At the heart of the peninsula are the magestic **Olympic Mountains**, snow-streaked even in summer. Long a subject of myth, these mountains remained unexplored until the 1890s, when an expedition from Seattle set off in search of man-eating savages. Even the peninsula's Native Americans avoided venturing into the interior, fearing the wrath of mighty Thunderbird, who was believed to reside atop Mount Olympus. Today the mountains are preserved and protected in a near-wilderness state as part of Olympic National

Park, which comprises 900,000 acres (365,000 hectares) of the peninsula, most of it inland but also including a 50-mile (80-km) strip of Pacific Ocean coastline. Only a few roads venture into the park, and these only peripherally. In fact, the park proper is surrounded by the **Olympic National Forest**, which makes it difficult to reach. Because the peninsula is largely under some form of Federal jurisdiction, there is considerable conflict with the lumber industry.

The Olympic Peninsula sustains the rainforests of the Hoh, Quinault, and Queets river valleys; the glacial peaks of the Olympics; and the rugged Pacific coastline as well as lumber towns, fishing villages, and nine American Indian reservations. Roosevelt elk, cougars, and bald eagles all reside here in greater concentrations than anywhere else in the land.

Charming **Port Gamble**, the first town along the route, calls itself "a permanent forest community," and so it is – an authentic lumber town reflecting a bygone era. Just beyond it, a bridge crosses the Hood Canal – the work of glaciers rather than men. At the town of **Discovery Bay** (a good place to buy fresh oysters, clams, and herring), State 20 veers off and up to Port Townsend.

## Victorian town

**Port Townsend** ⑩, first settled in 1851, is the peninsula's oldest town and an attractive base. Sea captains and storekeepers from back East made their homes here, and it was quick to become a boomtown, built in anticipation of being linked with the Union Pacific Railroad and consequently becoming the major seaport of the Northwest. All this came to pass – for Seattle, not Port Townsend. After the bust, settlers tore up the train tracks, closed down the banks, and departed for more prosperous parts.

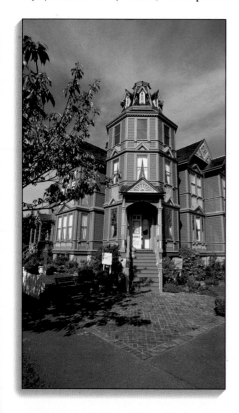

**BELOW:**
Victorian B&B in Port Townsend, Olympic Peninsula.

Left behind is the best example of a Victorian seacoast town north of San Francisco. Declared a National Historic District, Port Townsend has become a haven for artists and is also the headquarters of the **Northwest School of Wooden Boatbuilding** (tel: 360-385-4948), where a dying art has been revived. Free tours are offered to the public on weekdays throughout the year.

US 101 loops around the peninsula like a misshapen horseshoe, open at the bottom. In the north it passes through Olympic National Forest and on to the lumber towns of the "West End." The region between Discovery Bay and Port Angeles has been called the "banana belt," sitting as it does in the rain shadow of the Olympics. Farmers here see an average rainfall of only 17 inches (43 cm) compared with upwards of 140 inches (355 cm) on the other side of the mountains. Irrigated farms are a common sight along this part of US 101, as are madrona trees, twisted and terracotta in color.

## Small and distinctive

The towns along the way are small and distinctive. **Blyn** is gone before you can say "Little Brown Church of Blyn," its one and only landmark. **Sequim** (pronounced *skwim*) is a bigger town with a sense of humor about its name. Just north of here, on the Strait of Juan de Fuca – explorer De Fuca thought this was the Northwest Passage – is **Dungeness**, where the Dungeness crabs are landed.

Port Angeles, next settlement to the west, is called the "big town." The plants of several major lumber companies are located here, and the smell of wood permeates the air; it's also here that you catch big cruise boats to Victoria, British Columbia on gorgeous Vancouver Island. From Port Angeles, the road traces Elwha Creek, enters the National Forest, and winds down to crystalline Lake Crescent within the National Park. The highway is lined with towering evergreens, the roadside carpeted with ferns, as you continue west toward the ocean and the rainfall amounts suddenly begin rising again.

Map on page 144

## West End

Logging is a way of life in the peninsula's "West End." US 101 passes through the towns of **Sappho** and **Forks**, the latter calling itself "logging capital of the world," and evidence of this dubious activity is everywhere: clearcut hillsides denuded of all trees, logging trucks barreling down the roads, brawny lumberjacks, and cafés that request all patrons to remove their spiky, tree-climbing boots before entering the premises. Most of the big timber is long since gone now, and what remains is usually – though not always – off-limits to these lumber companies.

The temperate rainforests west of the mountains are the most beautiful of all the sights in **Olympic National Park ⓲**. They are the only ones in North America and contain some of the tallest timber in the world. Most accessible of these awe-inspiring forest is the **Hoh River Valley**, located south of Forks and inland on Hoh River Road: the embodiment of the "forest primeval" immortalized by Henry Wadsworth Longfellow. Most awesome are the ancient evergreens –

*The peninsula's town of Dungeness is the place to find the famous crabs.*

**BELOW:**
Second Beach at sunset, Olympic National Park.

**Map on page 144**

western redcedar, Sitka spruce, Douglas fir, and western hemlock – shrouded with club moss, filtered by light, surrounded by ferns and the sound of the river. It is an eerie, overgrown, magical place, barely touched by the presence of man – with one exception.

John "The Iron Man of Hoh" Huelsdonk came to the Hoh Valley from Iowa in 1891. Discouraged by all who met him, he nevertheless poled his canoe up the wild river and made his home in this forest. What he could not carry by canoe, such as his cast iron stove, he strapped to his back. Hence the nickname – and the birth of a legend. The Iron Man died and is buried in the forest he so loved, as is his wife.

The village of **La Push,** on the **Quilayute Indian Reservation,** is reached by way of La Push Road (Route 110) from Forks. Those who live here fish for a living, and those who visit here visit for the fishing. If La Push were not so unpretentious, it would surely proclaim itself driftwood capital of the world: its beach is beautiful at night, a string of warming campfires and sea-stacks visible through the perpetual mist.

## Land's end

**BELOW AND RIGHT:** Henry Wadsworth Longfellow called woods like the Olympic Peninsula's Hoh Rainforst the "forest primeval."

You can't get any farther northwest in the continental United States than isolated **Neah Bay**. Forking off the loop of US 101 at Sappho, State 113 and then State 112 winds its way to the ocean along the strait. Vancouver Island is now visible in the distance. Neah Bay is the ancestral and current home of the fine **Makah Indian Nation**, whose presence here for at least 3,000 years has been confirmed by archeologists. Once renowned whale hunters who took to the sea in cedar canoes, they still live off the ocean, though the catch today is more likely to be salmon. Entering town, a sign proclaims: "Makah Nation – a treaty tribe since 1855." The Makah do not underestimate the importance of this treaty, which guarantees their territorial and fishing rights, which to them means survival.

Neah Bay is also a gateway to one of America's most splendid stretches of wilderness coastline. A network of gravel and dirt roads goes part of the distance, but to reach land's end it is necessary to go on foot. If you want some adventure, drive as far as you dare and then hike the precipitous trail down to pretty **Shi-Shi Beach** and simply gaze out to sea. Be aware of time – and tide-tables– as the water rushes in quickly around here.

The trail to **Cape Flattery** is shorter and less dangerous. It descends an intricate stairway of tree roots through the forest, a clearing and a stand of huckleberry bushes before reaching the cliff's edge. Look out over Cape Flattery, knowing you stand as far northwest as possible in the lower 48 states of the USA – and that you have reached the end of a journey that began, thousands of miles ago, beside a different ocean in busy Boston Harbor.

Then retrace your steps back to Seattle, or follow US 101 around the rest of the peninsula and down to the town of Aberdeen, where you can, if you wish drive all the way to Mexico on US 101 and Highway 1 (*see the Pacific Route, page 382*).

# A SHORT STAY IN SEATTLE

*Seattle is youthful and friendly, business-minded, busy, and booming:* the *city for the 21st century. Here's a list of the not-to-be-missed attractions:*

◆ The Space Needle is only one aspect of the huge and impressive Seattle Center; other things to see and do include the opera house, an IMAX theater, a children's museum, a laserium, a fun fair, and the excellent Pacific Science Center.

◆ The Seattle Aquarium features 200 varieties of fish native to Puget Sound, plus environments simulating rocky reefs, sandy seafloors, eelgrass beds and tide pools. It's one part of the vibrant Waterfront area, which also has ships, piers, stores, and restaurants.

◆ Filled with shops and food, food, food, Seattle's International District shows off the city's unique mixture of Asian cultures. Beyond Chinatown lies the Curry Triangle, filled with Thai, Laotian, and Cambodian shops and restaurants.

△ **SPACE NEEDLE SKYLINE**
Built for the 1962 World's Fair, the Space Needle offers the best views of the city and surrounding hills. Relax in the revolving lounge at the top.

▽ **SEATTLE ART MUSEUM**
Designed by Robert Venturi, the museum holds a highly regarded collection of Northwest Indian art, with paintings by the Mystics group

◆ Experience Music Project (EMP) is a rock music museum conceived by Paul Allen of Microsoft fame, featuring artifacts like Eric Clapton's guitar, state-of-the-art technology, interactive exhibits, and architecture by Frank Gehry.

◆ Beautiful bodies bounding on sandy beaches aside cyclists, joggers and volleyball players make Alki Beach Seattle's answer to southern California. Alki Point Lighthouse looks postcard-perfect in front of Puget Sound.

◆ "The mountain" (as it is known by locals) is in Mount Rainier National Park, just outside of the city. A single road loops through miles of park-land and timbered canyons. South of Seattle is Mount St Helens; its crater (caused by a far-reaching 1980 eruption) can be accessed via roads with views of Spirit Lake.

▷ **PIKE PLACE MARKET**
Started in 1907 as a farmers' market, Pike Place still sells local produce and the freshest of fish, but they have now been joined by crafts people, street muscians, restaurants, cafés, and coffee-houses.

For visitors interested in staying longer in the big city, pick up a copy of *Insight Guide: Seattle*. This is a companion to the present volume, and is packed with insightful text and stunning pictures.

## THE EMERALD CITY

Seattle is constantly rated as one of the most livable cities in the US. With a diverse population, rich cultural life, and booming industries (Boeing and Microsoft), all situated amid awesome scenery, who wouldn't want to live here? Named for Native American chief Sealth, the laid-back lifestyle associated with the city has long been in place; tribes like the Salish and the Duwamish had been living peacefully in the hills for years. As do its residents now, surrounded by water and mountain peaks, working hard, playing easy, and drinking gallons of strong coffee. If the future of America is anywhere, it is probably right here.

▽ Red arrows on the map indicate routes from the city detailed in this book

△ **PIONEER SQUARE**
The oldest part of the city, Pioneer Square's 19th-century buildings are now showcases for shops and bars.

▷ **WATERFRONT**
A vintage streetcar serves the Seattle Waterfront, transporting tourists and locals alike.

## Important Information

**Population:**
540,000.

**Dialing code:**
206

**Website:**
www.seeseattle.org

**Tourist information:**
800 Convention Place, Washington State Convention & Trade Center, 98101 Tel: 206-461-5840

Seattle Throughways

0    5 miles
0    5 km

# THE CENTRAL ROUTE

*A detailed guide to the Central US, with principal sites
clearly cross-referenced by number to the maps*

It is perhaps fitting to begin a journey across America from the nation's capital of Washington, DC; the many museums and famous landmarks that give a glimpse into the country's past do much to set the scene for the rest of your trip west. In fact ,there are a few routes you could choose to head west from here, but for our purposes we've chosen a "south-central" course that combines enough history and beauty to sate any traveler's appetite.

The history lesson begins as soon as you leave Washington, heading first west and then sharply south along the beautiful Skyline Drive and the Blue Ridge Parkway through the Appalachian Mountains of Virginia. This was Stonewall Jackson territory; the route is sprinkled with Civil War sites as well as a myriad of caverns. Interstate 40, which we'll be following for much of the trip west, continues into North Carolina and through the Great Smoky Mountains, taking you past the charming old homes of Knoxville Tennessee and Andrew Jackson's home, The Hermitage, before heading into Nashville, capital not only of Tennessee but of country music.

From there it's truly into small-town America as you hit Arkansas, stopping for a time in Little Rock, with its impressive state capitol building and Historic District and Hot Springs. Then roll on into Oklahoma, where we pick up legendary Route 66 – which originates in Chicago – a highway that crosses eight states and all three time zones *(see also "Route 66" essay, page 35)*. Some know Route 66 from legend, others from childhood, when every mile with its weathered telegraph poles and zany-shaped motels were milestones on an exciting journey into a wonderland whose roadside attractions included snake pits, live buffaloes, and Indian dancers.

Oklahoma's piece of Route 66 passes through many interesting small towns, but also some bigger ones, such as Tulsa, with its Art Deco downtown, and Oklahoma City. You'll cut across the Texas Panhandle before heading into New Mexico, visiting the attractive cities of Santa Fe and Albuquerque. The state has a wealth of ancient pueblos; homes of early inhabitants that are well worth visiting. As you cross into Arizona you enter the Navaho Nation; the route passes by the Petrified Forest National Park before reaching Flagstaff, the largest city in the northern part of the state and the jumping-off point for the incomparable Grand Canyon. You'll cross some pretty desolate countryside in western Arizona, and again in eastern California's Mojave Desert, before you start seeing signs of "civilization" as you head into the urban sprawl of Los Angeles. With some 2,900 miles (4,700 km) now behind you, the Pacific Ocean beckons. ❏

**PRECEDING PAGES:** Route 66 memorabilia in Seligman, Arizona; McLean, Texas.
**LEFT:** heading straight for Monument Valley in the colorful Southwest.

# A SHORT STAY IN WASHINGTON, DC

*Planned as a city of monuments and memorials, the nation's capital is also one of its most beautiful. Here's a list of the not-to-be-missed attractions:*

◆ The Capitol Building is the home of America's national legislature, and stands as a symbol of Washington, DC.

◆ Whether you wish to retrace the path of Martin Luther King Jr, whose "I Have a Dream" speech came from these steps, or simply take a look at the huge statue of Abraham Lincoln, the Lincoln Memorial celebrates the liberty that the founding fathers hoped the US would provide.

◆ In keeping with the classical motif of the city, the domed Jefferson Memorial honors the third US president and chief author of the Declaration of Independence.

◆ The Vietnam Veterans Memorial lists the names of all known American soldiers killed in the 1960s conflict. It is also a personal monument, as families travel from across the US to find the names of relatives who never returned.

◆ At first a strategic stronghold in the Civil War, the Arlington National Cemetery contained 16,000 headstones by the end of the struggle. The eternal flame at the grave of John F. Kennedy honors the fallen president, and the Tomb of the Unknowns commemorates the nameless soldiers felled in battles over the last 100 years.

◆ Housing the most impressive collection of air and space artifacts in the world, the National Air and Space Museum combines these with hands-on experiments and audio-visual exhibits.

◆ The Library of Congress, founded by Jefferson, is now the largest library in the world. Assistants are sometimes able to give tours to visitors.

 Visitors staying longer in the big city should pick up a copy of *Insight Guide: Washington DC*. This is a companion to the present volume, and is packed with insightful text and stunning pictures.

▷ **THE WHITE HOUSE**
Self-guided tours of the President's home are popular, so be prepared to wait in line.

▽ **WASHINGTON MONUMENT**
The Washington Monument towers 555 feet (170 meters) above the city. In 70 seconds you can be at the top.

◁ **NIGHTTIME REFLECTIONS**
At dusk, Washington changes from a political town into a monumental city of beauty. From left to right: the Capitol, the Washington Monument, and the Lincoln Memorial.

△ **SMITHSONIAN INSTITUTE**
Sometimes called "America's attic," the Smithsonian is actually several buildings, and traces developments in diverse fields, particularly science.

# THE NATION'S CAPITAL CITY

A visit to Washington, DC is nothing less than a lesson in history, literally a living history, since the President of the US lives here. The city also has a unique beauty, the credit for which should go to George Washington. The new president insisted on creating a new city as the nation's capital, a place as grand as Paris or London. With this in mind, he hired French architect Pierre Charles L'Enfant to create a "city of magnificent distances." L'Enfant's plan was only partially realized, but Washington *is* magnificent and the distances between monuments deceptively large; bring a good pair of walking shoes.

△ **NATIONAL GALLERY OF ART**
I.M. Pei designed the east wing *(shown)*, which houses a collection of 20th-century art. The neo-classical west wing includes works by Da Vinci and Raphael.

## Important Information

| Population: | Tourist information: |
|---|---|
| 600,000 | 1300 Pennsylvania |
| **Dialing code:** | Avenue NW, |
| 202 | Washington, DC |
| **Website:** | 20005 |
| www.washington.org | Tel: 202-789-7000 |

▽ Red arrows on the map indicate routes from the city detailed in this book

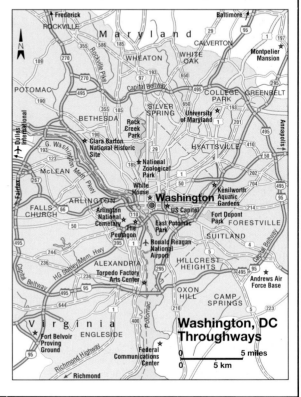

# Washington, DC Throughways

0 — 5 miles
0 — 5 km

# WASHINGTON, DC TO ARKANSAS

*From Ashville, North Carolina to Nashville, Tennessee and beyond, this route takes in Virginia, Memphis, and the scented highways of Arkansas to Little Rock*

Map on page 184

Washington

**O**ur route begins in **Washington, DC ❶** *(see page 180)*, the first leg of which runs to Winston-Salem, North Carolina, along Interstate 66, and then I-81 south. The interstate will take you to the town of Front Royal and then the Skyline Drive, which runs south along the eastern rampart of the Blue Ridge Mountains, mountains so pine-scented and peaceful we always recommend this drive as the preferred route into North Carolina. On the way to Front Royal, you may want to cruise past the town of **Fairfax**, where, a few miles west is the **Virginia Visitors' Center**, with hundreds of brochures covering every facet of Virginia tourism. Stop in for schedules of current events and festivals throughout the "Old Dominion."

At some point, if you have time, you can change from I-66 to Virginia 55, which runs parallel, as both roads head for the mountains. The pace of life begins to slow almost immediately as you drive along increasingly serpentine roads with vistas opening to reveal the majestic Blue Ridge Mountains looming in the distance. Cumulous clouds hover over the dark peaks to the west. Small waterfalls slide down rock faces along the road. Beautiful pink and purple crown vetch, dandelions, and goldenrod grow wild on the hillsides.

**LEFT:** Grand Ole Opry, Nashville.
**BELOW:** flying the flag on a bus.

## Moving site for Southerners

The fast track on Interstate 66 weaves through a tangle of ever-growing suburbs around Washington, DC, practically obscuring a moving site for Southerners. A detour from I-66 onto the smaller SR 234 leads to **Manassas National Battlefield Park ❷** (tel: 703-361-1339; open daily until dusk), the spot of two great Confederate victories during the Civil War – the First and Second Battles of Manassas (or locally, Bull Run). Ten hours of deadly fighting on July 21, 1861 resulted in a Union defeat, and it was at this battle that General Thomas J. Jackson earned the nickname "Stonewall." The second battle, one year later, proved the genius of Confederate General Robert E. Lee. Driving and walking tours are available, and the visitor center has a museum and slide program. Be warned, however, that even though the site is well signposted, finding the correct turn-off can be maddingly confusing – drive slowly and be alert.

The Civil War looms large in these parts, as Virginia was the site for more than half of its major battles (as an example, the Shenandoah Valley town of Winchester changed hands 74 times). At Front Royal you can take orientation tours of several Civil War sites, and at **Strasburg,** famous since 1761 for its pot-

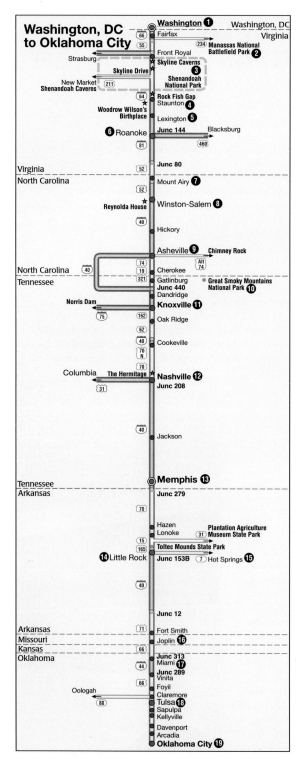

**Washington, DC
to Oklahoma City**

Washington ①
Fairfax
Front Royal
Skyline Caverns ③
Shenandoah National Park
Rock Fish Gap
Staunton ④
Lexington ⑤
Roanoke ⑥
Junc 144
Junc 80
Mount Airy ⑦
Winston-Salem ⑧
Hickory
Asheville ⑨
Cherokee
Gatlinburg
Junc 440
Dandridge
Knoxville ⑪
Oak Ridge
Cookeville
Nashville ⑫
Junc 208
Jackson
Memphis ⑬
Junc 279
Hazen
Lonoke
Little Rock ⑭
Junc 153B
Junc 12
Fort Smith
Joplin ⑯
Junc 313
Miami ⑰
Junc 289
Vinita
Foyil
Claremore
Tulsa ⑱
Sapulpa
Kellyville
Davenport
Arcadia
Oklahoma City ⑲

Washington, DC
Virginia
Manassas National Battlefield Park ②
Shenandoah National Park
Blacksburg
Reynolda House
Chimney Rock
Great Smoky Mountains National Park ⑩
The Hermitage
Plantation Agriculture Museum State Park
Toltec Mounds State Park
Hot Springs ⑮

Strasburg
New Market
Shenandoah Caverns
Skyline Drive
Woodrow Wilson's Birthplace
Virginia
North Carolina
North Carolina
Tennessee
Norris Dam
Columbia
Tennessee
Arkansas
Arkansas
Missouri
Kansas
Oklahoma
Oologah

tery, there's the **Stonewall Jackson Museum** (tel: 540-465-5884; open daily). Memorabilia of the famous Confederate general includes a bullet-pierced coat worn during his brilliantly flexible 1862 campaign defending the strategic north–south Shenandoah Valley (an "avenue of invasion") against Federal army troops.

"There are two things never to be lost sight of by a military commander," General Thomas J. "Stonewall" Jackson declared. "Always mystify, mislead, and surprise the enemy if possible… Such tactics will win every time." Strasburg is also home to the **Museum of American Presidents** (tel: 540-465-5999; open daily), eight of whom were Virginians.

## From the earth to the sky

Nestled in the foothills of Virginia's Blue Ridge Mountains – amid farms and woodlands, battlefields, riverbeds, streams, and tiny hamlets – are the **Crystal Caverns** (tel: 540-465-8660; open daily), one of a series of cave complexes carved out of the limestone cliffs at each side of the valley. The caverns are near the Stonewall Jackson Museum, also on the battlefield of Hupps Hill. The **Skyline Caverns** (tel: 800-296-4545) are 1 mile south of Front Royal; the **Endless Caverns** (tel: 540-896-2283), **Luray Caverns** (tel: 540-743-6551), and **Shenandoah Caverns** (tel: 540-477-3115) are all open daily and are near **New Market**, whose other attractions include a State Historical Park and museum on the site where Confederate troops routed a superior Union force in 1864, using teenage cadets from the Virginia Military Institute in Lexington.

**Front Royal** is a fairly ugly little town full of chain stores and fast-food restaurants crammed into a few town blocks. Luckily, you are not far away from the north entrance of **Shenandoah National Park** ③, where the 105-mile (169-km) **Skyline Drive** begins. Established in 1926 by an act of Congress, the park was an experiment in land reclamation. At the time, the region was overpopulated and the land was eroding. President Franklin Roosevelt ordered the Civilian Conservation Corps to build recreation facilities and complete construction of the Skyline Drive in 1939. During the decades since, the forests have revived and are once again densely overgrown with oak, hickory, pine, and locust trees.

Map on page 184

The **Dickey Ridge Visitors' Center**, open from April to October, is 4½ miles (7 km) down the road. Here you can pick up maps of the park, guides to local vegetation and wildlife, and information about camping and lodging. If the pioneer spirit of "roughing it" doesn't strike your fancy, there are still informative hikes and talks on the natural life of the park led by rangers; you will undoubtedly be tempted to get off the road awhile and hike some of the beautiful forest trails. Even if you don't, at least pack a meal to eat *al fresco* at one of the seven picnic locations.

Although the earliest access to the Skyline Drive through the park is at Front Royal, the road may be closed in winter, necessitating a drive further south as far as Swift Run Gap, east of **Elkton**, where US 33 crosses southbound US 340.

*The speed limit in the park is a leisurely 35 miles an hour – the perfect pace to enjoy the silence, the view, and the deer.*

## Oh Shenandoah

Immediately upon entering Shenandoah National Park, the speed limit slows to 35 miles an hour (55 kph), and the lumbering pace of your fellow cars sets the mood for a leisurely drive. Initially, it's a two-lane, winding road covered with dense trees on both sides. As the road ascends, however, you begin to get magnificent glimpses of the **Shenandoah Valley** and **Shenandoah River** to the west. Stop at one of the many overlooks, get out of the car, and take in the majesty of the sight. Almost as noticable as the view is the silence; stop frequently, turn off the engine and make the most of it. As you continue south, you'll see **Massanutten Mountain** between the north and south forks of the

**BELOW:** Luray, Virginia in the Shenandoah Valley.

Shenandoah River and then, after about 10 miles (16 km) more, the road switches angles to give you an eastern view of Piedmont country.

At Mile 50.7 (Km 82), stop for a short round-trip hike to **Dark Hollow Falls**, the closest waterfall to the drive. Water tumbles 70 feet (21 meters) over its greenstone face. Nearby Big Meadows is – along with Dickey Ridge – one of the two main visitors' centers in the park. For those wishing to stay overnight, the **Big Meadows Lodge and Campgrounds** are a convenient stop.

Hundreds of miles of hiking trails lead off the drive into a wilderness dotted with hickory, white pine, red spruce, and chestnut trees, some of which was earlier cleared and planted by the original settlers. After extending their farms onto the hillsides from the fertile Shenandoah Valley, the settlers bragged of being "the breadbasket of the Confederacy."

## Natural state

Thousands of tons of grain, leather, and iron were left here to support the Southern forces in the Civil War, nourished by the meat from hogs and cattle and equipped with uniforms from the wool of thousands of sheep. Memories of the Civil War are everywhere, and 400 Confederate soldiers are buried at **Mt Jackson**, a town near the Shenandoah Caverns.

In a novel experiment, almost a century after the conflict, President Franklin D. Roosevelt allowed the over-used foothills to return to their natural state. Pastures and croplands gradually became overgrown with shrubs and trees, creating a wilderness to which hundreds of species of birds, deer, bear, bobcat, and other creatures returned (although few of these can be seen). The Skyline Drive ends at **Rockfish Gap**, where US 64 leads to **Staunton ❹**, a pleasant former

**BELOW:**
Roanoke, Virginia, is known as the Capital of the Blue Ridge.

Map on page 184

mining town with buildings dating to the 18th century, some of which are B&Bs. Yet another president, also known for his pursuit of peace, is remembered at Staunton, where the **Woodrow Wilson Birthplace and Museum** (tel: 540-885-0897, open daily) illustrates local living conditions in the mid-19th century and portrays the 28th president's political career and eight-year (1913–21) White House stint.

West of I-81 is the attractive town of **Lexington ❺**, where ol' Stonewall was teaching cadets at the state-supported Virginia Military Institute (VMI) shortly after its founding in 1831. You can see the **Stonewall Jackson House** (tel: 540-463-2552; open daily). Jackson's Confederate colleague General Robert E. Lee also lived in Lexington and taught at the college founded by George Washington, known ever since as Washington & Lee University. Both universities welcome visitors. The latter has a chapel containing Lee's office and artifacts, while VMI's museums include one devoted to George C. Marshall, the politician and diplomat who won a Nobel Peace Prize at the end of World War II.

## Blue Ridge Mountains

Virginia's alluring landscape is a welcome diversion from the trials of the highway. The air is suddenly refreshingly clear, and the famous blue haze shrouding the Blue Ridge Mountains hoves into view. **Roanoke ❻** (pop. 97,000), known as the "Capital of the Blue Ridge" for its proximity to the Blue Ridge Parkway – the connecting link between Shenandoah and Tennessee's Great Smoky Mountains – is a pleasantly relaxed city famous for a downtown **Farmers Market** that has been operating for 120 years. Adjoining the market is a multi-cultural complex known as **Center in the Square** (tel: 540-342-5700), a

**TIP**

Leave yourself plenty of time to enjoy the walking and hiking excursions offered along the Blue Ridge Parkway; even a tiny walk to a beautiful waterfall can relieve the tedium of driving.

**BELOW:** the Blue Ridge Parkway was built along the top of the mountains.

vibrant collection of shops, restaurants, art galleries, and a planetarium. There are also history and science museums, as well as the **Harrison Museum of African American Culture** (most are closed Mon). Mill Mountain, topped by the huge, illuminated **Roanoke Star**, overlooks the city and is the site of the **Zoological Park** (tel: 540-343-3241; open daily), whose main attraction is a Siberian tiger called Ruby. **Virginia's Explore Park** (tel: 800-842-9163; closed Sun), just off the Blue Ridge Parkway (its junction is with State Road 116), is an environmental and historical site containing a re-created 17th-century village and exhibits dating back to 1000 AD.

Interstate 81 continues south, flanked by the vast Jefferson National Forest offering access at **Blacksburg** to the **Cascades National Recreation Trail**, a picturesque gorge that ends in a waterfall (a 4-mile/6-km hike, round trip). There's another access point farther along I-81 at Wytheville, where US 77 heads north to a campground in the park. But our route turns south just before that on US 52, which crosses the North Carolina border and takes us through the small town of **Mount Airy ❼** *(see page 69)*, home of the homespun 1960s TV situation comedy *Mayberry RFD*.

## Museum of living history

Continue south on US 52 to **Winston-Salem ❽** (pop. 144,000), founded by Moravian immigrants in 1766. The area where it all began, **Old Salem,** is now a museum of living history. "After traveling through the woods for many days … the first view of the town is romantic, just as it breaks upon you through the woods; it is pleasantly seated on a rising ground and is surrounded by beautiful meadows, well-cultivated fields, and shady woods," wrote William Loughton Smith in his journal of May 1791.

**BELOW:**
pickin' session
at Mount Airy,
North Carolina.

Arriving in Winston-Salem definitely gives one a sense of having "landed" in North Carolina, and the miles of highway driving start to pay dividends. Old Salem is possibly one of the most authentic and inviting living history towns in the US. Its old tavern is an upscale restaurant, and the simple timber homes contain their original furnishings. The printing shop of John Christian Blum, founding publisher in 1811 of *The Farmers' and Planters' Almanac*, is now a souvenir shop selling quill pens as well as cider and cookies. There is a **Children's Museum** (closed Sun morning) with hands-on exhibits. A remarkable timber bridge stands next to the **Frank L. Horton Museum Center**, containing paintings, textiles, ceramics, silver, and other 19th-century creative works. And what of the giant-size metal coffee pot standing on the village green? Built by the sons of Salem's founders, Samuel and Julius Mickey, it was used to advertise their tinsmith's shop.

Costumed guides roam another restored Moravian village, **Historic Bethabara Park** (tel: 336-924-8191; closed Sat and Sun morning) in a pleasant green setting off University Parkway.

The city's **Visitor Center** at 6th and Cherry streets (tel: 800-331-7108) distributes a free map of a downtown walking tour that includes the **City Market** – where a farmers market is held on summer Tuesdays and Thursdays – and such interesting structures as the Georgian Revival *Winston-Salem Journal* building (a replica of Philadelphia's Independence Hall), the Renaissance Revival Our Lady of Fatima Chapel, and the Art Deco R.J. Reynolds Building (whose New York architects Shreve and Lamb used it as a prototype for their subsequent Empire State Building.) Numerous old brick buildings in nearby streets are being transformed into galleries and artist studios.

**Reynolds House**, the former 1914 home of Katharine Smith and Richard Joshua Reynolds (founder of the giant R. J. Reynolds Tobacco Company) – along with its gardens and adjoining Reynolds Village, in which the former buildings have been converted into shops, offices, and restaurants – is open to visitors (tel: 336-726-5325; closed Mon). *The New Yorker*'s Brendan Gill praised the modesty of the mansion, adding "the intention here is plainly not to show off but to be happy among friends…"

From Winston-Salem we join I-40, which remains our route for most of the journey. About 73 miles (117 km) along the route is the town of **Hickory**, which is famous for its furniture: 100 such stores are gathered together in one center, and there is even a **Furniture Museum** (tel: 800-462-6278; open daily).

## ASHEVILLE TO NASHVILLE

The Blue Ridge Parkway sweeps across I-40 just before Asheville, home to a popular winery. "More scenery, more music, more country on Country 92 FM," sings the jingle on the car radio, and indeed, when you begin to get a sense of being enveloped by mountains, you've probably arrived. There are vistas around almost every street corner, and the mighty Mount Pisgah to the west signals the beginning of the Great Smokies.

Exuding a certain amount of small-town charm, **Asheville ❾** is architecturally diverse. Besides Queen Anne, Romanesque, and Revival styles, the town also has one of the largest collections of Art Deco architecture in the Southeast, outside of Miami Beach. You'll find the winery, along with shops and restaurants, in the immense landscaped gardens of the 250-room **Biltmore Estate** (tel: 800- 624-1575; open daily), America's largest privately owned home. George Vanderbilt's 250-room vision took root in 1887, when he visited Asheville on vacation and became enchanted by the mountain scenery. Vanderbilt set out to create a mansion modeled after the French Loire Valley chateaux, and equipped it with many state-of-the-art luxuries. Today visitors can enjoy the estate virtually as it was. The estate was a backdrop for *Being There*, one of several movies shot locally, along with *Thunder Road* and *28 Days*.

The natural beauty of Asheville, North Carolina's largest city, is emphasized in its botanical gardens, an arboretum with miles of walking trails, a nature center interpreting the area's plant and wildlife, the park-like Riverside Cemetery, and the river itself – perfect for white-water activities. Entry to all of these is free, as is the delightfully named **North Carolina Homespun Museum** (tel: 828-523-7651), which offers weaving demonstrations, and the **Folk Art Center** (tel: 828-298-7928).

Map on page 184

*Coffee break: this gigantic pot sits on the village green in Old Salem.*

**BELOW:** Biltmore is the largest private residence in the US.

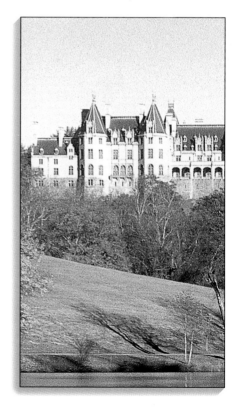

## Muse of the mountain

Asheville's beauty has attracted its fair share of literary giants, including F. Scott Fitzgerald and the influential author Thomas Wolfe. Wolfe spent his childhood in his mother's sprawling Queen Anne-style boarding house on Market Street, which is now the **Thomas Wolfe Memorial** (tel: 828-252-8171; closed Mon and in winter). A fire destroyed the roof in 1999, but the house is being restored. Despite being banned from the town's public library for seven years, Wolfe's *Look Homeward Angel* has never been out of print since it was first published in 1929. Before he died, aged 37, in 1938 he wrote about his old home: "And again, again, in the old house, I feel beneath my tread the creak of the old stair, the worn rail, the whitewashed walls, the feel of darkness and the house asleep, and think, 'I was a child here; here the stairs, here was darkness; this was I, and here is Time.'"

Southeast of Asheville, near the intersection of US 64 and 74A, is privately owned **Chimney Rock**, a 1,000-acre (405-hectare) Natural Heritage Site including Chimney Rock itself, and the bottomless pools and waterfalls of magestic **Hickory Nut Gorge**, a backdrop for the climactic scenes in the movie *The Last of the Mohicans*. Visitors can take an elevator 26 stories up inside a mountain to emerge on its flat rocky top, 1,200 feet (366 meters) above the river, to enjoy spectacular views stretching for up to 75 miles (120 km).

*The town of Gatlinburg, Tennessee is a popular place to get married; over 10,000 couples tie the knot here each year.*

## THE GREAT SMOKIES

**Great Smoky Mountains National Park ❿**, 16 of whose peaks exceed 6,000 feet (1,800 meters), sprawls majestically over the North Carolina and Tennessee borders. Access, on the North Carolina side, is gained from the Blue Ridge Mountain Parkway town of **Cherokee**, reached by taking US 74 east from Asheville and then branching off onto US 19 (also eastbound). The highest point in Tennessee, 6,642-foot (2,025-meter) **Clingmans Dome** (access closed in winter) is on the ridge-clinging Appalachian Trail midway between Cherokee and **Gatlinburg**, the Smoky Mountains gateway town on the Tennessee side of the park.

Abundant rainfall keeps the park rich in wildflowers and other plant life; bears and white-tailed deer can sometimes be spotted. An **aerial tramway** (tel: 865-436-5423; open daily) runs from downtown Gatlinburg to Ober Gatlinburg, a ski resort and amusement complex offering fun-but-dumb games and stupendous views. Gatlinburg has become a popular marriage venue, with over 10,000 couples taking their wedding vows here each year.

The more direct route from Asheville into Tennessee is simply to take Interstate 40 north, and then follow it as it turns west toward Knoxville. Just after this turn, on the shore of Douglas Lake, is **Dandridge** (named after George Washington's wife Martha Dandridge), with plenty of boat docks and campgrounds. A scenic route into the Smokies leads from here to Sevierville and Gatlinburg along State Route 92 and then US 411.

Just before Knoxville, the **Armstrong-Lockett House** (tel: 423-229-9422; closed weekends), with its

**BELOW:**
Pee-Wee League cheerleaders dressed in the colors of the University of Tennessee.

collection of 18th-century furniture and ancient English silver, presides over the former Crescent Bend plantation. There are also many interesting old homes in the former state capital, **Knoxville ⓫** – among them the **William Blount Mansion** (tel: 423-525-2375; closed Mon) built in 1792 by the governor of the Southwest Territory; the 1797 **Ramsey House** (tel: 423-546-0745; closed Mon); and the 1858 **Mabry-Hazen House** (tel: 423-522-8661; open Mon, Wed, Fri), which served as headquarters on different occasions for both sides in the Civil War. **James White's Fort** (tel: 865-525-6514; guided tours Mon–Sat) is a re-creation of the region's first pioneer structure.

## Celebrating his roots

Victorian art and architecture are plentiful in the serene and rural **Old Gray Cemetery** on North Broadway, named for the English poet, Thomas Gray, author of *Elegy Written in a Country Churchyard*. Tennessean and Pulitzer Prize-winning Alex Haley, best known for *Roots* and *The Autobiography of Malcolm X*, is celebrated with a larger-than-life bronze statue in Morningside Park. Among the many museums, worth noting is the unique **Women's Basketball Hall of Fame** (tel: 423-633-9000; open daily), where you can watch videos of past moments of glory, as well as shoot some hoops.

North of the city on I-75, the **Norris Dam** was the first to be built by the vast Tennessee Valley Authority, which brought electric power to this region in the 1920s. **Norris Lake**, acclaimed as one of the cleanest in North America, hosts several marinas and supports houseboats, fishing, and jet skiing. There are trails and campgrounds in the surrounding woods, and a Rice Grist Mill as well as several other museums. The **Museum of Appalachia** (tel: 423-494-7680;

**BELOW:** Clingmans Dome straddles both Tennessee and North Carolina.

*Nashville's Greek Revival-style state capitol building was used as a fortress during the Civil War.*

open daily) calls itself "a living mountain village" and does a superlative job of interpreting rural Tennessee, with a pioneer school, a dirt-floor cabin (used in the *Daniel Boone* TV series), and spinning and weaving among its many exhibits.

West of Knoxville, on State Route 162, **Oak Ridge**, the "secret city" built in 1942 to work on production of the first atomic bomb, today invites visitors to explore historic sites such as the **Graphite Reactor** that formed part of what was known as the Manhattan Project. Somewhat ironic icons are the **International Friendship Bell and Pavilion** intended to serve "as an expression of hope for everlasting peace," and the **New Bethel Church**, which was the wartime meeting place for scientists and engineers planning the Big Bang. At **Cookeville,** which is farther west of Knoxville along State 62, the **Depot Museum** (tel: 931-528-8570; closed Sun, Mon) occupies a station built by the Tennessee Central RR in 1909. Fun, faded, and aged cabooses are on display in the grounds.

Continue west on US 70N, but consider stopping just before you get into Nashville for a visit to President Andrew Jackson's gracious and beautiful mansion, **The Hermitage** (tel: 615-889-2941; open daily), extensively furnished and on whose grounds still stand some of the cabins in which Jackson lived before becoming America's seventh president. He died there in 1845.

## Nashville

After the peace and tranquility of Virginia and North Carolina, it's into Tennessee and the "country music capital of the world." **Nashville** ⑫ isn't too much of a shock to the senses, however, being a compact and pleasant town to walk around, and it's certainly a good stop for a decent cup of coffee after days on the "filter trail." By this stage in the drive *all* roads, it appears, lead to Nashville – where Interstates 40, 24, and 65 intersect at what likes to term itself "the Athens of the South."

This moniker is supported by the **Parthenon** (tel: 615-862-8431; closed Mon), a same-size replica built for the Tennessee Centennial Exposition in 1897. Originally constructed of wood, it was rebuilt in the 1920s of more sturdy concrete and is used for art exhibitions and other events in the popular Centennial Park. Fifty years before the Centennial, architect William Strickland had anticipated the style with his Greek Revival **State Capitol**, sturdy enough to be used as a fortress during the Civil War. Also worth seeing is the **Athenaeum** (tel: 615-381-4822; closed Mon–Tues), which began as a home for President James K. Polk's nephews but later became a school for the affluent offspring of planters and bankers. Polk's own ancestral home is at **Columbia**, on I-31, southwest of Nashville.

### Follow the green line

A City Walk wends through the downtown area, marked by a painted green line on the sidewalk. It includes the **Beaux Arts Hermitage Hotel**, where suffragist groups and their opponents gathered to lobby the state legislature in 1920 – their target being the 19th Amendment to the US Constitution. This gave women the right to vote and was duly ratified by Tennessee's vote. Also on the route is **Printers Alley**, the pre-World War II center of Nashville nightlife, with venues featuring Waylon Jennings, Chet Atkins, Hank Williams, and others. There's a life-size bronze statue of a guitar player outside the Bank of America at 5th and Union streets.

Nashville-born Red Grooms, the whimsical artist and sculptor who made his name in New York, created the city's most popular artwork – a working carousel on the waterfront whose painted figures all depict well-known local characters. They include the late sportscaster Grantland Rice; frontiersman Davy Crockett; musician Chet Atkins; Belle Kinney and her husband Leopold Scholz, who worked on the city's Parthenon; and millionaire socialite Adelicia Acklen.

## Tennessee State Museum

Centerpiece of the **Tennessee State Museum** (tel: 1-800-407-4324; closed Mon) is an illustrated history of the Civil War – which killed 600,000 Americans – accenting the role that Tennessee, a Confederate state, played in it. Occupying an entire floor are interactive exhibits with sound effects, film, battle flags, a Confederate cannon, Davy Crockett's powder horn, and an old Conestoga wagon in which some long-forgotten family from Virginia migrated to the state in about 1800.

Most of the Civil War battles in Tennessee took place along what is now known as the **Antebellum Trail**. A free leaflet listing battlefields (as well as a score of different old mansions) within a 90-mile (145-km) roundtrip loop, south of Nashville to the Natchez Race Parkway, is available from the

Map
on page
184

**BELOW:**
Tootsies Orchid
Lounge, Nashville.

Tennessee Department of Tourism (P.O. Box 23170, Nashville, 37202, tel: 800-836-6200).

Across the street from the State Museum in the 18-story state building is the **Military Museum**, exhibiting pictures and artifacts from America's subsequent wars. The **Tennessee Historical Commission** operates out of an outstanding 1850s mansion (open weekdays). The **Carl Van Vechten Gallery of Art** (tel: 615-329-8720; closed Mon), one of three university art galleries housing the Alfred Stieglitz collection of modern art, has a notable collection of photographs and paintings by major figures.

## Nashville's Scarlett O'Hara

Once a famous stud farm and thoroughbred nursery (from which came Iroquois, the 1881 winner of England's Derby), **Belle Meade Plantation** (tel: 615-356-0501; open daily) still displays the opulent lifestyles of a century-and-a-half ago, with tour guides in period costume. The 1853 Greek Revival mansion, elegantly restored, presides over what was once a 5,400-acre (2185-hectare) plantation whose grassy acres now house Nashville's most impressive homes in a multitude of "neo-anything" styles. At one end of the park, **Cheekwood** (tel: 615-353-2162; open daily), the immense home of the founder of Maxwell House Coffee, has botanical gardens, a restaurant, and an art gallery. Outdoor concerts take place in summer.

Sometimes regarded as the model for Scarlett O'Hara, Nashville's Adelicia Acklen (1817–89) built the Italian-style **Belmont Mansion** (tel: 615-386-4459; closed Sun, Mon), now on Belmont University campus, whose grand salon always incites awe and admiration.

**BELOW:** Nashville's numerous honky tonk bars were where musicians headed straight for after a gig.

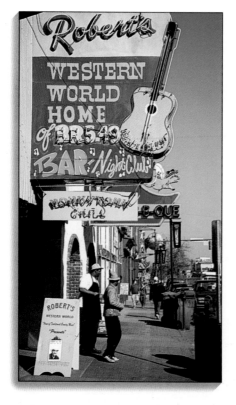

## Grand Ole Opry

Almost one-third of the 400-plus record companies in the US are situated in Nashville, so it's no surprise the city has a self-proclaimed **Music Valley**, the area lying between Briley Parkway and the Cumberland River. The "valley" contains at least 100 shops, restaurants, hotels, and other attractions, including the famous **Grand Ole Opry** (tel: 615-889-6611) and its adjoining museum.

Until recently, the Grand Ole Opry – the country's longest-running live radio program, which began in 1925 – was broadcast from Ryman Auditorium ("the Carnegie Hall of the South"), which, since it opened in 1892, has played host to everybody from Enrico Caruso, Rudolf Valentino, and Mae West to Bruce Springsteen and the Vienna Choirboys. There's a self-guided tour between 8:30am and 4pm any day of the week. Behind Ryman Hall were (and still are) a row of honky-tonk bars where the country and western stars would throw back a few beers after a foot-stomping gig.

From the Belmont Mansion, tree-lined 16th Avenue leads to the **Country Music Hall of Fame** (tel: 615-256-1639; open daily) – many of its old houses now converted into recording studios and record labels. Among them is Studio B, where Elvis Presley cut a platter. Do you know which was the most successful song in country and western history? Find the answer

Map
on page
184

at this mecca for country fans, which contains a floor segment from the old Ryman Auditorium on which visitors can pose and impress their friends. Like Hollywood's Walk of Fame, the museum's lobby has floor tiles of country singers as well as enlargements of the postage stamp series that included Patsy Cline (a sentimental favorite who died young and in mid-career after a plane crash) and Hank Williams. An entire showcase is devoted to Williams who, along with fellow musician Ernest Tubb, is credited with inventing the honky-tonk style developed in roadside taverns and dancehalls prior to World War II.

## The King's Cadillac

Other exhibits include Elvis Presley's solid gold Cadillac and his grand piano; George Strait's hat and jacket; a roomful of guitars from famous owners; and the1962 Pontiac – with pistols for door handles and steer horns mounted on the front bumper – owned by Webb Pearce. A chart listing facts about songwriting informs visitors that the standard royalty paid to song writers is 4¢ a record, half of it going to the publisher. There is also an incomparable collection of pictures and posters as well as the working print shop, which has been producing classic posters for a century.

If you're ready to hit the road to visit another famous city of the south, head east out of Nashville on I-40. Some 128 miles (205 km) farther on you'll come to **Jackson**, and just beyond that is a great family stop at **Casey Jones Village** (tel: 800-748-9588; open daily), with country stores, lavish buffets, an old-fashioned ice cream parlor, train rides, and a caboose to sleep in. But if that doesn't suit your fancy, keep headin' on down the highway straight on into **Memphis** ⓭ *(see page 196)*.

*Almost one-third of the 400-plus record companies in the United States are located in Nashville.*

**BELOW:**
the interior has a Country Music Walk of Fame.

# MEMPHIS: MUSIC CITY USA

*The gateway to the Mississippi Delta is the home of blues, Beale Street and the site of two kings: Elvis and Martin Luther*

The guest list at Memphis's ornate and venerable Peabody Hotel (pronounce it **ho**-tel) has included US presidents Andrew Johnson and William McKinley as well as the Confederate hero Robert E. Lee, but infinitely more popular today are the Peabody ducks, who live on the roof. Every day at 11am they take a ride in the elevator to the lobby, walk across a red carpet and, to the strains of John Philip Sousa, climb into the fountain, where they remain until 4pm when the performance is repeated in reverse.

Memphis is best known, of course, for Graceland (tel: 800-238-2000; open daily; mansion tour closed Tues Nov–Feb), about

10 miles (16 km) south along Elvis Presley Boulevard, where there are permanent lines to join variously priced tours to view the late singer's home, grave and assorted collections.

Sun Studios (tel: 800-441-6249; open daily) was where "the King" recorded, but BB King, Ike Turner, and many other artists preceded him here. In recent years Bono, U2, and Paul Simon have been clients. Hourly tours are given, and for an extra $20 you can record a tape of your own.

There are plenty of other music venues, among them the Memphis Music Hall of Fame (tel: 901-525-4007; closed weekends) which has Elvis paraphernalia as well as early band instruments and a re-creation of the Pee Wee Saloon, where W. C. Handy (1873–1958) wrote "St Louis Blues."

Beale Street is where it all began, and this is where Handy set to music the songs of the cotton pickers and "inscribed for ever in the heart of the nation his immortal songs," as the inscription reads on his statue here. The bars, nightclubs, restaurants, and stores of today's Beale Street all take second place for many visitors to the oldest establishment on the street – Schwab's, a general store that's been around since 1876 selling hardware, 99¢ neckties, handcuffs, clerical collars, voodoo powders, and tools.

Six blocks south is the National Civil Rights Museum (tel: 901-521-2699; closed Tues), located in the former Lorraine Motel where Dr Martin Luther King, Jr was tragically assassinated on April 4, 1968. Even today, the sight of the rumpled bed, breakfast tray, and a few simple objects in Room 306 – the last things Dr King saw before stepping onto the balcony – bring a tear to the eye. Other rooms of the fascinating museum feature a variety of art, artifacts, and powerful films relating to the Civil Rights movement.  ❑

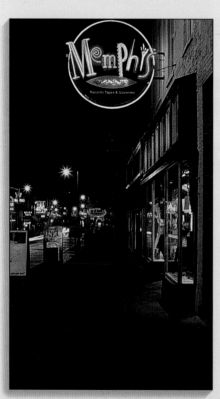

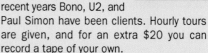

**LEFT:** Beale Street, where W.C. Handy wrote "St Louis Blues;" Music City USA.
**ABOVE:** Elvis drove here; Elvis recorded here.

## ARKANSAS

After the excitement of Nashville and Memphis, the next part of the journey takes us straight back to small-town America, where Interstate 40 crosses the **Mississippi River** and cuts into the middle of Arkansas. Roadsides in Arkansas are often gloriously colorful, testament to the state's extensive wildflower program, which has lined more than 1,000 miles (1,600 km) of highway with colorful banks of purple larkspur, black-eyed Susan, Indian Paintbrush, goldenrod, pink primrose, and bright red cardinal flowers – a native perennial that attracts hummingbirds. The Arkansas highway department claims that almost a quarter million acres of its highways have been graced with 600 species of flowers.

Map on page 184

Paralleling the interstate between Memphis and Little Rock is US 70, where along the way you will find **Hazen**, with its wildlife preserve, and **Lonoke**, which houses one of the country's largest fish hatcheries. Southwest of Lonoke, just off US 165, are the **Plantation Agriculture Museum** (tel: 501-961-1409; closed Mon), which tells the story of cotton production in the South, and the **Toltec Mounds State Park**, a sprawling prehistoric site.

US 70 turns southwest at Little Rock, heading through **Benton** with its bauxite deposits. This earthy substance from which aluminum is made is responsible for much of the area's wealth – justification enough for the world's only bauxite building to be constructed here.

The Arkansas River carves a gateway between the Ouachita and Ozark mountains to the delta at **Little Rock ⑭**. The city is, therefore, first and foremost a river city; an amalgamation of the Old South and the Southwest. The downtown area of Little Rock extends south from the Arkansas River. Beside it, under the Union Pacific Railroad Bridge, is the "Little Rock" that lent the city its name,

**BELOW:**
steaming down the Mississippi River.

and it's also the first visible rock outcrop to hove into view when traveling up from the Gulf of Mexico. **Riverfront Park**, with its pleasure boat wharf and extravagant fountain, is the site of an amphitheater and an outdoor film festival.

An extensive area called the **River Market**, flanked at the western end by the Convention Center, comprises businesses, shops, bars and cafés, two hotels, the library, and a Farmers' Market (closed Sun, Mon). There's ample parking at the eastern end, where there are plans to open the **Clinton Presidential Library**, and there's also a transit trolley making life even easier for out-of-towners. Heading back inland, the **Convention & Visitor Bureau** at the corner of Markham and Main streets (tel: 501-376-4781) is a good starting point to acquire information.

*The greyhound has been the symbol of US bus travel for many decades.*

## Yogurt tower

Across the street is the restored historical **Capital Hotel** where President Ulysses S. Grant stayed in 1877, four years after it opened. The interior and exterior are equally interesting. Note its four-story cast-iron front and an elegant 1908 interior by Little Rock architect George R. Mann. At Second and Center streets is the 10-story Southern Trust Building (now called **Pyramid Place**), the city's first skyscraper when it was built in 1907. Times have changed, and today's Downtown is dominated by the TCBY Tower, that TV and yogurt fans will recognize as being the headquarters of "The Country's Best Yogurt."

Two museums are located on Markham Street: the **Museum of Discovery** (tel: 501-396-7050; open daily) and the **Children's Museum** (tel: 501-374-6655; open daily). A number of venerable old buildings located in downtown streets include the Romanesque Revival **Pulaski County Courthouse**

**BELOW:** parades are an American institution.

(Markham and Spring streets) with its Classical Revival domed annex, and the **Arkansas Territorial Restoration** (tel: 501-324-9351; open daily). Inside is the **Hinderliter Tavern**, the city's oldest building.

The impressive **State Capitol** (tel: 501-682-5080; guided tours Sun–Fri) in which Bill Clinton served five terms as governor and where he gave his election-night victory speeches, lies at the western end of Capitol Avenue. Its design details include six brass doors purchased from Tiffany's in New York. Flying atop the building is the state flag, which has a diamond in the center to mark the fact that Arkansas is the only state with a diamond mine (at Murfreesboro).

## Grand old dames

Little Rock is understandably proud of its plethora of wonderful old houses – most of them funded and built by successful bankers, cotton brokers, or other successful merchants in the 19th century. These interesting mansions are listed in several free books and pamphlets, which offer mapped routes through the various historical districts. A few of the homes have been converted into striking bed and breakfasts. Opening times vary and few of the houses are actually open to the public, so if you do have time for a lengthy tour be sure to collect some of this literature from the visitor's bureau before setting out.

A brief drive around the quiet, tree-lined streets might begin in the **Governor's Mansion Historic District** at the mansion itself (18th and Center streets) and concentrate on the streets between 18th and 15th streets bordered by Louisiana and Gaines. In this area alone, 35 buildings are listed in the Bureau's Tour Number Three. The Queen Anne or Colonial Revival styles, and sometimes a combination of both, predominate in this district and though varying consid-

**Map on page 184**

**BELOW:** beauty contests are a Southern institution.

erably in appearance, many of the buildings were designed by the same architect, Charles L. Thompson, who practiced in Little Rock from 1885 for more than 50 years. The sumptuous **Governor's Mansion**, where the Clintons lived for 12 years, boasts a dramatic curving, walnut staircase and is stylishly furnished with Hepplewhite and Chippendale antique furnishings. A bust of Bill sits by the gate. Down the street are the **Cathedral Park Apartments** at 15th and Center, converted from a one-time Episcopal church, and four blocks west on Arch Street is the English Revival-style **Cornish House**, with its magnificent third-floor ballroom in which Ed Cornish, a prominent banker, and his wife staged lavish parties.

### More than bed and breakfast

At 2120 Louisiana Street, the **Hornibrook House** was built by successful saloon owner James Hornibrook who, after a social snub, was determined to build something to make the neighbors gasp. The result is a house known as the "Empress of Little Rock," a Queen Anne-style home with concave front doors, a stained glass skylight, turrets, gables, and a wrap-around porch. Inside is a series of luxuriously furnished parlors replete with lace cloths, tasseled lampshades, a dollhouse, antique chairs, and divans. The house now serves as an attractive B&B, with eight octagonal rooms named after some of the state's historical characters – such as John Edward Murray, the youngest general in the Confederate army.

Another B&B worth staying the night for is **Hotze House**, at 1619 Louisiana Street. This one was the monumental home of a cotton broker and has a Colonial Revival exterior with 20-foot (6-meter) high pillars. Beneath the stenciled ceilings are walls covered with tapestry and green damask shot with gold thread.

**BELOW:**
Capitol building, Little Rock, where Bill Clinton served five times as governor.

There are equally impressive homes to be found in the **MacArthur Park** district. The 1881 Italianate **Villa Marre** at 1321 Scott Street was named for another successful saloon keeper, Angelo Marre, about whom one of the local guidebooks writes: "Initially known for his quick temper and shady past, Marre eventually became a respectable member of the City Council." The distinctive **Hanger House** at number 1010 on the same block, which looks like a vision from a fairy tale, owes its earthy shade to Frances Hanger, who remodeled the house herself after researching decorating books. She remarked in a letter to a friend that red seemed to be "about as popular as ever for painting houses."

Next to a refurbished 1957 Mobil gas station (with its pumps frozen at 22.5 cents per gallon) at 2125 W. 14th Street is the **Central High Museum** (tel: 501-374-1957; open daily) opposite the (still operating) school that provoked the dramatic desegregation confrontation of 1957.

Photos and other visuals depict the scene when Governor Orval Faubus called out the National Guard to bar admittance to nine black students. Three weeks later President Eisenhower called out the US Army to escort the students into the school. The legal case remained in the courts for an entire year, during which time Little Rock high schools remained closed. At the time the Mobil station, with the only pay telephone in the area, was the scene of some unseemly competition among the visiting press.

## Hot Springs

About 50 miles (80 km) west of Little Rock, in the Diamond Lakes Region off SR 7, is the resort of **Hot Springs ⓯**, which has been a recreational area for hundreds of years. The springs have played a large part in Arkansas politics – not least for being the boyhood home of Bill Clinton. A lakeside resort city surrounded by low-lying mountains, it offers historic buildings, an alligator farm and petting zoo, spas, ranches, an aquarium, a wax museum, and all of the additional resort amenities. There are hundreds of accommodations ranging from hotels and lakeside cottages to campgrounds and houseboat rentals. (Information from 888-SPA-CITY.) One of the resort hotels claims that although Arkansas is famous for its unspoiled beauty, "we're famous…for our spoiled guests." From Little Rock, I-40 heads northwest and crosses the Oklahoma border at the rather unattractive **Fort Smith**. While the old Fort Town might be worth a quick visit on the way through, much of the new town of Fort Smith is memorable only for its used car lots and heavy traffic.

Although I-40 will carry you all the way through the state of Oklahoma and on westward, if you're interested in a more colorful journey, we suggest heading north just before Fort Smith on I-540, which becomes US 71 as it crosses into the southwest corner of Missouri and leads you to the city of **Joplin ⓰**, where you can pick up America's "Mother Road" – Route 66 – which will cut across the southeast corner of Kansas before heading into Oklahoma.  ❏

Map on page 184

**TIP**

You may want to roll down your windows when traveling through Arkanas: a highway department program has resulted in the planting of 600 kinds of wildflowers, some of which attract hummingbirds.

**BELOW:**
Mother Nature statue in Hot Springs, Arkansas.

# OKLAHOMA TO NEW MEXICO

Map on page 184

*Take "a stroll on wheels" along Route 66 through Oklahoma and the Texas Panhandle, then cruise through Santa Fe and Albuquerque. The highway anthem begins here*

**O**klahoma was the site of one of the most dramatic land rushes in the country. The new towns of Oklahoma City and Guthrie became home to more than 10,000 residents in the space of a day. The state is where we finally get to know the 2,448-mile (3,940-km) long Route 66 *(see essay on page 35)*. If your plan is to follow the "Mother Road" for most or all of the way, a word of advice: time is of the essence. Staying on the road is not as easy as it sounds, and having just enough – or even worse, *not* enough time – as opposed to having ample time could be the difference between a thoroughly enjoyable road trip and a disappointingly frustrating one. Advocates of the famous route claim that half the fun of Route 66 lies in the adventure of finding it, so plan ahead if it is to be a focal point of your drive. On the plus side, dipping in and out of it is relatively easy because of its proximity to the interstate, so even those with less time on their hands should see something of it.

## Exile on Main Street

Route 66 is a serious business – "business" being the operative word. Real fanatics will arm themselves with maps and guide books, motel directories, and red-hot tips gleaned avidly from their *Route 66 Magazine* subscription. Some might even drink coffee from their "Main Street, USA" mug while wearing an "I drove the Mother Road" T-shirt.

Fanatic or not, getting lost is inevitable, as you will come across stretches of the route that are maddeningly difficult to find. In some cases the not-so-trusty brown "Historic US 66" signs vanish, with little or no indication as to where it has gone, or whether it has been subsumed by the nearby interstate. In many places it runs parallel with the major highway for mile after mile, sometimes marked and sometimes not. Even experienced map-readers will have their competence sorely tested by some of the numerous maps claiming to trace the entire route. Time, patience, and – at the occasional unmarked crossroad – a little bit of guesswork are the keywords to a successful trip.

Paul Taylor, publisher of the aforementioned and intriguing *Route 66 Magazine*, maintains that with sufficient time to explore, driving the route presents only minor setbacks. Owners of some of the Route 66 landmark attractions and memorabilia stores along the way say that one of the reasons travelers lose their way is because too many people steal the signs. "They are popular souvenirs." So, however tempting – leave that sign alone!

**LEFT:** the best way to travel down Route 66.
**BELOW:** historic road fans stay here.

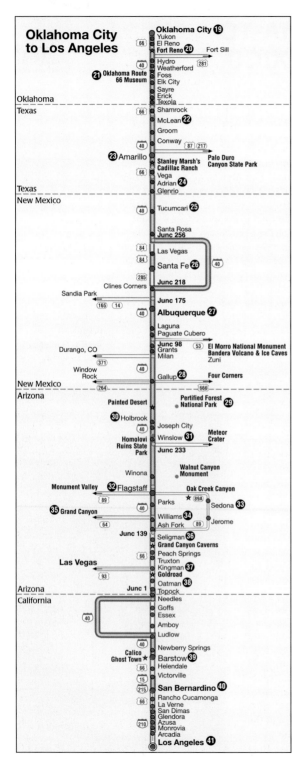

**Oklahoma City to Los Angeles**

Oklahoma City **19**
Yukon
66 El Reno
Fort Reno **20**    Fort Sill
Hydro   281
Weatherford
**21** Oklahoma Route 66 Museum   Foss
Elk City
Sayre

Oklahoma
Texas    66
Erick
Texola
Shamrock
McLean **22**
Groom
Conway   87   217
**23** Amarillo   Stanley Marsh's Cadillac Ranch   Palo Duro Canyon State Park
66 Vega
Adrian **24**
Glenrio

Texas
New Mexico
40   Tucumcari **25**

Santa Rosa
**Junc 256**
84 Las Vegas
84 Santa Fe **26**   40
285 **Junc 218**
Clines Corners
Sandia Park
165   14   **Junc 175**
40   **Albuquerque 27**
Laguna
Paguate Cubero
Durango, CO   **Junc 98**   53   El Morro National Monument
Grants   Bandera Volcano & Ice Caves
371   Milan   Zuni
Window Rock   40
**Gallup 28**   Four Corners
New Mexico
Arizona   264   666

Painted Desert   Pertified Forest National Park **29**
**30** Holbrook
40   Joseph City
Homolovi   Winslow **31**   Meteor Crater
Ruins State Park   **Junc 233**
Winona   Walnut Canyon Monument

Monument Valley   **32** Flagstaff
89   Oak Creek Canyon
Parks   89A
**35** Grand Canyon   40
Williams **34**   Sedona **33**
64   Ash Fork   89   Jerome
**Junc 139**
Seligman **36**
**Grand Canyon Caverns**
66   Peach Springs
Truxton
**Las Vegas**   Kingman **37**
93   **Goldroad**
Oatman **38**
Arizona   **Junc 1**   Topock
California   Needles
Goffs
Essex
40   Amboy
Ludlow
40   Newberry Springs
Calico
Ghost Town ★   Barstow **39**
66   Helendale
15   Victorville
215   **San Bernardino 40**
66   Rancho Cucamonga
La Verne
San Dimas
Glendora
210   Azusa
Monrovia
Arcadia
**Los Angeles 41**

Wondering how long it will take to drive all, or most of the route? This depends on many factors, not least whether you are what author Tom Snyder defines as: "Late starter, get loster, honky tonker, sensitive browser, coffee hound, museum freak, postcard looker." A reasonably fast trip, he estimates, would be at least eight days – from its origin in Illinois to the final mile in California.

Route 66 enters Oklahoma at **Quapaw** in the northeast corner, traversing 400 miles (643 km) of the state, for much of the way running parallel to (or being replaced by) I-44.

## Oklahoma's origins

The creation of the Oklahoma Territory following the Land Rush 50 years later shrank Indian territory by half, forcing Native Americans to abandon communal ownership in favor of small individual plots. Nevertheless, more than 30 Native American tribes are still represented in the state, and one of the first more major towns you'll come to after entering the state, **Miami** ❶, is named after one of these communities.

One of the earliest sections of the highway is found in the vicinity; you'll also find some Route 66 exhibits in the restored **Coleman Theater** in the town.

Just after Miami is one of those places where Route 66 sort of "disappears" – so don't feel you've cheated here by jumping on I-44 for a short stretch. This section of the interstate (up to Tulsa) is also known as the Will Rogers Turnpike (Woody Guthrie wrote a song about it), in memory of the famous homespun comic and No. 1 box office star. You can pick up Route 66 again a little farther on at **Vinita**, which gets its name from Vinnie Ream, who sculpted Washington, DC's Abraham Lincoln statue. The town stages a Will Rogers Memorial Rodeo every August and also lays claim to the world's largest (29,135 square feet/2,706 square meters) McDonald's.

Farther southwest, in Galloway Park near **Foyil**, is the world's largest totem pole, at 90 feet (27 meters) tall. Foyil's main street is named after Andy Payne,

$25,000 winner of the 84-day "Bunion Derby" in 1928, whose contestants hiked 2,400 miles (3,862 km) from New York to Los Angeles, mostly along Route 66. Less than half of the route had been surfaced by then: it was not until 1938 that the entire route was finally paved. "In those days," Tom Snyder writes, "even Lindbergh's solo flight over the Atlantic was easier than a cross-country trek by automobile in the same year."

A few miles farther on is **Claremore**, with a memorial to Will Rogers; his 1879 birthplace is memorialized at **Oologah**, just to the north. After Foyil, Route 66 continues to head southwest to Tulsa – with the route again joining up with I-44 just as you reach the outskirts of the city.

**Tulsa** ⓲ (pop. 380,000), with its downtown Art Deco buildings and a wonderful 1950s-style diner on East 11th Street, was once known as the "Oil capital of the world." Here, Cyrus Avery was a co-founder and booster of the fledgling Highway 66 Association. Of the hundreds of drive-in movie houses along Route 66 only a handful remain – and one is right here in Tulsa.

Continue to follow I-44 out of the city; you can return to Route 66 by getting off at exit 220. The Mother Road again runs parallel to the main highway between Tulsa and Oklahoma City; the interstate on this stretch is also known as the Turner Turnpike. You'll pass through a string of small towns: **Sapulpa**, where aspiring Western star Gene Autry once sang in the local ice cream parlor, and which has an interesting historical museum; **Kellyville** (look for the Cotton Gin Diner); **Stroud** (order buffalo burgers at the 60-year-old Rock Café); **Davenport**, known for Dan's Bar-B-Q, run by a former trucker; and – as you approach Oklahoma City – **Arcadia**, with its distinctive Round Barn.

## Crystal bridge

**Oklahoma City** ⓳ blossomed overnight on April 22, 1889, when the Land Rush opened up the adjoining territory to settlement – attracting 50,000 hopeful prospects. The appeal of today's Oklahoma City owes much to the planning talents of architect I.M. Pei, whose development scheme produced an elegant mix of lakes, parks, landscaped hills, and stylish buildings. The centerpiece is **Myriad Botanical Gardens** (tel: 405-297-3995; open daily), a 17-acre (7-hectare) oasis in the heart of Downtown, its seventh-floor Crystal Bridge housing a plant- and tree-filled tropical conservatory and waterfall.

Oil derricks near the State Capitol are a reminder that the city's wealth stemmed from a major gusher 75 years ago. A score of major producing oilfields still operate in the state. Cotton was once king here, but it's cattle ranching that predominates today, and this great heritage is celebrated at **Stockyards City**, where ranchers and real cowboys have been coming since its inception in the early 1900s for apparel, equipment, supplies, and a good meal. A "gaslight district" features a variety of western-oriented shops, galleries, and restaurants, but the place is still all about cattle: cattle auctions are held Mon–Wed each week, with tours available on Mondays from 8 am throughout the day at the Oklahoma National Stockyards Company.

More sobering is the site of the April 1995 bombing

*Throughout the Southwest, be sure to book rooms way ahead during the summer months.*

**BELOW:**
Red Earth festival, Oklahoma City.

Maps on page 184 & 204

of the Federal Building at which 168 people were killed. The site has now become a poignant memorial, with 168 empty chairs – reminding visitors of those who died – arranged on a grassy slope under a canopy of trees, facing a shallow reflecting pool.

**TIP**

Oklahoma City's Cowboy Hall of Fame is one of the best of its kind. It's also huge, so leave plenty of time to look through all the attractions.

## Cowboys on parade

One of Oklahoma's major attractions is the **National Cowboy Hall of Fame** (tel: 405-478-2250; open daily), just north of I-44 as you come into Oklahoma City (exit 129), whose wide, marble-tiled corridors are flanked with giant landscape paintings and photographs depicting cowboy life. This excellent museum has broad appeal, and even those with no interest in the Wild West might find themselves pleasantly surprised. Movie posters of Gene Autry, Tom Mix, and John Wayne decorate the theater, close to a larger-than-life statue of Ronald Reagan and a huge statue titled *The End of the Trail*, by James Earle Fraser. It is matched by his wife Laura's bas-relief of the Land Rush.

Visitors can stroll through the streets of an old Western town with church, dry goods store, and blacksmith's shop, while children can don chaps, boots, and spurs in the Cowboy Corral, before dismounting and hiding away in a range tent.

Among the hundreds of unique action photographs shot with a converted 1880 Graflex camera by rodeo's first professional photographer, Ralph Russell Doubleday (1881–1958), is one of movie cowboy Hopalong Cassidy leading a small-town parade. Postcards of pictures by "Dub," often created in the bathroom of whatever hotel in which he was staying, sold by the millions.

**BELOW:** the *Welcome Sundown* statue at the National Cowboy Hall of Fame.

You can continue to head west either on Route 66 or on I-40 (the two become one some 40 miles/64 km out of the city anyway). The Chisholm Trail ran along what is now Ninth Street in tiny **Yukon** – just outside the Oklahoma City limits on Route 66 and hometown of country star Garth Brooks. Both Sid's Café in this town and Johnnie's Grill in neighboring **El Reno** claim to be the home of that distinctive Oklahoma treat – the onion-fried hamburger. Dustin Hoffman and Tom Cruise shot a scene of *Rain Man* in the Big 8 Motel (now renamed DeLuxe Inn) here. More famous, though, is the El Reno Hotel (now a historical museum), built in 1892 when rooms cost all of 50¢ a night.

## Chisholm Trail

**Fort Reno** ⑳ (tel: 405-262-3987; open daily) displays exhibits from the days when it served as a cavalry post in the Indian wars. El Reno is now the headquarters for the Cheyenne-Arapaho tribe.

If you take exit 108 off I-40, a short detour north on US 281 leads to **Geary**, bypassed by Route 66 in 1933 despite the locals' work in grading and graveling the road in the hope of enticing the route, and its dollars, through their town. Not far away is **Left Hand Spring Camp**, where Jesse Chisholm, who gave his name to the famous Chisholm Trail, is buried. The trail, which stretched 250 miles (400 km) from San Antonio to Abilene, was first laid in 1860 when buffalo still roamed nearby. Twenty years later, when the trail was more or less abandoned, it had seen the passage of more than 10 million cattle. If you head south on US 281, about 78 miles (125 km) later you'll come to **Fort Sill**, where the Apache chief Geronimo died in captivity in 1909.

## Driving backwards

Just near where I-40 intersects with US 281 is the 4,000-foot (1,220 meter) long "pony bridge" crossing the South Canadian River, a multiple simple-span bridge typical of the type used in the construction of Route 66. In addition to offering superb vistas of the river, the bridge starred in a scene in John Ford's 1940 movie version of *The Grapes of Wrath*.

The hill leading up to the bridge is so steep that Model T Fords – their engines generating more power in reverse – had to climb it backward. Continuing west on I-40, just north of exit 89 is Lucille's gas station and store at **Hydro** – marked by the plaster animals out front. It is a favorite with Route 66 regulars, some of whom have been buying gas and groceries here since 1941. Other local landmarks include a building with Greek columns (formerly a bank, now a dress shop) and, a little farther along, the century-old Cotter's Blacksmith Shop at **Weatherford**, where the **General Thomas P. Stafford Museum** (tel: 580-772-6143; open weekends) with space suit and moon rocks commemorates Oklahoma's premier astronaut.

One really begins to get a feel of traversing the old road at **Clinton** (pop. 9,300), where the state-sponsored **Oklahoma Route 66 Museum ㉑** (tel: 580-323-7866; open daily) is the most comprehensive – and memorable – of many similar places found along the famous highway. Each era is presented in its individual room, with photographs of the road's construction in the 1920s.

Map on page 204

**BELOW:** Clinton, Oklahoma, has one of the best 66 museums along the historic route.

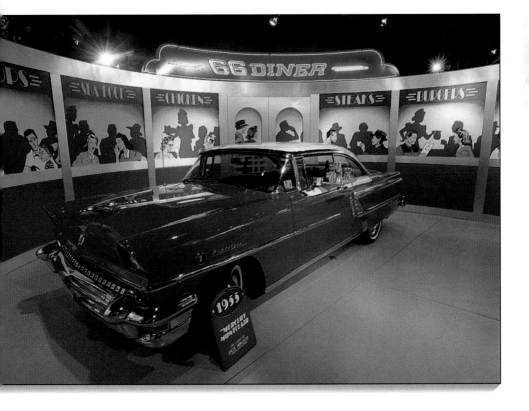

*The sounds commonly associated with a trip on Route 66 usually came from wonderful jukeboxes like this one.*

**BELOW:** some of the buildings in Texola, straddling the Oklahoma/Texas border, have seen better days.

Oklahoma was still "dry" in the 1930s, and the rise of the bootlegger prompted a corresponding increase in the number of law enforcement officers who are pictured in their intimidating uniforms.

## Mother Road memories

A typical garage from the same era – with its glass-topped Red Crown gasoline pump – flanks pictures of a few of the three million migrants in their battered trucks bearing "California or Bust" signs. The photos of trucks, crammed with furniture, bedding, pots and pans, and crated chickens typify the Dust Bowl years, when parched farmlands induced the westward-flight of almost one-fifth of the state's population. "66 is the path of people in flight, refugees from dust and shrinking land," wrote John Steinbeck in the book that produced the 1940 Academy Award-winning *The Grapes of Wrath*.

"We'll go on forever, Pa, cuz we're the people," declared the movie's Ma Joad. A World War II jeep, a Greyhound bus, and a VW bus evoking the hippies-on-the-road era are among the vehicles on show, the "bug" illuminated by fluorescent lighting in a room whose walls display '60s album covers from Sinatra and Dina Shore to Hank Williams and Chuck Berry. A poster promoting a one-time rattlesnake show, a map made by a retired postmaster with franking stamps from every post office along the route, a glass case of souvenirs from long-vanished gift shops, and a video running quaint family movies on an endless loop are also part of the museum tour, which climaxes with an absorbing movie depicting the route's history.

"We heard many years ago in New Zealand Nat King Cole singing 'Get Your Kicks on Route 66'," writes one visitor. "So we came to see it."

## Diner lingo

In the museum's replica of a 1950s diner, complete with a 1951 Ford parked out front and interior cozy booths, a jukebox playing Elvis Presley, and plastic donuts and coffee displayed on the Formica counter, is a translation of "diner lingo" – the shorthand used by waitresses when shouting orders to the kitchen. Some examples: "Drown one, hold the hail" (Coke, no ice); "Boiled leaves" (hot tea); "Rubber in a bun" (steak sandwich).

Until 1999, Clinton's historic Pop Hicks Restaurant was the oldest continuously operating restaurant along the entire route, but in that year it burned down and owner Howard Nichols has no plans to rebuild. Instead, check out Jiggs Smokehouse, just west on I-40 for delicious barbecue food.

West of Clinton, Route 66 parallels I-40, which is only a stone's throw away, and the advantage of traveling along the almost empty Mother Highway is summed up by a Burma Shave aphorism painted on the wall of a local café: *The Guy Who Drives/So Close Behind/Is He Lonesome/Or Just Blind? (see page 38).*

The ghost town of **Foss**; the Cotton Boll at **Canute** (now a private home but sign still extant); and the complex at **Elk City** of relocated old buildings, plus another Route 66 museum might draw you off the road after leaving Clinton. When the US Highway 66

Map on page 204

Association held its convention in Elk City's Casa Grande Hotel in 1931, more than 20,000 enthusiasts attended. The hotel is now the **Anadarko Basin Museum of Natural History** (tel: 580-243-0437; tours by appointment). Songwriter Jimmy Webb ("Up, Up and Away") was born here.

**Sayre**, a little bit farther on, is also alarmingly empty these days, but shows traces of having once been a prominent feature along the route. Its Owl Drugstore has a gleaming '50s soda fountain where you can have a root-beer float or a chocolate malt, and the town also has a rather grandiloquent courthouse, which featured fleetingly in the movie *The Grapes of Wrath*. The small, fairly ordinary towns of **Erick** and **Texola** have each – at different times by different surveys – been declared to be sitting on the 100th meridian, the longitudinal arcs running through both the North and the South poles that are used as geographical definitions.

Heading through Erick, Route 66 is renamed Roger Miller Boulevard – a tribute to its songwriting ("King of the Road") native son. Route 66 historian Tom Snyder says that Erick was once one of the nation's worst speed traps, but now behaves itself because its severity caused tourist traffic to dry up.

## THE TEXAS PANHANDLE

As you progress west through the high plains of Oklahoma, which merge into the Texas Panhandle, the grass becomes shorter and the hills begin to turn into small buttes and mesas. There's an overwhelming sense of insignificance in the face of the wide, open space stretching as far as the horizon. As might be expected in Texas, there is also a palpable feeling of having arrived in the real West, reflected in the confident pride of most residents. "Character traits, like an independent spirit, found expression in the West," explains the University of Oklahoma's Peter Hassrick. "By going West you escape the social restraints of the East. That same independent spirit could be seen in the mountain man and later the Forty-niners and finally the American cowboy."

Along this route you'll perhaps get your first glimpse of the impressive mile-long freight trains snaking their way along the Santa Fe tracks, usually paralleling the road but sometimes causing lengthy delays at road crossings. *Slow Down, Pa/Sakes Alive/Ma Missed Signs/Four and Five,* the Burma Shave signs used to admonish.

At **Shamrock**, Texas – where travelers are invited to experience 4 miles (6 km) of historic 66 – is the **Pioneer West Historical Museum** (tel: 806-256-3941; open Mon–Fri). Don't miss the abandoned lime-green and sand-colored Art Deco masterpiece, the U Drop Inn Café and adjoining gas station with matching tower. The pump's gasoline sign is frozen at a nostalgic 79¢ per gallon.

Early gas stations had to fight hard for custom in a highly competitive market and the filling pump station took many forms. One, on the site of Albuquerque, New Mexico's present-day Lobo movie theater, was shaped like a giant chunk of ice. Companies made a big deal of cleanliness. Texaco, for example, established its White Patrol in 1938 – a team of inspectors

**BELOW:** Art Deco U Drop Inn Café, Shamrock, Texas.

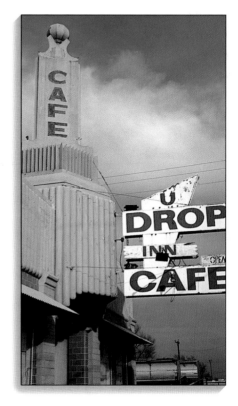

*Gas stations were highly competitive during the heyday of Route 66. In 1939, Phillips 66 hired registered nurses to inspect the cleanliness of the restrooms. These "Highway Hostesses" also carried ice water, and were told to be of assistance to motorists in trouble.*

in white coupés who toured the highways inspecting the company's rest rooms. The following year Phillips followed suit, hiring registered nurses and sending them out on a similar mission as Highway Hostesses who were mandated to carry ice water and render assistance to motorists in trouble. The Union Oil Company countered with its Sparkle Corps.

At picturesque, sleepy **McLean** ㉒ (pop. 850), which describes itself as "the heart of old Route 66," an old Phillips 66 gas station has been restored by volunteers, one of a surprisingly small number along the route (there are none at all in Arizona). The Phillips Petroleum Company records some of the many erroneous explanations people have offered for the "66" in the company's name, for example: there are 66 books in the Bible; the company's founders were down to their last $66 when they drilled their first successful oil well; or that founder Frank Phillips was 66 years old when he founded the company (he was actually 44).

## The Devil's Rope

The **Devil's Rope Museum**, formerly a brassiere factory, is here (tel: 806-779-2225; open daily) – the "rope" in question being barbed wire, a large rusty ball of which sits outside. Although the museum has a relatively small selection, there are as many as 8,000 different types of barbed wire in existence. Oklahoma's Cowboy Hall of Fame *(see page 206)* has the largest collection, including the popular "Dodge Spur" with its single line. In the mid-19th century there were hundreds of competing designs, but it was Joseph F. Glidden's patent for fencing material, consisting of barbs wrapped around a single strand of wire, that eventually predominated.

**BELOW:** heart-felt wall mural, Texas.

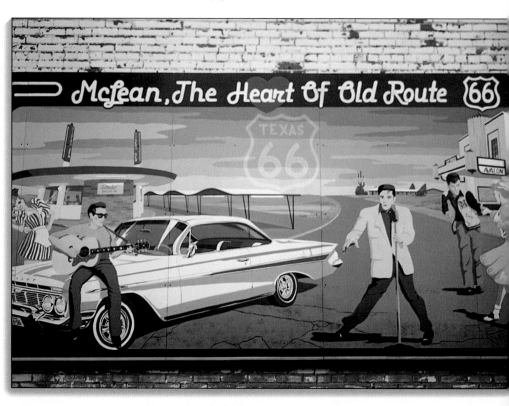

Map on page 204

## Towards Amarillo

As you drive out of McLean, look for the large wall mural depicting Elvis performing next to a yellow Cadillac, on whose hood sits a guitar player. The unpaved section of Route 66 between Alanreed and **Groom** has always been a problem for unwary drivers. Bob Moore and Patrick Grauwels, the acknowledged experts on the road, write that the section, once known as Jericho Gap, "was notorious for bogging down cars and trucks in a black, gumbo mud every time it rained." Their *Illustrated Guidebook to the Mother Road,* with pictures by Yannis Argyropoulos, is indisputably the most comprehensive of the many guides available: a spiral-bound, mile-by-mile summation, it has sold more than 50,000 copies. Moore points out that despite their years of research errors do occur "because Route 66 is still a living entity, and as such, changes are constantly taking place."

The route, which mostly parallels I-40 in this part of Texas, and sometimes merges with it, is hard to follow between here and Amarillo. At the entrance to many towns it's safer, when in doubt, to take the off-ramp road labeled *Business I-40,* which usually follows the old Route 66 through town. This is the case at **Conway**, recognizable by its huge grain elevators and decrepit, old motels. Located on the route as you head toward Amarillo is the 24-hour Cattleman's Club & Café, with a large steer on its sign. An interesting breakfast stop, this place is about as Western as you'll find, with half the customers of both sexes wearing Stetsons, rows of slot machines to keep them occupied, and gigantic rubbery omelets big enough to feed a ravenous cowpoke.

## Palo Duro Canyon

Just before Amarillo (where local rancher J.F. Glidden invented his barbed wire) you could turn south on US 87 to visit the vast **Palo Duro Canyon**, closely associated with the legendary Charles Goodnight. Goodnight – inventor of the chuckwagon and once owner of the largest ranch in Texas – was the first rancher to move into the Panhandle in the 1870s. A musical named simply *Texas* takes place at the Canyon nightly in summer (tel: 806-655-2181) against a steep cliffside backdrop. Chuckwagon tours beginning or ending with "cowboy" breakfast or dinner are offered on the rim of the canyon, where part of an Indiana Jones movie was filmed (tel: 800-658-2613).

**Amarillo ㉓** itself, always a major shipping point for cattle, stages regular rodeos (for information tel: 806-374-1497) and is the home of the **Big Texan Steak Ranch and Opry**, a world-renowned restaurant offering 72-ounce steaks free to anybody who can eat one within an hour. A unique natural resource found locally is helium, a monument to which sits on Streit Drive near the Botanical Gardens.

The city's one-way traffic system can be confusing, but you'll be back on Route 66 proper if you follow 6th Street, which leads into "**antique row**," where plenty of Route 66 shops and modern cafés entice visitors with their colorful signage, such as Smoky Joe's, Cup A Java, and Amigo's Café. It's worth parking the car to take a closer look at some of the

**BELOW:** stop for a cup of java in Amarillo's "antique row."

brightly-colored wall murals harking back to the good ol' days. There are three churches on one block, which ends with the San Jacinto Apartments, San Jacinto Heights being the old name for this particular suburb.

South of I-40 just outside town is **Cadillac Ranch**, the much-photographed and often repainted line of ten Cadillacs, their rear ends sticking out of the earth to make some kind of sculptural statement by art financier Stanley Marsh. This is one of those experiences that, sadly, is better in photographs; if you blinked, you probably missed it. The fleeting view from the highway is as close as you can get, too, as the Cadillacs are literally in the middle of a field.

## Death by highway

There's not much to see at the ghost town of **Vega**, except the vintage Vega Motel (tel: 806-267-2205). By 1928 motels were breeding fast along the fledgling Route 66, but in 1956 the creation of the Interstate Highway System sounded the death knell for scores of businesses, which suddenly found themselves bypassed by the traffic that for more than a quarter of a century had brought them prosperity. "As the world changes," says Joe Kisicki of Oklahoma's Route 66 Association, "so do things along the Mother Road. It mirrors life both modern and nostalgic, tacky and clever, restless and changeless."

Tiny, and, in parts, dilapidated **Adrian ㉔** declares itself to be at the exact center of Route 66, with a sign announcing that it is 1,139 miles (1,833 km) to Chicago and 1,139 miles to Los Angeles. There are other, more curiously philosophical signs dotted around its handful of streets – *You Will Never Be the Same* and *If A Man Could Have Half His Wishes He Would Double His Troubles* – but it is unlikely you will find anybody in the deserted streets to ask about them.

**BELOW:**
the Cadillac Ranch is just outside Amarillo, Texas.

Abandoned buildings such as the "First in Texas/Last in Texas Motel" dot **Glenrio**, the last Texas town you'll come to on this route and another virtual ghost town, although the four-lane Route 66 highway sits invitingly (albeit starting to disintegrate) at the edge of town.

## NEW MEXICO

However well prepared you think you might be for New Mexico, no amount of reading can dull the initial, and rather pleasant, shock of finding the aesthetic beauty of Spanish South America dropped right in the middle of this vast, though sometimes bland, scenescape. It feels oddly surreal. In some parts of the state you won't see a gaudy neon sign, motel chain, or a pair of golden arches for miles. Make the most of it.

Route 66 is heavily promoted throughout New Mexico, where it extends more than 300 miles (483 km) across the state. The State Fairgrounds in Albuquerque is the site of the 2001 75th anniversary celebration of Route 66 – which includes a photographic exhibit of historic buildings (a score of them in Albuquerque itself), a vintage automobile show, a "Poetry Slam," roadside diner cook-off, and many other events. An excursion along the route was once made by members of a European travel club in 30 vintage American cars that were shipped from Europe. Rich Williams, president of the state's Route 66 Association, says the road "still vibrates" and embodies "a kind of mythology, the best of American culture. And everybody wants to experience that – the authentic American spirit that really created this country."

Map on page 204

A sign outside the drive-in tourist information and rest area just across the border in New Mexico informs drivers that the surrounding terrain, the Llano Estacado (Staked Plain) – a high plateau covering 33,000 square miles (85,500 square kilometers) – is one of the flattest areas of the continental United States. Spanish explorer Francisco Vasquez de Coronado unsuccessfully combed the region for the fabled Seven Cities of Cibola back in 1540, expecting to uncover unimaginable hoards of gold and silver. Instead he discovered innumerable Indian pueblos, where the glitter came from beautiful jewelry shaped by native craftsmen. Nineteen of the pueblos still exist and can be visited today (phone ahead, tel: 800-747-0181 or 505-552-6654).

Route 66 crosses and re-crosses I-40 before running through **Tucumcari** ㉕ ("two miles long and two blocks wide") where the Tee Pee Curio Store (*circa* 1944) is one of the oldest souvenir shops along the route. Every conceivable type of souvenir item turns up here, and in dozens of independently-run shops in one small town after another along the route: pop-up art of paper buildings, old postcards, caps, jackets, scarves, traffic signs, sheriff's badges, playing cards, mugs, glasses, paperweights, ashtrays, earrings, belt buckles, money clips, and even baby bibs bearing the 66 logo. Almost everywhere can be found either original or reproduced Burma Shave signs: *Be a Modern/Paul Revere/Spread the News/From Ear to Ear/Burma Shave.*

*Cow's Skull: Red, White and Blue by Georgia O'Keeffe; visit a museum devoted to the artist in Santa Fe, NM.*

Tucumcari once advertised it had 2,000 motel rooms and watched a nonstop stream of traffic pass by. Not the case today, but keep an eye out for such veterans of the highway as the historic Blue Swallow Motel, its characterful rooms replete with flowered pillows, and the Safari Motel with its neon sign of a man on a camel. Among Route 66's achievements was the molding of the bus and trucking industries, both able to supply essential transportation in an era of wartime gasoline rationing. A museum in Oklahoma City is devoted to Lee Way, one of the more famous freight companies along the route. Parking meters also began to make an unwelcome appearance in the main streets here and in other towns along the route.

**BELOW:** smiles near Santa Fe.

It's worth turning off Tucumcari's main highway to sip a malted milkshake at the long-standing Big Dipper Café, situated near the Spanish Revival railroad station, and there's a wide variety of fascinating old artifacts and Route 66 memorabilia worth looking at in the **Historical Museum** (tel: 505-461-4201; closed Sun).

## Santa Fe

Farther along the route, just past **Santa Rosa** at exit 256, you can swing north on US 84, crossing the Pecos River to Las Vegas (not to be confused with the Nevada city of the same name), and then follow the highway as it turns sharply west to **Santa Fe** ㉖, one of the oldest and best-known Western cities by virtue of the Santa Fe Trail. The trail ran from here almost 800 miles (1,280 km) to Kansas City and was

the major western trade route in the 18th and 19th centuries. Less a road than a beaten track for freight wagons across the Plains, it segued into El Camino Real, which led into central Mexico. The capital of New Mexico was on the original Route 66 until 1938 when a straighter route superceded it and cut 126 miles (200 km) off the journey.

Today's Santa Fe, its central buildings in matching adobe shades (coated with stucco instead of the traditional, yet fragile, mud plaster), is chic, tasteful, and expensive, with sleek hotels filled with affluent boutique shoppers. There are exceptions, though – such as the charming El Rey Motel (tel: 505-982-1931) with its 1940s ambience and more moderate rates, and there are numerous cheaper but very pleasant and quite homey B&Bs sprinkled among the more expensive hotels.

*Whoever designed the streets of Santa Fe must have been drunk and riding backwards on a mule.*

— WILL ROGERS

## Archbishops and artists

Santa Fe's impressive historic center and plaza is designed for relaxed strolling, but if you are intending to conduct a more thorough walking tour, it might be a good idea to arm yourself with one of the free local maps. Will Rogers once said: "Whoever designed the streets of Santa Fe must have been drunk and riding backwards on a mule." An alternative is to take one of the organized walking tours or take the narrated Open Air Tram City Tour. This covers a 10-mile (16-km) loop through historic and residential areas.

A landmark is **St Francis Cathedral**, whose archbishop, Jean Baptiste Lamy, buried below the altar, was the model for Willa Cather's novel, *Death Comes to the Archbishop*. The **Museum of New Mexico** is actually several museums, including the **American Indian Arts Museum** (tel: 505-988-6281; open daily). Fans of Georgia O'Keeffe will find plenty of the artist's work in the **Georgia O'Keeffe Museum**, a few blocks from the plaza (tel: 505-995-0785; closed Mon) and designed by Richard Gluckman, who was responsible for Pittsburgh's interesting Andy Warhol Museum.

**BELOW:** Southwest style, Santa Fe.

Artists have always loved Santa Fe, and many of them live in historic adobes along **Canyon Road**, off Paseo de Peralta south of the river, once a burro track but now a chic area of art galleries, restaurants, and shops. Look for **El Zaguan** and the **Rafael Borrego House**, both charming haciendas; the **Cristo Rey Church**, filled with Hispanic religious art; and the boutiques of **Gypsy Alley**. The **Old Santa Fe Trail** (now US 285) was, in 1821 the channel of communication between the Spanish Rio Grande and America. It crosses the Paseo, and on the trail are historic sites like the San Miguel Mission, the **Loretto Chapel** with its "Miraculous Staircase," and the **State Capitol**.

Gene Autry made his film debut in 1935 with *In Old Santa Fe* and the city has since decorated many titles – *Santa Fe Stampede* (with John Wayne), *Santa Fe Passage* (Slim Pickens), *Santa Fe Trail* (Ronald Reagan and Errol Flynn) – in addition to providing the setting for Hollywood movies as wide-ranging as the 1958 *The Left-Handed Gun* (Paul Newman) and the more recent 1988 *Twins* (Danny De Vito and Arnold Schwarzenegger).

## Towards Albuquerque

You can take US 285 south to connect up with the main route west again, and just before the intersection with I-40 you'll come to **Cline's Corner**, which founder Roy Cline subsequently described as "the coldest, the meanest, the windiest place on Highway 66." The town features in many of the tales told by Howard Subtle in his *Behind the Wheel on Route 66*. Subtle spent 28 years as a Greyhound bus driver heading back and forth along the highway, and his book is a ragbag of reminiscences about mislaid children, garrulous passengers, and the occasional stowaway hiding behind the rear seats. On one occasion he spotted an elephant tied to a tree; it turned out the beast had not been abandoned, but had been left with food and water after the truck that was transporting it broke down.

At Tijeras, east of Albuquerque, is the turn-off through Cedar Crest to the 10,700-feet-high (3,260-meter) **Sandia Mountains**, which offer fabulous panoramic views and one of the world's longest (2¾ miles/4 km) aerial tramways (open Thur–Sun in summer). The Sandia Ranger Station is open daily (tel: 505-281-3304).

In **Albuquerque** ㉗, the old Route 66 runs along what is now Central Avenue, where the Civic Center, the tourist office, and a handful of vintage buildings lie across the Atchison, Topeka, and Santa Fe railroad tracks just past Second Street. Local Route 66 revitalization projects are very much in evidence along this stretch of the route, where shops and businesses seem to be doing a roaring trade. Note the elaborate Rococo KiMo Theater; the Avalon Restaurant with its arresting cowboy sign; and the 1880 railroad symbol carved into the metal fretwork street lamps.

Map on page 204

**BELOW:**
Christmas Eve
in Albuquerque's
Old Town.

## Albuquerque's Old Town

Two miles further west, on the other side of the Rio Grande, the **Old Town** with its attractive shops and restaurants is one block to the right of Central Avenue, its ancient plaza grandly dominated by the adobe **San Felipe Church** (1706). Five flags have flown over this plaza: Spanish, Mexican, Confederate, the Stars and Stripes, and that of New Mexico. Allow at least an hour to wander around Old Town and try to time it with lunch or an early dinner to take advantage of one of the many cafés.

The **Albuquerque Biological Park** (tel: 505-764-6200; closed Mon) with its aquarium, zoo, and botanical garden, is at 2601 Central Avenue, and nearby are the **Science Center and Children's Museum** (tel: 505-842-1537; closed Mon), the **Albuquerque Museum** (tel: 505-243-7255; closed Mon), the **Museum of Natural History & Science** (tel: 505 841-2800; open daily), and the shuddery **Rattlesnake Museum** (tel: 505-242-6569; open daily). One block north, on 12th Street, the **Indian Pueblo Cultural Center** (tel: 505-843-7270; open daily) has galleries, a museum, gift shop, restaurant, and free traditional dance performances on weekends.

Albuquerque, like so many places in the state, has been popular with moviemakers. Mary Pickford was there in 1912 to appear in an early silent movie, *The Old Actor*. Leaving town along Central Avenue, look out for the venerable El Vado and DeAnza Motels, relics of the 1950s when there were almost 100 motels in Albuquerque. There are now half as many, and old neon motel signs have become collectors' items as valuable Art Deco artifacts.

Eric Szeman, co-owner of the Route 66 Malt Shop in Albuquerque, made the cross-country trip with his parents almost 50 years ago. "America became

**BELOW:**
Southwestern cities often have breath-taking settings.

more mobile than it ever had been," he recalls. "The mass migration westward was pretty much handled by Route 66."

Westward, Route 66, running side by side and sometimes absorbed by Interstate 40, passes through **Laguna** with its early 18th-century church, **Paguate Cubero** (near which novelist Ernest Hemingway settled in to write *The Old Man and the Sea*), and past the gas station and casino below **Acoma Sky City** which, perched on a mesa 367 feet (112 meters) overhead, is the oldest continuously occupied village in the country. **Grants** (named after three brothers) actually *looks* like a street from the mid-20th century with its Zia and Franciscan motels, Grants Café, El Jardin, and Monte Carol Restaurant – all of which date from that era.

## Volcanos and ice caves

Interesting side trips can be made to the dormant **Bandera Volcano** and nearby **Ice Cave** (tel: 888-ICE-CAVE, open daily), 25 miles (40 km) south on Highway 53; and to **El Morro**, or Inscription Rock, 28 miles (45 km) farther along. The sandstone pillar is a written history of those who have passed by, from Native Americans, Spanish explorers, and the US Army Camel Corps to pioneers heading west in the mid-19th century.

For most of the way between Grants and Gallup, Route 66 and the interstate are only a few yards apart, with **Milan**'s funky Crossroads Motel (*circa* 1948) the first landmark and – 15 miles (24 km) farther west – the Continental Divide marked by a roadside café of the same name. The **Prewitt Trading Post**, once called the Zuni Mountain Trading Post, dates back to 1946. An unbroken chain of steep, red rock mesas flank the highway to the north.

Map on page 204

*Route 66 gas stations were made as pretty as possible in a competitive marketplace.*

**BELOW:** picking up groceries.

Map on page 204

## Gallup's movie-star hangout

One of the high spots of the entire route is surely the **El Rancho Hotel and Motel** (tel: 800-543-6351) at **Gallup** ㉓, built in 1937 by Raymond E. Griffith, who passed himself off as the brother of movie pioneer D. W. Griffith. This town is worth an overnight stay as Gallup is very appealing as a genuine New Mexico town. At first glance it's not nearly as pretty to look at as picture-perfect Santa Fe or Albuquerque, but it has lots of character and plenty of lingering remnants of the Route 66 era. There's definitely a sense here of a place that gets on with everyday life, rather than one which is filled with admiring tourists, or one that is now deserted following the route's demise. The hotel was a favorite with movie stars from the beginning; by the 1960s at least 15 movies had been shot using the hotel as headquarters, among them *Sundown*, *Streets of Laredo*, and *The Hallelujah Trail*.

El Rancho is enormous and resembles everybody's dream of a huge ranch house with its Navajo rugs, solid Western furniture, wagon wheels, and mounted moose heads. Its wooden staircase is distinctive enough to bear a designer credit and leads to a balcony decked out with signed photographs from Ronald Reagan, Rosalind Russell, Paulette Goddard, Humphrey Bogart, Jack Benny, and a host of others. Off the immense lobby is a charming restaurant and bar, and burgers and sandwiches are named after the likes of Doris Day, Errol Flynn, and Burt Lancaster. The "Mae West" sandwich is cheeerfully defined as "stacked beef or ham."

Gallup tags itself "where the Indian southwest begins" and remains, as it has always been, a major trading post for the native peoples – these days as many as 200,000 of them – who live on the 17½-million-acre (708,000-hectare) **Navajo Nation**. This sprawls across the distinctive **Four Corners** region to the north where the states of New Mexico, Arizona, Colorado, and Utah meet. The percentage of Native-American owned land is second only to Arizona.

## Indian territory

The Navajo capital of **Window Rock** is 25 miles (40 km) from Gallup (and *just* across the border in Arizona) on State Route 264. The largest pueblo in the state, that of **Zuni** (tel: 505-782-4481) with its Our Lady of Guadeloupe Mission (1629) is 40 miles (64 km) south on Highway 53. Zuni artisans are famous for their intricate silver jewelry skillfully inlaid with turquoise and coral. If you shop around, Zuni pieces can look surprisingly contemporary.

Indian artifacts such as rugs, jewelry, and other crafts can be bought at many stores along Route 66, which happens to be Gallup's main street, the center of town being located in a 12-block area around Hill Avenue and Fourth Street.

The century-old **Rex Hotel** is now a museum, and a new cultural center staging ceremonial dances nightly in summer occupies the historic railroad station. **Red Rock Museum** (tel: 505-863-1337), with its Indian handicrafts, is 20 minutes' drive to the east in the park of the same name. There is a balloon rally in Red Rock Park every December. ❑

**BELOW:** on the road in the desert.
**RIGHT:** scaling a Southwest slot canyon.

# ARIZONA TO LOS ANGELES

*Wigwam motels, gorgeous gas stations, soda fountains that work –
the cruise along Route 66 continues, taking in ghosts
and the Grand Canyon along the way*

Map
on page
204

The Mother Road becomes difficult to follow just over the border from New Mexico into Arizona, so if cruising the length of Route 66 is not a priority, you can remain on Interstate 40 through Holbrook, Arizona. About 25 miles (40 km) inside the state, exit 330 from I-40 leads into **Petrified Forest National Park ㉙**, whose 100,000 acres (40,500 hectares) are littered with giant petrified logs. More than 200 million years ago the region was a swampy, tropical zone whose mineral-rich soil helped to preserve the fossilized bones of prehistoric animals. In the northern section of the park is the **Painted Desert Inn National Historic Landmark** (tel: 520-524-6228), now a museum.

Dinosaur statues line the road on the way to **Holbrook ㉚**, whose outstanding attraction is the roadside **Wigwam Motel**, a long-standing favorite (particularly with kids) on Route 66 (tel: 520-524-3048). A collection of 15 cozy rooms, each one is inside its own tall, stone teepee built by owner John Lewis' father in the 1940s from plans by architect Frank Redford. He allowed seven similar motels around the country to be built from his plans, stipulating only that each be equipped with a radio that played 30 minutes for 10¢.

Parked outside the teepees is the family collection of '50s Fords and Buicks, while inside the main building a small museum exhibits chunks of petrified trees, Indian artifacts, and rifles and powder horns from the frontier days. A Visitor Center and historical museum can be found in the **Old Navajo Courthouse** (*circa* 1898) on Navajo Boulevard (Route 66), which runs through the center of town.

**LEFT:** the
Wigwam Motel,
Holbrook, Arizona.
**BELOW:** "It's
a rough life,
but somebody's
gotta do it."

## Pony Express

Holbrook's evocatively named Butterfield Stage Co., a contemporary of the Pony Express, is a good spot to stop for barbecue food. The spirit of the short-lived but legendary Pony Express, whose demise was induced by the telegraph system some 150 years ago, is kept alive in the town by the Navajo County Sheriff's posse, who carry mail to Scottsdale (near Phoenix) in late January every year.

Under a contract with the US Postal Service, the 40-strong "Hashknife Posse" carries out a tradition begun in 1954, when a similar posse carried to the state governor an invitation to attend a stampede. An estimated 15,000 letters (sent in by admirers throughout the world) are hand-stamped with the official ride logo and franked with a Pony Express postmark before being sent off in mail bags relayed by the riders every few miles in the course of the 200-mile (320-km) journey.

The posse's name is derived from The Hash Knife Outfit, a branch of the third-largest cattle company in the country, which began shipping out thousands of

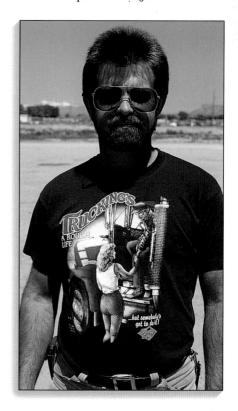

cattle after 1881 when the life-changing railroad began to go through here.

Holbrook's preserved **Blevins House** across from the Santa Fe depot was the scene of a spectacular shoot-out on September 4, 1857, when the county sheriff went to arrest a horse thief and survived after being shot at by several members of the thief's family. Nearby are the notorious Bucket of Blood Saloon, the 1910 J&J Trading Post, and the one-time Campbell's Coffee House (now a Rexall's drug store), which became famous for its "Son of a Bitch stew."

## Anasazi ruins

Five miles (8 km) off I-40 near **Joseph City** ("Joseph Small Town" would be more appropriate) is the Jackrabbit Trading Post, with its original crouching rabbit sign, while 16 miles (26 km) farther on, a turn north on State Route 87 – just before you get to Winslow – will take you to the extensive 14th-century Anasazi site of **Homolovi Ruins State Park** (tel: 520-289-4106).

**Winslow ❸** achieved fame from its inclusion in the pop song "Take It Easy" by Jackson Browne. The Eagles' hit single refers to "Standin' on a corner in Winslow, Arizona," and visitors pour into town to do just that at Standin' on the Corner Park (Kinsley and Second streets), where there is a 6-foot (2-meter) high bronze statue of a man with a guitar. The lyric goes: *Well, I'm standing on a corner in Winslow, Arizona/Such a fine sight to see/It's a girl, my Lord/In a flatbed Ford/Slowing down to take a look at me.*

Until the 1960s, Winslow, born with the arrival of the railroad in 1880, was the largest town in northern Arizona, but business began to fade when it was bypassed by the interstate. Its rebirth began with the renovation of Downtown, and notably that of a former 1930 Fred Harvey hotel, **La Posada** (tel: 520-289-4366). Three popular eating places long-associated with the highway (around Second and Third streets) have evocative names: the Whole Enchilada, Miss Zip's, and the Falcon Restaurant.

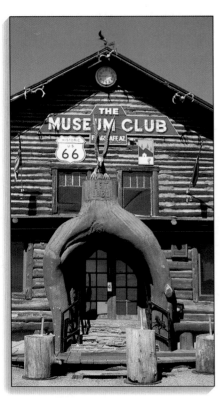

South of Winslow off SR 99, Anasazi petroglyphs can be admired in **Chevelon Canyon**, west of town, to which tours are conducted from Rock Art Canyon Ranch. Anglers know the area well for its rainbow and – more enticingly – brown trout that live in the lake and creek here.

About 20 miles (32 km) west on I-40, Exit 233 leads south to **Meteor Crater**, a 600-foot (183-meter) deep hole almost a mile across created by the impact of a meteorite nearly 50 centuries ago. Astronauts were trained here before the moon visit, and an Astronaut Hall of Fame and Apollo Space Capsule are on display in the museum (tel: 800-289-5898; daily tours). Back on the main road heading west, the ghost town of **Two Guns** sits on an abandoned portion of Route 66.

Although **Winona** features in Bobby Troup's "Route 66" song, it's actually a dead-end, and what Route 66 historian Tom Snyder calls "a one-blink town." Near Winona, 7 miles (11 km) before Flagstaff, is the **Walnut Canyon National Monument** (tel: 520-527-0246), where a short hike down a paved trail reveals ancient cliff dwellings that fell into disuse hundreds of years ago.

## Flagstaff

The only large town in northern Arizona, **Flagstaff**  (pop. 58,900) is a staging point for trips to the Grand Canyon, 80 miles (129 km) to the north. The trip up US 89 and then along State Route 64 is longer, but more scenic, than the shorter route from Williams farther along the highway. Two of Flagstaff's museum attractions, the **Pioneer Museum** (tel: 520-774-6272; closed Sun) and the **Museum of Northern Arizona** (tel: 520-774-5213; open daily), are not far apart on Fort Valley Road, or from US 180, which also leads to the canyon. Flagstaff's other attractions are either in or near the historic and attractive downtown railroad district, through which Route 66 runs. The city stages a Route 66 Celebration each June with live music, a parade of classic cars, and displays of arts and crafts.

On the way into Flagstaff from the direction of the east, be sure to stop by the **Museum Club**, a 1931 roadhouse which in Prohibition days began as a "zoo" filled with stuffed animals. This is now supplemented with more bizarre exhibits and, more importantly, the memories of dozens of country-music legends that have performed in the Southwest's largest log cabin. Nearer to Downtown are the **Lowell Observatory** (tel: 520-774-2096; open daily) and the richly furnished 40-room **Riordan Mansion** (tel: 520-779-4395; open daily), set in an attractive park.

Leroux Street is opposite the train station, and is where you'll find the remarkable **Weatherford Hotel** (tel: 520-774-2731), which opened its doors on the first day of 1899. That day it welcomed among its scores of distinguished guests the publisher William Randolph Hearst, President Theodore Roosevelt, and lawman Wyatt Earp. The bar boasts an antique counter that came from Tombstone,

Map on page 204

**BELOW:** the Hotel Weatherford played host to presidents, publishers, and Wyatt Earp.

## MONUMENT VALLEY

A 182-mile (293-km) journey from Flagstaff, Arizona leads to one of the most famous sights in the Southwest. Monument Valley is easily recognized from far away *(see picture on page 178)* thanks to scenes from countless Westerns, especially those by director John Ford, who often used the valley as the backdrop for his movies. With its serene rock formations dominating the surrounding barren desert plains, the valley's mesas were not just attractive to Hollywood, but also served as significant religious monuments for local Native Americans. Medicine men once climbed the Rain God Mesa – home to a sacred burial ground – to pray for rain. The Totem Pole formation served as a center for mythical incidents in folklore, while the Yei-Bi-Chei resembles holy Navajo figures performing a traditional dance. Like the Grand Canyon or Sedona, the timeless mystery of these rocks are humbling in their presence. What seems an impossible creation is the result of ageless erosion of the sandstone and shale, which leaves the harder stone intact. Monument Valley lies entirely within the Navajo Nation reservation, and the tribe conducts tours through its desolate beauty. Telephone 435-727-3255 for more information.

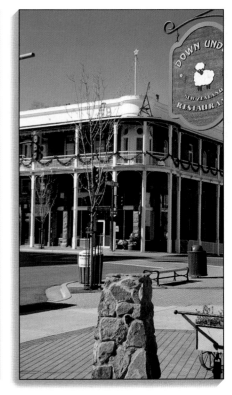

*Native American sign near Williams, Arizona.*

and the ballroom is named for Western author Zane Grey, who stayed here while writing *Call of the Canyon*.

A young reader of Zane Grey's books was one Cecil B. De Mille, who concluded that Flagstaff sounded like a good place to launch his movie career. When he arrived in the town from the East however, it was snowing, and De Mille decided to continue on the train to Los Angeles, thus altering the course of movie history forever.

An attractive side trip from Flagstaff is along State Highway 89a through the red rocks of spectacular **Oak Creek Canyon** to the artist community of **Sedona** ㉝, 28 miles (45 km) south. A daily shuttle service (tel: 520-774-2200) connects the two communities. Further south is another artist's haven, **Jerome**, a former ghost town named after a defunct copper mine.

## Back on Route 66

Between Flagstaff and Williams, Route 66 is mostly unsurfaced and not very well maintained, but has the distinction of containing the highest point of the route at 7,300 feet (2,225 meters) above sea level, about a mile or two before **Parks**. The Parks in the Pines general store has been in business for more than 80 years. Nearby are the remains of the **Beale Wagon Road Historic Trail**, a sturdy 120-foot (36-meter) wide track constructed in 1857 on which pioneers could safely travel as far as the Colorado River.

**BELOW:** Navajo women on their Arizona reservation.

Back on I-40, the next town, **Williams** ㉞, with its main street on Route 66 and nearby mountain were all named after Bill Williams (1787–1849), an early fur trapper whose statue stands at the west end of town. The excellent *Route 66 Magazine* is published here, the last town on Route 66 to be bypassed by I-40

Map on page 204

and the main departure point for the Grand Canyon. The Grand Canyon Railway (tel: 800-THE-TRAIN) departs here for the canyon every morning. The five-hour round-trip – by vintage steam locomotives in summer, diesel locomotives the rest of the year – allows for three hours' sightseeing at the canyon, but is a worthwhile trip in itself (particularly for families), complete with strolling cowboy musicians and, on the return trip, a "train robbery."

## The Grand Canyon

The South Rim of the **Grand Canyon** ❸❺ (which can also be reached by traveling about 40 miles/64 km north on US 180 from Williams) is open around the clock every day of the year, although the Visitor Center and most park facilities operate only from 8am to 5pm. Free canyon shuttle buses operate between mid-March and mid-October, allowing visitors access to different points so that they can hike along the rim of the canyon. (To reserve accommodation at one of the lodges tel: 303-297-2757 or 800-528-6367; be sure to book early.)

Near the Williams railroad depot (which also houses an interesting museum) is the restored **Fray Marcos Hotel** (tel: 520-635-4010), originally a unit of the once-ubiquitous Harvey House chain, which an English immigrant, Fred Harvey, established in the 1880s along the route of the Santa Fe line, revolutionizing the then-abysmal standards of railway food. One of Harvey's basic rules was that the coffee – served by smiling "Harvey Girls" in black dresses and spotless white aprons and bows – was re-made every two hours, even if the urn was still full. For 75¢, customers could choose from seven entrees and take second helpings, too.

*The Grand Canyon is more than 270 miles (435 km) long and averages 10 miles (16 km) in width. It passes through five of the seven temperate zones at which different species flourish.*

**BELOW:**
the Grand Canyon is open around the clock, every day of the year.

A tan-colored 1953 Cadillac and life-size cutouts of James Dean and Marilyn Monroe sit outside **Twisters**, a self-proclaimed "back-to-the '50s diner" that displays hundreds of snapshots of families taken along the route, along with an old glass-topped Sky Chief gasoline pump that has been converted into a holder for typical road souvenirs.

Sit here for 20 minutes or so and immerse yourself in pure, unadulterated kitsch. A menu offers a dozen different shakes, malts, floats, and cherry phosphates. For those seeking more conventional fare, the best-known restaurant in town, **Rod's Steak House**, has been serving customers along Route 66 for more than half a century.

### Beyond Williams

From Williams, 19 miles (30 km) west along Interstate 40, it's worth getting off the busy road to visit somnolent **Ash Fork**, which was a stage coach depot until the arrival of the railroad in 1882. This was also a regular stop along Route 66 until the town was bypassed by the bigger thoroughfare; a Confederate flag flies over the Route 66 Grill. One of the adorable Harvey Girls *(see page 230)* lived nearby until her death, and she donated several artifacts from the defunct Harvey House chain to a fledgling museum located in a vast, empty warehouse beside the tourist office.

A former railroad dispatcher, Dan Ayres, who has a print shop in town, is the author of a series of "railway novels," which are highly regarded locally. Half a dozen sandstone companies, whose flagstone wares are piled high around the station, mine the surrounding mountains for an earth-colored stone that is shipped nationwide.

**BELOW:**
Seligman Suzy Q.
**RIGHT:**
buy malts and
soda pop here.

## Toward the California border

Returning briefly to the interstate, it's advisable to leave it again at the Crookton Road exit for the longest and most nostalgic section on the entire Historic 66 Highway. It's quite simple to remain on it all the way to the California border at Topock, a distance of about 180 miles (290 km).

You won't miss **Seligman ③**, whose main thoroughfare resembles a permanent state of Christmas. The solitary main road and Route 66 are lined with strangely compelling gift shops devoted to the highway's history. One of these is run by Myrna Delgadillo, whose father, Angel, is a hero to fans of the road. The walls of his barber shop (which doubles as a Visitor Center), are covered with business cards from all over the world, and a day rarely passes without a stranger seeking him or the shop out. It was Angel who got the state's Historic Route 66 Association off the ground and who revived attention in a dying Seligman after the town was bypassed.

Born and raised in the town, Angel is apt to reminisce about the early days, recalling that when migrants came through he could guess their relative wealth by how many mattresses sagged over the sides of their overloaded trucks. Angel's brother Juan operates the Snow Cap Drive-In next door, at the rear of which lies a "garden" of oddities, including two old-fashioned wooden outhouses equipped with modern plumbing. Seligman's gift shops carry every conceivable type of souvenir, from US 66 highway signs, Mother Road license tags and oil company signs, to old Coca Cola posters and bottles – as well as the now-familiar inscribed mugs, glasses, and T-shirts. There's a vast range of books about the road, some esoteric like the *Gas Pump Collectors' Guide* and, of course, Frank Rowsome's *The Verse by the Side of the Road*.

Map on page 204

*Stomachs and gas tanks fueled here.*

**BELOW:** local hero Angel Delgadillo, whose Seligman barber shop doubles as a 66 Visitor Center.

**TIP**

Travelers might care to visit Oatman *outside* the summer months, when temperatures are hot enough to hold an annual Sidewalk Egg Fry at high noon, right in the middle of Route 66.

Small as it is, Seligman includes enough sites to offer a 20-minute walking tour, for which a free leaflet is available at Angel Delgadillo's barbershop. Visitors might note the 1932 Deluxe Motel on the main street, Black Cat Bar (1936) at the western end of town, and the boarded-up, pseudo-Tudor Harvey House beside the rail track. Twenty-five miles (40 km) west of Seligman is the deep **Grand Canyon Caverns** (tel: 520-422-3223; open daily), into which early visitors paid 25¢ to be lowered 150 feet (46 meters) by rope. Today, there's an elevator and illuminated paths on which to walk.

## Kingman and good cooking

The oldest operating garage on the route, together with some abandoned motels and the Hualapai Tribal headquarters, are in **Peach Springs**, and good cooking can be found at the Frontier Café at **Truxton**. At **Hackberry**, the owners of the general store (which doubles as a Visitor Center) have established a Bobby Troup Memorial Oasis. These are the main points of interest along 66 until **Kingman ❸**, where the tubby, gruff-voiced movie star Andy Devine was born. The main street is named after him, and on this and the adjoining Beale Street are the oldest buildings, including the old Beale Hotel where Clark Gable and Carole Lombard were married in March, 1939.

The **Mojave Museum of History and Arts** (tel: 520-753-3195; open daily) displays attractive turquoise jewelry and a recreated Hualapai dwelling, among other historical artifacts.

Heading west, the highway takes on a desolate, rocky wilderness appearance – an indicator of what's to come; be sure you have good breaks on the car. Before long the road is climbing between jagged peaks in a series of seemingly endless switchbacks and scary, blind curves to the 3,500-foot (1,067-meter) high summit at **Sitgreaves Pass** (named, like the Beale Wagon Trail, for a mid-19th-century Army surveyor), before beginning an equally twisting and turning segment down into the tiny town of Oatman.

### Haunted hotel

On the way down into Oatman, you'll pass **Goldroad**, the site of a mine that produced $2-billion-worth of gold in its early years, but closed down in the '90s when gold prices dropped. The mine is open every day to tour groups from Oatman (tel: 520-768-1600), with transportation provided.

Hundreds of wild burros turned loose by early miners roam the mountains, occasionally straying across the highway and wandering into **Oatman ❸**, proving irresistible camera fodder for photographers. Oatman looks exactly the way you'd imagine an ancient Western town to look, with sagging wooden shacks lining the solitary unpaved street on which amusing mock gunfights are conducted daily.

Across the street from Fast Fanny's (selling clothes, sunglasses, and postcards), a bed on wheels promotes the annual Great Oatman Bed Races, which are held every January. Summer temperatures can reach 118°F (48°C), prompting the annual Sidewalk Egg Fry. The 1926 Mission Inn, located next to a sidewalk display

**BELOW:** Clark Gable and Carole Lombard were married in Kingman, Arizona.

of life-size wooden bears, is a popular local place to eat; it serves substantial tasty, cholesterol-laden breakfasts of the sort that fat-obsessed and health-conscious Californians can only dream – or have nightmares – about.

The worn and characterful 1902 **Oatman Hotel** (tel: 520-768-4408), its walls plastered with photographs, newspapers, and movie posters, makes no concession to such modern comforts as television, or even running water in the rooms, but is nonetheless an irresistible place to stay. History rules here, not luxury, and the hotel even has its own ghost called Oatie, supposedly the spirit of a lonely and homesick drunken Irishman who lay undiscovered at the hotel for three days before being kicked into a shallow grave.

## Honeymoon hideaway

A very much alive Clark Gable and Carole Lombard spent their honeymoon night in Room 15, after being married in Kingman, and the simple room is preserved as a sort of shrine to the glamourous Hollywood couple with pictures of the pair on the walls and a pink nightdress draped over a chair.

The "honeymoon suite" and Oatie the ghost's room cost an extra few dollars to stay in, in addition to the suggested (inexpensive) donations for the other rooms. There's a cozy, fairly "local" bar downstairs where the talk is good, but no food after 6pm when (for much of the year) restaurants and shops close up tight as soon as the tourists have left.

Twenty miles (32 km) of desert scrub land lies between Oatman and **Topock**, where the Colorado River marks the California border. Route 66 comes to a dead-end at Moabi Regional Park with its lake and boat rentals – a refreshing stop after the long drive in the hot sun.

Map on page 204

**BELOW:** Viva Las Vegas!

# DETOUR – LAS VEGAS

A desert drive of 101 miles (163 km) from Kingman, Arizona on US 93 leads straight to Sin City. Each year 12 million visitors empty their pockets of $4.2 billion in a time-honored homage to frivolity, greed, and gluttony – not to mention plain old fun. For a long time after gambling was legalized in 1931, Las Vegas remained a sleepy desert town. It took visionary underworld hit man Bugsy Siegel to free this seething neon dragon. In 1946, Siegel opened the Flamingo Hotel, sparing no expense in mob finances for its plush interior, which sported a flashing pink neon facade and set a new standard in sheer swank. From a high-roller's point of view, Las Vegas is divided into two parts. First is the Strip, where modern hoteliers vie with each other to offer the latest in accommodation extravaganzas, replicating Venice, Paris, Rome, ocean liners, and Egyptian pyramids. Then there's Downtown – the original Vegas – also known as Glitter Gulch. As for gambling, either way you lose, but Downtown casinos are said to afford better odds. The best advice is simply enjoy it: win, lose or draw, there's nothing quite like the Strip at night, ablaze with electric light and self-indulgence. The Las Vegas Tourist Board is on 702-892-0711.

## CALIFORNIA

As the car heads ever closer toward the setting sunset, spare a though for the former migrants, for whom crossing the border into the "promised land" was not always a pleasant experience in the early days of Route 66. Swamped by a tide of refugees from the Dust Bowl states, Californians were worried what might happen to property prices or already low-paid jobs. It's a story that is still familiar today, albeit at a different border.

Sadly, once in California, much of the old Route 66, apart from a few parched stretches through the Mojave Desert, has been largely supplanted and is submerged beneath a welter of busy freeways to re-emerge only in occasional short stretches or as the main routes through towns such as Barstow, Victorville, and Rancho Cucamonga. In the first town you'll come to in California, **Needles**, Route 66 passes through the business section and along Broadway where, across from an old covered wagon at the junction of Front Street, the vintage 1930s Palms Motel is now a bed and breakfast renamed the Old Trails Inn.

*Don't Take A Curve
At 60 Per We Hate to
Lose A Customer.*
— BURMA SHAVE

### Needles and grins

There are more historic motels past the Amtrak terminal, where the defunct 1906 Fred Harvey House, known as El Garces and regarded as the crown jewel of the chain, is now just a part of the station. Harvey Girls lived in the upper floors. Trained in neatness and courtesy, the girls signed a contract of employment agreeing not to marry for a year, and lived on the upper floors of the hotel.

The **Needles Regional Museum** (tel: 760-326-5678; closed Sun) has a fanciful collection of stuff guaranteed to raise a grin: vintage clothes, old jars and bottles, obsolete currency, pictures curling with sepia, cartridge shells, and Indian artifacts. The **Mojave Tribal Center** with its **Indian Village** sits near the Needles Bridge, and there's a marina park and golf course near the river.

**BELOW:**
motel signs
from the Mother
Road are now Art
Deco collectibles.

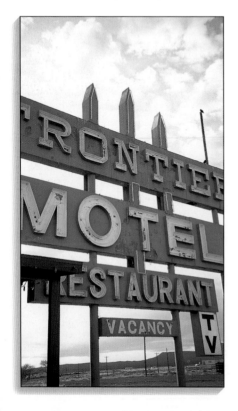

In World War II, General George Patton established an army training center in the Mojave, realizing that a familiarity with its harsh terrain would prepare the troops for the forthcoming Africa campaign, and indeed, conditions are similar. The US Army National Training Center is still headquartered at Barstow, 145 miles (233 km) due west of Needles.

The route from Needles to Barstow can be traveled swiftly on I-40, but the old Route 66 runs north of the interstate and heads through **Goffs** before diverting south through the barely existing communities of Essex, Amboy, and Baghdad (famous for its landmark café and, earlier, another Harvey House). Bob Moore recalls in his guidebook that **Essex** (pop. 35) appeared on NBC's *Tonight Show* in 1977, claiming to be the only town in America without television. A Pennsylvania company promptly donated the necessary equipment. About a mile from **Amboy** (where the venerable 1930s Roy's Café, serving typical '50s diner food, is a favorite with filmmakers) is an extinct volcano known as the **Amboy Crater**.

**Ludlow**, where Route 66 links up once more with the interstate, was once a boom town served not only by the Santa Fe railroad, but also by two others (local lines bearing ore from Death Valley), and in fact was named for a Central Pacific repairman. The 1940s Ludlow Cafe building is derelict, as is the abandoned Ludlow Mercantile Building (1908) down by the railroad tracks, but the newer Ludlow Coffee Shop is usually bustling with activity. Water, always scarce in these parts, was at one time brought in to fill the steam trains by tank cars from **Newberry Springs**, 40 miles (64 km) to the west. There really are springs here, and they supplement the water supply from the region's numerous artesian wells.

The State Agricultural Inspection Station, which tended to hassle visitors in the early days, more often that not these days just waves cars through. Just before Barstow is **Daggett**, whose landmark **Stone Hotel** (beside an old alignment of the route) was popular with Tom Mix and other movie cowboys. On show in the fledgling museum (tel: 760-254 2629; open weekends) is a scale model of the California Edison Company's Solar One thermal plant out in the desert. Giant mirrors focused the sun's energy on tanks of nitrate salt intended to convert water into the steam required to power a turbine generator.

## Barstow

The Mojave Desert was a forbidding, yet paradoxically inviting place in the 1870s when gold, silver, and borax were among the valuable metals and minerals that drew prospectors and miners from all over the country. The arrival of the Santa Fe railroad in 1883 connected up – and in many cases created – isolated small towns, and the Mediterranean-style Santa Fe Depot at **Barstow ③** and renovated 1911 Casa del Desierto, a former Harvey House, give some idea of the forgotten splendor of the times. Gift shops and a McDonald's, at which customers eat in converted railroad cars, are among the station's attractions.

Map on page 204

*Remember This If You'd Be Spared Trains Don't Whistle Because they're Scared.*

— Burma Shave

**BELOW:** "As the world changes, so do things along the Mother Road. It mirrors life both modern and nostalgic..."

With the arrival of the pre-World War II National Old Trails Highway, the predecessor to Route 66, Barstow's importance as a transportation center was quite literally cemented. Sitting at the major junction of I-15 and I-40, it has shown little sign of decline. Midway between Los Angeles and Las Vegas, it is a convenient rest stop for drivers on their way to and from the resort city. The older Route 66 motels are to the west end of town. Watch for the splendid El Rancho, built with railroad tiles, and whose 100-foot (30-meter) high neon sign has been a landmark since the early days of the highway.

The **Mojave River Valley Museum** (tel: 760-256-5452; open daily) and the **California Desert Information Center** (tel: 760-255-8760; open daily) will together answer all your questions about the desert – past and present.

### Side trips from Barstow

One worthwhile side trip from Barstow is to the **Rainbow Basin** (for information, tel: 760-252-6000) where a 4-mile (6-km) loop road circles an area filled with fossilized animal remains and fringed by multi-colored cliffs; another is to **Calico Ghost Town** (tel: 800-TO CALICO; open daily), 11 miles (18 km) to the east, whose prosperity between 1881–96 came from mining a $12-million seam of silver, a boom that was supplemented by the discovery of borax nearby

When both "cash crops" gave out, the town's 22 saloons closed one after another as the population drifted to other areas to seek their fortunes, but many of the old buildings have been rehabilitated, and such tourist attractions as wagon rides, mock gunfights, and gold panning were introduced. A few miles to the east at the town of **Calico**, the **Early Man Site** (tel: 760-252-6000; open Wed–Sun) displays relics from the Pleistocene era, which was approximately 50,000 years ago.

**BELOW:** you can take all sorts of desert rides at Calico Ghost Town.

Apart from one small diversion, it's an uneventful 40-mile (64-km) drive on a good road (which parallels I-15) to Victorville, where Route 66 is merely another city street. A suggested stop-off is at the town of **Helendale** to see the **Exotic World Museum** (tel: 760-243-5261; open daily), a collection of burlesque souvenirs assembled by curator Dixie Evans, a one-time performer and Marilyn Monroe impersonator. A bawdy comedy show of the late 19th and early 20th centuries, the striptease eventually became one of burlesque's main elements.

The incomparable *Route 66 Magazine* ran a story about Dixie's collection of costumes, fans, photographs, and performance bills. "People went to the theater to have a good time," she told writer Dan Harlow, "and burlesque gave them that. It's as American as apple pie."

### Roy Rogers Museum

**Victorville** (pop. 68,800), now a big city, began as a mining camp in the 19th century and became a magnet during Hollywood's golden age for movie-makers attracted by its "Western" feel. It thus became the perfect venue for the **Roy Rogers-Dale-Evans Museum** (tel: 760-243-4547; open daily), whose vast galleries warrant at least an hour. The sight of Roy's sequined costumes and silver-studded saddles, along with dozens of guns, boots, walls of magazine covers, cereal packets (containing Roy Rogers collector cards), photographs, movie posters, jeeps, an old Wells Fargo wagon, and a stuffed Trigger (1932–65) – the horse that starred in 188 movies – is positively awe-inspiring. For children, there's a Kids' Corral of their own where they can mount model horses.

"Our place isn't a typical museum," Rogers wrote in his autobiography, *Happy Trails*, "it's personal… all the stuff I had saved… Dale and I think that it will be a place for people to come and have fun and learn about our lives and also to remember what America was like so many years ago." Rogers died in July 1998, aged 87.

The **California Route 66 Museum** (tel: 760-951-0436; open daily) offers a final chance for westbound travelers who haven't yet had their fill of ephemera from the Mother Road to dose-up. Among the free tabloids available in Victorville is a *Desert Survival Guide*, but don't take it seriously, as it's merely an advertising give-away containing no specific information whatsoever about survival in the desert, at the grand old age of 87.

## San Bernardino

South of Victorville, I-15 heads over the 4,300-foot (1,310-meter) Cajon Summit, which, after taking the Oak Hill exit, brings you to Mariposa Road and the **Summit Inn**, a longtime Route 66 landmark where waitress Hilda has been serving diners for more than 30 years. Apart from a brief stretch, I-15 has subsumed much of the old route, but you're on it if you follow Cajon Boulevard into **San Bernardino ㊵**, a Mormon town in the 1850s, and once a major citrus center. It's the gateway to the mountainous **San Bernardino National Forest**,

Map on page 204

*Black beetle on white sand.*

**BELOW:** the Mojave Desert was a forbidding place when gold was discovered in the 1870s.

Map on page 204

more than 600,000 acres (243,000 hectares) of wilderness plus well-known resorts such as **Big Bear** and **Lake Arrowhead**, all dominated by 11,500-foot (3,350-meter) high Mt San Gorgonio, the highest in Southern California. State Route 18, romantically known as the **Rim of the World Drive**, is the lofty 40-mile (64-km) highway that leads to these destinations.

## Final stage

In San Bernardino, the classy old (1928) **California Theater**, on West Fourth Street, is worth noting. Restored and still active, it was used in the 1920s to preview new movies and became the last stage on which Will Rogers appeared before his death in 1935.

Head out of town on Mt Vernon Avenue past some aged motels and a hard-to-miss Santa Fe railroad smokestack, and eventually you'll pass another Wigwam Motel (1950) along Foothill Boulevard. This leads into **Rancho Cucamonga** and begins with a series of large and anonymous shopping malls, but at the corner of Vineyard Avenue there's a glimpse of earlier times, with an old-fashioned Mobil station from the 1920s sitting on the opposite corner to the Thomas Winery. A radio museum is located nearby.

Further down is the historic **Sycamore Inn**, a huge, rustic log palace on the site of an 1848 trailside inn that catered to the Gold Rush adventurers. In 1858 it became a stop along the route of the Butterfield Stage.

Past **Claremont**, where the old route suddenly moves upscale with a grassy median and eucalyptus trees, are a few eating places that old-timers might remember. There's Wilson's restaurant (now La Paloma) at **La Verne**; the Pinnacle Peak Steak House, where they cut off customers' ties, at **San Dimas**; and the Golden Spur Restaurant (which began as a hamburger stand 70 years ago) in **Glendora**.

There are many of old motels and an early example of a McDonald's (sans arches), prettily tiled in red-and-white, located west of the drive-in movie theater at **Azusa**; the Derby Restaurant and Rod's Grill at **Arcadia**; and at **Monrovia,** the distinctive one-story Aztec Hotel (tel: 626-358-3231). This hotel dates from 1925, when it was built by architect Robert Stacy-Judd in a pseudo-Mayan style to catch the attention of motorists along the route.

## The end of the road

Just before **Los Angeles** ④ proper *(see page 236)*, Route 66 becomes what is now the Pasadena Freeway, but which started life in the closing days of 1940 as the Arroyo Seco Parkway, the first freeway in a bold, new experiment that was eventually to cover the entire state of California with a network of similarly fast motorways. Continue driving and take the Sunset Boulevard exit, then head west along Sunset until it joins Santa Monica Boulevard, which runs all the way to the Pacific Ocean.

Nobody can recall ever seeing a Burma Shave sign in Santa Monica itself, where Route 66 ends, but if the company had ever put one there it would probably have been the one that read *If You/Don't Know/Whose Signs/These Are/You can't Have/Driven Very Far!* ❏

**BELOW:**
diamondback
rattlesnake
in strike pose.
**RIGHT:**
Calico Ghost Town,
near Barstow.

# A SHORT STAY IN LOS ANGELES

*The city of fantasy and film, LA has endless sun,*
*an easy ambiance and, of course, Hollywood.*
*Here's a list of the not-to-be-missed attractions:*

◆ The Hollywood Entertainment Museum is the place to pay homage to the achievements of the silver screen. Included are displays on history, personalities, and technological innovations.

◆ Part amusement park, part working film studio, Universal Studios is one of the most visited sites in LA. Sensational stunts and special effects are just some of the attractions; simulations of earthquakes, shark attacks, and infernos are others.

◆ Lined with jewelers, designer studios, upmarket fashion, and accessories boutiques, Rodeo Drive in Beverly Hills is one of the most exclusive temples to commerce in the world.

◆ Backdrop to a million holiday snapshots, the Hollywood sign is now a protected monument. Behind it, Griffith Park extends for miles and has (smog permitting) wonderful, far-reaching views over LA and the San Fernando Valley.

◆ With a church-like entrance hall crowned by an impressive dome, and a floor in shades of marble, City Hall was constructed in 1928.

◆ Art lovers should not miss the Los Angeles County Museum of Art. Costumes and pottery, gold and silverware are displayed, as well as paintings and sculpture from all eras.

◆ The Hollywood Bowl, a natural amphitheater for outdoor concerts, plays host to some of the best acts in the world.

◆ Historic and modern-day injustices of racism and prejudice are the focus of the thoughtful Museum of Tolerance on West Pico Boulevard.

For visitors interested in staying longer in the big city, pick up a copy of *Insight Guide: Los Angeles*. A companion to the present volume, it is packed with insightful information and stunning pictures.

△ **MANN'S CHINESE THEATER**
Sidney Grauman, the man who "invented" the movie premiere, designed this in the 1920s. Its main attraction is the forecourt, with hand- and foot-prints of the stars.

▷ **GETTY CENTER**
Architect Richard Meier's fabulous building on top of a hill with stunning views almost distracts from the collection of treasures inside.

# HOLLYWOOD

## CITY OF ANGELS

In 1781, Father Junípero Serra named a dry, dusty settlement after St Francis of Assisi's first church, St Mary of the Angels. No one could have conceived that hot, arid place would turn into glittering Los Angeles, the capital of moviedom and a world-famous synonym for glamor and fun. Residents of most big cities pretend to be blasé in the presence of celebrities, but Angelenos really are: movie stars are the stock-in-trade here, as common as scarlet-suited guardsmen in London or yellow cabs in New York. LA is also a city of adventure and innovation: Disneyland, rollerblading, beach culture, rap music – it all started here first.

▽ **DISNEYLAND**
The first Magic Kingdom, in nearby Anaheim, opened in 1954. Plans are afoot to make it bigger and better than ever.

△ **UNIVERSAL STUDIOS**
The theme park's spoof of attractions like the Hollywood sign and early star Betty Boop keep the crowds coming.

▽ Red arrows on the map indicate routes from the city detailed in this book

▷ **STARS AT THEIR FEET**
The Walk of Fame on Hollywood Boulevard commemorates stars from James Dean to Tom Cruise.

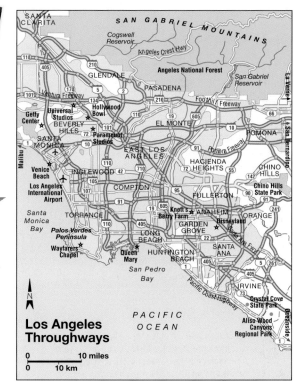

**Los Angeles Throughways**

## Important Information

| | |
|---|---|
| **Population:** | **Tourist Information:** |
| 3.5 million | LA C & V Bureau |
| **Dialing codes:** | 685 Figueroa Street |
| 213, 310, 323 | CA 90071 |
| **Website:** | Tel: 213-689-8822 |
| www.lacvb.com | Fax: 213-624-1992 |

# THE SOUTHERN ROUTE

*A guide to the South and the Southwest, with principal sites
clearly cross-referenced by number to the maps*

**S**it back, relax, and enjoy the ride if you've chosen the Southern
route across the continent: this is a laid-back land that just cries
out to be explored, absorbed, and not rushed through. Even if
you're not ready to, you'll probably adapt to the pace soon enough
as you meander down a Georgia street lined with trees draped in
Spanish moss, tour a gracious antebellum mansion, sit down to a
plateful of down-home cookin' (yes, they really *do* eat fried green
tomatoes), relax on a Texas beach, or kick up your cowboy boots in
a turn-of-the-century saloon in Tombstone, Arizona.

Our nearly 2,500-mile (3,900-km) journey through America's
South kicks off in Atlanta, unofficial capital of the "New South,"
dynamic home to some well-known global corporations but still
blessed with enough of the equally well-known "Southern hospitality" to make it a pleasant and very liveable city. After a detour in
Macon – to get a taste of the "Old South" – your trip west begins,
moseying through Alabama and its true southern cities of Montgomery and Mobile and on into Mississippi for just a spell before hitting Louisiana and its belle of a city: New Orleans, full of fabulous
food, unforgettable music, and unique architecture.

Our route then takes you through the boggy bayous of Louisiana
and across America's largest swamp (watch out for those 'gators)
before dipping into Texas – so that *you* can dip your toes into the
warm Gulf of Mexico in between catching some rays on one of
Galveston's gorgeous beaches. Then we jog north to Houston –
known for its space connections but with much, much more to please
the visitor – before continuing west to Austin, the Texas capital, and
charming San Antonio, with its history (remember the Alamo) and
delightful Paseo del Rio (River Walk).

It's a long haul, then, to the next major city – El Paso – but we keep
things more interesting by avoiding the interstate and instead following the winding Rio Grande at the Mexican border. There's a
worthy detour on the way to beautiful Big Bend National Park before
you hit El Paso and its infinitely more interesting Mexican "sister
city," Ciudad Juárez, across the border.

New Mexico's next, with its high-tech weaponry and missile sites,
but also home to the natural beauty of White Sands National Monument and some ancient cliff dwelling sites. You'll cross the Continental Divide before entering Arizona, where the "Old West" really
comes to life in places like Tombstone and Bisbee. The state's "big
cities" of Tucson and Phoenix also have much to keep you busy
before continuing on west into California to your ultimate destination: sunny San Diego. ❏

**PRECEDING PAGES:** the best American cars – ever; everybody's somebody in the
Texas town of Luckenbach.
**LEFT:** sax appeal on a soft Southern night.

# A SHORT STAY IN ATLANTA

*Atlanta is bold, brash, and self-confident, a cosmopolitan island surrounded by rural Georgia. Here's a list of the not-to-be-missed attractions:*

◆ The World of Coca-Cola Atlanta *(shown right)* houses everything you ever wanted to know about this fizzy drink – except, of course, its secret ingredient. There are free samples, too, dispensed from a space-age soda fountain.

◆ Underground Atlanta is the shopping, eating and entertainment center of Downtown. Filled with shops and watering holes, the complex stretches six blocks above and below ground.

◆ Sometimes called the "Beverly Hills of the South," Buckhead contains more than beautiful homes. It also serves as the dining room of Atlanta and the shopping center of the Southeast, not to mention being good for nightspots.

◆ Consisting of many acres of gardens, trails and woodlands, Buckhead's Atlanta History Center makes for a wonderful day hike, taking in along the way the Tullie Smith farmhouse and the impressive Swan House mansion.

◆ If eclecticism interests you, don't miss Little Five Points. This area's shops specialize in everything from New Age crystals and vintage clothes, to music and books. It's good for art, too.

◆ Architecture, sculpture and art come together at the High Museum of Art. The building, designed by Richard Meier, has a sculpture by Rodin outside, while inside, works by Picasso, Matisse, and that all-American favorite, Norman Rockwell, line the museum walls.

◆ If you need to cool down fast, head for the outskirts of town and White Water Atlanta, then plunge down the Cliffhanger waterslide.

▷ **SKYSCRAPER CITY**
Atlanta's skyline is filled with gleaming, state-of-the art skycrapers, many designed by local boy John Portman, the architect of modern landmarks in many countries.

▽ **MARTIN LUTHER KING, JR**
Retrace the life of the Civil Rights leader in the Freedom Walk, a four-block area that includes King's birth home *(shown)*, his gravesite and the church in which he preached.

For visitors interested in staying longer in the big city, pick up a copy of *Insight Guide: Atlanta*. This is a companion to the present volume, and is packed with insightful text and stunning pictures.

## CAPITAL OF THE NEW SOUTH

Atlanta has always been a city alert to opportunity. Many think this determination to succeed is a consequence of being burned down during the Civil War – but, in fact, Atlanta has always been this way. It's an urban phenomenon, a new city in microcosm, with the air of a prosperous, self-confident, and self-absorbed town inventing itself every day. Winning the bid for the 1996 Olympics was just the beginning; now Atlanta wants to take on the world. It's not the easiest of towns for visitors – streets are confusing, signs non-existent – but the longer you stay, the better it gets.

▽ Red arrows on the map indicate routes from the city detailed in this book

△ HERE'S THE NEWS
A 45-minute studio tour allows you to watch the professionals at work; the weather map is unmissable.

▷ GONE WITH THE WIND
author Margaret Mitchell came from Atlanta, and her home and other locations are now museums.

## Important Information

**Population:**
400,000
**Dialing codes:**
404
**Website:**
www.atlanta.com

**Tourist information:**
Atlanta C & V Bureau,
233 Peachtree Street,
Suite 100, GA 30303
Tel: 404-521-6600
Fax: 404-577-3293

# ATLANTA TO NEW ORLEANS

*The mournful whistle of freight trains, small towns on hot summer nights, and grand, glorious antebellum towns highlight this trip through Georgia and Alabama*

 Map on page 248

**A**mong all the states of the "Deep South," **Georgia** has been the most successful in keeping pace with, and even outstripping, its rivals in the North and West. For more than a century after its cataclysmic encounter with historical destiny – as the focus of the Confederacy during the American Civil War (1861–65) – the South continued to set itself apart from its conquerors (the Federal Government, or Union), stubbornly maintaining its identity with the antebellum days on the Cotton Belt. Finally, however – and in part unwillingly, as a result of the changes forced upon it by the civil rights campaigns of the 1950s and 1960s – a "New South" has begun to emerge. While there's still truth in the popular image of the region as a poor, undeveloped, and un-educated rural backwater, many of its urban communities have recast themselves beyond recognition, as high-tech high-achievers to match any in the nation.

## Georgia on my mind

Nowhere is that more true than in the cities of Georgia, and above all in its dynamic capital **Atlanta** ❶ *(see page 244)*, on the broad Piedmont Plateau of its north-central region. Home to global corporations from Coca-Cola to CNN, Atlanta can justly claim to be the heart of the "New South." Nonetheless, it has managed to retain the more appealing aspects of its past, such as the South's traditional mannered gentility and famed flair for hospitality. Macon, too, on the "fall line" that runs from Augusta to Columbus to separate northern Georgia from the Coastal Plain, has prospered without losing sight of its heritage, while Savannah, on the Savannah River close to the Atlantic Ocean, surrounds its stunning, antebellum city center with modern industry and shipping activity *(see "Atlantic Route," page 78)*.

Banking, manufacturing, media, military installations, and tourism may have come to dominate its cities, but much of the rest of Georgia remains rural. Agricultural produce such as the state's trademark peaches and sweet Vidalia onions, together with lumber, cattle and poultry, continue to figure prominently in the economy.

Throughout Georgia, you can expect hot days and pleasant nights from May through September, temperate comfort in April and October and cool to cold temperatures November through March. Georgia blooms most beautifully in the spring, which is ideal visiting season. Southern Georgia, on the Coastal Plain, is balmiest, often sweltering in summer.

If finding parking in downtown Atlanta leaves you crying for escape, take a trip 7 miles (11 km) east of I-285 on US 78 to **Stone Mountain Park**, a recreation complex including an ice rink, golf course,

**LEFT:** Stone Mountain Park, outside Atlanta. **BELOW:** dressed with finesse.

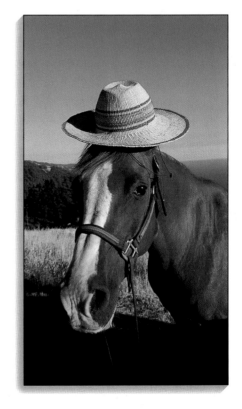

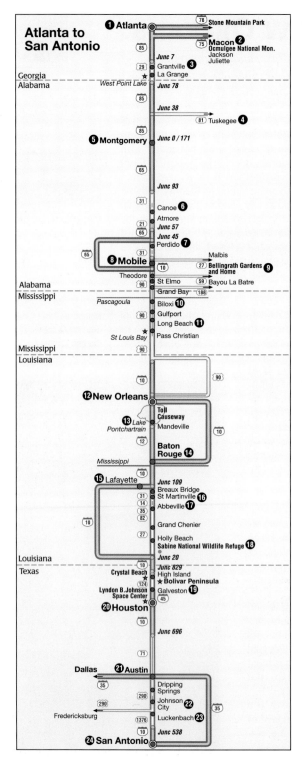

**Atlanta to San Antonio**

campground, waterslides, boating, fishing, tennis, wildlife trail, "Scenic Railroad" ride, and reconstructed plantation. Stone Mountain's plantation showcases buildings imported from points throughout the state.

The park sprawls around the central figure which gives the area its name: **Stone Mountain**. The exposed portion of this granite giant occupies a volume of 7.5 trillion cubic feet (213 million cubic meters) and is thought to be almost 3 million years old. Its gestation period was long, as igneous rock struggled to push through the surface. Stone Mountain's thrust to the sky is a fine metaphor for the concrete explosion of modern Atlanta after its razing by the Union army.

The mountain itself, smooth but for light pocks in the surface, is spectacle enough. However, its focus has become the **Stone Mountain carving**, 50 years in production, depicting the Confederate leaders Jefferson Davis, Robert E. Lee, and "Stonewall" Jackson. The sculpture, which spreads 147 feet (45 meters) across and towers 400 feet (122 meters) above the ground, was completed in 1972.

## Macon

Heading southeast out of Atlanta on I-75 – one of the major north–south arteries in the United States – you'll begin to encounter what the Federal Writers' Project called "the rolling character of the land [which] makes for undulations in the roadways, the fields and the pine forests that border them. The clay hills are deeply gullied by erosion and their red color against the dark pines of the wooded regions creates a perpetually vivid landscape." Some 80 miles (128 km) after leaving the "big city," I-75 takes a sharp turn to the south and straight into the heart of **Macon ❷** (pronounced to rhyme with "bacon"); you can venture into the city from either I-75 or I-16, which continues southeast to Savannah. Don't expect any classic skyline views: downtown Macon has long since ceased to be the commercial center, and those few skyscrapers it does hold, such as the **Liberty Federal** and **Hilton Hotel** buildings, are if anything eyesores rather than symbols of prosperity. First impressions can be misleading, however, and while Downtown may not be exactly bustling, Macon itself has experienced something of an economic boom in recent years.

The effect of industry – together with any number of huge shopping malls – taking over green-field sites all around the periphery of the city has been to spare Downtown from large-scale "development," while generating the capital to restore the treasures of the past. Macon's marvelous antebellum mansions and civic buildings were spared destruction during the Civil War by a simple ruse. When in 1864 General Sherman and his troops launched shots into the city across the Ocmulgee River, they were met with return fire suggesting a substantial resistance force. However, the troops that turned Sherman and his all-too-tragic torch down in the direction of Savannah were not Confederate regulars, but old men and young children.

## The Old South

The architecture that has been preserved and restored is incredibly diverse, yet thoroughly Southern. As one resident puts it: "When people from outside the South come to find the "Old South," it's not in Atlanta, which is too new, nor is it in Savannah, which by virtue of its settlers and design is closer to a European city. The Old South is right here in Macon."

During the "cotton boom" of the early 19th century, cotton kings built lavish homes in the early Federal style with classical touches. These were followed by structures in the Greek Temple style adapted to the climate. Over the years, waves of commercial expansion inspired forays into new styles for mansions and civic and commercial buildings. Italianate Revival, Roman Revival, and

Map on page 248

*Georgia Time*

*Georgia's best-loved local hero*

**BELOW:** Macon is the epitome of the Old South.

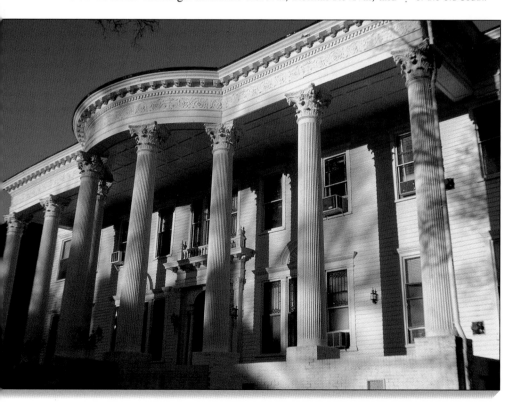

Academic Revival experiments carried through to the 1920s. Among fine examples open daily to visitors are the huge **Hay House** (tel: 912-742-8155) on Georgia Avenue, and the **Cannonball House** (tel: 912-745-5982) on Mulberry Street, scarred by a shot from Sherman's artillery and now appropriately housing a **Confederate Museum**.

All can be enjoyed at their best in March each year, when the Cherry Blossom Festival celebrates the simultaneous flowering of Macon's pride and joy, the incredible 150,000 Japanese cherry trees that have been planted along the downtown streets.

Macon's visitor center, on Cherry Street, can provide detailed walking tours to aid explorations of the city's architectural heritage. Next door, the **Georgia Music Hall of Fame** (tel: 912-750-8555; open daily) pays tribute to the state's many musical heroes, from Johnny Mercer to Little Richard and James Brown.

If you wish to step farther into the past than 1800, take the short trip to **Ocmulgee National Monument**, crossing the Ocmulgee River from Downtown by means of a drab concrete bridge named in honor of Macon-born soul-music legend Otis Redding. The monument conserves traces of the civilizations that populated the plateau from 8000 BC.

The greater part of the exhibits in the Visitor Center and out on the trails reconstruct the life of the Mississippian Indians in the 10th to 13th centuries. At Ocmulgee, they painstakingly erected huge mounds of sand and clay; many were used for ceremonial purposes, as evidenced by the altar-like structure inside the largest mound. Regrettably little is known about the mounds, but their very presence is fascinating.

**BELOW:**
The Whistle Stop Cafe in Juliette, Georgia was built for the movie *Fried Green Tomatoes*. The food is filling and not to be missed.

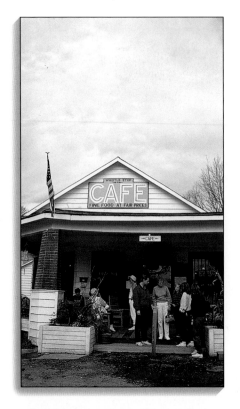

## Backwoods whistle-stop

Taking US 23, which winds northward from Macon along the approximate line of the Ocmulgee River, enables you to get an appealing taste of rural Georgia. Tiny **Juliette**, 20 miles (32 km) along, was reinvigorated in the early 1990s, when its air of picturesque deep-woods dereliction made it the perfect location for the movie *Fried Green Tomatoes at the Whistle Stop Cafe*. A **Whistle Stop Cafe**, built for the film beside a still-used country railroad station and across from an ivy-covered abandoned mill, does indeed dish up copious platefuls of fried green tomatoes. Another traditional Southern delicacy is available on the outskirts of the peaceful county town of **Jackson**, 15 miles (24 km) farther on, where the roadside **Fresh Air Barbecue** serves succulent barbecued pork; ask to peek into the giant ovens, bursting with whole, slow-roasting hogs.

US 23 rejoins I-75 10 miles (16 km) north of Jackson, but the lull of simple highway cruising is cruelly shattered 7 miles (11 km) south of Atlanta as you reach I-285, the **Atlanta ByPass**, which rings the sprawling Atlanta metropolitan area, appearing deceptively on the map as the quiet fringe outside the bustling city. But the eye of a hurricane is calmest, while its perimeter spins fastest.

The Atlanta ByPass is this city's answer to the Indianapolis 500. It's an almost mythical, lawless road-rally in which Southern gentlemen and ladies vent their frustrations on the way to and from their suburban homes. In the words of one southern Georgina, "If you do 55 in Atlanta the way they do up North, you'll get blown off the highway." Nowhere is this truer than on I-285. Average speed can reach 75 mph (120 kph); top speed goes up from there. Fortunately, to continue your journey west, you only have to endure the ByPass for a short stretch before turning off on I-85 southwest to Alabama.

## ATLANTA TO SOUTHWEST ALABAMA

Alabama and much of the land to its west passed through several hands before it was taken over by the United States in the late 18th century. Labyrinthine Colonial struggles involving the Indian "Five Nations" (Cherokee, Seminole, Muscogee, Chickasaw, and Choctaw) mark Alabama's early history, and its coat-of-arms displays the emblems of the five non-native nations that successively held sovereignty over it: France, Great Britain, the United States, the Confederacy, and again the United States.

The last two of these regimes, of course, have left the clearest stamp on Alabama, named for the Alabama River, itself named after an Indian tribe. Alabama rose to its economic apex during the cotton boom of the 19th century, and has been markedly reluctant to let go of the memory of its Confederate heyday. Only following bitter campaigns in the 1990s did the state capitol building in Montgomery finally cease to fly the Confederate flag. The state has seen better days, economically and socially, but its natural resources, hard-working citizenry, and enduring pride refuse to admit decline.

From downtown Atlanta, I-85 cuts a sure path southwest to the heart of Alabama. It's a slightly hair-raising drive at first, as airplanes pass alarmingly

Map on page 248

**TIP**

A memorable experience is to attend a Southern church service. Locals can be wary of "foreigners," however, so be prompt, well-dressed, and respectful.

**BELOW:** Sunday morning in a small Southern town.

*Sign of the South:*
*This climbing vine,*
*known as kudzu, was*
*brought from Asia*
*and used by the*
*government to stop*
*soil erosion. It is now*
*virtually unstoppable,*
*smothering thousands*
*of acres of land.*

**BELOW:**
Tuskegee, Alabama.

close overhead as they descend into the airport, but the interstate soon becomes an attractive parkway through the rolling Piedmont highlands, with woods to either side and a grassy central median erupting with wildflowers. "Alabama the Beautiful" is barely an hour's drive away, but there's potential for a last dip into rural Georgia. Leaving I-85 to join US 29 at **Grantville ❸**, 50 miles (80 km) out, offers an undulating ride through characterful little towns such as **LaGrange**, and also takes you along a brief stretch of the 525-mile (845-km) shoreline of **West Point Lake**. Engineered under the Flood Control Act of 1962, this enormous power source features 43 recreational areas for fishing, swimming, boating, hunting, and general relaxation.

## State line

Although in principal the **Chattahoochee River** delineates the boundaries of Georgia and Alabama, in fact at this point you cross the Alabama state line a short way west of the river. Even then, you don't join the rest of Alabama on Central Time – one hour earlier – until you're beyond the Lanett Valley here. The vigorous promotion of the state by the Alabama Welcome Center, just across the state line on I-85, stands in sharp contrast to Georgia's *laissez-faire* attitude. This distinction is certainly attributable to Alabama's image as a backwater state with little to offer either the traveler or the prospective settler.

After rolling through a forested area along I-85 westbound, you can turn off at exit 38 to **Tuskegee ❹** via State 81 south and State 126 west. Tuskegee is the site of Booker T. Washington's **Tuskegee Normal and Industrial Institute**, which is one of the few institutions of higher learning for American blacks that existed during the 19th century.

In the words of the leading black intellectual, W. E. B. DuBois, Washington was "the greatest man the South produced since the Civil War." Politically deft and enormously inspired, Washington believed in cooperation with the ruling whites and in practical education to serve the needs of the black masses concentrated in the South. Washington's policy of avoiding confrontation made enemies among other educated blacks and "liberal whites," but he kept Tuskegee alive.

While the institute remains very much active, much of its historic campus has been preserved with the aid of the National Park Service. Its centerpiece is the **Carver Museum** (tel: 334-727-6390; open daily), named after the black agricultural chemist George Washington Carver, who worked and taught on campus from 1896 until his retirement to **The Oaks** in Tuskegee, where he died in 1943.

He had abandoned artistic aspirations to forge the pioneer science of industrial agriculture, and his discoveries literally saved the Southern economy from collapse after the boll weevil infestation of 1919 destroyed the cotton industry. Many of his "bulletins" (pamphlets) are displayed in the museum; through such works as *How To Grow The Peanut and 105 Ways of Preparing It for Human Consumption*, a black man saved a region whose elite had oppressed and would continue to oppress his race. The museum also shows a well-made documentary film entitled *Up from Slavery*, which details the history of the institution and of Washington's struggle without shying away from the controversies that surround them.

Map on page 248

## Old Acres and Pecan Grove

Back on I-85 south, travel 41 miles (66 km) from Tuskegee to the boundary of **Montgomery ❺**. Montgomery consists of a small, quiet downtown area surrounded by wide outlying neighborhoods whose names smack of agricultural gentility: Old Acres, Pinedale, Pecan Grove, Open Acres, Spring Valley, and Park Manor. While the prairie muds are still rich, Montgomery bases its livelihood on government services, construction, and manufacturing. Montgomery also benefits from the patronage of the US Air Force, whose elite members are frequently assigned to **Maxwell Air Force Base** on the site of famed aviators Wilbur and Orville Wright's flight school.

Although Montgomery is not exactly unattractive, little about it is glamorous. By and large, no one in the city seems all that excited about selling its image to outsiders – except those who enthusiastically maintain and promote the city's "rich heritage." They are not exaggerating when they use this term to describe the marble-columned **State Capitol** on Goat Hill and the surrounding historic sites. Two grand structures stand across Washington Street from the Capitol: the quiet **First White House of the Confederacy** (tel: 334-242-1861) and the imposing **Alabama Archives and History** building (tel: 334-242-4435; open daily). The White House, moved next to the Archives from its original site at Bibb and Catoma streets, was the home of Confederate president Jefferson Davis during Montgomery's stint as first capital of the Confederate States of America. This rebel nation was comprised of the 13 states and territories that seceded from the United States in 1860 and 1861 over the issue of states' rights – among them the right to maintain slavery. Davis has been eclipsed in history by Confederate General Robert E. Lee, but in the South he is still revered as an emblem of distinction and self-determination, as evidenced by the frequently-seen bumper sticker "Don't Blame Me – I Voted For Jefferson Davis."

**BELOW:**
Montgomery,
Alabama.

## Civil rights sites

The neo-classical Archives Building is a rich storehouse of Native American arts, Confederate history and state development. From relics of the "first Alabamians," the Shell Mound Indians of the 10th century, to the Hank Williams Collection of the great Alabamian country singer's clothing, the Archives pieces together the multi-textured story of "Dixie."

Barely a hundred yards down from the Capitol is the **Dexter Avenue King Memorial Baptist Church**, whose 26-year-old pastor, Rev Martin Luther King Jr, was thrust somewhat unwillingly into the limelight in December 1955 when he was invited to spearhead the civil rights campaign known as the Montgomery Bus Boycott. A mural inside the church, "Montgomery to Memphis, 1955–1968," commemorates the long struggle for dignity and equality. Outside the Southern Poverty Law Center nearby, the moving

**Civil Rights Memorial**, designed by Maya Lin (who was also responsible for the celebrated Vietnam Veterans Memorial in Washington, DC), honors King and 40 other martyrs of the movement. The most significant cultural event in Montgomery is **Jubilee CityFest**, a springtime community celebration held on the third weekend of May. During the rest of the year, the zoo, historic districts, riverboat ride, and fine arts museum do nicely.

## Another Alabama

I-85 into Montgomery dovetails into I-65 and continues south into the rural glades of southwestern Alabama. Along the way, the radio bands are striped with black contemporary music, pop, country, gospel, sermons, and jazz.

Skid marks that swerve off to the shoulder suggest high-speed highway adventure. The soil deepens again to red where it had been sandy and gray in the "Black Belt" through the midsection of the state. Deeper exploration of rural Alabama is definitely recommended, and US 31 is a good place to start. Branching away from the interstate near the cute little town of **Evergreen**, US 31 arcs through Escambia and Baldwin counties, grazing the northwesternmost edge of Florida near Atmore and Perdido. The land surrounding towns such as Castleberry – "Home of the Alabama Strawberry" – is dotted with small green ponds and spread with groves of pine and oak. Cattle graze on the muddy soil, and farmhouses call forth images of peaceful backwaters.

Before reaching **Atmore**, you pass through **Canoe ❻**, Alabama, where you might see a horse and buggy along one side of the road as a 100-car-long freight train whistles by on the other. Atmore is weary-palmed, open-fielded, and railroad-tied, with churches signposted in all directions off the highway. If you

**BELOW:**
the right side of the tracks, Evergreen, Alabama.

head back up to the interstate on State 21, close to the intersection you'll come to the invitingly named Good and Plenty Restaurant, Bakery and Gift Shop run by Mennonites transplanted from Pennsylvania. Religious books, cookies, breads, and buffet lunch and dinner are served.

Continue on I-65 along a 13-mile (22-km) stretch before the next exit (exit 45) to **Perdido** ❼. Just south of the highway, the fruit of Jim and Marianne Eddins' gumption and perseverance continues to thrive: **Perdido Vineyards**.

## 'Bama wine

Winemaking in Alabama, once a great domestic industry, was effectively killed by Prohibition. Even afterward, Baptist leaders maintained that drinking – let alone manufacturing – alcohol was next to ungodliness. The Eddins family dared the opposition and began their muscadine vineyard in 1971, marketing the grapes to a Florida winemaker. When that arrangement fell through, the Perdido Vineyard began producing its own wine in 1979.

The muscadine varieties grown at Perdido – scuppernongs, higgins, nobles, and magnolias – are from a tough vine indigenous to the southeastern United States. Perdido's table wines, which may be sampled at the vineyard, are mostly sweet wines with a few drier varieties, including an extra-dry white which is reminiscent of some California wines.

The Perdido venture met with initial hostility from the community, but its success and the subsequent attention it brought to Baldwin County considerably warmed their reception. But as one disgruntled entrepreneur put it: "Sometimes you gotta get down on your hands and knees and pray for deliverance from the Christian businessmen."

Baldwin County is subject to a "pressure-cooker" climate, hot and prone to extremes of humidity. Nature has been hard on American farmers for centuries, but the environment was very attractive to a settlement of Greeks who came to the shores of Mobile Bay before World War II. Under the leadership of a Greek Orthodox priest named Malbis, the community established the lushest plantation in the county. When Malbis died in Nazi hands after he returned to Greece, the community carried out his plan to build an Orthodox Church in what is now the town of **Malbis**, between US 31 and I-10, 4 miles (6 km) east of Mobile Bay. The church was constructed from materials imported from Greece and includes stunning tile work and stained glass.

## MOBILE TO NEW ORLEANS

The coastline of the Gulf of Mexico, arcing from northwest Florida to southeast Texas, can well lay claim to the title of "the American Riviera" – though less reverently, it's also known as "the Redneck Riviera." Not so much a Cote d'Azur as a Cote de Blanc, the Gulf Coast spreads its white sands beside warm waters stocked with fine shrimp, oysters, and other delicacies. While never quite ranking as an international destination, the superb beaches of Gulf-Coast Alabama, Mississippi, and Texas have attracted vacationers from the South and Midwest since the

Map on page 248

*The Gulf of Mexico arcs from northwest Florida to southeast Texas. One of its many names is "the Redneck Riviera," a derogatory title that locals find funny but gets "correct" Yankees writing hotly to newspapers.*

**BELOW:** the beaches of the Gulf coast have attracted visitors since the mid-19th century.

*Crest of the Historic Development Commission in Mobile, Alabama.*

**BELOW:** Mobile's visitor center is housed in this replica of the town's Fort Condé.

mid-19th century. Tourism and fishing remain the economic mainstays of the region, but they have been impinged upon by the growth of the oil industry, which often drills and explores within sight of the sunbathers. Whatever the ecological effects of oil retrieval may be, the petrochemical industry has been crucial to the survival of cities such as Mobile, Alabama.

## Former French capital

Interstates 10 and 65 and US 90 (which pick up from US 31) all straddle the mouth of the Mobile River as they cross westward from Baldwin County into the port of **Mobile ❽** (pronounced *Mo-beel*). Mobile's locale on river and gulf has made it the most contested area in all of Alabama's twisted power struggles, and to this day it feels resolutely atypical of a state that outsiders regard as the most insular in the South. That sense of cosmopolitan diversity is hardly surprising; after all, Mobile began life in 1706 as the capital of the French colony of Louisiana, which covered a far larger, if not all that precisely defined, area than the modern state of the same name.

Mobile is the most attractive destination for visitors in what might otherwise be dismissed as a "pass-through" state. Its Colonial past remains evident everywhere, while parallels with Louisiana in general, and New Orleans in particular, range from the intricate iron grill-work that adorns the city's balconies to the oysters and gumbo sold in its restaurants. Most striking of all is Mobile's Mardi Gras, which – say locals – pre-dates its more famous counterpart in New Orleans. Arrive in the week before Lent, and you'll be dazzled by the parades and costumes, but throughout the year tell-tale strings of colored Mardi Gras beads festoon the live oaks and telephone wires Downtown.

A stroll along downtown avenues such as lower **Government**, **Church**, and **Dauphin streets** is much the best way to get a flavor of Mobile. Start at the south end of Royal Street, where the city's visitor center is housed in a faithful replica of **French Fort Condé**. The original was built from 1724 onwards; this version, on the same site, was constructed to mark the Bicentennial in 1976. Its cannons now point forlornly across a concrete underpass, but the chambers below serve as a good museum of local history, and feature a fine photo gallery of recent carnival queens, the vast majority of whom appear to be called "Tammy." From there, a short walk will take you through stately historic districts that flourish with magnolia, azalea, and oak, all of which thrive in the semi-tropical climate. Yet again, serious commerce has fled to the outlying malls, so the old department stores have closed down, but cafés, clubs, and restaurants are present in abundance.

## Semi-tropical jungle

Government Street becomes US 90 as it pulls away from Mobile Bay and widens into the usual mall-motel-and-fast-food sprawl. On reaching the town of **Theodore**, you'll spot a huge billboard directing you south on State 59 to **Bellingrath Gardens and Home ❾** (tel: 334-973-2217; open daily), "The Garden For all Seasons." All the hype – "Incomparable," "One of the World's Most Beautiful Year-Round Gardens" – turns out to be pretty much true. Originally a semi-tropical jungle on the Isle-aux-Dies River, the land was purchased by Walter Bellingrath, who made his fortune as the first bottler of Coca-Cola in Alabama. Mr and Mrs Bellingrath landscaped 65 acres (26 hectares) of the 905-acre (366-hectare) plot, sculpting an evolving, living work of art to surround

Map on page 248

**BELOW:** the Japanese section of Bellingrath Gardens.

their magnificent riverfront home. Azaleas, roses, hibiscus, chenille, chrysan-themums, poinsettias, lilies, violets, and dogwood are all part of the "rapturous floral beauty." The Oriental-American Garden, honking geese, flamingos, and teeming bayou will charm where the gift shop and restaurant depress; renting a taped tour is an unnecessary distraction. The mapped walk is well-designed, but its much more fun to let yourself wander aimlessly, dream by the ponds and waterfalls, and lounge languidly in the gazebos.

## Town life in the Deep South

US 90 is the "old highway" along the Gulf Coast from Florida to Louisiana, and it's recommended over the bald interstate. The going is generally slower, and traffic lights are more frequent in places. Nevertheless, US 90 offers a glimpse of town life in the deepest South.

Out of Mobile and Theodore, US 90 passes in a dispiriting blur through dreary **St Elmo**, where the only relief from the endless succession of trailer parks are a couple of large dragway stadiums. Five miles (8 km) westward, you arrive in **Grand Bay**, "home of the world's largest watermelon festival." At Grand Bay, State 188 swoops south into State 16 to **Bayou La Batre**, an oil, shipbuilding, and shrimping town where the Blessing of the Shrimp Fleet in early May and the Seafood Festival in late July are two of Mobile County's big attractions. About 5 miles (8 km) outside Grand Bay, US 90 crosses with remarkably little ceremony into the state of Mississippi. The highway crawls through the towns of Pecan, Orange Grove, and Kreole before skirting **Pascagoula**, one of the three major Mississippian anchors on the Gulf Coast (the two that follow are Biloxi and Gulfport). Although the "old highway" is

**BELOW:** born again in the eyes of the Lord.

immediately announced as the "Scenic Beach Route to New Orleans," it takes about 27 miles (43 km) of unattractive inland commercial districts and malls to get from state line to scenery. A billboard puns that Jackson County is a "shipshape community" before you climb onto the drawbridge over the ship-dotted **Pascagoula River**. The land from Gautier to Biloxi is swampy, and the gray-blue skies are crystal clear. Another drawbridge delivers you into Harrison County, and straight into the resort city of **Biloxi ❿** (pronounced locally: *Bluxi*).

## Mississippi resort

Biloxi was the second base of operations for the French government of the Louisiana Territory, following Mobile. Founded in 1699 across the Biloxi Bay from its present location, the city sits on a peninsula cut by two bays and the Gulf of Mexico, providing a brilliant and popular beach. The somewhat forlorn slogan with which it celebrated the tercentenary of its "discovery" in 1999 – "Rediscover Biloxi" – owes much to the extent to which Biloxi has transformed itself since the legalization of casino gambling in Mississippi. Several huge new casinos – superficially eye-catching, but far from architecturally distinctive – now dominate the Biloxi shoreline.

The 19th-century stately homes on which Biloxi's reputation as a posh winter resort had rested have largely disappeared, though most of the credit for that rests with a succession of severe storms that have swept in from the Gulf. The worst damage was wrought by the vicious onslaught of Hurricane Camille in 1969, but a head-on hit from Hurricane Georges in 1998 also caused widespread destruction.

The extent to which gambling can be credited with turning around the

Map on page 248

*Mailbox with tiny Confederate flag at the Jefferson Davis home in Biloxi, Mississippi.*

**BELOW:** fat crabs from the warm waters of the Gulf.

Map on page 248

economy of Mississippi as a whole is debatable, but there's no disputing its impact on Biloxi. That said, it's so hedged around with arcane restrictions as to make Biloxi a peculiar hybrid. First of all, casinos can only be built on existing commercial property, so long swathes of pristine beach still survive, and in the quest for room to build, some of the largest casinos have located themselves facing inland on the previously sleepy Back Bay.

Secondly, state laws only allow for gambling on boats, not on land, so the huge structures you see from the road are in fact just the hotel and restaurant segments of the operation, while the actual gaming takes place on "barges" situated behind. Once inside, however, you can't tell where building ends and barge begins. As with much of the Gulf, the appeal of Biloxi remains more for weekenders from adjoining states than international travelers; the casinos may be glitzy but they have none of the flair of their Las Vegas equivalents, and the fact that you can see beautiful expanses of ocean through their floor-to-ceiling windows merely serves – except to die-hard gamblers – to make them feel all the more claustrophobic.

## Gulfport and Long Beach

Biloxi does at least hold one genuine historical attraction. The white-columned oceanfront mansion of **Beauvoir** (tel: 228-338-9074; open daily), the last home of Confederate president Jefferson Davis, now serves as a showcase for his furnishings and other possessions, and also as a wide-ranging Confederate museum. Davis's continuing appeal for diehard Southerners is demonstrated by a recent addition to the no-expense-spared **Jefferson Davis Presidential Library**.

If it's beach fun you're after, continue along the coast on US 90, where the golden strands of **Gulfport** and **Long Beach** ⓫ are lined with kiosks that rent out jet-skis, beach tractors with colossal inflatable wheels, or simply multi-colored beach parasols. One final community, the intriguingly named **Pass Christian**, harks back to more gracious days in Mississippi, with an avenue of live oaks whose branches intertwine above the highway to create a cool green tunnel, but by the same token its lack of commercial development means that it offers little incentive for drivers to get out of their cars.

US 90 then curves sharply away from the coast and crosses the St Louis Bay, where a bridge terminates in **Bay St Louis**, "Gateway to the Gulf Coast." With little warning, the road forks: State 609 takes the northwestern way toward I-10 and a National Aeronautics and Space Administration (NASA) test site; US 90 slides southwestward. Both bring you shortly to Louisiana. In the late afternoon, the skies over Lake Pontchartrain are gauzy and wide. Eight miles (13 km) of bridges form Interstate 10 from shore to shore – from St Tammany "Parish" (as counties are called in Louisiana) into Orleans Parish. As the car crosses on **Lake Pontchartrain Causeway** *(see page 265)*, you feel you're dipping and climbing through the water itself. Suddenly, wistful **New Orleans** ⓬ *(see page 262)* rises from the opposite shore of **Lake Pontchartrain** ⓭, a crescent of skyscrapers amid a green lake of oak. ❑

**BELOW:** gambling has transformed the Mississippi resort of Biloxi. **RIGHT:** the Lake Pontchartrain Causeway, gateway to New Orleans.

LEVEL
5

# NEW ORLEANS: THE BIG EASY

*Anchor of the Gulf Coast, cradle of jazz, home of exotic food – this is without doubt the most fascinating city in the South*

**C**urling sinuously and luxuriantly around a mighty bend in the Mississippi, New Orleans is known as the "Crescent City" – the home of jazz, blues and great food. It is also synonymous with Mardi Gras. Since 1857, Carnival has been the unbridled expression of New Orleans' spirit: at the private balls, in the wild parades, behind masks and under the glitter of costume jewelry, locals and visitors join together to celebrate. With the advent of Lent, it's back to business as usual, which, at least in the rowdier parts of Bourbon Street, is simply a muted version of the same.

The first stop for most visitors is the Vieux

Carré ("Old Square"), otherwise known as the French Quarter. Occupying the site, and still following the gridded street pattern, of the original walled French settlement, the Vieux Carré rests beside the Mississippi River between what are now Canal Street and Esplanade Avenue. Due to a series of disastrous fires in the early days, only one building survives from the city's first, French, incarnation – the Ursuline Convent (1750) at 1114 Chartres Street (tel: 504-529-3040; closed Mon) – but in its exquisite harmony and display, the entire ensemble of buildings works wonderfully in this haunting locale.

The heart of the French Quarter is Jackson Square, the true "old square" fronted by St Louis Cathedral (1794). The flagstones immediately outside the cathedral are the domain of street musicians, portrait artists, and transparently fraudulent but flamboyant fortune tellers – not to mention the "Lucky Dog" hot-dog sellers, their carts shaped like garish giant sausages, immortalized in John Kennedy Toole's comic masterpiece *A Confederacy of Dunces*. To either side, the red-brick Pontalba Buildings (1849), with their fine cast-iron balconies, are considered the oldest apartment buildings in the US. Two excellent museums flank the cathedral itself, housed in cupola-topped Colonial structures known as the Cabildo and the Presbytere.

The main drag (in every sense) of the French Quarter is high-spirited Bourbon Street, a pedestrian circus at all hours and in every season. In contrast to Bourbon, one block toward the river, parallel Royal Street plays host to an array of classy galleries and antique shops, interspersed with formal restaurants such as Brennan's – legendary for its breakfasts – and the Court of Two Sisters, whose spacious, well-shaded courtyard makes it the ideal spot for a leisurely "jazz brunch."

The architecture along Decatur Street, the main riverfront thoroughfare, is less fascinating. Tourists continue to flock to the old French Market, and the Jackson Brewery a block away, but both have recently lost so much of their original identity in the process of "restoration" that they amount to little more than shopping centers. The Mississippi itself lies on the far side of a high levee. For an appealing half-mile or so, the aptly-named

"Big Muddy" is lined first by a wooden boardwalk known as the "Moonwalk," then by grassy parks, one of which contains the well-stocked Aquarium of the Americas (tel: 504-861-2537). Free ferries cross to the quiet suburb of Algiers on the far side, while replica sternwheelers offer longer sightseeing cruises.

Well-meaning but misguided regulations have ensured that while no developer can tamper with the gorgeous facades of the French Quarter, almost any degree of re-building is permitted inside. However, Lafitte's Blacksmith Shop at 941 Bourbon Street, the tumbledown brick smithy where the pirate Lafitte plotted many a high-seas escapade, is an atmospheric if almost impenetrably gloomy bar that makes an appropriate starting point for nightly walking tours of "Haunted New Orleans," while the stately Napoleon House at 500 Chartres Street, allegedly the focus of a scheme to rescue the exiled emperor from St Helena and bring him to the United States, is another ravishingly Stygian bar with its own courtyard café.

Traditional jazz can be heard in nightspots such as Preservation Hall (tel: 504-522-2841), a dilapidated wood and concrete structure on St Peter Street, or the more upmarket Storyville development on Bourbon Street, a complex of bars and restaurants that aims to recall the spirit of New Orleans' early 20th-century Red Light district. A more youthful form of brass-band music, often incorporating soul, reggae, and rap, is played in clubs such as Tipitina's on Decatur Street and Donna's on Rampart Street, while truly excellent house bands entertain diners at countless cafés and restaurants.

Best with Creole food is a cold draught of Dixie beer, New Orleans' own brew. The definitive local liquor drinks are Sazerac and Ramos Gin Fizz; a rum-based Hurricane at Pat O'Brien's; or a cooling Pimm's Cup at the Napoleon House. New Orleans is also famous for its chicory coffee. The home of the rich *cafe au lait*, the sidewalk Café du

Monde in the French Market, also serves the sweet local speciality, *beignets* – doughnut-like pastries heaped with powdered sugar.

Away from the Vieux Carré, the Continental influence decreases, as New Orleans merges the Old South with the New. The perfect way to explore it is on the St Charles streetcar, which trundles through the Central Business District, the home of the Louisiana Superdome, to the lush and wealthy Garden District, where you can find antebellum

houses standing amid the azalea and dog-wood, and baroque oak trees shading marvelous structures built in Greek Revival, Renaissance, and Victorian styles. ❑

**LEFT:** fabulous food found here; Jazz Fest in the spring is the best time to hear the best music.
**RIGHT:** tomb of a voodoo queen; elegance in wought-iron; St Louis Cathedral, Jackson Square.

Map
on page
248

# NEW ORLEANS TO SAN ANTONIO

*Cruising across what claims to be "the longest bridge in the world,"*
*take an alligator-enhanced trip through Cajun Country*
*and end up in cowboy country*

San Diego

This route from New Orleans to the Texas border takes in, first, Cajun country and then the state's capital. Leaving the city and driving north, Lake Pontchartrain is spanned by **Lake Pontchartrain Causeway**, "the world's longest bridge." The causeway is a 24-mile (39-km) double stripe of highway propped above the surface of the lake. For miles, nothing can be seen on the horizon, and the camelback plunge into the void is akin to crossing the barren yet subtle plains of Texas *(see picture on page 261)*.

On the trip north over the causeway to **Mandeville**, land initially appears as a thin blue sliver on the horizon, an airy gray-blue strip melting off the murky waters into the sky. Gradually, the land becomes more distinct, broader and deeper in color until it becomes the interface of two great azure bodies: sea and sky. If you choose to cross the Lake Pontchartrain Causeway, it might be best to do so on your way out of the city.

A round-trip across the lake may be a little overwhelming, and concentration sometimes tends to falter on the second stretch. When the Causeway touches land in Mandeville, it becomes US 190. Four miles (6 km) north of the lakeshore it interchanges with I-12, which runs 61 miles (98 km) west to the capital of Louisiana, Baton Rouge.

**LEFT:** Cajun music in Breaux Bridge.
**BELOW:** Vermilionville museum, Lafayette.

## Acadian bayous

Alternatively, if you follow the efficient I-10 out of New Orleans, you cut through the boggy, baroque bayou country on the southwest bank of Lake Pontchartrain in St Charles and St John the Baptist parishes. The highway is stilted out of grass-fringed still water where the thin trunks that disappear into the mire mimic the somber poles that support the parallel powerlines.

Bayous – narrow, sluggish rivers usually surrounded by wetlands – run in veins throughout southern Louisiana, otherwise known as Acadiana. This expansive region is named after the Acadians, Catholic French refugees driven out of Nova Scotia by the British in the late 18th century. Settling the Louisiana lowlands, mostly Spanish dominions, they were joined by Frenchmen fleeing the Revolution, and created a culture known as "Cajun" (a corruption of "Acadian").

Acadiana, stretching along the Gulf Coast to Texas and west from the Mississippi River up to Avoyelles Parish, has been described as "South of the South," although in many ways it's more conspicuously akin to the societies of the French and Spanish West Indies than to the traditional American South.

## The land of the Kingfish

I-10 meets the Mississippi River at the city of **Baton Rouge ⓐ**, capital of Louisiana and the state's major port. That name, in French, means "red stick." It's generally agreed that the "stick" was a tree, red either from the blood of animals hung there by Indians or from the stripping of its bark. In the latter case, the tree may have been used to mark the boundary of Houma and Bayou Goula Indian land. Although Baton Rouge abuts Acadiana, it has little to do with it, except for governing it and shipping its oil. The ambience is definitely "Southern," and you'll notice, in comparison to New Orleans, a deepening of accent and of provincial ways. The rather quiet, laid-back tempo of the streets belies the intense industry and politicking at the city's heart.

The principal sights of Baton Rouge are the old and new trappings of government. The **Old Capitol** building (tel: 225-342-0500; closed Mon), a Gothic folly constructed beside the Mississippi in 1849, attracted the full force of Mark Twain's considerable scorn. Blaming the "debilitating influence" of Sir Walter Scott for the antebellum South's obsession with notions of "chivalry," he charged "It is pathetic enough that a whitewashed castle, with turrets and things, should ever have been built in this otherwise honorable place; but it is much more pathetic to see this architectural falsehood undergoing restoration and perpetuation in our day, when it would have been so easy to let dynamite finish what a charitable fire began."

In contrast, the skyscraping Art-Deco **New Capitol** commands an eminence at the north end of town. Resembling a scaled-down Empire State Building, it was built in 1932 during the regime of legendary governor Huey Long, the so-called "Kingfish" who reigned supreme over Louisiana through the Great Depression. By all accounts a distasteful and corrupt man, Long was nevertheless an enlightened despot who brooked no opposition to his semi-socialistic rule for the "common man." Highways, schools, and hospitals were built; the unemployed put to work; the privileged heavily taxed. He was gunned down in the capitol in 1935 – a case of memorabilia on the exact spot admits that he may have been killed by his own bodyguards as they panicked in the face of a supposed assassin who never fired a shot – and is now buried in the adjacent garden, alongside a larger-than-life statue. Despite the lessons of Long's death, security in the Capitol is refreshingly minimal; tourists are free to ride the elevator to its topmost tower for wonderful views, or to join Louisiana's political elite for lunch in the basement canteen.

To the outsider, Baton Rouge is largely impenetrable and culturally poor, but it's worth a stop to savor the Mississippi River breeze that cuts the unusually balmy air. The twin foundations of the city's wealth are best appreciated as you leave. From the huge **Baton Rouge Bridge**, on which I-10 crosses the river, you can see belching petrochemical refineries stretching away into the distance they help make so hazy. Down below stands Baton Rouge's port, the fourth most active in the nation thanks to being the farthest inland of all deep-water ports serving the Gulf of Mexico. That status was not achieved by chance; one

**BELOW:**
Baton Rouge's Old Capitol was constructed along the Mississippi in 1849, causing great scorn.

of Long's most brilliant ploys to boost his own state was to build this very bridge too low for ocean-going vessels to continue any farther upstream.

West of the Mississippi, you re-enter Acadiana in West Baton Rouge Parish, and soon pass beyond into Iberville Parish. For the first time in this trip – but not for the last, as you head toward the open spaces of the West – you're treated to spectacular scenery without having to leave the interstate. Here it becomes the **Atchafalaya Swamp Freeway**, crossing America's largest swamp, dividing into two separate highways, supported on precarious concrete stilts, and separated by an expanse of soupy open water that holds lozenge-shaped islets.

## Drowned forests

To either side, the landscape is a magical melding of water and drowned forest, punctuated by clumps of trees, telegraph poles, and strangely-shaped cypress "knobs" (those parts of the root systems of cypress trees that poke out of the morass). Locals fish sedately, or even race speedboats, just below the highway, and every unidentified piece of flotsam may potentially be an alligator. Not a place to run out of gas, let alone to take your eyes off the road and go over the edge. On the far side of the 20-mile (32-km) wide swamp, you find yourself safely back on terra firma. Louisiana natives draw a distinction between the Prairie Cajuns, who farm the soil of south-central Louisiana, and the Bayou Cajuns, the "half-man, half-gator" shrimp-fishing river-dwellers of the marshlands closer to the Gulf. In terms of what the rest of the world thinks of as being Cajun culture, like the accordion- and fiddle-based Cajun music, or the spicy food, the two are not far apart.

**Lafayette ⓯**, 50 miles (80 km) west of Baton Rouge, is the largest city in

Map on page 248

**ALLIGATOR CROSSING**

**NEXT 7 MILES**

*Now crossing alligator land, Atchafalaya Swamp, Louisiana.*

**BELOW:** 'gator in a glade, Atchafalaya.

Acadiana, and standing close to the hypothetical line that divides the prairies from the bayous, makes an ideal hub for exploring the region. It's a sprawling and far from prepossessing city, but in addition to some excellent restaurant-cum-music-clubs, such as **Prejean's** and **Randol's**, it also holds a couple of entertainingly informative "living museums."

## Land of the Cajuns

The best, **Vermilionville** (tel: 318-233-4077; open daily), consists of an idealized village of restored and transplanted 19th-century buildings where experts demonstrate traditional Cajun crafts. Quilter Nell Barron, for example, painstakingly stitches together authentic century-old patterns, dismissing visitors' awe at the sheer work entailed: "This isn't work; to me work is what you don't like to do. I don't count the hours; it's not a nine-to-five job."

If you're pressed for time and decide to stick to the interstate, the Texas border is barely 100 miles (160 km) west of Lafayette. The temptation to explore Cajun country in more depth, however, is liable to prove irresistible. A short excursion north, for example, leads to the welcoming real-life prairie town of **Eunice**, and to **Opelousas**, home of Cajun music's blacker, bluesier, counterpart, zydeco. More ambitious travelers can add half a day or so to the long haul westward by taking the longer detour south to parallel the more interesting coast along the **Jean Lafitte Scenic Byway**. Start by backtracking slightly from Lafayette on I-10, leaving at exit 109 to little **Breaux Bridge**, where **Mulates Restaurant** justly claims to be the "most authentic Cajun restaurant in Louisiana." State 31, briefly renamed Main Street as it passes through Breaux Bridge, follows Bayou Teche another 11 miles (18 km) south to St Martinville.

*Acadiana is named after the Acadians, Catholic French refugees driven out of Nova Scotia in the late 18th century. Joined by a few French fleeing the Revolution, they created a culture known as "Cajun," a corruption of "Acadian."*

**BELOW:** eat catfish *etouffée* at Mulates in Breaux Bridge.

## Paris to the paddy-fields

St Martinville ⓰ is one of the most unspoiled towns you will find in your travels in America. A former indigo plantation and Spanish holding, it was populated by Acadians and Frenchmen in the late 18th and 19th centuries, an era when its culture was so rich that its inhabitants nicknamed it "Petit Paris." After its transformation to a minor port on the bayou, St Martinville settled into its current form of small agrarian center, with visible Cajun and French roots.

Locals are glad to recite half-remembered and half-invented histories in small cafés, which might serve Coca-Cola and catfish *etouffée*. The town is thoroughly infused with the legend of Evangeline (subject of a well-known Henry Wadsworth Longfellow poem), who allegedly walked from Nova Scotia to St Martinville in search of her lover.

The venerable **Evangeline Oak** beside the **St Martin de Tours** church (1765), where she arrived only to hear that her faithless sweetheart had married another, is now a riverside beauty spot where Cajun couples hold their wedding services, while the **Longfellow-Evangeline State Commemorative Area** preserves Acadian history in the interesting Acadian House Museum.

South of St Martinville, State 675 and then State 14 will take you west into Vermilion Parish and the attractive parish seat, **Abbeville** ⓱. Home to the Great Omelette Celebration in November, Abbeville consists of three interlocking and very sleepy squares, as well as a couple of oyster restaurants. Picking up State 82 west here, you're swiftly carried down toward the Gulf, as the distinction between land and water grows increasingly blurred.

Grazing cattle indicate solid ground, but the next field along may be a waterlogged rice paddy through which cranes and herons meticulously pick their

Map
on page
248

**BELOW:**
the musicians
at Mulates play
authentic Cajun
sounds.

*Spanish moss is found draped over live oak trees. It is not really Spanish nor is it really moss; it is an air plant and a member of the pineapple family.*

**BELOW:** paddling a *pirogue* (canoe) at Vermilionville.

long-legged way. Locals fish patiently in the channels that run alongside the roadway, or wade through with shrimping nets.

The farther you go, the fewer signs of human life there are along this bleak and windswept drive, but the birds are a constant source of delight. The trees are bent at ever more acute angles as you approach the Gulf, and in places it feels as though you're having to force yourself through the thick tangles of Spanish moss that hang from overhead. This wispy, gray, romantic shroud is not a parasite but an epiphyte, which means it draws no sustenance from its host, and is therefore equally at home dangling from telephone wires. Turn on the radio for company, and you'll find French- and English-language stations in equal measure, together with Spanish baseball commentaries from Houston as you come within earshot of that city.

## Marsh trail

Seventy-two miles (113km) from Abbeville, highway signs announce that you're arriving in **Grand Chenier**, but apart from a few trailer parks, or a Catholic church surrounded by praying statues, no recognizable town ever appears. Another 30 miles (48 km) on, beyond a straggle of run-down motels and rudimentary restaurants catering to workers in the occasionally-glimpsed oil refineries, the highway is interrupted by an on-demand platform ferry that shuttles a dozen vehicles at a time across the outlet of **Lake Calcasieu**. On the far side, the open ocean lies barely 50 yards (45 meters) off to your right, and mighty drilling rigs are visible far out to sea. It's said that early Spanish explorers would beach their vessels here to caulk their hulls with the mysterious black substance found oozing on the beaches; a boon for Louisiana, perhaps, but no

incentive for a quick dip at **Holly Beach**. In any case, it's time to turn your wheel back inland. The coastal road ahead has been closed by one Gulf storm too many, and to reach Texas you'll have to head 35 miles (56 km) north to rejoin the interstate. One final highlight remains, however, in the shape of the **Sabine National Wildlife Refuge ⑱**, 9 miles (15 km) up State 27. As you walk the short, paved Marsh Trail here, which starts beside the **Intracoastal Waterway** – a mind-boggling canal that spans almost the entire length of the state – close-up sightings of alligators are all but guaranteed.

Map on page 248

## EAST TEXAS TO SAN ANTONIO

Few people who haven't been to, say, Idaho have a clear image of that state. But everyone has at least one picture of Texas. Tumbleweeds and cacti, oilfields, cowboy millionaires, humming border towns, cattle ranches: popular culture has disseminated a rugged, romantic vision of the largest of the "lower 48" states. Such familiar cultural snapshots, however, both over and underestimate the sprawling diversity and vitality of Texas. This *is* where the West begins, but it is a West with no coherent definition. At the risk of over-simplifying, one can think of a passage through Texas as a micro-cosmic passage from East to West, with the point of transition coming at San Antonio, the westernmost of the state's major cities.

Within the compact urban triangle of Houston, Dallas-Fort Worth, and San Antonio is centered Texas' vast wealth and power. From Galveston through Houston to Austin, the Southern tour arcs through the heart of East Texas – its resort, its port, and the state capital. Wherever you go, note the change in the triangular yellow signs that elsewhere in the South advise motorists to "Drive Safely." Here they read: "Drive Friendly." The name "Texas," after all, is derived from "Tejas," meaning "friendly" – the name given by the Spanish to the Native Americans whom they encountered.

**BELOW:** the "drowned forests" of Louisiana's swamplands.

### Port Bolivar ferry

From the moment you enter Texas on I-10 from Louisiana, highway signs start to count down the mileage to New Mexico. The magnitude of what lies ahead is clear; shortly after the state line, exit 877 branches off to the town of Orange, and the first sign you'll see for El Paso shows it as an incomprehensible 857 miles (1,370 km) distant. The chances are, however, that you'll feel ready to leave this nondescript stretch of highway long before the first city of any size – Houston, 110 miles (177 km) in. The best, and most obvious alternative, is to return to the Gulf coast as soon as possible, and head for the resort community of **Galveston ⑲**.

Halfway to Houston, as you approach exit 829, look out for the billboard that lets drivers know whether the Port Bolivar ferry is in operation. Assuming that it is, pick up State 124 at Winnie, which runs due south to the ocean. En route, as you cross first Spindletop Bayou and then Elm Bayou, little about this marshy landscape suggests that you've left Louisiana. Rice and even crawfish farms stand on either side of the highway, while indefatigable little oil pumps diligently bob away, atop mounds of scrubby vegetation. About 20 miles (32 km) down from the interstate, a steep humpback bridge crosses the Intracoastal Waterway at **High Island**, a dismal little town where the only sign of life is a junkyard advertising "Kahla's Fresh Junk." At the time of writing, State 87 east of here was closed due to storm damage, but to the west it runs the full 27-mile (43-km) length of the slender spit of land known as the **Bolivar Peninsula**.

For much of the way, all that separates State 87 from the ocean is a low sandbank held together by bedraggled wind-battered telegraph poles; through the occasional gaps that permit beach access, you'll catch glimpses of the churning muddy waves beyond. Little by little, the closer you get to Galveston, beachfront structures grow grander and more numerous. Flimsy trailer parks give way to ambitious real estate developments with names like "Copacabana By The Sea." The only genuine town is **Crystal Beach**, near the western end, which celebrates the Texas Crab Festival in mid-May. A couple of miles beyond that, State 87 ends at the terminal of the **Port Bolivar Ferry**, a free 24-hour shuttle service provided by two or three large vessels that take 20 minutes to traverse the busy mouth of Galveston Bay.

## Pirate on the beach

Galveston initially impresses with an air of southern California as you roll down Ferry Road (Second Street) to Seawall Boulevard. The spacious streets, salmon colored buildings, and regal palms have a West Coast feel that extends up Broadway (Avenue J) past Avenues O 1/2 and N 1/2. Farther Downtown, however, the Victorian/neo-Classical aspect brings you back to the South, while along Seawall Boulevard, the feel is more Gulf Coast than Long Beach.

**BELOW:** seagulls on the beach along Seawall Boulevard, Galveston, Texas.

Galveston first came to prominence during the early 19th century as a seaport that served as headquarters for the pirate Jean Lafitte, whose name may also be familiar from his activities in New Orleans. In the local economic boom that followed the Civil War, it flowered into a fully-fledged city, becoming Texas' leading manufacturing center and, by 1899, the largest cotton port in the world. Galveston had the first telephone system in Texas, the first newspaper, electric lights, golf course, brewery, and Ford dealership, while the Strand, thanks to its profusion of great commercial houses, was renowned as "The Wall Street of the Southwest."

Galveston remains an active shipping center, but Houston's port has entirely over-shadowed the island's, and these days it's more involved with the vacation industry. Of it 32 miles (51 km) of beach, the most popular stretch lies on the Gulf side of the island, along **Seawall Boulevard**. This broad thoroughfare is lined on its inland side by sprawling motels and fast-food restaurants, while the beach itself is interrupted by a succession of privately-owned piers that jut out into the ocean and offer competing attractions and diversions. The waters are not as temperate as the southern Gulf Coast beaches, but the grayish sands might as well be gold to vacationing Houstonians. Remarks one Galvestonian, "You'd think they'd never seen a beach before."

## Old wealth

Galveston's acclaimed **East End Historical District**, bounded roughly by Broadway, Mechanic Street, 19th Street, and 11th Street, is where the Victorian homes stand, intermixed with buildings that betray neo-Classical, Renaissance, and Italianate influences. Bungalows rest in the shade cast by oleanders, oaks, maples, and palms, and are slightly raised from the ground out of respect for the gulf. A walk in this district, especially down Post Office and Church streets, gives a glimpse of how the first rich Texans displayed their wealth. Downtown, **The Strand** has undergone the familiar renovation-into-tourist-attraction, arguably losing its soul in the process of gaining a money-spinning assortment of galleries, cute shops, and Art-Deco restaurants.

Renovation projects have managed to preserve a few marvelous structures, like the beautiful Italianate **Ashton Villa** (1859; tel: 409-762-3933; open daily), Broadway at Tremont, but a truer Galveston rises in the form of the eyesore **American National Insurance Company** at 19th Street between Mechanic and Market. This shamelessly ugly monstrosity is the legacy of William Lewis Moody, Jr, the founder of that company, as well as Galveston's City National Bank and many other enterprises in the early 20th century.

From a glance at the map, Galveston appears to lie a full 50 miles (80 km) south of Houston. In fact, however, the build-up to the megalopolis begins as soon as you cross back to the mainland on the I-45 Causeway, to be confronted by massed ranks of smoke-belching oil refineries.

From there on in, strip malls and garish billboards line the interstate for the full 27 miles (44 km) up to the Sam Houston Tollway, which circles the entire city at a distance of around 20 miles (32 km). As you pass beneath its stacked

Map
on page
248

*"Galveston" is an anglicized version of "Galvez," the original Spanish name for the island settlement. It was named for Bernardo de Galvez, the Spanish Governor of Louisiana.*

**BELOW:**
dining room of Galveston's Ashton Villa, built in 1859.

# HOUSTON:
# SPACE AGE CITY

*Once an oil town, Houston now houses
a wide range of high-tech industries
and quintessentially Texan self-confidence*

**H**ouston boasts that the first word uttered by the first man on the moon was – you guessed it – "Houston." Mission Control Center, receiver of the greeting, is the city's prime tourist attraction. Officially the Lyndon B. Johnson Space Center (tel: 281-483-8693), it's located on NASA Road 1 off I-45, approximately 25 miles (40 km) south of Houston. Displays commemorate milestones in the US space program, and a tour takes visitors through a campus of structures containing moon rocks and astronauts, into the Mission Control Center, and full-scale replicas of the Space Shuttle used for training. Follow I-45 straight into downtown Houston for Tranquility

Park. Named in reference to the July, 1969 *Apollo* moonshot, the park at Bagby and Walker streets is a landscaped monument to the space race. Craters encircle the focal point of the park: five golden phalluses cascading water in the image of a takeoff.

More deserving of the name "Tranquility" than the park is the hushed, tranquil Rothko Chapel located in the Museum District at the southwestern corner of the city. American abstract-impressionist Mark Rothko created this chapel for non-denominational worship and meditation. Inside, it houses 14 large Rothko canvases. Outside rises Barnett Newman's disturbingly moving *Broken Obelisk*, dedicated to Martin Luther King, Jr. The worthy Museum District houses many collections, all interesting in their ways, as is the Victorian Romanesque campus of Rice University,

The galleries of Houston show how "black gold" has enriched the state through the purchase of works of art. On Sul Ross Street, the Menil Collection houses arts and artifacts of mankind from the earliest days in the Near East to contemporary abstract pieces. The Matisse bronzes that turn their backs to you at the Museum of Fine Arts (tel: 713-639-7300; closed Mon) at Main and Bissonet streets, make their case about Houston's attitude toward the norm. The collection is particularly strong in American paintings. Across the street is the Contemporary Arts Museum (tel: 713-284-8250; closed Mon), dedicated to current works. At Hermann Park is the Museum of Natural Science (tel: 713-639-4600; open daily), with a walk-through greenhouse aflutter with butterflies.

An emblem of Houston's appreciation for huge size is the unbelievable Astrodomain, comprised of the Astrodome stadium (Eighth Wonder of the World); Astroworld (a 100-ride amusement park); and Astrohall (the world's largest one-level convention facility). ❑

**LEFT:** Museum of Medical Science exhibit; Johnson Space Center on NASA Road.
**ABOVE:** the Astrodome; Rice University.

Map on page 248

and spiraling freeways and connecting concrete loops, **Houston's** ㉒ *(see page 274)* futuristic downtown skyline finally rises on the northern horizon.

If you see Texas as a microcosm of the whole country, then it's as you head west of Houston that you leave the South behind and enter the Great Plains. The state capital, **Austin** ㉑, is approximately 150 miles (240 km) west, but as I-10 runs directly to San Antonio instead, along a slightly more southerly route, reaching Austin entails at least 40 miles (64 km ) of driving off the interstate. Whichever route you choose will be much the same, a mildly attractive but far from enthralling cruise through the lush plains and gently rolling hills of the "ranch country" that lies within the Houston–Dallas–San Antonio triangle. Probably the most bucolic option is to leave I-10 at exit 696, near little Columbus, and join State 71 as it meanders back and forth across the equally sinuous Colorado River – not the one in Colorado – all the way up to Austin.

## Well-sheltered Austin

Austin itself nestles amid verdant woodland in the middle of an agricultural paradise that's unique among the many Texan climates and terrains. Sheltered from the humid heat that sweeps in waves over Houston, this locale makes a pleasant ideal for ranching and recreation. Unlike Houston, and despite having experienced similarly phenomenal growth, Austin is fairly well contained. Exit between Martin Luther King, Jr Boulevard and Eighth–Third streets from I-35, and you'll be in the middle of a walkable Downtown. For most visitors, the experience of the city is confined to the area from First Street and the Colorado River up to 24th Street and the heart of the **University of Texas** (UT) at Austin along Guadalupe Avenue.

**BELOW:** the tower of the University of Texas at Austin glows orange (the school color) after sports victories.

## High tech and outlaws

Austin manages the difficult double act of being not only Texas' political capital, but also its true cultural capital. Having attained that distinction during the 1960s, when it was a hippy mecca, it went on to spearhead the "outlaw country" movement of the 1970s, when musicians such as Willie Nelson and Waylon Jennings first came to prominence. Its reputation as a center for live music and the arts no doubt contributed to its 1980s growth as "the Silicon Valley of Texas," when more and more high-tech and financial firms relocated here. That process, of course, brought with it an influx of young urban professionals, and one need look no farther than **Sixth Street** to see the impact of aggressive consumerism on the culture. Experiencing the same gentrification as San Francisco's Haight Street, formerly gay-dominated Sixth Street is still a good place to bar-hop, but not nearly so much of a community as it used to be.

Despite its changing face, Austin retains much of its spirit. At the University of Texas – with over 50,000 students, the largest university campus in the state – the counter-cultural element will always have its place. At heart, it's still got long hair and a beard, though it might also have a Mercedes and a kid, and its image as a hotbed of new ideas sits uncomfortably with its dubious claim to fame as the place where the determinedly dumbed-down "slacker" student ethos of the 1990s first emerged.

Austin also continues to rock. Nightclubs abound, offering a nightly wide-ranging choice between hard-edged country, "new music," ska, classical, blues, R&B, or jazz. Theater and literary events are numerous, while good bookstores, record stores, cafés, and tiffany-glass restaurants intermix with low-down, funkier spots. Above all, local legends have persisted despite the changes – for

**BELOW:** Austin's Sixth Street is for entertainment and shopping trips.

## DETOUR – DALLAS

A 195-mile (314-km) drive along Interstate 35 from Austin leads to the glittering town of Dallas. With just over a million residents, Dallas attracts visitors with its sky-high architecture, quality art collections, and high-class shopping malls. The city began with the cabin of trapper John Neely Bryan beside the Trinity River, which Bryan believed to be navigable for trade all the way to the Gulf of Mexico. It wasn't, but the Houston and Texas Railroad brought people and commerce soon enough. The most extravagant of local institutions is Neiman Marcus department store, whose Christmas catalog once contained a page entitled "how to spend a million dollars." Fortunately, the penchant for extravagance extends to wonderful art collections bought with the revenues of black gold. Darker history also plagues Dallas: the most visited site is the former Texas School Book Depository, where Lee Harvey Oswald shot President John F. Kennedy in 1963. The Sixth Floor Museum overlooks Dealey Plaza, through which the president was riding when he was assassinated. The Conspiracy Museum records developments, while across the road stands a memorial to the fallen president. The Dallas Visitor's Bureau, tel: 214-746-6677.

Map on page 248

example, **Scholz Garden**. "The most historic restaurant and beer garden in Texas," Scholz Garden was founded in 1866, 16 years before work began on the capitol building. Through various ownerships, additions, retractions, rowdies of all ages, and storms of legislative dispute, Scholz has kept its original front room and unspoiled diversity. You can find good food here with unpretentious charm and heartfelt – if stumbling – music; you may even care to dance on occasion. Try the chicken-fried steak, a Texas favorite.

## Lone star capitol

Scholz Garden is a few blocks from the **State Capitol** (tel: 512-463-0063; open daily for tours) and the lower edges of UT, two major sources of business. The capitol itself is unmistakable, a red-granite version of the nation's capitol in Washington, DC. Its white, classical interior focusses on the great rotunda, commemorating the six governments that reigned supreme over Texas (Spain, France, Mexico, the Confederate States, the United States, and, most proudly, the Republic of Texas). Above, at the apex of the dome, is the lone star that is the state's emblem: independence, self-determination, and singularity.

Portraits of the state's governors ring the rotunda and, to all sides, wings lead to the offices of state legislators. *The Surrender of Santa Anna*, a painting at ground level, captures the dramatic moment when Mexico's "Napoleon of the West" surrendered to Sam Houston, "Liberator of Texas" and commander-in-chief of its forces during the Texas Revolution against Mexico. Among the monuments to Texas' glory in that war and in the War Between the States (Civil War) is the quiet sculpture by Bill Bond, *150 Years of Texas*, which honored the state's sesquicentennial in 1986.

*You know you're in Texas when... the State Capitol is the largest of all the state capitols in the US. On completion, it was thought to have been the seventh biggest building in the world.*

**BELOW:** Austin has more than its share of young urban professionals.

*Exhibit from the LBJ Library, Austin. This part of Texas is full of tributes to the locally born 36th President of the US.*

**BELOW:** restaurant in Johnson City.

## Hill Country

Historic San Antonio is barely an hour's drive southwest of Austin on I-35, but there's a diverting half-day's sightseeing to be had if you make your way between the two along the **Texas Hill Country Trail** to the west instead. At first, leaving Austin, the "trail" – in reality, US 290 – crosses a somewhat dreary Western landscape of thin grassland.

Beyond **Dripping Springs**, however, which calls itself the "Gateway to the Hill Country" but has nothing more to offer than an ugly stone-clad high school, the road starts to climb through a rich rolling terrain of open meadows, scattered with a delightful profusion of wildflowers. By the time it reaches **Johnson City** ㉒, 50 miles (80 km) west of Austin, it's undulating through pastoral countryside. Johnson City acquired its name long before local boy Lyndon Baines Johnson became the 36th President of the United States, following the assassination of John F Kennedy in 1963. However, the downtown birthplace of "LBJ," who shared his initials with his wife Lady Bird Johnson, and the nearby LBJ Ranch to which they retired after the Vietnam War put an end to his political career, are now major tourist attractions in the area.

This very middle-European region must have seemed almost heavenly to early European immigrants, and it's hardly surprising that it attracted hundreds of German settlers during the 19th century. The Main Street of the town of **Fredericksburg**, another 32 miles (48 km) west, for example, is labeled "Haupstrasse" and lined with pseudo-Teutonic beer gardens and bakeries, while numerous German-named farms along the intervening highway, like "Der peach garten," sell German-style wines and liquors.

To get a real feel for the best of the Hill Country, take the lesser State 1376

down to San Antonio. Cutting away south from US 290 just south of the Pedernales River, 4 miles (6 km) east of Fredericksburg, this route passes within a few feet of the tiny village of **Luckenbach** ㉓, another 4 miles (6 km) on. Unless you know where to look, however, you'll miss it altogether; the unmarked turning comes immediately before South Grape Creek. A much-loved ghost town – more of a joke town, really – Luckenbach was bought in its entirety by humorist Hondo Crouch in 1970, and made famous by a No. 1 Country & Western hit, recorded in 1976 by Willie Nelson and Waylon Jennings, that featured the refrain "Let's Go To Luckenbach Texas."

Map on page 248

## Country music town

Hundreds of country fans now do just that, to while away an afternoon in the diminutive post office as the postmaster cracks corny jokes and sings songs, and perhaps buy a souvenir such as a stuffed armadillo drinking a bottle of Luckenbach beer. Willie Nelson hosts a picnic here on July 4th each year, while most summer weekends there's some sort of large-scale concert in the dancehall. From Luckenbach, State 1376 continues south toward San Antonio by way of some beautiful hills, where you're liable to startle wild deer grazing beside the highway. Ten miles (16 km) northeast of the city limits, it meets I-10/US87 at Boerne.

**San Antonio** ㉔ at first seems deceptively pastoral; not far from the interstate, luxurious Italianate villas perch on isolated rocky knobs that look like Tuscan hill towns. Soon enough, however, you're forced to run the gauntlet of manic freeways entailed in reaching every large American city; just before it finally spits you out into Downtown, the interstate for no reason splits alarmingly into two separate highways, one stacked on top of the other. ❏

**BELOW:** Luckenbach was put on the map by a Willie Nelson/ Waylon Jennings C&W song.

# SAN ANTONIO TO SOUTHERN NEW MEXICO

*Davy Crockett and Billy the Kid are only two of the people who left their mark on the lands that border Mexico and the Rio Grande*

Map on page 282

O f all the major cities in Texas, El Paso and San Antonio are the oldest. El Paso began as the first Spanish mission in the future state, while it was in San Antonio that American Texas was born and nearly slaughtered by the Mexicans at the Alamo. Stretching between the two is the vast expanse of **Trans-Peco Texas**, a largely barren yet subtly beautiful mountainous desert. There is a timeless quality to the landscape that stands in most marked contrast to the booming spectacle of the metropolitan east.

In the anchor cities, Hispanic culture has consistently revitalized itself, much more effectively than in Galveston, Houston, or Austin. El Paso and sister city Juárez are bound as a Mexican/American metropolis, the gateway to the American Southwest.

## Cradle of Texas liberty

San Antonio ㉔, the "Cradle of Texas Liberty," was the capital of Texas before Mexico won its independence from Spain in 1821 and opened the territory to settlement by anyone who would develop the land. After Stephen Austin led the first wave of pioneers into the new land, the floodgates were open. Just before Austin's pilgrimage, there were 2,500 persons of European descent in Texas. By 1836, 30,000 Anglos, 5,000 blacks, and 4,000 Mexicans populated the area.

**LEFT:** mountain lions are fairly common in the wild Southwest.
**BELOW:** Texas is the gateway to Mexico.

When Spaniards first came in the late 1680s to the San Antonio River Valley, which cradles modern San Antonio, they found it occupied by the Payaya Indians, hunters who supplemented their catches with the fruits of the pecan and mesquite trees and the prickly pear cactus. The Payaya cooperated readily with the Europeans, but the Apache, who controlled the plains to the north, took more convincing, and the nomadic Comanche were always a threat.

Intent on securing their claims in the area and on taming the godless heathens, the Spanish established a mission on the west bank of the San Antonio River in 1718. Mission San Antonio de Valero, later known as **The Alamo** (tel: 210-225-1391; open daily), was relocated to the east bank and then closed down in 1793. Mexican troops were transferred there to protect the pueblo that had grown around the riverbanks. Renamed *El Alamo* (the Cottonwood), it became a crucial fortification.

The dubious glory of the converted mission arises from an ill-conceived standoff with the forces of Mexican president General Antonio Lopez de Santa Ana, the self-styled "Napoleon of the West," on March 6,

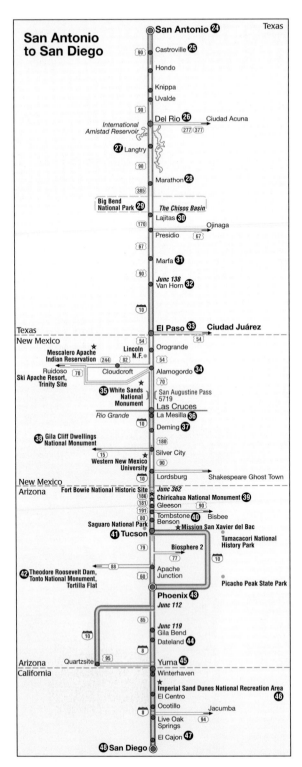

San Antonio
to San Diego

San Antonio **24**    Texas
Castroville **25**
Hondo
Knippa
Uvalde
Del Rio **26**    Ciudad Acuna
International Amistad Reservoir    277  377
**27** Langtry
Marathon **28**
Big Bend National Park **29**    The Chisos Basin
Lajitas **30**
Presidio  67    Ojinaga
Marfa **31**
Junc 138
Van Horn **32**
Texas
New Mexico
Mescalero Apache Indian Reservation  244   82    Lincoln N.F.
Ruidoso Ski Apache Resort, Trinity Site  70    Cloudcroft
**35** White Sands National Monument
Rio Grande
Gila Cliff Dwellings National Monument **38**
Western New Mexico University
New Mexico
Arizona    Fort Bowie National Historic Site
Saguaro National Park
**41** Tucson
**42** Theodore Roosevelt Dam, Tonto National Monument, Tortilla Flat
Arizona    Quartzsite
California
El Paso **33**    Ciudad Juárez
Orogrande
Alamogordo **34**
San Augustine Pass 5719
Las Cruces
La Mesilla **36**
Deming **37**
Silver City
Lordsburg    Shakespeare Ghost Town
Junc 362
Chiricahua National Monument **39**
Gleeson
Tombstone **40**    Bisbee
Benson
Mission San Xavier del Bac
Tumacacori National History Park
Biosphere 2
Apache Junction
Picacho Peak State Park
Phoenix **43**
Junc 112
Junc 119
Gila Bend
Dateland **44**
Yuma **45**
Winterhaven
Imperial Sand Dunes National Recreation Area
El Centro    **46**
Ocotillo    Jacumba
Live Oak Springs  94
El Cajon **47**
**48** San Diego

1836. Mexico's 5,000 troops were met by 187 (or 186, depending on who you ask) "Texian" martyrs-to-be. In the words of memorializer Frank J. Davis, "All dead within one sanguinary hour; yet the heroes of the Alamo are deathless."

## Remember the Alamo

"Remember the Alamo!" was adopted as the Texan battle cry, and revenge came swiftly. Seven weeks later, Santa Ana was defeated within a mere 18 minutes at the Battle of San Jacinto, whereupon the Texas Revolution culminated with the declaration of the newly independent Republic of Texas.

Riddled though it is with as many contradictions as bullet holes, the Alamo today is an essential pilgrimage destination for tourists. Its defenders during the battle were, after all, recent arrivals from foreign countries that included England, Ireland, Scotland, and even Denmark – as well as the United States – while their 26-year-old commander, William B. Travis from South Carolina, wrote three days before he died that "the citizens of this municipality are all our enemies."

## Davy Crockett

His associates included opportunists such as Jim Bowie, remembered for his namesake knife (though the museum here can only rustle up one of his less celebrated spoons), and the legendary Davy Crockett, a three-term Congressman from Kentucky who sought his fortune in the West after the evaporation of his presidential ambitions. The independent Texas for which they fought and died survived just nine years before being subsumed by the United States.

A plaque on the front door of the grafitti-etched **Alamo Shrine**, originally the mission's chapel, requests "Be quiet friend, here heroes died to blaze a trail for other men." The request is roundly ignored.

Because the taking of photographs in the shrine is prohibited, most visitors raise their brief squall, then retire first to the lovely garden, shaded by everything from myrtles to a mescal bean tree, and then on to the very busy gift shop. On sale are such reverent mementos as Alamo mugs, belts, patches, playing cards, pencils, plaques, postcards, dishware, license-plate frames, keychains, banners, bells, pins, coasters, caps, tote-bags, and erasers.

Map on page 282

## A river runs through it

That San Antonio ranks second only to New Orleans as the loveliest city on the Southern Route is largely due to its delightful and distinctive **Paseo del Rio**, otherwise known as the **River Walk**. This highly original and elegantly simple concept, instigated in 1939 as part of Franklin Roosevelt's New Deal, consists of confining the San Antonio River into a tight and very narrow little channel as it loops through the city center, paving and landscaping both banks, and garnishing them liberally with restaurants, patio cafés, stores, and gardens.

Though San Antonio is in truth a large, sweltering city, you'd never know it as you amble along the shaded, lively, and completely pedestrianized River Walk, which stands roughly 10 feet (3 meters) lower than the busy Downtown streets. Flat-bottomed cruise boats ply gently along the river itself, and at night, in particular, the effect is quite magical. There's even an open-air theater, the ingenious **Arneson River Theatre**, where the stage is arranged on one side of the river while the audience watches from a stucco Spanish-style amphitheater of benches on the opposite bank.

*Mural along the River Walk in San Antonio.*

If you can bear to tear yourself away from the pleasures of the River Walk, downtown San Antonio holds several other worthwile attractions. The beautifully restored **Spanish Governor's Palace** (tel: 210-224-0601; open daily), a tranquil little gem, is located near to the original site of Spain's Presidio de Bexar (1722), the **Plaza de Armas**, where a sign notes that in the Republic of

**BELOW:** the Alamo, symbol of the Republic of Texas.

**TIP**

Once past San Antonio, this route skirts the Mexican border all the way to California. Roadblocks and stop-checks by the US Border Patrol are commonplace, so foreign travelers should always keep their papers handy. Passports or green cards are required if you cross into any Mexican border town.

**BELOW:** San Antonio's River Walk at nighttime.

Texas era, running from 1836 to 1845, the grounds had already become a busy market teeming with "noisy vendors of vegetables, fresh eggs, chili peppers, and live chickens. Strolling guitarists, tourists, and girls selling songbirds mingled with pickpockets…"

**Hemisfair Park**, not far southeast of the Alamo, is dominated by the slender, Space Needle-like **Tower of the Americas**, but trips to its 75th floor observation deck are rewarded only with fairly dull views of monotonous plains. Even the Hill Country amounts to little more than a few vague bumps on the horizon. Nearby, however, the **Institute of Texan Cultures** (tel: 210-458-2300; closed Mon) takes an entertaining look at the many different peoples, from Comanches to Czechs, who have contributed to the cosmopolitan blend of modern Texas. Perhaps the least-known group are the Wends, 600 of whom arrived from Prussia in 1854; their descendants have maintained their identity ever since. There's also a glorious evocation of the cowboy past; one early African-American *vaquero* is quoted as saying "we loved to work cattle so much we'd just be sittin' around cryin' for daylight to come."

## Miles, mesas, and mountains

You're going to have to devote at least a day of your life to driving the 500-mile (800-km) distance between San Antonio and El Paso, so it makes sense to make the most of what this largely desolate expanse has to offer. Rather than stick to I-10, which plots a northerly course across the barren plains, head due west on US 90 to meet up with the legendary Rio Grande at Del Rio. Following the Mexican frontier from there enables you to relish the magnificence of Big Bend National Park, among the most remote yet stunning national parks in the US.

Almost as soon as you leave San Antonio on US 90, there's a parched quality about the roadside grasslands even in springtime that presages the dessication ahead. At first, however, agriculture maintains a foothold. **Castroville ㉕**, 40 miles (64 km) out, proclaims itself to be "A Touch of Alsace France," and has several Alsatian restaurants (catering to humans, not dogs), while **Hondo** just beyond has the feel of the Great Plains, with huge fields of corn and wheat.

Next come **Knippa** – "Go Ahead and Blink, Knippa is Bigger than You Think" – which is devoted to stone quarrying, and **Uvalde**, where unless you need to rent a tractor, there's no imaginable reason to stop. This region seems to be the spiritual home of the Drive-Thru Beverage Barn, where locals can stock up on hard liquor without having to peel themselves off the leatherette seats of their pick-up trucks.

## The Rio Grande

By now, you'll almost certainly have logged your first sighting of the agents and vehicles of the US Border Patrol, who are going to remain an ever-vigilant presence for the rest of your trip. Across most of Texas, the desert makes a far more effective barrier against illegal entrants from Mexico than does the Rio Grande. Rather than monitor every inch of the river, therefore, the Border Patrol simply erects roadblocks along the few highways that lead away from it; be sure to have your papers to hand at all times.

Once past Uvalde, US 90 dwindles to a single lane in either direction. The only distraction in the 72-mile (114-km) stretch to Del Rio is Bracketville, where the set used by John Wayne to film *The Alamo* will no doubt confuse future archeologists. **Del Rio ㉖** itself comes as an anti-climax; it's home to the large Laughlin Air Force base, and any number of shopping malls catering to daytrippers from the adjacent Mexican town of **Ciudad Acuna**, but apart from a couple of 19th-century buildings, there's not much to divert tourists.

A further 12 miles (20 km) northwest, **Amistad Lake** carefully claims to be the "third largest international man-made lake in the world." It was created by the completion of the Amistad Dam, a huge curving wall of concrete jointly dedicated by the presidents of the US and Mexico in 1969. Above this point, the Rio Grande is officially designated in the finest American tradition as a "Wild and Scenic River," but the dam firmly puts paid to any remaining wildness. At the monument in the middle you can stand with a foot in either country, watching anglers and even scuba-divers as they sport in the waters below.

Another 30 miles (48 km) northwest, the highest highway bridge in Texas crosses the deep gorge of the Pecos River, just before its confluence with the Rio Grande. The stern "No Diving From Bridge" signs seem somewhat superfluous, but it's worth stopping to admire this first of the many Western canyons to come, and envy the eagles and falcons that soar so majestically above it.

Beyond the Pecos, there's no longer any doubt that you've reached true desert, while confirmation that you're in the Wild West soon comes with your arrival

Map on page 282

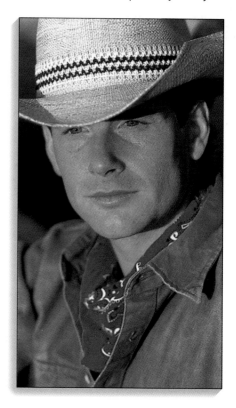

**BELOW:** welcome to cowboy country.

*British actress Lily Langtry, for whom the eccentric Judge Roy Bean named the tiny Texas town of Langtry.*

**BELOW:** Big Bend National Park.

in **Langtry ㉗**. This tiny hamlet is celebrated as the home of Judge Roy Bean, the "Law West of the Pecos." Judge Bean was a storekeeper who was appointed as a Justice of the Peace in 1882, despite an ignorance of all legal matters that he never attempted to rectify. His saloon-cum-courtroom, a hundred yards shy of the dry-as-bones canyon of the **Rio Grande**, is now a museum and information center.

Until you come to **Marathon ㉘**, 120 empty miles (193 km) west of Langtry, you've added no extra mileage to your trip by taking US 90 rather than I-10. This is where you'll have to decide whether to detour down to Big Bend, however – a decision best contemplated in the luxury of the restored **Gage Hotel**. (Most of the towns *en route* have had a handful of rundown motels, but this is the first really appealing accommodation since San Antonio.)

## Bears and mountain lions

It would be hard to recommend **Big Bend National Park ㉙** too highly. Even the 40 mile (64 km) drive south to the park entrance on US 385 is a delight, as you head straight toward a mysteriously misty wall of mountains, centering on one giant pyramidal peak, only to shimmy around them at the last minute to find yourself confronted by another equally alluring range on the horizon. Once inside the park, 30 more miles (48 km) brings you to the main visitor center, but the prime destination, the **Chisos Basin**, lies another 12 miles (20 km) beyond that. A truly glorious dead-end road – too narrow for large RVs – climbs steeply into the park's central cluster of mountains. It feels for all the world as though you're entering another kingdom. Tall yucca plants stand like sentries to either side as the road picks its way through a labyrinth of towering rocks, where

wonderful pink-blossomed cacti and other desert succulents look down from the high scree slopes. Finally, you drop down a succession of tight hairpin bends into the basin itself, a grassy bowl ringed by mountains that holds the park's lodge, campsite, and other visitor facilities. This is bear and mountain lion country, so you may prefer to stay close to your motel-style room, but even in these there's a risk you'll find a rattlesnake coiled on your doorstep. Marked hiking trails enable the more intrepid to explore the wilderness; the best trail winds 3 miles (5 km) down to the **Window**, a natural gap in the circle of mountains that looks westward across an eerie desert landscape of buttes and mesas.

Map on page 282

## River-rafting trips

State 170 west of the park, also known as the **River Road**, is one of Texas' most attractive highways, providing a rare opportunity to drive along the Rio Grande in all its glory. It reaches the river 41 miles (66 km) west of the Chisos Basin at the small resort town of **Lajitas** ㉚, which specializes in offering river-rafting trips through high-walled Santa Elena Canyon into the park. Until recently, Lajitas was noteworthy for having a goat as its mayor – and not just any goat at that, but Clay Henry, the Beer-Drinking Goat. Sadly, however, Clay has come to prefer beer to politics; stripped of his civic responsibilities, he's now a sorry specimen. For 50 miles (80 km) from Lajitas, the River Road sticks close to the river, sometimes scrambling over high sandstone outcrops, at others meandering through well-watered fields. Cattle can often be seen grazing in Chihuahua, Mexico, and in several places the river is shallow enough for them to wade across. If you're tempted, there's another chance to cross into Mexico at **Presidio**, where **Ojinaga** on the far side holds a couple of seafood restaurants – you'd have to wonder how fresh their supplies can be – plus cut-rate opticians and pharmacies.

From Presidio, a 61-mile (98-km) drive north on US 67 enables you to rejoin US 90 at **Marfa** ㉛, known for its highly-regarded contemporary art musuem – a legacy of the NewYork-born artist Donald Judd – as well as its mysterious lights illuminated in the sky, which most people think are UFOs, and as the place where the 1956 movie *Giant* was filmed. For almost all the 74-mile (119 km) drive northwest to I-10, the road is paralleled on one side by an endless procession of telegraph poles, and on the other by a railroad along which colossal freight trains – larger than any of the settlements *en route* – drag themselves toward California. Little "dust devils," created by local air disturbances, swirl in the fields in the distance, while frail tinder-box tumbleweeds blow in from the desert when you least expect them. It may seem Texan through and through, but the tumbleweed is in reality the Siberian thistle operating under a homely alias, and as such is an unwanted foreign pest.

**Van Horn** ㉜, 120 miles (193 km) east of El Paso on I-10, is a typical interstate pit-stop whose fast-food restaurants, motels, and gas stations nonetheless make it seem like a land of plenty after the austerity of the desert crossing. Even the long radio silence comes to a sudden end, with four different stations devoted to the weather alone; the one snag is that there's no

**BELOW:** Marfa is known for its mysterious lights; some people think they are UFOs.

weather to speak of. As you continue westward, there's an additional bonus in the form of an extra hour to your day, gained when you enter the Mountain Time Zone close to Allamore. This final stretch into El Paso passes through perhaps the most featureless landscape it's possible to imagine. Its sheer emptiness induces a sort of meditative calm, leaving you free to ponder such eternal questions as, why does everyone seem to be towing gigantic ocean-yachts across this infinite sandscape, when the tide went out for the last time approximately 60 million years ago?

## Border town

Where San Antonio has profited from redeveloping historic districts and monuments, the city of **El Paso** ③ has failed. Of course, San Antonio has the Alamo; nothing in El Paso is comparable as a marketable emblem. Nevertheless, San Antonio has made exceptional efforts to upgrade and maintain its attractions while injecting romance into its riverfront. El Paso, on the other hand, has left the excitement and romance (well, excitement anyway) to its much larger sister city *across* the riverfront. That city is **Ciudad Juárez** (*see below*), and the river is the Rio Grande, separating the United States and Mexico.

El Paso, which spreads around the base of the Franklin Mountains, lies in the oldest European-settled area of Texas. In the 16th century, Spaniards first crossing the Rio Grande to explore their territories in New Mexico headed along *El Paso del Norte* – the Pass of the North – which sent the river through a break in the mountain ranges. Soon *El Camino Real* was extended from south of Chihuahua City, Mexico, to what is now Santa Fe, New Mexico, by conquistador Juan de Oñate. When the Spanish colonists were driven out of Santa

**BELOW:** Eagle Dancer statue outside the Speaking Rock Casino, El Paso.

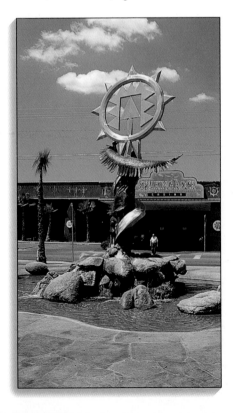

## DETOUR – MEXICO

Ciudad Juárez, across the bridge from El Paso, Texas, is probably the most interesting Mexican border town outside of Tijuana, south of San Diego. But whereas San Diego is sleek and efficient, confirming the US's superior grasp of the modern world, the difference between El Paso and Ciudad Juárez is definitely in Mexico's favor. El Paso is gray, grim and depressing, whereas Juárez, the biggest city in the state of Chihuahua, is vibrant and colorful. Bullfights and bright souvenirs to take home make a strong impression right away. The Juárez Museum of History traces the area's development, with special attention paid to the Mexican Revolution and the Mexican hero (American criminal) Pancho Villa. Our Lady of Guadalupe Mission explores the rich religious tapestry of the country. Juárez's food is wonderful and spicy, but don't drink the water, or eat ice cream or ice cubes (an urban myth recommends a shot of tequila with each meal to kill impurities). It's certainly worth a day trip to experience another country, but don't be fooled by the ease of crossing to Ciudad Juárez; the Border Patrol is much more strict in the other direction, and a passport, green card, or other paper work might be required to get back into Texas.

Fe by the Pueblo Indian Revolt of 1680, a dispirited column of refugees regrouped here, around an adobe Franciscan mission they called Ysleta del Sur. It took 12 long years before the Spaniards returned in force to reconquer New Mexico, by which time the towns of Ysleta and El Paso had sprung up around the mission. El Paso gradually absorbed Ysleta, but was itself split in two after the designation of the Rio Grande as the United States–Mexico border. The US city remained El Paso and the Mexican city was dubbed Juárez.

El Paso's strategic location has made it a travelers' stop for centuries. The Gold-Rush '49ers passed through on their way to fortune in California. Refugees, desperados, and tourists have all met here. Much of the commemorated history invokes gunfights, with the notorious Marshall Dallas Stoudenmire and John Wesley Hardin on many a winning end before finally biting the dust. There's a lot of dust to bite. El Paso's climate is singularly dry, although rain is not unknown. But the rain just wets down the dust and refuses to be kicked up by the winds which herald it. Watering holes are few in the city proper, which is underdeveloped and unremarkable.

The Rio Grande in El Paso these days is more of a fortified moat than a river. In a sad parody of San Antonio, what water it holds is compressed into the narrowest of cement channels, but here the aim is very decidedly to keep visitors away, and the channel is lined on both sides not by peaceful walkways but by high, barbed-wire fences.

Until 1994, when the Border Patrol instigated "Operation Hold The Line" to halt the perceived flood of illegal immigrants from Mexico and beyond, El Paso had been notorious as one of the weakest links in the "Tortilla Curtain" between the United States and Mexico. Now it's a sulky, shame-faced kind of city, professing friendship for neighboring Ciudad Juárez while demonizing the mass of its inhabitants as would-be "wetbacks" to be corralled like cattle.

## Back in the USA

Coming back across the bridge from Ciudad Juárez, it's America, alright, but Mexico hasn't ended. In fact, save for the ghost-town feeling, it's really the same city as Juárez. The Mexican population of El Paso is large, and it's focused at the border. But the Latino presence is felt everywhere. It's said that English is spoken as widely as Spanish in Juárez; the statement is equally true in El Paso.

Due to its geographic and commercial situation, El Paso is an inexpensive city, but an unexciting one. Tourism is ultimately channeled to its environs and up to **Ranger Peak** in the Franklin Mountains. The **Tigua Indian Reservation**, a living pueblo of the oldest identifiable Indian tribe in Texas, is on the eastern edge of the city, while the **Ysleta Mission** (converted) is in the Ysleta neighborhood in western El Paso, between Zaragosa and Old Pueblo roads. And that's about it, apart from **Fort Bliss** in the northeast, the site of the largest Air Defense School in the "free world," which is also home to the **US Border Patrol Museum** (tel: 915-759-6060; closed Mon). So, after a brief nod and an *adios* to "old Mexico," it's time to cross over into that bright, shiny state, New Mexico.

Map on page 282

*Only a bridge over the Rio Grande separates El Paso, Texas and Mexico's Ciudad Juarez.*

**BELOW:** down Mexico way.

## NEW MEXICO

New Mexico is among the youngest of the United States (as the 47th to be admitted to the Union), but it has had one of the longest histories. At its northeastern edge, near Folsom, archaeologists have dug up spearheads at least 10,000 years old, and by the time the first Spanish conquistadores reached the valley of the Rio Grande, in 1540, the region held as many as 100 separate village communities – "pueblos" – each home to a distinct Native American tribe. The Spaniards named the infant colony New Mexico in the misplaced hope that it might yield similar treasures to the Aztec empire of Mexico.

By the late 16th century, the *Camino Real* (now US 85) extended along the Rio Grande from Mexico to Santa Fe, site of the oldest government building in north America and the oldest US capital. However, although New Mexico covered an area far greater than the modern state, including all of modern Arizona and much of Nevada, California, and Utah, until the Yankees arrived in 1846 it remained an impoverished provincial backwater, whose farmers had to battle against, not only the unforgiving desert environment, but also Navajo, Apache, and Comanche raiders.

Under American rule, New Mexico has attended to its somewhat mundane motto: *Crescit Eunde* ("It grows as it goes"). Railroading, ranching, and mining have all thrived on the state's rocky surface, warm valleys, and subterranean waters. A deliberate US policy during World War II of siting defense installations in remote land-locked locations has also brought unexpected dividends. It was in New Mexico that scientists developed and tested the first atomic bombs, and military facilities continue to play a major part in the state's economy. New Mexico is sparsely populated by approximately 1.3 million people, roughly 11 per sq. mile (4.2 per sq. km). Among its notable residents have been sworn enemies Pat Garrett and Billy the Kid, "king of the innkeepers" Conrad Hilton, novelist D. H. Lawrence, artist Georgia O'Keeffe and firefighting legend Smokey the Bear.

New Mexico promotes itself as "The Land of Enchantment." Its natural beauty and the mysteries of its landscape have captivated all who come here, from prehistoric Indians, via generations of Hispanics, to modern new-age tourists drawn to cities such as Santa Fe, Albuquerque, and Taos. Even little green men from outer space seem to love it here; supposedly drawn by the first signs of mankind's nuclear capability, they've been flocking to places such as Roswell ever since.

Exiting El Paso, US 54 east skirts the eastern slopes of the Franklin Mountains. As soon as you leave the city, you find yourself in an absolute wasteland; there are virtually no services in the entire 83-mile (134-km) stretch to Alamogordo and the Tularosa Valley. New Mexico arrives, with the minimum of ceremony, 10 miles (16 km) out of El Paso, at which point US 54 contracts to a two-lane undivided highway. These dusty plains appear totally uninhabited, but they're no stranger to modern man.

As you ride the gorge between the Organ Mountains that lie to the west and the Hueco Mountains that lie to the east, you will soon be passing through

**BELOW:** Harley-Davidson at the Aspenfest Motorcyle Rally held in Ruidoso, New Mexico.

the **Fort Bliss Military Reservation**, home of the **McGregor Missile Range**. Beyond that, you nick the edge of the **White Sands Missile Range**. Roadside signs warn of unexploded ammunition lying in the desert, and advise you not to leave the highway.

## A store that sells rocks

A barely perceptible wiggle in the road announces **Orogrande**, 46 miles (74 km) from El Paso, where the only distraction apart from two gas stations and a barbecue joint is a store that optimistically attempts to sell rocks. After all that emptiness, **Alamogordo** ❸ itself feels like a major metropolis, though a sojourn of any length soon reveals that there's not actually all that much behind the bonanza of billboards and signs lining the highway. A small but fascinating museum next to the visitor center displays artifacts allegedly made by the pygmy Indians who once inhabited the area. What's more certain is that Alamogordo was explored by ancestors of the Navajo and Apache before the Spanish passed through, naming it for its "fat" (*gordo*) cottonwood trees and eventually settling on the Tularosa River at La Luz.

The locale of the present-day town was left virtually untouched before two enterprising brothers from the East, C. B. and John A. Eddy, founded Alamogordo as a stop on their railroad line. Seduced by the forestland in the valley and its commercial potential as a rich source of lumber, the Eddys sold the railroad and settled down in Alamogordo to reap their riches from the indigenous resources. Alamogordo grew as a trade center, but the development of the White Sands Proving Ground and nearby Holloman Air Force Base radically recast the contours of the city. In the words of one local historian, "No longer was it a

Map
on page
282

*Local boy William H Bonney, otherwise known as Billy the Kid, looms large in these parts. Cattle rustler and killer, the Kid escaped capture several times before being gunned down, at the age of 21, by Sheriff Pat Garrett.*

**LEFT:** Billy the Kid gift shoppe.
**RIGHT:** the badge says it all.

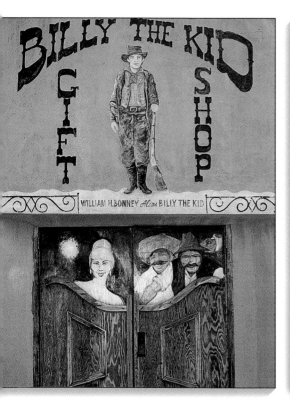

sleepy, peaceful land of *mañana* [tomorrow], but a hustling, bustling, fast-growing city." Still a trade and manufacturing center, Alamogordo is dominated by the high-tech weaponry community. It also harbors, however, a tribute to the peaceful uses of technology in the exploration of space, in the shape of the **Space Center** (tel: 505-437 2840; open daily), standing prominently on the foothills at the edge of the valley.

This well-conceived museum chronicles the international race for the stars, featuring a "Hall of Fame" of pioneers in space exploration, from early dreamers to the moon-walking astronauts of NASA's Apollo missions. After admiring space shuttle models, a lunar TV camera, and samples of foods brought aboard *Apollo* and *Skylab* missions (e.g., canned vanilla ice cream and dehydrated peach ambrosia), you can watch a video presentation of highlights from the *Apollo* 11, 12, and 14 moon landings.

## Land of many uses

Although attractions in Alamogordo proper are relatively sparse, oases of natural beauty abound in the Sacramento Mountains to the east. In summer, these well-wooded hills provide a welcome cool relief from the heat of the plains, attracting visitors from all over southeastern New Mexico and west Texas. In winter, when top-class skiing is on offer, the appeal is even more compelling. A scenic half-day's driving tour from Alamogordo begins by taking US 82 to **Cloudcroft**, 19 miles (31 km) northeast of Alamogordo. The highway swiftly climbs through scrubby reddish-tinged sandstone hills to reach the tree-covered slopes of the **Lincoln National Forest**.

**BELOW:**
White Sands
Missile Range.

As highway signs inform you, the US government sees a national forest as a "Land of Many Uses." They're not nearly so protected as national parks, so commercial logging, ranching, and even mining is often allowed. None of which mars the beauty of this particular stretch. Cloudcroft is an attractive little faux-Western town filled with rental cabins, snackeries, and souvenir stores, and there's good hiking in the hills nearby.

Just north of Cloudcroft is the southern edge of the **Mescalero Apache Indian Reservation**. A 28-mile (45-km) drive northward through the reservation on State 244 takes you through some delightful Alpine scenery, complete with shimmering little lakes and flower-filled meadows, where you're likely to see Apache cowboys riding the range. Any notions you may have of Native American reservations as desolate or depressing places will soon be shattered.

The Mescalero are in fact prosperous entrepreneurs; while parts of the reservation are closed to outsiders, the tribe operates some very successful commercial enterprises on adjoining lands.

These include the region's grand resort hotel, the **Inn of the Mountain Gods**, which shares its lovely lakeside setting with a yet greater money-spinner, the glitzy **Casino Apache**. Even more incongruous is the tribe's luxury winter-sports venue, **Ski Apache**. The ski resort is set above the fast-growing mountain town of **Ruidoso**, which is home to the Ruidoso Downs racetrack and a newer year-round attraction, the

**Museum of the Horse**. From Ruidoso, US 70 drops back down to the Tularosa Valley by way of the principal reservation community, **Mescalero**, to reach Alamogordo in 46 miles (74 km).

Map on page 282

## Blinding white gypsum

Taking the optional detour described above, you'll enjoy long-distance views of the most unique and spectacular feature of the region. Glimpsed at first as a dazzling white line on the western horizon, **White Sands National Monument** ③ is located 15 miles (24 km) southwest of Alamogordo. This stunning 144,458-acre (58,460-hectare) expanse of gypsum sand dunes is carved out of the otherwise off-limits White Sands Missile Range. The only access road, US 70–82, is regularly closed for up to two hours at a time so the military personnel can drive their strange top-secret cargoes along it in peace; enquire at local visitor centers before you set off. As you approach White Sands, jets no doubt roaring overhead, the glowing dunes rise from the base of the San Andreas Mountains. Upon arrival, stop at the information center for some background on the formation of the dunes and on their stubborn inhabitants.

Gypsum is one of the most common compounds found on earth, but it's rarely seen on the surface because it dissolves readily in water. Surface sand elsewhere is almost always composed of quartz. The Tularosa Basin, however, is all but unique in having a climate dry enough, and winds strong enough, to produce the rare, surreal dunes of powdered gypsum crystal.

White Sands is breathtaking at any time of day, but especially so toward sunset. In the middle of the day, the sands are a beautiful, blinding, pure white, reflecting so strongly they sting the naked eye. As you clamber over the dunes,

*Would-be cowboys should visit the Museum of the Horse in Ruidoso.*

**BELOW:** White Sands National Monument.

occasionally marked by the pawprints of nocturnal wanderers, you should periodically remove your sunglasses to appreciate the hallucinatory expanse fully. As the afternoon cedes to evening, the sands begin to refract the light, breaking it down into a rainbow. The park is open until 10pm, and with care you might observe some of the 500 different animals that populate the dunes, from coyotes and roadrunners to owls and skunks. There is also a sparse scattering of beautiful plant life, including the hedgehog cactus with its brilliant red flowers.

A paved driveway, equipped with spacious parking and picnicking areas, loops through the dunes. The deeper it penetrates into the heart of White Sands, however, the more liable the road surface is to be obscured by drifts of gypsum sand. The effect is both disorienting and remarkable.

Concealed amid the roadless wastes to the north, the **Trinity Site** is the awesome crater that was created in July 1945, when the United States detonated the first atomic bomb. Public access to this sobering site is only permitted on the first Saturdays in April and October, when convoys of vehicles set off from an inconspicuous gateway north of Alamogordo. Check with the town's visitor center for details.

## The Wild West

US 70–82 slowly but surely rises out of the Tularosa Valley as you continue west toward Las Cruces. For almost 30 miles (48 km), as you drive in a dead straight line towards the sheer wall of the San Andreas Range, it seems impossible that there could be any way through these mottled peaks. Eventually, the highway jinks to the right and climbs to reach its apex at the **San Augustine Pass**, 5,720 feet (1,700 meters) high and overlooking the valley that holds Organ and, beyond it, Las Cruces. After taking the pass, you plunge down an exhilarating 3-mile (5-km) slope to find yourself back in the beautiful low valley of the Rio Grande, where greens and browns evolve through shades and mixtures below the pearly blue peaks in the distance.

The route briefly engages **Las Cruces** before hooking into I-10 to Deming. Las Cruces is unremarkable; in fact, it's downright ugly. Nevertheless, a degree of historic significance lies buried beneath the unrelenting mallscape; human occupation of the Mesilla Valley has been shown to date back to the 4th century. Under Spanish rule, the valley was forever liable to the depredations of Apache raiders. Las Cruces – "the crosses" – acquired its name in 1830, after a caravan of travelers coming from Taos were ambushed and slaughtered, and white crosses were erected to mark their graves.

The town of **La Mesilla** ㊱, a short drive from downtown Las Cruces on State 28 and State 292 (Motel Boulevard), has made greater efforts at historical preservation. Its restored **Plaza**, dominated by its old gazebo, offers a real taste of the Wild West. This was where the Gadsden Purchase was sealed in 1854, establishing the current boundaries of Mexico and the United States, while a gift store in one corner was originally the courthouse where the notorious outlaw Billy the Kid was tried and sentenced to hang for murder in 1881. The Kid managed to escape before his hanging, but subsequently met his maker at the hands of Pat Garrett, who was in turn murdered near Las Cruces in 1908. Crafts and curios merchants have now taken over most of the plaza, selling rugs and wind chimes, Indian jewelery and ceramic ornaments, though the "Emerald Isle" Irish shop strikes a discordant note. At least there's still room for the historic **Double Eagle Restaurant**, which is not only attractive but has tasty food.

## Across the Great Divide

A short distance out of Las Cruces on I-10 west, a double ribbon of landscaped orchards lines the narrow Rio Grande, which flows here from its source in Colorado by way of Santa Fe and Albuquerque. Beyond the shallow sandy ridge on the far side, the highway levels out to cross the windblown chapparal of Luna County, where more and more specimens of the ostrich-like state plant, the yucca, scrutinize travelers as they make their way westward. From here to the Arizona state line, freeway exits are commonly marked with frontier-style outlets for supposedly characteristic goods. Behind false façades spring a trading post, Wild West town, or teepee where moccasins, cactus jelly, and plant candy are available to tourists.

Fifty-six miles (90 km) out of Las Cruces is **Deming ③**, which is enriched by four short mountain ranges: the **Florida Mountains** to the southeast, the **Little Floridas** to the east, the **Tres Hermanas** to the south, and **Cooks Range** to the north. Cooks Range is the largest of these, and its highest point – Cooks Peak, about 8,400 feet (2,560 meters) in elevation – commands an impressive vista. The Cooks Range was once in the heart of Apache lands and served as an

Map on page 282

*Billy the Kid's tombstone in Fort Sumner, New Mexico.*

**BELOW:** the historic Double Eagle Restaurant in La Mesilla, NM.

ideal lookout. Before there was Deming, there was New Chicago, an "end of the track" railroad town with a supply of water – crucial to locomotives – in the subterranean **Mimbres River**. Relocated 10 miles (16 km) west of its present site, Deming was of great strategic importance to railroad magnate Charles Crocker, who joined his Southern Pacific line to the Santa Fe Railroad at the site. Early settlers included soldiers, professionals, merchants, and a large population of gunmen who dominated local affairs until the town was "cleaned up" in 1883. There's a fine museum of local history and Mimbres crafts located in central Deming in the former **National Guard Armory** (1916). One exhibit recreates frontier life, which, in the words of one guide, was "as you can see just by looking around, not easy here. This wasn't a luxury place." Today, Deming is an easy-going, temperate city of about 10,000 where everybody seems to know everyone else, folks drive and walk slowly, and shade trees throw up their defenses against the sun.

Deming has become popular as a retirement settlement because of its dry climate, 98 percent sunshine and relatively mild temperatures. Agriculture, however, remains a real struggle. As you look out across the valley, it's not unusual to see up to a dozen separate "dust devils"– swirling little clouds of desert detritus – spinning across the barren fields.

## Relics of the Mimbres

Rather than stay on dreary I-10 for the 60 miles (97 km) west to Lordsburg, it makes sense to veer northward on US 180 towards the Gila Mountains. Between the 10th and 12th centuries, this region was roamed by the Mimbres Indians, a peaceful people noted for their exquisite ceramics. Author J.W. Fewkes has claimed that "no Southwestern pottery, ancient or modern, surpasses that of the Mimbres; and its naturalistic figures are unexcelled in any pottery from prehistoric America."

The Mimbres take their name from the Mimbres river, which at lower elevations remains a bone-dry sandy wash for much of the year. US 180 crosses it repeatedly *en route* to **Silver City**, 53 miles (85 km) out of Deming. This rough-and-tumble Wild West settlement has successively been the base for Indian turquoise miners, Hispanic silver miners, and modern copper conglomerates. Billy the Kid lived here as a child, but most of the town he knew was wiped out by a cataclysmic flood in 1895.

The **Western New Mexico University Museum** (tel: 505-538 6386; open daily), 12th and Alabama streets, holds the world's finest collection of Mimbres pottery, decorated with elegant animal designs and abstract patterns. They're considered priceless by collectors, not least because perfect specimens are all but unknown. Each pot is thought to have belonged to a single individual, and to have been buried with its owner, having first had a symbolic "kill hole" punched through its base.

With half a day to spare, it's well worth taking a laborious 88-mile (142-km) round-trip drive up into the Gila Mountains. The exhilarating scenery *en route* culminates at the **Gila Cliff Dwellings National**

**BELOW:**
Silver City has historically been the base for Indian turquoise miners and Hispanic silver miners.

Monument , where intact adobe dwellings used by the Mimbres people or their immediate successors still nestle in caves above the Gila River. Many centuries later, around 1829, this beautiful and remote spot was also the birthplace of legendary Apache leader Geronimo.

State 90 runs 44 miles (69 km) southwest from Silver City to rejoin I-10 at **Lordsburg**. Along the way, it surmounts the Continental Divide, then descends slowly and gloriously to the vast sagebrush sea in which Lordsburg seems to float alone. The largest settlement in Hidalgo County, Lordsburg sprawls languidly beside the interstate and the Southern Pacific railroad tracks at the northern edge of the Pyramid Mountains. The train tracks themselves tell the story of modern Lordsburg, which eventually eclipsed neighboring **Shakespeare**. Shakespeare had been a stop on the great Butterfield Stagecoach Line run by the post office from St Louis, Missouri, to San Francisco, California, at the time Charles Crocker laid his railroad tracks.

## This town's got ghosts

Today, Shakespeare is a ghost town, privately preserved in its current state of decay after being abandoned for more profitable pastures. (Aside from the glaring Motel Drive, you might think Lordsburg is the ghost town.) Shakespeare, a short drive south on Main Street from Lordsburg, is the genuine item, although it *is* inhabited. As a rule, residents and owners Rita and Janaloo Hill open up the town for two weekends each month, conducting anecdote-peppered tours at 10am and 2pm on Saturday and Sunday. Several notable characters are known to have graced the dining room of its **Stratford Hotel**, including an escapee from Silver City jail: Billy the Kid. ❏

*Near the town of Shakespeare is a cemetery that claims to be the oldest of its kind in the Southwest. According to a handpainted sign, one of its "residents" is the outlaw Sandy King, convicted of being a "damned nuisance" and hung by committee.*

**BELOW:** Gila Cliff Dwellings National Monument, NM.

# SOUTHERN ARIZONA TO SAN DIEGO

Map on page 282

*From its ponderosa pine forests and saguaro-studded deserts to modern cities and ancient reservations, this part of the Southwest has made the most of its gifts*

To most English speakers, the word "Arizona" suggests one image: aridity. Yes, water is indeed precious here – "Arizona's most precious resource, next to its people" – but the name has nothing to do with lack of water. It is in fact derived from a far less familiar tongue – either from the Pima Indian word for "little spring place," or from the Basque *arritza onac*, meaning "valuable rocky places." The latter perhaps rings truer, as Arizona's first industry was silver mining.

But there *are* "little spring places" in Arizona, as well as just about every climatic, topographic, and ecological variant known to America. From its ponderosa pine forests and saguaro-studded deserts to modern cities and reservations unchanged since ancient times, exquisite Arizona has made the most of its natural gifts.

Arizona would not be what it is today, however, without irrigation and air conditioning. Technology has tamed the desert, although a great deal of arid land remains untouched. Though beautiful, the desert can be unbearable in the summer. Winter is "the season" in most parts of Arizona, particularly in the south and west, although prices tend to rise, also.

**LEFT:** Yaqui deer dancer; Yaquis live in the Phoenix and Tucson areas. **BELOW:** chilis are local staples.

## Stone spirirts

Leaving Lordsburg, New Mexico on Interstate 10, there's one final 20-mile (32-km) stretch of desiccated grassland to cross before you reach the Arizona state line. The serried ranks of mountains that then confront you on the western horizon were in the 19th century the stronghold of the Chiricahua Apache, whose chief, Cochise, memorably declared "When I was young I walked all over this country, east and west, and saw no other people than the Apaches."

Two sites indelibly associated with the tragic confrontation between the Apache and the US Army stand just inside the border: Fort Bowie and Chiricahua National Monument. Both can be reached by taking exit 366 from I-10 at the run-down little pitstop of Bowie, then heading south on Apache Pass Road. For its first 3 miles (5 km), this skirts some meticulously groomed pistachio orchards, but it then climbs through much scrubbier ranching country, to become an unpaved but well-maintained gravel road 12 miles (19 km) out of Bowie.

Soon after that, a small parking lot marks the start of the wonderful hiking trail up to **Fort Bowie** (tel: 520-647-2500; open daily). Built in 186 following two bloody clashes between the Route Army and the Chiricahua, the fort was the headquarters for the next

25 years of a campaign that eventually drove the Apache from this region altogether. As you walk the 3 miles (5 km) up to its evocative ruined adobe walls, you seem at first to be in a dry, bowl-shaped depression entirely ringed by mountains. Eventually however you come to tranquil, well-wooded Apache Spring, teeming with wildlife, which made this spot so precious to the Apache, and then to the fort, commanding wonderful views out across the valley below.

## Stacks of rocks

Another 8 miles (13 km) of easy driving beyond the parking lot, the unpaved road reaches State 186. Head west from here to I-10 if you're in a hurry to reach Tombstone, by way of Willcox and Benson, but **Chiricahua National Monument** ㊴ (tel: 520-824-3560; open daily) lies a mere 14 miles (23 km) east. Chiricahua may be a little off the beaten track, but it's a magnificent spot, ideal for hiking, camping, and scenic drives. From the informative visitor center close to the park entrance, Bonita Canyon Drive climbs to an elevation of 6,870 feet (2,100 meters). All the way up, alarmingly balanced stacks of rock loom precariously above the road, while the viewpoint at the top surveys a panorama of bizarrely shaped stone towers and columns. This unique landscape has taken shape over a period of 27 million years, as deposits of ash left by volcanic eruptions have been eroded by water, wind, and ice. Benefitting from twice the rainfall received by the yellowed, dusty plains and gorges below, the Chiricahua highlands provide a rich environment for juniper, fir, piñon, yucca, oak, cypress, and sycamore, and harbor many rare species of birds and animals. This petrified maelstrom can be explored along several well-marked hiking trails; an easy half-hour stroll along **Echo Canyon Trail**, for example, will take you through a forest of weird formations.

The most direct route between Chiricahua and Tombstone is to thread your way steadily westwards on State 181, which has the advantage of passing the rattlesnake craft shops, saloons, and crumbling buildings on the main drag of an old copper-mining town called **Gleeson**. Just outside of town on the opposite side of a curvy hillside, the town of **Tombstone** ㊵ can be seen shining in the distance.

## Tales from Tombstone

Tombstone was whimsically named by founder Edward Schieffelin after he was advised that the only thing he would find on his mad hunt for silver would be exactly that, his own tombstone. The most famous of "Wild West" mining towns, Tombstone did indeed sit in the heart of lands rich in silver. Its dizzying growth and wealth in the early 1880s attracted more than its share of troublemakers, but Tombstone's decline was every bit as precipitous. Its main silver mine was flooded in 1886, and the town has barely changed since then. Today it's a tacky but undeniably endearing tourist trap, happy to provide visitors with a sanitized and glamorized taste of the lawless days of the Wild West.

Tombstone might well be forgotten now had it not played host to the quintessential frontier "showdown" at the **OK Corral**, which pitted Wyatt Earp,

**BELOW:** real-life victims of the OK Corral shootout are buried in Tombstone's Boothill Cemetery.

his brothers, and the consumptive dentist Doc Holliday against the Clanton and McLaury brothers. The latter were at the forefront of a "cowboy" gang that allegedly engineered a series of stagecoach robberies, while the Earps – themselves no angels – represented "establishment" Tombstone. Political and personal clashes culminated in the legendary, bloody "Shootout at the OK Corral" on October 26, 1881, which left three men dead.

Map on page 282

## The OK Corral

The OK Corral still stands on Allen Street, preserved as it looked on the fateful day. Mannequins of the various participants pose in its yard, guns in hand, despite the general agreement of historians that the shootout in fact took place on neighboring Fremont Street. Alongside, the former studio of Wild West photographer Camillus Fly showcases some of his finest work, including shots of Apache warrior Geronimo. In season, as many as three rival groups of gunfighters roam the streets of Tombstone looking for customers for their staged gunfights; so far, however, there's been no showdown to thin their ranks. Stagecoaches clatter evocatively past landmarks like the Bird Cage Theatre and Tombstone Courthouse, as well as some very ritzy galleries of Western art. The real-life victims of the shootout rest in **Boothill Cemetery** at the edge of town, on a dusty hillside where the peace of their slumbers is disturbed by loudspeakers concealed amid the boulders that play mournful country music.

Another 24 miles (38 km) south of Tombstone on State 80, the more sedate but equally attractive former mining town of **Bisbee** squeezes into a cleft in the Dragoon Mountains. Those of its Victorian mansions that don't house comfortable hotels and B&Bs are instead home to intriguing little crafts and antique

*Wyatt Earp, one of his brothers, and Doc Holliday were the "good guys" in the OK Corral saga.*

**BELOW:** Tombstone storefront.

stores. The one drawback is having to negotiate all the steep stairways that connect streets at widely varying elevations.

From Bisbee, you can either retrace your steps along State 80 (through Tombstone) or take State 90 (which initially heads west and then takes a jog north in Sierra Vista) to meet up with I-10 at **Benson**. Whichever way you choose, a worthy stop before you head off down the highway is a recent Arizona attraction: **Kartchner Caverns State Park**, just 9 miles (14 km) south of I-10 off of State 90. Already hailed by many to be the best of Arizona's state parks, its focal point is the recently discovered (1974) "living" cavern – its formations inside are still growing – with its miles of surveyed passages.

Tours are given daily, but numbers are limited so as to protect the cave's environment, so it is necessary to book ahead (tel: 520-586-2283). In addition to the cave, there is a world-class Discovery Center, 5 miles (8 km) of hiking trails, a picnic area and campground, and a hummingbird garden.

## Tucson

From Benson there are another 43 miles (69 km) to go before you reach the city of **Tucson** ㊶ (pronounced *too-sawn*) to the west. Tucson is a classic sprawling "boom" city, which has had so much room to expand in the prosperous years since World War II that it has been able to do so without destroying the evidence of its 18th-century Hispanic origins. Having been founded in 1776, it's exactly the same age as the United States, though it only passed into American hands with the Gadsden Purchase of 1854.

Downtown Tucson still centers on the narrow area that was originally contained with the adobe walls of the Spanish *presidio*. This delightfully spacious

**BELOW:** vivid video shop, Tucson.

area is now dotted with artisans' shops, cafés, several good shade trees, and some extremely interesting architecture, anchored by **St Augustine Cathedral,** built in 1897. An attraction for tourists here is the **Tucson Museum of Art** (tel: 520-624-2333; open daily), whose collection concentrates especially on pre- and post-Colonial Mexican artifacts.

Map on page 282

## Emblem of the West

As a whole, however, Tucson is a somewhat formless city, far too large to explore on foot, whose appeal lies less in its modern buildings than in the fantastic scenery that surrounds it. **Saguaro National Park** occupies two separate tracts of land to either side of the city proper. As its name suggests, it was established to protect dramatic expanses of multi-armed saguaro (pronounced sah-WA-row) cacti. Although it's often considered emblematic of the Wild West, the saguaro – which can live for 200 years, and grow to the height of 50 feet (16 meters) – is in fact a native of the Sonoran Desert, only a small portion of which extends into Arizona from Mexico. Tucson is thus one of the few places in the US where you can see this fascinating cactus. The western segment of the park, the **Tucson Mountain District,** holds an extraordinary "forest" of towering saguaros, which take on an other-worldly magnificence at sunset.

*Car advertising a cowboy museum, Arizona.*

Nearby, the **Arizona-Sonora Desert Museum** (tel: 520-883-2702; open daily) holds showpiece gardens of cacti and desert plants of all kinds, as well as desert mammals from prairie dogs to mountain lions. Its real highlights, however, are its walk-through aviaries alive with darting, iridescent hummingbirds.

The Mexican border at Nogales, 100 miles (160 km) south of Tucson, is perhaps too much of a diversion for travelers heading west, but no one should visit

**BELOW:** reflection of St Augustine Cathedral, Tucson.

**TIP**

October is the month for the Tucson Heritage Experience Festival, a melange of dance, music, and good food.

Tucson without venturing at least a short distance down the **Mission Trail** that served as the city's original lifeline. Just 9 miles (14 km) out of Downtown, the **Mission San Xavier del Bac** (tel: 520-294-2624; open daily) is renowned as the most beautiful of all the Spanish missions in North America. It was established at the end of the 17th century near the village of Bac ("where the water emerges"), inhabited by a people the Spanish called the Pima – who are now known by the name they call themselves, Tohono O'odham. Its showpiece, the ornate whitewashed mission church, dates from around 1783. Both its resplendent façade and its imposing baroque interior have recently been restored to their full glory by the Tohono O'odham, working with experts from the Vatican; its soubriquet of "Sistine Chapel of the Southwest" has never seemed appropriate. Especially on Sunday mornings, the windswept, cactus-studded plaza in front throngs with tourists and Indians intently studying each other. As one O'odham writer put it, "sometimes just 'hanging out' in front of the mission and looking at the tourists is a good way to pass the time."

## Missions and missiles

There's another wonderful mission church, this time abandoned in ruins, at **Tumacácori National Monument**, 53 miles (85 km) south. Much closer at hand, however, is a relic from more recent times. The **Titan Missile Museum** (tel: 520-625-7736; open daily Nov–Apr, Wed–Sun May–Oct), near Green Valley 16 miles (25 km) south of San Xavier, preserves the only one of the 27 US Titan Missile II sites not to have been dismantled at the end of the Cold War. In the 20 years between going into operation in July, 1963 and being decommissioned in November, 1982, it held two missiles, capable of being fired over

**BELOW:**

Mission San Xavier del Bac is called the "Sistine Chapel of the Southwest."

5,000 miles (8,000 km) in less than 20 minutes. Gung-ho guides lead equally gung-ho tour parties down into the underground silo and through subterranean passages to reach its control room, which was designed to remain functional even in the event of a direct nuclear hit on the surface above. What they can't tell you, however, is where the missiles were aimed; each was trained on a specific, unchanged target for all its active life, but that information remains Top Secret. The whole installation is eerie and unsettling, and nowhere more so than its restrooms, which feature prominent "watch for rattlesnakes" signs.

## Onward to Mars

For lovers of the truly bizarre, the Tucson area has one final, unmissable curiosity to offer: **Biosphere 2** (tel: 800-828-2462; open daily), just outside **Oracle**, 32 miles (48 km) north of the city on State 77. Completed in 1991, Biosphere 2 was designed as an hermetically sealed replica of Biosphere 1 – the planet Earth – albeit cunningly disguised as a giant greenhouse. Its aim was nothing less than to pave the way for the colonization of Mars. To that end, a group of ex-actors and scientists were locked into it for two full years, to see whether they could survive in a closed and self-sufficient environment. Detractors were quick to point out the obvious flaws in the experiment, such as the fact that it had an external power source, and gleefully noted such ironies as the chopping down of the "rainforest" inside the capsule to grow more crops.

To counter those criticisms, Biosphere 2 has scaled down its ambitions; now operated by Columbia University, it holds no permanent residents, and is used for more closely controled scientific programs. All the publicity, however, has turned it into a major tourist attraction. Tours are inevitably less exciting now

**BELOW:**
Biosphere 2, a hermetically sealed environment, was home to ex-actors and scientists for two years.

that there are no "Biospherians" to be glimpsed through the windows, but by way of compensation you can at least go inside the huge and oddly beautiful structure, including its luxurious living quarters.

## The Apache Trail

The most direct route between Tucson and Phoenix is I-10, on which the long, flat 100-mile (160-km) drive takes well under two hours. The main visual distraction along the way, **Picacho Peak**, looks like a double-pronged molar tooth as it looms up 30 miles (48 km) out of Tucson, but then resolves into two separate sharp fangs. At its foot, the **Rooster Cogburn Ostrich Farm** just off the highway provides an unexpected photo opportunity, selling bags of seed that you can feed to the aggressive and ungainly birds, as well as feather dusters and colossal eggs.

Alternatively, State 79 sets off from close to Biosphere 2 to follow a parallel and similar course that ends up by approaching Phoenix from the east rather than the south. Known as the **Pinal Pioneer Parkway**, it's lush with native vegetation, from the prickly pear and saguaro cactus to the catclaw and mesquite tree.

It eventually brings you to **Apache Junction**, due east of central Phoenix, which is the start of the **Apache Trail**. This modern road was constructed in 1905 to provide access to **Theodore Roosevelt Dam ㊷**, the first of the great dams of the West, built to quench the ever-growing thirst of nearby Phoenix. Named the Apache Trail in the hope of encouraging tourism, it was hailed by President Teddy Roosevelt, when he dedicated the dam in 1911, as combining "the grandeur of the Alps, the glory of the Rockies, and the magnificence of the Grand Canyon." Although the president made a wide-sweeping overstatement, it is indeed a ravishing drive.

Shortly after leaving Apache Junction, the Apache Trail passes the enjoyably (albeit touristy) ramshackle **Goldfield Ghost Town**, where you can take horse or jeep rides amid the abandoned mine machinery and falsefront stores, or simply pick up a snack at the bakery. Beyond that comes your first clear sighting of the **Superstition Mountains**. The Spanish called these peaks the "Mountains of Foam" because of their effusive volcanic ridges, but they're best known for the legends that surround the Dutch prospector Jacob Walz. He seems to have struck a huge lode of gold in the Superstitions in the late 19th century, but no one who followed him on his expeditions was ever seen again, and the "Lost Dutchman Mine" remains hidden to this day. The Superstition Mountains have taken the life of many an overly curious fortune-seeker.

The Apache Trail cuts into **Tonto National Forest**, where vistas and foot trails skirt the highway. The fun really begins as it winds its narrow way into the highlands. Drivers beware: you'll have to keep your eyes more on the road than the alpine rises, glorious vistas, and lush canyons. Saguaros and mesquite, dry riverbeds, and wave upon wave of mountain ridges follow a scenic overlook of the **Canyon River**. When you descend into the valley, pull up and strip down, because the blue waters are irresistible.

The trail is well-paved for the 18 miles (29 km) up

*Dutch prospector Jacob Walz allegedly struck a lode of gold in the Superstition Mountains, but no one from his mining expedition was ever seen again; the Lost Dutchman Mine remains hidden to this day.*

**BELOW:** learning the ropes at an Arizona pow-wow.

to **Tortilla Flat**, a required stop for lovers of desert lore and witty western character. The essence of Tortilla Flat is sold in two forms: a postcard reading *Tortilla Flat/Pop. 6/30 Miles from Water/2 Feet from Hell!*; and the hokey cans of Jack Rabbit Milk, "a balanced diet for unbalanced people." One of the six residents remarks: "Oh, it works wonders. Especially that vitamin P."

Map on page 282

## Best chili in the West

A hotel, post office, café/restaurant, gift shop, riding stable, curio shop, a legend, and a marvelous view – Tortilla Flat is a great place to stop for "the best chili in the West" and a "Howdy" from "the friendliest town in America." Admire the hundreds of dollar-bills tacked under business cards on the ceiling and walls of the café before you exit back to the sun-drenched desert. Roosevelt Dam lies another 30 miles (48 km) up the precipitous but passable dirt road beyond Tortilla Flat. Above and behind it spreads **Roosevelt Lake**, the reservoir it created. The best views are from a steep hiking trail in **Tonto National Monument**, just west of the dam on State 88.

That short but grueling hike culminates in a "cliff-dwelling" once occupied by the Salado Indians, who disappeared from this area before the Apache arrived. Retrack State 88 back into the valley. You'll pass through two unique suburbs, as State 88 becomes Main Street in Mesa, then Apache Boulevard in Tempe. **Mesa** contains Arizona's largest Mormon community and you'll pass by the beautiful **Latter Day Saint Temple**. Things change as you pass into **Tempe**, home of Arizona State University, and its young student population (over 40,000). Turning left on University, you'll come to I-10, which quickly whisks you into the heart of **Phoenix ㊸** *(see page 308)*.

**BELOW:** Wishing Shine, El Tiradito.

# PHOENIX:
# VALLEY OF THE SUN

*Business is booming in Phoenix, with plenty of industry, tourism, and golf courses. Just be sure to come in winter*

**P**hoenix may not have had any real *ashes* to rise from, but its founders were inspired by the knowledge that the merciless heat of the Salt River Valley had been overcome before. Between approximately 1100 and 1450, the Hohokam people successfully irrigated this region by means of over 300 miles (480 km) of canals, while Jack Swilling, in 1867, established modern Phoenix by simply re-digging the waterways.

In World War II the military, utilizing the desert for aviation training, revolutionized Phoenician life further with air-conditioning. Suddenly, life in the great hot desert became a year-round possibility, and the great migra-

tion was on. Now, Phoenix, a city of nearly 3 million people, is booming.

It's hard not to impressed by the city's setting. To the east soar the massive Four Peaks and Superstition Mountains, while the Sierra Estrella rides the southeast horizon. Hemming in the city north and south are lower mountain ranges, framing Camelback Mountain. All of these make for excellent day-hikes, and provide the visitor with an opportunity to witness the beauty (and silence) of the Sonoran desert.

But beware: the average high temperature June through August is 103°F (39°C); May and September aren't much better. Peak tourist season is the winter, when daily maximum temperatures hover around 70°F (21°C) and the valley's resorts and 190 golf courses fill up with tourists.

Phoenix is easily divided into urban districts. Downtown holds the skyscrapers, and the modern Arizona Center mall, home to the city's main visitor center. Once lacking a strong downtown character, Phoenix invested considerable energy in locating museums and cultural venues in the city center.

Heritage Square (tel: 602-262-5029; open Tues–Sun), just east of the Civic Plaza, remains from the city's Victorian days and forms part of Downtown's Heritage and Science Park. Rosson House, a striking red Victorian home built in 1895, stands out from the square's 11 buildings.

The Phoenix Museum of History (tel: 602-253-2734; open daily), with interactive exhibits of the city's development, and the Arizona Science Center (tel: 602-716-2000; open daily), a $50-million hands-on funhouse of science, embellished with a planetarium, attract the scientific and the simply curious to Heritage Square.

The beautifully designed and organized Heard Museum (tel: 602-252-8848; open daily), is near Downtown at 22 East Monte Vista Road. The Heard focuses on Native American arts and crafts, both ancient and modern. Extensive galleries cover the long-vanished Anasazi, Hohokam, and Mogollon groups as well as the still-thriving Navajo and Apache tribes. Former Republican senator Barry Goldwater gathered and donated the exquisite and fascinating collection of Hopi *kachina* dolls. The museum complex is worth visiting in its own right, with its older structures arrayed around a quiet courtyard planted with orange trees which manage to blend seamlessly in with the newer state-of-the-art facilities.

If you see nothing else, visit the Arizona Biltmore Hotel (tel: 602-955-6600) at 24th Street and Missouri, 5 miles (8 km) northeast of Heritage Park. Phoenix owes the arrival of the renowned American architect Frank Lloyd Wright to this hotel. Built in 1929, Albert Chase McArthur, a former student of Wright, originally designed the building, but found himself in trouble and summoned the master for help.

Wright probably gave more help than required, for the hotel is a delightful masterpiece from Wright's middle period. Gutted by fire in 1973, refurbished furniture and textile designs from all periods of Wright's career now decorate the interior.

Wright stayed on in Phoenix to found his architectural school and residence, Taliesin West (tel: 602-860-2700; open daily), hidden in the desert beyond the upscale suburb of Scottsdale, in the northeast.

Wright intended the buildings and facilities to be an ongoing, hands-on educational exercise for architectural and design students. A variety of different tours give visitors an insight into Wright's visionary architectural style, as well as the facility's interesting "apprentice" program.

Scottsdale is known for its abundance of luxury resorts, such as the ravishing Phoenician at the foot of Camelback Mountain, which caters to travelers visiting Arizona for sun and sport rather than pure scenery. Scottsdale also spawned some swish shopping malls, like Fashion Square, while its "Hometown USA" central streets are, in fact, filled with expensive galleries of so-called Western Art.

At the southern end of Scottsdale lies the Phoenix Zoo (tel: 602-273-1341) as well as the compelling Desert Botanical Gardens (tel:

602-941-1225; open daily). The arid gardens located in Papago Park display plants from the world's deserts, including half the known species of cactus. The excellent landscaping, and the exotic power of these acres cannot fail to impress.

South of the zoo and gardens lies Tempe. Home of Arizona State University and an artificial lake under a picturesque, old (but still in use) railroad bridge, Tempe is perhaps the most attractive of all of Phoenix's areas, and definitely the most self-contained. The city's active nightlife centers on Mill Avenue, which is within easy walking distance of both the hotels and the lake. ❑

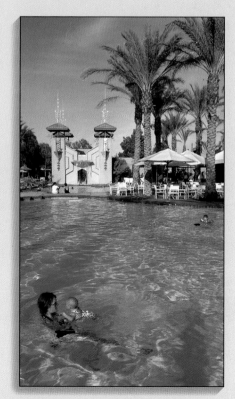

**LEFT:** Frank Lloyd Wright fell in love with the desert and moved here in 1937; a view of the skyscrapers in downtown Phoenix.
**RIGHT:** Hopi doll from the Heard Museum; Frank Lloyd Wright's home and studio, Taliesin West; the pool area of the architect's Biltmore Hotel.

## PHOENIX TO SAN DIEGO

The 150 miles (240 km) between Phoenix and the Colorado River, which marks the border with California, include some of the bleakest desert terrain in the entire Southwest. Taking the southern route to San Diego, you have a choice between sticking with I-10 as far as Quartzsite and then changing to US 95 south, or dropping south much earlier, to meet I-8 at Gila Bend. Either way, your final destination in Arizona will be the state's third largest city, Yuma, which is even hotter than Phoenix and Tucson.

**Quartzsite** is only really worth visiting if you're passing through in January or February, when up to 750,000 sun-seeking, northern "snowbirds" (most in RVs) descend on the town for a sort of mineralists' convention – a huge, open-air "flea market" for seekers and sellers of precious, semi-precious, and not-under-any-circumstances-even-slightly-precious stones and gems of various shapes and sizes. In a miracle on a par with the loaves and the fishes, Quartzsite's three motels and half-dozen restaurants somehow cope with this rock-hungry throng of oldsters.

Otherwise, you'd do better to turn off I-10 25 miles (40 km) west from Phoenix, and take State 85 down to the I-8 truckstop of **Gila Bend.** (For that matter, if you're in a hurry to get to the beach from Tucson, I-8 enables you to bypass Phoenix altogether.) Named, logically enough, for its location on a big bend in the Gila River, Gila Bend holds a predictable array of fast-food restaurants and motels, plus one outstanding exception. The **Best Western Space Age Lodge** is a marvelous 1950s-style folly, kitted out with kitsch Sputnik-shaped neon signs. Its **Outer Limits Coffee Shop**, which features a dazzling lunar-exploration mural, is well worth a stop for a bite to eat. The visitor center nearby, which doubles as a museum of local history, will confirm your suspicions that not a lot happens in Gila Bend.

**BELOW:** tarantula: a creature of the desert.

Signs on the interstate near Gila Bend warn that this is a "Blowing Dust Area," while bridges repeatedly cross "rivers" that are in truth little more than scrubby strips of sand. Somehow, however, **Dateland** ⓪, 50 miles (80 km) west of Gila Bend, manages to grow a bumper annual crop of dates. If you're desperate for a diversion, stop for a date shake or whatever other date-related product may strike your fancy in Dateland's solitary diner.

### The Devil's road

Surprisingly soon after you leave Dateland, you begin to be aware that you're approaching **Yuma** ⓺. The city avenues are numbered a mile apart, corresponding to the signs on the interstate that count the mileage down to California, and thus you pass an Avenue 51E that's a full 50 miles (80 km) east of downtown Yuma. In reality, Yuma is large, but it's not *that* large. There's still a long way to go, including the final climb over the ridge of the Gila Mountains and descent into the Colorado River Valley, before there's any sign of life. That is, apart from the low-flying jets that screech overhead. Southwest Arizona is another proving ground for the US military, and the latest top-secret warplanes are constantly being tested above the barren desert that lies between I-8 and the Mexican border. It has to be admitted that even most Arizonans roar with laughter at the very notion of anyone choosing to go to Yuma. Combine its somewhat shame-faced claim to be the hottest place on earth with its long-standing reputation as one of the worst hell-holes in the Wild West, and it makes an unlikely tourist destination. When Padre Eusebio Kino, the most tireless of all Spanish missionaries to the American Southwest, opened a trail in 1699 from Sonoita, Mexico, to what is now Yuma, he called the trail *El Camino del Diablo* – the Devil's Road. It seemingly led straight into the inferno. Yuma smolders to this day, but it's been tamed by the air conditioner into a city fit for human beings.

Map on page 282

## Starry-eyed gold diggers

Set just below the confluence of the Gila and Colorado rivers, Yuma has been known for centuries as the site of the only natural ford on the southern trail to the Pacific. As such, it was a crucial way-station on the road to California even before the Gold Rush of 1849. Originally, local Quechan Indians kept a monopoly on the lucrative river crossing, but as ever greater numbers of starry-eyed miners demanded to be ferried across into gold country, control was wrested away in some astonishingly bloodthirsty conflicts. When gold was discovered to the *east* of Yuma as well, in 1858, the city duly blossomed as a port, where ore was transported by steamboat down the Colorado River and into the Gulf of California.

After the mines dried up and the river was dammed, Yuma converted itself into an agricultural center, with help from irrigation technology. But it's still a crossroads, where Interstate 8 from San Diego meets US 95, replete with an

*Space cowboys should take a break from the road at the Outer Limits Coffee Shop, part of the Best Western Space Age Lodge, Gila Bend.*

**BELOW:** watermelon-eating contest; no spitting allowed.

*The slow road to Yuma – camels have been in the Wild West since the 1850s.*

**BELOW:** a resident of the Saihati Camel Farm in Yuma, Arizona.

international airport. During the winter, it's heavily trafficked by sun-seekers.

Thanks to diminished water flow, the Gila and Colorado now meet 5 miles (8 km) upstream from downtown Yuma. The high bluff that once overlooked their intersection remains occupied by **Yuma Territorial Prison State Historical Park**. This surprisingly interesting museum (tel: 520-783-4771; open daily) preserves the remaining structures of the infamous prison of the Arizona Territory, which closed in 1909 three years before Arizona achieved statehood. These include its guard house, courtyards, cell block, and notorious "Dark Cell" for solitary confinement.

## Rogues gallery

All the lawlessness of Arizona a hundred years ago is on show in the rogues' gallery of former inmates that decorates the central building. Larcenists, adulterers, manslaughterers, outright murderers, rapists, and criminals "against nature" all found a home here by the Colorado. You can rest assured the cells weren't air-conditioned, so Yuma Prison must have been a fate so dreaded that at least a few desperadoes thought twice before pulling the trigger.

The gray railroad bridge that spans the Colorado close to the prison was completed in 1915 as the "Ocean to Ocean" bridge that finally spared travelers the ferry ride across the river. The point from which the ferries once set off, down below on the fringes of Downtown, is now occupied by **Yuma Crossing State Historical Park**. Assorted overworked wagons, carriages, and even locomotives have been put out to pasture in this pleasant but not wildly exciting open-air park, which is perhaps more interesting simply for providing a spot where you can walk along the riverbanks.

At the core of downtown Yuma, "**Old Yuma**" consists of a few blocks of sleepy but atmospheric Victorian-era buildings. Lutes Casino, on South Main Street, resembles a featureless barn on the outside, but you'll find the interior is positively busting with memorabilia and bric-a-brac, as well as dispensing drinks and snacks.

The rest of the city sprawls for several miles south and east from Downtown, though it seems to hold almost nothing apart from motels, fast-food outlets, and a giant Air Force base. However, an enjoyable little echo of an earlier era does lurk south of the airport on Avenue 1E, in the shape of the bewildering but fun **Saihati Camel Farm** (tel: 520-627-2553; open daily; closed June–Sept).

## Miniature pyramids

Camels have, surprisingly enough, been a feature of the Western landscape since the late 1850s, when the US Army imported a batch of the beasts to see whether they were any better equipped than horses and mules to negotiate Arizona's rough terrain. Though the camels produced amazingly high scores on their "tests," they were prone to stampede, and smelled atrocious. After the Civil War put them out of a job, they were set free, and became a nuisance until camel hunting enjoyed a brief but effective fad.

Their Syrian driver, incidentally, Haiji Ali, is buried beneath a miniature pyramid in Quartszite under the name of "Hi Jolly." The Saihati Camel Farm maintains that tradition by breeding a herd of drooling, slobbering, one-humped dromedaries. If you'd like to acquire such skills as closing your nostrils against the gritty desert wind, or going a week without water, you can inspect them on tours that leave daily at 10am and 2pm sharp.

**BELOW:** Apache girl at Arizona rodeo.

## EUREKA! CALIFORNIA

Over the Colorado River, the down-at-heel community of **Winterhaven** provides a deceptively low-key introduction to California, the third largest and most populous state in the nation. Northwest of here, the **Imperial Valley** – thanks to extensive damming and irrigation – is one of the most agriculturally productive regions on earth. As you follow I-8 to the coast, however, where the Pacific laps on the forever-sunny beaches, it takes a while before the myth of California begins to be fulfilled. First, there is the desert to deal with.

The **Algodones Dunes**, immediately west of the Colorado, were every bit as much of an obstacle to early travelers as the river itself. This strip of deep, shifting sands stretches 40 miles (64 km) north to south. It's only around 6 miles (10 km) wide at this point, but for the first motorists to attempt to cross this might as well have been the Sahara Desert. In 1915, a "**Plank Road**" of railroad ties was laid down to enable automobiles to rumble their way over. By 1925, when as many as 30 cars were using the road each day, it had deteriorated alarmingly. A two-lane paved highway, California State Route 80, finally opened in August 1926, and has long since been superceded in turn by I-8.

A small segment of the original plank road can still be seen by leaving the interstate 20 miles (32 km) west of Yuma on Grays Well Road, to enter the **Imperial Sand Dunes National Recreation Area** ㊻ immediately south. Roughly 4 miles (6 km) along, parallel to the interstate and also to the very long **All American Canal**, the dried-out old planks descend a short slope. These arid dunes are now a raucous playground for the Californian youths who race their dune buggies and other off-road vehicles over the razor-edged inclines, while older "snowbirds" tan themselves sleepily beside their RVs. Incongruously, however, they're also closely monitored by the US Border Patrol, who – besides digging out hapless tourists who attempt to drive their rental vehicles over the sand – reckon on arresting around 300 illegal immigrants per day. As one officer remarked, they're not hard to spot as they plod the 5 miles (8 km) from the Mexican border across the white sands, and "they pretty much know what to expect."

Islands of irrigated green, dotted with palms, spell "oasis" at the end of the 58-mile (93-km) tumble from Yuma to **El Centro**. Supposedly the largest city below sea level in the Western hemisphere, and definitely the birthplace of the entertainer Cher, El Centro prospers quietly as a supply center for the Imperial Valley, but has little to detain the average tourist.

To the west, high winds howl across the valley, kicking up a dusty haze around the straggling palms. Beyond the reach of the canals, the vegetation all but disappears, and you enter the bare **Yuma Desert**. Scattered with only the occasional 14-foot (4-meter) orange-blossomed ocotillo cactus, the desert floor appears to have undergone an unsuccessful hair transplant. The appropriately named **Ocotillo**, 28 miles (45 km) west of El Centro, is no more than a flyblown little hamlet.

The mountain ranges that sweep down from the northwest just past Ocotillo are at first obscured by the dust, but soon you find yourself embarking on the

*A grand garden, the like of which in sheer pattern does not exist, I think, in the world.*

– FRANK LLOYD WRIGHT
ABOUT THE DESERT

**BELOW:** purple prickly pear cactus.

very steep climb up their rocky flanks. The east- and westbound lanes of the interstate divide at this point, each plotting its own course across a terrain that consists of no more than piles of rust-colored boulders. Every few hundred yards stand roadside barrels filled with "Radiator Water," as the risk of overheating is so high. Atop a minor eminence at an elevation of 3,000 feet (923 meters), 5 miles (8 km) out of Ocotillo, the **Desert View Tower** commands a stunning view back across Imperial Valley. Constructed in 1922 using blocks of hewn granite, it holds an enjoyable jumble of exhibits on local history. Entering San Diego County at Mountain Spring, I-8 pulls south to skirt the Mexican border; a minor turn-off leads to the border town of **Jacumba**.

## San Diego revealed

Near **Live Oak Springs**, 27 miles (43 km) west of Ocotillo, the winds die down and the rises level off. Interstate 8 soon swoops to green valleys and into the **Cleveland National Forest**, winding through Pine Valley and Alpine. As you drop toward Alpine, you should get your first glimpse of the Pacific Ocean, glinting on the horizon ahead. **El Cajon** ❹, 43 miles (69 km) beyond Live Oak Springs, is a nicely landscaped city that marks the first major outpost of the San Diego metropolitan area. **La Mesa** follows, set picturesquely amid the hills that rise on El Cajon's western outskirts.

Past La Mesa, traffic on I-8 becomes increasingly congested; the overpass of I-15 is the portal to San Diego. As the interstate pushes out to the Pacific beaches, its shoulders open up onto shopping malls and skyscraper hotels. To the south, buildings arched by trees glimmer on the slopes. Behind them lies the sunny city of **San Diego** ❹ *(see page 322).* ❏

Map on page 282

*El Centro is an oasis surrounded by the California desert. The singer Cher is from El Centro.*

**BELOW:** the long arm of the desert.

# THE PACIFIC ROUTE

*A guide to the Pacific Coast, with principal sites
cross-referenced by number to the maps*

**A**merica's historic US 101, which stretched from San Diego all the way up the coast through Oregon and Washington to the Canadian border, and eventually became in part today's California Highway 1, has a history which is comparable with its more famous companion, Route 66. It began with joint financing from the state of California, San Diego, and the city of Oceanside, which from 1909 to 1918 financed the concrete and macadam road. Up until then it had been a narrow, bumpy, dirt-surfaced track on which horse-drawn wagons and primitive autos competed for space.

The spiffy new road stimulated the rise of a new phenomenon known as "car culture," epitomized in sunny California, and which spawned all the enterprises that subsequently came to be associated with travel along the road, such as gas stations, garages, automobile dealers, hotels, motels, cafés, and even auto laundries.

The highway led visitors from all parts of the Pacific Coast to San Diego's Balboa Park for the 1915–16 Panama-California Exposition, enticed movie stars and others from Hollywood and elsewhere to its pristine beaches, and lured those in search of a good time during Prohibition to Mexico's Tijuana, where, as one historian put it, "booze flowed freely, horses raced continuously and one could gamble and dance the night away."

In 1925, the new road officially became US 101 and served the military in World War II, when it became a major conduit for the country's largest Marine Corps base at Camp Pendleton. Increased traffic spelled its doom, however, and by the end of the war a new four-lane highway, eventually to become Interstate 5, bypassed the old route. Today, the Pacific Coast Highway, often abbreviated to "PCH," and also known as the El Cabrillo Trail, is a sometimes-scrappy, often sea-scented mixture of the old US 101, California Highway 1, and roaring, ever-busy Interstate 5. We have followed it here as faithfully as possible, stopping off at breathtaking sites like California's San Juan Capistrano Mission, Big Sur and Hearst Castle, and Oregon's Oregon Sand Dunes Recreation Area, and only diverting inland and away from its old-fashioned charms to visit not-to-be-missed places like Portland and Seattle.

The Pacific Coast Highway's villages and towns – as well as much of its old structure – is still here, and for those travelers who have time, gasoline, and a romantic desire to reclaim an earlier America, following Highway 1 and historic 101 along the Pacific Coast to Seattle can lead to unimaginable pleasures. ❑

**PRECEDING PAGES:** rustic living in beautiful Big Sur; Huntington pier at sunset, southern California.
**LEFT:** the California dream, on wheels.

# A SHORT STAY IN SAN DIEGO

*San Diego is a busy, elegant harbor town with a history unsurpassed in the state of California. Here's a list of the not-to-be-missed attractions:*

◆ The Mission San Diego (1769) offers a peaceful sanctuary with fragrant gardens. A museum and a walking tour tell the story of the mission, while Mass is still celebrated in the church.

◆ Old Town is where Spanish soldiers and their families lived until the 1800s; Old Town Historic State Park preserves much of the original settlement and, through its structures, adobes, and shops, offers a glimpse of California as it was in the Mexican and early-American periods.

◆ Board at Broadway Pier for a harbor excusion: choose between a one-hour cruise or a two-hour cruise, or take a dinner-dance excusion in the evening. Whale-watching cruises in season, too.

◆ From Dixieland jazz to haute cuisine, the old, restored Gaslamp Quarter offers some of the city's best entertainment and nightlife, as well as interesting Victorian architecture. Shopaholics should make a beeline for nearby Horton Plaza, which has around 150 upmarket shops.

◆ Situated in the heart of San Diego is Balboa Park: over a thousand acres with seven museums, theaters, flora and fauna, art galleries, and more. A pass at the park's Hospitality Center allows admission to up to four of the museums, some of which are housed in old buildings. Have lunch at the Sculpture Garden, visit the Spanish Village Art Center, and afterward, soak up some culture at the Starlight Bowl or Old Globe Theatre.

◆ Tijuana is just a hop, skip and a jump from San Diego, the perfect distance for a day trip. Shop for leather and silver, then lunch on spicy-hot tortillas washed down by tequila.

**△ SAN DIEGO HARBOR**
Much of the harbor is centered around Seaport Village, which has an antique carousel, shops and cafés.

**△ TROLLEY TOURS**
There's a real trolley that ends at the Mexico border, and there are trolley tours by bus where you can get on or off at any stop along the way.

**▷ SAN DIEGO ZOO**
This highly regarded zoo is home to over 800 species of animals, including cute panda bears. The walk-through Owens Rain Forest Aviary simulates a Southeast Asian jungle environment.

**▽ HOTEL DEL CORONADO**
A dozen presidents have stayed in this Victorian resort; it also featured prominently in the movie *Some Like It Hot.*

 **For visitors interested in staying longer in the city, pick up a copy of *Insight Pocket Guide: San Diego*. This includes the recommendations of the local author and contains a full-size fold-out map.**

# THE BIRTHPLACE OF CALIFORNIA

California began at San Diego's Presidio Hill on July 16, 1769, when Father Junípero Serra conducted a mass dedicating the newly created Mission San Diego de Alcalá; the mission was moved to its present site in Mission Valley only five years later. History and luxury can be found in many parts of this harbor city, which has more than its fair share of upscale shops, plus at least 80 golf courses. Although San Diego's harborfront, the Embarcadero, can be tacky and touristy, there are enough historic sites, shady walks, harbor cruises and sandy beaches to appeal to the most discerning of visitors.

△ **SEAWORLD SAN DIEGO**
Killer whales *(shown)* have always been popular; now there's adventure rides, a 3D movie and special effects.

◁ **NATIVE AMERICAN ART**
Buy local arts and crafts, and then learn about the craftsmens' ancestors in Balboa Park's Museum of Man.

▽ Red arrows on the map indicate routes from the city detailed in this book

**San Diego Throughways**

Salk Institute
Oceanside
Escondido
University of California San Diego
Scripps Institution of Oceanography
LA JOLLA
La Jolla Blvd
Santee Lakes Regional Park
SANTEE
Fortuna Mountain 1291
Mission Trails Regional Park
EL CAJON
El Centre
Mission Bay Park
Mission Bay
Tesolote Canyon Natural Park
Sea World
Mission San Diego
Lake Murray
Mission Freeway
Fletcher Pkwy
Point Loma Nazarene University
Old Town State Historic Park
El Cajon Blvd
LA MESA
SPRING VALLEY
Jamacha Blvd
Rosecrans St
Lindbergh Field
Zoo
Balboa Park
Mt. King Jr Freeway
Maritime Museum
San Diego
Seaport Village
NATIONAL CITY
Sweetwater Reservoir
Hotel del Coronado
Cabrillo National Monument
San Diego Bay
Silver Strand Boulevard
S. Bay Freeway
Jacob Dekema Freeway
CHULA VISTA

**PACIFIC OCEAN**

0 ———— 5 miles
0 ———— 5 km

IMPERIAL BEACH
Otay
Otay Mesa Rd
Tijuana

## Important Information

**Population:**
1.25 million

**Dialing codes:**
619, 858, 935

**Website:**
www.sandiego.org

**Tourist information:**
401 B Street,
Suite 1400, San
Diego, CA 92101
Tel: 619-232-3101
Fax: 619-696-9371

# SAN DIEGO TO LOS ANGELES

*Beach towns, beach facilities and beaches themselves –*
*more than 20 of them – line this short stretch of coastline.*
*Is it any wonder the bikini first became famous here?*

Map on page 326

T he journey from seaside **San Diego ❶** *(see page 322)* to glittering Los Angeles is only around 125 miles (200 km), but following the ragged coastal roads can take much longer than that short distance implies. It's also much more rewarding, as the coastal route meanders past southern California's best beaches, prettiest towns, and most exclusive residential areas. For navigational purposes, the road signs along the way go by a variety of names – Highway 1, US 101, Interstate 5 – but to most Californians, this mix of roads paralleling the ocean is known simply as the Pacific Coast Highway.

## LA JOLLA TO OCEANSIDE

The first stop out of San Diego is **La Jolla ❷** (pronounced *la-hoy-ya*), a seaside community that once boasted "the richest zipcode in America." This college community and upscale town can be reached in a few minutes by heading north up Interstate 5, but a more scenic way is to start the drive to Los Angeles as you intend to proceed – using water as your navigator. From Sea World, take the road called Sea World Drive to West Mission Bay Drive, routes which curl along the bottom of **Mission Bay** itself. The road turns north (changing into Mission Boulevard) to parallel Mission Beach, then the livelier Pacific Beach, before rolling into La Jolla. La Jolla has beautiful homes and a downtown area – which calls itself "the village" – filled with expensive shops , as well as a contemporary art museum. Described by writer Raymond Chandler as "a nice place for old people and their parents," La Jolla featured in Tom Wolfe's 1960s surfer novel *The Pump House Gang*. On the campus of the University of California is the La Jolla Playhouse, whose forerunner was founded by local actor Gregory Peck. The caves carved into its coastal bluffs have long been a paradise for both deep-sea divers and cliff divers, and nearby **Black's Beach** was once legally – and is now illegally – a nudist beach.

**LEFT:** romance under the sun.
**BELOW:** Legoland, Carlsbad, California near San Diego.

### Architecturely awesome

At the north end of town above Point La Jolla is the renowned **Scripps Institution of Oceanography**, whose well-stocked **Stephen Birch Aquarium** (tel: 858-534-3474; open daily) offers whale-watching cruises in season. Among the 33 sea-filled tanks is a two-story tank that replicates a kelp bed with all its familiar and unfamiliar creatures. Farther north and also by the sea is the **Salk Institute**, designed by the late Louis I. Kahn, perhaps one of America's most admired contemporary architects. The institute is named after its famous resident scientist, Jonas Salk, who devised the polio vaccine.

La Jolla Shores Drive parallels Torrey Pines Road,

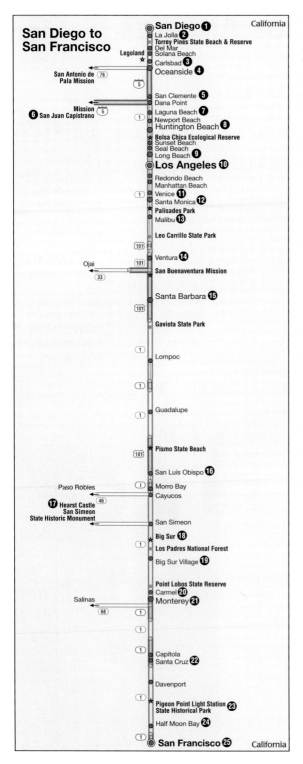

a winding hill out of La Jolla through the affluent suburb of the same name where the trees are environmentally protected. The road gives access to **Torrey Pines Scenic Drive**, off which is a windswept hillside used by flying enthusiasts for launching gliders over the ocean since the 1930s. The **Torrey Pines Gliderport** (tel: 888-452-9858) offers introductory lessons in paragliding and hang-gliding; spectators are welcome. There's also a restaurant and flight sport shop at the site. The **Torrey Pines State Reserve** and **Torrey Pines State Beach** are two places perfect for picnics.

## Del Mar and Solana Beach

A series of small coastal roads, which together make up US 101, parallel I-5 as far as the town of Oceanside, where the mighty interstate takes over until it reaches Dana Point. From then on the Pacific Coast Highway becomes Highway 1, and more or less stays Highway 1 until San Francisco.

Both the coast road and the interstate lead to the community of **Del Mar**, which has an Amtrak Station and has attracted crowds since the 1930s with its famous racetrack, which was rescued from collapse by actor Pat O'Brien and singer Bing Crosby. The entertainers turned the track into one of America's most popular racing circuit venues. The season begins in July, a week after Del Mar's big fair ends, and runs until mid-September.

The track's sandy-colored main building, in a sort of California-meets-Mediterranean style, can be seen from the interstate, but much of the town itself lies farther down the hill beside the coast road. Along the roads storekeepers favor a pseudo-Tudor style, with the upper part of the buildings displaying a brown-and-white timbered look.

The communities of **Solana Beach** – with its futuristic-looking railroad station; Cardiff-by-the-Sea, Encinitas, and Leucadia run into each other along this stretch of coast, and a profusion of stop signs and red lights can slow progress. Otherwise it is a pleasant stretch to drive with plenty of roadside trees, the beach, and the railroad track both near the road, and here and there a "Historic US 101" sign. Watch for the 101 Cafe (built in 1928) as you drive through Oceanside. The **Quail Botanical Gardens** (tel: 760-436-3036; open daily) at **Encinitas** may be worth a stop to admire the waterfall and extensive collection of exotic plants. The **San Dieguito Heritage Museum** (tel: 760-632-9711; open Wed–Sat) specializes in the history of the area – from the Diegueno Indians of 10,000 years ago to the present day – and includes a fine collection of more than 8,000 photographs. The beach is a few blocks away; the railroad parallels the road to the east. At the north end of the community are the golden domes of the Self Realization Fellowship temple.

## Making music

At **Carlsbad ❸** the road runs along the beach and heads past an ugly pink power plant with a tall stack, and then through a town whose Germanesque-looking buildings reflect the heritage of its German spa namesake. The region is known for flower growing, its bulbs being sold widely throughout the country, and almost 50 hillside acres are resplendent with bright colors. (To visit the gardens, telephone 760-431-3532.) The **Museum of Making Music** spans a century of music-making in America. Exhibits include vintage instruments, samples of popular music from each era, and historic photographs and paintings.

Carlsbad's 128-acre (52-hectare) **Legoland California** (tel: 760-438-5346; open daily), is the first of these amusement parks in the US. It used 120 million of its signature toy plastic bricks to depict such scaled-down landmarks as New York City, a New England harbor, and Washington DC – as well as Castle Hill with an "enchanted walk" where children can search for hidden treasure.

**Map on page 326**

**TIP**

San Diego's Scripps Institution of Oceanography offers whale-watching cruises December to March through its highly regarded aquarium. Tel: 858-534-3474 for more information.

**BELOW:** these waters form part of the migratory path for whales.

### Let's go surfing now

With almost 4 miles (6 km) of white, sandy beaches and "world-class surf," **Oceanside** ❹ is an appropriate place to find – on the main street opposite the Longboarder Café – the **California Surf Museum** (tel: 760-721-6876; open daily; closed Tues in fall and winter), which displays the evolution of surfboards from 16-footers weighing 200 pounds (90 kg) to fiber-glass creations known as potato-chip boards. There's a huge market among surfing dudes for memorabilia and thus much of the museum's collection is priceless. Surfing veterans such as Olympic-medal swimmer Duke Kahanamoka are honored here.

Other interesting museums include that of the **Historical Society** (tel: 760-722-4786; open Thur–Sat); **Oceanside Museum of Art** (tel: 760-721-2787; closed Mon) and **Buena Vista Audubon** (tel: 760-439-2473; closed Mon) beside a lazy lagoon on the highway south of town. Four miles (6 km) inland from the beach is the lovely **Mission San Luis Rey de Francia**, near which is **Heritage Park** (tel: 760-433-8297; park open daily, buildings open Sun) whose old buildings include the cottage that was once Oceanside's post office.

Oceanside has cafés and shops located in a pleasant man-made harbor, with a lighthouse that serves as a marina for several hundred boats at the north end. From here, boats run across to **Santa Catalina Island** (for information contact the Catalina Visitors Bureau and Chamber of Commerce, tel: 310-510-1520). Oceanside's pier, just north of Mission Avenue, is the longest recreational wooden pier on the West Coast. Hundreds of Downtown walkways are marked with the mysterious O.U. MIRACLE, the name of contractor Orville Ullman Miracle, whose construction company submitted the winning bid in the 1920s to improve the community's streets.

**BELOW:** granddads make waves, southern California.

## OCEANSIDE TO LOS ANGELES

An interesting diversion from Oceanside is to drive inland along State Route 76 for a few miles to **San Antonio de Pala Mission**, on the Pala Indian Reservation. This is the only Californian mission still serving Native Americans. San Antonio has celebrated its Corpus Christi Festival, with an open-air mass, dances and games, on the first Sunday of every June since 1816.

The United States Marine Corps occupies the coastal area north of Oceanside, where the coast road is incorporated into I-5 and the sea is half a mile away. Just north of the controversial San Onofre Nuclear Power Plant is **San Clemente ❺**, where former US president Richard Nixon, an Orange County native, set up a western White House on his 25-acre (10-hectare) estate, and where he lived until moving to New Jersey in 1980. This attractive town, with its Spanish-looking tiled roofs and white stucco walls, prompted the *Los Angeles Times* to write in 1927: "If the charms of this place could be shown to the poor, snow-bound, wind-beaten people back East, there would be an exodus so great the hills above San Clemente would be covered like mushrooms."

The **Heritage of San Clemente Visitor Center** (tel: 949-369-1299; open daily) has exhibits from Nixon's western White House and also has some surfing history. The town's founder, a former mayor of Seattle named Ole Hanson, is memorialized in **Casa Romantica**, his old home near the Parque Del Mar, as well as the Ole Hanson Beach Club and Ole's Tavern. In 1925, Hanson purchased and designed a 2,000-acre (800-hectare) community on what was then empty space. His instincts were sound then and even sounder now; San Clemente's population is expected to double over the next 20 years.

Writing in the *San Clemente Journal*, Ann Batty claimed that it was San Clemente designers who first popularized the bikini on local beaches, of which there are many (bikinis *and* beaches). San Clemente and Doheny beaches allow camping for a small fee, and Doheny, Dana Point, Laguna Niguel, Irvine Coast, and Newport Beach all have marine life preserves (patroled by state fish and game wardens) that are open to the public.

### Festival of Whales

Capistrano Beach and Doheny State Beach lie astride the San Juan Creek just before **Dana Point**, where most of the buildings in the harbor complex are a lot younger than they look – although the overall effect is quite attractive. There are dozens of places to shop and eat, and whale-watching excursions depart from here in season (December–March). Dana Point's annual Festival of Whales is a well-attended, amusing event with its imaginative whale costumes, and a parade of clowns, jugglers, and antique cars, as well as a lively street fair.

The **Orange County Marine Institute** (tel: 949-496-2274; open daily) at the northern end of the harbor commemorates Richard Henry Dana, whose seafaring exploits from here resulted in the novel *Two Years Before the Mast,* which became a 1946 movie starring Alan Ladd. **Santa Catalina Island** can be reached from here, too, in daily trips that take 90 minutes each way (tel: 877-447-5263).

Map on page 326

*It was the resort of Oceanside, along with San Diego and the state of California, that financed historic US 101 in the early 1900s. The improved road allowed visitors from up the coast to spend time in the sunny south.*

**BELOW:** lapping up the sunshine.

*Sometime it's pigeons, rather than swallows, that arrive at Capistrano.*

**BELOW:**
Capistrano's bells are among the mission's most valued treasures.

## San Juan Capistrano

Interstate 5 now veers away from the coast and heads inland to the town of San Juan Capistrano. Following it into town, Del Obispo Street leads to Camino Capistrano, on which sits the famous **San Juan Capistrano Mission ❻** (tel: 949-248-2048; open daily), seventh in the chain of 21 established by Franciscan padres late in the 18th century. There's a statue of Father Junipero Serra, who founded this and eight other California missions.

The Serra chapel behind the church is the oldest building still in use within the state of California. Pick up a free map that identifies and dates the chapel's treasures, including the bells to the left of the church, and also tells where the swallows' nests can be found during their residence between their scheduled arrival on St Joseph's Day (March 19) and their departure for the warmer climate of Argentina on October 23. By some mysterious alchemy the swallows have almost always been on time; their arrival here is marked by a week-long festival with mariachi bands leading a parade. Nevertheless, disappointed tourists sometimes arrive to find only pigeons.

## Highway 1

Back on the coast, the Pacific Coast Highway now officially becomes Highway 1. It's been a while since the long-gone Serpentarium at **Laguna Beach ❼** used to advertise that *rattlesnake à la Maryland* would be on the reptile zoo's menu, but this community still has more attractions than you would expect in a beach city. Laguna was always a favorite of Hollywood's movie colony, and Mary Pickford, Bette Davis, Judy Garland, and Rudolph Valentino were just a few of the movie stars who maintained homes here.

The resort has established a worldwide reputation with its annual **Pageant of the Masters** each summer, at which well-rehearsed volunteers take up their roles in living reproductions of famous paintings.

On specific evenings of each month, the popular **Laguna Art Museum** (tel: 949-494-8971; closed Mon) organizes the Art Walk, which includes visits to 40 local galleries. The Visitors Bureau located at 252 Broadway (tel: 949-497-9229) offers guidance on numerous other "heritage tours," which might include the **Murphy-Smith Historical Bungalow** (tel: 949-497-4439; open Thur–Sun afternoons), one of the few houses in downtown Laguna Beach remaining from the 1920s.

For lovers of the outdoor life there are many choices in addition to the annual whale-watching safaris. These include the **Sanctuary** (tel: 949-494-7734), a native plant and wildlife refuge about a mile inland on Laguna Canyon Road; the worthwhile **Marine Mammal Rescue Center** for sick and injured seals (tel: 949-494-3050; open daily); plus the excursions to inspect tide pools (tel: 949-874-6620; transportation from all hotels) and the **Glenn E. Vedder Ecological Reserve** at the north section of the main beach, where marine life can be explored by divers.

There are thousands of acres of wilderness parks surrounding Laguna Beach, and maps are available at the Visitors Bureau.

## Balboa peninsula

The upscale **Balboa peninsula**, with its 6 miles (10 km) of sandy shore, encloses a harbor that is usually filled with yachts, with a large paddle-wheeler moored beside the highway bridge. Newport Boulevard becomes Balboa Boulevard and, at its intersection with Washington Street, the Bon Appetite Bakery is a pleasant stop for lunch. Given pride of place on Main Street, it's hard to miss the **Balboa Pavilion**, built in 1905 as a railroad terminal, with its distinctive but totally unnecessary steeple. Behind it, if you get here early enough, you'll find fishing boats unloading their daily catch. Almost as old is the ferry that makes the 3-minute trip from the end of Palm Street to **Balboa Island**, with its million-dollar homes and classy shops and cafés.

On your way back across the water someone will surely point out, on nearby islands, the former homes of John Wayne and cowboy hero Roy Rogers. From **Balboa Pier** you can admire the kite-flyers, frisbee-throwers, and body-surfers. Check out Ruby's, a 1950s-theme restaurant at the end of the pier before finishing up at the Balboa Fun Zone with its rides and video arcades.

Depending on the month, if you stay a couple of weekday nights in pretty **Newport Beach**, the tourist office (800-942-6278) will give you round-trip tickets on the *Catalina Flyer*, yet another way to reach Santa Catalina. Waves cascade over the breakwater here, so it's not a great place for swimming; expert bodysurfers are the only people to truly excel in the water. The town does have other things to offer visitors, though, including a **Nautical Museum**; the well-stocked **Orange County Museum of Art** (tel: 949-759-1122; open Tues–Sun afternoons) or the shopping paradise of Newport Center Fashion Island, which the Irvine Company built when there was barely the population to support it. The shopping center sits on the right-hand side of the road, past Avocado Drive, as you leave town. In Corona del Mar, just to the south, the attractive gardens of the Sherman Library and Roger's Gardens are both pleasant places to pause.

## Beaches and birdwatching

Many of the communities around here are in dispute about which most deserves the desirable southern California title "Surf City," but **Huntington Beach ❽** claims to have the best case; in 1994 the town inaugurated a sidewalk **Surfers Walk of Fame** in the presence of its surf fanatical congressman, Dana Rohrabacher.

The highway heads along the coast past the state's longest municipal pier, rebuilt in concrete after the original was destroyed by a fierce storm. Three blocks up Main Street and directly opposite the pier is Plaza Almeria, with an attractive collection of shops, restaurants, and homes. Farther uptown another old mall, the Huntington Beach Center, is an entertainment and shopping complex.

Rail tycoon Henry Huntington first brought the railroad here late in the 19th century, and a subsequent oil boom introduced prosperity to a town that ironically is now best known for its environmental awareness. Its 350-acre (140-hectare) Central Park, 50 percent of which is devoted to wildlife and greenery, is nothing

Map on page 326

**BELOW:** San Juan Capistrano, 7th in the chain of 21 missions founded by Father Serra, is the most famous in California.

but a taster compared with the sprawling **Bolsa Chica Ecological Reserve,** a vast coastal salt marsh that serves as a resting place for birds migrating between North and South America.

The best spot for birdwatchers is on the inland side of the highway between Golden West Street and Warner Avenue, opposite the entrance to the state beach. There are walking trails and plenty of parking. The **Interpretive Center** (open Tues–Fri), which offers bird checklists, is at Warner Avenue. Not far away, between Warner and Heil avenues, is the **Monarch Butterfly Habitat**, where rare butterflies gather in the eucalyptus trees between November and March. Passing through the small, waterside community of **Sunset Beach**, you cannot help but notice a huge wooden water tower beside the highway that became a residence some years ago. Although the tower is private, it is a local landmark for miles around.

### Life's a beach

At the Los Angeles County line, **Seal Beach**, an unspoiled enclave with an 80-year-old inn and a lengthy pier uncluttered with modern diversions, is the last place at which the ocean can be seen from the highway for many miles. To the right of the highway at **Belmont Shore** you can make a diversion along Second Street, which skirts the beach of Alamitos Bay. Gondola Getaway on East Ocean Beach Boulevard operates hour-long tours in real gondolas along canals which pass the elegant homes of neighboring **Naples**. Operating from 10am–midnight daily, the gondolas carry from two to six people.

Highway 1 goes inland here, bypassing Long Beach, San Pedro, and the Palo Verdes Peninsula to hit the coast again just south of Redondo Beach.

**BELOW:**
each beach in
southern California
has its own fans
and habitués.

## Long live the Queen

Although the Pacific Coast Highway bypasses **Long Beach ❾**, it's worth passing through town to see some of its attractions, which includes the world's largest mural, a panorama of marine life that covers the entire surface of the Long Beach Arena on Ocean Boulevard. Other sights include the magnificent **Aquarium of the Pacific** (tel: 562-590-3100; open daily) and the venerable ship the **Queen Mary** (tel: 562-435-3511; open daily) – which made 1,000 trans-Atlantic crossings and was a hero of World War II before ending its journey here – moored in the harbor. The ship's history is a starry one, having been the carrier of choice for both celebrities and royalty; visitors can pretend to be the same by staying overnight in a cabin, or dine in the elegantly restored Art Deco restaurant.

*The famous Art Deco ocean liner, the Queen Mary, is now a restaurant and hotel in Long Beach.*

Long Beach has positioned itself as a sleek, modern city in recent years, and it certainly has a number of architecturally chic new structures. But it's also anxious to promote its historic downtown buildings from the early part of the 20th century. A walking tour map of more than 40 of these landmarks is available from the Visitors Bureau (tel: 562-436-3645; 1 World Trade Center). Anyone traveling with kids might like to know that State Highway 22 east from Long Beach hooks up with I-5 and leads to Anaheim, where the attractions include **Disneyland**, Knotts Berry Farm, and the Movieland Wax Museum.

## Harbor tours

Headquarters of southern California's fishing fleet, **San Pedro** once carried the distinction of being a genuine fishing port. The old town is now long gone, replaced by an imaginatively-designed pseudo-19th-century construction called Ports O'Call Village. Several blocks of saltbox-type weathered-looking shops – 75 in all, plus numerous restaurants – are a pleasure to walk around. Harbor tours and fishing trips leave from here (as well as the *Catalina Express* and a beautiful classic sailing ship), and there's masses of free parking space. Green and white trolleys run along the waterfront, stopping at the World Cruise center, the maritime museum, Ports O'Call Village, and the Frank Gehry-designed Cabrillo Marine Aquarium.

**BELOW:** gondolier in Naples.

San Pedro's **Cabrillo Beach** has earned a reputation as one of the best places in the area to go windsurfing, and beginners especially favor the sheltered waters inside the harbor breakwater. Between March and September – twice a month, like clockwork – milky-white grunion fish ride in by the thousand on the tide to deposit their eggs in the sand.

On the **Palos Verdes** peninsula are multi-million dollar Italianate villas and French chateaux overlooking the ocean. Abalone Cove, the beach west of Narcissa Drive, is an ecological preserve at the end of a steep path; perfect for divers and tide-poolers. Just past the Golden Shores mall is a lighthouse beside which, at the **Point Vicente Interpretive Center** (open daily), are long-lens telescopes for sighting passing whales (December to April), and an exhibit in which visitors can don earphones to hear the mournful voices of these loveable mammals.

About a mile farther on is the wood-and-glass **Wayfarers Chapel,** designed by Frank Lloyd Wright's son, whose inspiration is said to have been northern California's majestic redwood trees. The chapel was built in 1951 as a memorial to the 18th-century Swedish theologian Emmanuel Swedenborg. Walking around the peaceful gardens to the sound of songbirds, a fountain, and the gurgling stream is a very tranquilizing experience. There are services in the chapel at 11am every Sunday.

## Walking on water

By now we are well and truly in **Los Angeles ❿** *(see page 236)*, although most of this sprawling city's inland tourist attractions lie quite a ways farther north. LA's southern beaches are varied and linked by a combination of Highway 1 and minor roads. After its chances of becoming a major port were wrecked by its vulnerability to severe storms, **Redondo Beach** turned its attention to tourism. A Pacific Electric Railway developer hired a Hawaiian teenager to demonstrate surfing, and before long visitors were flocking to watch "the man who can walk on water."

In the 1930s even bigger crowds were lured by the gambling ships moored offshore – the most famous being the *Rex* – which could accommodate 1,500 customers, who took 25¢ rides out to the boat from the town pier. Offshore gaming was outlawed by Congress in 1946, but a pier remains at the center of the town's colorful boardwalk. The current pier is horseshoe-shaped, after several predecessors were destroyed by storms, while Redondo Beach itself is a big draw for bodybuilders.

**BELOW:** boardwalk.

Following Catalina Avenue from Redondo Pier leads to **Hermosa Beach**, an

inland road leading past Kings Harbor Marina, opposite which an enormous ocean mural is painted on the wall of the power plant. Hermosa Avenue continues for quite a way one block from the beach. The beach itself stretches for 8 sandy miles (13 km) between Kings Harbor and **Marina Del Rey**, the longest uninterrupted stretch in Los Angeles County. There are pedestrian-only streets leading from Hermosa Avenue to the beach at every block.

At 22nd Street a good neighborhood place to sit outside and watch the locals while drinking a cup of coffee is Martha's Corner. Hermosa is known for its nightclubs, Marina Del Rey for its child-friendly beaches.

In between the two is **Manhattan Beach**, whose name came about because of a homesick New Yorker, who was living in the area in 1902 when just a dozen families made up the community. Its population grew dramatically during World War II when aircraft plants sprang up along Avalon Boulevard. In recent years the Disney company has erected a dozen huge sound stages in what is still largely a commuter community of LA.

But in the last few years, this part of Orange County has become second only to Hollywood as a venue for moviemakers, with its coastal piers especially attractive to the makers of television commercials. The scene down by the water resembles an episode of *Baywatch*, with plenty of bronzed and beautiful joggers, rollerbladers, and volleyball players.

## Venice

Just north of Marina Del Rey, the long pedestrian and bicycle path linking **Venice ⑪** (and **Venice Beach**) with Santa Monica is a lively hub of activity, especially in Venice itself, where you'll encounter skimpily-attired rollerbladers

Map on page 326

*Manhattan Beach was named by a homesick New Yorker in 1902. Hermosa Beach stretches for 8 miles (13km) between Kings Harbor and Marina Del Rey, making it the longest in LA County.*

**BELOW:** roller-dancers, Venice Beach.

*Near Muscle Beach.*

**BELOW:** castles in the sand, Santa Monica.

of both sexes, rainbow-haired punks, magicians, fortune tellers, itinerant musicians, and pumped-up bodybuilders flexing their biceps at **Muscle Beach**. You can rent rollerblades on Windward Avenue or a bicycle on Washington Street (opposite the abandoned pier) or just sit at one of the sidewalk cafés and admire the passing parade. The most interesting place to grb a snack in Venice is probably the art- and artist-filled Rose Café on Rose Avenue. If you feel like getting away from the noise and the rentlentless body-beautiful activities, this is also a good spot from which to begin exploring Venice proper, which is surpringly different from the image normally associated with the place.

## Canals near the coast

The lesser-visited town of Venice is much more charming than the beach. Take a stroll through the residential area around the inland canals, where a proliferation of bright flowers tumbles over sagging fences and ducks nestle under upturned boats on tiny jetties. Visitors can pick their way along rutted paths, over gentle hump-backed bridges, and past lovingly tended gardens, admiring the variegated architecture, numerous birds, and floral displays.

More than 70 years after the death of Abbott Kinney, who acquired and reclaimed what was worthless marshland in anticipation of creating an "Italy in California," some of his vision still remains in what is probably the most pleasant walk in urban Los Angeles. The original circulation system for the canals – which envisaged seawater pulsing through 30-inch (76-cm) pipes with every fresh tide – proved unworkable, and the canals themselves became sand-clogged and stagnant. In 1993 a $6 million overhaul dredged and refilled the canals, repaired the adjoining paths, and rebuilt some of the bridges.

## LA's Auto Museum

Lovers of automobiles and travel will want to make a sidetrip into Los Angeles to visit the Petersen Museum, one of the world's largest museums devoted exclusively to the history and cultural impact of the car. For when it comes to vehicles, no city knows them like Los Angeles, and no one can know Los Angeles without a vehicle. This city, unlike few others, was designed for the car and its endless miles of freeway tie it together the way rivers tie together London or Paris. With a board of advisors comprising high-profile enthusiasts like actor Paul Newman and racing ace Parnelli Jones, the four floors of this $40 million museum detail everything you ever wanted to know about four wheels, and the culture that rides above them. The second floor houses racing and classic cars, hot rods, movie-star cars, and vintage motorcycles. But the Petersen is not just about transportation; it's also about style. Although the museum has yet to do an exhibition on why balding old men buy flash red sports cars, it does have rotating cultural exhibitions covering such novelties as low-riding cars, and the history of that quintessential American icon: the pick-up truck. The Petersen Museum is at 6060 Wilshire Boulevard, tel: 323-930-2277.

## Movie-star coast

Santa Monica ⑫ is a seaside resort where Los Angeles's West Side meets the ocean. In the streets behind and the canyons above lie the most famous of LA's attractions: Hollywood, Beverly Hills, Rodeo Drive. But down near the water-side, the "Bay City" of Raymond Chandler's novels is a pleasant place to be. The boulevards and side streets are attractive places to stroll and shop; a wide pedestrian mall at Third Street leads down to the sparkling Frank Gehry-designed **Santa Monica Place**, which is flanked by department stores. The trendy **Third Street** pedestrian mall, lined with restaurants, stores, and movie theaters, is usually filled with street performers, while the waterside, century-old **Santa Monica pier** offers a predictable assortment of amusement arcades, souvenir stands, snack bars, and sedentary fishermen. There's also a wonderful carousel with 44 hand-carved horses which featured in the 1973 film *The Sting*.

Good places to spend a couple of quiet hours in Santa Monica are the library, where there's an extensive collection of current magazines and a well-lit read-ing area, and the clifftop **Palisades Park**, a eucalyptus-fringed grassy stretch along Ocean Avenue that offers views of boats and sunsets. In recent years the park has proved to be a popular venue for the homeless – though their presence should not deter you from visiting. To one side is an information cabin for brochures and useful tips on where to catch local buses.

The mansions along the seashore at the northern end of Santa Monica were mostly built by moviedom's former elite. The grandest, at 415 Pacific Coast Highway, was the 118-room compound designed for William Randolph Hearst and his paramour, Marion Davies. The house was sold to the owner of the Hotel Bel Air, who turned it into a beach hotel and club. ❑

Map on page 326

**BELOW:**
the 100-year-old
Santa Monica pier
is lined with shops
and cafés.

# LOS ANGELES TO SAN FRANCISCO

*This legendary stretch of Highway 1 takes in
the California coast's most famous attractions:
extravagant Hearst Castle and fog-shrouded Big Sur*

Map on page 326

**T**he distance from Los Angeles to San Francisco is 380 miles (611 km). Taking Interstate 5 all the way means a city-to-city trip can be accomplished in around six hours, but that would be a pity. Highway 1 hugs the coast almost the entire way, presenting heart-stopping curves, breath-taking scenery, pretty inns, scenic sites, and two of California's best attractions – Hearst Castle and Big Sur. With all of this to savor, allowing three days rather than six hours makes far more sense.

## LOS ANGELES TO SANTA BARBARA

The Pacific Coast Highway out of Los Angeles cruises along **Malibu** ⓭ with the ease that community's name implies. Despite its worldwide reputation for hi-jinks and hedonism, the area is largely a private residential community where much of the beach has been cordoned off (at the junction with Webb Way) into the exclusive Malibu Colony. The must-see place in Malibu is **Adamson House**, built in 1929 for May Ridge, the widow of the man who bought most of what now comprises Malibu back in 1897. The richly decorated house, replete with tiles from the Ridge's short-lived Malibu Pottery, is a fascinating repository of history about the early Hollywood crowd, who were perfectly content with ocean-front shacks.

North of Malibu the beaches are more accessible and there's a string of them – **Point Dume**, **Zuma**, and **Leo Carrillo** – until the highway turns inland toward Ventura. Highway 1 is submerged into US 101 here, and you must leave it to visit the town of **Ventura** ⓮ itself, which has a huge city hall perched on the hillside and a heavily restored "Olde Towne." The 1782 **San Buenaventura Mission** (tel: 805-648-4496; open daily) is pretty and worth a visit, and Ventura's harbor area has lots of seafood restaurants. Most of the town's sites are connected by trolley.

Inland along State Route 150, hidden away on the edge of the Los Padres National Forest, is **Ojai** (pronounced *O-hi*), a sleepy artists' and writers' colony near which the 1926 movie *Lost Horizon* was filmed. The town is centered around a main street on which a graceful tower offsets a row of unpretentious shops built under a covered veranda. Artifacts in the Historical Society Museum include those from Chumash Indian times through the ranching period to the days when heavyweight champion Jack Dempsey cleared rocks from what became "Pop" Soper's training ranch. Dozens of boxers trained here, including hero Dempsey himself, while preparing for his fight against

**LEFT:** Santa Barbara's Spanish-style architecture.
**BELOW:** hitting the highway *à deux*.

Gene Tunney in 1926. On the outskirts of Santa Barbara, the charming **Montecito Inn** (tel: 805-969-7854) has been popular with refugees from Hollywood since the 1920s, when one of its original owners was Charlie Chaplin and guests included Fatty Arbuckle, Fred Astaire. and Will Rogers. More than 1,000 two-reeler movies were shot in the Santa Barbara area, most of them between 1913 and 1918; Chicago producer Samuel S. Hutchinson's Flying A Studios alone brought in such silent-screen film celebrities as Mary Pickford and D. W. Griffith. Because of its lower costs and proximity to Los Angeles, many movies and television shows continue to be shot in the region today.

Montecito's legendary **San Ysidro Ranch** (tel: 805-969-5046), in a canyon lined with sycamore and eucalyptus trees, was where John F. Kennedy honeymooned with his wife Jackie; where Lauren Bacall says she fell in love with Humphrey Bogart; and where Laurence Olivier and Vivien Leigh had a midnight wedding in 1940. Once owned by Ronald Colman, the ranch celebrated its centenary in 1993 by refurbishing its guest rooms and cottages.

## Santa Barbara

The most striking aspect of **Santa Barbara ⑮** is its distinctive Mediterranean architecture: the ubiquitous white-washed adobe, tiled roofing, and iron grillwork permeate a city in which, as one local writer noted, "its architects were able to create a myth of a tradition, which turned out to be far more believable than the realities of factual history." There are miles of enticing wide beaches; the coast's "queen of the missions," arguably the most beautiful in the state – the **Santa Barbara Mission** (tel: 805-682-4713; open daily); and **Stearns Wharf**, the oldest pier on the California coast, The pier contains an aquarium, wine-tasting rooms, fishing facilities, and seafood stands. A waterfront shuttle tram operates between the wharf, Downtown, and the zoo, connecting the beaches which line the shore with volleyball courts on both sides of the pier, and with the expensive hotels at the eastern end.

Two blocks from the Greyhound bus station in the town's center is the handsome 1929 Spanish-Moorish **Court House** (open daily). Its lobby is lined with mosaics and murals, and there's a lovely view from the top of gently sloping roofs and the multi-level lawn below. Turn up State Street to reach the area where the city began around the old **Presidio**. Inspect 18th-century adobes, and have lunch in the charming, cobbled street called **El Paseo**, where the local theater once featured a dancer named Rita Cansino, later to become better known as Rita Hayworth.

## Channel Islands

Between Christmas and late March there are daily excursions into the offshore Santa Barbara Channel for whale watching. Year-round trips are also made to Santa Barbara Island, whose desolate 640 acres (260 hectares) are a haven for birds, sea lions, 10,000 breeding seals, and other marine life. None of the **Channel Islands** is inhabited, but all can be visited at various times of the year when island rangers conduct tours.

**BELOW:**
Santa Barbara's architects "were able to create a myth of a tradition."

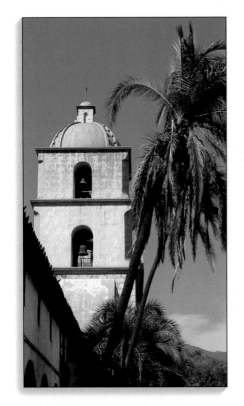

## SANTA BARBARA TO BIG SUR

After meandering through **Gaviota State Park**, Highways 1 and 101 split apart, but both turn inland. It's most fun to continue driving on Highway 1, the road nearest the coast, which heads through sleepy **Lompoc**, ennobled by the presence of the **La Purisima Concepcion** (tel: 805-733-3713; open daily), the state's 11th mission. North of town, the road passes through an immense area of agri-business-dominated land, irrigated fields used for growing broccoli, cauliflower, and strawberries as well as extensive fields of flowers, which in season offer an extraordinary display of magentas, pinks, golds, and purples. These supply most of the floral seeds that color the fields of the entire USA.

Vast fields continue past **Guadalupe,** a quiet, old-fashioned town with an Amtrak station and one-story buildings dating to the turn of the 20th century. Eighteen miles (29 km) north, an enormous oil refinery dominates the landscape. **Pismo State Beach**, once famous for its huge clams (still celebrated with a Clam Festival every October) has fabulous sandy shores stretching all around the bay and leads directly into San Luis Obispo, which is more or less the midway point between Los Angeles and San Francisco. Pismo is one of the few beaches where driving is allowed, so look out for dune buggies. Just before San Luis Obispo, keep an eye open for the extraordinary **Madonna Inn** (tel: 805-543-3000), each of whose 109 rooms are individually decorated in memorably kitsch fashion. The "old English" suite is large enough for two families to move into for the night.

*The Santa Lucia mountain range is a successful wine-producing region.*

The attractive, low-key college town of **San Luis Obispo** ⑯ (SLO) also has an 18th-century mission (tel: 805-543-6850; open daily), with a downtown community located around its plaza. There's an Art Center (closed

**BELOW:** Firestone Vineyards near Santa Barbara.

Mon), the adjoining County Historical Museum (open Wed–Sun), and the Apple Farm Mill House on Monterey Street – an authentic working gristmill set in scenic gardens with waterfalls. Every Thursday night, part of Higuera Street is closed to traffic to facilitate a farmers market and street fair along with bands and entertainment.

## Morro Bay

**Morro Bay** is dominated by its 576-foot (175-meter) high rock, whose aeries now shelter the endangered peregrine falcon, the 175-mph (282-kph) dive-bomber that feeds on live game. There's an excellent beach, and the restaurant-fringed harbor is an attractive place to walk around – but be aware that the harbor drive dead-ends in both directions and parking can be difficult. The beach is busy long before the tourists arrive, however – ubiquitous are the coastal snowy plover, "those little cupcake-sized birds that run along the beach looking for something to eat." Alas, the snowy plover is a threatened species. The **Museum of Natural History** (tel: 805-772-2694; open daily) contains exhibits that deal with coastal animal, marine, and plant life, including the Monarch butterfly. This short-lived beauty, with its amber and black wings, can be seen near Pacific Grove (up by Monterey) during the winter months.

At the pretty town of **Cayucos** you'll say good-bye to the ocean, which remains out of sight almost to **Cambria**, a pleasant little place just off the highway. In between the two towns, State Highway 46 winds east through the barren but beautiful hills of the Santa Lucia mountain range, linking up to US 101 and **Paso Robles**. This is a charming, small, wine-producing region where most of the wineries offer free daily tastings. A map of local wineries is available from

**BELOW:** Roman pool, Hearst Castle.

the Visitor and Conference Bureau (tel: 800-406-4040) in Paso Robles, where the **Pioneer Museum** (tel: 805-239-2740; open Thur–Sun afternoons) provides a little lesson in local history.

## Hearst Castle

Back on the coast, the hamlet of **San Simeon** is the nearest community to the house of San Simeon, more famously known as **Hearst Castle ⓱** (open daily). For many years Hearst Castle was the largest private residence in the US; now it vies with Disneyland for the title of "the state's most popular attraction." Perched over the sea on a hill so high the house is often wreathed in fog, its construction began in 1919, financed by newspaper and movie tycoon William Randolph Hearst. Craftsmen labored for 28 years to create the twin-towered home on *La Cuesta Encantada*, "the Enchanted Hill," which Hearst then filled with carvings, furnishings, and works of art from European castles and cathedrals. (During his lifetime, Hearst accumulated one of the largest collections of private art in the world, with a value measured in the hundreds of millions of dollars.) All materials for the house had to be brought up the coast by steamer, then hauled up that impossible hill. San Simeon's grounds were stocked with animals from all over the world, and Hollywood's elite, like Jean Harlow and Clark Gable, were invited to stroll through the beautiful gardens or enjoy the magnificent indoor and outdoor swimming pools.

Reservations for Hearst Castle (tel: 800-444-4445) are virtually mandatory to secure a place on one of the five daily tours, some of which include the home movies of Hearst, whose lonely, lavish lifestyle was the subject of Orson Welles' most celebrated movie, *Citizen Kane*. Tour 1 is probably the best for first-time

**Map on page 326**

*She was very nice and I liked her. She didn't have an awful lot to say... all the men used to flock around her. She was very attractive in an evening dress because she never wore anything under it.*

– MARION DAVIS ON JEAN HARLOW

**BELOW:** the Assembly Room decorated for Christmas, Hearst Castle.

visitors, as it gives the best overview of the castle and main rooms. Although Hearst Castle is very well visited, especially during the summer months, the estate is efficiently run, and timed entry means you can go away and have a picnic on the beach below if the wait proves to be a long one. Unmissable.

## Big Sur

The 94-mile (150-km) stretch of coastline between San Simeon and the Monterey Peninsula is known as **Big Sur** ⑱, a legendary wilderness of holistic healing retreats and remote homesteads inhabited by third-generation pioneers. The area was barely inaccessible to traffic until 1937, and even now the sheer cliffs of the Santa Lucia Mountains hugged by the highway occasionally slide into the sea, leaving residents in complete isolation until the road is rebuilt. There have been numerous occasions in recent years when Highway 1 has been closed for months at a time due to landslides, and as there are no roads inland between Cambria and Monterey, it is wise to check the situation at a gas station before proceeding.

The dark, thicketed mountains rise steeply to the right; the foamy sea to the left constantly changes shape and color. Only the two-lane road separates the two, which means the curling ribbon of road has its own distinct weather pattern. For this read: fog. Although the sun may be shining brightly on the other side of the mountain, and can often be seen slatted through the trees, Highway 1 can be distinctly chilly, and the fog comes on quickly, obliterating the world for unexpected moments. Infrequent guard rails, looking suspiciously flimsy, are small comfort in the face of the menacing rocks below. Driving along Big Sur is not for the faint-hearted *(see photograph on page 42),* but for those with a

**BELOW:** the best way to experience Big Sur is in a convertible or on a Harley. Be sure to wrap up, as the fog is chilly, even in the summertime.

sense of adventure and time on their side, this stretch of the California coastline is one of the most exhilarating routes in the US. For added excitement, try it in a convertible or – better yet – on a motorcycle, preferably a Harley-Davidson (which can be rented in either Los Angeles or San Francisco). Traveling non-stop with good weather, you could arrive in Carmel in about 3 hours, but the best way is to pause, then pause again, then stay at least for lunch or dinner. This is especially important for the person doing the driving, as the view is so fabulous, but the road so hazardous, it can be frustrating for the person at the wheel if frequent stops are not taken. Overlooks are numerous.

Coming from San Simeon, the hills begin gently enough, and the road fairly easy to navigate. The first sight on the right is **Los Padres National Forest**, the southern tip of the coastal redwood belt, which contains several almost preternaturally beautiful state parks. **Julia Pfeiffer Burns State Park** and **Pfeiffer Big Sur State Park** have wonderful trails that lead up into the mountains or down toward the sea, the former park with a waterfall near McWay Cove that rewards the completion of a (non-demanding) hike.

## The long and winding road

As the road twists and turns northward, anybody on a motorcycle will wish they had worn a heavy sweater. Arriving at **Big Sur Village** ⑲ confirms it is really little more than a huddle of shops and a post office. Places to stay are few and far between; if you're planning to be in Big Sur overnight during the summer months or on *any* weekend, be sure to book well in advance. The range of accommodation embraces the private campgrounds of Fernwood (tel: 831-667-2422) and Big Sur (tel: 831-667-2322) to the extravagant **Post Ranch Inn** (tel:

Map
on page
326

*Highway 1 runs almost the entire length of California. The Big Sur stretch is not for the faint-hearted.*

**BELOW:** Post Ranch Inn, Big Sur.

**BELOW:**

sea lions and birds, a common sight on this part of the Pacific Coast.

831-667-2200), an architectural gem set high on a hill, or the four-star, hot-tub haven of **Ventana** (tel: 831-667-2331) with its award-winning restaurant. A handful of motels and inns complete the picture.

Big Sur has always attracted unusual people. Until 1945 it was mainly populated by ranchers, lodgers, and miners, but soon after literary people turned up to stay. The **Henry Miller Memorial Library** near **Nepenthe restaurant**, where everybody goes for sunset, has works by and about this local literary hero, who called the area "the face of the earth as the creator intended it to look." In the 1960s, New Agers began communing at the hot spring called Esalen, named after the Native Americans who discovered it. Now the spring is owned by the **Esalen Institute**, where New Agers still congregate. North of the village is the area's crowning man-made achievement, the **Bixby Bridge**. Spanning the steep walls of Bixby Canyon and often obscured by fog, the bridge was called an engineering marvel when it was constructed in 1932.

## BIG SUR TO SAN FRANCISCO

Leaving the lush lands of Big Sur for the cities on the Monterey Peninsula can be a shock to the system. A way to ease this uncomfortable transition is to visit one last natural wonder on the way, the undramatic but still lovely **Point Lobos State Reserve** (tel: 831-624-4909; open daily). Miles of trails with glimpses of deer, rabbits, sea lions, and sea otters are gentle features that children will love. So did Robert Louis Stevenson, who is said to have been inspired to write *Treasure Island* while at Point Lobos. Several short footpaths traverse the rock-strewn headland, on which is one of two existing groves of ghostly Monterey Cypress trees.

## Carmel and Monterey

**Carmel** ❷⓿ ("Gateway to the Monterey Peninsula") has gained a reputation as being something of an artists' and writers' haven, but – due to the cost of local real estate – is really more a place for selling creative works than making them. Carmel is a classically beautiful little town that has outlawed high-rises, neon signs, traffic lights, parking meters – anything possessing the foul taint of city life, including artificial house plants. Although Carmel is undeniably attractive, the town's postcard-prettiness can be cloying, its prices inflated, and the snooty attitude of some of its residents (which include Hollywood's Clint Eastwood and Doris Day), does not inspire one to linger. **Carmel Mission** and **Carmel Beach** are very appealing, though; and just to the north is justly famous **Pebble Beach**, home to the challenging golf course of the same name.

Be warned: motorcyclists are not allowed on the peninsula's **17-Mile Drive**, which even charges an entrance fee to drive around admiring its luxurious private homes. These look, in fact, much like any other affluent American neighborhood, and given the proximity to the exquisite Big Sur coast, the shoreline along this private road is pretty expendable.

Cannery Row in **Monterey** ❷❶ at the north end of the peninsula basks in the glow of John Steinbeck's brilliant novel of the same name. What Steinbeck celebrated, however, were "weedy lots and junk heaps, sardine canneries of corrugated iron, honky tonks, restaurants and whore houses," not a tacky tourist trap. Steinbeck's world withered with the mysterious disappearance of the sardines in the mid-1940s, about the time the movie version of Steinbeck's *Sweet Thursday* was filmed here. A visit is redeemed, however, by a few hours spent at the excellent **Monterey Bay Aquarium** (tel: 831-648-4800), California's

Map on page 326

**BELOW:** statue of Father Serra in front of Carmel Mission.

Map
on page
326

finest and one of the best in the world, which explores to admirable effect the marine life found in a Grand Canyon-sized trench just offshore. Wall-length tanks house solitary sharks, regal salmon, and schools of tiny fish amid beds of kelp that writhe with the simulated tides. Keepers in glass tanks talk to spectators through underwater microphones during feeding times. Definitely a place to visit. In **Salinas**, Steinbeck's life is celebrated at the **National Steinbeck Center Museum** (tel: 831-796-3833; open daily), whose films and exhibits are devoted to the author's life.

## Half-moons and lighthouses

Traffic on this stretch of coast towards San Francisco is usually horrendous, with a virtually permanent traffic jam both sides of and within the resort of Santa Cruz, which sits at the head of Monterey Bay. The road is a divided highway, four-lanes bordered by flat agricultural fields. Although the beach town of **Capitola** is cute in a noisy sort of way, the main things to alleviate the disappointment about this stretch is the sunshine, welcome after the chilly fog of Big Sur, and the freshest of produce sold along the roadside: California's finest artichokes, cherries, and strawberries. Santa Cruz is a mile from the highway, and driving there is such a chore that you might want to continue up the coast through fields of artichokes to the attractive wide beach at **Scott Creek**, north of **Davenport**. On State Highway 156 to **Castroville**, the "Artichoke Capital of the World," is the Giant Artichoke Restaurant, which serves delicious deep-fried leaves. If you do choose to stop off in **Santa Cruz ㉒**, you can console yourself with a visit to the surfing museum or the **Boardwalk Amusement Park** (with scary roller coaster), or dine on yummy Dungeness crab in one of the restaurants on the pier, watching the pelicans play with swimmers in the sea.

Tan, black and white cows graze together in fields high up on the cliffs before Highway 1 swoops down to **Waddell Creek** and the driftwood-lined beaches (such as Bean Hollow State Beach) all the way up to the Santa Cruz county line. Thin slivers of fog can sometimes obscure the view, but when it shifts (which it does every few minutes), drivers are rewarded by views of **Pigeon Point Lighthouse ㉓**, which can be seen from the highway in both directions. Weekend tours are available; enquire locally.

Heading toward San Francisco, wide, flat fields lie between the highway and the coast. For a change of pace, horses can be rented at the coastal Seaview Riding Stable Ranch. Attractive **Half Moon Bay ㉔** is only half an hour's drive from the city, but is famous – not only for its pumpkins – but for the huge waves that pound its shores. Surfers from all around come to tackle the big ones – up to 40 feet (12 meters) high – and the talk in the bars is all of "mavericks" and "tubes." Sunday lunchtimes at Half Moon often include jazz or rock concerts.

With the suburbs of the city on the horizon, the coastline becomes rocky and untrafficked again. **Gray Whale Cove State Beach** or **Big Basin Park** are peaceful places for a final walk or picnic before hitting the big time – **San Francisco ㉕** *(see page 350).* ❑

**BELOW:** Monterey's Fisherman's Wharf.
**RIGHT:** Bixby Bridge, Big Sur, was called an engineering marvel in 1932.

# SAN FRANCISCO: CITY BY THE BAY

*Fisherman's Wharf, Chinatown, the Golden Gate Bridge – this city wins hearts straightaway and effortlessly*

**E**ach visitor takes a different memory away from San Francisco: the steep street that drops off toward the bay, the fog drifting through the Golden Gate Bridge, the dishes expertly blended making the perfect meal, or the simple fun of a cable-car ride, admiring Victorian houses along the way.

Begin at Union Square, where a winged statue commemorates Admiral George Dewey's naval victory over the Spanish in 1898. Chinatown Gate appears just to the northeast. While it is no secret to tourists, the crowds of Chinese residents vying for space on the sidewalk show the area still caters to locals. Tiny cluttered herb shops in

mysterious alleys promise everything from rheumatism relief to headache cures to the restoration of sexual prowess.

Chinatown ends where North Beach begins. While a few seedy clubs still promise lap dances, critically acclaimed restaurants and posh nightclubs entice a different crowd altogether. This old-fashioned Italian neighborhood still attracts writers and artists, however, particularly to the City Lights bookstore.

To the east, Telegraph Hill rises above North Beach, offering spectacular views across San Francisco Bay. Coit Tower (tel: 415-362-0808), with its momentous views and frescoes, crowns the hill and can be climbed.

Follow Columbus Avenue to Fisherman's Wharf. The fishing boats put out before dawn; their catch determines the "special of the day" at the numerous restaurants clustered around the wharf. Lined with shops and ready to please tourists, this is a "must" stop for all; even locals eat here.

A mile offshore from San Francisco is windswept Alcatraz (tel: 415-773-1188). Once home to such hardened criminals as Al Capone and the notorious Machine Gun Kelley, officials closed the prison in 1963 when repair costs grew too great. A tour of the prison is surprisingly rewarding; be sure to bring a sweater for the breezy boat ride over.

A ride on the Powell-Hyde cable car begins two blocks inland from Hyde Street Pier, offering a tour of Russian Hill's high-rise apartments and mansions. The cable car passes near the curvy section of Lombard Street often seen in movies and continues on to Nob Hill, called the "hill of palaces," by Robert Louis Stevenson.

At the corner of Washington and Mason streets, the Cable Car Barn Museum exhibits the city's transit history alongside the operating machinery that pulls the glamorous transportation through town.

The Financial District holds three impressive landmarks. The Embarcadero Center, the Bank of America building – so tall its roof sometimes disappears in the fog, and the distinctive Transamerica Pyramid, with 48 floors the tallest building in San Francisco.

"South of Market," or SoMa, is a focal point for art galleries, cafés, nightclubs, and local theaters. The San Francisco Museum of Modern Art (tel: 415-357-4000) spearheads the attractions of this area, which also include the Yerba Buena Gardens, the Center for the Arts, the Cartoon Art Museum, the Museum of the California Historical Society, and the Ansel Adams Center for Photography.

Mission Street heads south into the heart of the Mission district, San Francisco's melting pot of Latin American cultures. The thick adobe walls of Mission Dolores, built in 1776, still form the oldest building in San Francisco, which can be visited.

To the west lies the celebrated gay community of Castro. Same-sex couples and rainbow flags fill the streets lined with table-hopping bars, and such poignant landmarks as the Names Project Aids Memorial Quilt Visitors Center (tel: 415-863-1966).

Farther west is the Haight-Ashbury district. Haight Street was once so gaudy and bizarre that tour buses full of goggle-eyed tourists ran up and down it. Like most such radical departures from the social norm, the hippie experiment fell victim to time and fashion. The neighborhood still retains its anti-establishment roots, but today piercing shops and tattoo parlors replace flower power. It's still a lively, colorful stretch, however, with great shopping and a wide range of good, inexpensive restaurants and cafés.

Golden Gate Park (tel: 415-831-2700), 3 miles (5 km) long and almost half a mile wide, consists of tree groves dotted with lakes, meadows, and dells. Despite the thousands of visitors, it's easy to find tranquility here. In addition to peace, the Conservatory of Flowers offers botanical beauty, and the Music Concourse holds Sunday concerts.

The California Academy of Sciences (tel: 415-750-7145; open daily) includes animal dioramas, 16,000 specimens of marine life at the Steinhart Aquarium, and a laser light show at the Morrison Planetarium.

The Asian Art Museum (tel: 415-379-8800) contains 10,000 Asian artifacts dating back 3,500 years; the Japanese Tea Garden

claims to be the birthplace of the fortune cookie.

The beautiful, neoclassical California Palace of the Legion of Honor (tel: 415-863-3330) is unmissable. At the entrance is one of five bronze casts of Rodin's *The Thinker*.

The Golden Gate Bridge extends beyond the wonderful Golden Gate National Recreation Area. A promenade goes through Crissy Field, an airfield-turned-picnic area that belongs to the 1,480-acre (600-hectare) Presidio. In it stands The Plaster Palace, the classic rococo rotunda of the Palace of Fine Arts, housing the hands-on exhibits of the Exploratorium (tel: 415-561 0360).    ❑

**LEFT:** a cable car trundles up Nob Hill; the landmark Transamerica Pyramid was ridiculed when it was built in 1972.
**RIGHT:** follow the seagull signs for the best drive in town; Pacific Heights' Haas-Lilienthal House; the fabulous Golden Gate Bridge.

SHRINE
DRIVE-THRU TREE

5000          HEIGHT 275 FT.
21 FT.       CIR. 64 FT.
RS FLAT, CALIFORNIA

# SAN FRANCISCO TO OREGON

*The Pacific Coast Highway threads its way
past golden beaches, hot-tub hideaways,
good wineries, and the tallest living things on earth*

Map
on page
354

F rom San Francisco to the town of Crescent City, which is itself about half an hour's drive from the Oregon border, is 363 miles (584 km). Coastal beaches, wineries, and redwood forests are the attractions of this beautiful journey, with trees so massive you can even drive through one of them.

A trio of "goldens" marks the contributions of **San Francisco ㉕** to the Pacific Coast Highway, as Highway 1 passes straight through the city's Golden Gate Park, across the Golden Gate Bridge, and flirts with the southeastern edge of the Golden Gate National Recreation area. The pretty little harbor of **Sausalito ㉖** is located just off the highway, over the fabled golden bridge, with a turn-off to the right. The waterside shops, the warrens of pricey but perfect boutiques, and the houses perched behind them on a steep slope draw comparisons to Mediterranean villas of the Riviera. As there is little to do except stroll around or eat and drink, Sausalito might best be visited on a day trip by ferry from San Francisco, leaving you free to cruise westward toward the coast, passing near **Mount Tamalpais**, with its gorgeous views of the city in the far distance; the giant redwoods of 300-acre (120-hectare) **Muir Woods**; and **Stinson Beach**, the city's favorite destination on the few occasions it gets hot enough to swim. The coast road bypasses the town of **Bolinas**, on a thin sliver of a peninsula, which tries so hard not to attract visitors that a hard-core body of locals keeps stealing the highway signs.

The gorgeous **Point Reyes National Seashore** stretches northward for miles along a peninsula off which is the **Point Reyes Lighthouse** (visitor center open on weekends). On the way, the highway passes through tiny Olema; north of here it's possible to make a short (dead-end) diversion into the peninsula to attractive **Inverness**, which has a couple of pleasant eating places.

## Coastal drama

The road then travels lazily through pretty, upscale Marin County ("hot tub capital of the world") and out the northern end. A carved wooden fisherman in a bright yellow waterproof jacket sits outside Candy & Kisses as the road enters **Bodega**, which has a prominent sushi restaurant in midtown.

It's no coincidence that Alfred Hitchcock filmed his 1963 movie *The Birds* around **Bodega Bay ㉗**, where hundreds of bird species can be found. Brown pelicans are especially abundant.

After **Sonoma Coast State Beach** another really dramatic portion of the California coast begins, where Rivers End sits overlooking the mouth of the Russian River at **Jenner**. For miles Highway 1 snakes around the canyon at ascending levels. The top of a subsequent canyon has been plugged with stone, making a

**LEFT:** bikers love this big tree.
**BELOW:** Russian chapel, Fort Ross.

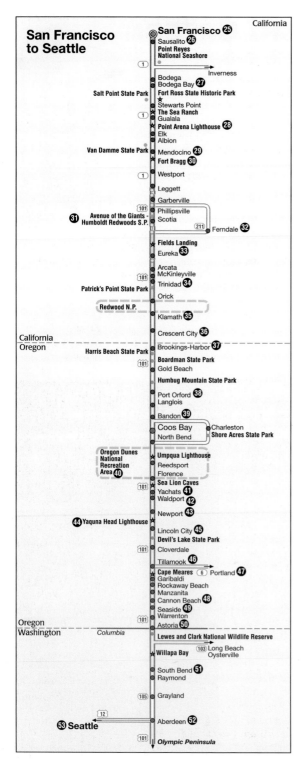

**San Francisco to Seattle**

California

San Francisco 25
Sausalito 26
Point Reyes National Seashore
Inverness
Bodega
Bodega Bay 27
Fort Ross State Historic Park
Salt Point State Park
Stewarts Point
The Sea Ranch
Gualala
Point Arena Lighthouse 28
Elk
Albion
Van Damme State Park
Mendocino 29
Fort Bragg 30
Westport
Leggett
Garberville
Phillipsville
Scotia
Avenue of the Giants - Humboldt Redwoods S.P. 31
Ferndale 32
Fields Landing
Eureka 33
Arcata
McKinleyville
Trinidad 34
Patrick's Point State Park
Orick
Redwood N.P.
Klamath 35
Crescent City 36
California
Oregon
Brookings-Harbor 37
Harris Beach State Park
Boardman State Park
Gold Beach
Humbug Mountain State Park
Port Orford 38
Langlois
Bandon 39
Coos Bay
Charleston
Shore Acres State Park
North Bend
Oregon Dunes National Recreation Area 40
Umpqua Lighthouse
Reedsport
Florence
Sea Lion Caves
Yachats 41
Waldport 42
Newport 43
Yaquna Head Lighthouse 44
Lincoln City 45
Devil's Lake State Park
Cloverdale
Tillamook 46
Cape Meares 6 Portland 47
Garibaldi
Rockaway Beach
Manzanita
Cannon Beach 48
Seaside 49
Warrenton
Oregon
Washington
Astoria 50
Columbia
Lewes and Clark National Wildlife Reserve
Willapa Bay 103 Long Beach
Oysterville
South Bend 51
Raymond
Grayland
Aberdeen 52
Seattle 53
Olympic Peninsula

bridge on which to site the road. The unfenced parts of the road are genuinely disconcerting; not a drive you'd want to make on a foggy night when – in any case – the fabulous views would be wasted.

The road goes right past the timbered stockade of **Fort Ross** (tel: 707-847-3286; open daily), but for history buffs it's worth exploring the cannon-studded fort with its church and blockhouses – if only to muse on how those early 19th-century Russian otter hunters withstood the rugged winters in flimsy wooden buildings on one of the windiest parts of the coast. So well fortified were they that their Indian and Spanish neighbors left them strictly alone until, in 1842, after 30 years of relentless otter hunting (for furs), they sold the place to rancher John Sutter and left. Between the fort and the sea is the former home of rancher G.W. Call, who farmed the area from 1873, shipping vast cargoes of potatoes, cattle, sheep, and wood products to San Francisco in his own coastal boats. The rear garden is a popular picnic spot.

## Look but don't swim

Back on the highway, the road descends to a dramatic cove before ascending once more. **Stillwater Cove Ranch** (tel: 707-847-3227) atop the hill is a delight – imaginative architecture and a stylish lobby whose gift shop features Ansel Adams books, paintings of blue cranes, and stuffed-wool racoons (whose real-life counterparts live in the hotel grounds). A number of sensationally situated inns, lodges, and ranches can be found around here, among them **Timber Cove Inn** (tel: 707-847-3231), "a place to be in love," according to the owners. They could be right, if its giant stone fireplace in a high-ceilinged lounge facing a beautiful bay is any indication.

At **Salt Point State Park** the trees march down to the water's edge. Off the highway, other beaches abound – such as Stump Beach and Fisk Mill Cove, the former being closer to the road, though suitably remote. Much of the time you'll find yourself a solitary visitor, as swimming is unsafe because of rip tides and what the coast guards call "sleeper waves." **Stewarts Point** was once a "doghole" for schooners, so-called because of its anchorages so tiny "only a dog could fit into them." This region was once part of the 5,000-acre (2,024-hectare) Rancho de Herman sheep farm, and sheep still graze south of **The Sea Ranch**, which – apart from being an irresistibly luxurious resort – is also a self-contained community with its own post office where locals come to pick up their mail. It's a popular place for weddings and other celebrations, for which there is a separate function space beside the ocean.

The Annapolis Winery announces itself with a sign at the beginning of a road of the same name, after which come Pebble Beach, Stengel Beach, and 8 more miles (13 km) of a winding two-lane road. Signs warn of deer crossing, and a bridge across the Gualala River marks the end of Sonoma County.

Map on page 354

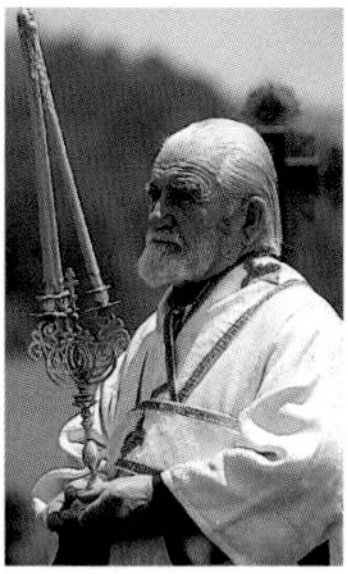

*Russian Orthodox priest at Fort Ross.*

## Mendonoma

Mendonoma, a name derived from the adjoining counties of Sonoma and Mendocino, identifies the coastal region between the Russian River at Jenner and the Navarro River, north of Point Arena. They'd like to share one telephone area code, but sadly the split was recently defined here at the Gualala River.

A heterogeneous mix of Russians, Germans, and Spaniards settled **Gualala** (pronounced *wah-***lah***-lah*) in the 1800s, which by the middle of the last century had four sawmills and four bars. Wells Fargo and Western Union had offices in the Gualala Hotel, built by the town's founder in 1903 when rooms with bath and ocean view cost $5. The writer Jack London stayed here a century ago, and things don't appear to have altered much. Since the last mill closed, upscale tourism has filled the gap.

**BELOW:** Bodega Bay at dawn.

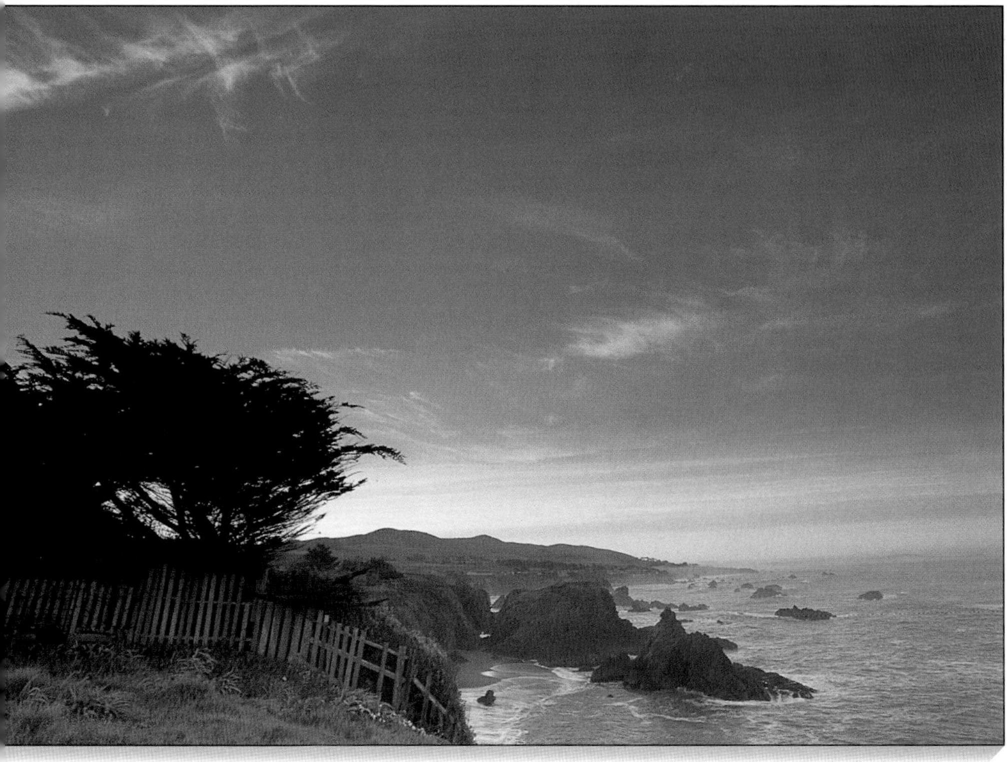

On the first Saturday of each month people come from far and wide to attend the rummage sale in the **Gualala Arts Center**, where they sometimes find pleasant surprises. A recent visitor ran across a small wooden owl collage her mother had made years before and which, as part of her vast collection of owl pictures, figurines, greeting cards, and jigsaw puzzles, had been sold for charity at her death. "I picked it up out of habit thinking fondly of Mom and how this was something she would really have liked," she told the *Coast Observer*. "Words cannot describe the feeling that came over me when I turned it over and found, in Mom's unmistakable handwriting, *Put together by me, 12/15/77.*"

A distinctive wooden Olde West structure with a tower marks **Anchor Bay**. Farther along, a carved blue-striped white wooden horse sits in a field, after which the coast-hugging, sometimes lonely road seems mostly deserted. Fifteen miles (24 km) of winding two-lane highway allow ample time to contemplate that state law decreeing that slow-moving vehicles must use a turn-off if five or more vehicles back up behind them.

One of the truly great coastal experiences is **Point Arena Lighthouse** ㉘, the tip of which can be spotted at the beginning of the 2-mile (3-km) diversion. A classically beautiful 111-foot (34-meter) high white tower with 145 steps, it replaced an earlier lighthouse damaged by the 1906 San Francisco earthquake. Its 2-ton (2,000-kg) French-made Fresnel lens (floating on a tub of mercury) was itself replaced in the 1970s with an aircraft-type beacon. It is maintained by a non-profit group of local citizens and takes 5 minutes to climb to the top.

**BELOW:** shave and a haircut, Mendocino.

Miles of open pasture dotted with ramshackle barns and grazing cows follow Point Arena. Then the road dips, turns, climbs, and dives, punctuated by fancy hostelries with such names as the Inn at Schoolyard Creek and Little River Inn. These types of bed and breakfast inns, plus restaurants serving high-level "California cuisine," are also features of tiny **Elk** and **Albion**, pretty roadside communities on either side of the Nararro River, with sloping tracks down to the beach. Soon after crossing the river, the highway twists and turns around high cliffs before descending to a leafy stretch past **Van Damme State Park** (which contains a "pygmy forest" of pines and cypresses), offering occasional glimpses of the sea. Keep an eye out for the colorful steel sculptures on the lawn of the Stevenswood restaurant to the right.

## Mendocino

The lovely old town of **Mendocino** ㉙, which lacks motels, supermarkets, and fast-food joints, is one of the most admired places on the coast and thus is usually filled with tourists, most of whom are just passing through. If you choose to stay the night after they have gone, you'll be rewarded with great restaurants (some with health-obsessed menus), and numerous small bed and breakfast inns, as well as art galleries and a Fetzer Vineyards tasting room adjoining the Mendocino Hotel. The entire village, established by New England whalers, is on the National Register of Historic Places. Among several Victorian homes, the 1854 **Ford House** and the 1861 **Kelley House** (both open daily in summer) each contain small museums. Be warned: parking spaces in Mendocino are as rare as gold dust.

North of Caspar the delightful **Mendocino Coast Botanical Gardens** (tel: 707-964-4352; open daily) are worth a stop if only to walk through the aromatic pine forest to the sea, enjoying the interplay between light and shade. Plants can be bought here, too. Next comes Noyo Harbor, once the biggest lumber port between Eureka and San Francisco and now a marina for sports fishing boats along with a "fisherman's village" and plenty of restaurants.

## Shipwrecks and microbreweries

An 1820 shipwreck led to the founding of **Fort Bragg** ㉚, when treasure seekers came to loot the wreckage and discovered the redwoods. A fort was built and the Bureau of Indian Affairs established a reservation for the Pomo Indians. Lumber mills sprang up, along with a railroad to transport their product. When the 1906 earthquake devastated so much of San Francisco, it was Fort Bragg's mills that provided the wood for rebuilding. The famous old "**Skunk Train**" (tel: 800-777-5865) that once carried timber across the mountains to the sawmill at Willits has been a tourist favorite for years, and it still follows the same picturesque route along the Noyo River and through redwood groves.

What remains of the original fort, along with surviving Victorian buildings, can be seen one block east of Main Street (Highway 1) near the Skunk Train depot at Laurel and Franklin. Both the Guest House Museum (local history) and the North Coast Brewing Company (free tours, tel: 707-964-3400), one of America's best microbreweries, are on Main Street. The town also blossoms with nurseries, one of which grows millions of trees for reforestation projects.

Map on page 354

*The "Skunk Train" at Fort Bragg once carried timber; now it transports tourists through enormous redwood groves.*

**BELOW:** Mendocino.

**TIP**

If you don't feel like making the fairly arduous 4–5-hour round-trip drive to see the hidden attractions of the Lost Coast, you can hire a guide in Ferndale; enquire locally for details.

Fort Bragg is an unpretentious working town refreshingly free of the leisure chic that pervades the surrounding areas. After Fort Bragg, 22 miles (35 km) of incessantly twisting and winding tree-shaded, narrow road (30 mph/48 kph is the most you'll manage) are interspersed with sections of freeway. Gift shops selling carved wooden figures (Big Foot is a favorite) and gimmicky attractions such as the circular house carved from a single redwood log and **Confusion Hill** (tel: 707-925-6456) vie for attention. The latter really is pretty weird: water runs uphill here; there's also a wooden shack in which a golf ball climbs a slope and a chair prevents you from getting up without using your arms.

The guy who bought Confusion Hill discovered these apparent paradoxes when he first tried to build his home on the hillside, and although some of the effects are obviously optical illusions, the owner says there are things he still hasn't figured out. There's also a funicular ride up the mountain.

## The Lost Coast

A few miles north of **Westport**, Highway 1 takes a final look at the sea before heading 25 miles (40 km) inland. Here it merges with US 101 at Leggett and – apart from a brief stretch near Eureka – disappears forever. The relatively inaccessible (and often unpaved) coastal road leads up through the evocatively named Sinkyone Wilderness and beyond, onto the justly celebrated **Lost Coast**, which has gloriously and almost uniquely escaped development. It's an area of "black sand beaches and old-growth forests on a wall of windswept peaks," as one writer noted. There are 80 miles (130 km) of trails and six campgrounds under the aegis of the Bureau of Land Management (tel: 707-825-2300).

Once projected for an extension of Highway 1, the coast can be visited via a

**BELOW:** rustic residents of the Lost Coast.

loop road picked up at the town of Weott, north of Leggett. The narrow side road crosses the Mattole River at Honeydew, heads through Petrolia, the site of the state's first but disappointingly unproductive oil strike, and follows the coast north to Ferndale, where it veers inland again to rejoin US 101 (*see "Ferndale," page 360, for more about the Lost Coast*).

**Map on page 354**

## Avenue of the Giants

South again, Highway 1 merges into US 101 at **Leggett** ("a fern-carpeted setting," claims one local resident), followed by **Garberville**, a pleasant little town known for its good manners and even better marijuana. Containing several restaurants and motels, Garberville is an ideal place to break your journey before heading into redwood country proper. Farther north, at **Phillipsville**, the 31-mile (50-km) **Avenue of the Giants** ❸ offers an irresistible alternative to US 101, to which it runs parallel, allowing occasional on-off access. There are trees here more than 300 feet (90 meters) high and up to 20 feet (6 meters) in diameter. "From them come silence," wrote John Steinbeck.

A handful of buildings are all that remain of two small towns that once straddled the route until they were washed away by floods in 1964. Otherwise the route in this stupendously awesome 50,000-acre (20,200-hectare) forest is untrammeled by human life. A series of small groves are dedicated to various groups and individuals that have fought to preserve this magnificent enclave. They are places for contemplation. "We do not see nature with our eyes," wrote William Hazlitt, "but with our understandings and our hearts." Many of the trees on the east side were planted in the 1980s under reforestation projects. Near the town of **Myers Flat** is the **Drive-Thru Tree**, a favorite with children and

**BELOW:** the Avenue of the Giants is a scenic drive of many miles.

tourists. Before Weott, the **Humboldt Redwoods State Park Visitor Center** (tel: 707-946-2263) is filled with explanatory exhibits about the magnificent redwoods, which attract tree fans from around the world.

## All about trees

*I never saw a discontented tree. They grip the ground as though they liked it, and though fast rooted they travel about as far as we do.*
— JOHN MUIR

Redwood has long been prized for its density and deep color, and despite slumps in the building industry and competition from more common trees such as cedar, it remains in demand. The logging industry, born in tandem with the Gold Rush, made hardly a dent in the redwood belt until the advent of power saws in the 1940s, which made it possible to clear acres in a single day. It takes 40 years to raise a stand of redwoods for such uses as pulp and press board, and 500 years to develop the fine grain and blood-red tint that have made the wood so popular: virgin forest remains at a premium. Conservationists estimate that trees are logged at two and a half times the rate of regeneration.

The company town of **Scotia**, built by the Pacific Lumber Company in 1869 entirely of ancient redwood, has a logging museum and fisheries exhibit and offers a self-guided sawmill tour (tel: 707-764-2222; closed weekends). This nature trail through a "Preservation Forest" is a skillful public relations ploy intended to ease visitors gently into the conception of this magnificent forest as a well-managed renewable resource. John Muir was not a friend to lumbermen. "Any fool can destroy trees," he commented. "They cannot defend themselves or run away… It took more than 3,000 years to make some of the oldest of the sequoias, trees that are still standing in perfect strength and beauty, waving and singing in the mighty forests of the Sierra."

**BELOW:** haunting Humboldt County.

The redwoods inspire not only passing tourists, but also the entire livelihood of the Humboldt community. Sculptors carve timbers into life-sized grizzly bears for sale at the roadside. Others, for a pretty hefty admission fee, show off the stout trunks growing in their backyards. Huge logging trucks carrying both raw timber and finished boards along the highway are a constant reminder that the trees in this area are an economic necessity as well as a natural wonder.

**Fortuna**'s **Depot Museum** features local logging and railroading history. Located on a back road between Fortuna and Eureka is minuscule **Loleta**, celebrated for cheese and ice cream production. Its factory, which starred in the 1982 movie *Hallowe'en III: the Season of the Witch,* makes supermarket ice cream in loads of varieties for 11 different companies.

## Fascinating Ferndale

The fascination of **Ferndale** ㉜, on the Eel River west of US 101 (reached by turning west off the highway just north of Fortuna), stems from its large numbers of garishly hued Victorian stores and houses, many of which have been converted into enticing bed and breakfasts. (The Creekside Inn advertises "Bed and No Breakfast" but does serve afternoon tea). The whole town, designated a State Historical Landmark, naturally attracts tourists by the thousand. The elaborately turreted and gabled **Gingerbread Mansion Inn** on Berding Street is outstanding, and the town's oldest building, the 18-room **Shaw House Inn**, is fashioned after Nathaniel Hawthorne's *House of the Seven Gables*. The year-round mild climate encourages productive gardening, and one is apt to see tamed cypresses shaped like giant gumdrops, or other evidence of extensive topiary work. At the head of Main Street, the 110-year-old **Victorian Inn** (tel: 888-589-1808) accurately boasts of its "luxurious comfort and exquisite craftsmanship;" also notable is the **Ferndale Emporium**, farther down the street, which serves genteel afternoon teas from Thursday to Saturday.

A top-hatted driver offers rides around town in a horse and carriage, while there's a genuine soda fountain on Main Street. Understandably, Ferndale attracts moviemakers, who use its setting for movie and TV dramas. Check out the **Kinetic Sculpture Race Museum** (tel: 707-786-9259; open daily) with its people-powered models used in the annual three-day race from Arcata.

## Wildcat Road

The drive south along the Lost Coast from Ferndale follows the old stagecoach route that's known locally as Wildcat Road, climbs high into the hills and then after 30 miles (48 km) of twists and turns, descends to cross the Bear River and arrives at the defunct community of Capetown. Off the deserted black sand beach is the immense Sugarloaf Rock and nearby Steamboat Rock, which resembles a big tanker stranded at sea. The **Cape Mendocino Lighthouse** – replaced in 1951 with an automatic beacon – had at least nine ships wrecked off this rugged shore during its 65-yer history. But it's not necessary to drive the 4- to 5-hour round trip to the Lost Coast if you hire the knowledgeable local guide and historian who has been transporting tourist groups around the region

**BELOW:**
Gingerbread
Mansion Inn,
Ferndale.

in his minibus for many years; it's worth checking while you're in Ferndale to see if he's available.

The biggest coastal city on the California coast north of San Francisco, **Eureka** ❸ (pop. 27,000) and its **Old Town** area on the waterfront has often stood in for the Bay Area city in movies. It has been anchored since 1922 by the **Eureka Inn** (tel: 800-862-4906), a massive Tudor Revival mansion whose early guests included Laurel and Hardy, Shirley Temple, John Barrymore, and Britain's Winston Churchill, who stopped by Eureka to visit an old friend who was editing the local paper. The town's distinctive 1886 **Carson Mansion** – built by a lumber baron with a yen for gables, towers, and turrets – is generally regarded as the handsomest Victorian building in the state, if not in the entire West. It is now a private club.

At the **Blue Ox Millworks** (tel: 707-444-3437; closed Mon), a working Victorian sawmill, visitors can watch craftsmen at work and see how much of the characteristic "gingerbread" ornamentation for such houses was crafted. The old Carnegie Library, with its wonderful balconies and redwood pillars, has been converted into an art museum; other attractions include the **Humboldt Bay Maritime Museum** with its lighthouse memorabilia, and the **Clarke Memorial Museum** with its collection of weapons, Native American crafts, and Victoriana.

**BELOW:** Eureka's Carson Mansion is one of the finest Victorian houses in California.

Across the bay on a peninsula is the famous **Samoa Cookhouse** (tel: 707-442-1659; open daily), which is the last remaining example of the 1890s lumber camp cookhouses, whose rules included eating as much as you could for a fixed price and helping yourself to anything within reach as long as one foot remained on the ground. Today, huge meals are served family style at long tables – and the same rules apply.

## EUREKA TO OREGON

Just north of Eureka, with a reputation for being "the Galapagos of North America," **Arcata** is famous for its birdwatching opportunities. Its variety of bird life is greater than anywhere else in the state, and Marbled Godwit, White-tailed Kite, and Cinnamon Teal are frequently observed. The Chamber of Commerce on G. Street, two blocks north of the plaza, publishes a free leaflet detailing all the different bird types and where to find them, as well as a self-guided walking map of old Victorian homes. Such establishments as Rookery Books and a coffee company advertising "our coffee is for the birds," are an indication of the level of interest in our feathered friends.

Birdwatchers from all over the country converge on the town for the annual Godwit Days in April to go on field trips and attend workshops with such intriguing titles as "Advanced Identification," and "Intermediate Owls." Adjoining the filtration plant on Arcata Bay (which produces more than half of California's oyster crop) is the main center of birding activity, the **Marsh and Wildlife Sanctuary**. Aleutian geese, once down to less than 1,000 in number, are now abundant after years of protection under the Endangered Species Act.

The town of Arcata, founded by a group of miners

from the Trinity River region in 1849, grew up around the **Jacoby Building** on the plaza. It was erected in 1857 of masonry, when wood usually sufficed, by a far-sighted merchant whose pack trains serviced the goldmines upriver. Elegantly restored and refitted, it now houses stylish shops, a railroad museum, and two of the town's best restaurants. On the ground floor is a store selling the stylish (and expensive) glassware made by Fire and Light, owned by a local group who conceived the company to take advantage of the huge amounts of recycled glass available. Their small factory offers demonstrations of the glass-making process.

Humboldt State University's **Natural History Museum** exhibits everything from butterflies to dinosaur tails. **McKinleyville**, the fastest growing town in Humboldt County, is also the nearest one to the misnamed Eureka-Arcata airport. It claims to have the world's tallest single-tree totem pole (at the shopping center). Its 30-acre (12-hectare) **Azalea Reserve**, which blooms in spring, can be reached via a trail off North Bank Road (Central Avenue exit from US 101; for information tel: 707-839-2449).

*A fine place to meet good swimmers.*

## Moonshine Beach and Wedding Rock

At **Moonshine Beach**, just north of the airport, Highway 1 detaches itself from US 101, under which it has been submerged for the past 100 miles (161 km). For a delightful stretch of 20 miles (32 km) or so it runs along the coast through the lovely clifftop village of **Trinidad ❸** (pop. 435), named by a Spanish explorer in 1775 and the site of a small museum. It is also the last gas station for 30 miles (48 km). Farther north is the entrance of **Patrick's Point State Park**, named for an Indian scout who settled here in 1851. Seals can be admired basking on the rocks off Rocky Point, and at low tide there are tide pools to explore.

**BELOW:** gathering seaweed is a good test for would-be mermaids.

*The lands within one mile of the Klamath River comprise the Yurok Reservation. Near Wedding Rock is the site of an old Yurok village, preserved with its sweat lodge, ceremonial dance pit and simple plank houses with circular doorways, through which women were obliged to enter backwards.*

**BELOW:** pretty as a picture of a picnic.

Farther north, **Wedding Rock** is a popular site for marriages conducted to the accompaniment of crashing waves below. The rock got its name from the park's first caretaker, Vieggo Andersen, whose marriage there to his housekeeper in 1933 began a popular custom. Scenes from Steven Spielberg's *Lost World* were filmed in the parking lot. Nearer to the highway, by the site of the old Yurok village, is an old canoe hollowed out by fire from a tree trunk, which sits near a native garden of indigenous plants. Camping is allowed and *yurts* (highly comfortable, wooden-floor tents) can be rented by the night.

About 25 miles (40 km) north of Patrick's Point on the highway before Orick, the **Redwood Information Center** (tel: 707-488-3461) distributes free maps depicting the various trails and camping sites of the redwood forests that extend northward from Crescent City. Seldom-seen black bears roam through the parks – as well as Roosevelt elk, which occasionally emerge onto the highway (don't get too close!) – but for the most part it's trees, trees, trees – the tallest living things on earth, which can reach heights of more than 360 feet (110 meters). Fossil records indicate that millions of years ago they blanketed the northern hemisphere when the climate was warmer and wetter. Today, only isolated patches of redwoods remain – mainly in California and China.

Judging by the stalls along the road, the main industry of **Orick**, once a major logging center, appears to be the sale of "burl slabs," which are grotesquely shaped redwood roots. Check out the venerable Palm Café and Motel (tel: 707-488-3381). When driving along, take the signposted Newton B. Drury Scenic Parkway through **Prairie Creek Redwoods Park**, a long avenue of incredibly tall trees. Somewhere along the way you'll probably see the resident herd of Roosevelt elk, which have a tendency to graze beside the highway. These animals should be treated with respect because they can be unpredictably dangerous. A worthwhile sidetrip is to drive down the narrow, pot-holed Coastal Trail along **Golden Bluffs Beach** through dense woodland to **Fern Canyon**; a ravine bordered on either side by sheer, fern-carpeted cliffs.

### Trees of Mystery

For a few miles before **Klamath** ⑮, US 101 runs alongside the broad **Klamath River**, crossed by a bridge marked at each end by life-size statues of golden bears. For a spectacular view of where the river meets the ocean, take the Requa Road on your left to an overlook 600 feet (183 meters) above the water. (This side road dead-ends after a few miles.) Gold mines farther up the Klamath River were once served via Klamath from steamers that brought supplies up the coast from San Francisco. Today the river is popular for jetboat tours from Klamath to see such wildlife as elk and bears. Huge "cartoon" figures herald the **Trees of Mystery** (tel: 800-638-3389; open daily). A trail leads past some unusual groupings: nine trees growing from one root structure to form the so-called **Cathedral Tree**; a dozen others growing from a single Sitka Spruce trunk. Admission is charged to each trail, but the absorbing museum, with its large collection of Indian costumes and crafts, is free.

US 101 hugs the coast around many attractive bays

before beginning a lengthy climb where traffic along the narrow road is controled by solar-powered lights. Tall trees flank most of the final 10 miles (16 km)
into Crescent City, until the sea comes into view once again just before town.

## Tallest living things on earth

Crescent City ㊱, named for the shape of the bay on which it sits, sprawls
somewhat unattractively behind an interesting harbor replete with restaurants,
a seafood market, and a **Marine Mammal Center** where distressed seals and
sea lions are rehabilitated. West of the harbor the **Battery Point Lighthouse** (tel:
707-464-3089; open Wed–Sun) can be visited at low tide and contains a museum
with photographs of some of the shipwrecks off this treacherous coast. When
John Muir visited Crescent City in 1896, he went out on a logging train to see
"the work of ruin going on." Some of the trees, he observed, were up to 200 feet
(61 meters) high and 20 feet (6 meters) in diameter and yet two men could
chop them down in a single day. His experiences doubtless led him to fight for
the redwoods' preservation. Crescent City has named a shopping center after
Jedediah Smith, the fur trapper who first explored the region in the 1820s, and
after whom the vast **Jedediah Smith Redwoods State Park** to the east is
named. The spectacular and turbulent Smith River, which runs through 300
miles (483 km) of wild scenery, offers white-water rafting between soaring
canyon walls. At **Gasquet**, on US 199, which runs through the **Smith River
National Recreation Area**, a Forest Service office (tel: 707-457-3131) provides maps, general information, and the opportunity to book a night in a remote
fire-lookout cabin atop Bear Basin Butte. Whether you head north from Crescent City or Gasquet, in less than 25 miles (40 km), you'll be in **Oregon**. ❑

Map
on page
354

*This huge tribute to
lumberjack Paul
Bunyan signals the
entrance to the
Trees of Mystery.*

**BELOW:** parade at
Klamath's Yurok
Salmon Festival.

# OREGON TO WASHINGTON

Map on page 354

*Oregon's rugged coastline stretches for 400 miles, offering wilderness glimpses of deer, elk, and bald eagles, before heading into the state of Washington for more of the same*

Trusty US 101 trundles all the way up the Oregon coast and into the state of Washington, serving the same function that Highway 1 served in California – offering some of the best coastal scenery in the United States. Rural and more rugged than much of its southern neighbor, Oregon's section of US 101, signposted as the Pacific Coast Scenic Highway, offers tantalizing views of elk and bald eagles.

## BROOKINGS-HARBOR TO WALDPORT

The southern part of the Oregon Coast – the **Siskiyou Coast** – begins calmly enough; a drive taking the car through relatively peaceful farmland after the turbulence of the Smith River near the state border. Ships pop up on dry land, first a huge one beached beside the appropriately named Ship Ashore Motel, and then an old tugboat beached and converted into a souvenir store just south of **Brookings-Harbor ③**. This is the town (although technically "towns": Brookings is the larger of the two side-by-side communities) where the sports fishing fleet anchors, and it also contains the local Visitor Information Bureau (tel: 800-535-9469).

At the mouth of the Chetco River, Brookings is a popular retirement spot because of its reputation as being in the "banana belt," with winter temperatures often reaching 65°F (18°C). The technical explanation for its moderate climate is that the town's southeast to northwest geographical layout combines with constant low-pressure thermal troughs that pull down the highly compressed air following a storm system. One consequence is that the region produces most of the country's Easter lilies, and visitors swarm in to see **Azalea State Park** (tel: 541-489-2063) in the springtime when the flowers are in bloom. There's an Azalea Festival on Memorial Day weekend. Some of the most spectacular scenery is to be found in coastal **Boardman State Park** just south of town. March brings daffodils, May the wild azaleas, and July the snow lilies, while every month of the year brings eager photographers.

**LEFT:** Yaquina Head Lighthouse, Oregon.
**BELOW:** windsuring is popular with Washingtonians.

### Anyone for gas?

As Oregon's coastline stretches for 400 miles (643 km), you won't be in the state for long before discovering that state law prohibits customers pumping their own gas, ostensibly to "boost the economy" by providing more jobs, but also because it is supposedly unsafe. This particular part of the Oregon Statute (unpopular with locals), cites 20 potential hazards, including the fact that customers are not trained in the safe handling of flammable liquids and that exposure to toxic fumes is a health hazard.

North of town past the large, green barns of the South Coast Lumber Company, and near the **Harris Beach State Park**, are numerous parking bays beside the highway from which to gaze at the ocean. Harris is one of 30 places on the Oregon coast designated as a whale-watching site, and is attended by trained volunteers on winter mornings to assist visitors.

Around 100 gray whales spend the summer feeding off the Siskiyou coast; the smaller mammals often nursing a calf. Larger gray whales can reach 45 feet (14 meters) in length – bigger than a Greyhound bus – and weigh up to 45 tons (45,720 kg). Their annual migration between the Bering Sea and Mexico is a gruelling 10,000-mile (16,000-km) round trip at a speed of around 5 mph (8 kph) heading southbound.

*Kissing Rock dates its name from 1850, when prospectors discovered that the sands surrounding the rock were sprinkled with gold dust.*

## Kissing Rock

US 101 soon crosses the **Thomas Creek Bridge**, the state's highest at 345 feet (105 meters), then a string of beaches begins just before Pistol River. The best of these are around the rather eye-catching **Kissing Rock**, popular with wind-surfers, between Meyers Creek and Gold Beach. The latter's name dates from the 1850s, when prospectors discovered that the sands around the mouth of the Rogue River were salted with gold dust.

Today, several companies offer excursions in powerful hydro jetboats up the river, whose upper reaches encompass dramatic canyons hundreds of feet deep. Sport fishing for salmon and steelhead trout can be arranged, as well as ocean fishing, and horses can be rented for riding on the beach. Stop for an espresso at **Gold Beach**, where you'll see the large mural on the side of the Soakery Coffee House, and make time to visit the Curry County Historical Museum

**BELOW:**
woman casting her nets wide and contributing to the local economy.

(tel: 541-247-6113; open Tues–Sat afternoons in summer). There are more farms and more cows north of town and there's even a pastoral community farther north called Denmark where, appropriately enough, cows appear to be the only visible inhabitants.

Seven miles (11 km) north of the Rogue River at **Nesika Beach**, the highway levels with the shoreline. Low-lying, tree-covered hills flank the right-hand side and marshland sits between road and sea. Massive moss and lichen-covered rocks stick out of the water, and around **Humbug Mountain** the scenery is particularly stunning. Towering mountains taper down to the road, which flanks a series of bays enlivened by crashing white surf. "The mountains are fountains of men as well as of rivers, of glaciers, of fertile soil," wrote John Muir. "The great poets, philosophers, prophets, able men whose thoughts and deeds have moved the world, have come down from the mountains – mountain dwellers have grown strong there with the forest trees in Nature's workshop."

## Westernmost city

Keep an eye out on the right for the painted dinosaur outside the **Prehistoric Gardens** in the rainforest. **Port Orford** ❸ ("a jewel-like coastal village perched on scenic bluffs," wrote one observer) is the westernmost city in the contiguous United States, and was a major lumber shipping port more than a century ago. Just offshore, past the battered shack that houses the Crazy Norwegians Café, is a wooded island called **Battle Rock**. In 1851 the island's original party of settlers was besieged by local Indians who resented their claim to the land. A month later a larger white group arrived and took possession.

Take a lingering look at Port Orford's lovely bay, because it will be your last

**Map on page 354**

**BELOW:**
logging pond full of rich timber destined for a large lumber mill.

uninterrupted view of the ocean for nearly 100 miles (161 km), although frequent "Coastal Access" signs dot the highway. Northeast of town on Elk River Road is the **Elk River Fish Hatchery**, where salmon smelts are raised.

## Lighthouses and lazy countryside

A 6-mile (10-km) side trip can be made to the cliffs of **Cape Blanco** to inspect the 1870 lighthouse (tel: 541-332-4248; open Thur–Mon in summer), which sits 245 feet (75 meters) above the sea. Next comes **Langlois**, with its half a dozen antique shops located in serene countryside filled with cows and sheep. In the surrounding hills are many lonely sheep ranches. Miles of bright yellow gorse line the approach to **Bandon ㊴**, twice destroyed by fire in the last century; a brick chimney on the site of the old bakery stands as a memorial just off the highway. Artists' homes and studios along with craft shops cluster around Bandon's **Old Town** area. The historical society's museum includes an exhibit about cranberry cultivation. This has been taking place in nearby bogs for more than a century, ever since the early settlers learned the technique from the Indians. The town celebrates with a Cranberry Festival every fall, and cranberry farms can be toured by appointment. Near Bandon is another lighthouse, the **Coquille River Lighthouse**.

**Coos Bay** is a major lumber shipping port, and the town itself, with warehouses and stacked timber lining the road, is not very attractive. Back in 1850, Asa Simpson established a sawmill and shipyard here, which built about 50 vessels before the end of the century. Tours can be made of the giant Weyerhauser Lumber Mill (where trees are stripped, sliced, and shaped) and also of the **Oregon Connection** factory, where myrtlewood logs are fashioned into bowls, goblets, and other products. To the east is **Golden and Silver Falls State Park** with its 100-foot (30-meter) waterfalls, and on the coast, south of the fishing village of **Charleston**, is **Shore Acres State Park**, once the gardens of the spacious house of lumber baron Louis J. Simpson, son of the legendary Captain Asa M. Simpson. New Englander Simpson founded an Oregon lumbering and shipbuilding empire.

## Dune walk

Across the long bridge spanning the Hayes Inlet is Coos Bay's neighbor, **North Bend**, where the useful Visitors Information Bureau (tel: 541-756-4613) sits opposite the ancient steam locomotive outside the Coos County Historical Museum (tel: 541-752-4847; open Tues–Sat).

The **Oregon Dunes National Recreation Area ㊵** begins at North Bend, a huge expanse of sand that blocks easy access to the sea for 40 miles (64 km) of coast. There are 11 different places offering beach access, at least one of which, **Spineel** (watch for the highway sign) offers a chance to rent dune buggies (tel: 541-759-3313) and cavort in the sandy wilderness. These dunes reach heights of several hundred feet, giving refuge to many types of flora and fauna, and are constantly sculpted into different shapes by wind and water. In addition to campgrounds and hiking trails, they are rife with wildlife and birds, as well

**BELOW:**
eat it now and
catch it later in
Bandon.

as red and yellow salmon berries, thimble berries (similar to raspberries), wild strawberries, and, in the fall, huckleberries.

Lower **Umpqua Bay** is said to be the most fertile place for big soft-shell clams, some weighing around half a pound (220 grams). The delicious Dungeness crab is found in the Winchester Bay area, where the Umpqua River meets the ocean. Shops sell crabbing equipment and bait.

At the Umpqua Dunes Trailhead (watch for the highway sign) you can park the car and climb the dunes. Camp facilities here include *yurts*: structurally supported domed tents with plywood floors, lockable doors, comfortable beds, and light and heating. Designed to withstand high winds and retain heat in winter, they are 126 feet (38 meters) in diameter with very high ceilings. Altogether the state of Oregon has 155 of them spread over 19 different parks, (tel: 800-551-6949 for information). In summer you might care to take a 5-mile (8-km) side trip to visit the **Umpqua Lighthouse** (open Wed–Sat afternoons), an 1894 replacement for the first one that had been built on the Oregon coast 37 years previously.

## Rusty frogs and bald eagles

Just before **Salmon Harbor** (unsurprisingly the largest salmon fishing port on the Oregon coast) watch for the Rusty Frog Gallery to your right and then cross the bridge into **Reedsport**, where an interpretive facility, the **Umpqua Discovery Center** (tel: 541-271-4816; open daily) explains the dunes and much else besides. An additional source is the **Dunes Visitor Center** on US 101, which publicizes preservation efforts, issues bird checklists (there are five different types of seagull alone), and books campground sites (tel: 877-444-6677). A

Map on page 354

*ATVs (all terrain vehicles) are the perfect way to play on the dunes; you can rent them in the town of Spineel.*

**BELOW:** the Oregon Dunes National Recreation Area.

*Many people not born near the sea confuse sea lions with seals. Sea lions have external ears, and can rotate their hind flippers to walk on land. Seals live exclusively on the edge of – or in – the water.*

**BELOW:**
watching boats, collecting driftwood, and studying tide pools are popular pastimes along this low-key coast.

mile or two to the east, visitors can admire herds of Roosevelt elk at the pleasant **Dean Creek Elk Viewing Area**, which is also a haven for bald eagles, osprey, and blue herons. Occasional signs warn that elk may stray into the road.

Continuing north, with water on both sides of the highway, the enormous plant of the International Paper Company stretches beside the Sound for half a mile. The road soon narrows to two lanes. "The law requires slow-moving vehicles to use turn-outs" is a sign frequently seen around these parts. A sensible law, indeed, you'll think when caught behind one of those huge family RVs ambling along at 30 mph (48 kph). There are numerous campgrounds in the flanking forest, and about a mile before the bridge into Florence is the **Siuslaw Pioneer Museum** (closed Mon), displaying old photographs and household items.

## Check the conditions

**Florence** has a picturesque harbor back-dropped by some ancient buildings, but it is not a place to detain the visitor for long except when the rhododendrons display their vivid pink blossoms in late spring. When landslides block US 101 to the north (as happened for months early in 2000), it's the last chance to turn inland before Waldport. If traffic conditions have been bad, check with the Oregon Department of Transportation (tel: 888-275-6368), because even when the road is "closed" it's sometimes open for an hour or two each day, usually early morning and early evening.

Eleven miles (18 km) north of Florence is the **Heceta Head Lighthouse**, which has been beaming its warning to mariners since 1894. Also, not far from Florence are the interesting **Sea Lion Caves** (tel: 541-547-3111; open daily) at the bottom of cliffs accessed by an elevator. Harbor seals (which have spotted coats) and elephant seals are the types most commonly found on this coast; neither has external ears – as opposed to sea lions. The latter can also rotate their hind flippers and thus walk on land.

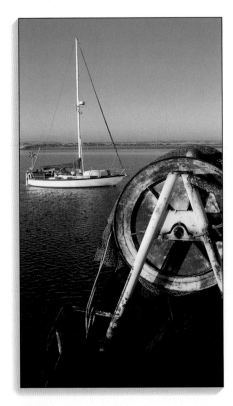

The curiously named **Yachats** ❹, a tourist resort nestled between the mountains and the sea, has beach trails, rewarding tide pools, and good fishing. Yachats is the only town between Florence and Waldport, and visitors come to watch smelts (a silvery sardine-like fish) when they gather to spawn in summer time. The tiny community celebrates rather ungratefully with an annual Smelt Fry every July, which is very well-attended, not least by classically trained musicians from San Francisco.

**Cape Perpetua** is the highest point (803 feet/245 meters above sea level) on the coast, and has a helpful **Visitor Center** that provides maps and advice for hikers bound for explorations along the trails of Siuslaw National Forest. From its overlook, the highway looks like a thin sliver of silver ribbon threading along the coast.

**Waldport** ❹ lies at the mouth of the Alsea River, which arrives at the ocean from its origin in Siuslaw National Forest, whose northern section is traversed by US 101, just before Neskowin. Waldport (pop: 1600) is mainly known for its fishing, crabbing, and clamming. It's also a particularly good base for anyone interested in hiking.

Map on page 354

## WALDPORT TO SEASIDE

Look to the right while crossing Yaquina Bay into the town of **Newport** ㊸. The section below the bridge is Newport's **Historic Bayfront**, whose attractions include old taverns, a harbor filled with fishing boats, and a trio of commercial attractions. There's the obligatory Ripley's Believe It Or Not Museum, and the Undersea Gardens (a below-the-surface aquarium where divers cavort behind glass). Across the bay, **South Beach** has the larger **Oregon Coast Aquarium** (tel: 541-867-4931; open daily), whose famous former resident, Keiko the Orca whale, starred in the film *Free Willy*.

To reach the Bayfront, turn off the main street at the traffic light (opposite the Mazatlan Mexican Restaurant in a gray, wooden building) and head down Hurburt Street. Farther on through town, several streets lead west to the seaport with its pedestrian promenade. Down Olive Street, just before the ocean, the Eager Beaver Secondhand Store sports an attractive mural on its sea side. One block farther, Third Street leads to **Nye Beach**, at one time the Oregon Coast's major draw. The Visual Arts Center (tel: 541-265-9231; open daily 12–4pm) is also here, while a boarding house from the 1890s forms part of the Lincoln County Historical Society Museum.

Just outside Newport is the much loved and much photographed **Yaquina Head Lighthouse** ㊹, built in 1873. Composer Earnest Block spent the last decades of his life at his home near here, and a memorial to him has been constructed. An interpretive center opened a few years ago.

About 5 miles (8 km) farther north of Newport, don't miss the signs for the **Devil's Punchbowl**, a couple of hundred yards off the highway. This is where a huge stone basin fills dramatically – and noisily – as the tide crashes in. Waves are higher in the Pacific than the Atlantic because the wind blows uninterruptedly over a larger distance, and the study of waves – whose height is measured as the distance between the highest point (crest) and lowest point (trough) – is understandably one of great interest to coastal communities. Tide tables are listed around here in local phone directories. A tide could be regarded as a very slow wave, with high tide representing the crest, and low tide the trough.

**BELOW:**
Heceta Head Lighthouse has been beaming its warning to mariners since 1894.

### Festival of glass

The coastal views from these cliffs and capes are spectacular, and sometimes whales can be spotted on their 12,000-mile (19,300-km) round trip between Alaska and Baja California. The awesome cliffs and headlands are basalt, formed by molten lava hitting the ocean aeons ago and hardening instantly. Sometimes this instant cooling creates oddly shaped rock structures known as pillow basalt, which can be seen offshore near Cape Foulweather and at **Depoe Bay**, a pretty place that claims to be the world's smallest navigable harbor. At high tide, seawater shoots skyward through two rock formations known locally as the **Spouting Horns**. Visitors get a close-up look at the wave action just by walking along the sea wall, which runs the full length of the town. When a storm is about to hit, everyone heads to a Depoe Bay restaurant for a full-frontal view, complete with sound effects.

Cape Foulweather was named in 1778 by the British navigator Captain James Cook. It was his first sighting of the American mainland following his return from discovering Hawaii. The winds here, 500 feet (150 meters) above the ocean, can reach 100 mph (160 kph), but don't seem to ruffle the friendly ginger cat that wanders around the cape's observation platform. Its home is the small gift shop with its collection of carved driftwood figures, kitschy souvenirs, and the much-prized green glass bubbles that have drifted here from fishermen's nets all the way from Japan. Lincoln City, also renowned for its kite flying, recently launched 2,000 floats of its own as part of a Festival of Glass.

## Pink starfish

Trawling for glass floats, collecting driftwood, and studying tide pools are all popular pastimes along this stretch of low-key coast. Tide pools could be regarded as miniature ocean habitats, where some creatures wait in anticipation for the waves to wash in their lunch. Orange and pink starfish, urchins, and sea anemones can usually be seen among the tiny fish that dart about the shallows, while rocky residents such as long-tapered mussels and white barnacles cluster on the rocks.

**BELOW:** the cheese factory at Tillamook offers free tours and samples; this is the place to learn "udderly amazing" facts about cows.

Lincoln City **⑮**, which has 7 miles (11 km) of beaches beginning with a half-mile-deep strand when the tide is out at Siletz Bay, also has 20 antique stores and several second-hand bookstores. There is the Chinook Winds Casino for night-time action and a **factory outlet** for daytime shopping, which, depending on the enthusiasm of the competition, is usually regarded as the largest in Oregon. Bus tours and tourists come in droves for great bargains from around 70 stores. The tiny D River links nearby **Devils Lake** with the ocean, providing both freshwater and oceanside fun.

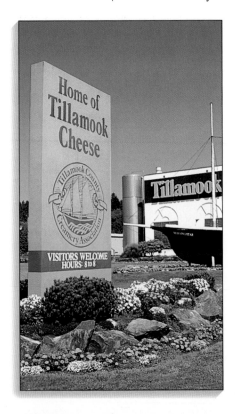

North of town, **Cascade Head** is the home of such raptors as falcons, hawks, and bald eagles – predators that deploy keen eyesight, outstanding hearing, and amazing speed to hunt and eat other mammals with their large clawed feet and hooked bills. Bird-watching is a popular local pastime and Lincoln City's Backyard Bird Shop is well stocked with books, tools, and birdhouses.

## Cows versus people

The highway skirts residential **Neskowin** and then heads inland, passing meadows of grazing cows (which outnumber people in this very pastural county) owned by the 180 working farms that provide the milk for the delectable Tillamook cheese. After colorful **Cloverdale**, with its big blue barn and bright yellow church, the highway traverses wonderful, fresh-scented **Siuslaw National Forest**, its highest peak, Mount Hebo, ascending to 3,000 feet (915 meters).

Sturdy wooden barns and springtime daffodils catch the eye before the towns of Hebo and Beaver appear. **Hebo** itself has houses that are set back beside the creek, and an airplane atop a pole that announces the **Blimp Hangar Air Museum** (tel: 503-842-1130; open daily), which is housed in an enormous hangar containing World War II vintage planes and a welcome 1940s-style café.

## Cheesy town

Tillamook ⓰ is justly famous for its huge, pristine cheese factory, which offers a free tour to inspect the manufacturing process and admire a life-size, painted plaster cow, beribboned with a computer chip that has replaced the old cow bell. A wall chart lists such "udderly amazing" facts as the fact that 2,600 pints of blood pass through the udder to produce one pint of milk and that a cow yields 10,000 gallons of milk in her lifetime. Help yourself to the free cheese samples, because it's a sure bet that you're bound to buy something in the tempting Aladdin's Cave that calls itself a gift shop. Not to be outdone, the **Blue Heron French Cheese** factory offers wine with its cheese tastings. Needless to say, the Dairy Parade is a major event each June.

West of Tillamook a sidetrip could be made along the 20-mile (32-km) **Three Capes Scenic Drive** to view the "Octopus Tree" – a Sitka spruce with multiple trunks – and the **Cape Meares Lighthouse**, built in 1890 with a lens imported from Paris. An early lighthouse keeper wrote of the harrowing all-night horse-and-buggy trip required to reach a doctor in Tillamook, a trip that today takes about 16 minutes.

Two miles (3 km) out to sea is the **Tillamook Lighthouse**, situated on a solitary rock amid crashing waves that in 1934 roared into a maelstrom, climbing more than 100 feet (30 meters) high to engulf the entire building. "Terrible Tilly" was how lighthouse keepers used to describe the building. Life on the rock was too hazardous to allow families to accompany staff to their jobs, who were routed every three weeks and allowed 96 days leave each year to recover. It was decommissioned in 1980.

For a taste of big city life, take a detour from Tillamook along State Route 6

Map on page 354

*Net gain. Some of the "bubble floats" from fishermen's nets have floated to Oregon all the way from Japan.*

**BELOW:** competitors for the day's catch.

# PORTLAND: CITY OF ROSES

*A ride-for-free transit system, stunning scenery, and microbreweries everywhere – no wonder Portland smells like roses*

Portland, voted one of America's best walking towns, has always prided itself on its pedestrian friendliness and trees-and-parks image. Its Forest Park is the largest urban wilderness in the US, and in the metro area alone there are 37,000 acres (15,000 hectares) of parks and gardens.

The Metropolitan Art Commission (tel: 503-823-5111) and Art Media (tel: 503-223-3724) have brochures locating museums and art galleries; the Portland Development Commission (tel: 503-823-3200) has a map showing interesting historical and architectural sites, and private guided walking tours are also available (tel: 503-227-5780).

Downtown Portland is focused around Pioneer Courthouse Square, where the Weather Machine, an earth-shaped sphere by local artist Terence O'Donnell on a 25-foot (8-meter) column comes to life with a musical fanfare at noon each day. Portland's efficient transit system is centered around a 300-block "Fareless Square" Downtown, the area where passengers ride free on buses or the light rail system. Washington Park subway is within easy access of many major attractions. These include the Oregon Zoo, the World Forestry Center, the Hoyt Arboretum, and the Children's Museum.

A streetcar system links the downtown area with the Pearl District (an area colonized by local artists) and the Nob Hill neighborhood with its fine Victorian and Georgian mansions. In the historic Skidmore District, there's a large weekend open-air market with live entertainment. Portland also has more microbreweries and brew pubs than any other city in the nation.

The state's history comes to life in the Oregon History Center and in the Pittock Mansion (tel: 503-823-3623), the 1914 home of the founder of Portland's well-regarded daily newspaper, *The Oregonian*. Various tour boats operate along the river, some venturing up the Columbia River as far as the Bonneville Lock and Dam, 40 miles (64 km) to the east. At the Oregon Museum of Science and Industry (tel: 503-797-4537; open daily) you can not only experience a simulated earthquake, but also board a jetboat for a worthwhile river excursion.

Two attractions are unique: the Church of Elvis (open 24 hours), a coin-operated shrine offering marriage counseling and more; and the American Advertising Museum (tel: 503-226-0000; weekends only), whose 200,000 artifacts include a complete set of Burma Shave signs (*see page 38*).  ❏

**LEFT:** sweetly-scented namesake; Mount Hood, the city, and gardens.
**ABOVE:** buy local; Pioneer Courthouse Square.

east to the "City of Roses," otherwise known as **Portland** ❼ *(see page 376)*. Past Tillamook, the highway hugs the 13-square-mile (34-sq-km) shallow bay, which is rarely deeper than 6 feet (2 meters). Estuaries such as this, where fresh water mingles with that of the ocean, are especially inviting to plant and marine life. Eelgrass provides shelter and nourishment to crabs as well as young salmon and other small fish; mudflats harbor gourmet treats for the stately great blue heron, which can often been seen rummaging. The Arago Cape is the home of the elephant seal, a deep-diving mammal that has been known to reach depths of 4,000 feet (1,200 meters).

Map on page 354

## Garibaldi and ghosts

Next on the Pacific Coast Scenic Highway, preceded by a giant, abandoned smokestack, comes **Garibaldi** (named for the 19th-century Italian liberator), which has a battered Ghost Hotel Tavern, a Lumberman's Memorial Park and Museum (tel: 503-322-0301), and the annual Crab Races, which presumably take place sideways.

At **Rockaway Beach**, a red caboose beside the highway is the tourist office (tel: 800-331-5928; open weekdays, albeit sporadically), run by volunteers. Freight trains loaded with lumber can occasionally be seen running on the roadside track, which follows the course of the Nehalem River. Tiny **Wheeler** has an art gallery that sponsors wine tasting, presumably from the winery at nearby **Manzanita**, a community that welcomes visitors with a brightly colored mural of a blazing sun and wave-lashed rocks.

After the long climb from Manzanita, there are spectacular views from an overlook above the sea where the **Oswald West State Park** begins. Down to the

**BELOW:** four-footed firmness required for this trip to the seashore.

*Haystack Rock at Cannon Beach.*

trestle bridge over the canyon, Tillamook County (which bills itself as "the land of cheese, trees, and gentle breeze") comes to an end just before the tunnel. A bridge over Arch Creek abuts a residential seaside community.

An unmistakable landmark at **Cannon Beach** ❹ is 235-foot (71-meter) high **Haystack Rock**, offshore. The very active community, an artists' haven with over 40 visual arts studios and galleries, is named after a cannon washed ashore after an 1846 shipwreck. It is another kite-flying paradise, where professionals turn up in April to perform at the annual Puffin Kite Festival.

The town also sponsors an annual Sandcastle Day in June and a dog show on the beach in October with contests for best bark, Frisbee catch, and owner/dog look-alike. There's even a Stormy Weather Festival (indoors) in November; the town publishes a chart of coastal tide tables with predictions for the entire year. If you can manage all this activity, telephone 503-436-0434 to request *Cannon Beach Magazine*.

## Seaside

Twenty-eight miles (45 km) north of Tillamook, US 101 descends into the town of **Seaside** ❹ (pop. 5,500), the largest resort on the Oregon Coast, and bisected by the Necanicum River, with its historic downtown area on the western side of Broadway. A wide sandy beach is flanked by a pedestrian promenade, along which is the **Aquarium** (open daily). Three blocks farther north is Seaside's **Historical Society Museum** (open daily). Note the attractive, blue, make-believe lighthouse of the Sundowner Inn on Oceanway, which is in the downtown area. Seaside's free *Visitors Guide* also includes annual tide tables (tel: 888-306-6825) for a copy, which also includes events.

**BELOW:** hitchhiking across America

It was at Seaside that members of the Lewis and Clark exploration party set up a camp to make salt by boiling seawater. For that first cold, wet winter of 1805 the expedition established – southeast of what is now **Warrenton** – **Fort Clatsop**, naming it for a local tribe of Indians who brought whale meat to trade (Clark cooked and ate some, describing it as "very palatable and tender").

A replica of the fort (tel: 503-861-2471; open daily) – a 50-sq-foot (5-sq-meter) stockade with a parade ground and two rows of small cabins – helps visitors to visualize the conditions. There's also a summer program in which buckskin-clad rangers offer demonstrations. Nearby **Fort Stevens** in the state park was built to defend the mouth of the Columbia River in the Civil War.

### ASTORIA TO ABERDEEN

**Astoria** ❺ – 22 miles (35 km) north of Seaside – was once known as the "the salmon canning capital of the world," and in an 1872 book, Frances Fuller Victor was able to write: "The immense numbers of all kinds of salmon, which ascend the Columbia annually, is something wonderful. They seem to be seeking quiet and safe places to deposit their spawn, and thousands of them never stop until they can reach the great falls of the Snake River, more than 600 miles (966 km) from the sea." As late as 1915, fishermen were taking

21,000 tons of salmon from the river. But then came the giant dams. The protest by the Cayuse Indians that it would abrogate their rights by eliminating most of the salmon sadly turned out to be true. Some salmon runs have declined 85 percent from what they once were, despite the production of 170 million fish each year by artificial hatcheries. In this place alone, at its mouth, is the Columbia River unchanged.

Map on page 354

## The mighty Columbia

Here, at its most powerful, the river thrusts 150 billion gallons (682 billion litres) of water a day through the sandbars into the Pacific Ocean, a torrent that has capsized 2,000 boats in the 185 years since John Jacob Astor's Pacific Fur Company created the first American settlement on shore. In recent years the Federal government has dredged a 40-foot (12-meter) channel and placed long jetties at each side to narrow the channel, but despite constant dredging and other attempts to tame the river at its mouth, it remains one of the most dangerous in the world. The weather so consistently stirs up stormy seas that the Coast Guard set up its National Motor Lifeboat School at the tip of Cape Disappointment; at times the waves reach as high as 30 feet (9 meters). Nevertheless, cruise boats regularly call at Astoria, depositing hundreds of passengers at the 17th Street Dock, used regularly by Coast Guard cutters.

The **Columbia River Maritime Museum** (tel: 503-325-2323; open daily) is all about shipwrecks, lighthouses, fishing, navigation, and naval history. Much of Astoria's history is reflected in its handsome old houses, which fall into particular styles: Italianate, whose overhanging eaves have decorative brackets and tall or paired windows and doors, or Queen Anne (multiple roof lines, tow-

**BELOW:** full moon over the gorgeous gorge of the Columbia River.

ers and turrets, paneled doors, and stained glass). An interesting example of the latter is the **Captain George Flavel House**, dating from the 1880s, on Eighth Street (tel: 503-325-2203; open daily).

It's a steep, winding drive past old Victorian houses up the hill on which sits the **Astoria Column**, with its 164 winding steps, each one individually sponsored. The Great Northern Railroad and Vincent Astor, great-grandson of fur-trading tycoon and town founder Jacob Astor, were responsible for the 125-foot (38-meter) high tower that was completed in 1926. The views, of course, are stupendous, but once back on the ground you'll be glad to warm up in the hut as you buy a postcard.

## WASHINGTON STATE'S DISCOVERY COAST

It was three weeks before the Lewis and Clark exploration party managed to cross the wide Columbia River, setting up another camp near today's **Chinook** on Washington state's west coast (publicized as the Discovery Coast). Here, US 101 continues past a bird-filled wildlife refuge to the pretty, unspoiled town of **Ilwaco** with its murals, carved wooden statues, and **Heritage Museum** (tel: 360-642-3446; closed Sun). The expedition stayed for three lonely months in this isolated area.

The 4-mile (6-km) long bridge that crosses from Oregon into Washington state is unusual in that it climbs steeply. Overhead seagulls swoop with keening cries and the wind is almost gale force. Be careful when driving.

Ilwaco sits at the bottom of the Long Beach peninsula – 28 miles (45 km) of uninterrupted sandy beach – which gets nicer the farther north you go. In the southwest corner, **Fort Candy** guarded the mouth of the Columbia for almost

**BELOW:** piano player at a party in a log cabin along the Pacific Coast.

a century before becoming a state park in 1957. It houses a very interesting **Lewis and Clark Interpretive Center** (open daily) where you can study biographies of members of the original party and entries from the actual journals they kept. **Cape Disappointment Lighthouse**, built in 1856, is less than a mile away at the southwestern-most tip, but such was the continuing toll of wrecked ships that it had to be supplemented before the century was out by another lighthouse at nearby **North Head**. This can be toured in summer (tel: 360-642-3078 for times).

Long Beach itself is a rather déclassé resort – its main street lined with tatty souvenir stores, a Ripley-style "museum," uninteresting restaurants, and numerous inexpensive motels. But it does have a pleasant boardwalk, as well as a 2-mile (3-km) Dune Trail. The peninsula's beaches are popular for clamming. **Nahcotta** and **Oysterville** at the northern end became prosperous from oyster gathering before the crop was over-harvested, but some fine Victorian homes remain from those days, and the **Willapa Bay Interpretive Center** (open weekends) at Nahcotta explains the history of it all. Leadbetter Park, at the northern tip, is also a wildlife refuge where birds stop over on their way south.

## Oyster capital

Back on "the mainland," US 101 crosses the Naselle River and a number of sloughs (inlets) before arriving at **South Bend ⑤**, which sits on a bay at the mouth of the Willapa River. Signs announcing oysters for sale in what calls itself the "oyster capital of the world" are a reminder that a century ago tons of these succulent bivalves were harvested by Native Americans, which all now find a ready and willing market in the gourmet restaurants of Seattle, Portland,

Map on page 354

*Pacific Ocean fish and oysters find a ready market in the watering holes of Seattle and Portland.*

**BELOW:** homesteaders at home.

Map
on page
354

and San Francisco. Also in search of the same is the black oystercatcher, a bird whose long red bill helps it open the shellfish once it has found them.

Two ancient wooden warehouses contain a shipwright and an iron works in South Bend, which stages its annual Oyster Stampede every May. South Bend's near neighbor **Raymond** is an unspoiled, un-touristy sort of place with a library built in the style of a timbered English cottage – its art-glass panes depicting fairy tale characters.

### Reckless extravagance

Architecturally, Raymond's pride and joy is the old courthouse, with its spiral staircase and stained glass dome. "A gilded palace of reckless extravagance" was how the local paper described it when the courthouse first went up in 1910. Life-size metal silhouettes of sculptured animals and local figures line the grassy verges around town. Four miles (6 km) east of Raymond on State Route 6 is the (marked) grave of Willie Kiel, a 19-year-old who died of malaria just before the family wagon train left Missouri in 1855. Preserved in whisky in a lead casket by his doctor father, the body came along for the trip and was buried atop a grassy knoll, now crowned with towering cedars.

Access to west coast beaches is via State Route 105, which runs past the Shoalwater Indian Reservation and the cranberry bogs between North Cove and Grayland. Cranberries blossom in late June, and **Grayland** holds its annual cranberry festival in October, following the harvest.

Between Raymond and Aberdeen, US 101 bends and twists through a glorious forest of mist-shrouded pines and other trees before emerging beside the smoke-belching, century-old Weyerhaeuser lumber plant, a mile or two south of

**BELOW:**
and then there
were three.
**RIGHT:**
dreaming of fish.

town. It is from Weyerhauser that the Federal government is buying a 274-acre (110-hectare) grove of cedars in a difficult-to-reach part of the peninsula. When the bridge over the broad Chehalis River is raised, vehicles must wait to continue their journey.

**Aberdeen 52**, a major lumber port for more than a century, is, like its Scottish namesake, at the meeting of two rivers. It is best known for **Grays Harbor**, the seaport around which the town grew after Robert Gray sailed in on the *Lady Washington* in 1788 to help arrange fur trading between the Pacific Northwest and China. A replica of the 170-ton ship is used for educational trips, but is usually on show in the harbor, and more about the town's early days can be explored in the **Aberdeen History Museum**. By the time the first mill was built in 1852, the government was making treaties with the Indians of the region and Aberdeen was developing into a rowdy, honky-tonk shipping town.

### San Diego to Seattle

US 101 reaches the end of the journey that began all the way south in sunny San Diego with a flourishy loop around the magnificent Olympic Peninsula *(see the Northern Route, page 167)*, ending up not far from Seattle. Alternatively, head straight for **Seattle 53** *(see page 172)* from Aberdeen by taking US 12 to **Olympia**, then Interstate 5.  ❑

# INSIGHT GUIDES
## TRAVEL TIPS

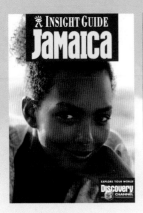

# CONTENTS

## Getting Acquainted

Time Zones ................386
Public Holidays............386
Electricity ....................386
Weights & Measures ..386
Business Hours ..........386

## Planning the Trip

Visa & Passports ........386
Tipping........................387
Health & Insurance.....387
Money Matters............387
Tax..............................387

## Practical Tips

Postal Services............387
Telecommunications ..388
Useful Numbers ..........388
Phone Codes ..............388
Embassies ..................388
Security & Crime ........388
Clothes Sizes Guide ....389
Smoking......................389

## Getting Around

Airports ......................389
By Train ......................389
By Bus ........................389
By Car ........................390
Disabled Travelers ......390

## Where to Stay

Hotels & Motels ..........391
Bed & Breakfasts ........391
Hostels and Camping ..391

## ATLANTIC ROUTE

NEW YORK CITY ..........392
New Jersey ................394
Pennsylvania ..............395
Maryland ....................396
Virginia........................396
North Carolina ............397
South Carolina ............399
Georgia ......................399
Florida ........................400
MIAMI ........................404

## NORTHERN ROUTE

BOSTON......................406
Massachusetts ............408
New Hampshire ..........409
Maine..........................409
Vermont ......................410
New York State............413
Pennsylvania ..............414
Ohio ............................415
Indiana........................415
Michigan ....................416
Illinois ........................416
Wisconsin ..................417
Minnesota ..................417
South Dakota ..............419
Wyoming ....................420
Montana......................421
Idaho ..........................423
Washington ................423
SEATTLE......................424

## Route 66

Museums....................438
State & National
Organizations ............438
Publications ................438

## CENTRAL ROUTE

WASHINGTON, DC ......426
Virginia........................428
North Carolina ............429
Tennessee ..................429
Arkansas ....................430
Oklahoma....................431
Texas ..........................432
New Mexico ................433
Arizona........................434
California ....................435
LOS ANGELES.............436

## SOUTHERN ROUTE

ATLANTA ....................439
Georgia ......................440
Alabama......................441
Mississippi ..................441
Louisiana ....................442
Texas ..........................444
New Mexico ................447
Arizona........................448
California ....................449

## PACIFIC ROUTE

SAN DIEGO .................450
California ....................451
Oregon........................457
Washington ................459

## Further Reading

General ......................460
On the Road ...............460
Fiction ........................460
Other Insight Guides....460

# Getting Acquainted

## Time Zones

The continental US spans four time zones. These are divided as follows:
- **Eastern** (Greenwich Mean Time minus five hours)
- **Central** (Greenwich Mean Time minus six hours)
- **Mountain** (Greenwich Mean Time minus seven hours)
- **Pacific** (Greenwich Mean Time minus eight hours)

### DAYLIGHT SAVINGS TIME

This begins each year at 2am on the first Sunday in April when clocks are advanced one hour, and ends on the first Sunday in October. Arizona and Indiana do not observe Daylight Savings Time.

## Electricity

Standard electricity in North America is 110–115 volts, 60 cycles AC. An adapter is necessary for most appliances from overseas, with the exception of Japan.

## Weights & Measures

The US operates on the imperial system of weights and measures. Metric is rarely used. Below is a conversion chart:
1 inch = 2.54 centimeters
1 foot = 30.48 centimeters
1 mile = 1.609 kilometers
1 quart = 1.136 liters
1 ounce = 28.40 grams
1 pound = 0.453 kilograms
1 yard = 0.9144 meters

## Public Holidays

As with other countries, the US has gradually shifted most of its public holidays to the Monday closest to the actual dates, thus creating a number of three-day weekends throughout the year.

Keep in mind that during public holidays, post offices, banks, government offices and many private businesses are closed. Holidays celebrated no matter on what day they fall in the year are:

- **January 1** New Year's Day
- **July 4** Independence Day
- **November 11** Veteran's Day
- **December 25** Christmas Day
Other holidays are:
- **Third Monday in January** Martin Luther King Jr Day
- **Third Monday in February** Presidents' Day
- **March/April** Good Friday, Easter Monday
- **May** May Day (first Monday)
- **Last Monday in May** Memorial Day
- **First Monday in September** Labor Day
- **Second Monday in October** Columbus Day
- **Last Thursday in November** Thanksgiving.

## Business Hours

**Banks** 9am–5pm, weekdays. Some stay open until 6 and Saturdays.
**Post Offices** 8am–4 or 5.30pm, weekdays, Saturday closing earlier and opening later.
**Shops** 10am–9pm generally.
**All-hours services** Most cities have 24-hour restaurants, convenience stores and supermarkets.

# Planning the Trip

## Visas & Passports

A passport, a passport-sized photograph, a visitor's visa, proof of intent to leave the US after your visit and (depending upon your country of origin) an international vaccination certificate, are required of most foreign nationals for entry into the US. Visitors from the UK staying less than 90 days no longer need a visa. Vaccination certificate requirements vary, but proof of immunization against smallpox or cholera may be necessary.

Canadian and Mexican citizens, and British residents of Canada and Bermuda, are normally exempt from these requirements. But it is wise to check for specific regulations on international travel in your country.
**Information** Up-to-date details on entry requirements may be found on the US State Department's website: www.travel.state.gov/visa_services.html.

### Extension of stay

Non-US citizens should contact US Immigration and Naturalization Service at 425 I Street, Washington, DC 20536
Tel: 202-514-4316
US Freephone: 800-755-0777

### Customs

For a breakdown of customs allowances write to:
**United States Customs Service**
P.O. Box 7407,
Washington, DC 20044,
Tel: 202-927-6724
Meat or meat products, illegal drugs, firearms, seeds, plants and fruits are among the prohibited goods. Also do not bring in any duty-free goods which are worth more

## Tipping

Although rarely obligatory, many service personnel in the US rely on tips for a large part of their income. Going rates are:
- **waiters & bartenders** 15–30 percent
- **taxi drivers** 15 percent
- **airport/hotel baggage handlers** around $1 per bag
- **chambermaids** for overnight stays it is not necessary to tip, for longer stays a minimum of $1–2 per day
- **doormen** 50¢–$1 for helping unload a car or other services
- **hairdressers, manicurists and masseurs** 15 percent

than $400 (returning Americans) or $100 (foreign travelers). Visitors over 21 may bring in 200 cigarettes, 3 lbs (1.3 kg) of tobacco or 50 cigars and 34 fl. oz (1 liter) of alcohol.

## Health & Insurance

Medical services are extremely expensive. Always arrange full and comprehensive travel insurance to cover any emergencies. Check the small print – most policies exclude treatment for water, winter or mountain sports accidents unless excess cover has been included. If you need medical assistance, consult the local Yellow Pages phone book for the physician or pharmacist nearest to you. In large cities, there is usually a physician referral service number listed. If you need immediate attention, go directly to a hospital emergency room (most are open 24 hours a day). You may be asked to produce proof of insurance cover before being treated.

Care should be taken to avoid dehydration and overexposure to the sun. In the desert, or at high altitude, this can happen rapidly even on cloudy days. A high-factor sun lotion, hat and water bottle are essential for outdoor excursions.

## Money Matters

### American visitors

**Credit cards** are accepted almost everywhere, although not all cards at all places. Most hotels, restaurants and shops take the major ones such as American Express, Diners Club, MasterCard, Visa and En Route. Along with out-of-state or overseas bank cards, they can also be used to withdraw money at ATMs.

**Travelers' checks** are widely accepted, although you may have to provide proof of identification when cashing them at banks (this is not required at most stores).

### Overseas visitors

Travelers' checks in US dollars are much more widely accepted than those in other currencies. The best rates of exchange for them are in banks. Take along your passport.

## Tax

Most states levy a sales tax. The amount varies from state to state, (up to around 8 percent in some) and is invariably excluded from the marked price. You may also have to pay a local sales tax on top of this.

When looking at prices, beware of other costs that may or may not be included in the stated price such as lodging or "bed tax" and taxes on restaurant meals, drinks and car rental. These are especially hefty in tourist towns like Miami. If in doubt – ask.

# Practical Tips

## Postal Services

### POST OFFICES

Even the most remote towns are served by the US Postal Service. Smaller post offices are limited to business hours (Monday to Friday 9am–5pm), although central, big-city branches may have extended opening times. Stamps are sold at all post offices, plus at some convenience stores, filling stations, hotels and transportation terminals, usually from vending machines.

### EXPRESS POST

For reasonably quick delivery at a modest price, ask for priority mail. For overnight deliveries, try US Express Mail or one of several domestic and international courier services, including:
**Fedex**, Tel: 800-238-5355
**DHL**, Tel: 800-345-2727
**United Parcel Service**, Tel: 800-272-4877

### POSTE RESTANTE

Visitors can receive mail at post offices if it is addressed to them, care of "General Delivery," followed by the city name and (very important) the zip code. You must pick up this mail in person within a week or two of its arrival and show some personal identification.

## Telecommunications

### TELEPHONE

Coin-operated telephones are ubiquitous: they are to be found in hotels, restaurants, shopping centers, gas stations and often in lighted booths on street corners. To call long-distance, dial 1+area code +local number. Have plenty of change with you to deposit on the operator's prompting.

#### Toll-free calls
When in the US, make use of toll-free (no-charge) numbers. They start with 800, 1-800, 888 or 877.

#### Cheaper rates
Long-distance rates are cheaper after 5pm on weekdays and throughout weekends.

### TELEGRAMS & FAXES

Western Union (Tel: 800-325-6000) takes telegram and telex messages, plus orders to wire money over the phone. Faxes can be found in most hotels and copy centers.

### EMAIL & INTERNET

Many public libraries, copy centers and hotels offer email and Internet access. Or visit a cyber café. Service providers such as Earthlink (www.i.e.w.com) and Hotmail (www.hotmail.com) offer web mail accounts that will enable access while traveling.

## Useful Numbers

- **Emergencies** 911 (the operator will put you through to the police, ambulance or fire services)
- **Operator** 0 (dial if you are having any problems with a line from any phone)
- **Telephone information**
Local: 411
Long-distance: 1+area code +555-1212
Toll-free directory: 800-555-1212

## Phone Codes

More than perhaps any other country, the United States has embraced the telephone. But now, with the proliferation of fax lines, modems and cellular phones, the system is seriously overloaded. To cope with these demands, the country has been forced to divide, then sub-divide its existing telephone exchanges, in some cases every six months. Although every effort has been made to keep the telephone prefixes listed here up to date, it's always a good idea to check with the operator if you're in any doubt.

## Embassies

**Australia**: 1601 Massachusetts Ave NW, Washington, DC 20036, Tel: 202-797-3000
**Canada**: 501 Pennsylvania Ave NW, Washington, DC 20001, Tel: 202-682-1740
**Denmark**: 3200 Whitehaven St NW, Washington, DC 20008, Tel: 202-234-4300
**France**: 4101 Reservoir Road NW, Washington, DC 20007, Tel: 202-944-6000
**Germany**: 4645 Reservoir Road NW, Washington, DC 20007, Tel: 202-298-4000
**Great Britain**: 3100 Massachusetts Ave NW, Washington, DC 20008, Tel: 202-462-1340
**Ireland**: 2234 Massachusetts Ave NW Washington, DC 20008, Tel: 202-462-3939
**Israel**: 3514 International Drive NW, Washington, DC 20008, Tel: 202-364-5500
**Italy**: 1601 Fuller St NW, Washington, DC 20009, Tel: 202-328-5500
**Japan**: 2520 Massachusetts Ave NW, Washington, DC 20008, Tel: 202-939-6700
**Mexico**: 1911 Pennsylvania Ave NW, Washington, DC 20006, Tel: 202-728-1600
**New Zealand**: 37 Observatory Circle NW, Washington, DC 20008, Tel: 202-328-4800

**Singapore**: 3501 International Place NW, Washington, DC 20008, Tel: 202-537-3100
**Spain**: 2375 Pennsylvania Ave NW, Washington, DC 20037, Tel: 202-452-0100

## Security & Crime

### ON THE ROAD

If you are driving, never pick up anyone you don't know. Always be wary of who is around you. If you have trouble on the road, stay in the car and lock the doors, turn on your hazard lights and/or leave the hood up to increase your visibility and alert passing police. It's well worth carrying a sign requesting help. Do not accept a rental car that is obviously labeled as such. Company decals and special license plates may attract thieves on the look-out for tourist valuables.

## Hitchhiking

Hitchhiking is illegal in many places and ill-advised everywhere. It's an inefficient and dangerous method of travel. Don't do it!

### IN THE CITY

Most big cities have their share of crime. Common sense is your most effective weapon. Try to avoid walking alone at night – at the very least stick to livelier, more brightly lit thoroughfares and move about as if you know where you are going. Keep an eye on your belongings. Never leave your car unlocked, or small children by themselves. Hotels usually warn that they do not guarantee the safety of belongings left in their rooms. If you have any valuables, you may want to lock them in the hotel safe. Take particular care when using bank ATMs at night. If you are in doubt about which areas are safe, seek advice from hotel staff or police.

## Clothes Sizes Guide

This table gives a comparison of American, Continental and British clothing sizes. It is always best to try on any article before buying it, as sizes may vary.

**Women's Dresses/Suits**

| American | Continental | British |
|---|---|---|
| 8 | 40/36N | 10/32 |
| 10 | 42/38N | 12/34 |
| 12 | 44/40N | 14/36 |
| 14 | 46/42N | 16/38 |
| 16 | 48/44N | 18/40 |

**Women's Shoes**

| American | Continental | British |
|---|---|---|
| 5½ | 37 | 4 |
| 6½ | 38 | 5 |
| 7½ | 39 | 6 |
| 8½ | 40 | 7 |
| 9½ | 41 | 8 |

**Men's Suits**

| American | Continental | British |
|---|---|---|
| 34 | 44 | 34 |
| - | 46 | 36 |
| 38 | 48 | 38 |
| - | 50 | 40 |
| 42 | 52 | 42 |
| - | 54 | 44 |
| 46 | 56 | 46 |

**Men's Shirts**

| American | Continental | British |
|---|---|---|
| 14 | 36 | 14 |
| 14½ | 37 | 14½ |
| 15 | 38 | 15 |
| 15½ | 39 | 15½ |
| 16 | 40 | 16 |
| 16½ | 41 | 16½ |
| 17 | 42 | 17 |

**Men's Shoes**

| American | Continental | British |
|---|---|---|
| 6½ | - | 6 |
| 7½ | 40 | 7 |
| 8½ | 41 | 8 |
| 9½ | 42 | 9 |
| 10½ | 43 | 10 |
| 11½ | 44 | 11 |

## Smoking

Smoking is banned on public transportation, domestic flights and in most cinemas and public buildings. Always check the policy in hotels and restaurants. Many have designated smoking areas; others – even bars – forbid smoking altogether.

# Getting Around

## Airports

If it is too impractical because of long distances to drive to the destinations listed here, an easy alternative is to fly. Airlines that serve the airports in the major hub cities include American, Delta, Continental, Northwest, Southwest, TWA, United and US Airways.

**California**: Los Angeles International; San Diego International
**Florida**: Miami International Airport
**Georgia**: Hartsfield International Airport (Atlanta)
**Massachusetts**: Logan International (Boston)
**New York**: John F Kennedy (JFK) International (New York City); La Guardia (New York City).
**Washington State**: Seattle-Tacoma International
**Washington, DC**: Reagan National, Dulles, Downtown Airport Terminal

## By Train

Although passenger services were greatly curtailed in the latter part of the 20th century, it is still possible to travel the length and breadth of the continent by rail. Amtrak is the major rail passenger carrier in the US. Its network links many cities, but sadly bypasses many more. However, there are still some excellent transcontinental routes that glide through breathtaking scenery. Not the fastest or cheapest way of getting around America, but riding the rails can be a leisurely and highly enjoyable experience if you have the time.

### Train passes

Passes for unlimited travel on Amtrak over a fixed period of time are available only from a travel agent in a foreign country. Proof of non-US residency is required. Be sure to ask about two- or three-stopover discounts, senior citizens and children's discounts, and also Amtrak's package tours.
**Information**: Details about Amtrak's train service may be obtained by calling 1-800-872-7245 or 215-628-1846, www.amtrak.com.

## By Bus

The national bus line, Greyhound, as well as a number of smaller charter companies, provide an impressive network of ground travel throughout the country, offering daily service to major towns and cities. Routes and schedules are subject to change; it is a good idea to check all arrangements with local stations in advance. Most cities also have municipal bus systems. As both Greyhound and municipal stations are often situated in somewhat squalid areas, try to stay alert and do not wander too far, particularly after dark. Plan your journey for daylight arrival if possible. On the whole, the buses themselves are safe and reasonably comfortable; choosing a seat near to the driver may discourage unwanted attention from any fellow passengers.
**Information**: reservations and local bus station details are available on Tel: 1-800-231-2222, or their website at: www.greyhound.com.

### Bus passes

An Ameripass offers unlimited travel to 2,600 destinations within 68 consecutive days. The pass may be purchased only outside the US. Details are available from the Greyhound bus company and most foreign travel agents.

## By Car

Car rental agencies are located at all airports and in cities and large towns. In most places you must be at least 21 years old (25 at some locations) to rent a car and you must have a valid driver's license and at least one major credit card. Be sure to check insurance provisions before signing anything. Cover is usually $15–25 per day. You may already be covered by your own auto insurance or credit card company, however, so check with them first.

## CAR RENTAL COMPANIES

**Alamo**, Tel: (US) 800-354-2322; (international) +1-305-522-0000
**Avis**, Tel: (US) 800-331-1212; (international) +1-918-664-4600
**Budget**, Tel: (US) 800-527-0700; (international) +1-214-404-7600
**Dollar**, Tel: (US) 800-800-4000; (international) +1-813-877-5507
**Enterprise**, Tel: (US) 800-325-8007; (international) +1-314-781 8232
**Hertz**, Tel: (US) 800-654-3131; (international) +1-405-749-4424
**National**, Tel: (US) 800-227-7368; (international) +1-612-830-2345
**Thrifty**, Tel: (US) 800-367-2277; (international) +1-918-669-2499

## RV RENTALS

No special license is necessary to operate a motor home (or recreational vehicle – RV for short), but they aren't cheap. When you add up the cost of rental fees, insurance, gas and campsites, you may find that renting a car and staying in motels or camping is less expensive. Keep in mind, too, that RVs are large and slow and may be difficult to handle on narrow mountain roads. If parking space is tight, driving an RV may be extremely inconvenient. Access to some roads may be limited. For additional information about RV rentals, call the **Recreational Vehicle Rental Association**, Tel: 800-336-0355

## AAA Membership

The Automobile Association of America (AAA) can help members with personalized itineraries. Benefits of AAA membership include a 24-hour emergency breakdown service, great road maps and travel literature. Insurance is also available through the association, which has a reciprocal arrangement with some of the automobile associations in other countries. Tel: 1-800-874-7532 or visit their website: www.aaa.com.

## DESERT & MOUNTAIN DRIVING

A word of caution for desert travelers: the single most important precaution you can take is to tell someone your destination, route and expected time of arrival. Check tires carefully before long stretches of desert driving. Heat builds pressure, so have them at slightly below normal air pressure. The desert's arid climate makes carrying extra water – both for passengers and vehicles – essential. Carry at least one gallon per person. Keep an eye on the gas gauge. It's a good idea to have more than you think you need. Remember, if you should have car trouble or become lost, do not strike out on foot. A car, visible from the air and presumably on a road, is easier to spot than a person, and it affords shelter from the weather. Wait to be found. Mountain drivers are advised to be equally vigilant. Winter storms in the Sierras occasionally close major roads, and at times chains are required on tires. Phone ahead for road conditions before you depart.

## Traveling with Children

Two words of advice about traveling with children: first, be prepared and, second, don't expect to cover too much ground.

Take everything you need: western towns may be small and remote with supplies limited. If you need baby formula, special foods, diapers or medi-cation, carry them with you along with a general first-aid kit. Games, books and crayons help kids pass time in the car. Carrying snacks and drinks in a day pack will come in handy when kids (or adults) get hungry on the road. Give yourself plenty of time, as kids do not travel at the same pace as adults. They're a lot less interested in traveling from point A to point B than in ex-ploring their immediate surround-ings. What you find fascinating (an art museum), they may find boring. And what they think is "really cool" (the game room at the hotel), you may find totally uninteresting. Be sure wilderness areas, and other back-country places are suitable for children. Are there abandoned mine shafts, steep stairways, cliffs or other hazards? Is a lot of walking necessary? Are food, water, shelter, bathrooms and other essentials available at the site? Avoid dehydra-tion by having children drink plenty of water before and during outdoor activities. Don't push children beyond their limits. Rest often, provide plenty of snacks, and allow for extra napping.

## Disabled Travelers

For general information on travel for the handicapped, contact **Moss Rehabilitation Hospital Travel Information Service**, 1200 West Tabor Road, Philadelphia, PA 19141, Tel: 215-456-9600, TDD 215-456-9602, or **The Information Center for Individuals with Disabilities**, 27–43 Wormwood St, Boston, MA 02210, Tel: 617-727-5540.

# Where to Stay

## Hotels & Motels

Chain hotels and motels are reliable and convenient but tend to lack unique character. You can, however, usually depend on a clean, comfortable room for a reasonable price. In general, prices range from $50 to $150 depending on the location, the season and additional amenities. When making reservations, ask specifically about special weekend or corporate rates and "package deals." Reservations staff in America are notorious for quoting only the most expensive rates, but many hotels offer a variety of discounts and promotions. Book your room by credit card and secure a guaranteed late arrival, in the foreseeable circumstance that your flight is interminably stacked up over the airport or your 40-minute limo ride from the airport turns into a two-hour nightmare of traffic jams. The telephone numbers listed below are the main numbers that should be dialed in order to make reservations once in the US.

## CHAIN HOTELS

**Best Western,** Tel: 1-800-528-1234
**Hilton,** Tel: 1-800-445-8667.
**Holiday Inn,** Tel: 1-800-465-4329
**Hyatt,** Tel: 1-800-228-9000
**La Quinta,** Tel: 1-800-531-5900
**Marriott,** Tel: 1-800-228-9290
**Quality Inn,** Tel: 1-800-228-5151
**Radisson,** Tel: 1-800-333-3333
**Ramada,** Tel: 1-800-272-6232
**Sheraton,** Tel: 1-800-325-3535

## MOTELS

**Budget Host Inns,**
Tel: 1-800-283-4678
**Comfort Inns,**
Tel: 1-800-221-2222
**Days Inns of America,**
Tel: 1-800-325-2525
**Econolodge,**
Tel: 1-800-424-7777
**Friendship Inns International,**
Tel: 1-800-453-4511
**Hampton Inns,**
Tel: 1-800-426-7866
**Motel 6,**
Tel: 1-800-466-8356
**Red Roof Inns,**
Tel: 1-800-843-7663

## Hostels

**Hostelling International/American Youth Hostels**
733 15th Street, Suite 840, Washington DC, 20005
Tel: 1-800-909-4776
Web: www.hiayh.org.
**YMCA**
YMCA of the USA, Association Advancement, 101 North Wacker Drive, Chicago, IL 60606
Tel: 312-977-0031
Web: www.ymca.com
**YWCA**
YWCA of the USA, Empire State Bldg, 350 Fifth Avenue, Suite 301, New York, NY 10118
Tel: 212-273-7800
Fax: 212-465-2281
Web: www.ywca.com
**Dude Ranchers Association**
PO Box 471, La Porte, CO 80535
Tel: 303-223-8440

## Bed & Breakfasts

B&Bs tend to be more personal than hotels. In some cases, you're a guest at a person's home where the accommodations are fairly simple; in others the rooms are in (large) historic homes or inns decorated with antiques, quilts, art and other period furnishings. Many do not allow smoking, so ask first. Before booking, also ask whether rooms have telephones or televisions and whether bathrooms are private. Inquire about breakfast, too. The meal is included in the price but may be anything from a couple of muffins to a multicourse feast. For more information contact:
**B&B Central Information**
PO Box 38279,Colorado Springs, CO 80937-8279;
Web: www.bbonline.com
**American Historic Inns**
Web: www.bnbinns.com

## Campgrounds

Most state and natural parks are seviced by campgrounds offering primitive facilities: a place to park, rest rooms and outdoor cooking. Fees are around $5 per site. Private campgrounds are usually a little more expensive and offer additional facilities such as hook-ups, coin laundries, pools and restaurants. Most are busy from mid-June to September and are allotted on a first-come-first-served basis. Camping space in popular national parks, like Yosemite and Yellowstone, should be booked up to a year in advance. For information on camping grounds call or write to individual parks and recreation departments or contact:
**American Park Network**
100 Pine Street, Suite 2850, San Francisco, CA 94111
Tel: 415-788-2228
Web: www.AmericanParkNetwork
**Kampgrounds of America (KOA)**
Tel: 406-248-7444
**National Park Service**
Department of the Interior
18th and C Streets NW
Washington, DC 20013
Tel: 202-208-4747
US Freephone: 800-365-2267
Web: www.nps.gov
**US Forest Service**
Tel: 202-205-1706
US Freephone: 800-280-2267
Web: www.reservusa.com
**Bureau of Land Management**
Tel: 202-452-5125

# Atlantic Route

## Useful Addresses

**New York City tourist information**
New York Convention and Visitors Bureau, 810 Seventh Avenue, NY 10019
Tel: 212-397-8222
Web: www.ci.nyc.ny.us
**New York State tourist information**
Empire State Development, Travel Information Center, 1 Commerce Plaza, Albany, NY 12245
Tel: 518-474-4116
US Freephone: 800-225-5697
**New Jersey tourist information**
New Jersey Chamber of Commerce, 50 W State St, Trenton, NJ 08608
Tel: 1-800-537-7397
Web: www.state.nj.us/travel
**Pennsylvania tourist information**
Chamber of Business and Industry, 417 Walnut Street, Harrisburg, PA 17120
Tel: 717-255-3252
US Freephone: 800-847-4872
Web: www.state.pa.us/visit
**Maryland tourist information**
Office of Tourism, 217 E Redwood Street, Baltimore, MD 21202
Tel: 410-767-3400
US Freephone: 800-543-1036
Web: www.state.md.us
**Virginia tourist information**
Division of Tourism, 901 East Byrd Street, Richmond, VA 23219
Tel: 800-847-4882
Web: www.state.sd.us/tourism
**North Carolina tourist information**
North Carolina Division of Tourism, 301 North Wilmington Street, Raleigh, NC 27601
Tel: 800-847-4862
Web: www.visitnc.com
**South Carolina tourist information**
Department of Tourism, Box 71, Columbia, SC 29202
Tel: 803-734-7000

US Freephone: 800-255-2059
Web: www.scci.com/sc
**Georgia tourist information**
Department of Industry, Tourist Division, Box 1776, Atlanta, GA 30301
Tel: 404-656-3590
US Freephone: 800-847-4842
Web: www.georgia.org/itt/tourism
**State tourist information:**
Visit Florida, PO Box 1100, Tallahassee, FL 32302
Tel: 850-488-5607
Web: www.flausa.com
**Miami tourist information**
Miami Visitor's Bureau, 701 Bricknell Avenue, Suite 2700, FL, 33139
Tel: 305-539-3063
Web: www.miami.com

## Hub City: NEW YORK CITY

### GETTING AROUND

#### Public transportation
**From the airport:** East of Manhattan on Long Island, New York's two major airports, John F. Kennedy International and LaGuardia, are respectively 15 and 8 miles (24 km and 13 km) from the city, with driving time from Kennedy estimated at just under one hour. In practice, heavy traffic can sometimes double this. Most charters and domestic flights and some international flights use LaGuardia. New York's third airport, Newark, is actually in New Jersey and, although further away from Manhattan than JFK and LaGuardia, can be easier to reach. New York Airport Service operates buses from both JFK and LaGuardia airports to Manhattan drop-off points, including Grand Central Terminal. New Jersey Transit and Olympia Trails Coach Service operate regular express buses between Newark airport and Manhattan, the former to the Port Authority Bus Terminal at Eighth Ave and 41st St, the latter to Penn Station, the World Trade Center and Grand Central Terminal.
**Rapid transit and buses** Subways and buses run 24 hours, less

frequently after midnight, with the fare (under $2) payable by token or (buses only) exact change, as well as by MetroCard pass (around $3 and up at subway ticket booths), which allows free transfers within two hours of use. Unlimited-ride passes are good for seven days or 30 day-passes are also available, as is a day pass sold at newsstands, hotels and electronic kiosks in some subway stations. For general bus and subway information and for details about the MetroCard pass call: 718-330-1234. Greyhound buses run from the Port Authority bus terminal, 41st and Eighth Avenue (Tel: 201-564-8484).
**Trains:** PATH (Port Authority Trans Hudson) trains run under the Hudson from six stations in Manhattan to New Jersey, including Hoboken and Newark. The fare is $1; Tel: 1-800-234-7284. National rail trains arrive and depart from Manhattan's two railroad terminals: Grand Central Terminal at Park Ave and 42nd St, and Pennsylvania Station at Seventh Ave and 33rd St. City buses stop outside each terminal and each sits atop a subway station. Amtrak information, Tel: 582-6875, or 1-800-872-7245.

#### Private transportation
Driving around Manhattan is not much fun although, should the need arise, there is a wide range of firms available at airports from which cars can be rented. Check the Yellow Pages for a list of local firms.
**Car Rental Companies**
Avis, Tel: 918-664- 4600
Budget, Tel: 214-404-7600
Hertz, Tel: 405-749 4424
Taxis, all metered, cruise the streets randomly and must be hailed, although there are official taxi stands at places like Grand Central Terminal. Be sure to hail an official yellow cab, not an unlicensed 'gypsy' cab. One fare covers all passengers up to four (five in a few of the larger cabs). After 8pm there is a 50¢ surcharge on all taxi rides. Telephone 302-8294 for lost property or to make a complaint.

## WHERE TO STAY

**Best Western Manhattan**
17 West 32nd Street
Tel: 736-1600 or 790-2705
US Freephone: 800-567-7720
Fax: 563-4007 or 790-2760
Web: www.applecorehotels.com
Like others in the Apple Core Hotels group (Quality Hotel East Side, etc.), rates at this 176-room hotel, a short walk from Macy's and Madison Square Garden, are extremely reasonable, especially considering that the comfortable rooms come with such conveniences as data ports and voice mail. There's also a lobby café with entertainment, a restaurant with room service, and an open-air rooftop bar where music and snacks can be enjoyed in summer, along with views of the Empire State Building. **$**

## Hotel Prices

Categories based on average cost of a double room for one night.
**$** = under $65
**$$** = up to $100
**$$$** = up to $150
**$$$$** = over $150

**The Carlyle**
35 East 76th Street
Tel: 744-1600
US Freephone: 800-227-5737
Fax: 717-4682
Posh, reserved and serene in its elegance, The Carlyle remains one of the city's most highly acclaimed luxury hotels. Home of Café Carlyle and Bemelmans Bar, two of the city's most enduring and upscale evening spots. The Carlyle is a favorite with visiting royalty. **$$$$**

**The Chelsea Hotel**
222 West 23rd Street
Tel: 243-3700
Fax: 675-5531
A red-brick, Victorian landmark of bohemian decadence, home to beatnik poets, then Warhol drag queens, then Sid Vicious, and now... some of all of the above. Accommodations vary from a few

inexpensive "student rooms" to suites. **$$–$$$**

**New York International Youth Hostel**
891 Amsterdam Ave, at W 103rd St
Tel: 932-2300
Fax: 932-2574
Accommodations in dormitory-style rooms range from $25–28 per person per night; $3 less for IYH members. **$**

**The Paramount**
235 West 46th St (between Broadway and Eighth Ave)
Tel: 764-5500
Fax: 354-5237
A New York fashion statement in the heart of Times Square (and one of former Studio 54 king – now hotel king – Ian Schrager's ever-growing roster of hotels). The Paramount's rooms and public spaces, designed by Philippe Starck, dazzle and amaze: amenities include beds with headboards made of reproductions of famous paintings, a fitness club, a supervised playroom for children, and The Whiskey, a trendsetting small bar. Rooms are also small, but well-equipped. **$$–$$$**

**Washington Square Hotel**
103 Waverly Place
Tel: 777-9515
Fax: 979-8373
An almost century-old hotel that offers the perfect Village locale. The rooms are small but nicely appointed. In a former incarnation, this was the seedy Hotel Earle, where Papa John wrote the 1960s rock classic *California Dreaming*. **$**

---

## WHERE TO EAT

There are literally thousands of restaurants in New York, of all sizes, specialties and qualities. The following does not even begin to hint at an "exhaustive" list. We cite here several of the best, those we recommend with few or even no qualms at all. Reservations are often necessary and almost always recommended.

**Carnegie Deli**
854 Seventh Ave at 55th Street
Tel: 757-2245

## Restaurant Prices

Categories based on average cost of dinner and a glass of wine, before tip.
**$** = under $15
**$$** = up to $30
**$$$** = over $30

A pilgrimage site in the heart of Midtown, this is one of New York's most famous Jewish delicatessens, where the corned beef sandwich is a must. No credit cards. **$$**

**Excellent Dumpling House**
111 Lafayette (just below Canal St)
Tel: 219-0212
Unpretentious, unadorned and on the outskirts of Chinatown proper; always packed with locals and devoted visitors who love its no-nonsense atmosphere, reasonable prices, and stellar dumplings (especially the vegetable dumplings, steamed or fried). No reservations, but there's sometimes a short wait; best for mid-afternoon lunch. No credit cards. **$$**

**Oyster Bar**
Lower level, Grand Central Terminal
Tel: 490-6650
A New York institution and a must for seafood lovers. The best fresh oysters and clam chowder in town, and you can sit at a counter, dining room or salon. **$$–$$$**

**San Domenico**
240 Central Park South
Tel: 265-5959
One of the most highly rated Italian restaurants in the city, this Central Park South establishment offers unusual Bolognese fare, with a wide variety of Northern Italian pastas and an extremely large wine list. A fine place to take a big party, but not necessarily for an intimate romantic meal. Reservations required. **$$$$**

**Totonno's Pizzeria**
1524 Neptune Avenue, Brooklyn
Tel: 718-372-8606
Totonno's freshly baked brick-oven pizzas may well be the finest in the five boroughs. **$**

**Union Square Café**
21 East 16th Street
Tel: 243-4020
Possibly the friendliest service in
New York and some of the best
new-American cuisine anywhere.
Reservations are difficult as this
very popular restaurant's innovative
menu attracts a hip, crowd.
Definitely call ahead. **$$$–$$$$**

## SHOPPING

Shopping is a major pastime in New
York: there isn't much to be found
anywhere that can't be found here,
and usually more of it. **Art**, of
course, is a good bet; apart from
the major auctioneers, **Sotheby's**
and **Christies**, where record prices
are set for world-famous works,
there are hundreds of art galleries
in which to browse (if not to buy).

**Antiques** can be found in
Greenwich Village along Bleecker St
and on side streets off University
Place; along Upper Madison Ave, on
60th St near Third Ave.

The city's famous **department
stores** offer something for almost
everyone but differ somewhat in
their clientele: the most famous are
the bustling **Bloomingdale's** (1000
Third Ave at 59th St) and **Macy's**
(151 West 34th St), which sell
everything from housewares to
furniture and clothing. **Lord & Taylor**
(424 Fifth Ave at 39th St); and **Saks
Fifth Avenue** (611 Fifth Ave)
concentrate on clothes, with the
latter offering the most upscale
fashions.

**Electronic and photographic
suppliers** can be found almost
everywhere, including Times Square
and on Lexington Avenue near
Grand Central Terminal. A few
outlets are less than scrupulous, so
it's best to do some comparison
shopping before actually buying. A
better bet might be in the downtown
City Hall district or on Fifth Avenue
between 37th and 40th streets.

The real bargains are often
downtown: along Orchard St on the
Lower East Side; in Chinatown; on
Canal St between Sixth and Third
avenues, and in the East Village,

particularly the cross streets
between First and Second avenues.
Savvy New York shoppers also flock
to Manhattan's **flea markets**,
including the eclectic weekend
**Chelsea antiques market** on Sixth
Ave between 25th and 27th streets
and the **Sunday flea market** at
Columbus Ave and 77th St on the
Upper West Side.

There are some excellent
antiquarian and second-hand
bookstores around town, especially
the **Strand Book Store**, 828
Broadway at 12th St, Tel: 473-
1452, which claims to have two
million volumes in stock and is a
wonderful place to browse.

## Hotel Prices

Categories based on average
cost of a double room for one
night.
**$** = under $65
**$$** = up to $100
**$$$** = up to $150
**$$$$** = over $150

## NEW JERSEY

### WHERE TO STAY

*LAMBERTVILLE*
**Apple Inn**
31 York Street, NJ 08530
Tel: 609-397-9250
Well-kept Victorian-style bed and full
breakfast in the heart of
Lambertville. Five nice rooms with
private baths. **$$$**
**Chimney Hill Farm Estate**
207 Goat Hill Road, NJ 08530
Tel: 609-397-1516
Fax: 609-397-1516
Web: www.chimneyhillinn.com
An impressive gabled fieldstone
house located in the hills 5 miles (8
km) from Lambertville. Candlelit
country breakfasts and many other
nice touches. **$$$$**

*MORRISTOWN*
**The Madison Hotel**
1 Convent Road, NJ 07960
Tel: 973-285-1800
US Freephone: 800-526-0729
Fax: 973-540-8566

Central, luxury accommodation with
indoor heated swimming pool,
Jacuzzi and sauna. Disabled
access. **$$$$**
**The Westin**
2 Whippany Road, NY 07960
Tel: 973-539-7300
Web: www.westin.com
Large, recently renovated hotel in
the heart of Morristown. Facilities
include 200 attractive guest rooms,
two restaurants and two lounges.
**$$**

*TRENTON*
**Best Western Bordentown Inn**
1068 Rt 206 Dunsmill, NJ 08505
Tel: 609-298-8000
US Freephone: 800-772-7083
Fax: 609-291-9757
www.bwnynjpa.com
This inn features attractive,
spacious rooms with movies,
cable TV, HBO and refrigerators.
Other amenities include an
attractive indoor pool, exercise
room, sauna, bar, free parking and
fishing. **$$$**
**Laurel Notch Motor Lodge**
US 206, Bordentown, NJ 08505
Tel: 609-298-6500
Simple but very clean rooms. Close
to local attractions. **$**

### WHERE TO EAT

*TRENTON*
**Mastoris Diner-Restaurant**
144 Hwy 130, Bordentown
Tel: 609-298-4650
Excellent prime rib and an
impressive 77 varieties of
sandwiches. For dessert choose
from the many pies baked on the
premises. **$**
**Sal Deforte's Ristorante**
200 Fulton Street
Tel: 609-396-6856
Romantic Italian – a little bit
northern, a little bit southern –
located in a century-old building
with a Victorian floral style dining
room and wood-paneled bar. **$$**

## PENNSYLVANIA

### WHERE TO STAY

#### LANCASTER
**The Gardens of Eden**
1894 Eden Rd, PA 17601
Tel: 717-393-5179
19th-century Victorian B&B with three rooms in main house and private guest cottage on 3-acre (1.2 hectare) garden spot overlooking the Conestoga River. Furnished with antiques and offering shared and private bath, full breakfast, free parking and tour guides. **$**
**Strasburg Village Inn**
1 W. Main St, Strasburg, PA 17579
Tel: 717-687-0900
Fully renovated 18th-century bed-and-breakfast inn with Colonial decor in the center of town. Amenities include: private bath, some rooms with Jacuzzi, complimentary full breakfast, air conditioning, TV, free parking. **$–$$**

#### PHILADELPHIA
**Best Western**
11580 Roosevelt Blvd, PA 19116
Tel: 464-9500
US Freephone: 800-528-1234
Good, clean, motel lodging at a decent price, about 25–30 minutes north of city center by car. Amenities: restaurant, lounge, fitness center, outdoor pool, game room and free parking. **$–$$**
**Omni Hotel at Independence Park**
401 Chestnut St, PA 19106
Tel: 925-0000
US Freephone: 1-800-843-6664
Plush hotel located in Old City adjacent to Independence National Park. Featuring Azalea, a gourmet restaurant and lounge; indoor pool, health club and sauna. **$$$$**
**Thomas Bond House**
129 S. 2nd St, PA 19106
Tel: 923-8523
US Freephone: 800-845-2663
A handsome, Federal-style B&B maintained by the National Park Service with 10 rooms and two suites in the heart of the historic district. Amenities: private and shared bath, some rooms with fireplace, whirlpool, sofa bed, free continental breakfast. **$$–$$$**

## Restaurant Prices

Categories based on average cost of dinner and a glass of wine, before tip.
**$** = under $15
**$$** = up to $30
**$$$** = over $30

### WHERE TO EAT

#### LANCASTER
**Market Fare**
25 W. King St
Tel: 717-299-7090
Classic American cuisine served in a relaxing establishment with 19th-century art, comfy armchairs, and upper level café. **$$–$$$**
**Olde Greenfield Inn**
595 Greenfield Road
Tel: 717-393-0668
Interesting, carefully prepared international seafood, poultry, steak and pasta in a historic farmhouse just outside of town. **$$**

#### PHILADELPHIA
**Le Bec-Fin**
1523 Walnut St
Tel: 567-1000
Regarded as one of the finest restaurants in the country, this very expensive French favorite near Rittenhouse Square garners rave reviews from critics and clients alike. Reservations required. A la carte menu served at the downstairs bistro. **$$$$**
**La Famiglia**
8 S. Front St
Tel: 922-2803
An Old City favorite for high-class Italian food in a lovely formal setting. **$$$–$$$$**
**Jim's Steaks**
400 South St
Tel: 928-1911
Many cheese-steak connoisseurs consider this funky little place the tastiest in town. **$**
**Joe's Peking Duck House**
925 Race St
Tel: 922-3277
Many think this Chinatown standard, with non-existent decor and crowded ambiance serves the best Chinese food in town. **$$**

## SHOPPING

#### PHILADELPHIA
Numerous **haute couture** boutiques line the streets around Liberty Place and Rittenhouse Square. The largest shopping district in the city is on Market Street east of Broad Street. Here you'll find **Lord & Taylor**, formerly John Wanamaker, (13th and Market), the grandad of Philadelphia department stores housed in a landmark building across from City Hall.

Farther east on **Market Street**, past discount shops, sporting goods, electronics, shoes and clothing stores, is **The Gallery**, a modern shopping mall which occupies three square blocks and four levels between 11th and 8th streets. There are over 200 shops and restaurants around the airy, sky-lit atrium including three department stores (**Kmart, J.C. Penney** and **Strawbridges**) and a surprisingly interesting food court that's convenient for quick and inexpensive meals or snacks.

**Market Place East** is next to **The Gallery** at 8th and Market streets. Housed in a magnificent cast-iron structure once occupied by **Lit Brothers Department Store**, this block-long mixed-use complex is now divided between offices and about 25 stores and restaurants.

For more adventurous tastes, **South Street** is the place to go. The shops and eateries on or near South Street from 9th to Front streets include everything from punk shops and art galleries to rock bars and fine restaurants. This is the hip, edgy part of town, popular with, but certainly not limited to, young people. It tends to be a bit of a carnival on Friday and Saturday nights, but it's almost always interesting. At one time, South Street ran through a large Jewish neighborhood. A remnant of those days can still be found on **Fabric Row**, which runs along 4th Street south of South Street. Mammoth **King of Prussia Mall** is beaten in size only by Minnesota's Mall of America.

## Hotel Prices

Categories based on average
cost of a double room for one
night.
$ = under $65
$$ = up to $100
$$$ = up to $150
$$$$ = over $150

## MARYLAND

### WHERE TO STAY

#### ANNAPOLIS
**Maryland Inn**
16 Church Circle, MD 21401
Tel: 410-263-2641
Web: annapolisinns.com
A pub and tavern with splendid
rooms, many dating to the
revolutionary era. The wooden
porches,and marble tiled lobby are
Victorian. $$$$

#### BALTIMORE
**Admiral Fell Inn**
888 South Broadway, MD 21283
Tel: 410-522-7377
US Freephone: 800-292-4667
Web: www.AdmiralFell.com
Pleasing proportions and
custom-crafted Federal-style
furnishings characterize this
well-preserved Fells Point inn.
The Admiral Fell has received
many accolades for its New
American cuisine and
award-winning wine cellar. Guests
are offered free parking and
transpor-tation to local attractions.
$$$$
**Celie's Waterfront B&B**
1714 Thames Street, MD 21231
Tel: 410-522-2323
Seven gorgeous rooms with private
balconies commanding superb
harbor views. $$$
**Hostelling International-Baltimore**
17 West Mulberry St, MD 21201
Tel: 410-576-8880
Fax: 410-685-3574
Email: baltimore.hostel@juno.com
Located within walking distance of
Inner Harbor's shops and
restaurants. Facilities include
kitchen, laundry, outdoor baggage
storage and travel center. $

## WHERE TO EAT

### ANNAPOLIS
**Carrol's Creek Restaurant**
410 Severn Avenue
Tel: 410-263-8102
Critically acclaimed waterfront
restaurant with fabulous views. $$$

### BALTIMORE
**Obrycki's**
1727 East Pratt Street
Tel: 410-732-6399
Rich, well-flavored seafood dishes.
Super-fresh Chesapeake Bay crab is
often the star of the show. $$
**Woman's Industrial Exchange**
333 North Charles Street
Tel: 410-685-4388
Well-prepared American home-style
cooking. Wonderful egg and bacon
breakfasts accompanied by fat
clouds of "scratch" biscuits. For
lunch try the well-seasoned crab
cakes or an old fashioned chicken
salad. Welcoming atmosphere. $$

## SHOPPING

### BALTIMORE
**Harborplace & The Gallery**
200 East Pratt Street
Over 100 shops, restaurants and
cafes in a sensational atrium mall.

## VIRGINIA

### WHERE TO STAY

#### BLACKSBURG
**Best Western Red Lion Inn**
900 Plantation Road, VA 24060
Tel: 540-552-7770
Fax: 540-552-6346
Close to Virginia Tech and
Smithfield Plantation. Cable TV,
lounge, pool, playground and
restaurant. $$

#### BUCHANAN
**Wattsull Inn**
130 Arcadia Road, VA
Tel: 540-254-1551
Spectacular vistas from this delight-
ful hilltop inn well-placed between
the Appalachians and the Blue
Ridge Mountains. Spacious
grounds, near Natural Bridge. $$

#### CHARLOTTESVILLE
**Best Western Cavalier Inn**
105 Emmett Street, VA 22905
Tel: 804-296-8111
Standard motel rooms in the university district. Complimentary breakfast, courtesy shuttle, seasonal
outdoor pool, and restaurant. $
**Clifton – The Country Inn**
1296 Clifton Inn Drive, VA 22911
Tel: 804-971-1800
Fax: 804-971-7098
US Freephone: 888-971-1800
Web: www.cliftoninn.com
Elegant Federal and colonial revival-
style historic manor house
surrounded by 40 wooded acres
(17 hectares). Guest rooms are
furnished with antiques and a wood-
burning fireplace. Facilities include
clay tennis courts, pool, whirlpool
and award-winning cuisine. $$$$
**Silver Thatch Inn**
3001 Hollymead Drive, VA 22911
Tel: 804-978-4686
Fax: 804-978-6156
Web: www.silverthatch.com
This delightful clapboard home is
one of the oldest buildings in
central Virginia. Accommodations
comprise seven guest rooms all
with private baths and several with
canopy beds and fireplaces. The
uniquely appointed rooms are
named after early Virginian-born
presidents. There are three dining
rooms and a bar. $$$–$$$$

#### LEXINGTON
**Historic Country Inns**
11 North Main, VA 24450
Tel: 877-463-2044
US Freephone: 877-463-2044
Fax: 540-463-7262
Web: www.innbrook.com/maplehtml
This firm runs three inns in the
area: two in the Lexington Historic
District – the Alexander Withrow
House and McCampbell Inn – and
Maple Hall 6 miles (9 kms) to the
north on 56 acres (22 hectares). All
inns feature fireplaces, fine dining,
trails and pool. $$$–$$$$
**B&B at Llewellyn Lodge**
603 Main Street, VA 24450
Tel: 540-463-3235
US Freephone: 800-882-1145
Web: www.Llodge.com
Six comfortable, individually

decorated rooms in an attractive gray brick colonial building. This inn is known for its tempting breakfast menu featuring the innkeeper's award-winning omelets. A health-conscious menu is also available. Other features include four poster beds, ceiling fans and a porch swing. Situated close to Downtown, this is the ideal base for visiting Lexington's attractions. **$$$**

## RICHMOND

**The Emmanuel Hutzler House**
2036 Monument Avenue, VA 23220
Tel: 804-353-6900
Web: www.bensonhouse.com
A large Italian Renaissance home with richly appointed interior. Each spacious room has its own private bath, a queen-sized bed and TV. Full breakfast included. **$$$**

**West-Bocock House**
1107 Grove Avenue, VA 23220
Tel: 804-358-6174
This elegant 19th-century historic house is well-placed for visiting the city's attractions. Guest rooms have private baths, fresh flowers and French linen. **$$**

## Restaurant Prices

Categories based on average cost of dinner and a glass of wine, before tip.
**$** = under $15
**$$** = up to $30
**$$$** = over $30

## WHERE TO EAT

## CHARLOTTESVILLE

**Blue Bird Café**
625 West Main Street
Tel: 804-295-1166
Appetizing lunches featuring steaks, fried chicken and crab cakes. **$$**

**C&O Restaurant**
515 East Water Street
Tel: 804-971-7044
Imaginative dishes with a French influence served in an attractively converted rail workers' layover. Try the sliced, marinated and seared flank steak. Elegant but casual atmosphere. **$$**

**Millers**
109 West Main Street
Tel: 804-971-8511
An old-style smokey atmosphere bar. Formerly a drugstore specializing in "Miller's Tonic" in the early 1900s. The current Millers' dispenses great cheeseburgers and a nice grilled chicken salad. Pleasant outdoor patio with fountain and live jazz. **$**

## FREDERICKSBURG

**Kenmore Inn**
1200 Princess Anne Street
Tel: 540-371-7622
Good steak and seafood restaurant with live entertainment. **$$**

## LEXINGTON

**Virginia House**
722 South Main Street, VA 24450
Tel: 540-463-3643
Mouth-watering southern cooking. **$**

## RICHMOND

**Bill's Barbecue**
5805 West Broad Street
Bill's is justly popular for lavish portions of succulent barbecue and excellent breakfasts. **$**

**Millie's Diner**
2603 East Main
Tel: 804-643-5512
Excellent New Southern cooking in a remodeled traditional diner. **$$**

**The Tobacco Company**
1201 East Cary Street
Tel: 804-788-4750
This restaurant features creative New American cuisine in a converted tobacco warehouse. **$$**

## ROANOKE

**Awful Arthur's**
108 Campbell Avenue
Tel: 540-344-2997
Much-loved seafood restaurant in an attractive historic location. Entrees include steamed crab, oysters, clams and fresh fish. **$**

**Roanoker**
2522 Colonial Avenue
Tel: 540-344-7746
Short on atmosphere but long on portions of delicious, southern cooking. A wide array of well-prepared vegetable side dishes, rich gravies, and other trimmings. **$**

## NORTH CAROLINA

### WHERE TO STAY

## CHAPEL HILL

**Carolina Inn**
211 Pittsboro Street, NC 27516
Tel: 919-918-2795
US Freephone: 800-962-8519
Fax: 919-962-3400
Web: carolinainn.com
This elegantly furnished historic inn provides a good base for exploring downtown Chapel Hill and the shops and restaurants of Franklin Street. Extras include complimentary breakfast and newspaper. The inn's Crossroads restaurant has been awarded a four diamond rating by the AAA. **$$$$**

## DURHAM

**Carolina Duke Motor Inn**
2517 Guess Road, NC 27705
Tel/Fax: 919-286-0771
US Freephone: 800-438-1158
Very reasonable rooms and suites. Amenities include pool and area transportation. **$**

## GREENSBORO

**Microtel Inn**
4304 Big Tree Way, NC 27409
Tel: 336-547-7007
Clean, comfortable, good-value motor inn. **$**

## MANTEO

**Tranquil House Inn**
405 Queen Elizabeth St, NC 27954
Tel: 252-473-1404
US Freephone: 800-458-7069
A pleasant waterfront inn with suites, rooms and a deck. Extras include a complimentary breakfast and wine & cheese evening. A good place to relax and renew. **$$–$$$**

## MT AIRY

**Mayberry Motor Inn**
1001US Hwy 52N, NC 27030
Tel: 336-786-4109
Email: mayberry@surrey.net
Well-kept, comfortable rooms. Very good value. Continental breakfast. Jogging and nature trail. **$**

## NAGS HEAD

**Carolinian Hotel**
2313 Virginia Dare Trail, NC 27959
Tel: 252-441-7171
Fax: 252-441-9514
Email: russ@carolinian.com
A rustic waterfront hotel with 86
rooms, cooking facilities. Amenities
include exercise and game rooms,
lounge, restaurant and pool. **$$$**

**First Colony Inn**
6720 S Virginia Dare Trail, NC
27959
Tel: 252-441-2343
Fax: 252-441-9234
Email: innkeper@firstcolonyinn.com
Handsome older inn, carefully
restored and furnished with
antiques. Babysitting services, two
Jacuzzis, pool. **$$**

## OCRACOKE

**The Island Inn and Dining Room**
PO Box 9, NC 27960
Tel: 252-928-4351
US Freephone: 877-456-3466
Fax: 252-928-4352
The characterful older section
(c.1901) offers rooms with
antiques, private baths and a
heated outdoor pool. The newer
motel-style section also has a pool
and welcomes families. Villa "full
efficiencies" with cooking facilities
are also available. The inn's dining
room is known for its fresh, well-
cooked seafood and hush puppies.
Guests may use the inn's canoes,
boats and rafts. **$$$**

## WILMINGTON

**Best Western Carolinian**
2916 Market Street, NC 28403
Tel: 910-763-4653
US Freephone: 800-528-1234
Between Downtown and the Atlantic
beaches. Recently remodeled
incorporating de luxe amenities,
and lovely mature gardens. Free
continental breakfast. **$$**

**The Inn on Orange B&B**
410 Orange Street, NC 28401
Tel: 910-815-0035
US Freephone: 800-381-4666
Fax: 910-251-1149
Web: www.innonorange.com
An historic Italianate Victorian home
located within walking distance of
the riverside and close to

Downtown. The inn features ceiling
fans, fireplaces and TVs on
request. Full breakfast is served on
the weekends; continental
breakfast is available on weekdays.
There is a two-night minimum stay
on the weekend. **$$–$$$**

## WINSTON-SALEM

**Tanglewood Manor House B&B**
Hwy 158W, 4061 Clemmons, NC
27012
Tel: 336-778-6370
Fax: 336-778-6379
Located in a country park with
fishing pier, horseback riding,
jogging and nature trail nearby.
Canoes, boats and rafts are
available for use by guests.
Restaurant, playground and some
rooms with fireplaces. **$$**

**Salem Inn**
127 South Cherry St, NC 27101
Tel: 336-725-8561
Well-maintained budget inn with
exercise room, lounge, pool, jogging
and nature trail. Continental
breakfast provided. **$**

## Restaurant Prices

Categories based on average
cost of dinner and a glass of
wine, before tip.
**$** = under $15
**$$** = up to $30
**$$$** = over $30

## WHERE TO EAT

## CHAPEL HILL

**411 West Italian Cafe**
411 West Franklin Street
Tel: 919-967-2782
Eclectic menu featuring
Mediterranean, Italian and
Californian dishes. The lemon
linguine with shrimp, scallops and
roast tomatoes is excellent, as are
the wood-burning fire pizzas. There
is a very pleasant glass domed
dining area with fountain. **$$**

**Spanky's**
101 East Franklin Street
Tel: 919-967-2678
Buzzing restaurant serving sandwiches, seafood and pasta. Spanky's
club sandwich is a favorite. **$**

## DURHAM

**Anotherthyme**
109 North Gregson Street
Tel: 919-682-5225
Innovative West Coast cuisine.
**$$**

## GREENSBORO

**Lo Spiedo di Noble**
1720 Battleground Avenue
Tel: 336-333-9833
A creative and diverse menu
strong on Italian and New
Southern dishes. Entrees range
from lobster steamed in banana
leaves to rack of lamb fillet. The
menu changes frequently and
fresh fish dishes feature in the
summer. **$$$**

## MOUNT AIRY

**Snappy Lunch**
125 North Main Street
Tel: 336-786-4931
The Snappy Lunch is known for its
hefty pork chop sandwich — a
cornucopia of juicy meat,
condiments and trimmings. Plenty
of atmosphere too. **$**

## WILMINGTON

**Crook's by the River**
138 South Front Street
Tel: 910-762-8898
Dishing up the best Southern
meals and Sunday brunches in
town. **$**

**Elijah's Restaurant**
2 Ann Street
Tel: 910-343-1448
Award-winning seafood
chowder and other delectable,
equally praiseworthy dishes. The
adjoining oyster bar with outdoor
covered patio faces onto Cape
Fear. **$$**

## WINSTON-SALEM

**Village Tavern**
221 Reynolda Village
Tel: 336-748-0221
Popular family restaurant offering
pub-style food and lively
atmosphere. **$$**

## SOUTH CAROLINA

### WHERE TO STAY

#### BEAUFORT
**Rhett House**
1009 Craven Street, SC 29902
Tel: 843-524-9030
Web: www.rhetthouseinn.com
Plantation house bordering the
Intercoastal waterway. Built in 1820
and restored following the Civil War,
the inn features stately white
columns, broad verandahs, rocking
chairs and period decor. Many
rooms have fireplaces, private
balconies and whirlpool baths.
Afternoon tea. **$$$$**

#### CHARLESTON
**Governer's House Inn**
117 Broad Street, SC 29401
Tel: 843-720-2070
US Freephone: 800-720-9812
Web: www.governorshouse.com
Attention to detail, elegant decor
and exceptional service are
hallmarks of this historic inn.
Originally the residence of Governor
Edward Rutledge, the youngest
signer of the Declaration of
Independence, the house still
retains an air of tradition with its
broad verandah, chandeliers,
numerous fireplaces and spacious
rooms. In the center of the historic
district and close to many
landmarks and restaurants. **$$$$**
**The Meeting Street Inn**
173 The Meeting Street, SC 29401
Tel: 843-723-1882
US Freephone: 800-842-8022
The distinguished sister of the
Governor's House. Built in 1844,
the inn originally housed a saloon
and restaurant. Having fallen into
disrepair after Hurricane Hugo it
has been lovingly restored. **$$-$$$**

#### GEORGETOWN
**Carolinian Clarion**
706 Church Street, SC 29440
Tel: 803-546-5191
Pleasant affordable rooms. Pool. **$**
**Harbor House Bed and Breakfast**
15 Cannon Street, SC 29440
Tel: 843-546-6532
US Freephone: 877-511-0101
Email: ino@harborhousebb.com

Large waterfront inn with distinctive
red roof. Built in 1740 as a
shipping warehouse. Lovely,
spacious rooms. **$$$**

#### MYRTLE BEACH
**Coral Beach Resort**
1105 South Ocean Blvd, SC 29578
Tel: 843-448-8412
US Freephone: 800-843-2684
Fax: 843-626-0156
Full service oceanfront resort
with nicely furnished guest
rooms and public areas.
Facilities include indoor and
outdoor pools, saunas, whirlpool,
restaurant and lounge. Disabled
access. **$$$**
**Compass Cove**
2311 S Ocean Blvd, SC 29577
Tel: 843-448-8373
US Freephone: 800-228-9894
Large family-friendly resort
situated 2½ miles (4 km)
from the Pavilion with ocean-front
rooms. The complex has pools,
Jacuzzis, restaurant and lounge.
**$$**

### WHERE TO EAT

#### BEAUFORT
**Anchorage House**
1103 Bay Street
Tel: 803-522-2090
Historic ambiance in waterfront
candlelit restaurant.
The low country specialties
include crab meat casserole with
sherry. **$$$**

#### CHARLESTON
**Alice's Fine Food**
468–470 King Street
Tel: 843-853-9366
Abundant portions of glorious fried
shellfish and the usual southern
comfort-food side dishes, served
cafeteria-style. **$**
**Pinckney Cafe and Espresso**
18 Pinckney Street
Tel: 843-577-0961
An imaginative menu featuring
fresh, well-cooked seafood
combined with a pleasant terrace,
relaxed atmosphere, fragrant
coffees and irresistible desserts
justify its popularity. **$**

#### GEORGETOWN
**Pink Magnolia**
719 Front Street
Tel: 843-527-6506
Fresh seafood salads, creole and
crab cakes served at your table
right on the harbor walk or indoors.
The non-seafood specialty is a fried
chicken salad. **$$**

#### JACKSONBORO
**Edisto Motel Cafe**
US Hwy 17
Tel: 843-893-2270
Luscious fried seafood in a casual
setting. **$$**

#### MYRTLE BEACH
**Omega Pancake and Omelet House**
2800 North Kings Hwy
Tel: 843-626-9949
Favorite breakfast spot for tourists
and locals alike. **$**

### Hotel Prices

Categories based on average
cost of a double room for one
night.
**$** = under $65
**$$** = up to $100
**$$$** = up to $150
**$$$$** = over $150

## GEORGIA

### WHERE TO STAY

#### BRUNSWICK
**Hostel in the Forest**
P.O. Box 1496, GA 31521
Tel: 912-264-9738
This hostel offers beds in tree
houses or geodesic dome.
Amenities include tranquility and
natural beauty. **$**

#### ST SIMONS ISLAND
**The Lodge on Little Simons Island**
PO Box 21078, GA 31522-0578
Tel: 912-638-7472
Web: LittleStSimonsIsland.com
This unique lodge, set on an un-
spoiled barrier hosts only 30 over-
night guests. The only way there is by
boat. Several cottages and lodges.
Price includes three southern meals
and on-island activities. Idyllic. **$$$$**

## SAVANNAH

**The Gastonian**
220 East Gaston Street, GA 31401
Tel: 912-232-2869
Fax: 912-232-0710
This 16-unit historic B&B
consists of restored, connected
late-1800s houses. Six rooms
with whirlpool bath. No pets
allowed. **$$$$**

**East Bay Inn**
225 East Bay Street, GA 31401
Tel: 912-238-1225
Fax: 912-232-2709
An historic bed-and-breakfast, this
28-unit restored 1853 warehouse
features large, Georgian-style
rooms. **$$$–$$$$**

**Hostelling International –
Savannah**
304 East Hall Street, GA 31401
Tel: 912-236-7744
Fax: 912-236-7744
An 1884 Victorian house in
the historic district. High
ceilings and slate fireplaces.
Amenities include kitchen,
baggage storage areas, laundry
and on-site parking. **$**

**Magnolia Place Inn**
503 Whitaker Street, GA 31401
Tel: 912-236-7674
Fax: 912-236-1145
A 12-unit restored Victorian
mansion, this historic B&B
has a hot tub in the courtyard
and whirlpools and
fireplaces in some rooms.
No pets. **$$$$**

**Olde Harbour Inn**
508 East Factors Walk, GA 31401
Tel: 912-234-4100
Fax: 912-233-5979
A 24-unit historic bed-and-
breakfast in the historic
riverfront district. River-view suites
with fully equipped kitchens.
**$$$–$$$$**

## WHERE TO EAT

### BRUNSWICK
**GA Pig**
Exit 29 off I-95
Tel: 912-264-6664
Expertly prepared barbecue dished
up in pleasant surroundings. A
mighty fine pit stop. **$**

## Restaurant Prices

Categories based on average
cost of dinner and a glass of
wine, before tip.
**$** = under $15
**$$** = up to $30
**$$$** = over $30

### MIDWAY
**Ida Mae & Joe's North Midway
Restaurant**
US Hwy 17
Tel: 912-884-3388
Very fresh, expertly fried fish. **$**

### ST SIMONS ISLAND
**Alfonza's Olde Plantation
Supper Club**
171 Harrington Lane
Tel: 912-638-9883
Glorious southern cooking served in
lush surroundings. **$$**

**Dressner's Village Cafe**
223 Mallory Street
Tel: 912-634-1217
A good choice for breakfast. **$**

### SAVANNAH
**The Chart House**
202 West Bay Street
Tel: 912-234-6686
Reserve a table and order the
prime rib in this three-story nautical-
themed restored warehouse. **$$**

**Mrs. Wilkes' Boarding House**
107 West Jones Street
Tel: 912-232-5997
Southern-style communal dining,
the old boarding house way. Pass
the biscuits and fried chicken, and
get there early. Lunch only. **$**

**The Pirates' House**
20 East Broad and Bay streets
Tel: 912-233-5757
Seafood galore at this Savannah
landmark. **$$$**

## SHOPPING

### SAVANNAH
**Oglethorpe Mall**
7804 Abercorn Street
**Savannah Festival Factory Stores**
11 Gateway Boulevard, South
**Savannah Mall**
Rio Road and Abercorn Ext

## FLORIDA

### WHERE TO STAY

### BAHIA HONDA STATE
### RECREATION AREA
For information about the park,
Tel: 305-872-2353.

**Big Pine Key Fishing Lodge**
33000 Overseas Hwy, Summerland
Key, FL 33048
Tel: 305-872-2351
Spick and span lodge rooms and
five canal-side motel rooms with
cooking facilities. **$$**

**Deer Run Bed & Breakfast**
Long Beach Road, FL 33043
Tel: 305-872-2015
Spacious guest rooms with ocean
views located in two houses near
the bay. Deer roam the
surrounding native wooded land
(also a good bird-watching area).
Amenities include a Jacuzzi on the
beach, porches and private
balconies. **$$**

### BRADENTON
**Silver Surf Motel and Efficiencies**
1301 Gulf Drive North, FL 34217
Tel: 941-778-6626
Fax: 941-778-4308
A de luxe waterfront hotel featuring
panoramic Gulf views, pool and
private sandy beach. **$$**

### CLEARWATER BEACH
**Belleview Biltmore**
25 Belleview Boulevard, FL 33756
Tel: 727-442-6171
US Freephone: 800-237-8947
Web: www.belleviewbiltmore.com
This grand old four season resort
has been welcoming guests since
1897. Recreational facilities
include red clay tennis courts, an
excellent golf course, a de luxe
spa and fitness center.
**$$–$$$$**

**Hostelling International –
Clearwater Beach**
606 Bay Esplanade, FL 33767
Tel: 727-443-1211
Fax: 727-442-1211
Email: magillr1@juno.com
Close to shops with pool,
landscaped courtyard, barbecue
and picnic area, kitchen, laundry
lockers and on-site parking. **$**

## Hotel Prices

Categories based on average cost of a double room for one night.

$ = under $65
$$ = up to $100
$$$ = up to $150
$$$$ = over $150

### EVERGLADES NATIONAL PARK

For information about the park, Tel: 305-242-7700.
40001 State Road 9336
Homestead, FL 33034

**Flamingo Lodge and Marina and Outpost Resort**
Tel: 941-695-3101
Simple, clean rooms and decent food in this remote Everglades outpost. $$

### FORT MYERS

**Mantanzas Inn**
414 Crescent Street, FL 33931
Tel: 941-463-9258
US Freephone: 800-462-9258
Nicely decorated rooms and close to the beach. Facilities include pool and restaurant. $$

### GAINESVILLE

**Village Lodge**
1900 Southwest 13th St, FL 32608
Tel: 352-372-1880
Clean and affordable rooms, some with microwaves and refrigerators. Facilities include pool, laundry facilities, airport transportation. $

### HOMESTEAD

**Everglades Motel**
605 South Krome Ave, FL 33030
Tel: 305-247-4117
Tidy rooms with pool and laundry facilities. $–$$

### ISLAMADORA

**Lime Tree Bay Resort Motel**
PO Box 839, Limekey 33001
Tel: 305-664-4740
Delightful cottages, apartments and de luxe motel rooms. Amenities include a private sandy area with beach chairs, hot tub, pool, small watersports rental concession and snorkeling. $$–$$$

### KEY LARGO

**Jule's Undersea Lodge**
From 51 Shoreland Drive, off MM 103.2, FL 33037
Tel: 305-451-2353
A unique two-bedroomed lodge 22 feet (7 m) beneath the sea. Originally a research facility, accommodations are basic, but comfortable. Each of the two bedrooms has a 42 inch (107 cm) round window looking into the sea, hot and cold shower, and TV/VCR. The only way to get there is by scuba diving. The price includes all gear and unlimited diving. Reserve well in advance. $$$$

**Kona Kai Bayfront Resort**
97802 Overseas Hwy, FL 33037
Tel: 305-852-7200
Waterfront resort with full kitchen facilities. $$$

### KEY WEST

**Hostelling International – Key West**
718 South Street, FL 33040
Tel: 305-296-5719
Fax: 305-296-0672
Located two blocks from the beach, this hostel offers scuba diving lessons, and snorkeling. There is an outdoor courtyard, barbecue pit, pool table, game room, laundry facilities and library. $

**The Marquesa Hotel**
600 Fleming Street, FL 33040
Tel: 305-292-1919
US Freephone: 800-869-4631
Fax: 305-294-2121
Web: www.marquesa.com
This late 19th-century landmark has been lovingly restored to its original splendor. Tucked in the heart of Key West's Historic District, four handsome buildings encircle two swimming pools and luxurious tropical gardens. Amenities include marble baths and fine dining in the adjoining Café Marquesa. $$$$

**Southernmost Motel in the USA**
1319 Duval Street, FL 33040
Tel: 305-296-6577
127 guest rooms in a beautiful old home. Two large pools and poolside bars, Jacuzzi, public beach access, bicycle moped rental and warm, friendly service. $$$–$$$$

### KISSIMEE

**Sevilla Inn**
4640 West Irlo Bronson Hwy, FL 34746
Tel: 407-396-4135
A well-maintained motor inn with pool. $

### MELBOURNE BEACH

**Hostelling International – Melbourne Beach**
1135 North A1A, FL 32903
Tel: 407-951-0004
Email: emccan@aol
Situated on the beach and convenient for area attractions. Amenities include kitchen, lockers, laundry and volleyball. Ocean kayaks and surfboards are available for guests' use. $

### MICANOPY

**Scottish Inns**
17110 SE CR 234, FL 32667
Tel: 352-466-3163
Squeaky clean budget rooms and a restaurant. $

### NAPLES

**Vanderbilt Inn on the Gulf**
11000 Gulf Shore Dr N, FL 34108
Web: www/vanderbiltinn.com
With a Caribbean flavor, this full-service Gulf resort features 300 feet (100 m) of fine sandy beach, restau-rant, lounge and beachside bar. Very comfortable rooms, with balcony or patio. $$$$

### OCALA

**Travelodge**
1626 SW Pine Ave, FL 34474
Tel: 352-622-4121
Well-fitted rooms some with microwaves and refrigerators. Pool and free continental breakfast. $

### ORLANDO

**Embassy Suites – Lake Buena Vista**
8100 Lake Avenue, FL 32836
Tel: 407-239-1144
Fax: 407-238-0230
Web: www.embassy-suites.com
Spacious suites with in-room movies, fitness center, whirlpool, steam room and family fun center. Free breakfast and transportation to Walt Disney World. $$$$

## Hotel Prices

Categories based on average cost of a double room for one night.
**$** = under $65
**$$** = up to $100
**$$$** = up to $150
**$$$$** = over $150

**Hostelling International –
Orlando/Kissimmee**
4840 West Irlo Bronson, FL 34746
Tel: 407-396-9311
hi-orlandoresort@compuserve.com
A stone's throw from Walt Disney World and close to other attractions. Facilities include air-conditioning, lake, en-suite bathrooms. Wheelchair accessible. **$**

**Sierra Suites**
8750 Universal Blvd, FL 32819
Tel: 407-903-1500
Fax: 407-903-1555
Web: www.sierra-orlando.com
Good-sized, family friendly suites. Conveniently located for all area attractions. Heated pool, exercise room and spa. Very good value. **$$**

**Walt Disney World
All-Star Resorts**
The cheapest rooms within Walt Disney World. **$$**

**All Star Movie Resort**
Tel: 407-939-7000. **$$$**
**All Star Music Resort**
Tel: 407-939-6000. **$$**
**All Star Sports Resort**
Tel: 407-939-5000. **$$**

### ST AUGUSTINE
**Kenwood Inn**
38 Marine Street, FL 32084
Tel: 904-824-2116
Web: oldcity.com/kenwood
This time-honored Victorian hotel is close to the seafront and other attractions. **$$–$$$**

### ST PETERSBURG
**Coral Reef Beach Resort**
5800 Gulf Boulevard, FL 33714
Tel: 727-360-0821
Fax: 727-367-3718
A first-class resort with de luxe suites and nicely appointed rooms. The pool is enormous. Beach bar and restaurant. **$$–$$$**

### SANIBEL ISLAND
**South Seas Plantation**
PO Box 194, South Seas Plantation Road, FL 33924
US Freephone: 800-237-3102
Sprawling resort occupying most of the island and Sanibel's first. Guests can choose from condominium style and well-fitted standard guest rooms. **$$$$**

### TAMPA
**East Lake Inn**
6529 E Hillsborough Ave, FL 33610
Tel: 813-622-8339
Clean and comfortable rooms, some with refrigerators. **$**

**Radisson Bay Harbor Inn**
7700 Courtney Campbell Causeway, FL 33607
Tel: 813-281-8900
Fax: 813-281-0189
Handsomely appointed rooms with balconies. The inn also has a restaurant and lounge, pool, private beach with watersports and exercise room. Close to local attractions. **$$$**

**Quality Suites – University of South Florida/Busch Gardens**
3001 University Center Drive, FL 33612
Tel: 813-971-8930
Nice rooms and lots of extras including complimentary beverages and snacks, a buffet breakfast. Pool and Jacuzzi. **$$$**

### TARPON SPRINGS
**Tarpon Shores Inn**
40346 US Hwy 19N, FL 34689
Tel: 727-938-2483
Good-value rooms, some with microwaves and refrigerators. Facilities include pool, Jacuzzi and laundry facilities. **$**

## WHERE TO EAT

### BRADENTON
**Crab Trap and Crab Trap II**
4814 Memphis Road, Ellenton
Tel: 941-729-7777
Hwy 19 at Terra Ceia
Tel: 941-722-6255
A local favorite for fine fresh-catch and game dishes. **$$**

**Sandbar Restaurant**
100 Spring Avenue, Anna Maria
Tel: 941-778-0444
Good food and excellent views. **$**

### CLEARWATER BEACH
**Kaiko Japanese Restaurant**
7245 McMullen Booth Road
Tel: 727-791-6640
First-rate sashimi, sushi and teriyaki. **$$**

### FORT MYERS
**The Veranda**
2122 Second Street
Tel: 941-332-2065
Continental cuisine served in a mellow old mansion with pleasant courtyard. Try the rack of lamb. Mellow atmosphere and steep prices. **$$$**

### GAINESVILLE
**Sovereign**
Southeast Second Avenue
Tel: 352-378-6307
Fine dining in a posh 19th-century carriage house. **$$$**

**Potlikker's Restaurant**
591 Washington Avenue
Tel: 305-248-0835
Tasty homestyle cooking. The barbecue is succulent and tangy. **$**

### ISLAMADORA
**Manny & Isa's Restaurant**
US Hwy 1 Mile Marker 81.6
Tel: 305-664-5019
Manny and Isa's is justly famous for mouthwatering key lime pie – possibly the best, certainly the freshest – to be had anywhere. The limes come from Manny's orchard. The spicy and savory dishes are seriously tempting as well. **$**

### JACKSONVILLE
**Matthews at St Marco's**
2107 Hendricks Avenue
Tel: 904-396-9922
Spare and chic interior – innovative menu. The five-course tasting menu is a good introduction to this innovative and varied menu. **$$$**

### Key Largo
**Crack'd Conch**
105045 Overseas Highway
Tel: 305-451-0732

## Restaurant Prices

Categories based on average cost of dinner and a glass of wine, before tip.
**$** = under $15
**$$** = up to $30
**$$$** = over $30

A sublimely relaxed venue for soaking up a few beers with the local atmosphere and tucking into a heaped plateful of fried conch. **$**

### KEY WEST
**Blue Heaven**
729 Thomas Street
Tel: 305-296-8666
Relaxed, time-worn and popular cafe serving West Indian-style breakfasts, lunches and dinners. **$**
**Pepe's**
806 Caroline Street
Tel: 305-294-7192
Excellent grilled steak, succulent oysters and fragrant, fresh-baked breads, indoor and outdoor dining and a very popular bar. **$$**

### MARATHON
**Herbie's**
Mile Marker 50.5
Tel: 305-743-6373
Great seafood and chowders. **$$**

### NAPLES
**Terra**
1300 Third Street South
Tel: 941-262-5500
Interesting menu of flavorful stews and shellfish risottos. Freshly baked breads with a Mediterranean accent. **$$$**

### OCALA
**Petit Jardin**
2209 East Silver Springs Boulevard
Tel: 352-351-4140.
Authentically French bistro dishes including *escargots*. **$$**

### ORLANDO
**Harvey's Bistro**
390 North Orlando Avenue
Tel: 407-246-6560
A Downtown eatery with a loyal following. Good soups, casseroles and pizzas. **$$**

**Pete's Bubble Room**
1351 South Orlando Avenue
Tel: 407-628-3331
Popular family restaurant. **$$**

### ST AUGUSTINE
**Fiddler's Green Oceanside Bar**
2750 Anahma Drive
Tel: 904-824-8897
Fine views and good food. **$$**
**Raintree**
102 San Marco Avenue
Tel: 904-824-7211
Very good seafood with freshly baked breads and pastries served in a restored older home. **$$**

### ST PETERSBURG
**Cafe Lido**
800 Second Avenue
Tel: 727-898-5800
Relaxing mainly Italian cafe with fine views. The wood-burning oven pizzas are excellent. **$$**
**Green Flash**
15183 Captiva Drive
Tel: 941-472-3337
Wide open ocean views and varied menu featuring fresh seafood. **$$**

### TAMPA
**Silver Ring Cafe**
1831 East Seventh Avenue
Tel: 813-248-4961
Heaped platters of authentic Cuban dishes. **$**

### VENICE
**Frenchy's Saltwater Café**
1071 Tamiami Trail South
Tel: 941-488-3775
Well-liked seafood restaurant. **$$**

## SHOPPING

If you are into kitsch – plastic flamingo ashtrays, canned sunshine, orange perfume – you will find Florida a veritable treasure house. From roadside shacks to massive, futuristic malls, stores carry plenty of traditional souvenirs. (Don't be surprised if your souvenir plate has a sticker on the bottom that says "Made in Taiwan.") And then, of course, there are the homegrown souvenirs like oranges, tangerines, limes, kumquats and grapefruits that can be shipped home for a small fee. But if you look a little harder, Florida also has an array of quality goods to take home from a trip. There are shops worth seeking out that sell designer clothing at factory prices, primitive Haitian art, Art Deco and old Florida antiques, Native Indian crafts, and shells that forever smell of the sea. For more humdrum shopping there is the usual array of convenience stores, drugstores, department stores and supermarkets. Many Floridians do their shopping in shopping malls, which contain the usual mix of department stores, boutiques, chain stores and one-of-a-kind shops. The **Gold Coast** has the biggest choice of malls, particularly Miami, Fort Lauderdale and Boca Raton. Just ask the staff in your hotel for details of the best malls in your area. Hours vary, but most shopping centers are open seven days a week. The following list highlights just a few of Florida's most famous shopping spots.

### Everglades National Park
**Miccosukee Indian Village**, west of the Shark Valley entrance, sells Native American crafts.

### Fort Lauderdale
**Fashion Mall** at Plantation's University Drive north of Broward Boulevard contains over 100 specialty shops and several nationwide outlets. The food court is a cut above the ordinary.

### Key West
**Gingerbread Square Gallery** at 1207 Duval Street sells works by local artists.

## Hub City: MIAMI

### GETTING AROUND

#### Public transportation

**From the airport:** Miami International Airport is 7 miles (12 km) from Downtown. SuperShuttle (Tel: 305-871-2000) operates between the airport and major hotels. Metrobus service departs from Level 1 next to Concourse E.

**Rapid transit:** Metrorail is an elevated rapid transit system connecting Downtown with Dadeland and Hialeah. The Metromover monorail system circles the Downtown area. Metro-Dade Transit runs both (Tel: 305-638-6700). Single fares under $2.

**City buses:** Metro-Dade Transit also runs the Metrobus fleet from stops indicated by distinctive blue and green signs. Single fares under $2.

**Intercity buses:** The main Greyhound terminal is at Bayside Station, 700 Biscayne Boulevard (Tel: 305-379-7403).

**Commuter rail:** The Tri-Rail (Tel: 800-874-7245) service links Miami-Dade with Palm Beach and Broward.

**Trains:** Amtrak trains run from the Miami Terminal (Tel: 305-835-1222).

#### Private transportation

Miami is not a difficult city to negotiate by car but try to avoid weekday rush-hour snarls. Parking in the Miami Beach area can be scarce and restrictions are stringently imposed by a fleet of super-efficient tow-trucks. Fortunately, Miami Beach is a delightful place to explore by foot. Most of the car rental companies have offices at Miami International airport or Downtown. Check the *Yellow Pages* for a full list of firms.

**Ports:** Florida has several major cruise ship ports, with Miami and Port Everglades leading with the most sailings. Others include Port Canaveral, Palm Beach, St Petersburg, Tampa, Port Manatee (in Tampa Bay), and Madeira

Beach and Treasure Island (just north of St Pete Beach). The Port of Miami is the largest cruise port in the world. Seven cruise lines carry more than 1.5 million passengers a year into the port, which represents over two-thirds of all cruise passengers worldwide. The port is just a five-minute ride from downtown and Miami Beach. Tel: 305 371-7678.

**Taxis:** Taxis are relatively plentiful in South Beach with fares under $3 per mile (1.6 km). They can also be found at airports, train stations bus terminals and the major hotels, or ordered by telephone. Call Yellow Cab Co (Tel: 305-633-0503); Metro Taxi (Tel: 305-888-8888); or Flamingo Taxi (Tel: 305-885-7000).

**Car rental companies**
Avis, Tel: 305-637-4908
Hertz, Tel: 305-871-0300

### Hotel Prices

Categories based on average cost of a double room for one night.
$ = under $65
$$ = up to $100
$$$ = up to $150
$$$$ = over $150

### WHERE TO STAY

**Astor**
956 Washington Ave, Miami Beach
Tel: 305-531-8081
US Freephone: 800-270-4981
Understated stylishness is the hallmark of this trendy deco hotel. Bedrooms – mostly suites – and their wall-to-wall marble bathrooms come in muted creams and beiges. The pool is striking, and Astor Place is one of South Beach's top restaurants. **$$$**

**Brigham Gardens Guesthouse**
1411 Collins Avenue, Miami Beach
Tel: 305-531-1331
Charming owner-run and homely little complex of 1930s buildings. Bedrooms are jolly and arty, and vary considerably in size according to price. The best feature is the large tropical garden, with its exotic caged birds. **$$**

**Cardozo**
1300 Ocean Drive, Miami Beach
Tel: 305-535-6500
US Freephone: 800-782-6500
Owned by Gloria Estefan, a Streamline Moderne Art Deco masterpiece that is bathed in purple neon at night. A lively bar, seductive dining terrace, and eye-catching bedrooms with hardwood floors, iron beds and zebra-striped furniture. **$$$**

**Hostelling International – Miami Beach**
1438 Washington Ave, FL 33139
Tel: 305-534-2988
US Freephone: 800-379-2529
Web: www.ClayHotel.com
Great location in the heart of the Old Miami Beach Art Deco District. Amenities include kitchen, laundry facilities, lockers/baggage storage and restaurant. **$**

**Marlin**
1200 Collins Avenue, Miami Beach
Tel: 305-531 8800
US Freephone: 800-688-7678
This much-photographed lilac-colored Art Deco building houses a very hip all-suite hotel and recording studios (U2 and Aerosmith have made albums here). Rooms are high tech and have outlandish "Afro-urban" decor (exotic furniture and stainless-steel kitchens). The Opium Den bar often has live music in the evenings. **$$$$**

**The Tides**
1220 Ocean Drive, Miami Beach
Tel: 305-531-8800
US Freephone: 800-688-7678
This sleek white oceanfront block contains a small luxury hotel of immaculate taste. The giant, minimalist bedrooms are really special. As well as a CD player, cordless phone and mischievous postcards with the message "Let's make love at The Tides," each has uninterrupted views of the ocean and the beach, with telescopes to spy on sunbathers. Also a good-sized swimming pool. **$$$$**

## Restaurant Prices

Categories based on average cost of dinner and a glass of wine, before tip.
**$** = under $15
**$$** = up to $30
**$$$** = over $30

## WHERE TO EAT

**Casa Juancho**
2436 Southwest Eighth Street
Tel: 305-642-2452
Authentic Cuban/Spanish fare. **$**
**Joe's Stone Crab Restaurant**
277 South Point Road
Tel: 305-673-0365
Regional specialties featuring the prized and delectably sweet stone crab. A Miami institution. **$$$**
**News Cafe**
800 Ocean Drive
Tel: 305-538-6397
Very fashionable oyster bar with outdoor dining. **$$**
**Wolfie Cohen's Rascal House**
17190 Collins Avenue
Tel: 305-947-4581
Ever-popular Miami Beach deli. **$**

## SHOPPING

**Aventura Mall**
19501 Biscayne Blvd, Aventura. One of Miami's newest malls. Over 200 shops with a half dozen of the major nationals including **Macy's Bloomingdale's**, and **Lord & Taylor**.
**Kafka's**
1464 Washington Ave, North Beach Wonderful new and second-hand bookshop with cafe.
**A&J Unique Deco**
2000 Biscayne Boulevard Exquisite, authentic Art Deco furnishings.

# Northern Route

## Useful Addresses

**Massachusetts tourist information**
*Boston*
Greater Boston Convention and Visitors Bureau, 2 Copley Place, Suite 105, MA 02116
Tel: 800-888-5515
Web: www.bostonusa.com
*State:*
Massachusetts Office of Travel and Tourism, 100 Cambridge Street, 13th Floor, Boston, MA 02202
Tel: 800-227-6277
Web: www.mass-vacation.com
**New Hampshire tourist information**
Division of Travel and Tourism Development, PO Box 1856, Concord, NH 03302-1856
Tel: 1-800-386-4664
Web: www.state.nh.us
**Connecticut tourist information**
The Connecticut Tourism Department, 505 Hudson Street, Hartford, CT 06106
Tel: 860-270-8081
US Freephone: 800-282-6863
Web: www.state.ct.us/tourism
**Maine tourist information**
The Main Publicity Bureau,Box 2300, 97 Winthrop Street, Hallowell, ME 04347
Tel: 207-287-5711
US Freephone: 800-533-9595
Web: www.visitmaine.com
**Vermont tourist information**
Vermont Tourist Information Office, 6 Baldwin Street, Montpelier, VT 05633
Tel: 802 828-3237
Web: www.travel-vermont.com
**Ohio tourist information**
Office of Travel and Tourism, PO Box 1001, Columbus, OH 43266
Tel: 800-282-5393
Web: www.ohiotoursim.com

**Indiana tourist information**
Indiana Division of Tourism, 1 North Capitol, Suite 200, Indianapolis, IN 46204
Tel: 317-232-8800
US Freephone: 800-289-6646
Web: www.state.in.us/tourism
**Michigan tourist information**
Michigan Travel Bureau, PO Box 3393, Livonia, MI 48151
US Freephone: 800-543-2937
Web: www.michigan.org
**Illinois tourist board**
Illinois Department of Commerce and Community Affairs, 620 East Adams Street, Springfield, IL 62701
US Freephone: 800-2-CONNECT
Web: www.state.il.us
**Wisconsin tourist information**
Wisconsin Department of Tourism, 201 W Washington Avenue, PO Box 7976, Madison, WI 53707
US Freephone: 800-432-8747
Web: www.tourism.state.wi.us
**Minnesota tourist information**
The State Office of Tourism, 121 E Seventh Street, St Paul, MN 55101
Tel: 612-296-5029
US Freephone: 800-657-3700
www.exploreminnesota.com/email
**South Dakota tourist information**
Dept of Tourism, Capitol Lake Plaza, 711 E Wells Avenue, c/o E Capitol Avenue, Pierre, SD 5701-5070
US Freephone: 800-732-5682
Web: www.state.sd.us/tourism
**Wyoming tourist information**
Wyoming Business Council, Tourism Division I-25 at College Drive, Cheyenne, WY 82002
Tel: 307-777-7777
US Freephone: 800-225-5996
Web: www.wyomingtourism.org
**Montana tourist information**
Travel Montana, 1424 Ninth Avenue, PO Box 200533 Helena, MT 59620-0533
Tel: 406-444-2654
US Freephone: 800-847-4868
**Idaho tourist information**
The Idaho Travel Council, Department of Commerce, 700 W State Street, Boise, ID 83720
US Freephone: 800-847-4843
Web: www.visitid.org
**Seattle tourist information**
The Seattle-King County Visitor's Bureau, 800 Convention Place, Washington State Convention &

Trade Center
Tel: 206-461-5840
Web: www.seeseattle.org
**Washington tourist information**
Washington State Tourism Division
PO Box 42500, Olympia, WA
98504-2500
Tel: 1-800-544-1800 ext. 101
State Parks and Recreation
Commission, 7150 Clearwater Ln,
Olympia, WA 98504
US Freephones:
800-452-5687 (reservations)
800-233-0321 (information)

## Hub City: BOSTON

### GETTING AROUND

#### Public Transportation

**From the airport:** Logan
International Airport, just 3 miles (5
km) from downtown Boston, is
closer to town than any other major
airport in the nation: this refers to
distance and not to time. Traffic
can back up at the tunnels under
the harbor connecting the airport
and city. The MBTA Blue Line from
Airport Station is the fastest way to
downtown (about 10 minutes) and
to many other places as well. Free
shuttle buses run between all the
airport terminals and the subway
station. Cabs can be found outside
each terminal. Fares to downtown
should average about $20,
including tip, providing there are no
major traffic jams. Airways
Transportation buses leave all
terminals every half hour for
downtown and Back Bay hotels, and
several major bus companies,
including Bonanza, Concord
Trailways, Peter Pan and Vermont
Transit, serve many outlying
suburbs and distant destinations.
**Rapid transit:** Boston is the only
New England city with a subway
system (the MBTA, or "T" for short);
the cost is relatively low. The
Boston Passport, offering one,
three or seven days of unlimited
rides, can be purchased at the
Boston Common Visitor Information
Center at 147 Tremont Street, Tel:
617-426-3115.
**City buses:** The majority of the

MBTA's 160-plus bus routes operate
feeder services linking subway
stations to neighborhoods not
directly served by the rapid transit
system. Some crosstown routes
connect stations on different
subway lines without going into
downtown. Only a few MBTA buses
actually enter downtown Boston,
and most of these are express
buses from outlying areas. The
basic MBTA bus fare is under $1.
**Intercity buses:** Several intercity
bus companies serve Boston. The
two largest, Greyhound (Tel: 526-
1800, US Freephone: 800-231-
2222) and Peter Pan (US
Freephone: 800-343-9999), have
frequent daily services from New
York City and Albany, NY, as well as
services from points within New
England.
**Commuter rail:** The MBTA Commuter
Rail extends from downtown Boston
to as far as 60 miles (100 km)
away and serves such tourist
destinations as Concord, Lowell,
Salem, Ipswich, Gloucester and
Rockport. Trains to the north and
northwest of Boston depart from
North Station, while trains to points
south and west of the city leave
from South Station. All south side
commuter trains, except the
Fairmount Line, also stop at the
Back Bay Station. For information
contact South Station (Tel: 345-
7456) or North Station (Tel: 722-
3600).
**National rail:** Amtrak Passenger
trains arrive at South Station
(Atlantic Avenue and Summer
Street, Tel: 482-3660; US
Freephone: 800-872-7245; TDD:
800-523-6590) from New York,
Washington, DC, and Philadelphia
with connections from all points in
the nationwide Amtrak system. They
also stop at Back Bay Station (145
Dartmouth Street, Tel: 482-3660).

#### Private Transportation

Boston, it is justly claimed, is a
walker's city – a good thing, for it is
certainly not a driver's city. The city
planners, as Emerson noted, were
the cows, and it has been
suggested that the Puritan belief in
predestination extended even to

### Hotel Prices

Categories based on average
cost of a double room for one
night.
**$** = under $65
**$$** = up to $ 100
**$$$** = up to $150
**$$$$** = over $150

urban design. Streets appeared
where Providence chose to lay them
– along cow paths, Native American
trails and colonial wagon tracks –
and are linked by crooked little
alleys. City planners, however, did
come into their own in the middle of
the 19th century, and the Back Bay,
South Boston to a lesser extent,
and the South End have impeccable
grid systems. If you attempt to drive
in the city, and feel frustrated and
inadequate, be consoled that many
Bostonians feel the same way.
Being faced by cars coming the
wrong way on a one-way street,
being stuck in a traffic jam, getting
lost and then being unable to find a
parking space is about par for the
course. It's said that indicating a
turn is considered "giving
information to the enemy." Most car
rental agencies have offices at the
airport and/or Downtown. Check
the *Yellow Pages* for a full list of
local firms.
**Car rental companies:**
Avis, Tel: 800-831-2847
Budget, Tel: 497-1800
Hertz, Tel: 527-0700
Conveniently located public parking
facilities are found at Government
Center; Post Office Square; the
Public Garden; the Prudential
Center; on Clarendon Street near
the John Hancock Tower; and
elsewhere. Private lots are
scattered here and there.
**Taxis:** Taxi stands are common at
popular tourist sites. Companies to
call include:
Bay State Taxi Tel: 617-566-5000
Boston Cab Tel: 617-262-2227
Checker Taxi Tel: 617-536-7500
Independent Taxi Operators
Association Tel: 617-426-8700
Metro Cab Tel: 617-242-8000
Red Cab Tel: 617-734-5000

## WHERE TO STAY

**Boston Harbor Hotel**
70 Rowes Wharf, MA 02110
Tel: 617-439-7000
Web: www.bhh.com
Board the airport water shuttle at Logan and, seven minutes later, step into the luxury of the city's foremost waterside hotel. Bedrooms all have either harbor or skyline views. Eighteen rooms are specially designed for the physically handicapped. A museum-quality art collection decorates the public areas. Across the road is the Financial District, while minutes away (on foot) is the Aquarium and Quincy Market. **$$$$**

**Boston International Youth Hostel**
12 Hemenway St, Fenway, 02115
Tel: 536-1027
Fax: 424-6558
Web: www.bostonhostel.org
Well located at the western fringe of the Back Bay. Very close to public transportation with 220 beds in 4–6 bed dormitories: bring or rent sheets. **$**

**Lenox Hotel**
710 Boylston Street, 02116
Tel: 617-536-5300
Fax: 617-267-1237
Web: www.lenoxhotel.com
Modest and moderate traditional family hotel built in 1900. Bedrooms, some with functional fireplaces, have been redecorated in French Provincial, Oriental or colonial decor. Just a few steps from the Prudential Center and the Public Library, and a block from the subway. **$$**

**Omni Parker House**
60 School Street, MA 02018
Tel: 617-227-8600
Fax: 617-227-2120
Web: www.omnihotels.com
Reportedly the oldest continuously operating hotel in America (since 1854); yet, the frequently renovated present building dates only from 1927. Some rooms have showers only. Malcolm X and (allegedly) Ho Chi Minh both worked here. A favorite with politicians, and possibly the most centrally located hotel in the city. **$$$**

## Restaurant Prices

Categories based on average cost of dinner and a glass of wine, before tip.
$ = under $15
$$ = up to $30
$$$ = over $30

## WHERE TO EAT

Many claim that Boston has the best seafood in the nation, and it is certainly a great town in which to indulge in all sorts of fish. Boston specialties include clam chowder (made with cream, not tomatoes), scrod (not a separate species of fish but the name given to small tender haddock or cod) and steamers (clams served with broth and melted butter). Baked beans, once synonymous with Boston, and Boston brown bread are not especially popular and may be difficult to find.

The Back Bay, especially Newbury and Boylston streets, has many sidewalk cafés and restaurants, pleasant for people-watching. A recent hotbed of haute cuisine, mainly contemporary American, is the South End. Other high concentrations of restaurants include Faneuil Hall Marketplace, Chinatown and the North End. Also, excellent international dining can be enjoyed in nearly all major hotels. The following are just a few of the many places worth seeking out:

**Ambrosia on Huntington**
116 Huntington Avenue
Tel: 617-247-2400
Anthony Ambrose is one of Boston's hottest young chefs, combining solid training with unflapping creativity. **$$$$**

**Durgin Park**
340 North Market Street (Faneuil Hall Marketplace)
Tel: 617-227-2038
Yankee cooking attracts flocks of tourists to this legendary old dining hall, where they are seated with others at long, picnic-cloth covered tables and insulted by the waiters. Try Brontosaurus-sized prime ribs. No reservations; long waits. **$$**

**Imperial Seafood**
70–72 Beach Street
Tel: 617-426-8439
Large, busy Cantonese restaurant. Main attraction: *dim sum*. **$–$$**

**Legal Seafoods**
26 Park Square
Tel: 617-426-4444
5 Cambridge Center, Kendall Square, Cambridge
Tel: 617-864-3400
Prudential Center
Tel: 617-266-6800
Copley Place, 100 Huntington Avenue
Tel: 617-266-7775
What started as a small Cambridge fish store now has a justly deserved international reputation. Enormous variety. No reservations and waits can seem interminable. **$$–$$$**.

**Parker's**
Omni Parker House
60 School Street
Tel: 617-227-8600
A New England tradition since 1854. Home of Parker rolls and Boston Cream Pie, with formal and attentive service. **$$$–$$$$**

**UVA**
1418 Commonwealth Ave, Brighton
Tel: 617-566-5670
A gem of a modern *trattoria*, with an enticing wine list. Reservations advised. **$$$**

## SHOPPING

**Downtown Crossing**, a pedestrian-only zone, is Boston's largest shopping area, complete with outdoor kiosks and street-vendors. The popular **Faneuil Hall Marketplace** has many small shops and foodstands. Boston's version of Fifth Avenue is **Newbury Street**, an 8-block stretch of expensive clothing stores, salons, and art galleries. Boston's **Copley Place** on Copley Square has almost 100 upscale stores and restaurants. Boston's historic **Haymarket**, selling inexpensive fruit and vegetables, meat and seafood, is open every Friday and Saturday near Faneuil Hall Marketplace. Boston and Cambridge are havens for buyers and browsers of new and used books. Check out **Wordsworth**'s **three stores in Harvard Square, Cambridge. For travel, nothing beats** Globe Corner Bookstore, 500 Boylston Street, Boston and 49 Palmer Street, Harvard Square, Cambridge. As for used bookstores, **Avenue Victor Hugo**, 339 Newbury Street and **Trident Booksellers and Cafe,** Newbury Street are both great. Two mammoth retailers worth checking out on Washington Street, Boston are **Filene's** and **Macy's.** For bargain hunters the floor below Filene's is the place to head for, a unique way of reducing prices. Boston's **Charles Street** has a number of antique dealers, including the **Boston Antique Co-op** on Charles Street.

## Hotel Prices

Categories based on average cost of a double room for one night.
**$** = under $65
**$$** = up to $100
**$$$** = up to $150
**$$$$** = over $150

## MASSACHUSETTS

### WHERE TO STAY

*CAMBRIDGE*
**The Charles Hotel**
1 Bennett Street, MA 02138
Tel: 617-864-1200
US Freephone: 800-882-1818
Fax: 617-864-5715
A modern hotel with 296 rooms in Harvard Square, with airy, neo-traditional rooms, some overlooking the river. Home to the popular Regatta jazz club which draws nationally known jazz artists. **$$$$**
**The Harvard Square Hotel**
110 Mount Auburn St, MA 02138
Tel: 617-864-5200
Fax: 617-864-2409
A six-floor motel in the heart of Harvard Square. All rooms with picture windows; a complimentary continental breakfast. **$**
**Mary Prentiss Inn**
6 Prentiss Street, MA 02140

Tel: 617-661-2929
Fax: 617-661-5989
Tastefully appointed Greek Revival B&B with a spacious deck. Some of the 18 rooms have antique armoires and four-poster beds. Situated on a residential street between Harvard and Porter Squares. **$$–$$$**

*CONCORD*
**Bass Rocks Ocean Inn**
107 Atlantic Road, MA 01930
Tel: 978-283-7600
A 48-room motel looking straight out to sea. **$$**
**Colonial Inn**
48 Monument Square, 01742
Tel: 978-369-9200
US Freephone: 800-370-9200
Fax: 978-369-1533
Web: www.concordscolonialinn.com
A 1716 inn on Concord's town common with 53 rooms. **$$**
**Harborview Inn**
71 Western Avenue, MA 01930
Tel: 978-283-2277
US Freephone: 800-299-6696
A comfortable house-turned-B&B near the Fishermen Memorial statue. Some of the nine rooms have an ocean view. **$–$$**
**Hawthorne Inn**
462 Lexington Road, 01742
Tel: 978-369-5610
B&B with seven rooms in the historic district, opposite Hawthorne's Wayside. **$$**
**Longfellow's Wayside Inn**
Wayside Inn Rd, S Sudbury, 01776
Tel: 978-443-1776
A mid-18th-century tavern with 10 rooms, near Concord. **$**

*GREENFIELD*
**Brandt House**
29 Highland Avenue, 01301
Tel: 413-774-3329
US Freephone: 800-235-3329.
Fax: 413-772-2908
www.brandt-house.com
Eight comfortable, simply decorated rooms, huge porches and a tennis court. **$$–$$$**

*DEERFIELD*
**Deerfield Inn**
81 Old Main Street, 01342
Tel: 413-774-5587

US Freephone: 800-926-3865
Fax: 413-773-8712.
Web: www.deerfieldinn.com.
A traditional inn surrounded by historic houses; 23 large rooms furnished with antiques and period reproductions. **$$$–$$$$**.

## WHERE TO EAT

*CAMBRIDGE*
**East Coast Grill**
1271 Cambridge Street (Inman Square)
Tel: 617-491-6568
A stylish, wildly popular spot for innovative grilled seafood (often topped with exotic spice rubs or fruit salsas), creative salads, barbecue and fiery "pasta from hell." Margaritas help ease the often long waits for a table. **$$$**
**Rialto**
Charles Hotel, I Bennett Street
Tel: 617-864-1200
Restaurateur Michela Larson and chef Jody Adams have earned international accolades for flavorful Mediterranean cuisine in a coolly elegant dining room. **$$$–$$$$**

*CONCORD*
**Colonial Inn**
48 Monument Square
Tel: 978-369-2000
A 1716 inn serving traditional New England fare as well as afternoon tea. **$$–$$$**
**Walden Grille**
24 Walden Street
Tel: 978-371-2233
Contemporary cuisine in an old brick firehouse. **$$–$$$**

*GLOUCESTER*
**Cafe Beaujolais**
118 Main Street
Tel: 978-282-0058
Upscale bistro with a popular wine bar, blending fresh fish and local produce into intriguing French creations. **$$$**
**Evie's Rudder**
73 Rocky Neck
Tel: 978-283-7967
A rollicking tavern in the Rocky Neck artists' colony. **$$**

**White Rainbow**
65 Main Street
Tel: 978-281-0017
Rich, evolved Continental in a dramatic granite-walled hideaway. **$$$**

## GREENFIELD
**Pete's Fish Market**
54 School Street
Tel: 413-772-2153
Local favorite for fish and chips. **$$**

## IPSWICH
**The Clam Box**
206 High Street
Tel: 978-356-9707
One of the best places in the region for fried clams. You can't miss the place – it's housed in a building shaped like a clam box. **$$**

## LEXINGTON
**La Boniche**
143 Merrimack Street
Tel: 978-458-9473
An intimate restaurant in a landmark Art Nouveau building with creative French fare. **$$–$$$**
**Dabin**
10 Muzzey Street (off Mass Avenue)
Tel: 781-860-0171
Traditional Japanese and Korean fare in a peaceful shelter from the bustle of Lexington Center. A small patio for outdoor dining. **$$**
**The Olympia**
453 Market Street
Tel: 978-452-8092
A friendly, family-run Greek restaurant. **$–$$**

## WILLIAMSTOWN
**The Orchards**
222 Adams Road
Tel: 413-458-9611
Accomplished New American cuisine in elegant setting. **$$$**

# SHOPPING

## CAMBRIDGE
The area in and around Harvard Square is chock-a-block with stores, most of which, not unexpectedly, have a youthful appeal. Some stores are gathered in mini-malls. Four such covered complexes are **The Garage** and the **Galleria**, both

on John F. Kennedy St, **Atrium Arcade** on Church St and **The Shops at Charles Pl** on Bennett St.
Those who want to show that they have been to Harvard – even if only as a tourist – will delight in the Harvard Shop, crammed with Harvard insignia merchandise.
It is claimed that here is the greatest concentration of bookshops in the nation. Most are in and around the Square, and some open until midnight. **Grolier** carries the largest selection of poetry books in the country; go to **Robin Bledsoe** for out-of-print books on art, architecture and design, and a large selection on women artists. The **Globe Corner Bookstore**, specializes in travel. For foreign books, used as well as new, visit **Schoenhof's Foreign Books**, more an institution than a bookstore.

# NEW HAMPSHIRE

## WHERE TO STAY

### CLAREMONT
**Claremont Motor Lodge**
On Beauregard Street, NH 03743
Tel: 603-542-2540
Refrigerators in some rooms and free continental breakfast. **$**

### MEREDITH
**Red Hill Inn**
RR 1 Hwy 25B, Center Harbor, NH 03226
Tel: 603-279-7001
This hillside farmhouse features lovely rooms, good food and fine views. Several snug cottages are also available. **$$$**

### PORTSMOUTH
**Inn at Strawbery Bank**
314 Court Street, NH 03801
Tel: 603-436-7242
An elegant older house with well-proportioned rooms. Great breakfasts. **$$**

### WOLFESBORO
**Wolfesboro Inn**
44 North Main, NH 03894
Tel: 603-569-3016
Picturesque 17th-century waterfront inn with an inviting tavern. **$$$**

# WHERE TO EAT

## MEREDITH
**George's Diner**
10 Plymouth Street
Tel: 603-279-8723
No-nonsense New England grub featuring such staples as corn chowder and red-flannel hash. **$**

## PORTSMOUTH
**Portsmouth Gas Light Company**
64 Market Street
Tel: 603-430-9122
In an attractive landmark building, this is a local favorite for its attractive surroundings and delicious brick-oven pizza. **$**

## WOLFBORO
**Bailey's**
South Main Street
Tel: 603-569-3662
Serving American-style food for over 60 years. The menu ranges from swordfish and prime ribs to peanut butter and jelly sandwiches. They freeze their own ice cream. **$$**

# MAINE

## WHERE TO STAY

### Cape Elizabeth
**Inn by the Sea**
40 Bowery Beach Rd, MN 04017
Tel: 207-799-3134
Large, rambling coastal resort with 43 luxury suites all with porch or deck with ocean view. **$$$–$$$$**

### CORNISH
**Cornish Inn**
Route 25 and Maine Street
Tel: 207-625-8501
Lovely colonial house at the base of the White Mountains.
*(see page 107)* **$$–$$$**

## KENNEBUNKPORT

**1802 House**
15 Locke St (PO Box 646A),
ME 04046
US Freephone: 800-932-5632
Web: www.1802inn.com
Warm, intimate guest rooms with
wood-burning fireplaces, antiques
and original artwork. The private
tiled bathrooms feature double
whirlpool baths. Secluded hideaway
minutes from Dock Square. **$$$**

**Maine Stay Inn and Cottages**
34 Maine St (PO Box 500A),
ME 04046
Tel: 207-967-2117
Fax: 207-967-8757
Web: www.mainestayinn.com
A graceful and distinctive mid-
Victorian house featuring wrap-
around porch, suspended staircase
and prominent cupola. Several of
the rooms have fireplaces.
Accommodation includes full
breakfast and afternoon tea. **$$$**

## OGUNQUIT BEACH

**The Beachmere Inn**
PO Box 2340, ME 03907-2340
Tel: 207-646-2021
US Freephone: 800-336-3983
Web: www.beachmereinn.com
Intimate and stylish Victorian inn
with wonderful coastal views and a
small private beach. Many rooms
have private balconies or decks and
several also have wood-burning
fireplaces. **$$$**

**The Dunes**
260 US Rt 1, Dunes Road, (PO Box
917), ME 03097
US Freephone: 888-283-3863
Established in 1936, The Dunes
features 17 well-kept guest rooms
and 19 traditional New England
cottages set in trim open grounds
overlooking the tidal river. **$$$**

## PORTLAND

**Hostelling International – Portland
Summer Hostel**
645 Congress Street, ME 04101
Tel: 207-874-3281
Fax: 207-874-3399
Web: www.tiac.net/users/hienec/
Located in downtown Portland.
Facilities include baggage storage,
cafeteria, kitchen, overnight parking
and vending machines. **$**

**Inn on Carleton**
46 Carleton Street, ME 04102
Tel: 207-775-1910
US Freephone: 800-639-1779
Web: www.innoncarleton.com
A beautifully restored Victorian
home in the center of
Portland's historical district.
**$$$–$$$$**

**Pomegranate Inn**
49 Neal Street, ME 04102
Tel: 207-772-1006
US Freephone: 800-356-0408
Fax: 207-773-4426
Web: www.pomegranateinn.com
A tranquil hideaway set in the
Western Promenade Historical
District. Downstairs guest room with
private terrace and a secluded
upstairs carriage house. **$$$**

## YORK

**Dockside Guest Quarters**
PO Box 205, ME 03909
Tel: 207-363-2868
Fax: 207-363-1977
Web: www.docksidegq.com
Situated on a private peninsula
surrounded by sweeping views
of Maine's scenic beauty.
**$$–$$$**

## Restaurant Prices

Categories based on average
cost of dinner and a glass of
wine, before tip.
**$** = under $15
**$$** = up to $30
**$$$** = over $30

## WHERE TO EAT

### KENNEBUNKPORT

**The Clam Shack**
Dock Square
Tel: 207-967-2560
Superlative fried clams and lobster
rolls dispensed to appreciative
locals from a simple hut. **$**

### OGUNQUIT BEACH

**Ogunquit Lobster Pound
Restaurant and Lounge**
Post Road
Tel: 207-646-2516
Grilled seafood and steak with
well-prepared pasta dishes. **$$$**

## PORTLAND

**Back Bay Grill**
65 Portland Street
Tel: 207-772-8833
In an attractive century-old building
with high pressed-tin ceilings.
Imaginative regional and New
American dishes are prepared fresh
daily in the open kitchen. The wine
list is extensive and the desserts
are exquisite. **$$**

**Becky's**
390 Commercial Street
Tel: 207-773-7070
Downtown diner with all-day
breakfasts and hearty homestyle
platters of fried seafood, turkey,
meatloaf, and lobster rolls. Small,
friendly and very popular. **$–$$**

## WELLS

**Barnacle Bill's**
Perkins Grove
Tel: 207-646-5575
Two restaurants side-by-side – one
specializing in lobster – the other in
steamed clams, mussels, and other
fresh local catch. **$$**

**Maine Diner**
Rt 1N
Tel: 207-646-4441
Excellent seafood menu with the
lobster chowder and lobster pie as
the twin crowning glories. **$**

## SHOPPING

### FREEPORT

Home of the famous outdoor
sportwear manufacturer **L L Bean**,
established in the early 1900s, now
a 24-hour megastore. Numerous
other factory outlets and swanky
fashion shops have sprung up along
Hwy 1 and in converted homes.

## VERMONT

### WHERE TO STAY

### ARLINGTON

**Arlington Inn**
Route 7A, VT 05250
Tel: 802-375-6532
US Freephone: 800-443-9442
Fax: 802-375-6534
An elegant Greek Revival mansion
with comfortable Victorian-style

interior furnishings in the 19 guest rooms. Located between Bennington and Manchester. **$–$$$**

**Arlington's West Mountain Inn**
River Rd (off Route 313), VT 05250
Tel: 802-375-6516
Fax: 802-375-6553
Web: www.westmountaininn.com.
A family-friendly 1840s farmhouse turned 18-room inn with mountain views on 150 country acres. Trails for hiking or cross-country skiing, game room and the resident llama ranch amuse all ages. **$$$–$$$$**

### BRIDGEWATER CORNERS
**October Country Inn**
Upper Road, VT 05035
Tel: 802-672-3412
US Freephone: 800-648-8421
A cozy farmhouse with 10 rooms on a back road, about 5 miles (8 km) from the Killington ski area. **$$**

### DORSET
**Barrows House**
Route 30, VT 05251
Tel: 802-867-4455
Fax: 802-867-0132
Web: www.barrowshouse.com
An 18th-century Federal-style inn and carriage house with homey touches in the 28 rooms and a well-regarded restaurant. Pool, tennis courts. Located 6 miles (10 km) north of Manchester. **$$$$**

**Cornucopia of Dorset**
Route 30, VT 05251
Tel: 802-867-5751
Fax: 802-867-5353
Web: www.cornucopiaofdorset.com
Five prettily appointed rooms; pampering services include champagne welcome, marvelous breakfasts (served by candlelight), cozy down comforters or quilts, and terry-cloth robes. **$$–$$$$**

**Dorset Inn**
Church and Main Streets, VT 05251
Tel: 802-867-5500
One of the state's oldest – and reliably enjoyable – inns, opened in 1796, with 31 rooms. **$$$–$$$$**

**Marble West Inn**.
Dorset West Road, VT 05251
Tel: 802-867-4155
An eight-room B&B in a marble-columned 1840s Greek Revival manse, elegantly decorated. **$–$$**

### Hotel Prices

Categories based on average cost of a double room for one night.
**$** = under $65
**$$** = up to $100
**$$$** = up to $150
**$$$$** = over $150

### FAIRLEE
**Silver Maple Lodge and Cottages**
520 US Rt 5 South, VT 05045
Tel: 802-333-4326
US Freephone: 800-666-1946
Web: www.silvermaplelodge.com
A handsome old farmhouse with comfortable lodge rooms and well-fitted rustic, knotty-pine cabins. **$$**

### KILLINGTON
**Cortina Inn**
Route 4, VT 05751
Tel: 802-773-3331
Fax: 802-775-6948
Ninety-seven surprisingly lush and spacious rooms; indoor pool, tennis courts, health club, ice skating, horseback riding. **$$–$$$$**

**Inn of the Six Mountains**
Killington Road, VT 05751
Tel: 802-422-4302
US Freephone: 800-228-4676
A 103-room modern hotel with a Rockies feel; everything, including the central fieldstone hearth, is lavishly overscale. **$–$$$**

**Mountain Meadows Lodge**
Thundering Brook Road, 05751
Tel: 802-775-1010
US Freephone: 800-370-4567
Web: www.mtmeadowslodge.com
A large lakeside farmhouse offering 18 rooms, with extensive cross-country trails. Child care center with a playground and farm animals. **$$**

### MANCHESTER
**1811 House**
Route 7A, VT 05254
Tel: 802-362-1811
US Freephone: 800-432-1811
Fax: 802-362-2443
A Federal manse that has been an inn/B&B for most of its history. Fourteen spacious, antiques-filled guest rooms. Located at the north end of Manchester Village. **$$–$$$**

**The Equinox**
Route 7A, VT 05253
Tel: 802-362-5700
US Freephone: 800-362-4747
Web: www.equinoxresort.com
A grand old hotel with 155 rooms, beautifully refurbished. **$$$$**

**Village Country Inn**
Route 7A, 05254
Tel: 802-362-1792
US Freephone: 800-370-0300
A rambling 33-room old inn with romantic country decor. **$$$–$$$$**

### MIDDLEBURY
**Swift House Inn**
25 Stewart Lane, 05753
Tel: 802-388-9925
Fax: 802-388-9927
An elegantly detailed 1815 Federal house with 21 luxurious guest rooms; the Carriage House features spacious suites with whirlpool baths. **$$–$$$**

**Middlebury Inn**
14 Court House Square, VT 05753
Tel: 802-388-4961
US Freephone: 800-842-4666
Web: www.middleburyinn.com
An 1825 inn (plus 1827 annex and modern motel extension, offering a total of 80 rooms) overlooking the village green. Dining room serves traditional New England fare. **$–$$$**

### NORWICH
**Beaver Meadow Bed and Breakfast**
319 Beaver Meadow Rd, VT 05055
Tel: 802-649-1054
Email: beamdw@valley.net
A cozy cottage and four comfortable bedrooms in a mellow farmhouse. Guests are invited to indulge in generous breakfasts and fine evening dining by candlelight. **$$**

### QUECHEE
**Quechee Inn at Marshland Farm**
Clubhouse Road, VT 05059
Tel: 802-295-3133
US Freephone: 800-235-3133
Fax: 802-295-6587
Web: www.pinnacle-inns.com
With Wilderness Trails, cross-country skiing, biking and canoeing, this inn has much to offer those seeking an active holiday. **$$$**

## RIPTON

**The Chipman Inn**
Rt 125, VT 05766
Tel: 802-388-2390
US Freephone: 800-890-2390
Email: smudge@together.net
Small, gracious historic inn with
appealing rooms and tranquil
atmosphere. **$$**

## WATERBURY

**Inn at Blush Hill**
Blush Hill Road, VT 05676
Tel: 802-244-7529
US Freephone: 800-736-7522
Fax: 802 244-7314
Web: www.blushhill.com
An exemplary B&B high on a hill
with sweeping mountain vistas. Five
cheerful rooms and gourmet
breakfasts in a 1790s room with its
original open hearth fireplace. **$–$$**

## WINDSOR

**Juniper Hill Inn**
Juniper Hill Road, VT 05089
Tel: 802-674-5273
US Freephone: 800-359-2541
Fax: 802-674-2041
A 100-year-old Greek Revival
mansion Bed and Breakfast set on
a broad lawn. Sixteen elegantly
appointed rooms furnished with
Queen Anne and Edwardian pieces.
Near Ascutney Mountain. **$$–$$$**

## WOODSTOCK

**Kedron Valley Inn**
Route 106, South, VT 05071
Tel: 802-457-1473
US Freephone: 800-836-1193
Fax: 802-457-4469
Heirloom quilts line the walls and
dress up the 27 prettily decorated
rooms of this Bed and Breakfast.
The restaurant is exceptional. The
ski lodge-style building behind the
main inn attracts families, who also
enjoy the swimming pond. **$$–$$$$**
**Three Church Street**
3 Church Street, VT 05091
Tel: 802-457-1925
Eleven-room B&B in a gracious early
19th-century house near the com-
mon, with tennis court and pool;
Well-priced elegance. **$**
**Woodstock Inn & Resort**
14 The Green (Route 4), VT 05091
Tel: 802-457-1100

US Freephone: 800-448-7900
Fax: 802-457-6699
www.woodstockinn.com
The Rockefellers' homage to
country inns past, full of Americana.
The decor is corporate/country with
modern furniture and patchwork
quilts. Facilities include 144
bedrooms, indoor and outdoor
pools, tennis courts, golf, health
club, racquet ball and squash
courts. **$$$–$$$$**

## Restaurant Prices

Categories based on average
cost of dinner and a glass of
wine, before tip.
**$** = under $15
**$$** = up to $30
**$$$** = over $30

## WHERE TO EAT

## ARLINGTON

**Arlington Inn**
Route 7A
Tel: 802-375-6532
Fairly formal candlelit restaurant
creating French Continental dishes –
rack of lamb, roast duck – pre-pared
with local meats and produce. **$$$**
**West Mountain Inn**
River Road (off Route 313)
Tel: 802-375-6516
New American fare in a low-beamed
paneled dining room at a romantic
and family-friendly inn. **$$$–$$$$**

## BRIDGEWATER CORNERS

**Blanche and Bill's Pancake House**
586 on Rt 4
Tel: 802-422-3816
Lovingly crafted pancakes and
waffles – ideal for maple syrup. **$**

## DORSET

**Barrows House**
Route 30
Tel: 802-867-4455
New American cuisine in an
intimate setting; the tavern serves
lighter fare. **$$$**
**Chantecleer**
Route 7A, East Dorset
Tel: 802-362-1616
Swiss and French provincial cuisine
in a former dairy barn. **$$$**

**Dorset Inn**
Route 30
Tel: 802-867-5500
Honest American cooking: a
choice of formal dining or
tavern feasting in a 1796
hostelry. **$$$**

## FAIRLEE

**Gilman's Fairlee Diner**
CR 82 Box 90, Bradford
Tel: 802-333-3569
Neat little diner with a nicely
balanced menu blending classic
and current fare. **$**

## KILLINGTON

**Cortina Inn**
Route 4
Tel: 802-773-3333
Chefs from the New England
Culinary Institute ensure deft and
innovative fare. **$$$**
**Hemingway's**
Route 4
Tel: 802-422-3886
Inspired regional cuisine,
consistently hailed as one of the
nation's best. **$$$$**

## MANCHESTER

**The Equinox**
Route 7A
Tel: 802-362-4700
Spectacular regional cuisine in a
formal barrel-vaulted dining room
looking out on Mount Equinox.
**$$$–$$$$**
**Bistro Henry's**
Route 11/30
Tel: 802-362-4982
A spacious dining room on the edge
of town preparing authentic
Mediterranean cuisine. Extensive
wine list. **$$$**
**Mother Myrick's Confectionery and
Ice Cream Parlor**
Route 7A
Tel: 802-362-1560
The place to indulge your sweet
tooth with a slice of freshly baked
pie, homemade fudge, or an ice
cream treat. **$**
**Up for Breakfast**
4235 Main Street
Tel: 802-362-4204
Fabulous pancakes, omelets and
baked goods. Jammed on the
weekends but worth the wait. **$**

## MIDDLEBURY
**Swift House Inn**
25 Stewart Lane
Tel: 802-388-9925
Elegant regional cuisine in a formal, paneled Federal dining room. **$$$**
**Woody's**
5 Bakery Lane
Tel: 802-388-4182
Unfussy Regional American cuisine with congenial crowd. Looking out on Otter Creek. **$$$**

## QUEECHEE
**Parker House Inn**
16 Main Street
Tel: 802-295-6077
Tasteful continental cuisine in a brick Victorian mansion with grand views. **$$$**
**Quechee Inn at Marshland Farm**
Clubhouse Road
Tel: 802-295-3133
Seasonal specialties in a tastefully restored tavern. **$$$**
**Simon Pearce Restaurant**
The Mill, Main Street
Tel: 802-295-1470
Fine country cuisine, with Irish touches set in an old riverside mill. Extensive wine list.
*(see page 109)* **$$$**

## WOODSTOCK
**White Cottage Snack Bar**
462 Route 4W
Tel: 802-457 2968
*(see page 111)* **$**

# NEW YORK STATE

## WHERE TO STAY

## BUFFALO
**Heritage House Country Inn**
8261 Main Street, Williamsville, NY 14221
Tel: 716-633-4900
Gracious old-style country inn with warm comfortable rooms. A good base for visiting Niagara Falls. Close to Downtown. **$$$**
**Hostelling International – Buffalo**
667 Main Street, NY 14205
Tel: 716-852-5222
Fax: 716-852-1642
Email: hibuffalo@juno.com
Convenient central location in the historic Downtown Theater District

## Hotel Prices

Categories based on average cost of a double room for one night.
**$** = under $65
**$$** = up to $100
**$$$** = up to $150
**$$$$** = over $150

with rapid access to shops and restaurants via the Metrorail Transit Line. Amenities include kitchen, bicycle/luggage storage, lockers and free linen. **$**
**Lenox Hotel and Suites**
140 North Street, NY 14201
Tel: 716-884-1700
Historic hotel offering luxury suites and guest rooms. **$$**
**Lord Amherst**
5000 Main Street, NY 14226
Tel: 716-839-2200
US Freephone: 800-544-2200
Well-maintained motel close to shopping malls. Exercise room and restaurant. **$$**

## CAMBRIDGE
**Blue Willow Motel**
51 South Park Street, NY 12816
Tel: 518-677-3552
Squeaky clean, standard motel rooms. **$$**

## CANANDAIGUA
**Morgan-Samuels Inn**
2920 Smith Road, NY 14424
Tel: 716-394-9232
Fax: 716-394-8044
Web: www.morgansamuelsinn.com
This stately English-style mansion with tree-lined approach invites you to unwind in civilized comfort. The inn stands in extensive wooded grounds and is furnished with oil paintings and antiques. **$$$$**

## COOPERSTOWN
**The Inn at Cooperstown**
Chesnut Street, NY 13326
Tel: 607-547-5756
Fax: 607-547-8779
Web: www.cooperstown.net/theinn
A distinctive Second Empire-style inn designed by Henry J Hardenbergh, known for his New

York City projects – the Dakota Apartments and Plaza Hotel. Built in 1874 as an annex to the plush Hotel Fenimore. **$$$**

## FREDONIA
**The White Inn**
52 East Main Street, NY 14063
Tel: 716-672-2103
US Freephone: 888-FREEDONIA
Fax: 716-672-2107
Email: inn@whiteinn.com
Dignified older inn tastefully furnished with antiques and reproductions. Restaurant offers excellent American cuisine with top-quality, fresh ingredients. **$$–$$$**

## GENEVA
**Canticleer Motor Inn**
473 Hamilton Street, NY 14456
Tel: 315-789-7600
US Freephone: 800-441-5227
Comfy and clean with free continental breakfast, pool and wheelchair accessible rooms. **$$**

## HAMBURG
**Knights Inn**
5245 Camp Road, NY 14075
Tel: 716-648-2000
Reliable chain motor inn with pool, airport transportation, laundry facilities, cable TV. Wheelchair accessible rooms. **$$**

## NIAGARA FALLS
**Clarion Hotel**
300 Third Street, NY 14303
Tel: 716-285-3361
Fax: 716-295-3900
Swanky and central. First-rate facilities include a hair salon, whirlpool and game room. And for those overcome by the romance of the Falls, there is a wedding chapel on the premises. **$$$$**
**Hostelling International – Niagara Falls**
1101 Ferry Avenue, NY 14301
Tel: 716-282-3700
The hostel occupies a historic Georgian-style home within walking distance of the Falls. Amenities include kitchen, TV room, on-site parking and laundry facilities. **$**

**ROME**
**Quality Inn of Rome**
200 South James Street, NY 13440
Tel: 315-336-4300
Comfortable, attractive rooms, with balconies and refrigerators. Restaurant, lounge and pool. Disabled access rooms. **$$**

**SARATOGA SPRINGS**
**Batcheller Mansion Inn**
20 Circular Street, NY 12866
Tel: 518-584-7012
Fax: 518-581-7746
www.BatchellerMansionInn.com
A marvelous High Victorian Gothic inn, impeccably preserved. The inn features 9 elegantly appointed rooms and 5 suites. Complimentary breakfast. **$$$$**

**SCHENECTADY**
**Ramada Inn and Convention Center**
450 Nott Street, NY 12308
Tel: 518-370-7151
Fax: 518-370-0441
Comfortable and central. Exercise room, whirlpool, lounge and restaurant. **$$**

**SYRACUSE**
**Hostelling International – Downing**
535 Oak Street, NY 13203
Tel: 315-472-5788
Fax: 315-426-0662
Attractive hostel occupies an enormous old house in the center of Syracuse. Amenities include equipment storage, laundry facilities and baggage storage. **$**
**The Radisson Plaza – Hotel**
500 South Warren St, NY 13202
Tel/Fax: 315-422-5121
Web: radisson.com/syracuseny
Very central historic hotel with many modern first-rate amenities. Pool, fitness center, sports bar & grill, restaurant and club. **$$$$**

**UTICA**
**Red Roof Inn**
590 Fairview Street, NY 13790
Tel: 607-729-8940
Email: i0203@redroof.com
Spotless, well-fitted rooms and friendly service. Restaurants and shopping close by. Children under 12 stay free. **$–$$**

**WATERLOO**
**Waterloo Motel**
989 Waterloo Geneva Road, NY 13165
Tel: 315-539-8042
Plain but comfortable rooms. **$–$$**

**WESTFIELD**
**The William Seward Inn**
6645 S Portage Road, NY 14787
Tel: 716-326-4151
Fax: 716-326-4163
Web: www.williamsewardinn.com
Fine old inn furnished with antiques and famed for its fine dining. **$$$$**

## Restaurant Prices

Categories based on average cost of dinner and a glass of wine, before tip.
**$** = under $15
**$$** = up to $30
**$$$** = over $30

## WHERE TO EAT

**BUFFALO**
**Anchor Bar**
1047 Main Street
Tel: 716-886-8920
*(see page 120)* **$$**
**Hemingway's**
492 Pearl St
Tel: 716-852-1937
This fun and vividly decorated restaurant serves snacks and salads to full entrees. **$**
**Lord Chumley's**
481 Delaware Avenue
Tel: 716-886-2220
Holding the cobblestone-street sidewalk cafe atmosphere alongside quality dishes from premium ingredients. **$$$**

**FREDONIA**
**Barker Brew Company**
34 West Main Street
A wide array of microbrews and hefty sandwiches served in attractive surroundings. **$**

**LOCKPORT**
**Garlock's Restaurant**
35 South Transit Street
Tel: 716-433-5595
Popular all-round restaurant. **$**

**ROME**
**Teddy's Restaurant**
851 Black River Boulevard North
Tel: 315-336-7839
Popular family restaurant. **$$**

**SARATOGA SPRINGS**
**Wheat Fields**
440 Broadway
Tel: 518-587-0534
Wholesome, fresh foods and good salads on a pleasant outdoor patio. **$$**

**SCHENECTADY**
**Blue Ribbon Diner**
1801 State Street
Tel: 518-393-2600
Much-loved diner. **$**
**Brandywine Diner**
970 Emmett Street
Tel: 518-372-6030
Italian-American diner fare. **$**

**SYRACUSE**
**Empire Brewing Company**
120 Walton Street
Tel: 315-475-2337
Housed in an smartly converted old grocery warehouse with much exposed stone and brick, this popular micro brewery has a long list of beers and an eclectic menu with the accent on Cajun. **$$**
**Hartford Queen Diner**
4783 Commercial Drive
Tel: 315-736-0312
Good value, constantly changing daily specials. The perennial favorite is "Chicken 'n' Biscuits," which features every Wednesday. Round it all off on any day with a slice of one of Hartford's many freshly made cream pies. **$**

## PENNSYLVANIA

### WHERE TO STAY

**ERIE**
**Erie Downtowner Inn**
205 West 10th Street, PA 16501
Tel: 814-456-6251
Clean and very central. Pool. **$**
**Super 8 Motel**
11021 Sidehill Road, PA 16428
Tel: 814-725-4567
Serviceable budget accommodations. Phone, cable. **$**

## WHERE TO EAT

### ERIE

**Smuggler's Wharf**
3 State Street
Tel: 814-459-4273
Very pleasant waterfront restaurant serving seafood, prime ribs, and creative appetizers. **$$$**

**Stonehouse Inn**
4753 West Lake Road
Tel: 814-838-9296
Upmarket and romantic. The Continental menu changes daily, and the wine list is one of the longest in the area. **$$$**

## OHIO

## WHERE TO STAY

### ASHTABULA

**Cedars Motel**
2015 West Prospect Rd, OH 44004
Tel: 440-992-45406
Good rooms with phone & cable. **$**

### CANTON

**Hilton Canton**
320 Market Ave South, OH 44709
Tel: 330-454-5000
Fax: 330-454-5091
Modern and central. Health club, large indoor pool, sauna, restaurant and lounge. **$$$**

### CLEVELAND

**Glidden House**
1901 Ford Drive, OH 44106
Tel: 216-231-8900
Attractive historic hotel on the Case Western Reserve campus and close to the city's museums. Amenities include pool, lounge, restaurant and children's playground. Wheelchair-accessible rooms. **$$$**

**Hostelling International – Stanford House**
6093 Stanford Road, OH 44264
Tel: 330-467-8711
Fax: 330-467-8711
Email: hi-stanfordhostel@juno.com
Housed in a Greek revival farmhouse, this hostel has kitchen and laundry facilities, parking, covered bicycle and motorcycle parking, piano and picnic table. **$**

**Wyndham Cleveland Hotel at Playhouse Square**
1260 Euclid Avenue, OH 44115
Tel: 216-615-7500
Fax: 216-615-7500
Adjacent to the theater district and convenient for local attractions. Nicely decorated rooms, restaurant, lounge, pool and fitness center. Wheelchair-accessible rooms. **$$$$**

### SANDUSKY

**Greentree Inn**
1935 Cleveland Road, OH 44870
Tel/Fax: 419-626-6761
Attractive, well-fitted guest rooms. Exercise room, pool, whirlpool, lounge, restaurant. **$$**

### TOLEDO

**Cross Country Inn**
1704 Tollgate Dr, Maumee, OH 43537
Tel: 419-891-0880
With 120 standard rooms with outdoor heated pool. **$**

**Crowne Plaza**
2 Sea Gate/Summit Street, Perrysburg, OH 43604
Tel: 419-241-1411
Fax: 419-241-8161
Plush riverview hotel in downtown Toledo. Exercise room, restaurant, grill and lounge. Wheelchair-accessible rooms. **$$$**

## WHERE TO EAT

### CANTON

**John's Bar and Grill**
2749 Cleveland Avenue Northwest
Tel: 330-454-1259
Good family restaurant. **$–$$**

### CLEVELAND

**Flat Iron Cafe**
1114 Center Street
Tel: 216-696-6968
Established in 1910 as a fisherman's cafe. Now folks come from miles around to indulge in the local delicacy – fried freshwater yellow perch. Also popular are the half pound hamburgers. Other menu items include pastas, salads and hot sandwiches. **$$**

**Hornblower's Barge and Grill**
1151 N Marginal Road
Tel: 216-363-1151
Take to the barge for brunch on this cosmopolitan floating restaurant with lake and city views. **$$**

**Ruthie and Moe's Diner**
4002 Prospect Avenue
Tel: 216-431-8063
Fine traditional diner fare with the emphasis on soups, stews and casseroles. **$**

### SANDUSKY

**Cedar Vella Restaurant**
1918 Cleveland Road
Tel: 419-625-8487
Italian-American food. Pastas, steaks, pizzas and seafood. **$**

### TOLEDO

**Tony Packo's Cafe**
1902 Front Street
Tel: 419-691-6054
Packo's hot dogs are a Toledo institution – don't leave uninitiated. **$**

## Hotel Prices

Categories based on average cost of a double room for one night.
**$** = under $65
**$$** = up to $ 100
**$$$** = up to $150
**$$$$** = over $150

## INDIANA

## WHERE TO STAY

### ANGOLA

**Inn at Amish Acres**
1234 West Market St, ID 46550
Tel: 219-773-2011
Web www.amishacres.com
A chance to enjoy some of life's quiet pleasures: porch rockers, checker boards, hot tub and twining flowers. Disabled-access rooms. **$$**

**Potawatomi Inn**
Pokagon State Park, 6 Lane, 100A
Lake James, ID 46703
Tel: 219-833-1077
US Freephone: 877-768-2928
Set in Pokagon State Park, overlooking Lake James, this inn features a tranquil landscaped

courtyard adjoining the pool and cafe. Other amenities include fitness room, recreation room, library, and gift shop. **$$**

### SOUTH BEND
**The Oliver Inn**
630 West Washington St, ID 46601
Tel: 219-232-4545
US Freephone: 888-697-4466
Fax: 219-288-9788
Web: www.lodging-south-bend.com
Very pretty early 20th-century house with corner porches, bay windows and trim gardens. The wood-burning fireplace and piano music add to the flavor of the common areas. **$$$**

### VALPARAISO
**The Inn at Aberdeen**
3158 SR 2, ID 46385
Tel: 219-465-3753
Web: www.valpomall.com/theinn
Comfortable guest rooms, some with hot tubs. Pool, full gourmet breakfast, evening dessert, unlimited beverages and snacks. Disabled access. **$$**

## Restaurant Prices

Categories based on average cost of dinner and a glass of wine, before tip.
**$** = under $15
**$$** = up to $30
**$$$** = over $30

## WHERE TO EAT

### SOUTH BEND
**Bonnie Doon Ice Cream**
52446 North Dixie Way
Tel: 219-272-2500
Great burgers rounded off with very fine ice cream to finish. **$**
**Miller's Home Cafe**
110 East Michigan St, New Carlisle
Tel: 219-654-3431
Home-style cooking featuring a popular all-you-can-eat buffet. **$**

### VALPARAISO
**Al's Diner**
**1084 Linwood Ave**
**Tel: 219-462-0055**
*(see page 129)* **$–$$**

**Strongbow Inn**
2405 Hwy 30
Tel: 219-462-5121
In business for over half a century. Good home-style steaks and seafood dishes and specializing in turkey. Imaginative vegetarian options are also available. **$$**

## MICHIGAN
### WHERE TO STAY

### DEARBORN
**Mercury Motor Inn**
22361 Michigan Avenue, MI 48124
Tel: 313-274-1900
Comfortable downtown motor inn. Kitchenette rooms available. **$**

### WHERE TO EAT

### DEARBORN
**Antonio's Cucina Italiana**
26356 Ford Road
Tel: 313-278-6000
Traditional Italian *trattoria*. **$$**
**Talal's Restaurant**
22041 Michigan Avenue
Tel: 313-565-5500
Popular Lebanese restaurant serving well-flavored kebabs with a good selection of side dishes. **$$**

## ILLINOIS
### WHERE TO STAY

### CHICAGO
**Blackstone**
636 S. Michigan Avenue, 60605
Tel: 312-427-4300
Fax: 312-427-4736
Plenty of gangster history and ambiance of bygone days. **$$$**
**Cass Hotel**
640 N. Wabash, 60611
Tel: 312-787-4030
US Freephone: 800-227-7850
Not special, but great location. **$$**
**The Drake Hotel**
140 E. Walton Place, 60611
Tel: 312-787-2200
Fax: 312-787-1431
Lavish lobby, worth a visit even if you're not staying. Shopping arcade and three restaurants including the Cape Cod Room. **$$$$**

**Whitehall**
105 E. Delaware Place, 60611
Tel: 312-944-6300
US Freephone: 800-323-7500
Fax: 312-573-6250
A 1920s hotel refurbished in the mid-1990s. **$$$–$$$$**

### WHERE TO EAT

### CHICAGO
**Everest Room**
440 S. LaSalle Street
Tel: 312-663-8920
One of the top restaurants (and views) in the country. **$$$$**
**Pizzeria Uno**
29 E. Ohio Street
Tel: 312-321-1000
Where Chicago pizza was born. **$$**
**The Pump Room**
1301 N. State Parkway
Tel: 312-266-0360
A Chicago institution and the place to celebrate that special occasion. Known since the 1930s for its "Booth One," which is reserved for celebrities. **$$$$$**
**Twin Anchors Restaurant and Tavern**
1655 N. Sedgwick Street
Tel: 312-266-1616
Among the best ribs in Chicago. Great burgers too. Pleasant neighborhood watering hole. **$$$**

### SHOPPING

Chicago has a number of vertical shopping malls, in particular along N. Michigan Avenue. It also has several of America's best department stores and a myriad of boutiques, fashion shops and discount houses. There's no shortage of manufacturers' outlets in the suburbs. Most stores and shops open at 9 or 10am and stay open until at least 6pm; many often remain open until 8 or 9pm. Here's a taster. State Street has two major department stores: **Carson Pirie Scott**, at State and Madison streets and **Marshall Field's**, at 111 N. State Street. **The Magnificent Mile** (Michigan

Avenue from Chicago River to Oak Street) is *the* glamorous shopping area including **Tiffany, Cartier, Saks Fifth Avenue**, and **Bloomingdale's. Chicago Place Mall** (700 N. Michigan Avenue) houses fifty specialty shops including **Saks Fifth Avenue** and **Williams-Sonoma**. The eighth-floor food court is in a tropical garden, and there's a European gourmet supermarket.

**Oak Street's** outstanding specialty shops emphasize diversity and quality. A fun place to window shop. The antique district is on the North Side in Lakeview and there are a number of stores and malls on **W. Kinzie** as well:

**Chicago Antique Center**
3045 N. Lincoln Avenue
**Wrigleyville Antique Mall**
3336 N. Clark Street

### Bookstores Include:
**Barbara's Bookstore**
Navy Pier and
1350 Wells Street
**Unabridged Books**
3251 Broadway

## WISCONSIN

### WHERE TO STAY

### DODGEVILLE
**Don Q Inn**
RR1 Box, 53533
Tel: 608-935-2321
*(see page 133)* **$$–$$$**
**Hostelling International –**
**Folklore Village Farm**
3210 County Hwy BB, WI 53533
Tel: 608-924-4000/608-924-2107
Best known for its folk music and dance program. Also has basic accommodations with kitchen and on-site parking. **$**
**House on the Rock**
3591 Hwy 23, WI 53533
Tel: 608-935-3711
US Freephone: 888-935-3960
Fax: 608-935-1691
Web: www.houseontherockinn.com
A modern inn situated a few miles south of the unique House on the Rock, echoing some of its features. An attractive lounge opens onto a deck overlooking the pool. **$$**

### MADISON
**Hostelling International –**
**Madison Summer Hostel**
126 Langdon Street. PO Box 260217, WI 53726
Tel: 608-285-8750 (5/20-8/21), 608-282-9031 (8/22-5/19)
Web: www.sit.wisc.edu/~hostel
Close to University of Wisconsin and the State Street pedestrian mall. Facilities include kitchen, lounge and TV. Disabled access. **$**
**Madison Concourse Hotel**
1 West Dayton Street, WI 53703
Tel: 608-257-6000
US Freephone: 800-356-8293
A smart, downtown hotel with indoor pool, fitness center, game room, bar and restaurant. **$$**
**Mansion Hill Inn & Governor's Club**
424 North Pinckney St, WI 53703
Tel: 608-255-3999
Fax: 608-255-2217
US Freephone: 800-798-9070
Web: www.mansionhillinn.com
A mid 19th-century Romanesque Revival mansion situated in the historic district. Tastefully furnished with fine antiques. Expect a warm welcome and attentive service. **$$$**

### RICHLAND CENTER
**Park View Inn**
511 West 6th, WI 53581
Tel: 608-647-6354
Fifteen well-maintained units some with kitchenettes. Playground. **$**
**Prairie House Motel**
East 4884, Hwy 14, WI 53588
Tel: 608-588-2088
Spacious, well-appointed rooms, fitness center, whirlpool, sauna and lounge area. **$$**

### WHERE TO EAT

### MADISON
**Dotty Dumpling's Dowry**
116 North Fairchild Street
Tel: 608-255-3175
Excellent burgers, fun decor and cheerful atmosphere. **$**
**Essen Haus**
514 East Wilson Street
Tel: 608-255-4674
Excellent German food and a long list of beers. Rollicking good fun. **$$**

**Sunporch**
2701 University Avenue
Tel: 608-231-1111
Interesting and well-flavored vegetarian food. **$**

## Hotel Prices

Categories based on average cost of a double room for one night.
**$** = under $65
**$$** = up to $100
**$$$** = up to $150
**$$$$** = over $150

## MINNESOTA

### WHERE TO STAY

### BLOOMINGTON
**Hotel Sofitel**
5601 West 78 Street, MN 55439
Tel: 612-835-1900
Luxury accommodation close to the Mall of America, with several French restaurants. **$$$**

### LE SUEUR
**Le Sueur Downtown Motel**
510 North Main Street, MN 56058
Tel: 507-665-6246
Clean, central and cheap. Wheelchair-accessible rooms. **$**

### MANKATO
**Riverfront Inn**
1727 N Riverfront Dr, MN 56001
Tel: 507-388-1638
Small, recently remodeled hotel. **$**

### MINNEAPOLIS
**Econ Lodge**
2500 University Avenue South East, MN 55414
Tel: 612-331-6000
Clean, affordable rooms in central Minneapolis. Swimming pool and coffee shop. **$**
**Evolo's B&B**
2301 Bryant Ave S, MN 55405
Tel: 612-374-9656
Pleasant bed and breakfast in Victorian house. **$$**
**The Marquette Hotel**
710 Marquette Avenue, MN 55402
Tel: 612-333-4545
Fax: 612-376-7419

De luxe boutique-style hotel. Pricey, but lower weekend rates are available. **$$$$**

**Nicollet Island Inn**
5 Merriam Street, MN 55401
Tel: 612-331-1800
Fax: 612-331-6528
Prime riverside location. Individually appointed rooms and top-notch restaurant featuring local cuisine. Valet service. **$$$**

**Rodeway Inn**
2335 Third Avenue, MN 55404
Tel: 612-871-2000
Well-maintained, comfortable rooms near city center. A Downtown shuttle service is provided. **$$**

### NEW PRAGUE

**Schumacher's Hotel & Restaurant**
212 West Main Street, MN 56071
Tel: 612-758-2133
Fax: 612-758-2400
Web: www.schumachershotel.com
A central European-style hotel with 16 uniquely themed rooms. Warm and cozy atmosphere with folk-painted furniture, billowing eiderdowns and pampering service. The inn is renowned for John Schumacher's award-winning central European cuisine. **$$$$**

### PIPESTONE

**Historic Calumet Hotel**
104 West Main Street, MN 56164
Tel: 507-825-5871
Fax: 507-825-4578
*(see page 137)* **$$**

### RED WING

**Parkway Motel**
3425 Hwy 61N, MN 55066
Tel: 651-388-8231
US Freephone: 800-762-0934
With twenty-seven simple, comfortable units. **$**

### ST PAUL

**Hostelling International – Caecilian Hall**
2004 Randolph Avenue, MN 55105
Tel: 651-690-6604
Fax: 651-690-6768
Located on the College of St Catherine campus. Information desk, kitchen, laundry, on-site parking, TV lounges. **$**

**The St Paul Hotel**
350 Market Street, MN 55102
Tel: 651-292-9292
Fax: 651-228-9506
Historic hotel located in city center, overlooking Rice Park. **$$$$**

## Restaurant Prices

Categories based on average cost of dinner and a glass of wine, before tip.
**$** = under $15
**$$** = up to $30
**$$$** = over $30

## WHERE TO EAT

### MANKATO

**Applewood**
Rural Rt 6, Box 52
Tel: 507-625-4105
Pleasant restaurant featuring excellent Sunday Brunch. **$**

### MINNEAPOLIS

**Buca**
11 South 12th Street
Tel: 612-638-2225
Generous portions of Italian fare. Friendly service; amusing decor. **$$**

**Buca de Beppo**
1204 Harmon Place
Tel: 651-638-2225
Critically acclaimed southern Italian restaurant. Enormous portions. **$$**

**Kramarczuk's East European Deli**
215 East Hennepin Avenue
Tel: 612-379-3018
Eastern European deli specializing in cheese and cabbage rolls, varenyky and sausages. The combination plate gives you a taste of everything. **$**

**Modern Café**
337 13th Avenue, North East
Tel: 612-331-9557
Hip crowd and huge servings of tasty grub. **$**

**Nye's Polynesian Room**
112 E Hennepin Avenue
Tel: 612-379-2021
Hearty Polish fare and live music in plush surroundings. **$$**

### ST PAUL

**Café Latte**
850 Grand Avenue
Tel: 651-224-5687

Soups, salads, stews and fragrant hearth-baked breads, as well as full afternoon tea and award-winning desserts. Pizzas available in the attached wine bar. **$**

**Mickey's Dining Car**
36 Seventh Street
Tel: 651-222-5633
Vintage diner in the heart of town serving up the usual fried and griddled fare. **$**

**St Paul Grill**
350 Market Street
Tel: 651-224-7455
Fine dining with great view of Rice Park. **$$$**

## SHOPPING

### BLOOMINGTON

**Mall of America**
Hwys 494 and 77
The largest shopping and entertainment center in the US. There are no fewer than 500 shops, an amusement park, a throng of restaurants and cafés. Wheelchairs and strollers are provided.

### MINNEAPOLIS

**At the Hop**
1752 Grand Avenue
Kitsch and trendy collectables.

**Gaviidae Common**
60 South 6th Street
Downtown shopping center featuring 50 shops and several restaurants.

**Ingebretsen's**
1601 East Lake Street
Scandinavian foods and crafts situated in a quaint marketplace.

**Nicollet Mall**
Downtown pedestrian avenue lined with boutiques, department stores and malls – links to further shops by means of the city skyway system.

### ST PAUL

**World Trade Center**
30 East Seventh Street
Specialty shops and restaurants.

## SOUTH DAKOTA

### WHERE TO STAY

**BADLANDS NATIONAL PARK**
Cedar Pass Lodge SD, 57750
Tel: 605-433-5460
Open mid-March to October. **$–$$**

**DEADWOOD**
**The Bullock Hotel**
633 Main Street, SD 57732
Tel: 605-578-1745
Fax: 605-578-1382
Well-decorated older hotel in historic town with 24-hour gaming, theater and gift shop. **$$**
**Franklin Hotel**
700 Main St, Deadwood, SD 57732
Tel: 605-578-2241
Located on Deadwood's historic Main Street, this lovely old hotel was built in 1903 and is now thoroughly restored. Amenities: air conditioning, television, parking, restaurant, bars, casino. **$$**
**Hostelling International –**
**Black Hills at the Penny Motel**
818 Upper Main Street, SD 57732
Tel/fax: 605-578-1842
Email: pennymot@mato.com
Minutes from historic downtown. Amenities include kitchen, bicycle rental, parking, patio, laundry facilities, luggage storage. **$**

**INTERIOR**
**Badlands Inn**
PO Box 103, SD 57750
Tel: 605-433-5401
Very comfortable rooms with Badlands views. Pool, restaurant. **$**

**MITCHELL**
**Anthony Motel**
1518 W Havens Street, SD 57501
Tel: 605-996-7518
Fax: 605-996-7251
Well-kept motel with pool, miniature golf, free movies, and laundry. **$**

**PIERRE**
**River Place Inn Bed and Breakfast**
Tel: 605-224-8589
Email: upland@cybernex.net
An attractive three-level home commanding magnificent views of the Missouri River. Full breakfast and evening snacks. **$$–$$$**

## Hotel Prices

Categories based on average cost of a double room for one night.
**$** = under $65
**$$** = up to $100
**$$$** = up to $150
**$$$$** = over $150

**RAPID CITY**
**Alex Johnson Hotel**
523 Sixth Street, SD 57701
Tel: 605-342-1210
Web: alexjohnson.com
Commissioned by rail tycoon, Alex Johnson, said to be a great admirer of Native American culture. An intriguing blend of German and Plains Indian influences. Don't miss the chandeliers fashioned from war lances or the portrait of Johnson in Sioux Indian apparel. **$$$**
**Stardust Motel**
520 E North Street, SD 57701
Tel: 605-343-8844
A newly remodeled motel with spacious rooms, queen-sized beds, outdoor heated pool and free continental breakfast. **$**

**SCENIC**
**Homestead Bed and Breakfast**
24880 Sage Creek Rd, SD 57780
Tel: 605-993-6201
The owners of this third-generation, 5,500-acre (2,226-hectare) working ranch invite you to enjoy a peaceful retreat on the edge of the Badlands. Ranch or continental-style breakfasts are offered and evening meals on request. **$$**

**SIOUX FALLS**
**Brimark Inn**
3200 W Russell Street, SD 57101
Tel/Fax: 605-332-2000
Good motor inn with Jacuzzi, pool and coin laundry. **$**

**SPEARFISH CANYON**
**Spearfish Creek Inn**
403 West Kansas, SD 57783
Tel: 605-642-9941
Email: kapust@trib.com
Peaceful and secluded creekside inn in the center of Spearfish. Heated pool. **$**

**WALL**
**Ann's Motel**
PO Box 431, SD 57790
Tel: 605-279-2501
Clean and comfortable rooms fitted with cable TV/Showtime. Tub/shower combos, microwaves, refrigerators and coffeemakers. Restaurants and lounges nearby. **$**

### WHERE TO EAT

**DEADWOOD**
**Jake's Atop the Midnight Star**
677 Main Street
Tel: 605-578-1555
Casual dining on the top floor of Kevin Costner's casino. Lounge. **$$**

**INTERIOR**
**A & M Cafe**
Hwy 44
Tel: 605-433-5340
Clean, friendly family restaurant with wonderful Badlands views. **$$**

**LEAD**
**Cheyenne Crossing Store & Cafe**
PO Box 1220
Tel: 605-584-3510
Scenic spot for tucking into a rib-sticking breakfast any time of day. **$**

**MITCHELL**
**Chef Louie's**
601 East Havens Street
Tel: 605-996-7565
Varied menu, mainly steaks. **$$**

**PIERRE**
**Town and Country Restaurant**
808 West Sioux Avenue
Tel: 605-224-7183
Popular homestyle restaurant. **$**

**RAPID CITY**
**Firehouse Brewing Company**
610 Main Street
Tel: 605-348-1915
Microbrewery serving 'pub-grub'. **$**

**SCENIC**
**Kristina's Café and Bakery**
334 S Phillips Avenue
Tel: 605-331-4860
Excellent baked goods. **$**

## SIOUX FALLS

**Minerva's**
301 Phillips Avenue
Tel: 605-334-0386
Prime-cut steaks, fish, pasta. **$$**

## SPEARFISH

**Bay Leaf Cafe**
126 West Hudson
Tel: 605-642-5462
Friendly and informal cafe in historic building serving a variety of well-prepared dishes from soup to buffalo steaks. **$$**

### Hotel Prices

Categories based on average cost of a double room for one night.
**$** = under $65
**$$** = up to $100
**$$$** = up to $150
**$$$$** = over $150

### WYOMING

### WHERE TO STAY

## BIGHORN

**Bozeman Trail Bed and Breakfast**
304 Hwy 335 (PO Box 416),
WY 82833
Tel: 307-672-2381
Web: www.thebluebarn.com
Spend some time in an old west homestead fitted out with modern comforts. Sweeping mountain views, hot tub and chuckwagon breakfast. Families welcome.
**$$–$$$**

## CODY

**Irma Hotel**
1192 Sheridan Ave, WY 82414
Tel: 307-587-4221
Built in 1902 by Buffalo Bill Cody for his daughter, Irma, the hotel still retains the flavor of the Old West. Amenities: air conditioning, television, restaurant. **$–$$**

## GRAND TETON NATIONAL PARK
**Park information:**
PO Box 170 Moose, WY 83012
Tel: 307-739-3399
Lodgings within the park include cabins at Signal Mountain Lodge

(**$$**) and the more luxurious **Jackson Lake Lodge. $$$–$$$$**
Both are managed by:
**Grand Teton Lodge Co.**
PO Box 240, Moran, WY 83013
Tel: 307-543-2811

## GILLETTE

**Deer Park Bed and Breakfast**
2660 Bishop Rd, (PO Box 1089),
WY 82717
Two nice rooms with private baths in an attractive historic home. **$$**
**Heartspear Hideaway**
425 Bowers Road, WY 82716
Tel: 307-682-0812
Fax: 307-685-6383
Web: www.heartspear.com
Expect stunning views from this guesthouse, which is located on a working cattle and horse ranch. Full or continental breakfast available. Guests may use the pool situated at the ranch house.
**$$$–$$$$**

## GREYBULL

**Yellowstone Motel**
247 Greybull Avenue, WY 82426
Tel: 307-765-4456
Warm, comfortable rooms. Putting green, heated pool and restaurant directly opposite. **$**

## JACKSON

**Buckrail Lodge**
110 E Karns Avenue, WY 83001
Tel: 307-733-2079
Fax: 307-734-1663
Large, comfortable cedar-log room with cathedral ceilings and western decor. Set in spacious grounds in quiet residential neighborhood. Good views. Jacuzzi, cable TV. **$–$$**
**Teton Inn**
165 W Gill WY 83001
Tel: 307-733-3883
Fax: 307-739-9351
Modest rooms and rates. Free local calls and newspaper. **$**
**Wagon Wheel Village**
435 N Cache Street, WY 83001
Tel: 307-733-2357
Fax: 307-733-0568
Log cabins in peaceful park setting near Elk Refuge and convenient to Town Square. Restaurant, saloon, gift shop, coin laundry. **$$**

## LOVELL

**TX Ranch**
PO Box 501, WY 82431
Tel: 406-484-6415
Guests help out with duties on this working cattle ranch situated at the foot of Pryor Mountain. Tents, horses, gear and food provided. **$$**

## SHERIDAN

**Sheridan Inn**
Guest House Motel
2007 North Main, WY 82801
Tel: 307-674-7496
Fax: 507-674-7687
Clean, good-sized, rooms. Amenities include free coin laundry, refrigerators in some rooms. **$**

## SUNDANCE

**Sundance Inn**
2719 E Cleveland Ave, WY 82729
Tel: 307-283-1100
Fax: 307-283-1104
This is a modest but pleasant inn. Amenities include free movies, breakfast, local phone calls and indoor pool. **$**

## YELLOWSTONE NATIONAL PARK
**Park information:**
WY 82190
Tel: 307-344-7381
Web: www.travelyellowstone.com
Amfac Parks and Resorts manages all lodgings within the park. Contact them well in advance as facilities are frequently fully booked up to a year in advance.
**Old Faithful Inn and Lodge**
Magnificent log inn built in 1903. Terrace Bar overlooks Old Faithful Geyser. Accommodation for most budgets, but early booking is essential. **$–$$$$**
**Old Faithful Snow Lodge**
Opened in 1999, this heavy timber lodge features a stone fireplace and hand-wrought iron details. The cabins are tastefully fitted with specially designed furnishings.
**$$$**
**Roosevelt Lodge Cabins**
Very basic, inexpensive. In wooden shelter. No bedding provided. **$**

## Restaurant Prices

Categories based on average cost of dinner and a glass of wine, before tip.

**$** = under $15
**$$** = up to $30
**$$$** = over $30

---

# WHERE TO EAT

### CODY
**The Noon Break**
927 12th Street
Tel: 307-587-9720
Cheerful breakfast and lunch spot serving Western, Mexican and Tex-Mex dishes. Beware of the chili. **$**

**Proud Cut Saloon**
1227 Sheridan Avenue
Tel: 307-527-6905
Local favorite for sandwiches, burgers and steak. **$–$$**

### GILLETTE
**Humphrey's Bar and Grill**
408 Juniper Lane
Tel: 307-682-0100
Lively sports bar with an excellent salad bar. **$**

### JACKSON
**Blue Lion**
160 North Millward Street
Tel: 307-733-3912
Long-established local favorite in an older, renovated building. Excellent regional and continental dishes including elk, chicken and vegetarian options. Dine indoors or al fresco. **$$$**

**Cadillac Grill**
55 North Cache Street
Tel: 703-733-3279
Lively atmosphere and decor with fashionable cuisine featuring seafood, game and pasta. **$$**

**Snake River Grill**
84 East Broadway
Tel: 307-733-0557
American seafood and steak grill with an Asian influence. The menu varies with the season. **$$$**

### SHERIDAN
**Melinda's**
57 North Main
Tel: 307-674-9188

Imaginative, appetizing fare with some unusual twists. **$**

### SUNDANCE
**ARO Family Restaurant**
205 Cleveland Avenue
Tel: 307-283-2000
Well-prepared food served in warm, friendly atmosphere. Excellent value. **$**

# MONTANA

## WHERE TO STAY

### BOZEMAN
**Gallatin Gateway Inn**
Hwy 191, Gallatin Gtwy, MT 59730
Tel: 406-763-4672
US Freephone: 800-676-3522
Web: www.gallatingatewayinn.com
Attractively decorated, light and spacious rooms in a beautifully restored historic railroad hotel. American cuisine fine dining by reservation. **$$$**

**Mountain Sky Guest Ranch**
Box 1128, MT 59715
Tel: 406-587-1244
US Freephone: 800-548-3392
The ranch overlooks the lovely Paradise Valley about 30 miles from Yellowstone National Park in southwestern Montana. Amenities: horseback riding and instruction, children's counselors, fishing, tennis, pool, hot tub. **$$$**

### COLUMBIA FALLS
**Meadow Lake Resort**
100 St Andrews Dr, MT 59912
Tel: 406-892-7601
Fax: 406-892-0330
Web: www.meadowlake.com
Luxurious resort comprising vacation homes, combos and inn rooms. Amenities include golf course, tennis and fitness center, Amtrak and ski shuttles, indoor and outdoor pools, restaurant and lounge. **$$$–$$$$**

**Plum Creek House**
985 Vans Avenue, MT 59912
Tel: 406-892-1816
US Freephone: 800-682-1492
Web: www.wtp.net/go/plumcreek
A ranch-style home perched high above Flathead River with stunning views from large windows. The inn

features five spacious luxury rooms with private baths, terry-cloth robes and a formal, elegantly furnished dining room. Heated pool and riverside Jacuzzi. **$$$**

### CORAM
**A Wild Rose**
10280 Hwy 2 East, MT 59913
Tel: 406-387-4900
Web: www.cyberport.net/wildrose
Cradled in stunning mountain scenery bordering Glacier National Park, this inn provides tranquility and pampering services with therapeutic spa and massage, whirlpool suites and gourmet breakfasts. **$$$**

### ESSEX
**Paola Creek**
HC 36 Box 4C, MT 59916
US Freephone: 888-311-5061
Web: www.wtp.net/go/paola
A rustic, handcrafted larch-log home featuring an impressive river rock fireplace and magnificent views of Mount St Nicholas. Sumptuous full breakfasts, sack lunches and dinners by reservation. **$$$**

### GLACIER NATIONAL PARK
**Park information:**
Glacier National Park
West Glacier, MT 59936
Tel: 406-888-7800
Web:www.nps.gov.glac
Lodgings within the park are managed by:

**Glacier Park Inc.**
May–September: East Glacier Park, MT 59434. Tel: 406-226-5551
October–April: Station 1210, Greyhound, Phoenix, AZ 85077
Tel: 602-207-6000

**Glacier Park Lodge**
PO Box 127, MT 59936
Tel: 406-387-5830
US Freephone: 800-841-3835
Fax: 406-387-5835
A chalet-style lodge constructed from hand-hewn logs and fronted by a broad verandah with dramatic views of Glacier National Park. Set in 240 private acres (97 hectares), and offering many civilized comforts, this is a fine wilderness retreat. Open May to September. **$$$**

## HELENA
**Appleton Inn B&B**
1999 Euclid Avenue, MT 59601
Tel: 406-449-7492
Fax: 406-449-1261
Century-old house on National
Historic Register, now a
comfortable B&B. **$$**
**Elkhorn Mountain Inn**
1 Jackson Creek, MT 59634
Tel: 406-442-6625
Fax: 406-449-8797
Attractively furnished and
affordable. Coffee makers, free
local calls and newspaper. **$**

## HUNGRY HORSE
**Hostelling International –
East Glacier Park**
1020 Montana Hwy 49, MT 59434
Tel: 406-226-4426
Occupying a pleasant two-story log
building with kitchen, equipment
storage, laundry facilities, linen and
bicycle rentals. **$**
**Mini Golden Inns Motel**
8955 Hwy 2E, MT 59919
Tel: 406-387-4313
Modern rooms with mountain
views. Amenities include
breakfast, coin laundry and free
local calls. **$**

## KALISPELL
**Kalispell Grand Hotel**
100 Main Street, MT 59901
Tel: 406-755-8100
Web: www.vtown.com/grand
Fine old historic hotel. **$$**

## LIVINGSTON
**63 Ranch**
Box 979, MT 59047
Tel: 406-222-0570
Founded in 1929, this working
ranch is set on 2,000 acres
(810 hectares) in the Absaroka
Mountains about 50 miles
(81 km) north of Yellowstone
National Park and is listed on the
National Register of Historic
Places. Amen-ities: horseback
riding and instruc-tion, fishing,
overnight trips. **$**
**The Murray Hotel**
201 West Park Street, MT 59047
Tel: 406-222-1350
Web: www.murrayhotel.com
Numerous celebrity guests have
stayed in this gracious old hotel –
from Peter Bogdonovich to the
Queen of Denmark. Elegantly
furnished rooms, a rooftop hot tub,
workout room and an excellent
cafe. **$$–$$$**

## MISSOULA
**DoubleTree Hotel**
100 Madison, MT 59802
Tel: 406-728-3100
Fax: 406-728-2530
Comfort and good service. Dining
room. **$$$**
**Downtown Motel**
502 E Broadway, MT 59802
Tel: 406-549-5191
Comfortable rooms in town center.
Reasonable rates. Coffee makers,
free movies. **$**
**Goldsmith's Bed and Breakfast Inn**
809 East Front, MT 59802
Tel: 406-721-6732
Fax: 406-543-0045
A quiet riverside B&B in an older
house, just a pleasant stroll away
from Downtown. **$$$**

## POLSON
**Best Western KwaTaqNuk Resort**
303 Hwy 93, MT 59860
Tel: 406-883-3636
US Freephone: 800-882-6363
Fax: 406-833-5392
This bayfront resort has many first
rate facilities including two pools,
whirlpool, marina, fine dining
restaurant and gift shop. **$$$**

## ST IGNATIUS
**Sunset Motel**
32670 Hwy 93, MT 59865
Tel: 406-745-3900
Well-placed small hotel newly
decorated in 'mountain theme.'
Cable TV and refrigerators. **$**

## WHITEFISH
**Duck Inn Lodge**
1305 Colombia Avenue, MT 59937
Tel: 406-862-3825
Fax: 1-800-344-2377
Web: www.duckinn.com
This is a pretty lodge by the river.
Fireplaces, patios, Jacuzzi, deep
soak tubs, breakfast. Courtesy
Amtrak van. **$$**

## WHERE TO EAT

### BOZEMAN
**John Bozeman's Bistro**
242 East Main Street
Tel: 406-587-4100
Eclectic menu featuring Thai and
Italian dishes. Relaxed, informal
atmosphere. **$$**

### Restaurant Prices

Categories based on average
cost of dinner and a glass of
wine, before tip.
**$** = under $15
**$$** = up to $30
**$$$** = over $30

### HELENA
**Frontier Pies Restaurant & Bakery**
1231 Prospect Avenue
Tel: 406-442-7437
Good food and freshly baked
pies worth traveling for. Western
decor **$**
**Windbag Saloon**
19 S Last Chance Gulch Street
Tel: 406-443-9669
Sample the lively atmosphere
and range of microbrewery
beers in this popular, local spot.
Good burgers and great pasta.
**$–$$**

### KALISPELL
**Moose's Saloon**
173 North Main Street
Tel: 406-755-2337
The genuine article. Good pizzas **$**

### LIVINGSTON
**The Sport Restaurant**
114 South Main
Tel: 406-222-3533
Juicy burgers with a wide
choice of toppings and great
slabs of toothsome, fresh pies to
follow. **$**
**Winchester Cafe**
201 West Park
Tel: 406-222-2708
This popular local meeting place
adjoining the Murray Hotel serves
fresh well-prepared fish, meat and
pasta dishes. Convivial
atmosphere – occasionally
rowdy. **$$**

## MISSOULA

**Food for Thought**
540 Daly Avenue
Tel: 406-721-6033
Great breakfasts, lunches and freshly prepared salads. **$**

**McKay's on the River**
1111 East Broadway
Tel: 406-728-0098
Excellent seafood, steaks, pasta. Sweeping view of the river. **$$$**

## POLSON

**Watusi**
308 Main Street
Tel: 406-883-6200
Delicious healthy lunches. **$**

## WHITEFISH

**Dos Amigos**
Wisconsin Avenue
Tel: 406-862-9994
Good choice of dishes. Mainly Mexican but with several Cajun and American dishes on offer. **$$**

## SHOPPING

## BOZEMAN

**Country Book Shelf**
28 West Main Street
Comprehensive collection of regional titles.

**Country Mall Antiques**
8350 Huffine Lane
Around two dozen stalls selling antiques and collectables.

## HELENA

**Reeder's Alley**
100 South Park Avenue
Specialty shops in a district that developed during the Gold Rush.

## MISSOULA

**Freddy's Feed and Read**
1221 Helen Avenue
Do exactly what it says on the sign. A pleasant bookstore with an in-house deli.

**Southgate Mall**
Highway 93 and South Avenue
105 shops.

**Grizzly Boot Company**
814 S. Higgins Ave

## IDAHO

### WHERE TO STAY

## BONNERS FERRY

**Best Western Kootenai River Inn and Casino**
Rt 4, Box 4740, ID 83805
Tel: 208-267-8511
US Freephone: 800-346-5668
Fax: 208-267-3744
Excellent facilities and beautiful view. Very reasonable. Pool, hot tub, waterfront access, exercise room. **$$**

## COEUR D'ALENE

**The Coeur d'Alene Resort**
On Lake Coeur d'Alene, 83814
Tel: 208-765-4000
US Freephone: 800-688-5253
Fax: 208-667-2707
Web: www.cdaresort.com
Luxury resort on scenic Lake Coeur d'Alene. The many first-rate amenities include a floating moveable golf green. Close to fishing, skiing and other area attractions. **$$$**

## NAPLES

**Hostelling International – Naples**
Hwy 2, ID 83847
Tel: 208-267-2947
Fax: 208-267-4118
*Circa* 1950s dance hall now a comfortable hostel. Amenities include kitchen, laundry facilities, baggage storage, on-site parking, basketball court and piano. **$**

## SANDPOINT

**Coit House Bed & Breakfast**
502 N Fourth Avenue, ID 83864
Tel: 208-265-4035
Fax: 208-265-4035
Web: www.keokee.com/bdgecenresv
Comfortable B&B at reasonable rates. Breakfast. **$$**

**Selkirk Lodge**
Schweitzer Mountain Resort,
10000 Schweitzer Mt Rd, ID 83864
Tel: 208-263-9555
US Freephone: 800-831-8810
Fax: 208-263-0775
Web: www.schweitzer.com
Cozy European-style ski lodge with sweeping views of Lake Pend Oreille

## Hotel Prices

Categories based on average cost of a double room for one night.
**$** = under $65
**$$** = up to $100
**$$$** = up to $150
**$$$$** = over $150

and the surrounding mountains. Hot tub, pool, mini-mart, cable TV. Breakfast included. **$$$**

### WHERE TO EAT

## BONNERS FERRY

**Alberto's**
6536 South Main Street
Tel: 208-267-7493
Authentic, first-rate Mexican fare in gaily decorated surroundings. **$$**

## COEUR D'ALENE

**Cedars Floating Restaurant**
1 Marine Drive
Tel: 208-664-2922
Warm and welcoming restaurant moored on Lake Coeur d'Lane affording panoramic views. Extensive, nicely balanced menu featuring very fresh, expertly prepared fish. **$$**

## SANDPOINT

**Hydra**
115 South Lake Street
Tel: 208-263-7123
Steak and seafood restaurant with cocktail bar. Sunday brunch. **$$**

## WASHINGTON

### WHERE TO STAY

## EDMUNDS

**Andy's Motel**
22201 Hwy 99, WA 98026
Tel: 425-776-6080
Simple and comfortable. Wheelchair accessible. **$**

## FORKS

**Miller Tree Inn**
654 East Division St, WA 98331
Tel: 360-374-6806
Nice and quiet. **$**

### INDEX

**Bush Country House Inn**
308 Fifth Street, WA 98256
Tel: 360-793-2312
Handsome century-old house. Good
rooms and restaurant. **$**

### LA PUSH
**La Push Ocean Park Resort**
PO Box 67, WA 98350
Tel: 360-374-5267
Recently remodeled resort complex
with very nice cabins and guest
rooms, some with fireplaces. **$$**

### LEAVENWORTH
**Alpenrose Inn**
500 Alpine Place, WA 98826
Tel: 509-548-3000
Intimate Bavarian-style B&B inn in
scenic alpine setting. **$$**
**Haus Rohrbach Pension**
2882 Ranger Road, WA 98826
Tel: 509-548-7024
US Freephone: 800-548-4477
Fax: 508-548-5038
Web: www.hausrohrbach.com
Cozy and convivial European-style
pension. High on a hill with views
across the valley. **$$–$$$**

### NEAH BAY
**Silver Salmon Resort**
Bay View Avenue, WA 98357
Tel: 360-645-2388
Web: www.silversalmonresort.com
Adjacent to the marina with 11
small rooms. Close to store,
restaurants and gift shop. **$**

### PORT ANGELES
**DoubleTree Hotel**
221 N Lincoln Street, WA 98362
Tel: 360-452-9215
Fax: 360-452-4734
Waterfront location with harbor
view. Some rooms have balconies.
Facilities include dining room, valet
service and laundry. **$$$**
**Uptown Inn**
101 E Second Street, WA 98362
Tel: 360-457-9434
Individually appointed rooms.
Whirlpool, free movies. **$$**

### PORT TOWNSEND
**Hostelling International – Olympic**
272 Battery Way, WA 98368
Tel: 360-385-0655

Web: www.washingtonhostels.org.
Located in Fort Worden State Park.
Sleeping bags allowed. **$**
**Palace Hotel**
1004 Water Street, WA 98368
Tel: 360-385-0773
Fax: 360-385-0780
Nicely restored historic
Downtown edifice. Decorated in
original Victorian style.
Restaurant. **$$$**
**The Tides Inn**
1807 Water Street, WA 98368
Tel: 360-385-0595
US Freephone: 800-822-8696
On the waterfront; some rooms
have kitchenettes, Jacuzzis. **$**

### SEQUIM
**Suntree 8 Inn**
123 South Post Street, WA 99201
Tel: 509-838-8504
Downtown chain motel. **$**
**West Coast Ridpath Hotel**
West 515 Sprague Ave, WA 99204
Tel: 509-838-2711
Fax: 509-747-6970
Elegant older hotel in a convenient
central location. Tastefully
decorated, well-equipped rooms.
**$$**

## Restaurant Prices

Categories based on average
cost of dinner and a glass of
wine, before tip.
**$** = under $15
**$$** = up to $30
**$$$** = over $30

## WHERE TO EAT

### FORKS
**Rain Drop Cafe**
111 South Forks Avenue
Tel: 360-374-6612
Good breakfasts. The international
lunch and dinner menu features
tacos, gourmet burgers, fish and
chips and very nice salads. **$**

### LEAVENWORTH
**Café Christa**
801 Front Street
Tel: 509-548-5074
A pleasant café right on the city
square. **$$**

### PORT ANGELES
**Destiny Seafood and Grill**
1213 Marine Drive
Tel: 360-452-4665
Mediterranean and Middle Eastern
cuisine. Nice baked goods. **$**
**First Street Haven**
107 E First Street
Tel: 360-457-0352
Sweet-smelling cakes, muffins and
scones baked in-house. Breakfast
served all day on Sundays. **$**

### PORT TOWNSEND
**Salal Cafe**
634 Water Street
Tel: 360-385-6532
Wholesome meals served in
pleasant surroundings. **$**
**The Silverwater Café**
237 Taylor Street
Tel: 360-385-6448
Well-prepared, fresh local seafood
and produce. Easy ambiance. **$**

### SEQUIM
**Three Crabs Restaurant**
113 Crabs Road
Tel: 360-683-4264
Fine view of the harbor and freshest
Dungeness crabs around. **$**

### SPOKANE
**Fugazzi Bakery and Cafe**
1 North Post Street
Tel: 509-624-1133
Nice sandwiches and pastries. **$**
**Niko's**
725 West Riverside Avenue
Tel: 509-624-7444
Excellent Greek food. **$$**
**Patsy Clark's**
2208 West Second Avenue
Tel: 509-838-8300
Acclaimed fine dining in a fabulous
old mansion with super fresh
salmon entrees and the sublime
President Steak. **$$$**

## Hub City:
## SEATTLE

### GETTING AROUND

#### Public transportation
**From the airport:** Seattle-Tacoma
Airport, known as Sea-Tac (Tel: 206-
431-4444, 800-544-1965) is 13
miles (20 km) south of Seattle.

Access to Sea-Tac is via I-5 (exit 154 from south I-5 or exit 152 from north I-5), or via Highway 99/509 and 518. Stop-and-go traffic on I-5 is not uncommon, especially during rush hours, so the alternate route on the highway is often quicker. Buses provide the least costly method of transportation. The 194 is the most direct, bringing passengers downtown in about 30 minutes. The 174 makes local stops on its way downtown. Bus or van companies that link the airport with metropolitan Seattle or Bellevue include:

The Grayline Airport Express (Tel: 206-624-5077)

Shuttle Express (Tel: 206-622-1424)

Metro Transit (Tel: 206-553-3000)

Quick Shuttle (Tel: 206-684-9373, 800-665-2122)

STITA (Tel: 206-246-9999) provides a taxi service to and from the airport. From the airport to downtown (or vice versa) costs about $30.

**National buses:** The Greyhound terminal is located at 811 Stewart Street (Tel: 800-231-2222).

**National trains:** The Amtrak station is at Third Avenue and S. Jackson Street (Tel: 1-800-872-7245)

**Commuter trains:** Metro Transit (Tel: 206-553-3000) provides a "Ride Free Area" in the downtown core bordered by the I-5 to the east, the waterfront to the west, Jackson Street to the south and Battery Street to the north.

**Streetcar:** Metro also operates a waterfront streetcar, a 1927 vintage trolley which runs 1½ miles (3 km) along the waterfront every 20–30 minutes from Myrtle, and from Edwards Park to the Pioneer Square district. The ticket requires exact change.

**Monorail:** The Monorail, which was built for the 1962 World Fair, runs every 15 minutes between Seattle Center and Fourth and Pine streets to Westlake Center. The ride is just under 1 mile (2 km) and takes only 90 seconds. It's clean and spacious with large windows.

**Ferries:** The Washington State Ferry system (Tel: 206-464-6400, 800-

843-3779), the largest in the country, covers the Puget Sound area, linking Seattle (at Pier 52) with the Olympic Peninsula via Bremerton and Bainbridge Island. State ferries also depart from West Seattle to Vashon Island and Southworth and from Edmonds, 7 miles (11 km) north of Seattle, to Kingston on Kitsap Peninsula. They also go from Anacortes, 90 miles (145 km) northwest of Seattle, through the San Juan Islands to Victoria, on Canada's Vancouver Island. Passengers to Canada need a passport. The Black Ball Ferry (Tel: 206-622-2222) departs from Port Angeles on the Olympic Peninsula to Victoria, BC, four times a day in summer and twice daily the rest of the year. Ferries carry cars.

### Private Transportation

When the weather is fine, Seattle is a very pleasant city to walk about in – it is hilly, but many of the sights may be toured comfortably on foot. Heavy traffic congestion and scarce, expensive parking make driving in the center a less attractive option. Many of the major car rental agencies have offices at Seattle-Tacoma Airport or in the downtown area. Consult the Yellow Pages for a full listing of rental firms.

**Car rental companies**
Avis, Tel: 206-433-5252
Budget, Tel: 206-431-8800 ext 870
Hertz, Tel: 206-248-1300

---

## WHERE TO STAY

**The Edgewater Inn**
Pier 67, 2411 Alaskan Way, WA 98101
Tel: 206-728-7000, 800-624-0670
Seattle's only downtown waterfront hotel. Atrium lobby, stone fireplaces and mountain lodge decor. Restaurant features northwestern cuisine. Rates vary depending on water- or city-view rooms. **$$$**

**Ben Carol Motel**
14110 Pacific Hwy S, WA 98168
Tel: 206-244-6464
The best of several cheap motels halfway to the airport, adjacent to a

family-type restaurant and a huge 24-hour supermarket. Pool. **$**

**Challenger Bunk and Breakfast**
1001 Fairview Ave N, WA 98101
Tel: 206-340-1201
Unusual tugboat-turned-B&B on Lake Union with rooms decorated with nautical charts and brass ornaments. The views alone are worth the stay. **$$$**

**Hostelling International – Seattle**
84 Union Street, WA 98101
Tel: 206-682-0462
Lounge, library and self-service kitchen, laundry available. **$**

**Inn At The Market**
Pike Place Market, 86 Pine Street, WA 98101
Tel: 206-443-3600
Web: www.innatthemarket.com
In Pike Place Market with splendid views of Elliott Bay. Surrounded by trendy shops, spa and restaurant, Free downtown shuttle. **$$$$**

**Shafer-Baillie Mansion**
907 14th Avenue East, WA 98112
Tel: 206-322-4654
Antique-furnished B&B in spacious grounds. Gourmet breakfast included. **$$$**

**University Plaza Hotel**
400 North East 45th St, WA 98105
Tel: 206-634-0100
In the heart of the University District, with 135 rooms. Pool, fitness center, beauty salon, laundry service, restaurant, lounge with entertainment. **$**

---

## WHERE TO EAT

**Campagne**
86 Pine Street.
Tel: 206-728-2800
In Pike Place Market, serving southern French cuisine with a rustic ambiance. Daily specials

from seafood caught that day
along with fresh local produce.
**$$$**

**The Gravity Bar**
Broadway Market, Capitol Hill
Tel: 206-325-7186.
Imaginative vegetarian dishes,
wheatgrass juice and espresso. A
great place to people-watch. **$**

**Macrina Bakery & Café**
2408 1st Avenue
Tel: 206-448-4032
Pleasant coffee house with eats.
**$**

**Ray's Boathouse**
6049 Seaview Avenue NW
Tel: 206-789-3770
Truly a local establishment from
the wonderful view of Puget Sound
to elegant preparation of local
ingre-dients in this upscale eatery.
**$$**

**Salty's on Alki**
1936 Harbor Avenue South West
Tel: 206-937-1600
Alder-smoked salmon stuffed with
Dungeness crab, but it's the view at
night that steals the show. **$$**

**Shanghai Garden**
524 6th Avenue South
Tel: 206-625-1689
Brightly painted pink restaurant.
Anything with the homemade
shaven noodles is a good bet. **$$**

**The Yankee Diner**
5300 24th Avenue NW
Tel: 206-783-1964
The food lives up to the name of
this casual cafe serving old-
fashioned meat and potatoes type
meals with an excellent view. **$**

# Central Route

## Useful Addresses

**Washington DC tourist information**
Washington DC Convention and
Visitors Association, 1212 New York
Avenue NW, #600, Washington DC,
20005
Tel: 202-789-7000
Web: www.washington.org

**Tennessee tourist information**
Department of Tourist
Development, Fifth Floor, Rachel
Jackson Building, 320 Sixth Avenue
North, Nashville, TN 37202
Tel: 615-741-2158
US Freephone: 800-836-6200
Web: www.state.tn.us/tourdev

**Arkansas tourist information**
Arkansas Department of Parks and
Tourism, One Capitol Mall, Little
Rock, AR 72201
US Freephone: 800-628-8725
Web: www.arkansas.com

**Oklahoma tourist information**
Tourism Department, PO Box
60789, Oklahoma City, OK 73146
Tel: 800-652-6552
Web: www.otrd.state.ok.us

**Texas tourist information**
Texas State Board of Tourism, PO
Box 5064, Austin, TX 78763-5064
Tel: 512-462-9191
US Freephone: 800-452-9292
Web: www.state.tx.us

**New Mexico tourist information**
New Mexico Department of Tourism
PO Box 20002, Santa Fe, NM
87503
US Freephone: 800-545-2040
Web: www.newmexico.org

**Arizona tourist information**
Arizona Office of Tourism, Suite
4015, 2702 North Third Street,
Phoenix, AZ 85004
Tel: 602-230-7733
Email: arizonaguide@guide.com

**Los Angeles tourist information**
Los Angeles Convention and
Visitors Burea, 633 W Fifth Street
Tel: 213-689-8822
Fax: 213-624-9746
Web: www.ci.la.ca.us

**California State tourist information**
The California Office of Tourism,
801 K Street, Suite 1600,
Sacramento, CA 95814
Tel: 916-322-2881
US Freephone: 800-862-2543
Web: www.gocalif.co.gov

## Hub City: WASHINGTON, DC

### GETTING AROUND

*Public Transportation*
**From the airport:** Transportation
between Washington's three
airports and downtown hotels is
good. National Airport, the airport
closest to the center of town, is on
the metro system. The metro
station is a short walk from the
arrivals lounges, but can also be
reached by regular shuttle buses.
SuperShuttle (Tel: 703-416-7873)
runs a door-to-door service from
between $10–$30. National Airport
shuttle buses run to the downtown
terminus at 1517 K Street NW. Taxi
fares into downtown Washington
are reasonably priced. Dulles
International has a shuttle bus
service to the downtown terminus
at 1517 K Street NW, as well as
shuttles to West Falls Church
metro station, which feeds right
into the metro system, and to
National Airport. The Washington
Flyer is a taxi service operated by
the Dulles Airport. Trips into
downtown Washington cost just
over double the amount from
National Airport. BWI Airport runs a
shuttle service into the downtown
terminus at 15th and K Street NW.
Taxis to central Washington are
also available. Amtrak runs a
service from BWI into Union Station.
**Rapid transit:** The Metrorail (Tel:
202-637-7000) subway service is
fast and efficient with stations
serving all of the major sights. A
single ticket is under $2.

**City buses:** Metrobus (Tel: 202-637-7000) operates a comprehensive network of routes covering the city and outlying areas. Single fares are under $1.50.
**National buses:** Greyhound buses operate out of the station at 1005 First Street NE.
**National rail:** Amtrak runs from Union Station, 50 Massachusetts Avenue NE.

### *Private Transportation*
Washington DC is compact enough to make it one of the best cities in the country for exploring on foot. Another good way to get around – particularly if you are interested in some of the worthwhile day trips – is to rent a car. You can do this at the airport, your hotel, or any car rental agency, checking the phone book under "Automobile Renting." Cars can often be delivered to you. Car rental companies all charge roughly the same price. Most hotels (but not all) offer free parking for their guests; if staying in the city for any length of time, leave your car in the garage. Parking around DC is difficult on the street and expensive in car parks. Some of the bigger companies are Avis, Budget, Hertz, Alamo and Dollar. All have numerous offices around the city, so consult the phone directory for the one nearest you. Most rental agencies require you be at least 21 years old and possess a valid driver's license. If you are insured in the US, you should not have to purchase insurance from the agency. If uninsured, read the rental agency's insurance policy carefully before purchasing the car insurance.
**Taxis:** Long-distance taxi fares are steep, but traveling inside Washington is cheaper than in other American cities and much cheaper than in some European capitals. For planned trips, reserve a taxi at least an hour in advance of departure. Some of the major taxi cab companies are:
**Taxi Transportation Service**, Tel: 398-0500
**Checker Cab Company**, Tel: 270-6000

Taxi cabs outside DC are all the same price – a fixed fare to get in the cab, then additional fees for every mile (or part of) thereafter. If you are going a long distance, you can usually negotiate with the cab driver to give you a fixed rate.

## Hotel Prices

Categories based on average cost of a double room for one night.
**$** = under $65
**$$** = up to $100
**$$$** = up to $150
**$$$$** = over $150

## WHERE TO STAY

**Allen Lee Hotel**
2224 F Street NW, 20037
Tel: 202-331-1224
Simple but clean hotel – some rooms share baths. Great for the young. Amenities: free coffee and cookies in lobby on Sunday mornings, maid service daily. All rooms have TV; some have baths. **$$**

**The Channel Inn**
650 Water Street NW, 20024
Tel: 202-554-2400
US Freephone: 800-368-5668
Washington's only waterfront hotel, close to the marina restaurants, with large and simple but comfortable rooms. Amenities: good seafood restaurant, coffee shop, outdoor pool, plus the Arena Stage, golf course, indoor and outdoor tennis courts are close by. **$$$$**

**The Jefferson**
1200 16th Street NW, 20036
Tel: 202-347-2200
US Freephone: 800-368-5966
A relatively small hotel, offering discreet and sensitive service in elegant surroundings. Amenities: restaurant, Saturday jazz, high tea, bathrobes, hair dryers, exercise and swimming facilities at University Club opposite, laundry, one-hour pressing, valet parking, pets accepted. **$$$$**

**Washington International Youth Hostel**
1009 11th Street NW, 20001
Tel: 202-737-2333
Located one block north of the Convention Center, with common areas for meeting other travelers, information desk, ride board, free tours and movies, tight security, large kitchen available for groups. **$**

## WHERE TO EAT

The benefit of Washington as a magnet to political refugees and other immigrants from around the world is that there is almost no cuisine that is not represented somewhere in the city and its surrounding suburbs. Everything from Ethiopian cooking to Nepalese, from British high tea to the best French cuisine, can be found somewhere. Reservations are strongly recommended:
**I Ricchi**
1120 19th Street NW
Tel: 202-835-0459
Traditional Tuscan restaurant serving fresh, simple and hearty cooking. Bread, meat and fish cooked and grilled in the dining room's wood-burning stove. Wonderful sage and ricotta-stuffed tortellini, flavorful sauces for pastas and risottos, and excellent seafood. **$$**
**La Brasserie**
239 Massachusetts Avenue NE
Tel: 202-546-6066
The menu ranges from luxurious lobster to a variety of thick quiches to devilishly rich creme brulee. In warm weather, the terrace makes a nice backdrop to the gastronomic delights. **$$$**
**Market Lunch**
225 7th Street SE
Tel: 202-547-8444
It's no surprise there's a fight to get in here for Saturday breakfasts. The crabcakes and homemade bread are superb, and the prices are cheap. You have a better chance of getting a seat for a weekday lunch. Don't expect to pay with plastic. **$**
**Meskerem**
2434 18th Street NW
Tel: 202-462-4100

Try for a table on the top floor, with basket tables under a tented ceiling. Best with a large group, so that many dishes can be ordered. For two, try the combination platter to sample an array of items presented on *injera*, the curious gray, spongy sourdough pancake bread that is ripped off and used as the utensil for the food. **$$**

**Nora**
2132 Florida Avenue NW
Tel: 202-462-5143
Sometimes trying a little too hard to be original, Nora's is nonetheless worth a visit for its audacious balancing of seemingly incompatible ingredients, served in an intimate dining room (and outdoor dining area in clement weather). It declares its produce organic and biodynamic, but those bored by the thought need not expect a diminution of interesting flavors. **$$**

## SHOPPING

Shopping ranges from the downtown and Chevy Chase outlets of international fashion names, to small specialty shops located all over town and the glitzy new shopping complexes and malls that have mushroomed both in the center and in the suburbs. One of the most individual of these in design is the renovated **Old Post Office Pavilion** at 1100 Pennsylvania Avenue NW. A glass-enclosed elevator carries visitors to the Observation Tower for a magnificent view over the city. In **Georgetown**, along Wisconsin Avenue and M Street, are smaller specialty fashion and accessory boutiques, like **Hugo Boss**. Top European designers, such as **GianFranco Ferre, Giorgio Armani, Byblos**, and **Gucci** can be found at the **Watergate complex**, the **Mazza Galerie** mall in Chevy Chase and on **Wisconsin Avenue** at Chevy Chase. Upscale department store **Saks Fifth Avenue** is found at 2051 International Drive, McLean, VA. **Montgomery Mall** has undergone a complete overhaul to bring it up to the glitzy standard of the White Flint

Mall and Tyson's Corner. A mall that because it has more shopping outlets than there are days in the year also provides hotel accommodation, for those who *do* want to shop until they drop.

## VIRGINIA

### WHERE TO STAY

#### FRONT ROYAL
**Relax Inn**
1801 N. Shenandoah Avenue, VA 22620
Tel: 540-635-4101
Situated on the Shenandoah River 2 miles (1.6 km) from the entrance to the Shenandoah Parkway, all 20 guest rooms in this well-maintained older motel have double beds, bathtub, shower, refrigerator, microwave. There is a pool and pleasant picnic area. **$**

#### LURAY
**Shenandoah River Inn B&B**
201 Stagecoach Lane, VA 22835
Tel: 540-743-1144
US Freephone: 888-666-6760
Web: www.washingtonpost.com/yp/bandbriver
This former stagecoach inn has been welcoming guests since 1812. Located on the river with fine mountain views. Facilities include private baths, king/queen beds, screened porches, and gourmet breakfasts. Cabins available. **$$$**

**The Mimslyn**
401 West Main Street, VA 22835
Tel: 540-743-5105
A handsome hotel set high on a hill in its own grounds. Sweeping dining room, rooftop solarium and secluded nooks and crannies convey an elegance not reflected in the price. Suites also available. **$$**

#### NEW MARKET
**Blue Ridge Inn**
2251 Old Valley Pike, VA 22844
Tel: 540-740-4136
Pleasant with cable TV and refrigerators. **$**

#### SHENANDOAH NATIONAL PARK
For information about the park, Tel: 540-999-2243
Lodgings within the park are managed by:
**ARAMARK Services**
Shenandoah National Park
PO Box 727, Luray, VA 22835
Tel: 540-743-5108
US Freephone: 800-778-2851
Web: www.visitshenandoah.com

**Big Meadows Lodge**
Tel: 540-999-2221
(Open mid May – late October)
An attractive oak and chestnut structure, built in 1939, adjacent to the grassy 'big meadow'. Disabled access. **$$–$$$**

**Lewis Mountain Cabins**
Tel: 540-999-2255
Open May – October. These historical cabins are reasonable and ideal for families. Facilities include sheltered outdoor cooking, recreation area with fireplace and picnic table. Wheelchair accessible. **$–$$**

**Skyland Resort**
Tel: 540-743-5180
Open March – early December. At 3,680 feet (1,122 m), this resort is located at the highest point of Skyline Drive. Fabulous views from airy suites and rustic cabins. Disabled access. **$–$$**

#### STRASBURG
**Hotel Strasburg**
213 South Holiday St, VA 22657
Tel: 540-465-9191
US Freephone: 800-348-8327
Web: www.svta.org/thehotel
Massanhutten Mountain forms the backdrop for this former hospital, converted into a lovely hotel in 1915. Featuring creative Southern-style fine dining. **$$**

## WHERE TO EAT

### FRONT ROYAL
**Sandy's Place**
117 E. Main Street 22630
Tel: 540-635-2911
Good food and friendly service. **$**

### NEW MARKET
**Southern Kitchen**
Hwy 11
Tel: 540-740-3514
Great fried chicken and regional
favorites. **$**

## NORTH CAROLINA

### WHERE TO STAY

### ASHEVILLE
**Richmond Hill Inn**
87 Richmond Hill Drive, NC 28806
Tel: 828-252-7313
US Freephone: 888-742-4550
Fax: 828-252-8726
Web: www.richmondhillinn.com
This romantic 19th-century
mansion commands fine
panoramic views from atop a
wooded hill. Quiet, individual
cottages and Garden Pavilion
rooms with a library, croquet
court, porch rockers and fine
dining featuring an extensive wine
list. A peaceful haven. **$$$$**

### CHEROKEE
**Best Western Great Smokies Inn**
441 North and Acquoni, NC 28719
Tel: 828-497-2020
US Freephone: 800-528-1234
Fax: 828-497-3903
Well-fitted guest rooms and
suites. Pool, laundry, restaurant
and movies. Near area attractions.
**$$**

## WHERE TO EAT

### ASHEVILLE
**Blue Moon Bakery and Cafe**
60 Biltmore Avenue
Tel: 704-252-6063
A popular all-rounder. Above-
average sandwiches, pizzas,
desserts and breakfasts. **$**

## TENNESSEE

### WHERE TO STAY

### DANDRIDGE
**Barrington Inn**
1174 McGuire Road, TN 37820
Tel: 423-397-3368
US Freephone: 888-205-8482
Set on 24 wooded acres (10
hectares). The inn comprises seven
guest rooms with private baths and
several with wood-burning
fireplaces. Full breakfast. **$$**
**Mountain Harbor Inn**
1199 Hwy 139, TN 37725
Tel: 865-397-3345
Fax: 865-397-0264
Nicely decorated rooms, all
with breathtaking mountain
and lake views. Extras include
fluffy quilts, antiques and good
food. **$$**

### KNOXVILLE
**Maplehurst Inn Bed and Breakfast**
800 West Hill Avenue, TN 37902
Tel: 865-523-7773
Elegant rooms, and a secluded
penthouse with private balcony,
fireplace and Jacuzzi. Marble tubs,
full breakfast. **$$–$$$**
**Wyndham Garden Hotel**
208 Market Place Lane, TN 37922
Tel: 865-531-1900
Fax: 865-531-8807
Web: wyndham.com
A full service hotel featuring
spacious guest rooms, cable TV, an
exercise room, three whirlpool
rooms and a restaurant.
Complimentary breakfast is offered
on weekends. **$$**

### MEMPHIS
**The Bridgewater House B&B**
7015 Raleigh La Grange Road,
Cordova, 38018
Tel: 901-384-0080
Email: kmistilis@worldnet.att.net
This intimate B&B is housed in a
century-old former schoolhouse
shaded by 2 wooded acres (1
hectare) of mature oaks. Many
pampering extras including
bathrobes, down comforters, and
a full gourmet breakfast. Ceiling
fans, antiques and hardwood
floors. **$$**

## Restaurant Prices

Categories based on average
cost of dinner and a glass of
wine, before tip.
**$** = under $15
**$$** = up to $30
**$$$** = over $30

**Heartbreak Hotel**
3677 Elvis Presley Blvd, TN 38116
Tel: 901-332-1000
Web: www.heartbreakhotel.net
Opened in 1999, adjacent to Grace-
land, owned and operated by Elvis
Presley Enterprises, Inc. Features
in-room Elvis movies. Packages
include Graceland tours. **$$–$$$**
**The Peabody**
149 Union Avenue, TN 38103
Tel: 901-529-4000
Web: www.peabodymemphis.com
(see page 196) **$$$**

### NASHVILLE
**Fiddlers Inn**
2410 Music Valley Drive, TN 37214
Tel: 615-885-1440
One of the district's more
affordable options. Clean rooms,
cable TV and pool. **$$**
**The Hancock House**
2144 Nashville Park, TN 37066
Tel: 615-452-8431
A Colonial Revival c. 1851, fur-
nished with period antiques, private
baths and fireplaces. The inn also
has a well-fitted cabin and Jacuzzi
suite. Full breakfasts include french
toast and freshly baked biscuits.
Fine dining by reservation. **$$$**
**The Beaux Arts Hermitage Hotel**
Corner of 6 and UNN, TN 37201
Tel: 615-244-3121
(see page 193) **$$–$$$**
**Opryland Hotel**
2800 Opryland Dr, TN 37214-1297
Tel: 615-889-1000
A Music City extravaganza with
Vegas-Disney overtones. Showy and
very pricey. **$$$$**

### OAK RIDGE
**Garden Plaza Hotel**
215 South Illinois Ave, TN 37830
Tel: 423-481-2468
Fax: 865-481-2474
Spacious, attractive rooms with

coffee makers and refrigerators. The hotel has an exercise room, indoor/outdoor pools and whirlpools, restaurant and lounge. **$$**

### SEVIERVILLE
**Blue Mountain Mist Country Inn and Cottages**
1811 Pullen Road, TN 37862
Tel: 865-428-2335
Fax: 865-453-1720
Lovely rooms and cottages furnished with antiques in beautiful mountain scenery. **$$–$$$**
**Hostelling International – Great Smokey Mountains**
3248 Manis Road, TN 37862-8224
Tel: 423-429-8563
Basic hostel accommodations in a simple building. Amenities include kitchen, laundry, piano, bonfire/barbecue, bicycle rentals and mini-store. **$**

## Restaurant Prices

Categories based on average cost of dinner and a glass of wine, before tip.
**$** = under $15
**$$** = up to $30
**$$$** = over $30

## WHERE TO EAT

### COOKEVILLE
**City Square Cafe**
453 East Broad Street
Tel: 931-528-9120
Fine homestyle cooking. Great breakfasts. **$**

### KNOXVILLE
**Calhoun's**
400 Neyland Drive
Tel: 423-673-3355
Enjoy excellent barbecue ribs and a fine river view. **$**

### MEMPHIS
**Buntyn Restaurant**
3070 Southern Avenue
Tel: 901-458-8776
Glorious home-style southern food featuring catfish, fried chicken, chicken fried steak and savory vegetables. They pile it high and serve it hot – you couldn't want for

more – but by all means ask for a dessert anyway. **$**
**Cozy Corner Restaurant**
745 North Parkway
Tel: 901-527-9158
Succulent hickory-smoked barbecue sandwiches, ribs and chicken with tasty sides. **$**
**The Dixie Cafe**
4699 Poplar Avenue 38117
Tel: 901-683-7555
A great little place for Americana, serving old-fashioned food and with a nostalgic soda fountain. **$**

### NASHVILLE
**Loveless Cafe**
8400 Hwy 100
Tel: 615-646-9700
Authentic southern cooking served family-style. With a choice of first-class preserves, grits, ham and red-eye gravy, breakfast is a real treat. Generous portions and abundant atmosphere. **$**
**Peaceful Planet**
1811 Division
Tel: 615-327-0661
Undoubtedly peace and love on earth would somehow include Elvis and fried chicken most places in Nashville. Here it's simple healthy food in a casual setting. **$**
**The Wild Boar Restaurant**
2014 Broadway
Tel: 615-329-1313
Creative French cuisine and courteous, helpful service. Excellent wine list. **$$–$$$**

### OAK RIDGE
**Village Restaurant**
123 Central Avenue
Tel: 423-483-1675
Tasty and affordable home-style cooking. **$$**

### SEVIERVILLE
**Applewood Farm House**
240 Apple Valley Road
Tel: 423-428-1222
Very pleasant and reasonable family restaurant. **$**

## ARKANSAS

### WHERE TO STAY

### HAZEN
**Super 8**
I-40 (Exit 193), AR 72064
Tel: 501-255-3563
Standard budget motel with pool and laundry facilities. **$**

### HOT SPRINGS
**The Arlington Resort Hotel and Spa**
239 Central Avenue, AR 71902
Tel: 501-623-7771
Fax: 501-623-6191
Web: www.arlingtonhotel.com
This full-service resort has been pampering visitors since 1873. Facilities include an on-premises bath house with thermal water baths and massages, twin cascading heated pools, shops, restaurant and beauty salon. **$$**
**Wildwood 1884 B&B Inn**
808 Park Avenue, AR 71901
Tel: 501-624-4267
Web: www.bbonline.com/ar/gablesinn
Carefully restored 1884 Queen Anne mansion with original woodwork, antiques and stained glass. Some rooms have porches. **$$**

### LITTLE ROCK
**Capital Hotel**
111 West Markham St, AR 72201
Tel: 501-374-7474
Handsome Victorian hotel. **$$$**
**The Empress of Little Rock**
2120 Louisiana Street, AR 72206
Tel: 501-374-7966
Web: www.TheEmpress.com
Impressive Gothic Queen Anne house featuring elegant double stairway and tower with poker room. Gourmet breakfast. **$$$**
**Pinnacle Vista Lodge**
7510 Highway 300, AR 72223
Tel: 501-868-8905
Web: www.pinnaclevista.com
Log house situated at the foot of Pinnacle Mountain in 23 acres (9 hectares) of grounds. Country breakfast served indoors or on the deck. **$$$**

# WHERE TO EAT

## HOT SPRINGS

**McClard's**
505 Albert Pike
Tel: 501-624-9586
Serving savory, well-seasoned barbecue since 1908. **$**
**Miller's Chicken and Steak House**
4723 Central Avenue
Tel: 501-525-8861
Long-standing favorite for freshly cooked country-style food. **$$**

## LITTLE ROCK

**Doe's Eat Place**
1023 West Markham Street
Tel: 501-376-1195
Choice-cut steaks. Famed locally for its burgers. Funky atmosphere. **$$**
**Faded Rose Restaurant**
1615 Rebsamen Park Road
Tel: 501-663-9734
Steaks, burgers and Yankee grub. **$**
**Franke's**
300 South University
Tel: 501-666-1941
Few better places to sample southern cooking cafeteria-style. Savory and satisfying. **$**

## Hotel Prices

Categories based on average cost of a double room for one night.
**$** = under $65
**$$** = up to $100
**$$$** = up to $150
**$$$$** = over $150

## OKLAHOMA

### WHERE TO STAY

## BRISTOW

**Carolyn Inn**
HWY 66N at I-44 exit, OK 74010
Tel: 918-367-2299
Simple, clean rooms, some with whirlpool tub. **$**

## CHANDLER

**Lincoln Court Motel**
740 East First Street, OK 74834
Tel: 405-258-0200
A well-maintained vintage Route 66 motor inn. **$**

## CLAREMORE

**Motel Claremore**
812 E Will Rogers Blvd, OK 74017
Tel: 918-341-3254
Small, clean motel with seven two-bedroom units and free movies. **$**

## CLINTON

**Best Western Elk City**
2015 West Third Street, OK 73644
Tel: 580-225-1811
Fax: 580-225-1277
Good-sized rooms with cable TV/HBO. Free continental breakfast, pool and airport transportation. **$$**
**Best Western Tradewinds Courtyard**
2128 Gary Boulevard, OK 73601
Tel: 580-323-2610
Comfortable and friendly motel with pool, whirlpool, free movies and laundry facilities. Ask to see #215 – the Elvis Room – graced by the King on four occasions. **$**

## MIAMI

**Best Western Inn of Miami**
2225 E Steve Owens Blvd, OK 74354
Tel: 918-542-5600
This inn is set in landscaped grounds with many mature trees. Good-sized rooms with free cable and refrigerators. **$**

## OKLAHOMA CITY

**Best Western Saddleback Inn**
4300 SW Third Street, OK 73108
Tel: 405-947-7000
Fax: 405-948-7636
Pool, hot tub, sauna, fitness center, restaurant. **$$**
**Carlyle Motel**
3600 NW 39th Exp, OK 73112
Tel: 405-946-3355
Central with pool, TV and free movies. **$**
**Hampshire Inn**
3501 S Prospect, OK 73129
Tel: 405-672-1193
Clean, comfortable rooms. Pool. **$$**

## STROUD

**Skyliner Motel**
717 West Main Street, OK 74078
Tel: 918-968-9556
Comfortable well-kept Route 66 establishment dating from 1950. **$**

## TULSA

**Lexington Hotel Suites**
8525 E 41st Street, OK 74145
Tel: 918-627-0300
Fax: 918-627-0587
A very clean and tidy motor lodge; each room with its own kitchen. With 162 rooms, you should always be able to fit in somewhere. **$$$**
**McBirney Mansion B&B**
1414 S Galveston, OK 74127
Tel: 918-585-3234
An elegant and cozy (only 8 rooms) mansion on lovely landscaped grounds overlooking the Arkansas river. **$$$$**
**Ramada Inn Downtown Plaza**
17 West Seventh Street, OK 74112
US Freephone: 800-585-5101
Above-average motor inn. Very comfortable rooms and good facilities. Complimentary breakfast. Pool, exercise room. Close to area attractions. **$$**

## VINITA

**Park Hills Motel and RV Park**
Southwest of Vinita, OK 74301
Tel: 918-256-5511
Modest, clean and serviceable. **$**

## WEATHERFORD

**Best Western Mark Motor Hotel**
525 East Main, OK 73096
Tel: 580-772-8950
Well-fitted guest rooms including free full breakfast, morning paper, and cable TV/HBO, in-room coffee and refrigerator. **$**

# WHERE TO EAT

## AFTON

**Route 66 Cafe**
5 Northeast First Avenue
Pull in for decent roadside grub and pleasant atmosphere. **$**

## ARCADIA

**Hillbillee's Cafe**
206 East Hwy 66
Tel: 405-396-8177
Good food and interesting surroundings in this former Route 66 garage. **$**

## CATOOSA
**Molly's Landing**
Hwy 66, OK 74015
Tel: 918-266-7853
Steak and seafood in a log cabin by the river with the Blue Whale landmark. **$**

## CHANDLER
**Martha's Cafe**
600 North Price
Tel: 405-258-2382
Top quality steaks, hamburgers and sandwiches. **$**

## CLAREMORE
**Hammett House Restaurant**
1616 West Will Rogers Boulevard
Tel: 918-341-7333
Tasty, freshly prepared grub. **$**

## DEPEW
**Spangler's General Store**
322 Main Street
Tel: 918-324-5472
Classic Route 66 landmark serving good burgers and sandwiches. **$**

## EL RENO
**Robert's Grill**
300 North Bickford Avenue
Tel: 405-262-1262
Home of the unique Fried Onion Burger and creators of the World's Largest Hamburger – annually on Memorial Day. **$$**

## ERICK
**Cal's Country Cooking**
I-40 (Exit 7)
Tel: 580-526-3239
Cal's has welcomed road-weary customers for over half a century. **$**

## OKLAHOMA CITY
**Cattleman's Steakhouse**
1309 S Agnew Avenue
Tel: 405-236-0416
Excellent steaks served up a stone's throw from the stockyards. Relaxed atmosphere. **$$**
**Classen's Grill**
5124 N Classen
Tel: 405-842-0428
Emphasis on southwestern and midwestern fare with a few creative twists. Portions are abundant. **$$**

**Sleepy Hollow**
1101 Northeast 50th
Tel: 405-424-1614
Superlative home-style fried chicken dinners. A local legend. **$**

## SAPULPA
**Norma's Diamond Cafe**
408 North Mission
Tel: 918-224-5798
Legendary Mother Road pit-stop. **$**

## SAYRE
**Owl Drug Store**
115 Main Street
Tel: 918-485-8408
*(see page 209)* **$**

## TULSA
**Ollie's Station Restaurant**
41st and Southwest Boulevard
Tel: 918-446-0524
Fun place with good food and a dozen or so model trains chugging merrily around. **$**
**Rib Crib**
1607 South Harvard Avenue
Tel: 918-742-6327
Southwestern and American grub, specializing in barbecue ribs. **$**
**Warren Duck Club**
6110 S Yale Avenue
Tel: 918-497-2157
This club is on the dressy side of Tulsa, serving a healthy and well-prepared menu to the heirs of oil barons no doubt, and with wonderful views of the manicured lawns. **$$**

## VINITA
**Clanton's Cafe**
319 East Illinois Street
Tel: 918-256-9058
Classic Route 66 eatery. **$**

## YUKON
**Johnnie's Grill**
442 West Main Street
Tel: 405-354-2030
*(see page 206)* **$**

## TEXAS

### WHERE TO STAY

## AMARILLO
**The Big Texas Motel**
7701 I-40E, TX 79120

Tel: 806-372-5000
Old West themed motel with good, clean rooms and continental breakfast. **$**
**Sleep Inn Amarillo**
2401 i-40 E, TX 79104
Tel: 806-372-6200
Fax: 806-372-6242
Perhaps too literal a choice for some, this clean and typical motor inn will live up to its name and even let you shower en-suite. **$$**
**Travelodge West**
2035 Paramount Drive, TX 79109
Tel: 806-353-3541
US Freephone: 800-578-7878
Fax: 806-353-0201
Comfortable rooms. Indoor pool and workout facilities. **$**

## CONWAY
**Budget Host S&S Motor Inn**
I-40 and Hwy 207 (Rt 2, Box 58)
Panhandle, TX 79068
Tel: 806-537-5111
Standard motel rooms and restaurant. **$**

## Hotel Prices

Categories based on average cost of a double room for one night.
**$** = under $65
**$$** = up to $100
**$$$** = up to $150
**$$$$** = over $150

## CANYON
**Buffalo Inn**
300 23rd Street, TX 79015
Tel: 806-655-2124
Run-of-the-mill rooms, free movies and restaurant nearby. **$**

## SHAMROCK
**Texan Motel**
Old Hwy 66, TX 79079
Tel: 806-256-3569
Classic Route 66 motel. **$**

## VEGA
**Vega Motel**
1005 Vega Boulevard, TX 79092
Tel: 806-267-2205
Another good example of a vintage Route 66 motel. Worth a look and maybe an overnight stop. **$**

## WHERE TO EAT

### ADRIAN
**Adrian Cafe**
HWY 66, TX 79092
Tel: 806-538-6379
Typical ranch fare. Steak burgers and homemade pies. **$**

## Restaurant Prices

Categories based on average cost of dinner and a glass of wine, before tip.
**$** = under $15
**$$** = up to $30
**$$$** = over $30

### AMARILLO
**Big Texan Steak Ranch and Emporium**
7701 I-40E
Tel: 806-372-6000
If you can eat a 72 oz steak, plus side dishes, in under an hour you don't pay for it. More modest por-tions of beef, buffalo, rattlesnake, etc. also available. **zero–$$**
**Calico County**
2410 Paramount Boulevard
Tel: 806-358-7664
Famed for its outstanding customer service, you'll be treated like a king as the staff makes all the delicious food from scratch. **$**
**Santa Fe**
3333 Coulter Drive
Tel: 806-358-8333
A southwestern oasis for the health-conscious, providing wonderful Mexican decor and food without all the lard. **$**

### GROOM
**Chalet Inn**
I-40 FM 2300, TX 79039
Tel: 806-248-7524
Unexciting, but serviceable enough if you are in need of a break from the road. **$**
**Mitchell's Restaurant**
I-40 and Hwy 83
Tel: 806-256-3424
Generous portions of honest home-style cooking and an abundant salad bar. **$**

## NEW MEXICO

## WHERE TO STAY

### ALBUQUERQUE
**Hi Way House**
3200 Central SE, NM 87106
Tel: 505-268-3971
One of the last in the old Hi Way House chain seen frequently on the old Route 66. **$**
**Hyatt Regency**
330 Tijeras South West, NM 87102
Tel: 505-842-1234
Elegant and contemporary downtown hotel. Pool, fitness room, restaurant, bar. **$$–$$$**
**La Puerta Lodge**
9710 Central Ave SE, NM 87123
Tel: 505-229-1770
Adobe-style 1940s; fab sign. **$**
**La Posada de Albuquerque**
125 2nd Street N. West, NM 87102
Tel: 505-242-9090
US Freephone: 800-621-7231
Comfortable old-fashioned hotel with nice architectural touches dating from the 1930s. Restaurant and bar. **$$**
**El Vado Motel**
2500 Central SW, NM 87104
Tel: 505-243-4594
(see page 216) **$**

### GALLUP
**El Rancho Hotel and Motel**
1000 E. Highway 66, NM 87301
Tel: 505-863-9311
(see page 218) **$–$$**

### GRANTS
**Best Western Inns and Suites**
1501 E Santa Fe Ave, NM 87020
Tel: 505-287-7901
Fax: 505-285-5751
Scenic location and excellent facil-ities. The restaurant features south-western food and western decor, a sports bar, free full breakfast and newspaper, game room, fitness center, sauna and Jacuzzi. **$$**
**Leisure Lodge**
1204 E Santa Fe Ave, NM 87020
Tel: 505-287-2991
Time-honored Route 66 landmark. **$**

### LAS VEGAS
**Plaza Hotel**
230 Old Town Plaza, NM 87701
Tel: 505-425-3591
US Freephone: 800-328-1882
A fine historical hotel with attractive restaurant and saloon overlooking the Old Town Plaza. **$$**

### MILAN
**Crossroads Motel**
1601 Old W Highway 66
Tel: 505-587-9264
(see page 217) **$**

### SANTA FE
**Alexander's Inn**
529 East Palace Ave, NM 87501
Tel: 505-986-1431
US Freephone: 888-321-5123
Fax: 505-982-8572
For a bit of romance off Route 66, try this quiet, but central B&B in Santa Fe. The owners have lovingly cared for this cottage and it shows, with their attention to detail becoming your nurturing atmosphere. **$$$**
**La Fonda de Santa Fe**
100 E San Francisco St, NM 87501
Tel: 505-982-5511
US Freephone: 800-523-5002
Historic Pueblo Revival-style hotel on the Plaza rebuilt in 1919. Amenities: air conditioning, television, parking, pool, restaurant, bars, nightclub, some rooms with fireplaces, shops. **$$$–$$$$**
**El Rey Inn**
1862 Cerrillos Road, NM 87505
Tel: 505-982-1931
US Freephone: 1-800-521-1349
Nice rooms at a reasonable price. **$**
**St Francis**
210 Don Gaspar Ave, NM 87501
Tel: 505-983-5700
US Freephone: 800-666-5700
Delightful older hotel built in the 1920s, fully restored with period decor. Restaurant, bar. **$$–$$$**

### TUCUMCARI
**Blue Swallow Motel**
815 E Tucumcari Blvd, NM 88401
Tel: 505-461-9849
(see page 213) **$**
**Safari Motel**
722 E Tucumcari Blvd, NM 88401
Tel: 505-461-3642
(see page 213) **$**

## WHERE TO EAT

### ALBUQUERQUE
**Avalon Restaurant**
(see page 215) **$$**
**Assets Grill Brewing Company**
6910 Montgomery NE
Tel: 505-889-6400
Mixed ethnic cuisine in a lively country setting; great selection of beers and brew made in-house. **$**
**M & J Sanitary Tortilla Factory**
Tel: 505-242-4890
Authentic and filling Mexican dishes in a casual diner-like setting. **$**
**66 Diner**
1405 Central Avenue NE
Tel: 505-247-1421
Spiffy old-time diner on old Route 66 near the university. **$**

### GRANTS
**Golden 50s/Uranium Cafe**
West Santa Fe Avenue
Tel: 505-287-7540
Cafe with good grub. **$**
**Grant's Cafe**
932 E. Santa Fe Avenue
Tel: 505-285-6474
(see page 217) **$**
**El Jardin Restaurant**
319 West Santa Fe Avenue
Tel: 505-285-5231
(see page 217) **$$**
**Monte Carlo Restaurant**
721 West Santa Fe
Tel: 505-287-9250
(see page 217) **$$**

### LAS VEGAS
**Landmark Grill**
230 Old Town Plaza
Tel: 505-425-3591
Very good regional dishes. **$**

### SANTA FE
**Coyote Cafe**
132 West Water Street
Tel: 505-983-1615
American and New Mexican fare served in an imaginatively decorated site (a former bus depot); its popularity is partly due to the owner's cookbooks. **$$**
**Geronimo**
724 Canyon Road
Tel: 505-982-1500
1756 adobe with intimate dining rooms and near the town's art

## Restaurant Prices

Categories based on average cost of dinner and a glass of wine, before tip.
$ = under $15
$$ = up to $30
$$$ = over $30

galleries. Food is diverse and delicious. **$$–$$$**
**Natural Cafe**
1494 Cerrillos Road
Tel: 505-983-1411
Healthy and vegetarian menu served in a cozy, arty setting. **$**
**Tomasita's**
500 South Guadalupe Street
Tel: 505-983-5721
Spicy New Mexican dishes at the former Santa Fe Railroad terminal; popular, lively and informal. **$**
**Villa Fontana**
Highway 522
Tel: 505-758-5800
Gourmet northern Italian cuisine at a lovely country restaurant. **$$**

### SANTA ROSA
**Joe's Bar and Grill**
865 Will Rogers Drive
Tel 505-472-3361
Regional dishes and good salad bar. A Route 66 classic. **$**

## ARIZONA

### WHERE TO STAY

### FLAGSTAFF
**Hotel Monte Vista**
100 N San Francisco, AZ 86001
Tel: 520-779-6971
US Freephone: 800-553-2666
Very central older hotel. Pleasant, simple rooms and dormitory accommodation. Very central, but affordable. **$**
**Jeanette's Bed and Breakfast**
3380 E Lockett Rd, AZ 86004
Tel: 520-527-1912
Fax: 520-527-1713
Pouring all their energy into just four Victorian rooms, the attention shows from the hand-made soap to the romantic fireplaces. **$$$**

**The Weatherford Hotel**
23 North Leroux Street, AZ 86001
Tel: 520-774-2731
(see page 223) **$$–$$$**

### GRAND CANYON
For park information: PO Box 129, Grand Canyon, AZ 86023
Tel: 520-638-7888
Web: www.thecanyon.com/nps
All lodgings are managed by:
**Amfac Parks and Resorts**
14001 E Iliff, No. 600, Aurora, CO 80014
Tel: 520-638-2631 (same-day reservations)
Tel: 303-297-2757 (advance reservations)
**Bright Angel Lodge**
W. Rim Drive
Tel: 520-638-2631
Old rustic lodge and bungalows with simple accommodation. Restaurant and bar. **$$**
**Grand Canyon Lodge**
Bright Angel Point
Tel: 520-638-2611
Basic accommodations and cabins on the North Rim; open seasonally. With a restaurant and bar. **$$**
**El Tovar Hotel**
Grand Canyon National Park Lodges.
Tel: 520-638-2401, 303-297-2757
This century-old rustic lodge is on the edge of the South Rim. Restaurant, bar, some rooms with balcony. **$$$$**

### HOLBROOK
**Wigwam Village**
811 West Hopi Drive, AZ 86025
Tel: 520-524-3048
Time your journey for an overnight stop in Holbrook and head for Wigwam Village. A night in a 1950s concrete teepee is a quinessential Route 66 experience. **$**

### JEROME
**Inn at Jerome**
309 North Main Street, AZ 86331
Tel: 520-634-5094
A small, friendly inn occupying the 1899 Frontier-style Clinksdale Building. Compact rooms attractively furnished with period antiques. **$**

## Hotel Prices

Categories based on average cost of a double room for one night.
**$** = under $65
**$$** = up to $100
**$$$** = up to $150
**$$$$** = over $150

### KINGMAN
**Hill Top Motel**
1901 E Andy Devine Ave, AZ 86401
Tel: 520-753-2198
Pleasant, well-maintained hotel accommodation with pool. **$**

### OATMAN
**Oatman Hotel**
HWY 66, AZ 86433
Tel: 520-768-4408
Characterful adobe hotel. **$$**

### PEACH SPRINGS
**Hulapai Lodge**
PO Box 538, AZ 86434
Tel: 520-769-2230
Basic but comfortable accommodation popular with rafters going down the canyon. **$**

### SEDONA
**Graham Inn and Adobe Village**
150 Canyon Circle Drive, AZ 86351
Tel: 520-284-1425
Fax: 520-284-0767
Web: www.sedonasfinest.com
A stylishly furnished inn commanding spectacular views of the red rocks. In addition to the six de luxe guest rooms, there are four romantic *casitas* (cottages) with waterfall showers, bathroom fireplaces, and breadmakers. Includes early morning coffee, full breakfast, afternoon refreshments and evening snacks. **$$$$**
**Historic Route 66 Motel**
500 West Rt 66, AZ 86337
Tel: 520-422-3204
Nice clean rooms with queen-sized beds and coffee makers. **$**
**Quality Inn – King's Ransom**
771 Hwy 170, OK 86336
Tel: 520-282-7151
Comfortable and affordable. **$$**

### WILLIAMS
**Fray Marcos Hotel**
163 Grand Canyon Blvd, AZ 86046
Tel: 520-635-4010
*(see page 225)* **$$**
**El Rancho Motel**
617 East Rt 66, AZ 86046
Tel: 520-635-2552
Clean rooms with free movies. **$**

### WINSLOW
**The La Posada Hotel**
303 East Second Street, AZ 86047
Tel: 520-289-4366
*(see page 222)* **$$**

## WHERE TO EAT

### ASH FORK
**Route 66 Grill**
322 Lewis Avenue
Tel: 520-637-2224
*(see page 226)* **$**

### FLAGSTAFF
**Black Bart's Steak House and Musical Revue**
2760 E Buner Avenue
Tel: 520-779-3142
Oh go on, you know you want a big steak and some country music over your gravy and potatoes. Indulge. **$$**
**Cottage Place**
126 West Cottage Avenue
Tel: 520-774-8431
Best fine dining. **$$**
**Kathy's**
7 North San Francisco Street
Tel: 520-774-1951
Friendly place for breakfast or lunch. Vegetarian dishes. **$**

### HOLBROOK
**Joe and Angie's Cafe**
120 West Hopi Drive
Tel: 520-524-6540
Good Mexican dishes. **$**

### JEROME
**English Kitchen**
119 Jerome Avenue
Tel: 520-634-2132
Since 1899. **$–$$**

### SEDONA
**L'Auberge De Sedona Restaurant**
301 L'Auberge Lane
Tel: 520-282-7131
So good they named a whole street (well, lane) after it. Still the French cuisine at this elegant restaurant is top notch. **$$$**
**Shugrue's Hillside Grill**
671 Highway 179
Tel: 520-282-5300
A health-conscious American menu in the ideal Sedona setting, looking onto the mountains. **$$**

### WILLIAMS
**Rod's Steak House**
301 East Bill Williams Avenue
Tel: 520-635-2671
Much-loved Route 66 dining landmark. **$**
**Twisters**
417 East Route 66
Tel: 520-635-0266
*(see page 226)* **$**

### WINSLOW
**Falcon Restaurant**
1113 East Third Street
Tel: 520-289-2342
*(see page 222)* **$**

## SHOPPING

### ARIZONA
One of the leading New Age centers in the US, which is reflected in the number of shops scattered throughout the state selling crystals, dreamcatchers and so on.
**Arizona Craftwork**
Native American arts and crafts, baskets, jewelry, blankets and so on are available at: **Cameron Trading Post**, Highway 89N, approximately 4 miles (7 km) outside Flagstaff. **Navajo Arts and Crafts Enterprises**, off route 264 adjacent to Navajo Nation Inn.

## CALIFORNIA

### WHERE TO STAY

### CLAREMONT
**Claremont Inn**
555 West Foothills Blvd, CA 91711
Tel: 909-626-2411
Nice rooms, some with refrigerators. Exercise room and whirlpool. **$$**

## MONROVIA

**Aztec Hotel**
311 W. Foothill Blvd, 91016
Tel: 626-358-3231
*(see page 234)* **$$**

**Best Western Colorado River Inn**
2371 Needles Hwy, CA 92363
Tel: 760-326-4552
Fax: 760-326-4562
Spacious rooms and mini suites
with large-screen TVs/HBO,
microwaves and refrigerators. Very
nice indoor pool, sauna and Jacuzzi
area. Restaurant adjacent. **$$**

**Four Points Barcello**
**Hotel-Sheraton**
700 West Huntington Dr, CA 91016
Tel: 626-357-5211
Comfortable rooms, some
with laundry, refrigerators and
micro-waves. The hotel has a pool,
three spas, whirlpool, exercise
room, a restaurant and a lounge.
**$$**

## SAN BERNARDINO

**San Bernardino Hilton**
285 East Hospitality Lane,
CA 92408
Tel: 909-889-8391
Web: www.hilton.com
Luxurious rooms. Fine dining, pool
and whirlpool. **$$$**

**Wigwam Motel**
2728 N. Foothill Blvd 92408
Tel: 909-875-3005
*(see page 234)* **$$**

## VICTORVILLE

**Best Western Green Tree Inn**
14173 Green Tree Blvd, CA 92392
Tel: 760-245-3461
Bright and cheerful decor. Over-
looks an 18-hole championship
golf course. Some rooms have
refrig-erators. Pleasant dining
room. **$$**

## WHERE TO EAT

## AMBOY

**Roy's Café**
National Trails Hwy
Tel: 760-733-4355
*(see page 230)* **$$**

**Trails Restaurant**
2519 Huntington Drive
Tel: 626-359-2850

Another classic roadhouse on Route
66 journey, *c.*1953. **$**

## NEWBERRY SPRINGS

**Bagdad Café**
46548 National Trails Hwy
Tel: 619-257-3101
Decent cafe rechristened after the
Peter Adlon film of the same name
was shot here. **$**

## OAK HILLS

**Alfredo's Pizza and Restaurant**
251 West Base Line Street
Tel: 909-885-0218
Excellent pizzas. **$–$$**

**Magic Lamp Inn**
8189 Foothill Boulevard
Tel: 909-981-8659
Another 66 landmark. **$–$$**

**Summit Inn**
6000 Mariposa Road
Tel: 760-949-1313
*(see page 233)* **$$**

## Hub City:
## LOS ANGELES

### GETTING AROUND

### Public transportation
This major city is notorious for its
lack of public transportation,
although the new Metro Rail
system is slowly nearing
completion. The primary public
transportation available is the
Southern California Metropolitan
Transit Agency bus company,
which everyone calls the MTA. MTA
offers a discount of about 10
percent if you buy booklets of 10
tickets or more. For information
and schedules, Tel: 213-626-
4455, or see www.mta.net.
Southern California is still in the
early stages of implementing its
most ambitious public transit

plans for half a century which,
when completed, will link areas as
far apart as Los Angeles port of
Long Beach and Palmdale, 50
miles (80 km) north of the city.
The 400-mile (645 km) system of
light rail, subway and other
transportation facilities will not be
fully in place until 2010, although
Metro's Blue Line between Long
Beach and Pasadena is already in
operation as is part of the Metro
Red Line from downtown heading
towards Hollywood, North
Hollywood and Canoga Park; and
the Metro Green Line to El
Segundo. Passengers for Long
Beach board at Pico and Flower
streets for the one-hour trip, with
the last train from LA at 9pm and
the last train from Long Beach at
7.50pm. Check the phone number
or website above for up-to-date
bus and rail schedules.

**From the airport:** Public
transportation is found on LAX's
lower level, which is where arriving
passengers claim baggage. At this
level, there are stops for taxis, LAX
shuttles, buses, courtesy trams,
and vans in front of each airline
terminal. Information boards about
ground transport are located in all
the baggage claim areas and they
are very easy to understand.
Shuttles from the airport are
reasonably priced, the fare varies
depending on your destination.
Among the companies operating
24 hours a day are Prime Time
Shuttle, Tel: 310-641-5039; LA
Xpress, Tel: 310-641-8000; Best
Shuttle, Tel: 310-783-4500, The
Super Shuttle, Tel: 310-782-6600
or 800-554-3146. Hopping in a
taxi at LAX should be avoided if at
all possible. Los Angeles' cabs are
very expensive – more so than
most US cities – and are almost
never found driving the streets
looking for customers. Free shuttle
service is now provided to the
Metropolitan Transit Authority –
Metro Green Line Light Rail's
Aviation Station. Pick up is on the
Lower/Arrival level under the LAX
Shuttle sign. Check out the MTA
bus and Metro Rail routes and
schedules at www.mta.net.

### Private transportation

**Taxis:** Taxis are fairly expensive and you will rarely find them cruising the streets. Nevertheless, they can be ordered or found at airports, train stations, bus terminals and at major hotels.

Try: Yellow Cab Co, Tel: 213-808-1000 or UITD, Tel: 213-462-1088. The LA Checker Cab Co, Tel: 310-330-3720 also offers vans with wheelchair lifts. An average fare from the Los Angeles Airport to Downtown Los Angeles would be at least $30.

The most efficient way to get around Los Angeles is to rent a car. Rental agencies may be found at the airport, your hotel, or any car rental agency (check the *Yellow Pages* under "Automobile Renting.") Cars often can be delivered to you. Car rental companies all charge basically the same price.

Avis Tel: 800-831-2847;
www.avis.com
Budget Tel: 800-221-1203;
www.budgetrentacar.com
Hertz Tel: 800-654-3131;
www.hertz.com

---

## WHERE TO STAY

**Argyle**
8358 Sunset Boulevard
Tel: 323-654-7100
Fax: 323-654-9287
www.argylehotel.com
Sixty three rooms, mostly suites. Art Deco landmark, formerly the Sunset Tower and one-time home of Harlow, Gable, Monroe and Flynn. Restaurant, butler service, pool, fitness center. **$$$**

**Hotel Oceana**
849 Ocean Avenue, Santa Monica,
Tel: 310-393-0486
Fax: 310-458-1182
www.hoteloceana.com
Sixty three suites. Mediterranean-villa like, across from the ocean, a short walk to pier and promenade. Room service by Wolfgang Puck Café. Pool, laundromat, fitness center, car rental. **$$$**

**Los Angeles Marriott Downtown**
333 S Figueroa Street
Tel: 213-617-1133

US Freephone: 800-228-9290
Fax: 213-613-0291
www.marriott.com.
Luxury hotel with 469 rooms on 4 acres (1.6 hectares) of landscaped grounds, near Music Center and Dodger Stadium. Executive floor, health club, business center, valet parking, airport bus service, restaurants, pool, courtesy coffee, babysitting, foreign currency exchange. **$$$**

**Orchid Hotel**
819 S Flower Street
Tel: 213-624-5855
US Freephone: 800-874-5855
Fax: 213-624-8740
Sixty-three rooms. Cozy. Transportation to LAX. **$**

**Residence Inn Santa Clarita**
2532 The Old Road
Tel: 661-298-2800
Fax: 661-290-2802
www.residenceinn.com
Ninety suites, close to Magic Mountain, 20 miles (33 km) to Downtown LA. Free breakfast, room service, pool, exercise room, full kitchens, some fireplaces. **$$**

**Venice Beach House**
15 Thirtieth Avenue, Venice
Tel: 310-823-1966
Fax: 310-823-1842
Pretty B&B near the beach built in 1911. Nine rooms, full breakfast, some share bathrooms. **$$**

---

## WHERE TO EAT

Southern Californians dine out an average of two or three times a week and variety is one of the main reasons. The most prevalent ethnic food you'll encounter here is Mexican, but the Golden State has also been the birthplace of several culinary trends over the years, including Szechuan, sushi, and of course, California cuisine. The best-known of the celebrity chefs are Wolfgang Puck (Spago, Chinois on Main) and Joachim Splichal (Cafe Pinot), but in a place where achievement equals celebrity there are many others. The following list is a mere

sampling of some notable restaurants across the city.

**Ciudad**
445 S. Figueroa Street
Tel: 213-486-5171
Latin and Southwest cross in a wild way. From Salvadorean *pupusas* (corn meal puffs with cucumber *curtido* and mango *rocoto* sauce) to Colorado lamb steak with sweet-roasted *poblano* chili. Incredible desserts and liqueurs. The new darling of downtown. **$$$**

**Grand Central Market**
317 S Broadway
Tel: 213-624-2378
Bustling shoppers, neon signs and varied produce – a feast for the eyes. Stalls offer fish tacos and other cheap street food. **$**

**Jiraffe**
502 Santa Monica Blvd
Tel: 310-917-6671
Innovative California cuisine at this hip scene. Good wine list. Interesting open architecture. **$$$**

**Mandarin Deli**
727 N Broadway
Tel: 213-623-6054
Worth going Downtown to sample these great Chinese dumplings. **$**

**Musso & Frank's**
6667 Hollywood Boulevard
Tel: 323-467-7788
A menu of old faithfuls that's basically unchanged since it began eons ago when Hollywood giants could be seen through the gloom (some still can). **$$**

**A Thousand Cranes**
120 S Los Angeles Street
Tel: 213-253-9255
The classiest of three restaurants in the New Otani Hotel, this one overlooks the lovely third-floor garden. Refined Japanese cuisine with sushi and tempura bars and tatami rooms. **$$$**

## Restaurant Prices

Categories based on average
cost of dinner and a glass of
wine, before tip.
$ = under $15
$$ = up to $30
$$$ = over $30

## SHOPPING

For intrepid shoppers, southern
California can be right up there with
the big guns like Paris and Hong
Kong. A recent press report
released by the tourist bureau
claimed that the area is becoming
"the unofficial seamstress to the
casually clad masses." Much of the
high-class fashion, of course, can
be found along that glitziest

shopping street, Beverly Hills'
renowned **Rodeo Drive**. While
Rodeo has now become quite a
tourist trap, with more people
window shopping than buying, some
of the world-class shops along the
drive include **Chanel**, **Armani**,
**Ungaro**, **Alaia** and **Bottega Veneta**.
A trip down **Melrose Avenue** is
essential. First there's the **Pacific
Design Center** – The Blue Whale –
with its 200 designers' showrooms
at the corner of San Vicente, and
then there are several blocks of
raffish shops between **Croft** and **La
Brea**. Lively **Chinatown**, rife with the
aromas of herbs, dried fish,
ginseng, and ginger is the primary
source of Asian imports. Try **F. See
On Company**, 507 Chungking, for
teak furniture and porcelain; **Fongs**,
939 Chungking, for antiques,

cloisonne, figurines, handpainted
bottles; **Win Sun**, 951 Chungking,
for jade and opal jewelry. All three
are in the **Chungking Mall**. It
mustn't be forgotten that for mall
lovers, Southern California is a
shopper's Valhalla. One of the
Southland's most famous
landmarks, the outstanding former
Uniroyal tire plant beside the Santa
Ana Freeway in the City of
Commerce has re-emerged as the
**Citadel Outlet Collection**, an
enticing shopping plaza whose 42
stores spread around a tree-flanked
courtyard.
    Further afield, the San Fernando
Valley is renowned for its malls, the
most famous and biggest of which
are the **Glendale Galleria** (270
stores, www.glendalegallerica.com),
the **Northridge Fashion Center**

## Route 66

### STATE AND NATIONAL ORGANIZATIONS
**Ash Fork Tourist Center**
Old Route 66, Ash Fork,
AZ 86320
**California Historic Route 66
Association**
2117 Foothill Boulevard #66,
LaVerne, CA 91750
Tel: 562-997-9817
**Historic Route 66 Association of
Arizona**
PO Box 66, Kingman, AZ 86402
**Oklahoma Route 66 Association**
PO Box 21382, Oklahoma City, OK
74834
Tel: 405-258-0008
Web: www.nowka.com/ok66html
**Old Route 66 Association of
Texas**
PO Box 66, McLean, TX 79057
Tel: 806-267-2828
**National Historic Route 66
Federation**
PO Box 423, Dept S, Tujunga, CA
91043-0423
Tel/Fax: 818-352-7232
Web: www.national66.com/
**New Mexico Route 66
Association**
1415 East Central, Albuquerque,
NM 87106
Tel: 505-832-4087

### MUSEUMS
**California Route 66
Museum/Victorville**
16849 D Street, Route 66,
Victorville, CA 92392
Tel: 760-261-8766
**National Route 66 Museum**
PO Box 5, Pioneer and Third
Elk City, OK 73644
Tel: 580-225-2207
**Route 66 Hall of Fame**
Dixie Trucker's Home, I-55 and US
136, McLean, IL 61754
**Route 66 Museum**
2229 Gary Boulevard, Clinton, OK
73601
Tel: 580-323-7866
Email: Jhill@
of-history.mus.ok.us

### RADIO
**KBLU 560 AM** – Yuma, Arizona
(news and golden oldies).
**KIXE 940 AM** – Douglas, Arizona.
**KAVV 97.7 FM** – Benson, Arizona
(news and Country & Western).
**KRCY 105.9** – Arizona (1960s
pop).
**KNFT 102.9 FM** – Deming, New
Mexico (Country).
**KDAP 96.5 FM**
**Radio Sonora 101.3 FM** Sonora,
Mexico.

### PUBLICATIONS
*Behind the Wheel on Route 66*
by Howard Suttle (Data Plus!
1993)
*The Grapes of Wrath* by John
Steinbeck, (William Heinemann,
1939)
*A Guide Book to Highway 66* by
Jack D. Rittenhouse (Originally
published 1946, now published in
facsimile edition by the University
of Mexico Press)
*Guide to Historic Route 66 in
California* by Vivian Davies & Darin
Kuna (California Historic Route
Assn, 1994)
*Historic Route 66*, a hard-bound,
fold-out map (Global Graphics)
*Route 66: An Illustrated
Guidebook to the Mother Road*
by Bob Moore & Patrick
Grauwels. Pictures by Yannis
Argyropoulos (Roadbook
International, 1998)
*Route 66 Magazine* quarterly from
326 W. Route 66, Williams AZ
86046
*Route 66 Travelers Guide &
Roadside Companion* by Tom
Snyder (St Martin's Press, 1995)
*The Verse by the Side of the Road*
by Frank Rowsome, Jr. (Penguin
Books, 1965, 1990)

(212 stores), and the **Sherman Oaks Fashion Square** (140 stores). A little further afield, in addition to Orange County's **South Coast Plaza**, are the **Del Amo Fashion Square** in Torrance, the 200 specialty shops in a Mediterranean-village type atmosphere of Newport Beach's **Fashion Island**, 1045 Newport Center Drive.

# Southern Route

## Useful Addresses

**Atlanta tourist information**
Atlanta Convention and Visitors Bureau Center, 233 Peachtree Street, GA, 30303
Tel: 404-222-6688
**Georgia tourist information**
*(see page 392)*
**Alabama state tourist information**
Bureau of Tourism and Travel, 401 Adams Ave, Suite 126, Montgomery, AL 36104
US Freephone: 800-252-2262
Web: www.touralabama.org
**Mississippi tourist information**
**Louisiana tourist information**
Louisiana Office of Tourism, P.O. Box 94291, Baton Rouge, LA 70804-9291
Tel: 800-677-4082
Web: www.louisianatravel.com
**Texas tourist information**
*(see page 426)*
**New Mexico tourist information**
*(see page 426)*
**Arizona tourist information**
*(see page 426)*
**California tourist information**
*(see page 426)*

## Hub City: ATLANTA

### GETTING AROUND

#### Public transportation
**From the airport:** Hartsfield International, the second busiest in the country, is located 10 miles (16 km) from Downtown. Many hotels offer courtesy buses from the airport. Atlanta Airport Shuttle is one of several companies providing service into the city. A single ticket is under $10.
Public transportation in the metropolitan area includes buses and MARTA trains, sublimely safe, swift, reliable and clean.
**Rapid transportation/buses:** MARTA (Metropolitan Rapid Transit Authority) is a rapid-rail system comprising north–south and east–west lines intersecting at the main Five Points Station in downtown Atlanta. Stations are designated N, S, E, W or P, denoting their compass relationship to Five Points. (P represents the current single-station Proctor Creek Line.) The Hartsfield International Airport Station is designated Airport S7.
**National buses:** Greyhound operates from the depot at 81 International Boulevard NW, Atlanta, Tel: 800-231-2222
**National rail:** Amtrak trains run from Peachtree Station, 1688 Peachtree Street NW, Tel: 881-3062 or 800-872-7245

#### Private transportation
Atlanta – sprawling, suburban and subject to extremes of weather – is not ideally suited for extensive walking tours. Should you decide to explore by car instead, car rental agencies may be found at the airport, and/or downtown. Check the *Yellow Pages* for a full list of firms.
Avis Tel: 800-331-1212
Budget Tel: 800-527-0770
Hertz Tel: 800-654-3131
**Taxis:** Taxi and limousine companies are numerous. Ask at a hotel for assistance; hotels are always good places to find a taxi. Tel: 658-7600 for information regarding taxi companies and fares. These fares are approximate: flag falling, $1.50; each additional ⅛ mile 20 cents; waiting, $12 an hour. Typical fare: airport to Buckhead, $25. Airport to downtown, $15. Fares are subject to 6 percent tax.

### WHERE TO STAY

**Atlanta Marriott Marquis**
265 Peachtree Center Ave, GA 30303
Tel: 404-521-0000
Fax: 586-6299

This whale of a hotel is another John Portman beauty: the atrium lobby has a volume of 9.5 million cu. ft (269,010 cu. meters), and visitors feel they've entered the rib cage of some mythical beast. Pool, sauna, whirlpool, steam room, health club – all the perks. **$$$$**

**Holiday Inn at Lenox**
3377 Peachtree Road, GA 30326
Tel: 404-264-1111
Fax: 404-231-7061
Dwarfed by adjacent high rises, this modest hotel has cool views of Lenox Square and suburban greenery, 300 rooms with in-room cable and HBO films on TV, in-room safes and coffee-makers. **$$–$$$**

**Hostelling International – Atlanta**
223 Ponce de Leon Ave, GA 30308
Tel: 404-872-1042
Email: rsvp@mindspring.com
Located in the heart of downtown Atlanta. Amenities include kitchen, parking, games and courtyard. **$**

**Terrace Garden Inn**
3405 Lenox Road NE, GA 30326
Tel: 404-261-9250
Fax: 404-848-7391
Southern hospitality comes to mind here, especially towards guests. Some 364 recently renovated rooms and suites, a health & racquet center, three dining venues; Marta and Lenox Square just across the street. **$$$–$$$$**

**Westin Peachtree Plaza**
210 Peachtree Street, GA 30343
Tel: 404-659-1400
Fax: 404-589-7424
With its 1,068 pie-shaped rooms, this 72-story, circular high rise is an Atlanta landmark, and the tallest hotel in America to date. Designed by famed architect John Portman, the structure is a must-see for visitors, whether checking in or not. Small pets allowed. **$$$$**

## WHERE TO EAT

If for some reason you were to randomly parachute into Atlanta, odds are you would land on a restaurant – and a good restaurant at that. The following list is nothing if not extremely limited and idiosyncratic. You should not leave Atlanta without stopping in at The Varsity on Spring Street (the world's largest drive-in), or that Jimmy Dean – Ford Fairlane dream of a diner on Ponce de Leon Avenue, the **Majestic**. Don't miss that other paean to junk food, on "Ponce" as well, the **Krispy Kreme** donut shop. But the following list should be one to keep body and southern soul together. Other restaurant listings are glossed in the text, and ethnic eateries are covered in *Atlanta Magazine* and *Creative Loafing* listings. For those interested in the up-to-the-minute southern best, the magazine *Southern Living* is a great reference.

## Restaurant Prices

Categories based on average cost of dinner and a glass of wine, before tip.
**$** = under $15
**$$** = up to $30
**$$$** = over $30

**Anthony's**
3109 Piedmont Road NE
Tel: 404-262-7379
Surely Atlanta's "Belle of the Ball," from the first cocktail on the verandah through "Roasts Carved From Our Silver Chariot," and on to a chocolate soufflé. The setting is antebellum plantation home; the service is Anglo-Atlantan. (Yes, one of the owners does have a Sheffield accent.) Reservations urged. **$$$**

**Buckhead Diner**
3073 Piedmont Road (at East Paces Ferry Road)
Tel: 404-262-3336
If Anthony's represents the Old South, the Buckhead Diner represents the New. See and be seen here, and enjoy the glorified pizza, hamburgers, soft-shell crabs, onion rings and tarted-up southern icons such as Banana Cream Pie. It's all "down home" – if home has a pair of BMWs parked out back. **$$**

**Dante's Down the Hatch**.
3380 Peachtree Rd NE, Buckhead,
Tel: 404-266-1600, and
60 Upper Alabama St
Tel: 404-577-1800
Twenty-three years in Atlanta, Danté Stephensen's fine fondue cuisine (using only Australian beef), 18th-century sailing-vessel decor, live jazz (and live crocodiles in the moat) have been turning heads and returning patrons such as Jimmy and Rosalyn Carter, Burt Reynolds and William Buckley. Keep your strawberry frozen daiquiri glass as a souvenir. Reservations urged. **$$**

**The Dining Room**
Ritz-Carlton Hotel, Buckhead, 3434 Peachtree Road
Tel: 404-237-2700
This five-star, four-course gem is probably Atlanta's top restaurant. Fantastic wine list, a once-in-a-lifetime dining pleasure. **$$$**

**Kamogawa Japanese Restaurant**
3300 Peachtree Road
Tel: 404-841-0314
This three-peach jewel is said to be local resident Elton John's favorite bite in town. Stunningly authentic Japanese cuisine in four unique settings: the sushi bar; white-linen-draped tables overlooking the Nikko's splendid Japanese garden; the teppanyaki grill; private tatami rooms. Reservations urged. **$$$**

**The Varsity**
61 North Avenue
Tel: 404-881-1706
One of Atlanta's most famous restaurants, a drive-in burger-and-Coke joint. Take antacid tablets before ordering the chili dogs, onion rings, fried fruit pies or fluorescent orange shake. **$**

## GEORGIA

### WHERE TO STAY

*LA GRANGE*
**Amerihost Inn**
107 Hoffman Drive, GA 30241
Tel: 706-885-9002
Fax: 706-885-1977
Web: amerihostinn.com
Pleasant rooms with continental breakfast and morning newspaper. Indoor pool, whirlpool suites. Close to shops and restaurants. **$**

## MACON

**1842 Inn**
353 College Street, GA 31201
Tel: 912-741-1842
Fax: 912-741-1842
A historic bed-and-breakfast.
Features 19th-century ambiance
with 21st-century perks. Some of
the 21 units have fireplaces and
whirlpool baths. **$$$$**
**Best Western-Riverside**
2400 Riverside Drive, GA 31204
Tel: 912-743-6311
Fax: 912-743-9420
A 125-unit motor inn with pool. **$**
**Courtyard by Marriott**
3990 Sheraton Drive, GA 31201
Tel: 912-477-8899
Pay movies, heated pool, exercise
room, 108 units. No pets. **$$**

---

### WHERE TO EAT

*JACKSON*
**Buckner Family Restaurant and**
**Music Hall**
I-75
Tel: 770-775-6150
Enjoy marvelous home-style
suppers with gospel music. **$**

*JULIETTE*
**Whistle Stop Cafe**
443 McCrackin Street
Tel: 912-994-3670
*(see page 250)* **$**

## ALABAMA

### WHERE TO STAY

*ATMORE*
**Royal Oaks**
5415 Hwy 21N, AL 36502
Tel: 334-368-8722
French-style country inn in a lovely
peaceful setting. **$$**

*BAYOUR LA BATRE*
**Best Western Bayou La Batre Inn**
13155 N Wintzell Ave, AL 36509
Tel: 334-824-2020
Fax: 334-824-1153
Close to the beach with 40
comfortable rooms. Continental
breakfast, pool, microwaves and
refrigerators. Hot tubs in some
rooms. Restaurant adjacent. **$**

## EVERGREEN

**Evergreen Inn**
I-65 and Hwy 83 (Mail: Rt 2 393-B),
AL 36401
Tel: 334-578-5500
Fax: 334-578-5168
Clean and comfortable. **$–$$**

*MOBILE*
**Riverhouse**
13285 Rebel Rd, Theodore,
AL 36590
Tel: 334-973-2233
US Freephone: 800-552-9791
Email: riverhsbb@aol.com
Designer house just south of
Bellin-grath Gardens. Light and
airy with its simple furnishings
and many glass doors. In-ground
hot tub. **$$$**
**Malaga Inn**
359 Church Street, AL 36602
Tel/Fax: 334-438-4701
US Freephone: 800-531-5900
This unique downtown inn is
set in a gas-lit courtyard.
The rooms are nicely decorated
and many feature hardwood floors.
**$$**
**Towle House**
1104 Montauk Avenue, AL 36602
Tel: 334-432-6440
US Freephone: 800-938-6953
Fax: 334-433-4381
A handsome Victorian home
situated in Mobile's historic
district. Gourmet breakfast
and evening cocktails are
included. **$$**

*MONTGOMERY*
**Lattice Inn**
1414 South Hull Street, AL 36104
Tel: 334-832-9931
US Freephone: 800-525-0652
Fax: 334-264-0075
A thoughtfully restored,
peaceful inn set in the Garden
District. **$$**
**Red Bluff Cottage**
551 Clay Street, AL 36104
Tel: 334-264-0056
US Freephone: 888-551-2529
Fax: 334-263-3054
A cottage with gazebo and
large porch commanding
excellent views of the Alabama
River and State Capitol. Pretty
rooms. **$$**

### WHERE TO EAT

*MOBILE*
**Dew Drop Inn**
1808 Old Shell Road
Classic American chili dogs and
chili cheeseburgers. **$**
**Roussos**
166 South Royal Street
Tel: 334-433-3322
Roussos is in the first rank of many
Mobile seafood restaurants. **$$**

*MONTGOMERY*
**Farmers Market Cafe and Pit** BBQ
315 North McDonough Street
Tel: 334-262-1970
They come in droves to this vast
and clamorous cafeteria for
excellent southern-style barbecue
and set-you-up breakfasts. **$**
**Moses Crawford Catering**
700 Columbus Street
Tel: 334-265-3520
Satisfying soul food in laid-back
atmosphere. **$**

### Hotel Prices

Categories based on average
cost of a double room for one
night.
**$** = under $65
**$$** = up to $100
**$$$** = up to $150
**$$$$** = over $150

## MISSISSIPPI

### WHERE TO STAY

*BILOXI*
**Father Ryan House**
1196 Beach Boulevard, MS 39530
Tel: 228-435-1189
US Freephone: 800-295-1189
Fax: 228-436-3063
Email: frryan@frryan.com
Formerly the home of Father Abram
Ryan, Poet Laureate of the
Confederacy. This 1841 beachfront
house has been converted into a
romantic inn. Spectacular views
from some of the rooms. *Travel
and Leisure* declares it to be
amongst "the best beachfront
resorts in the country. Disabled
access. **$$$**

### GREEN OAKS
580 Beach Boulevard, MS 39530
Tel: 228-436-6257
This elegant home was built on a
Spanish land grant in 1826. Now a
mellow inn graced with heirlooms
and surrounded by mature trees.
Full gourmet breakfast. **$$$**

### GAUTIER
**The Villas of Hickory Hill**
7900 Martin Bluff Road, MS 39553
Tel: 228-497-5150
US Freephone: 800-568-3155
Fax: 228-497-6427
Wheelchair-accessible rooms, pool,
exercise and game rooms, lounge.
**$$**

### GULFPORT
**Best Western Beach View Inn**
2922 West Beach Blvd, MS 39501
Tel: 228-864-4650
US Freephone: 800-748-8969
Fax: 228-863-6867
Very pleasant seafront hotel with
pool, lounge, free newspaper, guest
laundry, lounge and wheelchair-
accessible rooms. **$$**
**Crystal Inn**
9379 Canal Road, MS 39503
Tel: 228-822-9600
Fax: 228-822-0666
Attractive rooms and excellent
facilities including complimentary
hot breakfast, pool, spa. Close to
Gulf beaches and casinos. **$$$**

### LONG BEACH
**Red Creek Inn Vineyard and
Racing Stable**
7416 Red Creek Road, MS 39560
Tel: 228-452-3080
US Freephone: 800-729-9670
A late 19th-century French cottage
surrounded by 11 wooded acres
(4.5 hectares). The inn is fitted with
antiques, old-fashioned wooden
radios and porch swings. Generous
continental breakfasts. **$$$**

### PASS CHRISTIAN
**Harbour Oaks Inn**
126 West Scenic Drive, MS 39571
Tel: 228-452-9399
US Freephone: 800-452-9399
Fine views of the historic harbor and
beach from this elegant inn's porch
and second-story verandah. Five

rooms with private baths, a guest
kitchen and billiard room. Southern
breakfast included. **$$**

## Restaurant Prices

Categories based on average
cost of dinner and a glass of
wine, before tip.
**$** = under $15
**$$** = up to $30
**$$$** = over $30

## WHERE TO EAT

### BILOXI
**Fisherman's Wharf**
315 Beach Boulevard
Tel: 601-436-4513
Superb fresh fish in casual
surroundings. **$**

### GULFPORT
**Chappy's Seafood**
624 East Beach Boulevard
Tel: 228-865-9755
Popular restaurant with some
interesting regional specialties. Try
the frogs legs with a side order of
fried green tomatoes. **$**

### PASCAGOULA
**La Font Inn**
2703 Denny Avenue
Tel: 228-762-7111
Reliable steak and seafood
restaurant overlooking swimming
pool. Excellent prime rib. **$$**

## LOUISIANA

## WHERE TO STAY

### ABBEVILLE
**Sunbelt Lodge**
1903 Veterans Memorial Dr,
LA 70510
Tel: 318-898-1453
Standard rooms with free
continental breakfast, cable TV and
HBO. Near shops and restaurants.
The lodge has a pool and
wheelchair-accessible rooms. **$**

### BATON ROUGE
**Radisson Hotel and Conference
Center**
4728 Constitution Ave, LA 70808

Tel: 225-925-2244
Fax: 225-930-0140
www.radison.com/batonrougela
Attractive, comfortable rooms.
Amenities include: health club,
laundry, pool, restaurant and free
airport transportation. **$$$**
**The General Lafayette**
427 Lafayette Street, LA 70802
Tel: 225-387-0421
Basic rooms at reasonable rates. **$**

### BREAUX BRIDGE
**Bayou Cabins**
100 Mills Ave, Hwy 94, LA 70517
Tel: 318-332-6258
Atmospheric 19th-century Cajun
cabins with porches overlooking
Bayou Teche. **$**

### EUNICE
**The Seale Guesthouse**
125 Seale Lane, LA 70535
Tel: 318-457-3753
www.angelfire.com/lq2/guesthouse
Pretty guest house in tranquil
wooded grounds with large front
porch. Six rooms tastefully
decorated with antiques. **$$**

### LAFAYETTE
**Bois des Chênes**
338 North Sterling Drive, LA 70501
Tel: 318-233-7816
Lovingly converted Plantation
carriage house close to the city
center. Breakfast included. **$$**
**Lafayette Hilton and Towers**
1521 Pinhook Road, LA 70503
Tel: 318-235-6111
Fax: 318-261-0311
Luxurious rooms, some with views
of Vermillion Bayou. Pool, exercise
facilities, spa. **$$$$**

### NEW ORLEANS
**Bourbon Orleans**
717 Orleans Street, LA 70116
Tel: 504-523-2222
Fax: 504-525-8611
Web: www.bourbonorleans.com
Queen Anne furnishings and
marble baths. Phones and mini-
TVs are among the amenities in
this French Quarter hotel built
around an outdoor courtyard
where cabanas encircle the pool.
Rooms with balconies overlook
Bourbon Street, but it is quieter on

## Hotel Prices

Categories based on average cost of a double room for one night.
**$** = under $65
**$$** = up to $100
**$$$** = up to $150
**$$$$** = over $150

the courtyard side. Restaurant and lounge. **$$$$**

**Chateau Hotel**
1001 Chartres Street, LA 70130
Tel: 504-524-9636
Fax: 504-524-9636
A small, tastefully furnished motel with a charming courtyard, located in the residential Lower Quarter – a good choice for budget travelers. **$**

**Hostelling International – Marquette** 2253 Carondelet Street, LA 70130
Tel: 504-523-3014
The nation's fourth-largest youth hostel is set in a complex of century-old buildings one block from St Charles Avenue. There are dormitory rooms with bunk beds, private rooms and apartments. **$**

**Lafayette Hotel**
600 St Charles Avenue, LA 70130
Tel: 504-524-4441
www.neworleans.collection.com
A small gem, the very Gallic Lafayette's beautiful rooms have minibars, ottomans, easy chairs and bookshelves. Many have four-posters, and some on St Charles Avenue open on to balconies – great during Carnival season. **$$$**

**Le Richelieu**
1234 Chartres Street, LA 70116
Tel: 504-529-2492
Fax: 504-524-8179
This lovely 88-room hotel, consid-ered by many the best bargain in town, is in a restored macaroni fac-tory and 19th-century row of houses in the Lower Quarter. Large rooms are individually decorated, with balconies, brass ceiling fans and fridges. Paul McCartney stayed in one of the suites while cutting an album. **$$**

### OPELOUSAS
**Best Western of Opelousas**
1635 I-49 Service Road, LA 70570
US Freephone: 888-942-5540
Comfortable modern inn offering free continental breakfast, coffee and morning newspaper. Pool, cable TV. Disabled access. **$$**

### ST MARTINVILLE
**The Old Castillo Hotel**
220 Evangeline Blvd, LA 70582
Tel: 318-394-4010
Fax: 318-394-7983
Email: phulin@worldnet.att.net
Beautiful historic inn with excellent restaurant on Bayou Teche. **$$**

---

# WHERE TO EAT

### ABBEVILLE
**Black's Oyster Bar**
311 Pere Merget Street
Tel: 318-893-4266
Plump, fresh oysters – on the half shell, fried or po' boy style (tucked into crusty white bread). **$**

**Dupuy's Oyster Shop**
108 South Main Street
Tel: 318-893-2336
Highly acclaimed oyster and seafood restaurant. Since 1869. **$**

### BATON ROUGE
**Drusilla Seafood Restaurant**
3482 Drusilla Lane
Tel: 225-923-0896
Local favorite for seafood, steaks, Cajun food. Good atmosphere. **$**

### BREAUX BRIDGE
**Mulate's Restaurant**
325 Mills Avenue
Tel: 318-332-4648
Email: mulates@1stnet.com
Wildly popular Cajun food and music spot. **$$**

### EUNICE
**Ruby's Cafe**
221 West Walnut Avenue
Tel: 318-457-2583
Generous portions of well-flavored Cajun food for next to nothing. **$**

### LAFAYETTE
**Dean O's**
305 Bertrand Drive
Tel: 318-233-5446
Superb pizzas. **$**

**Old Tyme Grocery**
218 West St Mary Boulevard
Tel: 318-235-8165
Sample the famed po' boy sandwich. Crusty, fragrant white bread and an array of meat fillings. **$**

**Prudhomme's Cajun Café**
4676 North East Evangeline Thwy, Carencro
Tel: 318-896-1026
Excellent fried seafood. **$**

### NEW ORLEANS
New Orleans' extraordinary range of food includes everything from haute cuisine and Bananas Foster to blackened catfish and Creole soul. Unless it is otherwise noted in the description with words like "casual" or "informal", men are requested to wear a jacket and tie in the restaurants listed.

**Alex Patout's**
221 Royal Street, French Quarter
Tel: 504-525-7788
Fax: 504-525-7809
The chef-owner comes from a long line of Cajun culinary artists in South Louisiana. His stylish restaurant showcases seafoods enhanced by exotic sauces and seasonings. Fixed-price menus for lunch and dinner; reservations recommended for dinner; closed for lunch on weekends. **$$**

**Antoine's**
713 St Louis Street, French Quarter
Tel: 504-581-4422
Fax: 504-581-3003
This well-known French Creole restaurant has been run by the same family since 1840. Famous dishes such as Oysters Rockefeller originated at Antoine's. Many dishes are sensational, especially the Baked Alaska. **$$$**

**Camellia Grill**
626 S. Carrollton Avenue, Uptown
Tel: 504-866-9573
A New Orleans institution, the Camellia is famed for its burgers, waffles, chili and delicious pastries. Sometimes there is a wait. **$**

### OPELOUSAS
**Palace Cafe**
167 West Landry Avenue
Tel: 318-942-2142
A long-established Opelousas
favorite excelling in gumbo and
other Louisiana seafood staples. **$**

### ST MARTINVILLE
**Clambeaugh's Restaurant**
111 North Main
Tel: 318-394-8001
Creole cuisine in the historic district
bordering St Martin de Tours. **$**
**Josephine's Creole Restaurant**
830 South Main Street
Tel: 318-394-8030
Bona fide Creole and Cajun cooking
using time-honored family recipes.
Informal atmosphere. **$$**

## Restaurant Prices

Categories based on average
cost of dinner and a glass of
wine, before tip.
**$** = under $15
**$$** = up to $30
**$$$** = over $30

## SHOPPING

### Baton Rouge
**Mall of Louisiana**
6401 Bluebonnet Boulevard

### Lafayette
**Cajun Country Store**
401 East Cypress Street

### New Orleans
Royal Street is the place for
antiques, although the entire town
is great for shopping. Buy candy,
Carnival souvenirs or spices.

## TEXAS

## WHERE TO STAY

### ALPINE
**Sunday House Motor Inn**
E Hwy 90 (PO Box 578), TX 799831
Tel: 915-837-3363
US Freephone: 800-510-3363
Clean rooms, 24-hour restaurant,
club and pool. Rail station, bus and
airport shuttle available. **$**

### AUSTIN
**Austin Motel**
1220 S. Congress, TX 78704
Tel: 512-441-1157
Fax: 512-444-1157
Very central and a few blocks south
of Town Lake. Restaurant,
Laundromat, pool, spa, video rental
and library. **$**
**Driskill Hotel**
604 Brazos, TX 78701
Tel: 512-474-5911
US Freephone: 800-252-9367
Fax: 512-474-2214
Historic downtown landmark.
Includes workout facilities, suites
and a bar. **$$$**

### BANDERA
**Silver Spur Guest Ranch**
PO Box 1657, TX 78003
Tel: 210-796-3037
The ranch offers stone cottages in
the Hill Country outside San
Antonio. Amenities: horseback
riding and instruction, hayrides,
cookouts, pool, entertainment. **$**

### BIG BEND NATIONAL PARK
For park information, Tel: 915-477-
2251
Lodgings within the Park are
managed by: National Park
Concessions, Inc.
**Casa Grande**
Modern units with private balconies
overlooking the ruggedly beautiful
surrounding mountains. **$$**
**Chisos Mountain Lodge**
Tel: 915-477-2291
The lodge comprises four types of
accommodations:
**Lodge Units**
Situated on a wooded hillside in the
Chisos Basin. The lodge rooms are
equipped with private baths, ceiling
fans and electric wall heaters.
There is a common outlook porch
on each level of the building. **$$**
**Motel**
Comfortable rooms in one-story
units with mountain views and a
common porch. **$$**
**Stone Cottages**
Six historic stone cottages perched
on the Basin that can sleep up to a
maximum of seven. All cottages
have private baths, electric wall
heaters and large porches. **$$**

### CASTROVILLE
**Landmark Inn**
402 Florence Street, TX 78009
Tel: 830-931-2133
Fax: 830-538-3858
Originally a mail stop on the old
road to California and a hotel since
1870. Located in a state historical
park with good bird- and butterfly-
watching. The comfortable, simply
furnished rooms have been taken
back to their 1940s construction, a
few with private bathrooms. Very
good value. **$**

### COLUMBUS
**Columbus Inn**
2208 Hwy 71S, TX 78934
Tel: 409-732-5723
Fax: 409-732-60084
Standard motel rooms, some with
refrigerators. Amenities include pool
and laundry facilities. **$**

### CRYSTAL CITY
**Casa de Lorenzo Motel**
1800 Hwy 83N, TX 78839
Tel: 830-374-3483
Pleasant motel with restaurant,
playground, fitness and laundry
facilities. **$**

### EL PASO
**Camino Real Paso del Norte Hotel**
101 South El Paso St, TX 79901
Tel: 915-534-3000
Handsome and sophisticated
border hotel with some parts dating
to 1912. Pool, sauna and excellent
bar and restaurant. **$$$**
**Hostelling International –
Gardner Hotel**
311 East Franklin Ave, TX 79901
Tel: 915-532-3661
Fax: 915-532-0302
Email: epihost@whc.net
Housed in the landmark Gardner
Hotel. Amenities include kitchen,
equipment storage, laundry and
lockers. A few private rooms are
also available. No curfew. **$**

### FREDERICKSBURG
**Best Western Sunday House Inn**
501 E. Main, TX 78624
Tel: 830-997-4484
Efficient, popular hotel with clean
rooms. Offers breakfast coupons
for nearby Sunday Haus Café. **$$**

## Hotel Prices

Categories based on average cost of a double room for one night.
$ = under $65
$$ = up to $100
$$$ = up to $150
$$$$ = over $150

**Dietzel Motel**
909 W. Main (Jct. 290W and 87N), TX 78624
Tel: 830-997-3330
Simple and well-maintained rooms 1 mile (1.6 km) west of town center. $

### GALVESTON
**Gaido's Seaside Inn**
3828 Seawall, TX 77550
Tel: 409-762-9625
Fax: 409-762-4825
Many rooms have a seaview. There is also a tiered flower garden. $
**Hilltop Motel**
8828 Seawall Boulevard, TX 77554
Tel: 409-744-4423
Forty units. Gulf view rooms have private balconies. $

### HONDON
**Whitetail Lodge**
Hwy 90E (PO Box 110), TX 78861
Tel: 830-426-3031
Fax: 830-426-8662
Comfortable, well-maintained lodge with restaurant nearby. Free continental breakfast $

### HOUSTON
**Sara's Bed & Breakfast Inn**
941 Heights Boulevard, TX 77008
Tel: 713-868-1130, 800-593-1130
Fax: 713-868-1160
Victorian mansion with 14 rooms; VCRs and video library available. $$

**St Regis**
1919 Briar Oaks Lane, TX 77027
Tel: 713-840-7600
US Freephone: 800-241-3333
Fax: 713-840-0616
Luxury accommodation, including 52 suites adjacent to the exclusive River Oaks neighborhood. The Astro Floor features maître d' and butler service. Interpreters. $$$$

**Hostelling International – Houston International Hostel Inc.**
5302 Crawford, TX 77004
Tel: 713-526-8618
Pleasant house with tree-shaded porch, courtyard and gazebo. Close to NASA and other attractions. Facilities include kitchen, piano, laundry and bicycles. $
**The Westin Galleria**
5060 W Alabama, TX 77056
Tel: 713 960-8100
US Freephone: 800-228-3000
Fax: 713-960-6554
Stylish hotel in Galleria mall. Superb facilities, including ice rink, pool, restaurant, and gym. $$$

### JOHNSON CITY
**Save Inn Motel**
107 Hwy 281 and 290S (PO Box 610), TX 78636
Tel: 830-868-4044
Fax: 830-868-7822
Tidy, well-fitted rooms fitted with coffee makers. Pool. $–$$

### LAJITAS
**Lajitas on the Rio Grande**
Star Rt 70, Box 400, Terlingua, TX 79852
Tel: 915-424-3471
Fax: 915-424-3277
Web: www.lajitas.com
A reconstructed frontier town with spectacular mountain backdrop. On the edge of Big Bend National Park. The resort features an Old West hotel and saloon, pool, barbecues, float trips on the Rio Grande and Country and Western dancing. $$

### MARATHON
**Gage Hotel**
PO Box 46, Marathon, TX 79842
Tel: 915-386-4205
Built as a private lodge by rancher Alfred Gage in the 1920s, this charming little hotel, a Texas Historical Landmark, is replete with western antiques; a modern adobe building was added in the early 1990s. Amenities: air conditioning, restaurant, pool, shared baths, some fireplaces. $–$$

### NEW BRAUNFELS
**Gruene Mansion Inn**
1275 Gruene Road, TX 78130
Tel: 830-629-2641
Fax: 830-629-7375
Former cotton plantation home, with 25 rooms with antiques scattered in restored barns and sheds. Overlooks Guadalupe River, and is adjacent to Greune Hall, the oldest dance hall in Texas. $$$

### MARFA
**Arcón Inn**
215 North Austin, 79843
Tel: 915-729-4826
Fax: 915-729-3391
Email: arconinn@iglobal.net
This century-old adobe home has been an inn since the 1950s. The interior is a unique blend of Victorian and southwestern styles. Full southwestern breakfast and dinner by reservation. $$$

### PRESIDIO
**Three Palms Inn**
Old Hwy 67N, TX 79845
Tel: 915-229-3211
Well-kept motor inn with pool, cable. $

### SAN ANTONIO
**The Historic Menger Hotel**
204 Alamo Plaza, TX78205
Tel: 210-223-4361
US Freephone: 800-345-9285
Fax: 210-270-0761
Built in 1859 and located across from the Alamo. Several rooms have Jacuzzis and are furnished with antiques. Bar, Colonial Room restaurant, spa and fitness center. $$$–$$$$
**La Mansion del Río**
112 College, TX 78205
Tel: 210-25-2581
Fax: 210-226-0389
Spanish mission architecture on quiet portion of Paseo del Río. Interpreters. $$$
**Oge House on the Riverwalk**
209 Washington Street, TX 78204
Tel: 210-223-2353
Fax: 210-226-5812
An 1857 antebellum mansion with exquisite antiques. $$$

## TERILINGUA
**Big Bend Motor Inn**
PO Box 336, TX 79852
Tel: 915-371-2218
Fax: 915-371-2555
Minutes from the entrance to Big
Bend National Park, this inn offers
comfortable rooms with mountain
views, some with refrigerators and
microwaves. Pool. **$$**

## VAN HORN
**Best Western Americana Inn**
1309 Broadway, TX 79855
Tel: 915-283-2030
US Freephone: 800-621-2478
A welcome stop if you need a break
from the road. Free continental
breakfast, pool and cable TV/HBO.
Some rooms have fridges. **$**

## Restaurant Prices

Categories based on average
cost of dinner and a glass of
wine, before tip.
**$** = under $15
**$$** = up to $30
**$$$** = over $30

## WHERE TO EAT

Don't plan on dieting while in Texas.
Texans love their food, and a visit
here wouldn't be complete without
sampling a good portion of it. Tex-
Mex food has become synonymous
with the state, and it's not all fire-
breathing hot, so even the most
wary should give it a try. Another
Texas staple is the barbecue,
usually huge chunks of beef (but
sometimes pork and sausage)
which are cooked slowly for hours
over special wood such as hickory
or mesquite to add to the distinctive
flavor. One of the state's celebrated
barbecue joints is **The Salt Lick** at
Driftwood (Tel: 512-858-4959), 13
miles (20 km) west of Austin in the
Hill Country. The dish of Texas is
chili con carne, and you'll find it in
abundance throughout the state. On
average, some 15 chili compe-
titions are held each month. The
"runner-up" to the state dish must
surely be chicken-fried steak, an
inexpensive steak covered with
batter and fried, usually served with
gravy and found on Texan menus.
No matter how much you eat, leave
room to try the local pecan pie.

## ALPINE
**Outback Bar and Grill**
300 South Phelps and Avenue G
Tel: 915-837-5074
Eclectic menu featuring large
portions of steak, chicken, Mexican
and Italian seafood dishes. **$$**

## AUSTIN
**Cisco's Bakery and Coffee Shop**
East 6th Street
Tel: 512-478-2420
Fiery, hangover-busting Mexican
breakfasts. **$**
**Scholz Garden**
1607 San Jacinto Boulevard
Tel: 512-474-1958
(see page 277) **$$–$$$**
**Threadgill's**
6416 North Lamar
Tel: 512-451-5440
Famed Texan roadhouse café with
live music on Wednesday evening.
Lavish servings of southern cuisine,
Cajun and vegetarian. **$**

## COLUMBUS
**Schobel's**
2020 Milam Street
Tel: 409-732-2385
Nice range of well-prepared dishes
served in pleasant, informal
atmosphere. The salad bar and
noon buffet are very popular. **$**

## EL PASO
**The Dome Restaurant**
101 South El Paso Street
Tel: 915-534-3000
Located in the Camino Real Hotel.
Superb, innovative seafood and wild
game creations matched by the
majestic surroundings. **$$**
**Leo's Mexican Food**
5103 Montana Avenue
Tel: 915-566-4972
Reliable local favorite for authentic
Tex-Mex. **$**
**Smitty's**
6219 Airport Road
Tel: 915-772-5876
Divine Texas barbecue accompa-
nied by that stalwart trinity – potato
salad, beans and slaw. Not very
central but well worth a detour. **$**

## FREDERICKSBURG
**Altdorf Restaurant & Beer Garden**
301 West Main Street
German music, beer and grub. **$**
**Dietz Bakery**
218 Main Street
Tel: 830-997-3250
Delicious breads and pastries. **$**

## HOUSTON
**The Brownstone**
2736 Virginia
Tel: 713-520-5666
Top-notch food in opulent
surroundings. **$$$**
**Goode Company Texas BBQ**
5109 Kirby
Tel: 713-522-2530
Fabled barbecue place. **$$**
**Dessert Gallery**
3200 Kirby Drive
Tel: 713-522-9999
Sara Brook's sexy desserts plus
furniture as art. Lunch specials. **$**
**Pappadeaux Seafood Kitchen**
6015 Westheimer
Tel: 713-82-6310
Favored local Cajun spot. **$$**
**Rainbow Lodge**
1 Birdsall near Memorial Park
Tel: 713-861-6666
Classy fishing lodge with garden,
seafood and wild game. **$$$**

## JOHNSON CITY
**Hill Country Cupboard**
Hwy 290
Tel: 210-868-4625
Country-style lunch special. **$**

## MARFA
**Tumblewood Grill**
500 East San Antonio Street
Tel: 915-729-4065
Well-prepared regional cuisine in
attractive surroundings. **$$**

## NEW BRAUNFELS
**Krause's Café**
148 South Castell Avenue
Tel: 830-625-7581
Great German food Texas-style. **$**

## PRESIDIO
**El Patio Restaurant**
513 O'Reilly Street
Popular downtown restaurant
featuring tasty Mexican and
American entrees and salad bar. **$**

## SAN ANTONIO

**Casa Rio**
430 East Commerce St
Tel: 210-225-6718
This enduring Riverwalk favorite serves large portions of tasty, inexpensive Mexican food. **$**

**County Line**
111 W Crockett, on the Riverwalk
Tel: 210-229-1941
Popular barbecue parlor. **$$**

**Tower of the Americas**
222 Hemisphere Plaza
Tel: 210-223-3101
Spectacular views from the revolving tower. Classy food. **$$$**

## UVALDE

**Jerry's Restaurant**
539 West Main Street
Tel: 830-278-7556
Seafood, steaks and Tex-Mex dishes. **$**

# SHOPPING

## AUSTIN

Austin's biggest mall, **Highland Mall**, is at 6001 Airport Boulevard, but there are also numerous little specialty shops, such as the **Turquoise Trading Post**, Burnet Road at Koenig, which displays a large selection of Native American jewelry, including Zuni fetishes, Navaho Kachina dolls, medicine wheels and dreamcatchers. The more macabre-minded will enjoy the selection of skulls, hides and trophy mounts available at the **Corner Shoppe**, 5900 Lamar Street. As befits a college town – and state capital – Austin is proud of its literary leanings, pointing out that not only does it house branches of the big bookstore chains, such as **Borders** and **Barnes & Noble**, but also many independents, among them **Congress Avenue Booksellers Half Price Books** – which deals in used books and music – and three stores specializing in African-American literature: **Folktales**, **Just For Us** and **Mitchie's Fine Black Art Gallery & Bookstore**.

## EL PASO

El Paso is the home of the cowboy boot manufacturer, **Tony Lama**. There are four factory outlets in the city.

## SAN ANTONIO

Visitors to San Antonio's **North Star** mall (Loop 410 between San Pedro and MacCullough) are invited to begin their browsing with a visit to the information booth to pick up a free shopping bag and a coupon booklet offering discounts at many of the 200 stores. These include such big names as **Saks Fifth Avenue**, **Marshall Field's**, **Guess**, **Williams-Sonoma** and **Gap**. There are other malls, of which the most attractive architecturally is **Rivercenter**, 849 East Commerce, adjoining the restaurants and IMAX theater in the heart of downtown. **La Villita**, a recreated Mexican village, and **El Mercado** (514 West Commerce) both offer specialty shops with Mexican arts and crafts.

# NEW MEXICO

## WHERE TO STAY

### ALAMOGORDO

**Best Western Desert Aire Motor Inn**
1021 South White Sands Blvd, NM 88310
Tel: 505-437-2110
Close to White Sands National Monument. Guest rooms face onto a large attractive pool. Continental breakfasts included. Sauna, outdoor Jacuzzi and game room. **$**

### CLOUDCROFT

**The Lodge**
Corona Place, (PO Box 497), NM 88317
Tel: 505-682-2566

One of the last remaining hotels built during the region's timber industry boom in the late 19th/early 20th century. The Victorian-style lodge rooms are furnished with antiques. The Pavilion rooms are more simply furnished and include full breakfast. **$$**

### DEMING

**Butterfield Stage Motel**
309 West Pine Street, NM 88030
Tel: 505-544-0011
Basic but very clean and warm. **$**

### LAS CRUCES

**Royal Host Motel**
2146 West Pichaco St, NM 88005
Tel: 505-524-8536
Simple and well-maintained. Pool and cable TV. **$**

### LORDSBURG

**Best Western American Motor Inn**
2029 North Hwy 85, NM 87701
Tel: 505-425-5288
Attractive rooms and a pool. **$**

### MESCALERO

**Inn of the Mountain Gods**
PO Box 269, NM 88340
Tel: 505-257-5141
US Freephone: 800-545-9011
Owned by the Mescalero Apache tribe, this resort hotel is located on a lake in the Sacramento Mountains and offers a variety of recreational activities, including golf, tennis, pool, fishing and boating. **$$–$$$**

### RUIDOSO

**Best Western Swiss Chalet Inn**
1451 Mechem Drive, (PO BOX 759), HWY 48N, NM 88355
Tel: 505-258-3333
Fax: 505-258-5325
US Freephone: 800-477-9477
A Swiss-style hotel located in a cool, pine-clad forest with panoramic views of Sierra Blanca Mountain. Full breakfast, pool, hot tub, restaurant and tavern. **$$**

### SILVER CITY

**Bear Mountain Guest Ranch**
PO Box 1163, NM 88062
US Freephone: 800-880-2538

Web: www.BearMtGuest Ranch.com
Great for nature lovers, large
1920s ranch house charges all-
inclusive full board rates in its
very pleasant rooms and offers
guided bird-watching trips plus a
variety of activities including
mountain biking or cross-country
skiing tours. **$$$$**
**Hostelling International –
Carter House**
101 North Cooper St, NM 88061
Tel: 505-388-5485
Light and airy older home located
in the historic district with fine
moun-tain views from the
wraparound porch. Amenities
include kitchen, baggage storage,
lockers, cable TV/VCR and laundry
facilities. **$**

## Restaurant Prices

Categories based on average
cost of dinner and a glass of
wine, before tip.
**$** = under $15
**$$** = up to $30
**$$$** = over $30

## WHERE TO EAT

*LAS CRUCES*
**Nellie's Cafe**
1226 West Hadley Avenue
Tel: 505-524-9982
Excellent Mexican food laced with
fresh and fiery salsa. **$**

*MESCALERO*
**Dan Li Ka, Inn of the Mountain Gods**
PO Box 269
Tel: 505-257-5141
Excellent fine dining at the beautiful
inn. **$$**

*SILVER CITY*
**Drifter Motel**
711 Silver Heights Boulevard
Tel: 505-538-2916
Good-value breakfasts. **$**
**Silver Cafe**
514 North Bullard
Tel: 505-388-3480
Pleasant mid-town cafe. **$**

## ARIZONA

### WHERE TO STAY

*BISBEE*
**Bisbee Grand Hotel**
61 Main St, AZ 85603
Tel: 520-432-5900
Elegantly restored Victorian
hotel with period decor; in a
small southern Arizona mining
town. Amenities: parking, saloon,
billiard room and a free breakfast.
**$$**
**Copper Queen Hotel**
11 Howell Ave, AZ 85603
Tel: 520-432-2216
A turn-of-the century Victorian
landmark built during the heyday of
the Copper Queen Mine; guests in
the past have included John Wayne
and Teddy Roosevelt. Amenities:
parking, television, restaurant,
saloon, pool. **$$**

*GILA BEND*
**Best Western Space Age Lodge**
401 E Pima St, Box C, NM 85337
Tel: 520-683-2273.
*(see page 310)* **$**

*PHOENIX*
**Arizona Biltmore**
24th St & Missouri Ave, AZ 285016
Tel: 602-955-6600
Fax: 602-381-7600
An elegant grand hotel designed by
Frank Lloyd Wright in landscaped
grounds. Pools, fitness room, golf
courses, biking, restaurants, bars,
shops. **$$$$**
**Desert Rose**
3424 E. Van Buren St, AZ 85008
Tel: 602-275-4421
Modest but comfortable small hotel
with pool and restaurant a short
drive from downtown. **$**
**Maricopa Manor**
15 W Pasadena Avenue, AZ 85013
Tel: 602-274-6302
Spanish-style home built in the
1920s furnished with antiques and
art. All rooms are suites. With pool,
spa and gardens. **$$–$$$**

*SCOTTSDALE*
**Phoenician**
Tel: 602-941-8200
*(see page 309)* **$$$**

*TOMBSTONE*
**Tombstone Motel**
502 East Fremont St, AZ 85638
Tel: 520-457-3478
Clean, well-fitted rooms in historic
1880s building. **$**

*TUCSON*
**Hotel Congress**
311 East Congress, AZ 85701
Tel: 520 622-8848
US Freephone: 800-722-8848
John Dillinger and his gang stayed
here. Why shouldn't you?
Idiosyncratic and inexpensive. **$**
**Lazy K Bar Guest Ranch**
8401 North Scenic Drive, AZ 85743
Tel: 520-744-3050
US Freephone: 800-321-7018
Cabins in the Tucson Mountains.
Horseback riding, swimming
pool, spa, tennis courts,
volleyball and basketball.
Includes a ranch store and
entertainment. **$**
**Lodge on the Desert**
306 North Alvernon Way, AZ 85711
Tel: 520-325-3366
US Freephone: 800-456-5634
In-town resort restored to its
original casual allure. Most rooms
have red-tiled patios and
fireplaces. Its restaurant is
recognized as one of the best in
Tucson. **$$–$$$**

*YUMA*
**La Fuente Inn and Suites**
1513 East 16th Street, AZ 85365
Tel: 520-329-1814
Attractive contemporary inn with
nicely landscaped gardens and
pool. **$$**
**Yuma Cabana Hotel**
2151 South Fourth Ave, AZ 85364
Tel: 520-783-8311
Attractive little oasis. Very good
value. **$**

### WHERE TO EAT

*BISBEE*
**Dot's Diner**
1 Old Douglas Road
Tel: 520-432-2046
Superlative diner fare at absurdly
cheap prices. Adjacent to a unique
trailer park. **$**

## GILA BEND
**Outer Limits Coffee Shop**
(connected to the Best Western
Space Age Lodge)
401 E Pima St, Box C, NM 85337
Tel: 520-683-2273
*(see page 310)* **$**

## PHOENIX
**Aunt Chiladas**
7330 N Dreamy Draw Drive
Tel: 602-944-1286
Although its tamed-down Mexican
food compared with what you'd
find elsewhere, the flour tortilla
chips (available on request) and
fresh salsa more than
compensate. **$**
**Christo's**
6327 N 7th Street
Tel: 602-264-1784
One of the top Phoenix restaurants,
dishing up elegant Italian food in a
formal setting. **$$**
**Ed Debevic's**
2102 E Highland Avenue
Tel: 602-956-2760
Infamous (in a good way) for
their rude staff, this 1950's-style
diner dishes up excellent cafe
fare. **$**

## SCOTTSDALE
**Jean Claude's Petit Cafe**
7340 East Shoeman Lane
Tel: 602-947-5288
Contemporary French bistro
good for a romantic night out.
**$–$$**
**Shogun**
12615 North Tatum Boulevard
Tel: 602-953-3264
Good choice for sushi, tempura
and other Japanese specialties.
**$–$$**

## TOMBSTONE
**Nellie Cashman's Restaurant**
117 South Fifth Street
Tel: 520-457-2212
A long-running Tombstone favorite.
**$–$$**

## TUCSON
**Dakota Cafe**
6541 East Tanque Verde Road
Tel: 520-298-7188
Popular café with a broad menu and
vegetarian dishes. **$**

## Hotel Prices

Categories based on average
cost of a double room for one
night.
**$** = under $65
**$$** = up to $100
**$$$** = up to $150
**$$$$** = over $150

**El Minuto**
354 South Main Avenue
Tel: 520-882-4145
Spicy and filling Mexican food in a
stripped-down cantina. Popular with
locals. **$**
**Janos**
150 North Main Avenue
Tel: 520-884-9426
Inventive French-southwestern
cuisine served in a lovely 19th-
century adobe. **$$**

## YUMA
**Brownies' Restaurant**
1145 South Fourth Street
Tel: 520-783-7911
Good breakfasts and very
reasonable dinners. **$**
**Crossing Restaurant**
2690 South Fourth Avenue
Tel: 520-726-5551
Reliable if unexciting. **$**

## SHOPPING

### PHOENIX
The city has several large malls
located to the north, as well as
the **Arizona Center**, Van Buren
Street, in downtown. A number of
interesting shops are located in
**Heritage Square**, which is also in
the city center.
**Heard Museum Gift Shop**
2301 North Central Avenue
Exquisite Native American jewelry
and other crafts.

### SCOTTSDALE
**Fashion Square**
*(see page 309)*

### TUCSON
Tucson is a good center for
southwestern crafts. Try **Kaibab
Shops**, 2841–43 Campbell Avenue

or **Mark Subbette Medicine Man
Gallery**, 7000 East Tanque Verde
Road for Mexican and Native
American crafts.

## CALIFORNIA
### WHERE TO STAY

#### EL CENTRO
**E-Z Motel**
455 Wake Avenue, CA 92243
Tel: 760-352-8500
Clean, standard motel rooms with
free continental breakfast, pool and
laundry facilities. A few rooms are
equipped with kitchenettes. **$**

#### JACUMBA
**Jacumba Hot Springs Spa**
44500 Old US 80, CA 91934
Tel: 760-766-4333
Relaxing hot springs, pools and
private Jacuzzis. Very good
restaurant and bar. **$**

### WHERE TO EAT

#### EL CENTRO
**Mi Casita**
729 West Main Street
Tel: 760-353-8690
Very good Mexican food. **$**

#### LA MESA
**Marietta's Restaurant**
8949 La Mesa Boulevard
Tel: 619-462-3500
Southwestern dishes and friendly
service. **$$**

# Pacific Route

## Useful Addresses

**California tourist information:**
*(see page 426)*
**Oregon tourist information:**
Economic Development Department
775 Summer St. NE, Salem,
OR 97310
Tel: 800-547-7842
**Washington tourist information**
*(see page 406)*

## Hub City:
## SAN DIEGO

### GETTING AROUND

*Public transportation*
**From the airport:** San Diego
International Airport (Tel: 619-233-
8040) is located 3 miles (5 km)
from downtown. Various shuttle
services operate from the airport to
the center from under $10. The
Metropolitan Transit System bus
route 992 travels from the airport
to downtown for under $3.
**City buses:** City buses are run by
San Diego Metropolitan Transit
System (Tel: 619-685-4900). Call
619-233-3004 for route
information. The San Diego Trolley
System runs from the Santa Fe
Depot at 1850 Kettner Boulevard,
crossing into Mexico at San Ysidro.
The one-way fare is under $3.
**Intercity buses:** The Greyhound
depot is at Broadway and First
Avenue.
**Trains:** Amtrak services run from
the Santa Fe Depot at 1850 Kettner
Boulevard.

*Private Transportation*
Unlike Los Angeles, San Diego is a
relatively easy city to explore either
with or without a car. However, as in

most big cities, journeys are best
planned around the weekday early
morning and late afternoon crush.
Parking is generally easy to find and
for the most part moderately priced.
Most of the major car rental
agencies have offices at the airport
and in the downtown area.
**Car rental companies:**
Avis, Tel: 619-688-5000
Budget, Tel: 760-352-5550
Hertz, Tel: 619-220-5222
**Taxis:**
American, Tel: 619-234-1111
West Coast, Tel: 619-527-1077
Yellow Cab, Tel: 619-234-6161
**Traveling to Tijuana/Baja**
Non US citizens should bring their
passports or green cards. US
citizens don't need a passport
unless they're visiting for more than
72 hours, or plan to go beyond the
Hwy 1 checkpoint below Baja's
Ensenada. If so, they must acquire
a tourist visa in San Diego from any
travel agent, the Mexican Consulate
General, the Mexico Government
Tourism Office or the Automobile
Club of Southern California. Proof of
nationality must accompany the
visa. US insurance is not valid in
Mexico and it is definitely a wise
move to obtain short-term
insurance, obtainable at
innumerable sales offices just
north of the border. Crossing into
Mexico is easy, with immigration
officers at both sides usually just
waving you along. There are three
major crossings: at busy **San
Ysidro**, 18 miles (29 km) south of
downtown San Diego, which is the
gateway to Tijuana; at **Tecate** off
State 94, where there is rarely a
wait, although the solitary customs
officer tends to close the border in
early evening; and at **Mexicali**
(Baja's capital), a dreary industrial
city opposite the California town of
Calexico, which is about 90 miles
(144 km) to the east. Because
driving is not easy in Tijuana for
those unfamiliar with the city (and
the Spanish language), many
drivers park in San Diego's San
Ysidro, crossing into Tijuana via the
elevated pedestrian walkway. Avoid
leaving your car in the parking
places of merchants unless you

want to have it towed away by
police. There's an all-day secure lot
off the "Last Exit US parking" ramp
– turn right at the stop sign to the
Tijuana side. Cheap taxis and buses
are available.
**Crossing Back:** The return to
California can be a bit more tense
than the entry into Mexico, as US
Border Patrol officers take far more
interest in who's coming into the
country. During busy American
holiday periods, such as
Independence Day (July 4) and
Labor Day (early September),
waiting up to two hours to cross is
not uncommon.

## Hotel Prices

Categories based on average
cost of a double room for one
night.
$ = under $65
$$ = up to $100
$$$ = up to $150
$$$$ = over $150

---

### WHERE TO STAY

**Holiday Inn-Harbor View**
1617 1st Avenue
Tel: 619-239-9600
Fax: 619-233-6228
Close to I-5. Pool, restaurant,
laundromat. Shuttle to airport, zoo,
Sea World. **$$$**
**Horton Grand**
311 Island Avenue
Tel: 619-544-1886
US Freephone: 800-542-1886
Fax: 619-239-3823
Web: www.hortongrand.com
Elegant, historic Victorian hotel, in
Gaslamp District. Near Horton
Plaza, Marina Park, Seaport Village,
Convention Center. Fireplaces,
antiques. **$$–$$$**
**Hotel del Coronado**
1500 Orange Ave, Coronado,
CA 92118
Tel: 619-435-6611
Fax: 619-522-8262
Web: www.hoteldel.com
World-famous Victorian-era
landmark. Tennis court, pool, spa,
nearby golf, boating, beach,
restaurants. **$$$$**

**La Pensione Hotel**
1700 India Street
Tel: 619-236-8000
Fax: 619-236-8088
Web: www.lapensionehotel.com
A wonderful little secret, San Diego's best budget hotel, in Little Italy surrounded by cafes. Easy walk to downtown and harbor. Two blocks to trolley. European-style guesthouse, 80 units. **$**

**U.S. Grant Hotel**
326 Broadway
Tel: 619-232-3121
US Freephone: 800-334-6957
Fax: 619-232-3626
Web: www.grandheritage.com
Restored, grand old historic hotel in heart of business, shopping, nightlife. Near trolley and Convention Center. **$$$**

**Westin Horton Plaza**
910 Broadway
Tel: 619-239-2200
US Freephone: 800-643-7846
Fax: 619-239-0509
Web: www.westin.com
In the heart of downtown. Restaurant, pool, spa, lighted tennis courts, health club. **$$$$**

## Restaurant Prices

Categories based on average cost of dinner and a glass of wine, before tip.
**$** = under $15
**$$** = up to $30
**$$$** = over $30

## WHERE TO EAT

**Anthony's Star of the Sea Room**
1360 North Harbor Drive
Tel: 619-232-7408
Fabulous seafood served with dramatic flair. Located on the waterfront. Jackets and reservations required. Open for dinner only. **$$$**

**Casa de Pico**
2754 Juan Street
Tel: 619-296-3267
Located in the Bazaar del Mundo in Old Town. Reliable Mexican food and great margaritas. **$**

**The Marine Room**
2000 Spindrift Drive, La Jolla
Tel: 858-459-7222
At high tide the waves crash just outside the windows. **$$**

**Old Trieste**
2335 Morena Boulevard
Tel: 858-276-1841
Reputed to be one of the best Italian restaurants in town. Closed Sunday and Monday. **$$$**

## SHOPPING

San Diego's **Gaslamp Quarter**, a 16-block, 38-acre (17-hectare) district recommended for arts and crafts. In addition to its **Seaport Village** and the multilevel **Horton Plaza**, San Diego is also just a short hop away from the Mexican border town of Tijuana, where there are different souvenirs and lower prices

## CALIFORNIA

## WHERE TO STAY

### ARCATA
**Fairwinds Motel**
1674 G Street, CA 95521
Tel: 707-822-4824
Basic and clean. **$$**

### BIG SUR
**Pfeiffer Big Sur State Park**
For park information Tel: 800-424-4787
**Julia Pfeiffer Burns State Park**
For park information, Tel: 831-667-2377
**Big Sur Lodge**
State Route 1, Big Sur, 93920
Tel: 831-667-3100
US Freephone: 800-424-4787
Fax: 831-667-3110
Big Sur architect Mickey Muenning used the sea and the mountains as a backdrop to this lush resort. **$$**
**Big Sur River Inn**
Hwy 1 at Phenger Creek, CA 93920
Tel: 831-625-2700
Fax: 831-667-2743
Web: www.bigsuriverinn.com
Magnificent river views and warm welcoming rooms. Heated pool, restaurant, bar and patio. **$$**

### Ventana Inn
Highway 1, CA 93920
Tel: 831-667-2331
Fax: 831-667-2419
Quoted as America's most romantic resort, by an *LA Times'* writer. **$$$**

### BODEGA BAY
**Bodega Bay Lodge Resort**
103 Coast Highway 1, CA 94923
Tel: 707-875-3525
US Freephone: 800-368-2468
Fax: 707-875-2428
All rooms have panoramic ocean view and many have fireplaces. Romantic hideaway with restaurant, pool, fitness center and sauna. **$$**
**Inn at the Tides**
800 Hwy 1, CA 94923
Tel: 707-875-2751
Fax: 707-875-3285
US Freephone: 800-862-4945
Web: www.innatthetides.com
Impressive views from these hillside lodges featuring fireplaces and continental breakfast. **$$$**

### CARDIFF-BY-THE-SEA
**Cardiff-by-the-Sea Lodge**
142 Chesterfield, CA 92007
Tel: 760-944-6474
Fax: 760-944-6841
Neat, individual seaview rooms with fireplaces and whirlpool tubs. **$$$**

### CARLSBAD
**La Costa Resort and Spa**
US Freephone: 800-854-5000
A sprawling Southern Californian "total resort" well-known for its two PGA championship golf courses and de luxe facilities. The 500-room complex includes health spas, golf courses and tennis courts. **$$$$**
**Ocean Palms Beach Resort**
2950 Ocean Street, CA 92008
Tel: 760-729-2493
Fax: 760-729-0579
This full-service resort is minutes from the beach. The complex includes beachfront studios and suites with fully equipped kitchens, heated pool, and Jacuzzi. **$$$**

### CARMEL
**Cypress Inn**
Lincoln and 7th streets, CA 93923
Tel: 408-624-3871
Fax: 408-624-8216

Mission-style inn, warmly furnished with a garden courtyard and a restaurant/bar. **$$**

**La Playa Hotel**
Camino Real & Eighth St, CA 93923
Tel: 831-624-6476
Lush, prize-winning gardens surround this historic Mediterranean-style hotel, located two blocks from the stunning Pacific coast. **$$$**

**Vagabond's House Inn**
Fourth & Dollars
PO Box 2747, CA 93921
Tel: 831-624-7738
Fax: 831-626-1234
US Freephone: 800-262-1262
Web: www.carmelfun.com
Eleven uniquely-appointed rooms surround a tranquil stone courtyard, graced by mature oak tree and waterfalls. A short stroll to local shops. **$$$–$$$$**

### CAYUCOS

**Beachwalker Inn**
501 South Ocean Ave, CA 93940
Tel: 805-995-2133
Fax: 805-995-3139
Warm and welcoming rooms and suites with gas fireplaces. **$$$**

### ELK

**Harbor House by the Sea**
5600 South Hwy 1, PO Box 369,
CA 95432
Tel: 707-877-3203
Fax: 707-877-3452
Web: wwwtheharborhouseinn.com
Fine early 20th-century house over-looking magnificent rock forma-tions. The inn is fronted by beautifully landscaped gardens and pathways leading to the beach. The dining room offers Californian cuisine with Tuscan and Provençal accents. **$$$$**

### EUREKA

**Eureka Inn**
518 7th Street, CA 95501
Tel: 707-442-0116
*(see page 362)* **$$**

**Carter House Inn**
1023 Third Street, CA 95501
Tel: 707-445-1390
Renovated older home with comfortable, well-appointed rooms. Breakfast included. **$$$**

**A Weaver's Inn**
1440 B Street, CA 95501
Tel: 707-443-8119
Fax: 707-443-7923
www.humboldt1.com/~weavrinn
A pretty Queen Anne Colonial revival c.1883 building surrounded by a pristine white picket fence and furnished in period style. The attractive grounds feature a Japanese Contemplation Garden, cottage-style garden and croquet lawn. **$$–$$$**

### FERNDALE

**Gingerbread Mansion Inn**
400 Berding Street, CA 95536
Tel: 707-786-4000
US Freephone: 800-952-4136
Fax: 707-952-4136
Web: www.gingerbread-mansion.com
*(see page 360)* **$$**

**Shaw House Inn**
703 Main Street, CA 95536-1125
Tel: 707-786-9958
Fax: 707-786-9958
Web:
www.humboldt/.com/~shawhse
*(see page361)* **$$$**

**Victorian Inn**
400 Ocean Avenue, CA 95536
Tel: 707-786-4949
*(see page 361)* **$$$**

### FORTUNA

**Six Rivers Motel**
1141 North Main Street, CA 95437
Tel: 707-725-1181
Well-maintained, good-value rooms some with refrigerators and microwaves. **$**

### GARBERVILLE

**Best Western Humboldt House Inn**
701 Redwood Drive, CA 95542
Tel: 707-923-2771
US Freephone: 800-248-7234
Fax: 707-923-4259
An ideal base for touring the Redwoods. Spacious rooms, some with balconies and mountain views. Pool, spa, complimentary breakfast and newspaper. **$$**

**Historic Benbow Inn**
455 Lake Benbow Drive, CA 95542
Tel: 707-923-2124
Fax: 707-923-2122
This Tudor-style inn has been

welcoming guests for over 70 years. Three of the four spacious rooms have fireplaces and one of the three has a Jacuzzi as well. Extras include classic films in the library and afternoon tea and scones on the terrace overlooking Benbow Lake. **$$$**

### GUALALA

**Gualala Country Inn**
47955 Center Street, CA 95445
Tel: 707-884-4343
Fax: 707-884-1018
Web: www.gualala.com
Peaceful inn with ocean views. Several rooms with fireplaces and spas. **$$$**

## Hotel Prices

Categories based on average cost of a double room for one night.
**$** = under $65
**$$** = up to $-100
**$$$** = up to $150
**$$$$** = over $150

### GUERNVILLE

**The Willows**
15905 River Road, CA 95446
Tel: 707-869-2824
Elegant riverside inn. **$$–$$$**

### HALF MOON BAY

**Cypress Inn on Miramar Beach**
407 Mirada Road, CA 94019
Tel: 650-726-6002
US Freephone: 800-832-3224
Fax: 650-712-0380
Web: www.cypressinn.com
A light and airy inn featuring skylights and imaginative use of natural colors and materials. Full breakfast and dinner served by the fireside, only minutes to the fine sandy beach. **$$$$**

### HUNTINGTON BEACH

**Maxwell's By the Sea**
317 Pacific Coast Highway
Tel: 714-536-2555.
On the famous pier with good views as well as good food. **$**

## INVERNESS

**Hotel Inverness**
25 Park Avenue, CA 94937
Tel: 415-669-7393
Fax: 415-669-1702
Web: www.hotelinverness.com
In the historic section of Inverness, amidst lush woods, this hotel features stylish furnishings and a vibrant color scheme. **$$$–$$$$**

**Klamath**
15497 Hwy 101, CA 95548
Tel: 707-483-3152
US Freephone: 800-848-2982
Fax: 707-482-2005
Pleasant motel encircled by Redwood national and state parks with the unusual Forest Cafe opposite. Spick and span rooms, tennis court, king/queen size beds and cable TV/HBO. **$**

## LA JOLLA

**La Jolla Beach & Tennis Club**
2000 Spindthrift Drive, CA 92037
Tel: 619-454-7126
Fax: 619-456-3805.
On the beach, near Sea World. Restaurant with pool, golf, tennis, some disabled facilities. **$$$$**

**Torrey Pines Inn**
11480 N Torrey Pines Rd,
CA 92037.
Tel: 619-453-4420
US Freephone: 800-995-4507
Fax: 619-453-0691
Overlooks ocean, 1 mile (2 km) from beach, near Del Mar racetrack. Pool, restaurant, golf. **$$**

## LAGUNA BEACH

**The Carriage House-B&B**
1322 Catalina Street, CA 92651
Tel: 949-494-8945
Fax: 949-494-8945
A Charming B&B with en-suite rooms. **$$$**

**Hotel Laguna**
425 S Coast Highway, CA 92651
Tel: 714-494-1151
US Freephone: 800-524-2927
Fax: 714-497-2163
On beach. Near Pageant of Masters. Restaurants. **$$$**

**Inn at Laguna Beach**
211 N Coast Highway, CA 92651
Tel: 949-497-9722
Fax: 949-497-9972
Located on a bluff above the beach,

many of the inns offer patios with an oceanview. Heated pool and whirlpool also on grounds. **$$$$**

## LOMPOC

**Tally Ho Motor Inn**
1020 East Ocean Ave, CA 93436
Tel: 805-735-6444
Fax: 805-735-5558
Good facilities and well-kept rooms, some with microwaves and refrigerators. Sauna, indoor Jacuzzi, laundry facilities. Free breakfast. **$**

## MENDOCINO

**The Stanford Inn by the Sea**
PO Box 487, CA 95460
Tel: 707-937-5615
Fax: 707-937-0305
Web: www.stanfordinn.com
A unique hilltop inn overlooking (beautifully) landscaped gardens with marvelous open vistas across the fields to the bay. The well-furnished rooms and suites have sofas and wood-burning fireplaces. Sumptuous breakfasts, large pool, sauna, spa and exercise room. Wheelchair-accessible rooms. **$$$$**

## MORRO BAY

**Baywood Bed and Breakfast Inn**
1370 Second Street, CA 93402
Tel: 805-528-8888
Fax: 805-528-8887
Web: www.baywoodinn.com
Lovely suites with fireplaces, bay views and full breakfast. **$$**

**Embarcadero Inn**
456 Embarcadero St, CA 93442
Fax: 805-772-1060
This peaceful inn features luxury rooms with private balconies and attentive service. A good base for relaxing or touring local attractions. All rooms with bay view, many with balconies and fireplaces and two with hot tubs as well. **$$$**

## MONTEREY

**Hotel Pacific**
300 Pacific Street, CA 93940
Tel: 831-373-5700
Fax: 831-373-6921
Elegant adobe-style hotel. All rooms have deck and gas fireplaces for relaxing and free newspaper and breakfast for waking up in the morning. **$$$$**

**Monterey Plaza Hotel**
400 Cannery Row, CA 93940
Tel: 408-646-1700
US Freephone: 800-631-1339
Fax: 408-646-1339
Large hotel (285 rooms) with bellman, concierge and two restaurants in the heart of Cannery Row. **$$$**

**Old Monterey Inn**
500 Martin Street, CA 93940
Tel: 831-375-8284
US Freephone: 800-350-2344
Fax: 831-375-6730
Web: www.oldmonterey inn.com
This English Tudor-style inn is surrounded by oak-wooded grounds and fine, beautifully tended gardens. First-rate service and attention to detail. **$$$$**

## NEWPORT BEACH

**Newport Classic Inn**
2300 W Coast Highway, CA 92663
Tel: 714-722-2999
US Freephone: 800-633-3199
Fax: 714-631-5659
On bay, half a mile (1 km) from beach. Restaurant, pool, sauna. **$**

## OJAI

**Ojai Rancho Motel**
615 West Ojai Avenue, CA 93023
Tel: 805-646-1434
An attractive redwood motel in the town center. Guest rooms with fireplaces, kitchenette, coffeemakers, microwaves and refrigerators are available. **$$$**

## PESCADERO

**Hostelling International –
Pigeon Point Lighthouse**
210 Pigeon Point Road, CA 94060
Tel: 650-879-0633
Housed in an active 115 ft (35 meter) 19th-century cliff side lighthouse. An ideal vantage point for observing gray whales on their annual migration. Amenities include kitchen, outdoor hot tub, on-site parking and equipment storage. Wheelchair accessible. **$**

## PISMO BEACH

**Edgewater Inn and Suites**
280 Wadsworth Avenue, CA 93449
Tel: 805-773-4811
Fax: 805-773-5121

These spacious rooms and suites with fully equipped kitchens, heated pool and Jacuzzi are ideal for families. Situated on the beach. Free continental breakfast. **$$–$$$**

**Spyglass Inn**
2705 Spyglass Drive, CA 93449
Tel: 805-773-4855
Fax: 805-773-5298
Web: www.spyglassinn.com
Stylishly refurbished with panoramic ocean view, dining room and lounge. **$$$**

### REDONDO BEACH
**Best Western Sunrise Hotel**
400 N Harbor Drive
Tel: 310-376-0746
Fax: 310-376-7384
At the marina. Pool, spa, restaurant. **$$$**

**Portofino Hotel & Yacht Club**
260 Portofino Way
Tel: 213-379-8481
US Freephone: 800-468-4292
Fax: 310-372-7329.
Pool, restaurant, views over the marina and access to Gold's Gym nearby. **$$$$**

### REDWOOD NATIONAL PARK
**Hostelling International**
14480 California Hwy 101 at Wilson Creek Road, CA 95548
Tel: 707-482-8265
Email: redwoodhostel @mail.telis.org
Set in the Redwood National Park with grand views from the porches. Other features include an inviting common room, pellet stove, bicycle rack, laundry facilities and on-site parking **$**

### SAN CLEMENTE
**Hostelling International**
233 Ave Granada, CA 92672-4029
Tel: 949-492-2848
Web: www.hostelweb.com
Within walking distance of the beach and close to local amenities such as the Farmers' Market. Good atmosphere. Facilities include kitchen, patios, laundry, courtyard and lockers. **$**

### SAN FRANCISCO
**The Archbishop's Mansion**
1000 Fulton Street, CA 94117
Tel: 415-563-7872
US Freephone: 800-543-5820
Fax: 415-885-3193
Exquisite French chateau mansion in Alamo Square built in 1904 for the archbishop of San Francisco. An historical landmark. Complimentary breakfast and wine are served. **$$$**

**Hostelling International – Downtown**
312 Mason Street, CA 94102
Tel: 415-788-5604
One of the largest hostels in the country includes about 200 beds and community kitchens in its downtown location. **$**

**Hotel Boheme**
444 Columbus Avenue, CA 94133
Tel: 415-433-9111
Fax: 415-362-6292
An abundance of bohemian charm and bags of history. Wonderful black and white photographs line the hallway **$$**

**Red Victorian Inn**
1665 Haight Street, CA 94117
Tel: 415-864-1978
Perfect for the budget traveler. Friendly and casual with each room reflecting a different theme. **$**

**York Hotel**
940 Sutter Street, CA 94109
Tel: 415-885-6800
US Freephone: 800-808-9675
Fax: 415-885-2115
The setting for the Hitchcock movie Vertigo is both sophisticated and comfortable. The Plush Room Theater, which was once a Prohibition-era speakeasy now known for its cabaret, is also located here. **$–$$**

### SAN LUIS OBISPO
**Apple Farm Trellis Court**
2015 Monterey Street, CA 93401
Tel: 805-544-2040
US Freephone: 800-255-2040
Cozy rooms with fireplaces and pleasing decor. There is a good restaurant serving cider produced on-site by a water-powered apple press. **$$**

**Hostelling International**
1617 Santa Rosa Street, CA 93401
Tel: 805-544-4678

Categories based on average cost of a double room for one night.
**$** = under $65
**$$** = up to $100
**$$$** = up to $150
**$$$$** = over $150

Fax: 805-544-3142
http://internetcafe.allyn.com/SLO
Convenient location for downtown shops, restaurants, theaters, farmers' market and Amtrak station. Amenities include kitchen, bicycle rental, laundry, lockers, fireplace and piano. **$**

**Madonna Inn**
100 Madonna Road, CA 93405
Tel: 805-543 3000
Fax: 805-543 1800
Well known for its eccentricity and bizarre decor. The 109 rooms come dressed up in color-themed Western, Hawaiian, Austrian, etc. **$$**

### SANTA BARBARA
**The Chesire Cat B&B**
36 W Valerio Street, CA 93101
Tel: 805-569-1610
Fax: 805-682-1876
Ironically smoke free, this restored Victorian home offers a relaxed and pampered stay in the heart of Santa Barbara. **$$$$**

**Simpson House**
121 East Arrellaga, CA 93101
Tel: 805-963-7067
US Freephone: 800-676-1280
Fax: 805-564-4811
Web: simpsonhouseinn.com
A meticulously restored Victorian estate set in an acre of English gardens yet only a short stroll away from the downtown historic district and the beach. **$$$$**

**The Upham**
1404 De La Vina, CA 93101
Tel: 805-962-0058
US Freephone: 800-727-0876
Fax: 805-963-2825
Built in 1871, this is Southern California's oldest continuously operating hostelry. Charming garden cottages and main building furnished with antiques and period furniture. **$$$**

## SCOTIA
**Scotia Inn**
Main and Mill, CA, 95565
Tel: 707-764-5683
Tidy rooms; breakfasts. **$$**

## SEAL BEACH
**Seal Beach Inn and Gardens**
212 Fifth Street, CA 90740
Tel: 562-493-2416
Fax: 562-799-0483
Web: www.sealbeachinn.com
Refined and sophisticated with
peaceful public areas, library,
swimming pool, tearoom and
courtyard with French
Mediterranean flavor. **$$$$**

## SONOMA
**Sonoma Mission Inn and Spa**
Hwy 12 at Boyes Blvd, CA 95476
Tel: 707-996-5358
Web: www.sonomamisioninn.com
Pricey European-style spa in
the heart of the wine country.
Romantic, rooms and suites
with marbled baths and
plantation shutters. Acclaimed
fine dining and attentive service.
**$$$$**

## WESTPORT
**Howard Creek Ranch**
40501 North Hwy 1, CA 95488
Tel: 707-964-6725
Fax: 707-964-1603
Quiet rooms in historic farmhouse
surrounded by beauty. **$$–$$$$**

---

# WHERE TO EAT

## BIG SUR
**Big Sur River Inn Restaurant**
Tel: 831-625-5255
US Freephone: 800-548-3610
Relaxed and informal with river
views. **$$**

## CARMEL
**Pacific Edge**
Highlands Inn, Hwy 1
Tel: 408-624-3801
Best view, best regional. **$$**
**Papa Chano's Taqeuria**
462 Alvarado Street
Tel: 831-624-7500
Good value, filling and flavorful
Mexican food. **$**

---

## Restaurant Prices

Categories based on average
cost of dinner and a glass of
wine, before tip.
**$** = under $15
**$$** = up to $30
**$$$** = over $30

## CASTROVILLE
**Giant Artichoke Restaurant**
11221 Merritt Street, CA 95012
831-633-4259
*(see page 348)* **$$$**

## ENCINITAS
**Cilantro's**
3702 Via De La Valle, Del Mar
Tel: 619-259-8777
Good southwestern food. **$**
**Jake's Del Mar**
1660 Coast Boulevard, Del Mar
Tel: 619-755-2002
Outdoors and romantic. **$$**

## GUADALUPE
**Western Tavern**
899 Guadalupe Street
Tel: 805-343-2211
Top-quality steaks. **$$**

## HALF MOON BAY
**Papa George's Restaurant and Bar**
2320 South Cabrillo Highway
Tel: 650-726-9417
Antiques and memorabilia
accompany continental food. The
bar menu (**$**) is a less expensive
way to savor the feeling of being out
of San Francisco, but this is not too
far away in case you need to return
to the city soon. **$$**

## LA JOLLA
**The Cottage**
7702 Fay Avenue
Tel: 619-454-8409
The promise of a Cottage breakfast
should be enough to coax even the
worst sleepyhead into the daylight.
The fragrant, sweet pastries,
aromatic coffee and soothing
atmosphere revive gently. **$$**
**George's at the Cove**
1250 Prospect Street
Tel: 858-454-4244
Fresh, seasonal Californian cuisine
and marvelous views of La Jolla

---

Cove. The top floor is open-air and
casual; the first two floors are more
formal. **$$–$$$**
**Laguna Beach**
Las Brisas, 361 Cliff Dr,
Laguna Beach
Tel: 714-497-5434
Beside the sea. Mexican cuisine. **$**
**La Jolla Beach & Tennis Club**
2000 Spindthrift Drive
Tel: 619-454-7126
Fax: 619-456-3805
On the beach, near Sea World.
Restaurant, pool, golf, tennis, some
disabled facilities. **$$$$**
**Torrey Pines Inn**
11480 N Torrey Pines Road
Tel: 619-453-4420
US Freephone: 800-995-4507
Fax: 619-453-0691
Overlooks ocean, 1 mile (2 km)
from beach, near Del Mar racetrack.
Pool, restaurant, golf. **$$**

## LOMPOC
**Sissy's Uptown Café**
112 South I Street
Tel: 805-735-4877
A local favorite for baked goods and
desserts. Soup, sandwiches and
salads are also available. **$**

## MENDOCINO
**Café Beaujolais**
961 Ukiah Street
Tel: 707-937-5614
Upscale Californian cuisine. **$$$**

## MONTEREY
**Fandango**
223 17th, Pacific Grove
Tel: 831-372-3456
Italian, Basque and Spanish flavors,
with many seafood dishes, and a
mesquite grill. Paella from fresh
local catches. **$$$**
**Fresh Cream**
Heritage Harbor Building 100
Tel: 831-375-9798
Frequently listed as one of the top
100 restaurants in the country,
Fresh Cream's French/American
cuisine has rack of lamb and crisp
duck as specialties, as well as
many vegetarian dishes. Every table
with ocean view. **$$$**
**Sardine Factory**
701 Wave Street
Tel: 831-373-3775

Get in here if you can. Reservations are required at this semi-formal restaurant serving the health conscious and lovers of fresh seafood and pasta. **$$$**

### MORRO BAY
**Bayside Cafe**
State Park Road
Tel: 805-772-1465
A nifty little cafe situated in Morro Bay State Park serving well-cooked Californian and Mexican dishes. The char-broiled fish sandwich is very popular. Bay views. **$**

### NEWPORT BEACH
**Crab Cooker**
2200 Newport Blvd
Tel: 949-673-0100
Grilled seafood on paper plates, reasonable prices; no reservations. **$$**

### ORICK
**Palm Café and Motel**
21130 Highway 101, CA 95555
Tel: 707-488 3381
(see page 364) **$$**

### PACIFIC BEACH
**Ichiban P.B.**
1441 Garnet Avenue
Tel: 619-270-5755
Cheap and cheerful sushi and noodle house. **$**

### SAMOA
**Samoa Cookhouse**
Off Hwy 101 across the Samoa Bridge
Tel: 707-442 1659
Breakfast includes orange juice, scrambled eggs, pancakes, sausages, hash browns and coffee. Hefty lunches and dinners start with soup, salad and plenty of bread, and end with hot apple pie.
(see page 362) **$**

### SAN FRANCISCO
**A. Sabella**
2766 Taylor St, Fisherman's Wharf
Tel: 415-771-6775
Dungeness crab, a stunning Bay view, old-world hospitality and a renowned wine list combine with 110 years of experience. **$$**

## Restaurant Prices

Categories based on average cost of dinner and a glass of wine, before tip.
**$** = under $15
**$$** = up to $30
**$$$** = over $30

**Greens**
Building A, Fort Mason in the Marina district
Tel: 415-771-6222
Organic produce, seasonal specials and a mesquite grill are the cornerstones of this vegetarian restaurant. Plus spectacular views of the Golden Gate Bridge. **$$$**

**House of Nanking**
919 Kearny Street, Chinatown
Tel: 415-421-1429
The city's most popular and acclaimed Chinese, where the cramped seating and pushy service are part of the charm. Avoid weekend evenings. **$**

**Masa's**
468 Bush St, north of Union Square
Tel: 415-989-7154
Perhaps the most expensive and critically lauded restaurant in all of San Francisco. The perennial winner in the city's restaurant lists. **$$$$**

**Rose Pistola**
532 Columbus Avenue, North Beach
Tel: 415-399-0499
The ambiance and wood-fired oven have made this one of SF's hottest restaurants. Small dishes served family-style allow a wide variety of flavors. Do not pass up dessert. Heated sidewalk dining is perfect for watching the North Beach crowds stroll by. **$$**

**Tadich**
240 California St, Financial District
Tel: 415-391-1849
The oldest restaurant in San Francisco, Tadich has been serving fish, crab and oysters for a century and a half. **$$**

### SAN LUIS OBISPO
**Big Sky Cafe**
1121 Broad Street
Tel: 805-545-5401
A breakfast favorite. **$**

### SANTA BARBARA
**Acapulco**
1114 State Street
Tel: 805-963-3469
Artfully prepared and spiced Mexican food provided for almost three decades. **$**

**Brophy Brothers**
119 Harbor Way
Tel: 805-966-4418
Fried, sauteed, grilled and chowdered seafood, with marine views. The 1950s jukebox and the popularity of their hand-shaken *margueritas* combine to make it a very lively spot. **$$**

**La Marina**
Four Seasons Biltmore Hotel, 1260 Channel Drive, Montecito
Tel: 805-969-2261
Swanky hotel restaurant offering an excellent weekly five-course tasting menu that might include such entrees as roast Chilean sea bass, grilled pavé, lobster with sweet corn risotto or roast rack of lamb. You will also have the chance to sample five specially selected wines. **$$$**

**Montecito Inn**
1295 Coast Village Road
Tel: 805-969-7854
(see page 340) **$$**

**The Wine Cask**
813 Anacapa Street
Tel: 805-966-9463
Hundreds of wines from the adjoining shop to accompany delicious Californian cuisine, served in a lovely room with painted, beamed ceilings. **$$$**

### SANTA CRUZ
**Gabriella Cafe**
910 Cedar Street
Tel: 831-457-1677
Tasty seafood and pasta and pleasant atmosphere. **$**

### VENICE
**Rose Café and Market**
220 Rose Avenue
Tel: 310-399-0711
(see page 336) **$$**

**Wine tours**
For details on winery tours contact: Napa Valley Vinters' Association
PO Box 141, CA 94574
Tel: 707-226-7459
Fax: 707-255-2066

Most tours include free tasting and the chance to buy a few bottles – or a few cases.

## SHOPPING

### Santa Barbara
**La Arcada** shopping paseo is a cheerful Spanish-style courtyard adorned with tile, ornamental ironwork and bright flags.

### San Francisco
From elegant malls to farmers' markets, Northern California offers a wide array of shopping opportunities. In San Francisco alone, there are 20 distinct shopping areas. You might want to start by exploring some or all of the following:

**Union Square:** perhaps the most famous shopping area in San Francisco, the square includes the charming **Maiden Lane** with boutiques, galleries and a building designed by Frank Lloyd Wright (currently home to **Xanadu Tribal Art Gallery**).

**Chinatown:** between Stockton, Kearny, Bush and Broadway. Good for fresh produce, fish and poultry. Traditional herbalist, antiques, jewelry and souvenir shops vie for attention. The crowded streets flow into North Beach.

**North Beach:** this area offers a mix of book shops, Italian restaurants and delicatessens, cafés, vintage clothing and designer boutiques.

**Fisherman's Wharf:** shopping extends from **Pier 39** to **Ghirardelli Square** in **The Cannery**, a remodeled Del Monte peach canning plant; **The Anchorage**, a colorful, modern complex; and Ghirardelli Square itself. Along with unusual shops and galleries, each complex offers individual landscaping, live entertainment, open-air walkways and breathtaking views. Look for validated parking in marked structures if you're driving.

**Sacramento Street:** considered by locals to be a "secret" shopping district. Here, between Broderick and Arguello, the streets are often quiet and there's a concentration of upscale consignment and thrift stores, unusual children's and infant's clothing and toy stores, designer men's and women's clothing, furniture, fine linens and antiques for the house and garden. Bring your credit card as it's pricey.

## Hotel Prices

Categories based on average cost of a double room for one night.
**$** = under $65
**$$** = up to $100
**$$$** = up to $150
**$$$$** = over $150

## OREGON

### WHERE TO STAY

### ASTORIA
**Clementine's**
847 Exchange Street, OR 97103
Tel: 503-325-2005
Web: www.clementines-bb.com
A classic Italianate Victorian building with pretty English cottage gardens and a small library. The inn has five rooms with queen-sized beds, private bathrooms. One room has a gas fireplace. **$$**

**Crest Motel**
5366 Leif Erickson Dr, OR 97103
Tel: 503-325-3141.
Exceptionally nice motel with superb river views, hot tub on lawn under the gazebo and continental breakfast. **$$**

### BANDON
**Hostelling International – Sea Star**
375 Second Street, OR 97411
Tel: 541-347-9632
Fax: 503-363-5304
Web: www.SeaStarBandon.com/hi-sea.html
An attractive hostel located in the historic Old Town Waterfront District. Private rooms, skylights, exposed wood beams, cozy wood-burning stove and deck with harbor views. Also on the premises is the **Inn at Face Rock**
3225 Beach Loop Road, OR 97411
Tel: 541-347-9441
Fax: 541-347-2532

Good-sized rooms with restaurant, lounge and spa. Close to area attractions. Disabled access. **$$**

### BROOKINGS
**Pacific Sunset Inn**
HWY 101N, OR 97415
Tel: 541-469-2141
Basic motel accommodation. **$**

### COOS BAY
**Best Western Holiday Motel**
411 North Bayshore Dr, OR 97420
Tel: 541-269-5111
Fax: 541-269-7111
Well-appointed rooms convenient for local attractions. Cable TV/HBO, fitness center, guest laundry, pool, spa and continental breakfast. **$**

### FLORENCE
**Johnson House**
216 Maple Street, OR 97439
Tel: 541-997-8000
Web: www.touroregon.com/thejohnsonhouse
Very reasonable accommodations in this restored Victorian house in the old town Waterfront district. **$$**

### GOLD BEACH
**City Center Motel**
94200 Harlow Street, OR 97444
Tel: 541-247-6675
Comfortable, well-maintained motel. **$**

**Tu Tu' Tun Lodge**
96550 N Bank Rogue, OR 97444
Tel: 541-247-6664
Fax: 541-247-0672
Web: www.tututun.com
A contemporary lodge in tranquil riverside setting offering gourmet dining, white-water rafting trips, guided fishing and more. **$$–$$$$**

### LINCOLN CITY
**Salishan Lodge**
PO Box 118, Glen Eden Beach, CA 97388
Tel: 541-764-3600
US Freephone: 800-452-2300
Full service, four season resort set in 750 wooded acres (304 hectares) with golf, tennis, pool fitness centers, attic lounge, and an excellent restaurant. **$$$**

### NYE BEACH
**Penny Saver Motel**
710 North Coast Hwy, OR 97365
Tel: 541-265-6631
Well-fitted rooms, some with kitchenettes. Free continental breakfast. **$**

### PORTLAND
**The Benson Hotel**
309 SW Broadway, OR 97205
Tel: 503-228-2000
Fax: 503-226-2709
Web: www.citysearch.com
Kitchenettes, in-room spa, exercise room, tennis, restaurant. **$$$$**
**Gedney Gardens B&B**
2651 N.W. Cornell Rd, OR 97210
Tel: 503-226-6514
Fax: 503-228-8134
Three attractive rooms, full breakfast included. **$**
**Hawthorn Inn & Suites**
4319 N.W. Yeon Ave, OR 97210
Tel: 503-497-9044
US Freephone: 800-528-1234
Fax: 503-497-1030
Pool, spa, sauna. **$$**
**Mark Spencer Hotel**
409 SW 11th Avenue, OR 97205
Tel: 503-224-3293
US Freephone: 800-558-3934
Fax: 503-223-0522
Web: www.markspencer.com
Rooftop garden deck, some kitchenettes. **$$$**
**Shilo Suites Hotel**
11707 N.E. Airport Way, OR 97220
Tel: 503-252-7500
US Freephone: 800-222-2244
Fax: 503-254-0794
Pool, spa, exercise room, sauna, restaurant. **$$$**

### REEDSPORT
**Tropicana Motel**
1593 Highway Ave 101, OR 97467
Tel: 541-271-3671
US Freephone: 800-799-9920
Good-sized rooms with cable TV. Rooms with refrigerators, microwaves and kitchens are available. Free continental breakfast included. **$**

### ROCKAWAY BEACH
**101 Motel**
530 Hwy 101, OR 97136
Tel: 530-355-2420

---

## Restaurant Prices

Categories based on average cost of dinner and a glass of wine, before tip.
**$** = under $15
**$$** = up to $30
**$$$** = over $30

---

Well-fitted, good value motel rooms with nice views, fireplaces, kitchens and cable television. Hot tub. Wheelchair accessible. **$**

### SEASIDE
**Hostelling International – Seaside**
930 North Holladay Dr, OR 97138
Tel: 503-738-7911
Email: HISeaside@Transport.com
On the Necanicum River, four blocks from the ocean. Amenities include kitchen, outdoor decks and lawn on river, barbecue, laundry, kayak and canoe rental, espresso bar. **$**

### TILLAMOOK
**Tillamook Inn**
1810 Hwy 101N, OR 97141
Tel: 503-842-4413
Pleasant motor inn, some units with kitchenettes. **$**

### YACHATS
**Fireside Motel**
1881 North Hwy 101, OR 97498
Tel: 541-547-3636
Older, well-maintained motel. Some ocean-view rooms with balconies and a few with gas fireplaces. **$$$**

---

## WHAT TO EAT

### ASTORIA
**Columbia Cafe**
1114 Marine Drive
Tel: 503-325-2233
Buzzing atmosphere and gloriously fresh seafood. **$$**
**The Ship Inn**
1 Second Street
Tel: 503-325-0033
Decent English pub-style grub. **$**

### BANDON
**Bandon Boatworks Restaurant**
275 Lincoln Avenue SW
Tel: 541-347-9057

Excellent fresh seafood and lighthouse views. **$**

### BROOKINGS
**Wharfside Seafood Restaurant**
16362 Lower Harbor Road
Tel: 541-469-7316
Best casual. **$$**

### CANNON BEACH
**Lazy Susan Cafe**
126 North Hemlock
Tel: 503-436-2816
Excellent, filling breakfasts with a few lighter alternatives. **$**

### FLORENCE
**Blue Hen Cafe**
1675 Hwy 101
Tel: 5411-997-3907
Homely place dishing up generous servings of lovingly prepared food. Highlights are the crepes and the large, hot baking powder biscuits. **$**

### LINCOLN CITY
**Bay House**
5911 Southwest Hwy 101
Tel: 541-996-3222
Popular seafood restaurant. **$$**

### MANZANITA
**Blue Sky Cafe**
154 Laneda Avenue
Tel: 503-368-5712
Eclectic menu featuring fresh local produce, much of it organic. **$$**

### NEWPORT
**Canyon Way Bookstore and Restaurant**
1216 Southwest Canyon Way
Tel: 541-265-8319
Best lunch. **$**

### PORTLAND
**Bijou Café**
132 SW Third Avenue
Tel: 503-222-3187
Popular downtown café. Great breakfasts. **$**
**Bread and Ink**
3610 Hawthorne Boulevard
Tel: 503-239-4756
Well-prepared food cooked with fresh ingredients and cheerful service justify this café's popularity. Eclectic menu. **$**

**Café des Amis**
1987 NW Kearney Street
Tel: 503-295-9060
French bistro. Good wine list. **$$**

**Fullers Coffee Shop**
136 Northwest Ninth Avenue
Tel: 503-222-5608
No frills – just dependable, satisfying breakfasts and lunches. **$**

**Jake's Famous Crawfish**
401 SW 12th
Tel: 503-249-8486
Mouthwatering seafood. **$$**

*YACHATS*
**The Adobe Resort and Restaurant**
15555 Hwy 101
Tel: 541-547-3141
Good-quality, well-prepared steaks and fine views. **$$**

### SHOPPING

*PORTLAND*
**Saturday Market**
Food, arts and crafts stalls. Bustling, lively atmosphere. From March to December on Saturdays and Sundays.

**Powell's City of Books**
1005 West Burnside Street
Browse for hours.

**Old Town district**
Specialty shops in lovely setting.

**Portland Pendleton Shop**
900 South West Fourth Avenue
A good stock of the famous Oregon Pendleton shirts.

### WASHINGTON

#### WHERE TO STAY

*ABERDEEN*
**Flamingo Motel**
1120 East Wishkah, WA 98520
Tel: 360-532-4103
Clean, functional motel with 20 comfortable units. **$**

*CHINOOK*
**Hostelling International – Fort Columbia**
PO Box 224, WA 98614
Tel: 360-777-8755
Web: www.washingtonhostels.org/
Spectacular river views from this hillside hostel. Good spot for whale watching. Amenities include kitchen, laundry facilities, fireplace on-site parking and bicycles. **$**

*ELMA*
**Hostelling International – Grays Harbor Hotel**
6 Ginny Lane, WA 98541
Tel: 360-482-3119
Email: ghhostel@techline.com
Located halfway between Olympia and Aberdeen. Amenities include kitchen, library, hot tub, self-service bicycle repair shop and storage. **$**

*GRAYLAND*
**Walsh Motel**
1593 Hwy 105, WA 98547
Tel: 360-267-2191
With 24 standard units some with wheelchair access. **$**

*OLYMPIA*
**Cavanaughs at Capitol Lake**
2300 Evergreen Park Dr. SW, OR 98502
Tel: 360-943-4000
Fax: 360-357-6604
With a beautiful natural setting on the outside, the rooms inside offer whirlpools, balconies and all modern conveniences. **$$$**

*RAYMOND*
**Maunu's Mountcastle Motel**
524 Third Street, WA 98577
Tel: 360-942-5571
Spotless rooms, some with microwaves and refrigerators. **$**

#### WHERE TO EAT

*ABERDEEN*
**Bridges Restaurant**
112 N G Street
Tel: 360-532-6563
Fine dining in a relaxed setting of brass, glass and dark wood. Menu features steak and seafood. **$$**

*CHINOOK*
**Sanctuary Restaurant**
794 SR 101
Tel: 360-777-8380
Avoiding all innuendo's of sinful desserts and heavenly starters, you can pull up a pew to dine in this restored Methodist church. **$$**

### Hotel Prices

Categories based on average cost of a double room for one night.
**$** = under $65
**$$** = up to $100
**$$$** = up to $150
**$$$$** = over $150

*OLYMPIA*
**La Petit Mason**
101 Division Street
Tel: 360-943-8812
The French-country decor is quiet and will relax you so you can fully enjoy the menu of fresh seafood and decadent desserts. **$$**

**Santosh Restaurant**
116 Fourth Avenue
Tel: 360-943-3442
Serving the best north Indian cuisine in Olympia, Santosh also claims one of the trendiest settings in the city. **$$**

# Further Reading

## General

*American Diner: Then and Now* by J.S. Gutman. (Harper Perennial, 1993).

*Another Country* by James Baldwin. (Dell, 1988).

*The Book of the American West* ed. Jay Monaghan. (Julian Messner Inc, 1963).

*Great Plains* by Ian Frazier. (Farrar, Straus and Giroux, 1989).

*In Search of America* by John Steinbeck. (Viking, 1962).

*Legends of the American Desert* by Alex Schoumatoff. (Knopf, 1997).

*Native America*, by Christine Mather, photographs by Jack Parsons. (New York: Clarkson Potter, 1991).

*The Oxford Illustrated Literary Guide to the United States* by Eugene Ehrlich & Gorton Carruth. (Oxford University Press, 1982).

*Redwood Pioneer: A Frontier Remembered* by Andrew Genzoli & Wallace E Marin. (Schooner Features, 1970).

*Skid Road: An Informal Portrait of Seattle* by Murray Morgan. (University of Washington Press, 1988 ).

*Smithsonian Guide to Historic America*, Henry Wiencek, New York: Stewart. (Tabori and Chang, 1989).

*Still Life in Harlem* by Eddy L. Harris. (Henry Holt and Company, Inc, 1966).

*War So Terrible*, Sherman and Atlanta, by James P. Jones and James L. McDonough. (WW Norton and Co, New York, 1987).

*Webster's American Biographies* (G & C Merriam Co, 1974)

## Fiction

*Always Outnumbered, Always Outgunned*, Walter Mosley. (W.W. Norton & Company, 1977).

*Black Cherry Blues* by James Lee Burke, New York, (Random House, Inc).

*Bonfire of the Vanities* by Tom Wolfe. (Farrar, Straus, Giroux, 1987).

*The Border Trilogy* by Cormac McCarthy. (Alfred A Knopf, Inc. 1994).

*The Bostonians* Henry James. (Knopf, 1993).

*Brokenback Mountain*, Annie Proulx. (The New Yorker, October 13 1997; London, Fourth Estate Limited, 1998).

*Death Comes to the Archbishop*, Willa Cather. (Alfred A Knopf, 1927).

*The Friends of Eddie Coyle* by George Higgins. (Viking Penguin, 1987).

*Gone With The Wind*, by Margaret Mitchell. (MacMillan, 1936).

*Lake Woebegon Days* by Garrison Keillor. (Viking Penguin, 1985).

*Midnight in the Garden of Good and Evil*, by John Berendt. (Random House, 1994).

*My Antonia* by Willa Cather. (Houghton Mifflin, 1918).

*Riders of the Purple Sage*, by Zane Grey. (New York: Penguin, 1990).

*The Scarlet Letter* by Nathaniel Hawthorne. (Knopf, 1992).

*Tales of the City*, by Armistead Maupin. (Chronicle Publishing Company, 1978).

*Tortilla Curtain* by T Coraghessan Boyle. (Bloomsbury Publishing, plc, 1995).

*Where I'm Calling From*, Raymond Carver. (New York: Random House 1986).

*The Wrong Case*, James Crumley. (New York, Random House Ltd. 1975).

## On the Road

*Blue Highways: A Journey into America* by William Least Heat Moon. (Little, Brown and Company, 1982).

*The California Highway Book* by Rick Adams & Louise McCorkle. (Ballantine Books, 1985).

*Drive They Said: Poems About Americans and Their Cars* edited by Kurt Brown. (Milkweed Editions, 1994).

*Driving to Detroit: An Automotive Odyssey* by Lesley Hazleton. (The Free Press, 1998).

*Fear and Loathing in Las Vegas* by Hunter S Thompson. (Random House, 1972).

*The Lost Continent: Travels in Small Town America* by Bill Bryson. (Secker and Warburg, 1989).

*Lost Highway: Journeys and Arrivals of American Musicians* by Peter Guralnick. (Vintage Books, 1982).

*The New Roadside America* by Doug Kirby, Ken Smith and Doug Kirby. (Simon and Schuster1992).

*Open Road: A Celebration of the American Highway* by Phil Patton. (Simon and Schuster, 1986).

*Out West: American Journey Along the Lewis and Clark Trail* by Dayton Duncan. (Viking Penguin, 1987).

*An Overland Journey* by Horace Greeley (Knopf, 1963).

*Traveling the Oregon Trail* by Julie Fanselow. (Falcon Press, 1992).

*Travels with Charley: in Where the Road and the Sky Collide: America Through the Eyes of its Drivers* by K.T, Berger. (Henry Holt, 1993).

## Other Insight Guides

The book you are now holding guides you through the infinite variety of the United States. For more detailed information about particular cities, states and regions, Insight Guides publishes a comprehensive range of titles.

Companion titles to the present book include **Western United States, Alaska, American Southwest, Atlanta, Boston, California, Northern California, Southern California, Chicago, Florida, Hawaii, Los Angeles, Miami, New England, New Orleans, New York City, New York State, The Old South, Pacific Northwest, Philadelphia, The Rockies, San Francisco, Seattle, Texas,** and **Washington DC.** Thematic titles include **Native America, The Wild West, US National Parks East and US National Parks West.**

In addition, there are 14 **Insight Pocket Guides,** 16 **Insight Compact Guides** and 12 **Insight Maps.**

# ART & PHOTO CREDITS

The Art Archive 154T
Ellen Barone/Houserstock 281, 311, 332, 370, 373
Pat & Chuck Blackley 62, 62T, 66, 83, 83T, 96/97, 102, 103, 112, 142
Bruce Bernstein 23
Bodo Bondzio 165
Marcus Brooke spine bottom
Busch Gardens Tampa 87
Collection/Plains Indian Museum BBHC, Cody, WY 163T
Corbis 27
Courtesy of NY Public Library 30R, 31L, 31R
Alex Demyan/APA 259, 261, 262T, 262B, 263T, 263C, 263B
Vautier de Nanxe 22, 24/25, 235
Mark Downey 357T, 375
Courtesy of Fitzgeralds Casino 260
Michael Freeman 65T
Glyn Genin/APA 122, 130B, 130T, 131T, 131C, 233, 333T, 336T, 340, 350T, 350B, 351T, 351B
C. M. Glover 54, 185T
Carrie Grant 359
Kimberley Grant 111T
Andreas M. Gross back flap top, spine top, 16, 41, 79T, 79B, 91, 117T, 132, 134, 134T, 139, 146, 148T, 152, 169T, 174/175, 176/177, 183, 198, 198T, 220, 221, 224, 224T, 227, 232, 242, 252T, 258, 306, 315, 384
Blaine Harrington 44/45, 105, 145T, 178
Rankin Harvey/Houserstock 168, 212, 274TR
Christian Heeb/Look 148, 149
Jack Hollingsworth back cover centre left, 274BR, 283T, 287
Dave G. Houser/Houserstock 59T, 61, 74, 76, 77, 78T, 78B, 106, 107, 126, 155, 170, 264, 267, 270, 294, 295, 325, 330, 330T, 331, 335, 337
Jan Butchofsky-Houser/Houserstock 60BL, 60BR, 77, 78T, 78B, 121, 268, 269, 271, 296, 376TL, 376BR
Index Stock 274TL
Gavriel Jecan 219

Caroline Jones 5B, 15, 106T, 125
Catherine Karnow back flap bottom, back cover bottom left, front flap bottom, 2/3, 2B, 4/5, 4B, 6/7, 8/9, 10/11, 12/13, 14, 17, 42/43, 72, 90, 98, 143, 150, 153, 214, 216, 217, 218, 225, 247, 277, 280, 289, 302, 303, 307, 308T, 309C, 309B, 310, 313, 314, 316/317, 318/319, 320, 324, 328, 334, 336, 338, 339, 341, 341T, 342, 345, 352, 356, 357, 358, 360, 361, 363, 363T, 364, 365, 365T, 368, 369, 376TR, 377, 378, 380, 381, 383
Paul Karr/APA 81, 86T, 91T, 114T, 125T, 132T, 133, 141T
Dick Kent 215
Bob Krist 246, 249T
Las Vegas Convention & Visitors Bureau 229
Lyle Lawson 63, 65, 68, 71, 80, 182, 189, 190, 191, 199
Bill Lea 68, 187
Christina Lease 327
Don Leonard 362
Robert Llewellyn 63, 186
Teresa Machan back cover top right, 1, 189T, 192T, 194, 197, 202, 203, 208, 208T, 209, 210, 211, 217T, 222, 223, 226L, 226R, 227T, 228, 229, 230, 231
Fred W. Marvel 205, 206, 207
Robert P. Matthews 57, 57T
Buddy Mays/Travelstock 58, 115, 117, 119, 120, 128, 129,

Cartographic Editor Zoë Goodwin
Production Linton Donaldson
Design Consultants Carlotta Junger, Graham Mitchener
Picture Research Hilary Genin, Natasha Babaian
Proofreading Lisa Cussans
Indexing Elizabeth Cook

140, 141, 147, 151, 157, 158T, 159, 162, 163, 200, 201, 292, 297, 305, 308B, 309T, 366, 371, 371T, 374
Memphis City & Travel Visitors Bureau 196BL, 196BR, 197
Metropolitan Museum of Art 213T
Robert & Linda Mitchell 283, 288
Terrence Moore 160
Eleanor S. Morris 272, 273, 274BL
NY State Economic Development 116, 118
Laurence Parent 276, 278, 279, 284, 286
Brian Parker/Tom Stack & Associates 60TL, 60TR, 85TR, 89
Charlie Parker/Houserstock 290, 299
Christie Parker/Houserstock 293T, 295
Jack Parsons 291TL, 291BL, 291R, 295T
Peter Newark's American Pictures 286T
Sylvia Pitcher 55, 64, 69, 70, 70T, 185, 188, 192, 193, 195, 196TL, 254, 275
POVA 376BL, 379
Mark Read/APA 86, 255
Richard Weston Photography 38
The Ronald Grant Archive 29, 33
Route 66 Magazine 34, 35, 36, 37, 39, 40
John Running 298
Scott Rutherford 233T
David Sanger 343, 346, 347, 348, 353, 355, 355T, 367, 372, 375T, 381T, 382
William Schemmel 67, 249, 250
Stone 285
Texas Tourist Development Agency (Michael Murphy) 240/241
Tom Till 171, 257, 301
Tom Stack & Associates 88, 89, 234
Topham Picturepoint 18/19, 21, 30L
Stephen Trimble 164, 378T
Trip/K Cardwell 129T, 251
Trip/Tony Freeman 123
Trip/J Greenberg 114, 213
Trip/K McLaren 266
Trip/P Musson 238/239

# Index

## a

Abbeville, LA 269
Aberdeen, WA 170, 382
Acadiana, LA 265, 267–71
Acoma Sky City, NM 217
Adrian, TX 212
Alabama 251–8
The Alamo, TX 281–3, 285
Alamogordo, NM 290, 291–2
Albion, CA 356
Albuquerque, NM 36, 212, 215–16
Alcatraz, CA 350
Alcott, Louisa May 103–4
Algodones Dunes, CA 314
All American Canal, CA 314
Alligator Alley, FL 88
Amarillo, TX 211–12
Amboy, CA 230
Amboy Crater, CA 230
American Advertising Museum, OR
    376
American Indian Arts Museum, NM
    214
American Museum of Fly Fishing,
    VT 112
American Swedish Institute, MN
    136
Amish 128–9
Amistad Lake, TX 285
Anadarko Basin Museum of Natural
    History, OK 209
Anaheim, CA 333
Anchor Bay, CA 356
Anderson, Laurie 31
Angola, IN 127
Annapolis, MD 61–2
Antebellum Trail, TN 193
Apache Junction, AZ 306
Apache Trail, AZ 306–7
Appalachian Trail 110, 190
Aquarium of the Americas, LA 263
Aquarium of the Pacific, CA 333
Arcadia, CA 234
Arcadia, OK 205
Arcata, CA 362–3
Arizona 40, 174–5, 178, 218,
    220–29, 298–313
Arizona-Sonora Desert Museum,
    AZ 303
Arkansas 197–201
Arlington, MA 103
Arlington, VT 112–13
Ascutney, VT 108

Ash Fork, AZ 226
Asheville, NC 189–90
Aspenfest Motorcycle Rally, NM
    290
Astoria, OR 378–80
Astoria Column, OR 380
Astrodomain, TX 274
Atchafalaya Swamp, LA 267
Atlanta, GA 244–5, 247
Atlanta ByPass, GA 250–51
Atmore, AL 254–5
Austin, TX 275–7, 278
Avenue of the Giants, CA 359
Azalea Reserve, CA 363
Azalea State Park, OR 367
Azusa, CA 234

## b

Babe Ruth Birthplace, MD 60
Badlands, SD 139–141
Badlands National Park, SD 140
Bahia Honda State Recreation
    Area, FL 90
Balboa Peninsula, CA 331
Ballston Spa, NY 114
Baltimore, MD 60, 61
Bandera Volcano, NM 217
Bandon, OR 370
Barstow, CA 230, 231–2
Baton Rouge, LA 266–7
Battenkill River, VT 112
Battle Rock, OR 369
Bay St Louis, MS 260
Bayou La Batre, AL 258
Bayport, FL 86
Beale Wagon Road Historic Trail,
    AZ 224
Beaufort, SC 77
Belle Meade Plantation, TN 194
Bellingrath Gardens and Home, AL
    257–8
Belmont Mansion, TN 194
Belmont Shore, CA 332
Benson, AZ 302
Benton, AR 197
Big Basin Park, CA 348
Big Bear, CA 234
Big Belt Mountains, MT 161
Big Bend National Park, TX 284,
    286–7
Big Creek Baldy Mountain, MT 165
Big Horn Basin, WY 154
Big Horn County Museum, MT 153
Big Pine Key, FL 91
Big Sur, CA 42, 316–17, 344–6,
    349
Big Texan Steak Ranch and Opry,
    TX 211

Big Timber, MT 153
Bighorn Canyon, MT 153
Bighorn Mountains, WY 149, 153
Bighorn National Forest, WY 153
Billings, MT 153
Billings Farm and Museum, VT 113
Billy the Kid 290, 291, 294–5,
    296, 297
Biloxi, MS 259–60
Biltmore Estate, NC 189
Biltmore Hotel, AZ 309
Biosphere 2, AZ 305–6
Bisbee, AZ 301–2
Bitterroot Valley, MT 164
Bixby Bridge, CA 346, 349
Black Hills, SD 139, 144–8
Black Hills National Forest, WY
    149
Black Swamp, OH 126
Blackfeet Reservation, MT 163
Black's Beach, CA 325
Blacksburg, VA 188
Blimp Hangar Air Museum, OR 374
Blue Earth, MN 136, 137
Blue Ridge Mountains, VA 183,
    184, 187–8
Blue Ridge Parkway, VA 55, 66,
    67, 187, 189
Blyn, WA 168
Boardman State Park, OR 367
Bodega, CA 353
Bolinas, CA 353
Bolivar Peninsula, TX 272
Bolsa Chica Ecological Reserve,
    CA 332
Bonners Ferry, ID 165
Bonnie and Clyde 33
Boston, MA 100–101, 103
Bozeman, MT 153, 160
Bracketville, TX 285
Bradenton, FL 87
Breaux Bridge, LA 264, 268, 269
Bridgewater Corners, VT 110, 111
Brimfield, IN 127
British Columbia 167, 169
Brocton, NY 123
Brookings, OR 367
Browning, MT 163
Brunswick, GA 82
Buffalo Bill see Cody, William F.
Buffalo Bill Dam, WY 155
Buffalo Gap National Grassland, SD
    140
Buffalo, NY 120, 123
Buffalo, WY 150
Burgess Junction, WY 153
Burma Shave 37, 143, 208, 209,
    213, 230, 231, 376
Busch Gardens, FL 87

## c

Cabinet Mountains, MT 165
Cabrillo Beach, CA 333
Cadillac Ranch, TX 212
Cajun Country, LA 265–71
Calamity Jane 148
Calico, CA 232
Calico Ghost Town, CA 232, 235
California 6–7, 12–13, 230–37, 314–65
California Desert Information Center, CA 232
California Route 66 Museum, CA 233
California Surf Museum, CA 328
Calvin Coolidge Historic Site, VT 111
Cambria, CA 342, 344
Cambridge, MA 103
Cambridge, NY 113
Camelback Mountain, AZ 308, 309
camels 312, 313
Camillus, NY 118
*Camino Real* 290
Canandaigua, NY 118
Cannon Beach, OR 378
Canoe, AL 254
Canton, OH 125
Canute, OK 208
Canyon Ferry Lake, MT 161
Canyon River, AZ 306
Cape Blanco, OR 370
Cape Canaveral, FL 85
Cape Disappointment Lighthouse, WA 381
Cape Flattery, WA 170
Cape Foulweather, OR 374
Cape Hatteras National Seashore, NC 70
Cape Lookout National Seashore, NC 70
Cape Meares Lighthouse, OR 375
Cape Mendocino Lighthouse, CA 361
Cape Neddick Light Station, ME 106
Cape Perpetua, OR 372
Capistrano Mission, CA 330, 331
Capitola, CA 348
Carlsbad, CA 325, 327
Carmel, CA 347–8
Carmel Beach, CA 347
Carmel Mission, CA 347
Carson, Rachel 106
Carver Museum, AL 252–3
Cascade Range, WA 167
Cascades National Recreation Trail, VA 188

Casey Jones Village, TN 195
Castroville, CA 348
Castroville, TX 285
Cave of the Mounds, WI 132
Cayucos, CA 342
Cedar Point, OH 126
Center Harbor, NH 107
Chain O'Lakes State Park, IN 127
Channel Islands, CA 340
Chapel Hill, NC 70, 71
Charleston, OR 370
Charleston, SC 74–7
Charlottesville, VA 65–6
Chattahoochee River, GA 252
Cheekwood, TN 194
Cherokee, NC 190
Cherry Valley, NY 115
Chevalier, Michael 16, 23
Chevelon Canyon, AZ 222
Chicago, IL 122, 130–31
Chimney Rock Natural Heritage Site, NC 190
Chinook, WA 380
Chiricahua National Monument, AZ 299, 300
Chisholm Trail, OK 206–7
Chisos Basin, TX 286–7
Chittenango, NY 117
Chittenango Falls, NY 117
Church of Elvis, OR 376
Circle Trail, MN 138
Ciudad Acuna, Mexico 285
Ciudad Juárez, Mexico 288–9
Civil Rights Memorial, AL 254
Claremont, CA 234
Claremont, NH 108
Claremore, OK 205
Clark, William *see* Lewis and Clark
Clarke Memorial Museum, CA 362
Clearwater Beach, FL 86
Cleveland, OH 124–5
Cleveland National Forest, CA 315
Cline's Corner, NM 215
Clingman's Dome, TN/NC 190, 191
Clinton, OK 207–8
Clinton Presidential Library, AR 198
Cloudcroft, NM 292
Cloverdale, OR 374
Cody, WY 154–5
Cody, William F. "Buffalo Bill" 24, 151, 154–5
Coeur d'Alene, ID 164, 165–6
Colorado 150
Colorado River 314
Columbia River 167, 379–80
Columbia River Maritime Museum, OR 379

Concord, MA 103–4
Confederate Museum, GA 250
Confusion Hill, CA 358
Connor Battlefield, WY 152
Continental Divide, MT 161, 164
Continental Divide, NM 297
Conway, TX 211
Cookeville, TN 192
Cooks Range, NM 295–6
Coolidge, Calvin 111
Coon Valley, WI 134
Cooper, James Fenimore 115
Cooperstown, NY 115
Coos Bay, OR 370
Coquille River Lighthouse, OR 370
Corbin Covered Bridge, NH 108
Corn Palace, SD 138–9
Cornish, ME 107
Corona del Mar, CA 331
Cottonwood, SD 139
Coulee City, WA 167
Country Music Hall of Fame, TN 194–5
covered bridges 96–7, 108
Crazy Horse Memorial, SD 146–7
Crescent City, CA 365
Cross Creek, FL 84
Crow Agency, MT 153
Crow Indian Reservation, MT 152
Crystal Beach, TX 272
Crystal Caverns, VA 184
Cumberland Island, GA 83
Custer, George Armstrong 144, 152–3
Cuyahoga Valley, OH 125

## d

Daggett, CA 231
Dalí, Salvador 86
Dallas, TX 276
Dana Point, CA 329
Dandridge, TN 190
Darien, GA 81–2
Dartmouth College, NH 109
Dateland, AZ 310
Davenport, CA 348
Davenport, OK 205
Davis, Jefferson 248, 253, 259, 260
De Tocqueville, Alexis 16, 23, 26
Deadwood, SD 147–8
Dean Creek Elk Viewing Area, OR 372
Dearborn, MI 126
Del Mar, CA 326
Del Rio, TX 284, 285
Delaware River Valley, NJ 57
Deming, NM 295

Denver, CO 150
Depoe Bay, OR 373
Depot Museum, CA 360
Depot Museum, TN 192
Desert View Tower, CA 315
Detroit, MI 126
Devil's Gulch, SD 138
Devil's Punchbowl, OR 373
Devil's Rope Museum, TX 210
Devil's Tower, WY 149
Discovery Bay, WA 168
Disney World, FL 85
Disneyland, CA 333
Dodgeville, WI 132
Dorothea's Christmas, NY 116
Dorset, VT 112
Dripping Springs, TX 278
Drive-Thru Tree, CA 359–60
Dublin, NC 72
Dungeness, WA 169
Dunkirk, NY 123
Dunn, NC 72
Durham, NC 69, 70
Dylan, Bob 134

### e

Early Man Site, CA 232
Earp, Wyatt 300–301
Eastman, George 119
*Easy Rider* 32, 33
Echo Canyon Trail, AZ 300
Edison National Historic Site, NJ 55–6
Edison, Thomas 55–6, 87, 126
Edisto Island, SC 77
Edmonds, WA 167
Egypt, NY 119
El Cabrillo Trail 321
El Cajon, CA 315
El Centro, CA 314
El Morro, NM 217
El Paso, TX 288–9
El Rancho Hotel and Motel, NM 218
El Reno, OK 206
Elizabethtown, NC 72
Elk, CA 356
Elk City, OK 208–9
Elk River Fish Hatchery, OR 370
Elkton, VA 185
Emerson, Ralph Waldo 103, 104
Enaville Resort, ID 166
Encinitas, CA 327
Endless Caverns, VA 184
EPCOT Center, FL 85
Erick, OK 209
Erie, PA 124
Erie Canal, NY 114–20

Esalen Institute, CA 346
Esperance, NY 115
Essex, CA 230
Eunice, LA 268
Eureka, CA 362
Evangeline Oak, LA 269
Everglades, FL 88–9
Evergreen, AL 254
Exotic World Museum, CA 232
Explore Park, VA 188

### f

Fairfax, VA 183
Fairlee, VT 109
Fairmount Park, MD 61
Fayetteville, NC 72
Fern Canyon, CA 364
Ferndale, CA 359, 360–61
Finger Lakes, NY 117, 118
Flagstaff, AZ 223–4
Flathead Indian Reservation, MT 161
Flathead Lake, MT 162
Flathead National Forest, MT 162
Florence, MN 137
Florence, OR 372
Florida 8–9, 50, 83–93
Florida Keys 89–91
Folklore Village, WI 132
Ford, Henry 26, 87, 126
Ford, John 32–3
Forks, WA 169
*Forrest Gump* 29, 33
Fort Bliss Military Reservation, NM 289, 291
Fort Bowie, AZ 299–300
Fort Bragg, CA 357–8
Fort Candy, WA 380
Fort Clatsop, OR 378
Fort Herkimer Church, NY 116
Fort King George State Historic Site, GA 82
Fort Myers, FL 87
Fort Phil Kearny, WY 151
Fort Reno, OK 206
Fort Ross, CA 353, 354, 355
Fort Sill, OK 207
Fort Smith, MT 153
Fort Smith, OK 201
Fort Snelling, MN 135
Fort Stevens, OR 378
Fort Sumner, NM 295
Fortuna, CA 360
Foss, OK 208
Four Corners 218
Four Peaks, AZ 308
Foyil, OK 204–5
Franklin, Benjamin 61

Franklin Mountains, TX 289, 290
Fray Marcos Hotel, AZ 225
Fredericksburg & Spotsylvania County Memorial National Military Park, VA 62
Fredericksburg, TX 278
Fredericksburg, VA 62–3
Fredonia, NY 123
Front Royal, VA 184
Frost, Robert 111

### g

Gainesville, FL 84
Gallatin National Forest, MT 159
Gallup, NM 218
Galveston, TX 271–3
Garberville, CA 359
Gardiner, MT 159
Garibaldi, OR 377
Garretson, SD 138
Garrison, MT 161
Garryowen, MT 152
Gasquet, CA 365
Gatlinburg, TN 190
Gaviota State Park, CA 341
Geary, OK 206
Geneva, NY 118
George Washington National Forest, VA 66
Georgetown, SC 74
Georgia 77–83, 244–52
Georgia Music Hall of Fame, GA 250
Gibson Guitars 160
Gila Bend, AZ 310, 311
Gila Cliff Dwellings National Monument, NM 296–7
Gillette, WY 149
Gingerbread Mansion Inn, CA 360–1
Glacier National Park, MT 157, 162–3
Gleeson, AZ 300
Glendora, CA 234
Glenrio, TX 212
Goffs, CA 230
Going-to-the-Sun Road, MT 162–3
Gold Beach, OR 368–9
Golden Bluffs Beach, CA 364
Golden and Silver Falls State Park, OR 370
Goldfield Ghost Town, AZ 306
Goldroad, AZ 228
Goldston's Beach, NC 72
Gorham, ME 107
Graceland, TN 196
Grand Bay, AL 258
Grand Canyon, AZ 225

Grand Chenier, LA 270
Grand Coulee Dam, WA 166, 167
Grand Ole Opry, TN 182, 194
Grand Strand, SC 73
Grand Teton, WY 94–5
Grand Teton National Park, WY
  94–5, 157, 158, 159
Grants, NM 217
Grantville, GA 252
Graphite Reactor, TN 192
Gray, Thomas 191
Gray Whale Cove State Beach, CA
  348
Grayland, WA 382
Grays Harbor, WA 382
Great Plains, MT 157
Great Smoky Mountains National
  Park, NC/TN 190
Green Mountain National Forest,
  VT 111
Greenfield Village, MI 126
Greensboro, NC 70
Griffiss Air Base, NY 117
Groom, TX 211
Gros Ventre Mountains, WY 159
Guadalupe, CA 341
Gualala, CA 355–6
Gulf of Mexico, FL 86, 88, 255–6,
  258–61, 265, 269–73
Gulfport, MS 260
Guthrie, OK 203
Guthrie, Woody 15, 30, 31–2, 204

**h**

Hackberry, AZ 228
Haley, Alex 191
Half Moon Bay, CA 348
Hamburg, NY 105, 123
Hanover, NH 109
Harbor, OR 367
Harris Beach State Park, OR 368
Harris Neck National Wildlife
  Refuge, GA 81
Harrison Museum of African
  American Culture, VA 188
Hashknife Posse 221–2
Haystack Rock, OR 378
Hazen, AR 197
Heard Museum, AZ 308
Hearst Castle, CA 342, 343–4
Hearst, William Randolph 337,
  343–4
Heart Mountain, WY 154
Hebo, OR 374
Heceta Head Lighthouse, OR 372,
  373
Helena, MT 161
Helendale, CA 232

Hemingway, Ernest 91, 131, 217
Hemisfair Park, TX 284
Herkimer County Courthouse, NY
  116
Herkimer Home, NY 116
The Hermitage, TN 192
Hermosa Beach, CA 334–5
Hiawatha Lake, MN 138
Hickok, Wild Bill 148
Hickory, NC 189
High Island, TX 272
Hofwyl-Broadfield Plantation, GA
  82
Hoh River Valley, WA 169–70
Holbrook, AZ 221–2
Hole-in-the-Wall, WY 149
Holly Beach, LA 271
Homestake Mine, SD 147
Homestead, FL 89
Homolovi Ruins State Park, AZ
  222
Hondo, TX 285
Hot Springs, AR 201
House on the Rock, WI 133
Houston, TX 274, 275
Hudson River, NY 113
Humboldt Bay Maritime Museum,
  CA 362
Humboldt Redwoods State Park
  Visitor Center, CA 360
Humbug Mountain, OR 369
Hungry Horse, MT 162, 164
Huntington Beach, CA 318–19,
  331–2
Hydro, OK 207

**i**

Ice Cave, NM 217
Idaho 164, 165–6
Ilion, NY 116
Ilwaco, WA 380
Imperial Sand Dunes National
  Recreation Area, CA 314
Imperial Valley, CA 314–15
Independence National Historic
  Park, NJ 58
Independence (packet boat), NY
  117
Indian Museum of North America,
  SD 147
Indian Pueblo Cultural Center, NM
  216
Indiana 127–9
Indiana Historic Radio Museum, IN
  128
Interior, SD 141
International Museum of
  Photography, NY 119

Inverness, CA 353
Iron Mountain Road, SD 145
Islamadora, FL 90

**j**

Jackrabbit Trading Post, AZ 222
Jackson, GA 250
Jackson Hole, WY 159
Jackson, Thomas J. "Stonewall"
  183, 184, 187, 248
Jackson, TN 195
Jackson, WY 158, 159
Jacksonville, FL 83
Jacumba, CA 315
Jean Lafitte Scenic Byway, LA 268
Jedediah Smith Redwoods State
  Park, CA 365
Jefferson National Forest, VA 188
Jefferson, Thomas 23–4, 25, 64–5
Jenner, CA 353
Jewel Cave, SD 147
John Pennekamp Coral Reef State
  Park, FL 90
Johnson City, TX 278
Johnson, Lyndon B. 278
Johnson, Robert 31
Johnson Space Center, TX 274
Johnson, John "Jeremiah Liver-
  eating" 155
Joplin, MO 201
Joseph City, AZ 222
Juárez, Mexico 288–9
Jubilee CityFest, AL 254
Jules' Undersea Lodge, FL 90
Julia Pfeiffer Burns State Park, CA
  345
Juliette, GA 250

**k**

Kalispell, MT 162, 164
Kankakee River, IN 129
Kartchner Caverns State Park, AZ
  302
Kellyville, OK 205
Kennebunk, ME 106
Kennedy, John F. 276, 340
Kennedy Space Center, FL 85
Kerouac, Jack 30
Kettle Moraine State Forest, WI
  132
Key Largo, FL 90
Key West, FL 91
Killington, VT 111
Kinetic Sculpture Race Museum,
  CA 361
King, Jr, Martin Luther 196,
  253–4, 274

Kingman, AZ 228
Kingston, ID 166
Kingston, WA 167
Kissing Rock, OR 368
Klamath, CA 364, 365
Klamath River, CA 364
Knippa, TX 285
Knotts Berry Farm, CA 333
Knoxville, TN 190–91
Kodak/Eastman, NY 119
Kootenai Falls, MT 165
Kootenai National Forest, MT 164

**l**

La Crosse, WI 134
La Jolla, CA 325
La Luz, NM 291
La Mesa, CA 315
La Mesilla, NM 294–5
La Push, WA 170
La Verne, CA 234
Lafayette, LA 267–8
LaGrange, GA 252
Laguna, NM 217
Laguna Beach, CA 330
Lajitas, TX 287
Lake Arrowhead, CA 234
Lake Calcasieu, LA 270
Lake Erie 123–6
Lake Erie State Park, NY 123
Lake Geneva, WI 132
Lake Michigan 130, 131
Lake Okeechobee, FL 88
Lake Pend d'Oreille, ID 165
Lake Pontchartrain, LA 260, 261, 265
Lake Sunapee, NH 108
Lake Superior, MN 135
Lake Winnipesaukee, NH 107
Lambertville, NJ 57
Langlois, OR 370
Langtry, TX 286
Las Cruces, NM 294
Las Vegas, NV 229
Le Sueur, MN 137
Lead, SD 147
Leadbetter Park, WA 381
Leatherstocking District, NY 115
Leavenworth, WA 167
Lee, Robert E. 248, 253
Left Hand Spring Camp, OK 206
Leggett, CA 359
Legoland California, CA 325, 327
Lewis and Clark 15, 23–5, 157, 160–61, 378, 380, 381
Lewis and Clark Interpretive Center, WA 381
Lewis Rock, MT 160

Lexington, MA 103
Lexington, VA 187
Libby, MT 164–5
Ligonier, IN 128
Limberlost Historical Site, IN 127
Lincoln City, OR 374
Lincoln National Forest, NM 292
Little Bighorn Battlefield, MT 152–3
Little Falls, NY 115–16
Little Norway, WI 132
Little Rock, AR 197–201
Live Oak Springs, CA 315
Livingston, MT 153, 159
Lockport, NY 120
Logan Pass, MT 162
Loleta, CA 360
Lompc, CA 341
Long Beach, CA 333
Long Beach, MA 260
Long Beach, WA 380–81
Long Key State Recreation Area, FL 90
Long Sands, ME 106
Long Trail, VT 111
Longfellow, Henry Wadsworth 138, 169, 170, 269
Longhorn Saloon, SD 143
Lonoke, AR 197
Looe Key, FL 91
Lordsburg, NM 297, 299
Los Angeles, CA 234, 236–7, 334–7
Los Padres National Forest, CA 345
Lost Coast, CA 358–9, 361–2
Lovell, WY 154
Lowell Observatory, AZ 223
Luckenbach, TX 240–41, 279
Ludlow, CA 230–31
Luray Caverns, VA 184

**m**

McDonald Creek, MT 162
Macedon, NY 119
McGregor Missile Range, NM 291
McKinleyville, CA 363
McLean, TX 176–7, 210–11
Macon, GA 247, 248–50
Madison, WI 132
Maine 105–7
Makah Indian Nation, WA 170
Malbis, AL 255
Malibu, CA 339
Mammoth Hot Springs, WY 157, 158
Manassas National Battlefield Park, VA 183
Manchester, VT 112

Mandeville, LA 265
Manhattan Beach, CA 335
Manhattan Project, TN 192
Mankato, MN 137
Manzanita, OR 377
Marathon, FL 90
Marathon, TX 286
Marblehead Peninsula, OH 125
Mardi Gras 256, 262
Marfa, TX 287
Marias Pass, MT 164
Marina Del Rey, CA 335
Marine Mammal Rescue Center, CA 330
Marshes of Glynn, GA 82
Maryland 60, 61–2
Massachusetts 100–105
Massanutten Mountain, VA 185–6
Maxwell Air Force Base, AL 253
Medicine Wheel, WY 153–4
Medina, NY 120
Melville, Herman 29, 31
Memphis, TN 196
Mendocino, CA 356–7
Mendonoma, CA 355
Mendota, MN 136
Menlo Park Laboratory, MI 126
Meredith, NH 107
Mescalero Apache Indian Reservation, NM 292
Mesilla Valley, NM 294–5
Meteor Crater, AZ 222
Mexican border 284, 285, 287, 288, 289, 303, 314, 315
Miami, FL 89, 92–3
Miami, OK 207
Micanopy, FL 84
Miccosukee Indian Reservation, FL 88
Michigan 126, 130–31
Middlebury, VT 112
Midway, GA 81
Milan, NM 217
Miller, Henry 346
Miller, Roger 209
Mimbres River, NM 296
Minneapolis, MN 134–6
Minnesota 134–8
Minnesota State Fair, MN 136, 137
Minute Man National Historical Park, MA 103
Misery Bay, PA 124
Mission Bay, CA 325
Mission Dolores, CA 351
Mission San Luis Rey de Francia, CA 328
Mission San Xavier del Bac, AZ 304

Mission Trail, AZ 304
Mississippi 258–60
Mississippi River 133–6, 197, 262, 263, 266
Missoula, MT 161
Missouri 201
Missouri River, SD 139
Mitchell, SD 138–9
Mobile, AL 256–7
Mohawk, NY 116
Mojave Desert, CA 230–32, 233
Mojave Museum of History and Arts, AZ 228
Mojave River Valley Museum, CA 232
Mojave Tribal Center, CA 230
Monarch Butterfly Habitat, CA 332
Monrovia, CA 234
Montana 149, 152–3, 159–65
Montecito Inn, CA 340
Monterey, CA 347–8
Montgomery, AL 253
Montshire Museum of Science, VT 109
Monument Valley, AZ 178, 223
Moon, William Least Heat 30, 33
Moonshine Beach, CA 363
Moorcroft, WY 149
Moravians 188
Mormons 119, 164, 233, 307
Morristown, NJ 56–7
Morristown National Historical Park, NJ 56–7
Morro Bay, CA 342
Motown Historical Museum, MI 126
Mount Airy, NC 69, 188
Mount Equinox, VT 112
Mount Horeb, WI 132
Mt Jackson, VA 186
Mount Rushmore National Memorial, SD 145–6
Mount Tamalpais, CA 353
Mount Washington, NH 107
Movieland Wax Museum, CA 333
movies 28, 29, 32–3
Muir, John 360, 365, 369
Muir Woods, CA 353
Munson-Proctor Institute, NY 116–17
Murfreesboro, AR 199
Muscle Beach, CA 336
Museum of American Presidents, VA 184
Museum of Appalachia, TN 191–2
Museum Club, AZ 223
Museum of the Horse, NM 293
Museum of Making Music, CA 327

Museum of Northern Arizona, AZ 223
Museum of the Old West, WY 155
Museum of the Plains Indian, MT 163
Museum of the Rockies, MT 160
Music Valley, TN 194–5
Myers Flat, CA 359
Myrtle Beach, SC 74

**n**

Nahcotta, WA 381
Naples, CA 332
Naples, FL 87
Nappanee, IN 129
NASA 85, 274, 292
Nashville, TN 192–5
National Baseball Hall of Fame, NY 115
National Bison Range, MT 161
National Bottle Museum, NY 114
National Civil Rights Museum, TN 196
National Cowboy Hall of Fame, OK 206
National Elk Refuge, WY 158, 159
National Museum of Racing and Hall of Fame, NY 114
National Steinbeck Center Museum, CA 348
Natural Bridge, VA 66
Navajo Nation 218, 223, 224
Neah Bay, WA 170
Needles, CA 230
Needles Highway, SD 147
Nesika Beach, OR 369
Neskowin, OR 374
Nevada 229
New Hampshire 105, 107–108, 109
New Hope, PA 57
New Jersey 55–61
New London, NH 107–8
New Market, VA 184
New Mexico 212–18, 290–97
New Orleans, LA 262–3
New Prague, MN 137
New York City 52–3, 55
New York State 113–20, 123
Newberry Springs, CA 231
Newport Beach, CA 331
Newport, NH 108
Newport, OR 373
Niagara Falls, NY 120
*Niagara* (ship), PA 124
Night Rodeo, WY 155
Nixon, Richard 329
No Name Key, FL 90

Nogales, AZ 303
Norman Rockwell Exhibit, VT 112–13
Norris Dam, TN 191
Norris Lake, TN 191
Norskedalen, WI 134
North American Indian Days, MT 163
North Bend, OR 370
North Carolina 69–72, 188–90
North Carolina Homespun Museum, NC 189
North East, PA 124
North Head, WA 381
Northwest School of Wooden Boatbuilding, WA 168
Norwich, VT 109
Nubble Light, ME 106
Nye Beach, OR 373

**o**

Oak Creek Canyon, AZ 224
Oak Ridge, TN 192
Oatman, AZ 228–9
Ocala, FL 84
Oceanside, CA 326–8
Ocmulgee National Monument, GA 250
Ocotillo, CA 314
Ohio 124–6
Ojai, CA 339
Ojinaga, Mexico 287
OK Corral, AZ 300–301
Okeechobee, FL 88
O'Keeffe, Georgia 213, 214, 290
Oklahoma 201, 203–9
Oklahoma City, OK 203, 205–6, 213
Oklahoma Route 66 Museum, OK 207–8
Old Deadwood Trail, SD 139
Old Salem, NC 69–70, 188–9
Old Stone Face, MN 138
Old Stone Fort Museum Complex, NY 115
Olympia, WA 382
Olympic Peninsula, WA 167–70, 382
Oneida, NY 117
Oologah, OK 205
Opelousas, LA 268
Open Cut, SD 147
Oracle, AZ 305
The Oracle, MN 138
Orange County Marine Institute, CA 329
Orange County Museum of Art, CA 331

Oregon 366–80
Oregon Coast Aquarium, OR 373
Oregon Dunes National Recreation
   Area, OR 370–72
Oregon Trail 24
Orford, NH 109–10
Orick, CA 364
Orlando, FL 84–5
Orogrande, NM 291
Orondo, WA 167
Oswald West State Park, OR 377
Outer Banks, NC 70
Overseas Highway, FL 89, 90
Oysterville, WA 381

## p

Pacific Coast Highway, CA 321
Pacific Coast Scenic Highway, OR
   367
Pageant of the Masters, CA 330
Paguate Cubero, NM 217
Painted Desert Inn National
   Historic Landmark, AZ 221
*Pale Rider* 33
Palmyra, NY 119
Palo Duro Canyon, TX 211
Palos Verdes, CA 333
Parks, AZ 224
Pascagoula, MS 258–9
Paso Robles, CA 342–3
Pass Christian, MS 260
Passe-a-Grille Beach, FL 86
Patrick's Point State Park, CA 363
Pawlet, VT 112
Pawley's Island, SC 74
Paynes Prairie State Preserve, FL
   84
Peach Springs, AZ 228
Pebble Beach, CA 347
Pecos River, TX 285
Peninsula, OH 125
Pennsylvania 124
Pepin, WI 134
Perdido, AL 255
Petersen Museum, CA 336
Petrified Forest National Park, AZ
   221
Pfeiffer Big Sur State Park, CA 345
Philadelphia, NJ 58–61
Phillipsville, CA 359
Phoenix, AZ 307, 308–9
Picacho Peak, AZ 306
Pierre, SD 139
Pigeon Point Lighthouse, CA 348
Pinal Pioneer Parkway, AZ 306
Pine Ridge Indian Reservation, SD
   140, 143

Pioneer Museum, AZ 223
Pioneer West Historical Museum,
   TX 209–10
Pipestone, MN 137–8
Pismo State Beach, CA 341
Plank Road, CA 314
Plantation Agriculture Museum, AR
   197
Point Arena Lighthouse, CA 356
Point Lobos State Reserve, CA
   346
Point Reyes National Seashore, CA
   353
Point Vicente Interpretive Center,
   CA 333
Pollock, Jackson 155
Polson, MT 162
Pony Express 24, 221–2
Port Bolivar Ferry, TX 271, 272
Port Gamble, WA 168
Port Orford, OR 369–70
Port Townsend, WA 168
Portland, ME 106–7
Portland, OR 376
Portsmouth, NH 105
Potter Place, NH 107
Prairie Creek Redwoods Park, CA
   364
Prehistoric Gardens, OR 369
Presidio, TX 287
Presley, Elvis 195, 196, 211
Presque Isle, PA 124
Prewitt Trading Post, NM 217
Princeton, NJ 57
Pro Football Hall of Fame, OH 125

## q

Quail Botanical Gardens, CA 327
Quapaw, OK 207
Quartzite, AZ 310
Quechee, VT 109, 110
*Queen Mary* (ship), CA 333
Quilayute Indian Reservation, WA
   170

## r

Rainbow Basin, CA 232
Raleigh, NC 69, 70
Ranchester, WY 152, 153
Rancho Cucamonga, CA 230, 234
Ranger Peak, TX 289
Rapid City, SD 140, 144
Rattlesnake Mountain, WY 155
Rattlesnake Museum, NM 216
Raymond, WA 382
Red Rock Museum, NM 218
Red Rocks Amphitheater, CO 150

Red Wing, MN 134
Redondo Beach, CA 334
Redwood Information Center, CA
   364
Reedsport, OR 371
Remington Firearms Museum, NY
   116
Rendezvous Mountain, WY 159
Reynolda House, NC 189
Rice Museum, SC 74
Richfield Springs, NY 115
Richland Center, WI 133
Richmond, VA 63–4
Rim of the World Drive, CA 234
Rio Grande 284–90, 295
Ripton, VT 111
River Road, TX 287
road movies 28, 29, 32–3
*The Road Warrior* 33
Roanoke, VA 66, 186, 187–8
Robert Frost Interpretive Trail, VT
   111
Rochester, NY 119–20
Rockaway Beach, OR 377
Rockwell, Norman 112–13
Rocky Mountains 150, 154,
   157–64
Rogers, Roy 232–3, 331
Rogers, Will 204, 205, 214
Rome, NY 117
Roosevelt Lake, AZ 307
Roosevelt, Theodore 306
Roswell, NM 290
Rothko Chapel, TX 274
Route 66 35–41, 174–5, 179,
   201–37
Roy Rogers-Dale-Evans Museum,
   CA 232–3
Ruidoso, NM 290, 292–3
Ruskin, FL 87
Russell, Charles 157, 161
Rye Beach, NH 105

## s

Sabine National Wildlife Refuge, LA
   271
Saguaro National Park, AZ 303
Salem, MA 104–5
Salinas, CA 348
Salk Institute, CA 325
Salmon Harbor, OR 371
Salt Lake City, UT 164
Salt Point State Park, CA 354
Salvador Dalí Museum, FL 86–7
Samoa Cookhouse, CA 362
San Antonio, TX 278, 279, 281–4
San Antonio de Pala Mission, CA
   329

San Augustine Pass, NM 294
San Bernardino, CA 233–4
San Bernardino National Forest, CA 233–4
San Buenaventura Mission, CA 339
San Clemente, CA 329
San Diego, CA 315, 322–3, 325
San Dieguito Heritage Museum, CA 327
San Dimas, CA 234
San Francisco, CA 350–51, 353
San Juan Capistrano, CA 330, 331
San Luis Obispo, CA 341–2
San Pedro, CA 333
San Simeon, CA 343–4
San Ysidro Ranch, CA 340
Sandford, NC 72
Sandia Mountains, NM 215
Sandpoint, ID 165
Sanibel Island, FL 87
Santa Barbara, CA 340, 341
Santa Barbara Mission, CA 340
Santa Catalina Island, CA 328, 329, 331
Santa Cruz, CA 348
Santa Fe, NM 213–14, 290
Santa Fe Trail 213–14
Santa Lucia Mountains, CA 341, 342, 344
Santa Monica, CA 234, 336, 337
Santa Rosa, NM 213
Sappho, WA 169
Sapulpa, OK 205
Sarasota, FL 87
Saratoga National Historical Park, NY 113
Saratoga Springs, NY 114
Sausalito, CA 353
Savannah, GA 77, 78–9, 247
Savoy, SD 148
Sayre, OK 209
Scenic, SD 143
Schenectady, NY 114–15
Schohairie, NY 115
Scotia, CA 360
Scott Creek, CA 348
Scott, Ridley 33
Scripps Institution of Oceanography, CA 325
Sea Island, GA 82
Sea Lion Caves, OR 372
The Sea Ranch, CA 355
Seal Beach, CA 332
Seaside, OR 378
Seattle, WA 167, 172–3, 382
Second Gallatin City, MT 160–61
Sedona, AZ 224
Seligman, AZ 174–5, 226, 227–8

Seneca Falls, NY 118
Seneca Lake, NY 117, 118, 119
Seneca Wine Trail, NY 117, 118
Sequim, WA 168
Seven Mile Bridge, FL 90
Sevierville, TN 190
Shakespeare, NM 297
Shamrock, TX 209
Shark Valley, FL 88
Shenandoah Caverns, VA 184
Shenandoah National Park, VA 184–6
Sheridan, WY 151–2
Shi-Shi Beach, WA 170
Shore Acres State Park, OR 370
Shoshone Canyon, WY 155
Shoshone National Forest, WY 155
Sierra Estrella, AZ 308
Silver City, NM 296
Silver Creek, NY 123
Sioux Falls, SD 138
Siskiyou Coast, OR 367–8
Sitgreaves Pass, AZ 228
Siuslaw National Forest, OR 372, 374
Siuslaw Pioneer Museum, OR 372
Skew Arch Railroad Bridge, NY 123
Skunk Train, CA 357–8
Skyline Drive, VA 66, 184–6
Smith, Joseph 119
Smith River National Recreation Area, CA 365
Snake River, WY 159
Snoqualmie National Forest, WA 167
Solana Beach, CA 326–7
Solar One thermal plant, CA 231
Sonnenberg Gardens, NY 118
Sonoma Coast State Beach, CA 353
Sonora Desert Museum, AZ 303
South Bend, WA 381–2
South Carolina 73–7
South Dakota 138–149
Space Centers 85, 274, 292
Spearfish Canyon, SD 148
Spineel, OR 370–71
Split Rock Creek, SD 138
Spokane, WA 166
Spotted Horse, WY 149
Spouting Horns, OR 373
Springsteen, Bruce 31, 140
St Anthony Falls, MN 135
St Augustine, FL 84
St Elmo, AL 258
St Ignatius, MT 161–2
St Martinville, LA 269
St Mary, MT 163
St Paul, MN 134–6

St Petersburg, FL 86
St Simons Island, GA 82
Staunton, VA 186–7
Steinbeck, John 15, 26, 29, 31, 208, 347, 348, 359
Stewarts Point, CA 355
Stillwater Cove Ranch, CA 354
Stinson Beach, CA 353
Stockbridge, VT 111
Stockyards City, OK 205–6
Stone Mountain Park, GA 246, 247–8
Stonewall Jackson House, VA 187
Stonewall Jackson Museum, VA 184
Strasburg, VA 183–4
Stratton-Porter, Gene 127
Strong, Margaret Woodbury, NY 119–20
Stroud, OK 205
Sugarloaf Key, FL 91
Summit Inn, CA 233
Sun Studios, TN 196
Sunapee, NH 108
Sundance, WY 149
Sunset Beach, CA 332
Superstition Mountains, AZ 306, 308
Surfers Walk of Fame, CA 331
Swedenborg, Emmanuel 334
Sycamore Inn, CA 234
Syracuse, NY 117–18

**t**

Taliesin, WI 133
Taliesin West, AZ 309
Tamiami Canal, FL 88
Tampa, FL 87
Tar Heel, NC 72
Tarpon Springs, FL 86
Tennessee 190–96
Teton Range, WY *see* Grand Teton
Texas 176–7, 209–12, 240–41, 271–89
Texas Hill Country Trail 278–9
Texola, OK 208, 209
*Thelma and Louise* 33
Theodore, AL 257
Theodore Roosevelt Dam, AZ 306, 307
Thomas Creek Bridge, OR 368
Thoreau, Henry David 103, 104
Three Capes Scenic Drive, OR 375
Three Forks, MT 160
Tigua Indian Reservation, TX 289
Tijeras, NM 215
Tillamook, OR 374, 375
Tillamook Lighthouse, OR 375

Titan Missile Museum, AZ 304–5
Toledo, OH 126
Toltec Mounds State Park, AR 197
Tombstone, AZ 300–301
Tonto National Forest, AZ 306
Tonto National Monument, AZ 307
Topeka, IN 128
Topock, AZ 229
Torrey Pines Gliderport, CA 326
Torrey Pines Scenic Drive, CA 326
Torrey Pines State Beach, CA 326
Torrey Pines State Reserve, CA 326
Tortilla Flat, AZ 307
Tower of the Americas, TX 284
Townsend, MT 161
Trees of Mystery, CA 364, 365
Trenton, NJ 58, 59
Trinidad, CA 363
Trinity Site, NM 294
Troy, MT 165
Truxton, AZ 228
Tucson, AZ 302–4
Tucumcari, NM 213
Tularosa Valley, NM 290, 291–4
Tulsa, OK 205
Tumacácori National Monument, AZ 304
Tuskegee, AL 252
Twain, Mark 30
Two Guns, AZ 222

### u

Ucross, WY 149
Umpqua Bay, OR 371
Umpqua Discovery Center, OR 371
Umpqua Lighthouse, OR 371
Universal Studios Florida, FL 85
US Army National Training Center, CA 230
US Border Patrol Museum, TX 289
USS North Carolina Battleship Memorial, NC 72
Utah 164
Utica, NY 116–17
Uvalde, TX 285

### v

Valparaiso, IN 129
Van Damme State Park, CA 356
Van Horn, TX 287

Vancouver Island, Canada 167, 169, 170
Vanderbilt, George 189
Vedder Ecological Reserve, CA 330
Vega, TX 212
Venice, CA 335–6
Venice, FL 87
Ventura, CA 339
Vermilionville, LA 265, 268, 270
Vermont 96–7, 103, 108–9, 110–14
Victoria, BC 167, 169
Victorville, CA 230, 232–3
Vinita, OK 204
Virginia 54, 55, 62–6, 183–8

### w

Waddell Creek, CA 348
Walden Pond Reservation, MA 104
Waldport, OR 372
Wall Drug, SD 139, 143–4
Walnut Canyon National Monument, AZ 222
Walt Disney World, FL 85
Warrenton, OR 378
Washington, DC 26, 62, 179, 180–81
Washington, Booker T. 252
Washington Crossing State Park, NJ 57–8
Washington, George 63
Washington State 166–73, 380–82
Waterbury, VT 111
Wayfarers Chapel, CA 334
Weatherford, OK 207
Weatherford Hotel, AZ 223
Wedding Rock, CA 364
Weeki Wachee, FL 86
Wells Estuarine Reserve, ME 106
Wenatchee National Forest, WA 167
West Orange, NJ 55–6
West Point Lake, GA 252
West Woodstock, VT 111
Westfield, NY 123
Westport, CA 358
Westville, IN 129
Wheeler, OR 377
Whistle Stop Cafe, GA 250
White Lake, NC 72
White Sands Missile Range, NM 291, 292, 293

White Sands National Monument, NM 293–4
Whitewater, WI 132
Whitman, Walt 29, 31, 33, 59
Whitman, Walt 29, 31, 33, 59
Wigwam Motel, AZ 220, 2211
The Wild One 28, 33
Wildcat Road, CA 361
Will Rogers Turnpike, OK 204
Willapa Bay Interpretive Center, WA 381
Williams, AZ 40, 224–5
Williamsburg, VA 63
Wilmington, NC 72, 73
Wilson, Woodrow 26, 187
Wind Cave, SD 147
Window Rock, AZ 218
Windsor, VT 109
Winnewesa Falls, MN 138
Winona, AZ 222
Winslow, AZ 222
Winston-Salem, NC 69–70, 188–9
Winterhaven, CA 314
Wisconsin 132–4
Wolfe, Thomas 190
Women's Basketball Hall of Fame, TN 191
Women's Hall of Fame, NY 118
Woodenknife Drive-Inn, SD 141
Woodstock, VT 110
Wounded Knee Creek, SD 143
Wright, Frank Lloyd 131, 133, 147, 308, 309, 314, 334
Wyoming 94–5, 149–52, 153–5

### y–z

Yachats, OR 372
Yaquina Bay, OR 373
Yaquina Head Lighthouse, OR 366, 373
Ybor City, FL 87
Yellowstone National Park 156, 157–8
York, ME 105–6
Ysleta Mission, TX 289
Yukon, OK 206
Yulee, FL 83
Yuma, AZ 310–11
Yuma Crossing State Historical Park, AZ 312
Yuma Desert, CA 314
Yuma Territorial Prison State Historical Park, AZ 312
Zuni, NM 218

**66** I was first drawn to the
Insight Guides by the
excellent "Nepal" volume.
I can think of no book
which so effectively
captures the essence of
a country. Out of these
pages leaped the Nepal
I know – the captivating
charm of a people and
their culture. I've since
discovered and enjoyed
the entire Insight Guide
series. Each volume deals
with a country in the
same sensitive depth,
which is nowhere more
evident than in the
superb photography. **99**

*Sir Edmund Hillary*

# ☀ INSIGHT GUIDES

*The world's largest collection of visual travel guides*

## Insight Guides – the Classic Series that puts you in the picture

| | | | | |
|---|---|---|---|---|
| Alaska | China | Hong Kong | Morocco | Singapore |
| Alsace | Cologne | Hungary | Moscow | South Africa |
| Amazon Wildlife | Continental Europe | | Munich | South America |
| American Southwest | Corsica | Iceland | | South Tyrol |
| Amsterdam | Costa Rica | India | Namibia | Southeast Asia |
| Argentina | Crete | India's Western | Native America | Wildlife |
| Asia, East | Crossing America | Himalayas | Nepal | Spain |
| Asia, South | Cuba | India, South | Netherlands | Spain, Northern |
| Asia, Southeast | Cyprus | Indian Wildlife | New England | Spain, Southern |
| Athens | Czech & Slovak | Indonesia | New Orleans | Sri Lanka |
| Atlanta | Republic | Ireland | New York City | Sweden |
| Australia | | Israel | New York State | Switzerland |
| Austria | Delhi, Jaipur & Agra | Istanbul | New Zealand | Sydney |
| | Denmark | Italy | Nile | Syria & Lebanon |
| Bahamas | Dominican Republic | Italy, Northern | Normandy | |
| Bali | Dresden | | Norway | Taiwan |
| Baltic States | Dublin | Jamaica | | Tenerife |
| Bangkok | Düsseldorf | Japan | Old South | Texas |
| Barbados | | Java | Oman & The UAE | Thailand |
| Barcelona | East African Wildlife | Jerusalem | Oxford | Tokyo |
| Bay of Naples | Eastern Europe | Jordan | | Trinidad & Tobago |
| Beijing | Ecuador | | Pacific Northwest | Tunisia |
| Belgium | Edinburgh | Kathmandu | Pakistan | Turkey |
| Belize | Egypt | Kenya | Paris | Turkish Coast |
| Berlin | England | Korea | Peru | Tuscany |
| Bermuda | | | Philadelphia | |
| Boston | Finland | Laos & Cambodia | Philippines | Umbria |
| Brazil | Florence | Lisbon | Poland | USA: Eastern States |
| Brittany | Florida | Loire Valley | Portugal | USA: Western States |
| Brussels | France | London | Prague | US National Parks: |
| Budapest | Frankfurt | Los Angeles | Provence | East |
| Buenos Aires | French Riviera | | Puerto Rico | US National Parks: |
| Burgundy | | Madeira | | West |
| Burma (Myanmar) | Gambia & Senegal | Madrid | Rajasthan | |
| | Germany | Malaysia | Rhine | Vancouver |
| Cairo | Glasgow | Mallorca & Ibiza | Rio de Janeiro | Venezuela |
| Calcutta | Gran Canaria | Malta | Rockies | Venice |
| California | Great Barrier Reef | Marine Life ot the | Rome | Vienna |
| California, Northern | Great Britain | South China Sea | Russia | Vietnam |
| California, Southern | Greece | Mauritius & | | |
| Canada | Greek Islands | Seychelles | St. Petersburg | Wales |
| Caribbean | Guatemala, Belize & | Melbourne | San Francisco | Washington DC |
| Catalonia | Yucatán | Mexico City | Sardinia | Waterways of Europe |
| Channel Islands | | Mexico | Scotland | Wild West |
| Chicago | Hamburg | Miami | Seattle | |
| Chile | Hawaii | Montreal | Sicily | Yemen |

Complementing the above titles are 120 easy-to-carry Insight Compact Guides, 120 Insight Pocket
Guides with full-size pull-out maps and more than 60 laminated easy-fold Insight Maps

## Atlantic Route

| | New York, NY | Baltimore, MD | Roanoke, VA | Savannah, GA | Orlando, FL | Miami, FL | Key West, FL |
|---|---|---|---|---|---|---|---|
| New York, NY | | 202 | 543 | 811 | 1170 | 1597 | 1761 |
| Baltimore, MD | 202 | | 341 | 609 | 968 | 1395 | 1559 |
| Roanoke, VA | 543 | 341 | | 268 | 627 | 1054 | 1218 |
| Savannah, GA | 811 | 609 | 268 | | 359 | 786 | 960 |
| Orlando, FL | 1170 | 968 | 627 | 359 | | 427 | 591 |
| Miami, FL | 1597 | 1395 | 1054 | 786 | 427 | | 164 |
| Key West, FL | 1761 | 1559 | 1218 | 960 | 591 | 164 | |

## Northern Route

| | Boston, MA | Buffalo, NY | Chicago, IL | Pierre, SD | Cody, WY | Seattle, WA | Cape Flattery, WA |
|---|---|---|---|---|---|---|---|
| Boston, MA | | 872 | 1419 | 2309 | 2891 | 3961 | 4095 |
| Buffalo, NY | 872 | | 547 | 1437 | 2019 | 3089 | 3223 |
| Chicago, IL | 1419 | 547 | | 890 | 1472 | 2542 | 2676 |
| Pierre, SD | 2309 | 1437 | 890 | | 582 | 1652 | 1786 |
| Cody, WY | 2891 | 2019 | 1472 | 582 | | 1070 | 1204 |
| Seattle, WA | 3961 | 3089 | 2542 | 1652 | 1070 | | 134 |
| Cape Flattery, WA | 4095 | 3223 | 2676 | 1786 | 1204 | 134 | |

## Central Route

| | Washington DC | Memphis, TN | Joplin, MO | Amarillo, TX | Gallup, NM | Flagstaff, AZ | Los Angeles, CA |
|---|---|---|---|---|---|---|---|
| Washington DC | | 940 | 1371 | 1850 | 2270 | 2452 | 2922 |
| Memphis, TN | 940 | | 431 | 910 | 1330 | 1512 | 1982 |
| Joplin, MO | 1371 | 431 | | 479 | 899 | 1081 | 1551 |
| Amarillo, TX | 1850 | 910 | 479 | | 420 | 602 | 1072 |
| Gallup, NM | 2270 | 1330 | 899 | 420 | | 182 | 652 |
| Flagstaff, AZ | 2452 | 1512 | 1081 | 602 | 182 | | 470 |
| Los Angeles, CA | 2922 | 1982 | 1551 | 1072 | 652 | 470 | |

## Southern Route

| | Atlanta, GA | New Orleans, LA | Houston, TX | San Antonio, TX | Lordsburg, NM | Phoenix, AZ | San Diego, CA |
|---|---|---|---|---|---|---|---|
| Atlanta, GA | | 473 | 825 | 1070 | 1989 | 2213 | 2572 |
| New Orleans, LA | 473 | | 352 | 597 | 1516 | 1740 | 2099 |
| Houston, TX | 825 | 352 | | 245 | 1164 | 1388 | 1747 |
| San Antonio, TX | 1070 | 597 | 245 | | 919 | 1143 | 1502 |
| Lordsburg, NM | 1989 | 1516 | 1164 | 919 | | 224 | 583 |
| Phoenix, AZ | 2213 | 1740 | 1388 | 1143 | 224 | | 359 |
| San Diego, CA | 2572 | 2099 | 1747 | 1502 | 583 | 359 | |

## Pacific Route

| | San Diego, CA | Los Angeles, CA | San Francisco, CA | Eureka, CA | Crescent, OR | Newport, OR | Seattle, WA |
|---|---|---|---|---|---|---|---|
| San Diego, CA | | 124 | 504 | 785 | 867 | 1108 | 1399 |
| Los Angeles, CA | 124 | | 380 | 661 | 743 | 984 | 1275 |
| San Francisco, CA | 504 | 380 | | 281 | 363 | 604 | 895 |
| Eureka, CA | 785 | 661 | 281 | | 82 | 323 | 614 |
| Crescent, OR | 867 | 743 | 363 | 82 | | 241 | 532 |
| Newport, OR | 1108 | 984 | 604 | 323 | 241 | | 291 |
| Seattle, WA | 1399 | 1275 | 895 | 614 | 532 | 291 | |

**Atlantic Route**
New York (NY) - Key West (FL)

**Northern Route**
Boston (MA) - Cape Flattery (WA)

**Central Route**
Washington, DC - Los Angeles (CA)

**Southern Route**
Atlanta (GA) - San Diego (CA)

**Pacific Route**
San Diego (CA) - Seattle (WA)

# From Playpen To Podium

NOBLE

Noble Publishing Associates
1311 N.E.134th Street, Suite 2A
Vancouver, WA 98685
www.noblepublishing.com
800-225-5259

**From Playpen to Podium**
©1997 by Jeffrey L. Myers
Published by Noble Publishing Associates
1311 N.E. 134th Street, Suite 2A
Vancouver, WA 98685
Ph:800-225-5259

ISBN 1-56857-068-6

**Printed in China**

00 01 02 03 04 05 06 / 10 9 8 7 6 5 4 3 2

## DEDICATION

It requires patience and dedication to transform a self-conscious, shy and bumbling young person into a confident communicator. Jerry McCollough, H. Gene Specht, Louise Brokaw and David Boman all poured themselves into my life, and I am forever grateful. In addition, I have benefited from the ideas and encouragement of my mother and father ever since they talked me into taking a speech class in 9th grade. May all of their efforts bear fruit in the next generation of leaders!

# TABLE OF CONTENTS

Chapter One: Your Child: An Outstanding Communicator . . . . . 11

Chapter Two: How Communication Skills Relate
to Your Goals for Your Child . . . . . . . . . . . . . . . . . . . . . 15
The Communication Advantage
Goals Most Parents Have for Their Children
Reaching Your Goals Through Communication Training

Chapter Three: The Six Pillars of Communication Excellence . . . 21
The Spiritual Mantle of Family Communication
Building a Structure for Communication Excellence
How to Put the Six Pillars to Work in Your Home
Ready, Set, Grow!

Chapter Four: Adjusting Your Home Environment to
Focus on Communication Excellence . . . . . . . . . . . . . . 27
Communication Excellence Begins at Home
How to Create an "Over the T. O. P." Home Environment
How to Become More Aware of the Communication Environment
in Your Home

Chapter Five: Helping Strengthen Your Child's
Sense of Purpose in Life . . . . . . . . . . . . . . . . . . . . . . . 37
Sense of Purpose as a Foundation for Communication Development
Live as if Your Child has a Purpose
Helping Your Child Develop a Sense of Purpose
Helping Your Child Maintain a Sense of Purpose
Sense of Purpose: A Source of Energy

Chapter Six: Helping Your Child Become More Aware of
the World Around Him . . . . . . . . . . . . . . . . . . . . . . . . 47
The Importance of Awareness in Communication Development
Helping Your Child Become More Observant
Interpreting What You Observe
Evaluating What You Observe

Chapter Seven: How Your Child Can
Become a Better Learner . . . . . . . . . . . . . . . . . . . . . . . 57
How Learning and Communication Skills are Related
The Reading Road to Communication Excellence
How to Model Enthusiasm for Learning
How to Make Learning Fun
Learning Together Through Travel

**Chapter Eight: Help Your Child Become
a More Creative Thinker** . . . . . . . . . . . . . . . . . . . . . . 67

The Nature of Thought
The Nature of Creativity
Drama: Letting the Imagination Communicate
Storytelling: Can You Imagine...Can You Create?
We are Made in the Image of a Creative God

**Chapter Nine: Helping Your Child Develop
Poise in Social Situations** . . . . . . . . . . . . . . . . . . . . . 75

Have You Ever Been Embarrassed by Your Child?
The Breathtaking Significance of Social Skills
The Fear of the Unknown Makes Us Uncomfortable
How to Teach Your Child to Greet Others
How to Teach Appropriate Public Behavior
Rewarding Enthusiasm

**Chapter Ten: Helping Your Child
Relate to Others: A Life Skill** . . . . . . . . . . . . . . . . . . . 87

Empathy: A Character Quality of Christ
How to Teach Active Listening to Your Child
How to Teach Conversation Skills to Your Child
Empathy: Mission Impossible?

**Chapter Eleven: Communication-Building Activities
for Every Child** . . . . . . . . . . . . . . . . . . . . . . . . . . . 95

Now It's Time to "Get Practical"
Ideas that Work—From Playpen to Podium
How to Target Specific Skill Needs
Now It Starts...

**Chapter Twelve: Infant Communication** . . . . . . . . . . . . . . 101

Communication: A Breath of Life for Your Baby
How Important Is Communication With Your Baby?
Getting to Know Your Baby
Fourteen Powerful Ideas You Can Use Right Now
Where to Get More Information

**Chapter Thirteen: Toddler Communication** . . . . . . . . . . . . . 115

The Exciting New World of Toddlerhood
Why Is Communication Training Vital to Toddlers?
What Are the Stages of Speech Development in Toddlers?
Emphasize Talking!
Provide Stimulating Experiences
Require Communication
Read! Read! Read!
Patience Makes Perfect

**Chapter Fourteen: Ages Three to Seven** . . . . . . . . . . . . . . . . . **125**

How to Create a Desire for Communication
How to Use Play to Develop Communication Skills
Communication Development Between Ages Three and Seven
Six Areas of Vital Communication Development
How to Use the "Project Pages"
Project Pages:

Storytelling Puppets
Magnetic Stories Drama
Sequence Stories Recitation
Cartoon Stories Drawing
Situation Cards Journaling
Half-Told Story Copying
Story-Round-the-Family Tape Recorder Games

**Chapter Fifteen: Ages Eight to Twelve** . . . . . . . . . . . . . . . . . . **173**

What Will He Be Like?
Now You're Thinking!
I Know How You Feel!
How Well Can I Communicate?
Helping Your Child Understand His Behavior
What Kind of Activities Will Be Helpful?
Project Pages:

Observation Skills Discussion
Naming Games Question-Asking
Vocabulary Building Telephone Skills
Memory "Describe a Process" Speech
Listening Demonstration Speech
Tell Me How Mystery Projects
Expressiveness

**Chapter Sixteen: Ages Thirteen and Up** . . . . . . . . . . . . . . . . . **221**

Traits of a Socially Adept Adolescent
What Is My Role as a Parent?
Take Advantage of Real World Opportunities
Project Pages:

Getting to Know the Library Organizing a Speech
Critical Inquiry Informative Speech
Advanced Listening Skills Persuasive Speech
Interview Biographical Speech Project
Being Assertive Video or Radio Plays
Being Persistent Slide Show
Commonplaces Advertising Campaign
Impromptu Speeches

# CHAPTER ONE

# YOUR CHILD:
# AN OUTSTANDING
# COMMUNICATOR

The cardboard box full of small slips of paper moved slowly up and down the aisles of gleaming desks. On each slip of paper was a number, one through twenty-seven, which would determine the order of each student's demise; it was oral book report day. A very fair method, to be sure, was this teacher's way of determining the order in which each student would present. Trembling fingers reached into the box to pull out slips of paper. There were many sighs of relief as the box passed from one student to the next.

**You can teach your child to communicate effectively!**

One extremely shy young man was struck with horror. Not only had he forgotten that this was the day to begin oral book reports, he had forgotten to read his chosen book! Heart pounding, he reached into the box, hoping for a number which would allow him until the next day to prepare. Shaking hands unfolded the small paper scrap. *Number...* one. Terrified and embarrassed, he announced that he was unprepared, put his head on his desk, and wept.

Several years later, another young man of the same age walked confidently into a room full of stern-looking adults. He faced his audience squarely and delivered a five-minute oration with a clear, convincing voice, earnest gestures and a compelling story. When all twenty participants had given their speeches, the results were tallied. The young man was awarded first prize!

**This book will**

**help your**

**child become**

**the kind of**

**purposeful,**

**personable,**

**prudent,**

**polite and**

**persuasive**

**person he**

**was created**

**to be.**

I happen to know the difference between the two young men. The second young man began communication training at a much earlier age, at home, with the help of his parents. Although his parents possessed no formal speech training, they taught instinctively, using hints gained from years of helping their oldest child develop communication skills.

How do I know? Because the second young man was my brother, Tim. The first child? That was me.

After my awful experience, our parents made "communication building" a priority. They encouraged me to take a speech class, got me signed up for the high school debate team, volunteered their weekends to judge debates, drove vans of noisy high school students to speech tournaments, and became involved in communication activities themselves. The example, inspiration, advice, and persistence of my parents, speech teachers and debate coaches opened the door to my becoming a high school state debate champion and later a nationally ranked collegiate debater, as well as student government president of a university of 7,000 students.

Since that first experience, by the grace of God, I have delivered well over 2,000 speeches to audiences ranging from graduate classes to keynote addresses to thousands of professional people, as well as innumerable radio and television interviews. Learning to communicate well has allowed me to walk through doors that I might not even have *knocked* on otherwise.

One reason I'm excited about this book is that it contains the wonderful counsel and advice that changed my life so dramatically.

Another reason I am so enthusiastic about the material in this book is this simple, incredible premise: *everything my teachers did for me, you can do for your child, and you can do it even more effectively.* Your home can be a living, breathing communication workshop far better than any class your child will ever take. Moreover, there is no need to wait until your child is of high school age. Everything you need to know is right here, and you can start your child at birth.

Perhaps a disclaimer is in order here. Despite first appearances, the purpose of this book is not to turn young children into wondrous and charming public speakers, though I believe that skill will emerge in your child if you follow the strategies described here. The real purpose of this book is to help you provide a strong foundation for your child so that he will become an outstanding communicator in *every* area of life, throughout life, whether that is in one-on-one relationships or in front of huge audiences.

Just as I must disclaim something, I must also claim something. As a follower of Jesus Christ, I strive to base all of the principles in this book on God's Word, the Holy Bible (by the way, I *am* a fallible human being, so please don't take everything I say as gospel!). I say this so that fellow believers will understand the perspective from which I am writing: I believe God wants His people to lead by example, and this book will help your child become the kind of purposeful, personable, prudent, polite and persuasive person he was created to be. In short, this book will help your child develop *practical* leadership skills which glorify God.

When a craftsman sets his mind on accomplishing a large task, he first makes sure he has the necessary tools. This book contains all of the tools you need for the task of giving your child the communication advantage in every area of life. You will discover how to help your child

**Your home can be a living, breathing communication workshop far better than any class your child will ever take.**

become more comfortable in social situations, think more clearly, read and write more effectively, take a stand more boldly, analyze more carefully, and speak more articulately.

Here is what this book will do for you:

• Demonstrate how "communication building" fits into the goals that you have for your child.

• Show you the "six pillars" of communication success, and give you clear ideas on how to build them into the structure of your home.

• Give you dozens of easy-to-use ideas to build specific kinds of communication skills from infancy through the teen years.

• Demonstrate the most important things to know in preparing and giving a speech and how to make use of them.

This book is designed to help you pursue excellence, not perfection, for your child. You *can* help your child improve his ability to communicate so he can be what God wants him to be. And what better motivation can parents have than to see their children grow to be successful in the things that matter most? Proverbs 23:24-25 says, "The father of the righteous will greatly rejoice, and he who begets a wise child will delight in him. Let your father and your mother be glad, and let her who bore you rejoice." I pray this will come true for you and your family in a whole new way because of this book.

By the way, what *are* those things which matter most to parents? In the next chapter, I will discuss the goals which you as a parent probably have for your child and how communication skills will help you reach those goals.

# CHAPTER TWO

# HOW COMMUNICATION SKILLS RELATE TO YOUR GOALS FOR YOUR CHILD

## THE COMMUNICATION ADVANTAGE

In a complex and competitive world, children who possess excellent communication skills will have a tremendous advantage over those who do not. Most jobs, even so-called "unskilled" positions, require public speaking, and even companies hiring for jobs which focus primarily on technical skills are increasingly hiring those who possess strong communication abilities over those who do not. Currently, seven out of ten jobs require good speech skills.

Moreover, those who communicate their thoughts and ideas clearly and fluently are often chosen to be leaders. The great speakers in our nation's history, William Jennings Bryan, Patrick Henry, Abraham Lincoln, Martin Luther King, Jr. and hundreds of others, all recognized the creative power of words to reach deep into the hearts of their audiences.

Listed here are some of the goals parents have for their children which may be better reached through the communication skills emphasized in this book.

**Those who communicate their thoughts and ideas clearly and fluently are often chosen to be leaders.**

## GOALS MOST PARENTS HAVE FOR THEIR CHILDREN

*"I want my child to have a sense of purpose in life."* It has been said that the number one fear of youth today is that they will not discover their purpose in life. Hopelessness and boredom reign supreme among young people who live for the moment, having been convinced that life is really a big mistake and that existence is meaningless. Such is the natural consequence of a philosophy of life without God. The Christian life can and should be dramatically different. Jesus said, "I have come that they might have life, and have it to the full" (John 10:10, NIV). Moreover, Colossians 3:23 says that whatever we do, we are to do it "heartily," which literally translates "with all the life that is in us (NIV)."

Purpose emerges, in part, through action; we find our sense of purpose through *trying out* lots of things. A young person who knows how to communicate well with others and is willing to speak publicly will discover a whole new world of opportunities. I have seen young people develop communication skills and then start Bible studies, plan outreach crusades, testify before state legislatures, appear on television talk shows, conduct radio interviews, participate in press conferences, speak to community groups, and run political campaigns. Through such activities, your child will catch a vision for the world around him, and ultimately for the things of God. This book will give you dozens of ideas for how to use communication building to help your child discover a sense of purpose in life.

*"I want my child to be aware of the world around him."* Awareness is a foundational principle of good communication skills, and good communication skills lead to greater awareness. Unfortunately, many young people are unaware of the world around them and unconcerned that there is a world outside of themselves.

In his letter to the Philippians, the Apostle Paul calls us to do nothing out of selfish ambition, but to put the needs of others before ourselves (Philippians 2:3-4). As we learn to communicate more effectively, we become more sensitive to those around us, and more aware of significance of everyday events. Communication skills are closely tied to intelligence: not a higher I. Q., but "practical intelligence" or "common sense." Excellent communication skills will help your child use his five senses to become *aware* of the world around him. This book will give you creative ways to help your child in this area.

We learn primarily by reading, which allows us to absorb new information, and writing, which allows us **"I want my child to be a better learner."** to translate those thoughts into a meaningful new form. Poor oral communication skills are a significant reason for young people failing in reading and writing.

Conversely, learning to communicate well strengthens reading and writing skills. One study noted that students who display the greatest mastery of words exhibit a higher level of scholastic ability than their counterparts regardless of the area of study. Other studies simply show that children who are given the opportunity to communicate orally, and are encouraged to use language as a tool to satisfy their curiosity, develop a stronger foundation of language learning which ultimately makes the learning of reading and writing more profound. This book will show you how your child's improving communication skills will strengthen his reading and writing skills.

Communicating well helps children *think* more effectively, because there is a living connection between **"I want my child to be a creative thinker."** thoughts and words. Speech helps us create the structures in our mind that promote creativity and a quick wit. A whole host of academic studies have proven that confident communicators are those who can "think on their feet," that is, quickly and accurately understand a situation and formulate a response to it. This book will share some powerful secrets to boosting your child's ability to think well.

**"I want my child to be poised."** People expect good communicators to know how to act in a socially appropriate manner. If our behavior is awkward and embarrassing, or if we are not sure of how to communicate our thoughts clearly, we are seen as unintelligent by our teachers and bosses. On the other hand, polished communication skills open doors throughout life. Zig Ziglar quotes a series of studies in his book *Top Performance* which claim that 85 percent of the reason one gets a job, keeps a job, and moves ahead in that job has to do with *people skills and people knowledge!* Through training in communication skills, your child will become a more graceful and pleasant person. This book highlights some creative ideas that can make poise happen.

**"I want my child to relate well to others."** Dr. Frank Dance, an expert on speech development, believes that one of the main purposes of communication is to link us to our environment. Communication brings your child in contact with others, and allows him to listen and share with others. Children who "link-up" to their environment well find it easier to relate to others, and therefore enjoy smoother social interaction. Your child will attract others, because attraction is more a function of how well we relate to others and express concern for them than how physically beautiful we are. This vital skill is called empathy. This book will help you create a strong foundation for empathetic communication by focusing on the skills of listening and conversation.

### REACHING YOUR GOALS THROUGH
### COMMUNICATION TRAINING

Quite simply, the goals that parents have for their children are *integrally related* to communication skills. Armed with good communication skills, young people gain the confidence they need to take a stand for what is right, when everyone else is retreating. Communication training shows young people how to make contributions, exert influence, and create positive peer pressure, setting a good example that other children may be willing to follow. Using this book, you will be able to add a rich new dimension to your child training, imparting the skills that your child needs to survive and mature into a thoughtful, intelligent, caring and successful person.

Each of the significant communication skills we just discussed are pillars which, based on the foundation of a strong home environment, support the "roof" of communication excellence, no matter the age of your child. The next chapter will describe the foundation and the pillars to help you decide on a strategy for communication excellence.

# CHAPTER THREE

# THE SIX PILLARS OF COMMUNICATION EXCELLENCE

## THE SPIRITUAL MANTLE OF FAMILY COMMUNICATION

**Family communication in the home is the number one issue in the scholarly study of leadership.**

Henrietta Mears was perhaps one of the most gifted communicators of the twentieth century. Founder of the Sunday School movement as we know it, her influence on the Christian leaders of today was nothing short of profound. During the course of her life, she founded several ministries, including Gospel Light Publications and the Forest Home Conference Center. Among the hundreds of people she discipled were Billy Graham, Bill Bright of Campus Crusade International, and Richard Halverson, the late chaplain of the U. S. Senate.

Few individuals could serve as a better model of a confident communicator. Barbara Hudson Powers, in *The Henrietta Mears Story*, makes clear the key to Miss Mears' success:

One thrilling thing…about the life of Henrietta Mears is the great spiritual heritage she has received. The scope of her life has been tremendous; even more tremendous is the spiritual influence of her forebears, which can be traced back through at least five generations, and the spiritual 'mantle' that has been handed down on the maternal side from one generation to the next. Truly this is a witness to the scriptural promise "that it may go well with thee, and with thy children after thee."

Miss Mears' spiritual legacy was strong in large measure because her spiritual heritage was strong. The same is true in every area of life; every strong building rests on a solid foundation. According to Frank Pace, an expert on why people become leaders, family communication in the home is the number one issue in the scholarly study of leadership. If your family encourages communication and provides opportunities for reasoned discussion and influence, your child's influence on the world around him is almost certain to be greater.

### BUILDING A STRUCTURE FOR COMMUNICATION EXCELLENCE

Imagine it this way; the foundation of communication excellence, and indeed of your child's impact on the world, is a home environment conducive to developing strong communication skills. If this foundation is strong, then one can confidently place on it pillars strong enough to support the roof. If we put a strong foundation in place, and create a pillar to represent each of the six "goals that parents have for their children" as discussed in chapter two, the roof of communication excellence is well supported. It will be strong, stable and protective of the very elements that lend it support.

Just so we can better visualize the process, here is how the structure might look:

This first section of this book addresses the foundation and each of the six pillars, one chapter for each. It will show you, with dozens of practical, helpful ideas, how to enhance your child's communication skills in a way that builds a strong foundation for life-long communication excellence. Look for exciting, usable games and projects to help your child improve communicatively, no matter what his age. You can start with infants, teenagers or anywhere in between. It's that simple.

## HOW TO PUT THE SIX PILLARS TO WORK IN YOUR HOME

Here's how you can use this book: If you are looking for general improvement in your child's communication skills, read the first eight chapters, begin putting some of the ideas into practice, and then gradually begin trying out some of the projects geared toward the specific age of your child. If you desire to help your child "brush up" on a particular skill, look for the "stamps" which accompany each project, indicating which of the pillars addresses that skill most directly. Here are the stamps which you will find throughout these chapters, along with a brief description of each.

## *Home Environment*

*Home Environment* results from parents teaching and modeling communication skills in everything they do, often unconsciously, as a way of life. It supports the pillars of communication excellence in the same way that warm clothes, healthy food, and a clean, pleasant house support the health and happiness of your child.

## *Purpose*

*Purpose* results from a child's recognition of his parents' love, as well as a sense of the excitement and meaning of everyday life. It supports communication excellence by taking away fear and making your child's communication appealing to others. In turn, communication excellence generates enthusiasm for other areas of your child's life.

## *Awareness*

*Awareness* results from a child's curiosity about the world, and it supports communication excellence by giving your child the ability to become more aware of the experiences of others, how to reach the heart of an audience, and how to effectively translate his own experiences into meaningful information for an audience.

## *Learning*

*Learning* results from a child's love of gaining new information, and it supports communication excellence by giving your child a base of experience from which to speak. In turn, communication excellence generates a heightened sense of the importance of words, making a deeper level of expression possible.

# Creative Thinking

*Creative Thinking* results from experiences which allow your child to be creative and to think in interesting, exciting ways. It supports communication excellence by giving your child a unique, exciting perspective on life, spurring him on to a new level of quick, powerful thinking.

# Poise

*Poise* results from a child learning to be comfortable in a wide variety of settings. It raises your child's comfort level and skill in front of an audience or in any social situation in which he might find himself.

# Empathy

*Empathy* results from a child being trained to listen to and learn from the experiences of others. It improves your child's skill in relating to others, increasing his attractiveness to them and thus the power of his message.

## READY, SET, GROW!

This book is both a course of study and a reference tool. Use it however it works best for you, but *use it!* The impact on the life of your child will be profound *and* far-reaching.

# Chapter Four

# Adjusting Your Home Environment to Focus On Communication Excellence

## Communication Excellence Begins at Home

The home environment is the foundation on which communication success rests. People who believe that a classroom is the best environment for learning will consider this a radically unorthodox idea. However, child researcher Dr. Mabel Rice demonstrated that since communication skills are *natural* to a child, simply being in an environment where communication takes place is stimulation enough for a child to learn to communicate. There are certain foundations which even the best classroom teacher cannot create for you, and this is one of them. As far as communication skills are concerned, you are the best teacher your child will ever have.

Since communication skills develop and mature naturally in the home, any activity which creates a more stimulating home environment should result in better communication skills. Thus, the focus of this chapter is to suggest ideas which will help you create a home environment

**As far as communication skills are concerned, you are the best teacher your child will ever have.**

that fosters a dramatic improvement in your child's willingness and ability to communicate.

## How to Create an "Over the T.O.P." Home Environment

Three areas in which you can begin improving your home's communication environment include using your *time* wisely, creating an environment of *openness* to communication, and being *persistent* in the example you set through your own communication. These three areas form a memorable acrostic:

### T = Time
Use the time you have with your child wisely.

### O = Openness
Foster openness so that your family wants to communicate.

### P = Persistence
Persist in setting a good example of communication.

Let's take a few minutes and review each briefly.

### T = Time

How can your family, busy as it is, find time to foster better communication skills? Here are some ideas that fit into the schedule of things you already do:

1. **Eat meals together.** Dorthea McCarthy discovered that children who score highest on language tests usually come from families who have breakfast and supper together. Meal time is probably the best time for two-way conversation and family bonding. Try it out!

If you have a difficult time stimulating conversation, here are three simple ways to get things going:

- Bring something to share. Ask each family member to bring something to discuss, whether it is what happened at work, what was learned in math class, how the favored team fared in the "big game," or a question about a political candidate.

- Bring questions. Ask each family member to come to the table with a question they can ask another family member. This reinforces listening skills and stimulates general interest in other family members.

- Start a sharing sack. Ruth Beechick suggests that each person place a note in the sack before dinner. The note can be a Bible verse, joke, passage from a book, news article, cartoon, answer to prayer, etc. When conversation lulls, draw something out of the sack and let the contributor talk for awhile.

2. **Use car time wisely.** How much car time does your family spend with each person off in his own little world? Here are some ways you can utilize car time to stimulate communication:

- Listen to story tapes or a radio talk show and discuss it.

- Review what is expected of your child in an upcoming situation.

- Ask your newly reading child to call out words he knows on passing signs.

- Play a game in which you call out a word and the next person must think of a word which begins with the last letter of yours, and so on.

An easy way to

gain more time

together as a

family is to

limit television

viewing.

The average

American

watches

television 28

hours a week,

time that could

almost certainly

be better

invested.

- Speculate imaginatively about the place you are visiting. Make up stories about fictional characters who might have been there many years ago.

- Purchase pre-made car games, or modify games such as *Twenty Questions*.

- Play the alphabet game: compete to find the letters of the alphabet, in order, on passing road signs or billboards.

- Make up stories. One person starts the story, and each person adds a paragraph.

- Design a small song book with your family's favorite songs.

3. **Develop a family night each week.** Each family member can have the opportunity to decide what you should do during that time. Consider doing something outside the home once each month. The other nights, have fun at home and save money!

- Go see a play.

- Rent a movie and discuss it.

- Read aloud together.

- Visit friends.

- Have a game night.

- Play "Kick the Can" or a family sport.

Using activities like these, you will significantly increase the number of hours in each week when you can turn your attention toward communication skills. Yet there is one other suggestion, controversial as it may be. An easy way to gain more time together as a family is to limit television viewing. The average American watches television 28 hours a week, time that could almost certainly be better invested. At the same time, don't feel pressured to use every single minute productively. Just add a few simple activities here and there, and you will start getting results.

In order to make your family time together more productive, you will want to create an environment in which each member of the family feels comfortable communicating with the rest of the family. This aspect of the environment is called openness.

## O = OPENNESS

In *Six Weeks to Better Parenting*, Caryl Waller Krueger says that surveys of parents have revealed five areas where parents would like to improve relations with their children: finding the time and topics to discuss with their children, expressing patience and understanding, having time to enjoy children in a recreational way, following through on discipline, and giving children responsibilities that will help them grow. Amazingly, many of these desires may be reached through activities that also build communication skills. Here are some simple things you can do to open up the communication environment of your home and spend more time with your child in ways that make a difference:

1. **Create experiences through language.** Strive to put your thoughts and the experiences you have together with your child into words. For example, when driving over a railroad bridge, say things like, "We're going over a railroad track. What travels on the railroad track? Why do we have railroad tracks?" Talk about trains, discuss what they carry and share a story about the railroad or "the little train that could."

**Openness in**

**your home is**

**sometimes hard**

**to develop.**

**It may feel**

**awkward. Your**

**child may be**

**suspicious.**

**But stick**

**with it!**

2. **Affirm your love for your child.** Communicate the certainty of your love and acceptance of him. Do it even when you must communicate displeasure. Children have very short memories; they will easily interpret irritation or silence as a *withdrawal* of love.

3. **Organize family devotions.** Use family time to lead your children to a better understanding of God's Word. Occasionally ask an older child to read the devotional material (an excellent book is *Leading Little Ones to God,* published by Baker Bookhouse). Give that child the right to ask questions of other family members about the reading. He will not only reflect more carefully as he reads, he will also make sure the others are listening! When you read the devotional material, ask a question or two of the family before you begin and have them listen for the answer.

4. **Host family meetings.** Family meetings give your child a forum in which his input matters. It also encourages him to think through his comments, basing them on reasonable evidence, and taking the perspective of others. It can be an excellent time to read a book together, teach your child how to take a stand for his faith, discuss heroes, share vacation plans, address current events, make plans together, and work through problems. Some parents opt to present problems to the family and ask for possible solutions. However, those parents should check with each other before turning a problem over to the family to solve, and they should never burden their child with problems he cannot help solve (such as, "Where are we going to get money to buy food this month?"). Once concluded, the whole family must abide by the decision of the group, or your child will quickly begin to think of family decision-making as a waste of time.

Openness to communication in your home is sometimes hard to develop. It may feel awkward. Your child may be suspicious, but stick with it! Perhaps the most significant way to show that you're serious about openness to communication is to consider our next topic, how to be persistent in improving your own communication skills.

## P = PERSISTENCE

Parents are the most significant models for how children should act. Studies in behavior demonstrate that children will more frequently do as the parents do, rather than what the parents say, if the two are inconsistent. This is especially true in communication. As the *Becoming a Nation of Readers* report noted, "Language frames the world the child knows; the richer the language, the richer the child's world. Especially with a small child, it is better to say too much than too little." If you are not a talkative person, then concentrate on at least communicating more than commands and admonishments. Your persistence will reap meaningful benefits in the life of your child. Here are some ideas to consider:

1. **Express positive emotions.** Your child takes cues from you regarding how expressive he should be, so use a wide vocal range and let your voice convey what you feel, especially with positive emotions such as happiness, excitement, suspense, and joy. Point out to your child that certain situations demand certain tones of voice, and that vocal variety is useful for communicating in "real life."

2. **Send consistent messages.** A parent who maintains a smiling face while using an angry voice will confuse his child. The most clear message results when all aspects of your communication are giving the same message, so match your tone with your gestures, eye contact, and facial expressions.

*Studies in behavior demonstrate that children will more frequently do as the parents do, rather that what the parents say, if the two are inconsistent.*

3. **Make eye contact positive.** Eye contact is an extremely powerful means of communicating positively, yet it is often used in a negative way (as in, *"Look at me when I am talking to you!"*). Children who are asked for eye contact only when being reprimanded will view it as unpleasant. Instead, connect eye contact with a smile and pleasant words.

4. **Express your feelings carefully.** When you feel angry about your child's behavior, do not say, *"You make me so angry."* This rids you of responsibility for your own feelings, and indicates that the problem is a permanent part of the child. Try instead to describe his behavior to him by saying, *"I feel very frustrated when you behave that way."* This indicates to the child that you are *not* frustrated at who he is, but at his behavior *at that moment.* In addition, carefully control your voice during discipline. A parent who responds in a loud, irritable voice to even the most minor infraction will find himself not taken seriously in the event of a major infraction. Ask yourself: "Are my emotions in check?" Children will learn emotional control by your example.

5. **Be sensitive to the level of your child.** Don't assume that your child always understands what is said to him, or that he means what he says. The way children learn language varies: sometimes they understand words that they do not use, sometimes they form rough definitions of words based on the context in which they are used, and sometimes they simply parrot words they've heard. Often the best way you can help is to be patient with them!

6. **Communicate clearly.** Have you ever been frustrated when your child doesn't understand and act on what you say? Sometimes it is pure mischief. However, if there are a number of distractions in the environment, your communication will be unclear, somewhat

like trying to talk through a cheap set of walkie-talkies. The way to overcome noise is by saying the same thing in several different ways to ensure that your meaning is understood. The "70/30 Rule" was designed by George A. Miller, an expert on humans' capacity to process information. He concluded that the best way to make ourselves understood is to spend 30% of our time stating in simple terms what we want the other person to understand, and 70% giving examples and painting brief pictures of the outcomes we desire. This is true with parent-child communication as well. By making yourself clear, and asking your child to repeat back to you what you want him to do, you will minimize misunderstandings.

## How to Become More Aware of the Communication Environment in Your Home

Perhaps the best way to improve the communication environment of your home is to take a "self-test" each day. Ask yourself questions like, "Are my voice and facial expressions consistent?", "How can I set a better example of expressiveness for my children?", "When was the last time I used eye contact to communicate in a positive way with my child?", "Does my communication reduce uncertainty about my love and acceptance of my child?", "Do I communicate unconditional love even when I must punish my child?", "When was the last time I really *showed* my child that I love him?", "How can I use words to create new experiences for my child?", "What one thing can I do to make my child's language environment richer today?" "Have I communicated more than just short verbalizations with my child today?", or the ultimate, "If communication were a measure of wealth, would we be rich or poor today?"

These questions are important because they turn your attention to the home environment as the foundation of

*Model and teach your children to communicate more effectively, and the pillars which are built on this foundation will stand strong and true.*

communication excellence. Such a foundation is not built overnight, and it must be repaired frequently. The strength of the home environment is a meaningful, subtle and vital part of our relationship with the rest of the world. Model and teach your children to communicate more effectively, and the pillars which are built on this foundation will stand strong and true.

It is now time to move on to a discussion of the first pillar, purpose in life. Purpose, as we shall see, is not really a communication skill. However, a child who is developing a strong sense of purpose will be primed and ready to quickly learn whatever skills are necessary.

# CHAPTER FIVE

## HELPING STRENGTHEN YOUR CHILD'S SENSE OF PURPOSE IN LIFE

### SENSE OF PURPOSE AS A FOUNDATION FOR COMMUNICATION DEVELOPMENT

The first pillar that must be built on the foundation provided by the home environment is *purpose*. Purpose is the source of and motivation for all skills, especially communication skills. Great communication comes from the <u>heart</u>, not the head. Once when teaching a university speech class, I had a student who struggled terribly in the class; he was shy, unwilling to communicate expressively, and disorganized. One day he gave a speech warning of the dangers of alcoholism that caught me completely off guard. He violated virtually every aspect of the assignment, yet gave a truly tremendous presentation. I stood back and let him go; he had something that no instructor could teach in just one semester.

Later, I tried to pinpoint what had changed. It was as if the student had a *passion* for his subject; he really *believed* what he was saying. He saw significance in it. Based on whatever tragic life events compelled him to

**Great communication comes from the heart, not the head.**

give the presentation, he had *lived* the significance in it. Then it dawned on me; his speech was so infused with meaning that it was as if it was part of his very purpose for existence.

Then I understood. It *did* contain his purpose for existence. That is why it was truly great.

After thinking it through, I scrapped my old lecture on "overcoming fear" in public speaking, and replaced it with a new approach based on "purpose in life." If an individual can understand his purpose in life, and use that purpose to energize what he does, then whether it is in a speech or just in daily communication, he will advance far beyond what would otherwise have been thought possible.

There are many historical examples of a sense of purpose igniting the desire to communicate an important message to the world. William Wilberforce gave hundreds of speeches before Parliament, most of them urging his colleagues to abolish the immoral practice of slavery. He was a hated man. Wilberforce's speeches became so unpopular that members of parliament would file out of the chamber when he rose to speak. Ultimately, however, his burning passion for justice resulted in the abolition of the British slave trade.

Wilberforce's success was fueled not by his desire to put himself in front of lots of people, but by a holy passion and a love for those who could not help themselves. His epitaph in the Westminster Abbey bears witness to this fact, noting that he was "among the foremost to fix the character of his times."

Purpose in life cannot really be considered a communication skill, but it is so integral to communication that we dare not leave it alone. It is purpose in life which makes it easy to get up in the morning, to plan carefully the impact we wish to have on the world around us, and to stand courageously in spite of great difficulty. Purpose makes timid people strong, propelling them beyond the ordinary into a kind of greatness that few understand. D. L. Moody embodied this kind of purpose. He said, "The world has yet to see what will happen when a man will truly get on fire for God. By God's grace, I intend to be that man." Moody impacted the lives of tens and perhaps hundreds of thousands, and his legacy is still doing so today.

This chapter will give some rudimentary ideas about how to assist your child in developing a sense of purpose in life. If the lives of students with whom I've worked are any indication, the result will be a much stronger platform on which to build communication skills. The three points which I consider most important in developing purpose in life are these: live as if your child has a purpose, help your child develop a sense of significance, and be a cheerleader for your child.

## LIVE AS IF YOUR CHILD HAS A PURPOSE

Scripture is quite clear that human beings are endowed with purpose by their Creator. The psalmist writes:

"For you created my inmost being;
    you knit me together in my mother's womb.
I praise you because I am fearfully and wonderfully made;
    your works are wonderful, I know that full well.
My frame was not hidden from you when I was made
    in the secret place.
When I was woven together in the depths of the earth,
    your eyes saw my unformed body.
All the days ordained for me were written in your
    book before one of them came to be."

Psalm 139:13-16 (NIV)

It is purpose in life which makes it easy to get up in the morning, to plan carefully the impact we wish to have on the world around us, and to stand courageously in spite of great difficulty.

**Purpose in**

**life means**

*enthusiasm*

**based on the**

**realization**

**that our**

**lives have**

**meaning and**

**that every**

**event in**

**them is**

**infused with**

**significance.**

Purpose in life means *enthusiasm* based on the realization that our lives have meaning and that every event in them is infused with significance. We thus see the world in a meaningful way and recognize our importance in it.

I believe that above all else, to treat children *as if they have purpose* is the most significant way to help them develop a sense of purpose in life. Here are some questions you can use to help decipher that sense of purpose for your child:

1. **Questions to discover the significance of past events and present condition.**

   - Why do you suppose God chose to have you born when he did?

   - Why do you suppose God gave you the family that he did?

   - Why do you suppose God allowed you to grow up where he did?

   - Why do you suppose God allowed certain things to happen to you?

2. **Questions to discover the interests and abilities God has given you.**

   - Who are three people who have made an impression on your life? How did God work through them?

   - What sorts of things have you accomplished which gave you a tremendous sense of satisfaction?

   - What one thing would you share with an audience if you only had one speech left in life?

- When you think about the future of the nation, what is one area in which you can make a difference?

### 3. Questions to help you discern your ministry.

- What particular burdens for the ministry do you have?

- What special opportunities and needs are put before you?

- What do you feel called, compelled and obligated to do?

- What do you enjoy doing for the Lord?

- What talents and skills has God given you that can be dedicated to the Lord and his service?

- Who can you ask that might be able to help you discern answers to those questions?

### 4. Questions you can use with your child every day.

- What was the best thing that happened to you today?

- What happened during your day that was funny?

- What would you do differently if you had it to do over again?

- What was the strangest thing that happened to you today?

Questions that allow you to reflect on the meaning and significance of life are a significant step toward purpose in life. They give you a framework for interpreting what happens, no matter how mundane.

One caution: be careful not to give your child the impression that his answer is set in concrete and may never change. Questions such as these form a *benchmark* which helps us see more clearly how God works in our lives. Our understanding of our purpose emerges and becomes clearer as we grow older, so be patient!

### HELPING YOUR CHILD DEVELOP A SENSE OF PURPOSE

Often it is difficult for parents to keep the lines of communication open with their children. Whether through the stress and strain of everyday life, or simply being preoccupied, we unintentionally put our children on hold. Here are some powerful tips on imparting a sense of significance which take just a few moments but which your child will always remember:

- Tell him frequently that you love him and that you are glad he is in your family.

- Give him an idea of his "place" in the family by highlighting for him and other family members the role he plays, i.e., "No one else in our family would have noticed that. Think what we would have missed! I'm so glad you're part of our family!"

- Show him baby pictures and convey the sense of excitement you had while waiting to have him, as well as your thrill of holding him in your arms.

- Tell him stories about your family: the different places you have lived, things that happened to you or your relatives, and how you met your mate.

- Use "I can" language that demonstrates that you have responsibility for your life, that it is not out of your control. For instance, replace "I can't" with "I choose not to," "I'll try" with "I will" or "I won't," and "You make me so mad" with "I feel very angry when you do that." Encourage your child to make these changes as well.

- Let your child see you in action making a difference in the life of another person in your community or in a significant cause.

- Say, "I may not always like what you do or approve of it, but no matter what, I will never stop loving you."

- Focus on positive emotions: "Isn't it great to..."

- Make sure your child knows that the time you spend together is meaningful: "I would rather be spending this time with you than doing anything else in the world."

- Express interest in what is important to him: "I don't know very much about this, but I am interested in learning about what *you* are interested in!"

Simple adjustments such as these can have a profound, lasting impact in the life of your child.

## HELPING YOUR CHILD MAINTAIN A SENSE OF PURPOSE

The final role of parents in imparting a sense of purpose is that of cheerleader. A coach motivates his players to top performance by providing opportunities to practice winning strategies and then serving as cheerleader, applauding the team's success and helping its members work through the pain of failure.

Here are some ways you can be a cheerleader for your child:

- Reinforce your child's confidence in himself and give him opportunities to decide things on his own. Caryl Waller Krueger suggests that this may be as simple as appreciating his decisions: "You did the right thing to not open the door to that stranger" or "How wise of you to turn off the oven so the meat loaf wouldn't burn."

- Refrain from "managing" his communication. Dr. James Dobson says that children feel most confident when they believe their parents have confidence and trust in them. Do you become tense and nervous when your child speaks to others? Do you interrupt to explain what he was *really* trying to say, or do you let him speak for himself, even if he doesn't say it quite the way you would have wished?

- Reward your child for noticeable performance. When I was growing up, my parents rewarded my brother and me with a shiny quarter every time someone complimented *them* on *our* good behavior.

- Spend meaningful sharing time with your child. Find a time each day to visit. Share with him a letter you received from a missionary friend, or have him read it aloud to you. Help your child focus on the positive experiences of the day. Take him with you when you run errands, and use this time to listen to your child and find out more about his thoughts and interests.

- Focus your time and energy on positive people and characteristics. Your child should know that it is okay to admire the positive characteristics that another person possesses. In many of the summer camps at which I teach, we ask questions such as, "Who is one person you admire and why?" Sometimes I design questions to stimulate students' thinking such as, "If you had to go into hiding for being a Christian, who would you want to have with you to take care of you?" or, "If you could be Tonto, who would you have as your Lone Ranger?" Understanding the heroic is important to our own character development.

## SENSE OF PURPOSE:
## A SOURCE OF ENERGY

Your child's confidence level will increase as he sees the purpose in everyday events, and senses from you that his life has meaning and significance. He may feel more free to embrace hobbies or causes with gusto, having experiences that will be vital for future communication confidence.

The next step in building communication skills is to help your child become more aware of the world around. Awareness ties your child together with others and allows him to learn the lessons which are so vital to outstanding communication skill.

# CHAPTER SIX

# HELPING YOUR CHILD BECOME MORE AWARE OF THE WORLD AROUND HIM

## THE IMPORTANCE OF AWARENESS IN COMMUNICATION DEVELOPMENT

"I just started looking around," said my brother Tim. "I looked at billboards and thought, 'How *negative* they all seem to be. Companies using women in bikinis to sell beer, cigarettes and whiskey. I have got to get our community focused on *positive* media images.'" Tim didn't just look; he took action by starting a small billboard company, Positive Media, to create and place billboards with a positive message. Tim raised thousands of dollars to put up billboards. How did he, at age sixteen, raise the money? "I just observed people who had money, and I asked them for it," he explains, matter-of-factly. In starting Positive Media, Tim took action based on an awareness which escaped most adults, and ultimately developed a vision which significantly impacted his community.

**Great communicators cultivate an awareness of their surroundings.**

Observation: seeing what is going on around you. Awareness: knowing what it means. It's not just a gift for police detectives! Every child can benefit from becoming

**Great**

**communicators**

**harness the**

**powers of**

**physical**

**eyesight to**

**develop**

**spiritual**

**insight.**

aware of the world around. This chapter highlights aware-ness as a vital pillar in the building of communication. Here are some of the distinguishing marks of people who possess a greater awareness than those around them:

- They see more clearly into the needs and aspirations of others. They are more attuned to "unspoken" com-munication.

- They discern untruths more quickly.

- They sense possibilities which go unnoticed by others.

- They enjoy life more, because their senses are height-ened.

- They can quickly figure out solutions to difficult prob-lems.

- They drink deeply from the well of lessons that nature and other people have to teach.

- They develop a stronger sense about how others might be persuaded to change what they believe and do.

Great communicators cultivate an awareness of their surroundings. Everyday occurrences take on greater mean-ing; they harness the powers of *physical eyesight* to develop *spiritual insight*. The human condition and the search for meaning become eminently more understandable. Aware-ness helps writers be brilliant, speakers witty, and coun-selors adept at assessing the needs of clients.

In addition to being the source of great communication skill, awareness is a foundational principle of the Christian faith. The twenty-fourth proverb of Solomon, verses 11-12 says:

"Rescue those being led away to death; hold back those staggering toward slaughter. If you say, 'But we knew nothing about this,' does not he who weighs the heart perceive it? Will he not repay each person according to what he has done?" (NIV)

The implication is that we are to observe the world around us, and to act on what we observe to the glory of God and the benefit of others. Other passages of Scripture give the same message: "Where there is no vision, the people perish." Jesus said, in Matthew 15:14, "If the blind lead the blind, both will fall into the ditch." Being sensitive to the world around us often involves asking "What would Jesus do?" when we confront difficult issues.

Being aware of the world around him, your child can better understand its problems, relish its joys, and utilize its potential. Your child can rise above society's expectations and be truly set apart for a special purpose.

Two physical senses play into awareness: hearing and seeing. These senses become gateways to the mind. The key to raising awareness is intensifying your child's ability to get information and process it. What follows are some activities which will help you help your child in this regard.

### HELPING YOUR CHILD BECOME MORE OBSERVANT

You can help your child become more aware of the world around him through simple activities that focus on observation skills. Here are some activities that will work easily into your busy schedule.

- Develop special observation times. I occasionally take a child with me on errands, stopping for a soft drink on the way home. As we sit in the restaurant, we observe other people. I ask questions like, "What do you suppose that woman is like? Friendly? Unfriendly? Why do you think that?" or, "Why do you suppose that man looks happy? What might have happened that would put him in a good mood?" We also observe negative behaviors. "Why does that boy look down at the floor most of the time? What would make him want to do that? How can we make sure we don't act like that?" As you listen and respond, your child will develop a whole new repertoire of observation skills.

- Start a "Sense Journal." Ask your child for one observation each day that you can record in a journal for him. I often write my own observations on note cards, so I can file them for later use in speech or book illustrations. In fact, I encourage the college and seminary students that I teach to do the same thing. Lavish praise on your child for thorough, creative observations.

- Play "What can you see?" games. For a younger child, test his skills of observation through questions about things in his immediate environment. Ask questions like, "Which three items in this room are orange?" "Which of these three drinking glasses can hold more water?" Questions should emphasize three factors: perception (questions which ask, "Which is bigger, smaller, wider, longer, rougher, brighter," etc.), understanding (questions which ask, "Why, how, when, where, who"), and value (questions which ask, "Which of these do you prefer and why?").

- Involve the child in your activity. If you are looking at a magazine, show him some pictures and ask questions about them. If you are baking, ask your child to help make measurements.

- Play the "Block game." With one set of blocks, create a structure. Have your child observe the structure for a few seconds, then go in another room and recreate the structure with an identical set of blocks. Praise your child for accuracy and quickness in his reconstruction. Better yet, take turns, and allow him to test *your* observation skills.

- Play the "Selling game." Choose a household item and ask your child to develop a "sales pitch," pointing out the item's good qualities. This game is often funny, sometimes silly, but always creative!

- Encourage choice-making. Choices heighten the need for awareness. They require children to discern right from wrong and to distinguish between good and great, better and best. Caryl Waller Krueger suggests giving children as many choices as possible:

  "Of these three vegetables, which one do you want for dinner?"
  "Would you like to watch television program A or program B?"
  "Would you like to stay up late tonight or tomorrow night?"

Regardless of the choices made, be sure to enforce the consequences of the decision. Do not let your child talk you into allowing him to stay up late both nights! TIP: Limit the choices you offer to a very young child who may not understand that "choice" means one or the other, and may be baffled and upset as a result.

- Take a trust walk. In a trust walk, you blindfold your child and lead him around, giving him opportunities to touch, smell, listen and taste. Removing one of the senses, sight, will cause him to rely more on the others.

Developing an

awareness of

the world will

provide the

source of

information for

speeches, it will

help your child

understand

others more

clearly, and it

will deepen

the well of

resources from

which he can

draw as an

outstanding

communicator.

After about ten minutes, remove the blindfold and ask your child to identify what happened.

Observation games should be a source of challenge and fun. If you get to the point where you are "drilling" your child, or he loses interest, stop for a while. Gradually you will notice your child developing observation skills on his own.

### INTERPRETING WHAT YOU OBSERVE

*Interpreting* involves forming an image of the source's trustworthiness and competence, and detecting the message's emotional impact. Depending on the age of the child, use children's stories, magazine advertisements, pictures, television programs and news stories to demonstrate how to interpret the messages we receive.

Here are some ways to discuss interpretation:

- Discuss believability. Define and discuss what it means to trust. What makes a person trustworthy? How can *we* be more trustworthy? What evidence is there that a particular message is trustworthy? Is it good evidence?

- Consider the persuasive appeal. What is this particular story or advertisement or program trying to get you to feel or do?

- Discuss the motives to which the message is appealing. To what are the advertisers appealing in order to get you to buy their product? Do they claim that their product will make you more attractive, more outgoing, or more wealthy? Can they really deliver what they say? If not, how does that affect their trustworthiness?

Here are three print advertisements which are similar to those found in the classified section of many newspapers and magazines. Find some in your newspaper and discuss them with your child.

- WATCH FAT WASTE AWAY! New cream designed by a team of doctors and nutritionists will shrink unwanted fat cells and leave you with a beautiful body. No exercise or special diet needed. Just wait until your friends notice!

- FREE HAWAIIAN VACATION! Just come in and test drive any of this year's models, and receive a vacation for two in Hawaii. Round trip airfare for one and four nights' accommodations included. When you're dreamin' away in tropical paradise, you'll be glad you came in!

- GOVERNMENT SURPLUS AUCTION! Cars for $50, jeeps for $25. Boats, yachts, equipment; all dirt cheap! Send $25 plus $5 shipping/handling for catalog.

Interpreting a message is the first step in understanding it. The second step is to evaluate it. Evaluating information allows your child to develop impressions about the things he sees and make sense of them for his own life.

### EVALUATING WHAT YOU OBSERVE

*Evaluating* means testing ideas for truth or falsehood and deciding how much of a message to accept or reject. You can enhance your child's ability to evaluate messages by presenting "what if" scenarios geared to the age of the child. Here are some examples:

- "What should you do?" activities. Tell the story of a child who lies to his parents, or read "The Boy Who Cried Wolf." Your child can evaluate what the child in the story should and should not have done and why. Other scenarios could include:

What if...

— a stranger asked you if you wanted a ride?

— someone told you that God does not exist?

— you were a guest at someone's house and you spilled your drink?

• Evaluate advertising messages. Examine advertisements in the mail, in newspaper, and magazines and on television. Help your child discern, for example, the truth in an automobile advertisement. What does it mean to lease a car for $199 a month? What other costs might be hidden? When you see a television report about a news story which you know is slanted, quiz your child about what sort of questions he might ask the reporter. Consider questions such as, "How do you know that is true?" and "Where do you get your information?"

• Observe the folly of the wicked. In Proverbs 24:30-34, the author tells of observing and learning lessons from the mistakes of a lazy man: "I went past the field of the sluggard, past the vineyard of the man who lacks judgement; thorns had come up everywhere, the ground was covered with weeds, and the stone wall was in ruins. I *applied my heart* to what I *observed* and *learned a lesson* from what I *saw*" (NIV) (Italics mine). We learn much of our practical morality from observing how acting foolishly leads to horrible consequences. If you see a picture of someone who is being led away to prison, or if you see a drunkard on the street, discuss with your child how that person might have gotten himself into that situation. The ability to observe and then *avoid* actions with negative consequences is of lifetime benefit.

Developing an awareness of the world around is a skill with lifelong benefit to your child. It will provide the source of information for speeches, it will help him understand others more clearly, and it will deepen the well of resources from which he can draw as an outstanding communicator.

This "deep well of resources" will make learning an adventure. The next chapter will show how communication skills and a love of learning are tied together, serving as another strong pillar in our building of communication.

# CHAPTER SEVEN

# HOW YOUR CHILD CAN
# BECOME A BETTER LEARNER

## HOW LEARNING AND COMMUNICATION
## SKILLS ARE RELATED

Three-and-a-half-year-old Rebekah crawled into my lap with a second grade storybook. "May I read to you?" she inquired sweetly. Having never refused such a generous offer, I said, "You bet!" I awaited the typical "reading" of children that age, namely, an oral interpretation of the pictures. To my amazement, the book contained few pictures. I thought, "Boy, this must be a really dull book!" Much to my amazement, Rebekah slowly read, and I mean *read*, the story to me.

Without a doubt, Rebekah was an unusual little girl. There is something unique about her family which helps me understand her early advancement and obvious joy for reading. She lives in a family with parents who love to learn. Her parents communicate their love for learning in such a way that Rebekah naturally wants to learn more. In conversation around the dinner table they weave fantastic tales, share the exciting plot from the book they've been

*The foundation you build in your home for learning will provide a strong support for your child's developing communication skills.*

"The limits of

my language

mean the limits

of my world."

—Wittgenstein

reading, and create suspense about a story they will read as a family that night.

The third pillar of the building of communication is *learning*. The ability to learn, as well as the love of learning, provides lifelong tools for developing wisdom and knowledge. The foundation you build in your home for learning will provide a strong support for your child's developing communication skills, which will, in turn, give him further opportunities to learn. In this chapter we will discuss some easy-to-implement ideas to make your child *want* to learn! Let's begin by examining the connection between learning and communication skills.

We noted earlier that children who are given the opportunity to communicate orally, and are encouraged to use language as a tool to satisfy their curiosity, develop a stronger foundation of language learning which ultimately makes learning more profound. The philosopher Ludwig Wittgenstein explained it this way, "The limits of my language mean the limits of my world." Those with powerful communication skills will be granted access to the storehouse of knowledge that is the foundation of our civilization. Without that access, our civilization will not long be civilized, since citizens who cannot learn from the past cannot avoid its mistakes or plan thoughtfully for the future.

This chapter will present four ways you can create enthusiasm for learning in your home: reading, modeling enthusiasm for learning, making learning fun, and learning together.

## THE READING ROAD
## TO COMMUNCIATION EXCELLENCE

"The single most important activity for building the knowledge required for eventual success in reading is reading aloud to children," states the 1985 report of the

Commission on Reading. Top authorities in the study of reading skills appear to be in universal agreement on this point. Because reading is the means by which one acquires in-depth knowledge throughout a lifetime, it will never be a waste of time to emphasize reading in your home. This process begins when the child is very young and continues even after the child learns to read to himself. Reading together provides a vital bond between parent and child.

According to Mary Jo Puckett-Cliat and Jean M. Shaw, reading aloud to your child helps him understand how language is put together, forming the foundation for his own language use. He will learn thinking skills and develop an intuitive understanding of logical thinking and cause-and-effect relationships. This ultimately leads him to deep, rich "imagining" skills. The mind and imagination of children crave stimulation, and reading aloud or telling stories fulfills this need, motivating them to a life-long love of reading.

Here are some ways to inject your home with enthusiasm for reading:

1. **Start reading early.** Experts suggest that parents begin reading to children as young as a month or two old! Studies by child education experts show a direct and long-term benefit, demonstrating that if you can start the process early, the empty framework of your child's mind will fill up much more quickly.

2. **Read enthusiastically.** When reading to your child, play the role of each character, adding vocal inflection and actions to bring the characters to life.

3. **Read with suspense.** Create a sense of suspense and wonder through reading. If you are reading a book that will take more than one day, for example, don't stop reading at the end of the chapter. Stop at a

*The mind and imagination of children crave stimulation, and reading aloud or telling stories fulfills this need, motivating them to a life-long love of reading.*

highly suspenseful moment in the story. Both of you will have something to look forward to the next day!

4. **Read inquisitively.** Have characters in the book "ask questions" of the child, or have the child ask questions of the characters, to which you make up appropriate responses. While reading *Jack and the Beanstalk*, for example, say, "I have a question for Jack. 'Jack, what did you think when you saw how tall the beanstalk had grown?'"

5. **Make reading adventurous.** You can add a fun twist to reading and help your child grow in imagination by approaching reading in a larger context. If your child reads a book about another part of the world, help bring it to life by asking him to find that place on the map, draw pictures about various scenes, list questions to ask someone who has been there, or look up additional information in the encyclopedia.

6. **Use poetry.** Many adults have had bad experiences with poetry, but poetry reinforces the natural rhythm of life. King David filled his thoughts and worship with poetic songs and essays, reflecting on the nature of God and the world around him. In some inexplicable way, singing songs and reciting poems which have a strong meter actually help the mind become organized. This is especially true for young children. Second, poetry teaches intense language skills. It trains children to convey complex thoughts using few words. Find poetry books for children at a used bookstore. Encourage your child to memorize a poem or two if he is so inclined, or even write poetry of his own.

7. **Overcome the vocabulary barrier.** Be certain your child understands the vocabulary and ideas presented in the reading. Asking questions or making comments

about the reading lowers your child's level of frustration and creates additional interest.

Reading aloud is valuable for its own sake. It has the additional advantage of encouraging excellent oral communication skills. If you have time for nothing else, be sure to make time for reading!

The next step in creating enthusiasm for learning is to actually model *enthusiasm* for learning. Consider the eye-opening suggestions in this next section.

**Children who are good readers come from families where parents enjoy reading.**

## HOW TO MODEL ENTHUSIASM FOR LEARNING

Modeling good communication skills to your child will give him a significant boost toward becoming a curious, inquisitive learner. Consider this statement from Professors Kimmel and Segal:

> Several studies of children from widely varied backgrounds who learned to read early and remained good readers throughout their school years revealed that they had something in common. They all had been read to regularly from early childhood and had as models adults or older children who read for pleasure.

Some time ago I spent time with a family whose son had just turned two. Because of his mother's inquisitiveness about the world around them, he developed an enormous vocabulary for his age. I discovered this while taking a walk with him. "Look, Jacob, there is a flower," I commented as we passed a garden. He stopped, studied the particular flower I was pointing to and said, "Not flower, *rose!*" I stood corrected, and quite amazed. The child continues to be far ahead of his class not because his parents are more brilliant than other parents, but because they model good learning.

"Enforced

illiteracy,"

knowing how

to read but

not doing so,

is the second

greatest

educational

problem

facing our

nation, next

to not being

able to read

at all.

Here are some helpful ways to model learning in your home:

1. **Devote family time to learning.** Laura Ingalls Wilder told tales of earlier times, when fathers read to the family while the girls served or mended and the boys whittled or worked with leather. Give this old-fashioned idea a try. Sometimes you can read aloud to the whole family, other times you can make it a silent reading time when parents read the newspaper or magazine and children read their own books.

2. **Reinforce learning through activity.** Make homemade books for your young child, with pictures of family members, your house, car, dog, toys, and other recognizable items. As you read them, point out the real object so the connection between the picture and the real object becomes clear.

3. **Talk about learning.** Talk with your older child about the books he is reading. For a younger child, reinforce the words he knows or letters he recognizes. You can conduct this activity by watching signs while riding in the car.

4. **Focus on the interesting parts of learning.** While it will later be important for your child to understand why stories work the way they do, it is best to listen carefully, asking specific questions, but allowing your child to tell his version from start to finish. Moreover, avoid questions about vocabulary, sentence structure, plot, or anything that will diminish his enthusiasm for the excitement wrapped up in the story itself. As Ruth Beechick notes, focusing on such details is like an artist saying, "Don't get carried away, folks; it's really only oils and colors and brush strokes." Beechick suggests that you talk instead about the construction of the story and

how the characters manifested positive or negative character traits ("How did they demonstrate honesty, diligence, courage, kindness, or obedience?"). Your child can even project himself into the story and speculate about how he would act in a given situation.

It has been said that "enforced illiteracy," knowing how to read but not doing so, is the second greatest educational problem facing our nation, next to not being able to read at all. On the other hand, few things are more exciting than a family which models learning. The results are so *obvious*. Your child will not only stand out among his peers, he will have a strong foundation for the things that matter most in life.

## HOW TO MAKE LEARNING FUN

Children do not gain the ability to think abstractly until they are about thirteen years of age. Before that, their thinking is very concrete, craving practical application. Knowing this, you can structure activities to accompany learning which build enthusiasm and enhance your child's ability to retain key points. Here are some creative ideas, each of which is expanded in the projects section of this book:

1. **Reinforce the alphabet.** Sing through the alphabet, or stick some magnetic letters to the refrigerator. Your child can learn the letters and form words, even devising games to entertain himself while you are fixing dinner. Toy stores also sell foam letters which stick to bathtub tiles when wet, so you can turn bath time into learning time.

2. **Use art.** Allow your child to paint, mold, draw or construct scenes from a book he has read using the various art techniques at your disposal. These can be collected

**In the long**

**run, children**

**prefer toys**

**which allow**

**them to**

**create things.**

in a book or posted on the wall. *Any activity which enhances your child's imagination and ability to relate what he knows to reality will reinforce communication skills.*

3. **Create advertisements.** Ruth Beechick also suggests that you permit your child to develop written and oral advertisements about the book he is reading, with the goal of persuading someone else to read it. This is a fun way for the child to synthesize the main points of the book, deduce what makes the book suspenseful, and expand his imagination.

4. **Dictate stories and journals.** If your child is of pre-school age, he can "write" stories by dictating them to you. These stories may describe a vacation, an exciting day, or imaginative situations which you make up together. Illustrate the book with drawings, photographs, magazine pictures, or a greeting card. On really special occasions, you can have the book laminated and bound at a local photocopy store. These books will be treasured and re-read many times.

5. **Have the child read aloud to you.** The primary purpose of this activity is not to critique your child's reading level, but to have an opportunity to show how proud you are of his skills. There is absolutely nothing like a parent's encouragement to inspire a child to continue reading!

When buying toys for your child, remember that in the long run, children prefer toys which allow them to create things. These kinds of toys last longer and yield more benefits than battery powered cars or robots.

The final key to enthusiastic learning in the home is to learn *together* as a family. Since traveling as a family is a perfect opportunity for learning as a family, we will focus our attention on this point in the next section.

## LEARNING TOGETHER THROUGH TRAVEL

Traveling together as a family is often stressful, and many a parent has felt severe disappointment when the child does not seem as interested in a historical sight or nature exhibit as the parent does. Yet in spite of the downside, traveling is one of the most powerful ways to create enthusiasm for learning. Studies demonstrate that children who have had travel experiences have a larger vocabulary and better communication ability than those who have not.

Here are two ideas for making more of this potential learning time:

1. **Create enthusiasm for travel in advance.** Experiences are always more meaningful if your child is prepared for what he will see. Whether you plan to attend a play, visit a Civil War battlefield, or take in a major league baseball game, brief the child in advance. For a play, set up the plot in a way he will understand. For a battlefield, describe why it was important, borrow some mementoes from a friend, read stories about the battle or ones similar to it, and rent a film. For a game, give your child some idea of what to expect and be sure he possesses a rudimentary understanding of how the game is played. I knew of one college-age girl whose father had never explained the game of baseball to her. She grew up believing that a "strike" occurred when the batter flinched as the ball crossed the plate! Needless to say, she did not enjoy baseball.

2. **Make the most of travel.** Collect brochures in advance and set realistic expectations. Give your child his own set of maps so he can chart the family's progress (laminate them if possible), and ask him to help plan stops and decide which sights to see. You might even appoint an older child "tour guide" to "lead" small parts of the

Children who have had travel experiences have a larger vocabulary and better communication ability than those who have not.

trip. This will encourage him to observe much more than he might otherwise notice.

In conclusion, a love of learning and communication skills fit hand in hand. If your child comes to love learning, developing advanced communication skills will be no problem whatsoever. The result will be a child who is confident, knowledgeable, and more prepared to take on the challenges of life.

The ability to learn and the love of learning are enhanced by the techniques of creative thinking, the next pillar in the building of communication.

# CHAPTER EIGHT

# HELP YOUR CHILD BECOME A MORE CREATIVE THINKER

## THE NATURE OF THOUGHT

Contrary to popular belief, great thinkers are not necessarily like *Star Trek's* "Spock," thinking in a logical, computer-like fashion. Instead, the key to highly effective thinking is the ability to *think outside of the boundaries* which bind everyone else. Consider the following:

- Thomas Edison and physicist Richard Feynman both attributed their intellectual prowess to their ability to think in analogies, or creative word pictures, that simplified outrageously complex ideas.

- Albert Einstein, according to nearly all accounts, was extremely creative, almost childlike in his fascination with the creativity of nature. His creativity freed him from the strictures of thought which had bound physicists for centuries.

- A shockingly high number of computer programmers, mathematicians, engineers and physicists are also

**Those who learn to communicate well stand a better chance of learning to think more clearly and creatively than those who do not.**

**To the degree**

**that we are**

**made in the**

**image of**

**God, we can**

**think, speak**

**and create in**

**wonderfully**

**complex and**

**beautiful ways.**

highly accomplished musicians and artists, dispelling the myth that creativity and logical thought are somehow two separate phenomena. One of the computer programming companies in a city where I used to live encourages lunch-time classical music sessions. I'm told that these programmers are some of the most talented musicians in town.

L. S. Vygorsky, a Russian researcher, believed that the speech structures mastered by the child become the basic structures of thinking. In other words, those who learn to communicate well stand a better chance of learning to think more clearly and creatively than those who do not. In focusing on creative thinking, this chapter promotes the idea that as your child learns to communicate more effectively, he will become more *creative*, and that creativity is the key to higher order thinking.

## THE NATURE OF CREATIVITY

Thinking, creativity, and communication skills reflect the nature of God. The Gospel of John says, "In the beginning was the *Word*," or "*logos*," which in Greek means both *word* and *mind*. God *created* the universe in his *mind*, and then through the *Word* (personified in Jesus Christ) he *spoke* it into existence. To the degree that we are made in the image of God, we can think, speak and create in wonderfully complex and beautiful ways.

It seems perfectly natural, based on the above, to work on enhancing thinking skills through practicing communication skills. The best way to enhance creative thinking is through acts of creativity that employ thinking and communication skills in a unique, powerful way. Two practical ways of utilizing the creative principle are drama and storytelling.

## DRAMA:
## LETTING THE IMAGINATION COMMUNICATE

Drama is a natural way to get children to communicate in a fun, yet non-threatening manner. Caryl Waller Krueger explains that drama teaches skills of intelligence, conviction, clarity, imagination and creativity. While we will focus more intensely on drama in the practical application section of this book, it may be helpful to outline several different ways drama can be used to reinforce communication skills and allow children to work together to accomplish a goal.

1. **Act out reading.** Your child can *be* the "little engine that could" or David swinging the slingshot at Goliath. Acting out reading is a natural way to transfer "book" knowledge into actual experience.

2. **View professionally produced plays.** A play often costs less than a movie, provided it is performed by a community theater group or local high school or college. There is nothing like live theater to spark a child's interest in drama.

3. **Perform spontaneous plays.** Mrs. Krueger suggests that you set the scene by giving a few sentences of introduction, then having the child carry out the play without structure or script. This enhances his ability to think on his feet and develop plot structure creatively and intuitively.

4. **Enact plays about real world experiences.** Use a play to act out things such as attending a new church, going on an airplane, attending a party, or visiting someone your child doesn't know. In fact, drama can be used to reinforce visiting and conversation skills.

5. **Play charades.** Choose a character for each child to act out until the others in the room can guess what it is. This helps children learn to use their bodies in a dramatic way. It also shows them how to use their nervous energy to *boost* their performance rather than paralyze them.

6. **Host a neighborhood play.** Allow your child to gather neighborhood children for a production. Volunteer your backyard or garage, prepare snacks, and invite the other parents to watch. You will be amazed at the embellishment which children add to the set, comic relief, and fake fights!

7. **Present puppet shows.** Old socks, knickknacks such as sponges and yarn, and even paper sacks make great puppets. Give your child an old sheet or newspapers which he can paint or color for set design.

8. **Create Bible pantomimes.** Together you and your child can devise pantomimes of Scripture passages. Consider the possibilities of passages such as Proverbs 23:19-21, "Listen, my son, and be wise, and keep your heart on the right path. Do not join those who drink too much wine or gorge themselves on meat, for drunkards and gluttons become poor, and drowsiness clothes them in rags." (NIV) Your family will find new meaning in Scripture as you guess the story being acted out. Your child will *feel* the meaning as he or she acts out Moses' amazement at the parting of the Red Sea, Mary's gratefulness as she anointed Jesus' feet and wiped them with her hair, and Naaman's expression when the little slave girl told him that he could be made well by going to visit Elisha. Make it memorable!

The most enjoyable drama is spontaneous and evokes participation by lots of people. In her youth, my mother and her cousins put on plays and even imaginary marching band drills for all the family members gathered. One of her uncles reciprocated by dressing up like a tramp and limping toward the children once when they were just out of sight of Grandma's farmhouse. They ran screaming to the house and right under the bed! The "tramp" followed them, laughing uncontrollably. Drama will give your family many wonderful memories, bringing communication alive!

STORYTELLING:
CAN YOU IMAGINE... CAN YOU CREATE?

Storytelling takes the products of our imagination and recreates them for the enjoyment of others. The latest research in education confirms what the Bible demonstrates: stories are the best way to transmit values from generation to generation. The Old Testament narrated history in a timeless manner. Jesus continued a long tradition through the use of parables. As a parent, your stories connect your child to the past, teach the difference between right and wrong, help him develop godly character, and affirm that life is an exciting process of observation, discovery and imagination.

In addition, stories will exercise your child's memory. Study of oral cultures shows that "uneducated" people without a written language are often able to perform prodigious feats of memory with ease. Yugoslavian bards, for instance, can listen to a thirty-minute-long story, told musically, and then repeat it thought for thought and nearly word for word. The same principles apply to children; even before your child is reading you can use storytelling to enhance both his imagination and his memory.

Storytelling is vital for life, and it can be easily taught with just a little fore-planning. We will spend a great deal of time in the "Project Pages" section of this book discussing

**Even before he is reading, you can use storytelling with your child to enhance both his imagination and his memory.**

different tactics for teaching storytelling to your children, but it is vital to note here that the way you tell stories to your child will enhance his own storytelling ability.

Here are three ideas to enhance storytelling:

1. **Create a storyteller's chair.** Professors Huckleberry and Strother suggest that with some tin foil or gold spray paint and some inexpensive red or purple velvet, you can create a throne of honor in which the storyteller may sit. What a fun way to spark a desire to exercise imagination and creativity!

2. **Debrief stories well.** Most parents read or invent stories for their children. Although I suggested earlier that you not go overboard in "analyzing" stories, there are a few elements, an understanding of which makes it possible for your child to weave exciting tales for himself. You can help your child become aware of what makes stories exciting by asking such questions as, "Is the writer just trying to entertain us, or is she saying something about people?" "What do you like about this story?" "What have you learned from this story?" "How does the author convey action and suspense?" "Is the story boring? Why?" As you ask your child what makes the story interesting, you can point out things such as the characters speaking in dialogue form, how the action progresses and other elements which will ultimately help him create more interesting stories himself. Again, as noted earlier, a good story does not consist of the structure that pulls it together. However, a basic understanding of structure makes story construction easier for your child.

3. **Infuse stories with emotion.** Emotion draws your child into the story, generating curiosity. It also sets a positive example of how to communicate in a way that interests others.

## WE ARE MADE IN THE IMAGE OF A CREATIVE GOD

By now, you have access to a whole new repertoire of activities which you can work on with your child. When God created us in his image, he gave us the ability to use words to create. It is only fitting that we learn, and in turn teach our children, how to use this powerful gift as effectively as possible. The next chapter applies the lessons learned in the construction of the first four pillars to the area of poise, or how your child handles social situations in a way that demonstrates communication excellence.

# CHAPTER NINE

# HELPING YOUR CHILD DEVELOP POISE IN SOCIAL SITUATIONS

## HAVE YOU EVER BEEN EMBARRASSED BY YOUR CHILD?

Every parent has a story about a time when they were mortified by the behavior of their child. Whether it is a shy child hiding *underneath* your dress at church in front of about 20 people, or a teenager, upon meeting someone you greatly respect, mumbling a surly greeting and barely offering a limp handshake while avoiding eye contact.

This chapter tackles the fifth pillar in our building of communication: poise. The material contained herein is wildly popular with audiences to whom I speak. People seem incredulous to discover that you can train a child to be polite, respectful, and even engaging! In this chapter, you will learn how to teach your child the most significant social skills: greeting people, maintaining a conversation, behaving in public, expressing appreciation, answering the telephone, and answering the door. But first, let's discuss why social skills are so vital to your child.

## THE BREATHTAKING SIGNIFICANCE OF SOCIAL SKILLS

Speech links your child to his environment, bringing him into contact with others, and allowing him to learn and share ideas. Children who "link-up" effortlessly find it easier to relate to others, and therefore enjoy smoother social interaction. Even more significant, effective communication skills allow your child to influence, rather than be influenced by, the culture around him.

Most people assume that children excel in social skills because of physical attractiveness. Yet studies show that attractiveness has less to do with physical beauty than with how well one communicates with others. Professors Gottman, Gonso and Rasmussen studied the characteristics of popular children and discovered that children who know how to give and receive positive verbal reinforcement are popular with their peers and are better able to make friends. They can make contributions to conversation, exert influence, and be recognized in a social manner. Even as early as preschool, notes Professor Stohl, those who use communication skills to take charge of social situations become more noticeable to their peers, and are thus viewed as more attractive. In addition, a multitude of studies show that, unfair as it may seem, teachers spend more time with and give higher evaluations to children who communicate well.

Obviously, your child can benefit through stronger and smoother social skills. Most children, at one time or another, struggle with this. Some are too shy, and others are too hyperactive! Both of those responses, however, seem to originate in the same place, as we will now discuss.

## THE FEAR OF THE UNKNOWN MAKES US UNCOMFORTABLE

The fear of not knowing what to do in social situations seems to be the single greatest culprit in children's lack of comfort in such situations. Entering a social situation with an adult may seem as intimidating to a child as if *you* were entering a social situation with a well-known public figure. The President of the United States, to avoid awkward situations when visiting with foreign dignitaries, retains a staff of dozens of experts trained in the "protocol" of various nations. These experts brief the President on how to greet a dignitary according to that person's customs, explain which gestures are not acceptable (in some countries the common American gesture signifying "Okay" by making a circle with the forefinger and thumb, is a vulgarity), demonstrate how to sit properly (in some Mid-Eastern countries, showing the bottom of one's shoe is an unforgivable insult), describe what might be served and how to eat it, and suggest what constitutes proper topics of conversation.

If you can gently instruct your child on *how* to act appropriately, he will feel more comfortable, and in my experience, will respond with more pleasing behavior. You can help your child overcome his fear of the unknown by practicing social skills in the home before actually trying them out. As a parent, you will have to think ahead, never assuming that your child automatically knows how to behave. Here are some ideas about instructing your child in common social situations.

## HOW TO TEACH YOUR CHILD TO GREET OTHERS

Whether consciously or unconsciously, we view others based on first impressions. The first few seconds give us an impression that governs everything else we think about

Entering a social situation with an adult may seem as intimidating to a child as entering a social situation with a well-known public figure is to an adult.

**If you can**

**gently**

**instruct your**

**child on**

**how to act**

**appropriately,**

**he will feel**

**more**

**comfortable**

**and will**

**respond**

**with more**

**pleasing**

**behavior.**

that person. In fact, that first impression can last in your mind for several years! Teaching appropriate greeting skills is easy, but getting your child to follow through will take some practice.

An effective greeting contains two steps: first, the introduction, and second, the conversation stimulant. Let's say you wish to introduce your son to Horace Englebert, an associate from work. You would first say, "Excuse me, Mr. Englebert, this is my son Junior. Junior, Mr. Englebert is one of the men with whom I work." Train your son to offer a firm (not crushing) handshake while looking your colleague in the eye, and saying, "Hello, Mr. Englebert, I am pleased to meet you." Second, it is appropriate for you to stimulate conversation between the two. "Junior, you might be very interested in Mr. Englebert's hobby of gluing toothpicks into eight-inch-tall statues of the Alamo." (Okay, okay, so this example is *extremely* hypothetical.) Or, you could say, "Mr. Englebert, since you appreciate fine talent, you would be interested to know that Junior is an accomplished pianist. Why, he just finished learning Opus 360 by Klaus Swindlepucker."

Here are some of the finer points of greetings:

• Your child should not assume that the other person remembers him. If he is greeting someone he has not seen for a while, teach your child to reintroduce himself and give the person a brief recap of where they last met. Your child should *never* put someone on the spot by saying, "Do you remember me?" or, "What's my name?"

• Help your child learn to make the other person as comfortable as possible. Simple, appropriate greetings may include:

"How are you today?"

"How is your family?" (Ask by name.) "What have you been doing lately?"

If the person is a public figure, or is otherwise not known to your child, coach your child to say something like:

"I am very pleased to meet you."

"I would like to know more about you (your work, your family, etc.)."

Do not ask questions which might be too personal or put the person on the spot.

Help your child learn to disengage from the conversation when it is time to go. Except in extreme circumstances, it is polite to wait until the conversation seems to be near an end, extend your hand again, look the person in the eye, and say, "I am pleased to have met you," and then offer a pleasant goodbye such as, "Enjoy the rest of your day," or, "Have a wonderful day." If the person is long-winded and your child really needs to go, he can say, "I'm sorry, it is time for me to go," and offer his goodbye. Teach your child to offer a reason if possible, but never to lie. Good reasons would be things like, "I told my parents I would meet them at 12:30, and I have just enough time to get there" or, "I'm working right now so I must get back to the task at hand."

## HOW TO TEACH APPROPRIATE PUBLIC BEHAVIOR

It is vitally important to coach your child on what constitutes appropriate behavior in a public setting. Do not

*The first few seconds give us an impression that governs everything else we think about that person. In fact, that first impression can last for several years!*

assume that he knows what to do. The importance of this kind of training is highlighted in Caryl Waller Krueger's practical, idea-filled book, *Six Weeks to Better Parenting* (Pelican Press). Mrs. Krueger's advice is so common sense that it ought to be obvious. However, for most people, it is far from obvious. I once saw a young boy run up to a male adult speaker and punch him *in the groin*. He meant it as a gesture of play, I'm sure, but his mother nearly fainted dead away (and so did the speaker, by the way)! In turn, the mother nearly extinguished the life of the young boy, who, bewildered, failed to recognize that he had done anything inappropriate. The whole situation could have been avoided had he been coached in appropriate behavior in advance. On the other hand, I know a mother who *always* coaches her young son, even before something as routine as a church service. I have heard many people comment on that boy's incredibly polite behavior, never realizing that it is far from accidental. Such behavior may be attributed to the child, but reflects nicely on the parents, too!

## VISITING

Your child will benefit from opportunities to visit with adults, and you can manufacture situations in which to give him practice. For example, the next time you go to church, require your child to greet one or two adults and engage them in a conversation for at least one minute. It may seem artificial at first, but who knows? Maybe the conversation will last even longer. The child may even enjoy it. He will certainly learn from it! Afterwards, debrief the experience over dinner and praise your child for his efforts. Point out how special people feel when others acknowledge and appreciate their presence.

One of the objects of teaching visiting skills, at least initially, is to make your child feel comfortable. Practice visiting skills with guests in your own home first, where children feel more comfortable. Then move on to visits outside the home, brief ones at first—30 minutes or less. Mrs. Krueger suggests explaining the purpose of the visit and reviewing appropriate behavior before each visit. How should this person be greeted? If he or she is a close friend or relative, a kiss or hug may be more appropriate than a handshake. How should your child respond to an offer of food? How does he ask to use the rest room? How should he ask if he wants to play with the toys in the other room?

Another way to put your child at ease is for him to take something to share with the person being visited. A game, picture, small book, or snack are all appropriate. This puts the child on familiar turf in an unfamiliar place. Also, for every rule about what the child cannot do on the visit, think of a privilege which the child *can* exercise. At the end of the visit, debrief. Praise your child for good behavior and manners, discuss whether the purpose of the visit was achieved, and help him become satisfied with the results.

**Children often fall apart in conversation because they feel they have nothing valuable to say.**

## CONVERSATION WITH ADULTS

Ability to converse with adults is a mark of maturity in children. You can enhance your child's maturity by equipping him with strategies for difficult situations. Children often fall apart in conversation because they feel they have nothing valuable to say.

It is perfectly appropriate to prepare your child for specific situations. At a birthday party, make sure your child knows how to respond when given a gift. He should be able to say more than just "thank you," and should know how to respond when he receives a duplicate gift. The response should be gracious and appropriate (not, "Did you keep the receipt?").

Those who

make a habit

of blessing

other people

will find a

significant

mission field

right before

their very

eyes.

Your child will become more comfortable in social situations *outside* the home if you converse frequently *inside* your home. One excellent book which can help you converse with your child is Dr. Jane M. Healy's *How to Have Intelligent and Creative Conversations with Your Kids* (Doubleday). Dr. Healy suggests dozens of playful topics for conversation. Here are some of them for each age group:

## PRIMARY LEVEL (3-7):

If you could spend one day as an animal, which one would you choose to be? Tell about what you think your day might be like.

How can you tell if someone is your friend? What do you need to do to be a friend?

What if you found a secret passage in your house or apartment?

## MIDDLE LEVEL (8-12):

If you were asked to invent a new holiday, what would it be for? What would you call it? When and how would it be celebrated?

Pretend there is a robot standing in the room. What would you have to change about it so that you could call it human?

You have been invited to participate in an experiment with a newly developed time machine. You may choose to go forward or backward in time to any place you wish. Would you go? If so, what year or period would you like to land in? Why?

## UPPER LEVEL (13 AND UP):

Pretend you leave your bedroom one morning and close the door. Is your bed still there if no one can see it, touch it, or sense it in any other way? How could you prove it?

How might the course of human civilization have been different if people did not need to eat but could absorb all the nourishment they needed from air and water?

How is a game of football like the United States government?

You can probably think of other fun topics of conversation to use with your child and for your child to use with others. Topics such as these help acclimate him to the flow and pace of conversation.

### EXPRESSING APPRECIATION

Poised people know how to express appreciation to others for their kindness. Bennett Cerf offered the following advice:

> A very wise public-relations counsel cautions letter writers to delete the pronoun "I" as much as possible. "A weekend thank-you note that opens 'I had a wonderful time,'" he points out, "is not half so captivating as one beginning, 'You are a wonderful hostess.' Both say 'thank you,' but, ah, my friends, the second is the one that will get you asked back!"

As Christians, our purpose is not so much to get asked back, but to love others. The Bible commands us to encourage one another in the faith, spur one another on to good deeds, and love our neighbor as ourselves. Those who make a habit of blessing other people will find a significant

**Taught**

**properly,**

**young**

**children**

**enjoy**

**answering**

**the telephone**

**and will take**

**a great deal**

**of pride in**

**doing so.**

mission field right before their very eyes. Your child can participate in this blessing as part of his developing communication ability.

## ANSWERING THE TELEPHONE

Explain to your child that answering the telephone provides the opportunity to make an impression on someone, either negative or positive. Teach him to use a pleasant voice, inquire about the caller, and take messages. Have your child practice on a toy telephone to prove he can do it correctly.

I rediscovered the importance of telephone manners through a conversation with a four-year-old, home-school child named Kyle. I telephoned his family in reference to an upcoming conference, and the following conversation took place when Kyle answered the telephone:

"Smith residence, this is Kyle," he said distinctly. "Who would you like to speak to?"

"Hello," I said, taken aback, "I would like to speak to your father."

"My father is not available," replied young Kyle. "Would you like to speak to my mother?"

I said, "That would be fine."

"May I ask who's calling?" he inquired.

Caught off guard once again, I said, "Yes, this is Jeff," not bothering to overload him with additional information such as my last name.

"Hold one moment, please," he said, and dashed off. Then I heard him say, "Mom, there is a Jeff on the phone for you. He did not say what kind of Jeff he was!"

You can bet that I was impressed with the poise and skill that little Kyle demonstrated when answering the phone, and a little embarrassed that I underestimated his talent at doing so. Because I was impressed, my whole approach to Kyle changed, and our interaction rose to a new level. Both of us benefitted.

When teaching your child to answer the telephone, keep security concerns in mind. In our insecure and some-times dangerous world, it may be best for your child to not answer the telephone in your absence. If he must, teach him how to answer without indicating that you are gone. A proper response might be, "My mother cannot come to the telephone right now. May I take a message?" Be sure message paper and a pen are handy. Teach him to ask for the name, proper spelling, telephone number, and what the call is regarding, as appropriate. Designate a standard place where family members can pick up and leave messages. If you *are* home, but not available, saying, "My mother can-not come to the telephone right now. May I take a mes-sage?" will suffice. One young boy with whom I spoke indicated, much to his mother's embarrassment, that his mother was on the toilet right then and couldn't come to the phone!

Think of various situations your child might encounter on the telephone, and then test him once or twice by call-ing from a pay phone. Devise a reward system for proper responses to these surprise calls. Taught properly, young children enjoy answering the telephone and will take a great deal of pride in doing so. In return for answering pleasantly and appropriately, give your child the privilege of making telephone calls. Be sure to set up clear rules about what times of the day he may receive calls, how long the calls may be, and whether he needs to ask permission.

## ANSWERING THE DOOR

Answering the door is good practice for greeting others. The rules will differ from home to home depending on how safe your neighborhood is and whether the child can view the caller through the door. Teach your child to ask who it is before unlocking and opening the door. Clarify the rules as to who is to be let in; it is rude to leave friends and family standing outside, but it is perfectly appropriate for strangers. If the caller is unknown, your child should ask, "May I tell my parents who is here?" Again, in our sad days of high crime rates, it may be best for your children not to answer the door at all when you are not home.

## REWARDING ENTHUSIASM

Sometimes your child's enthusiasm may cause a mix-up. When he was six or seven years of age, my brother Tim once answered the door with his telephone greeting: "Hello, Myers residence." It is still an embarrassment to him many years later. Mix-ups are no big deal; they are part of learning. The skills your child can learn by completing these simple tasks, however, allow him to develop poise and confidence, and leave a positive first impression that can benefit him and encourage others for years to come.

# CHAPTER TEN

# HELPING YOUR CHILD RELATE TO OTHERS: A LIFE SKILL

## EMPATHY: A CHARACTER QUALITY OF CHRIST

Communication brings your child in contact with others, allowing him to listen, learn, and mature into a more well-rounded human being. It also gives him the opportunity to encourage others, contributing fullness and meaning to their lives. This ability to understand others and relate to their lives is called *empathy*. It forms the basis for the sixth and final pillar in the building of communication. Empathy means the ability to relate to others in such a way as to ensure that they know we really understand them. Empathy is the apex of all communication skill since it makes our relationships and impact on the world meaningful.

**Empathy: the ability to understand others and relate to their lives.**

Empathy is a quality displayed by Jesus in relation to us:

Since the children have flesh and blood, he too shared in their humanity so that by his death he might destroy him who holds the power of death—that is, the devil—and free those who all their lives were held in slavery by their fear of death...

**Empathy**

**shows the**

**other person**

**that you**

**understand,**

**not necessarily**

**that you**

**agree.**

For this reason he had to be made like his brothers in every way, in order that he might become a merciful and faithful high priest in service to God, and that he might make atonement for the sins of the people. Because he himself suffered when he was tempted, he is able to help those who are being tempted (Hebrews 2:14-18, NIV).

Jesus identified with our sufferings in part because he had suffered. Even though we may not have been through the same experiences as those around us, we should attempt to *identify* with them so we can more effectively *reach* them. To empathize does not mean the same thing as sympathize, which connotes more of a "feeling sorry for" or endorsing the beliefs, attitudes and values of others. Empathy shows the other person that you understand, not necessarily that you agree.

Two primary ways to develop the communication skill of empathy include active listening and advanced conversation ability.

## HOW TO TEACH ACTIVE LISTENING TO YOUR CHILD

King Solomon, the world's wisest man, warned in Proverbs 1:32-33, "For the waywardness of the simple will kill them, and the complacency of fools will destroy them; but whoever *listens* to [wisdom] will live in safety and be at ease, without fear of harm" (NIV). James 1:19 says, "Everyone should be quick to listen, slow to speak, and slow to become angry" (NIV). Proverbs 1:5 says, "Let the wise listen and add to their learning" (NIV). The Bible also calls those who do not listen fools.

Active listening occurs when the listener concentrates on feeling the emotion behind what the speaker says. Active listening requires the listener to overcome tiredness, to avoid preoccupation with other thoughts, to not get ahead of the speaker, and to avoid mentally formulating a response before the speaker is finished.

Practice active listening before teaching it to your child. When your child has something to say, stop what you are doing, get on his level, look him in the eye, and treat what he says as important by smiling, nodding and asking questions.

Active listening also means listening to *comprehend*. An active listener understands the central idea being expressed, identifies the arguments in support of that idea, and figures out what the *speaker* thinks is important. Every child can learn to comprehend the central idea expressed in conversation, or even in books, stories, movies and news items. Practice by giving your child the opportunity to listen to a speaker, story or song, and then testing him through a true/false quiz. For added realism, include *noise*, making it difficult to concentrate.

Here are the six steps to active listening:

1. **Be attentive.** Demonstrate attentiveness by looking the person in the eye, and sitting up straight. Lean forward instead of slouching, and uncross your arms to take a more open stance. Nod and smile when appropriate.

2. **Show interest.** Keep the discussion going with verbal responses such as, "I see," "Uh-huh," and "Yes, go on."

3. **Reflect back.** When the person pauses for a response, reflect his feelings back so he can hear them voiced. This convinces him that you are listening. You can reflect either the content or feelings the person is expressing. If the topic is emotional in nature, consider the person's feelings first. Common reflecting sentences include:

*Active listening occurs when the listener concentrates on feeling the emotion behind what the speaker says.*

**We model**

**one-way**

**communication**

**to our children**

**by avoiding**

**personal**

**involvement.**

- "Wow, it sounds like you're really…"

- "I hear how you feel."

- "If I'm hearing you correctly…"

4. **Clarify.** Question the statement until the person agrees that you understand fully.

- "Let me restate what you've said to make sure I understand."

- "Is there something else?"

- "Is the problem _____?"

5. **Re-state everything.** Especially in complex conversation, with difficult to understand material, it is important to make sure you are on the same wavelength.

- "If I understand you, you plan to _____."

- "Let me see if I understand the reasons for what you want to do…"

6. **Summarize.** Put together the essential facts and ideas.

## HOW TO TEACH CONVERSATION SKILLS TO YOUR CHILD

Conversation may be a lost art in our nation. Most people would rather *watch* something than engage in a social situation where the focus of attention is *each other*. We expect children to play with other children and leave adults alone. We model one-way communication to our children by avoiding personal involvement. One study showed that 94% of all questions refer to the immediate situation, reflecting on such valueless topics as the weather.

Fortunately, there are ways to solve this problem. Here are some unique approaches:

1. **Use a tennis ball to reinforce the importance of conversation.** The speaker holds a tennis ball while speaking, throwing it to someone else when finished. The second person says something and then throws the ball to someone else. Try this with your child to demonstrate the flow of conversation.

2. **"Prime" the pump.** Give your child conversation tips before going into unfamiliar territory. I travel several days each month, frequently meeting new people. I am always grateful to hosts who brief me about those whom we will be meeting. It makes conversation easier, allowing us to "hit it off" almost immediately. Your child will benefit from similar preparation. If you know with whom your child will be visiting, hint at possible topics of conversation. For instance, "What kind of dog is Sammy?" "Are you a war veteran?" or, "Did you remodel this room yourself?"

3. **Think of five topics.** Have your child think of five topics he would like to discuss with any given adult: his new bicycle, a current event, what he is learning in school, or a question about a sports team.

4. **Think of five questions.** Alter the "five topics" strategy for older children. At a retirement center, for instance, he may think of questions such as, "What was it like to live during the Great Depression?" "Will you tell me about your family?" "What is something that one of your children has done of which you are proud?" or, "What are some of your fond memories of childhood?" Usually, one of these topics sparks an interest, giving your child the chance to hear and appreciate history through the words of an older person.

**Asking questions is perhaps the most effective stimulus of good conversation.**

Here are some questions to use in other situations:

Tell me about...

...where you grew up.

...a favorite childhood memory.

...a good book you have read recently.

...one thing you would attempt if you knew you could not fail.

...an exciting place you have been.

- Describe your dream vacation.

- What is your favorite meal? Animal? Place in the world?

- If you could do one thing to change the world, what would you do?

- Describe the most adventurous thing you have ever done.

- Some people consider themselves to be introverts and some consider themselves to be extroverts. Which do you think you are and why?

- What is your hobby or what do you enjoy spending time on?

- If you could build your very own dream house, what would you put in it?

Asking questions is perhaps the most effective stimulus of good conversation. Moreover, it leaves a positive impression in the mind of the other person. I'll never forget my college roommate returning from a date exclaiming, "That was the most brilliant girl I have ever dated!" When I asked what gave him that impression, he could not think of an answer. It turned out, of course, that *she* asked *him* lots of questions, so he talked about himself the whole evening, coming away with the impression that *she* was brilliant!

## EMPATHY: MISSION IMPOSSIBLE?

Empathy is a communication skill in great demand. We talk but we do not really know how to empathize with one another. An eerie, uncomfortable silence has developed in our souls. Learning to listen and converse is important to fulfilling our mission on earth of reaching, touching and loving others as God loves us. If you and your family embrace this mission, your influence on this world will be far-reaching and profound.

Now that we have covered the foundation and all six pillars of communication success, it is time to begin building the roof! The next part of the book gives you hundreds of exciting communication-building ideas for children of all age ranges. It is time to get practical!

*Learning to listen and converse is important to fulfilling our mission on earth of reaching, touching and loving others as God loves us.*

# CHAPTER ELEVEN

# COMMUNICATION-BUILDING ACTIVITIES FOR EVERY CHILD

## NOW IT'S TIME TO "GET PRACTICAL"

The first part of this book offered dozens of ideas for improving the quality of communication in your family. This last section offers dozens more in the form of specific projects you can use to work on particular communication skills. Each project is tailored to a specific age group and categorized as to which communication skill it develops.

## HERE'S HOW!

Each project from age three and up is organized to maximize its usefulness. Here is an overview of how the projects are structured:

*Project Sketch* gives you an overview of each project.

*How-To* shows you what materials are needed and how to accomplish the project successfully.

*Timely Tip* provides special insight into field-tested ways to get the most out of each project.

*Future Adventure* offers variations of the project so that you can extend the life of those which work best for you.

*Make it Memorable* shows you a relationship-building key to each project that makes it something your child will never forget!

## IDEAS THAT WORK—FROM PLAYPEN TO PODIUM

In addition to being highly practical, each project is "age integrated" to work on skills specific to each developmental level. The projects are divided into sections as follows:

*Infants:* Communication with infants is extremely important; your child is born ready to communicate, and most of the "landmarks" in communication training have passed by three years of age! This section gives you 14 practical ideas you can start using right now, or give to a friend who has a baby.

*Toddlers:* Toddlers are human sponges. They absorb everything—especially communication. This chapter shows you how to take advantage of your child's natural inquisitiveness to stimulate his communication ability.

*Ages Three to Seven:* This is the age at which communication-building becomes really fun! You can create a desire for communication in your child through play activities, and this chapter shows you how. It also gives more ways to encourage storytelling than you probably have ever seen in one place!

*Ages Eight to Twelve:* During the pre-teen years, children can learn how to be confident in social situations and begin to learn basic speech skills.

This chapter starts at the very beginning, using creative ideas to make communication development fun.

**Ages Thirteen and Up:** This is the age at which young people have the opportunity to work on the leadership and communication skills they will use throughout life. In this chapter they will learn skills of critical inquiry, interviewing and listening, as well as different kinds of speeches that even the most shy teenager can accomplish.

Use these projects to their fullest potential by adding your own comments and variations on the blank "Notes" pages you will find throughout.

### HOW TO TARGET SPECIFIC SKILL NEEDS

Finally, each project is geared toward practicing some of the specific skills we discussed in the first section of the book: strengthening your child's sense of purpose, becoming more aware of the world around, becoming a better learner, thinking more creatively, developing poise, and relating to others. Each project is tagged with a primary and a secondary skill target. To review, here are the tags you will see for each skill:

*Purpose*

**Purpose** results from a child's recognition of his parents' love, as well as a sense of the excitement and meaning of everyday life. It supports communication excellence by taking away fear and making your child's communication appealing to others. In turn, communication excellence generates enthusiasm for other areas of your child's life.

## Awareness

*Awareness* results from a child's curiosity about the world, and it supports communication excellence by giving your child the ability to become more aware of the experiences of others, how to reach the heart of an audience, and how to effectively translate his own experiences into meaningful information for an audience.

## Learning

*Learning* results from a child's love of gaining new information, and it supports communication excellence by giving your child a base of experience from which to speak. In turn, communication excellence generates a heightened sense of the importance of words, making a deeper level of expression possible.

## Creative Thinking

*Creative Thinking* results from experiences which allow your child to be creative and to think in interesting, exciting ways. It supports communication excellence by giving your child a unique, exciting perspective on life, spurring him on to a new level of quick, powerful thinking.

# *Poise*

*Poise* results from a child learning to be comfortable in a wide variety of settings. It raises your child's comfort level and skill in front of an audience or in any social situation in which he might find himself.

# *Empathy*

*Empathy* results from a child being trained to listen to and learn from the experiences of others. It improves your child's skill at relating to others, increasing his attractiveness to them and thus the power of his message.

### NOW IT STARTS...

Please allow me to make a personal note here. The Apostle Paul says that we must be prepared to communicate with others in a gentle and respectful fashion, taking care that our speech is "seasoned with salt" (Colossians 4:6, NIV). Salt is both a preservative and a healing agent. In the same way, communication preserves and builds fragile human relationships.

I see these projects as more than just fun things to do with your child. They form the bedrock of his social impact on the world, showing him how to "salt" others in a way that causes them to grow and become what God wants them to be.

Each human being is made in the image of God, and we will all have to give account someday for how we bore that image. Yet, most people are terrified of communicating publicly. In one survey, adults listed "Speaking before a group" as their number one fear. It was named more often than financial problems, illness, and even death!

These projects will equip your child to take the higher ground, persevering where you might shrink in fear. Ultimately, young people who learn to communicate, and to do so truthfully and lovingly, will become the next generation of leaders. My prayer is that your child will be among them.

# CHAPTER TWELVE

# INFANT COMMUNICATION

## COMMUNICATION:
## A BREATH OF LIFE FOR YOUR BABY

Most people seem surprised to discover that how you communicate with your infant may have a long-term impact on his communication development, but it is true. This is not to say that a parent's influence at this age level is fully understood because it is not, even by researchers who have studied parents and children for decades. But researchers now recognize that infant communication is extremely important, and that infants do have the awareness and intelligence to process words and emotions.

A striking example of the horrible consequences of the old philosophy, that infant communication was irrelevant, was discovered in the ruins of the communist regime in Romania. Relief workers discovered thousands of small children who had been forcibly taken from their parents and raised by the government, some of whom were as old as five years, yet were the size and maturity level of infants. These children had been kept in large rooms full of dozens of cribs, with just enough nursing care to feed and sometimes clothe them, but not to communicate with or mother them. These poor children could not care for themselves or talk, and many experts wondered if they would ever be able to take a normal role in society. Clinging desperately to

**Babies not only**

**attempt to**

**speak, they**

**actually mimic**

**the "turn-taking"**

**which is**

**necessary for**

**conversation.**

their rescuers, these children experienced love, cuddling and communication for the first time in their short lives. Thankfully, most have been adopted into loving homes, providing the opportunity for somewhat normal development.

This chapter is not designed to teach you how to communicate with your baby—that comes naturally. However, it *will* enhance your ability to understand your baby's stages of communication development and deepen your ability to build a strong foundation for his future communication skills. As with all teaching tools, "balance" is very important. Chattering to your baby all the time, or creating "flash cards" and language drills would quickly become counterproductive! This chapter will help clarify what is appropriate and healthy.

### How Important Is Communication with Your Baby?

Oddly enough, the word infant literally comes from the Latin word "in" (meaning without) and "fan" (meaning to speak). It literally means "without speech." We now know that even though the physical structures for actual speech are not in place, your baby is trying out his inborn ability to speak from day one! According to Dr. Rachel Stark, an infant researcher, many of those who have studied each stage of speech development have concluded that infant vocalization is actually an attempt to mimic human speech. Moreover, according to Dr. Stark, babies not only attempt to speak, they actually mimic the "turn-taking" which is necessary for conversation.

Additionally, infants are sensitive to the communication of others from birth. According to Professor Baltaxe, another infant researcher, babies react to the quality of feelings expressed in the voice and can even discern emotions in the voice and match them to facial expressions. Most infants desire communication so strongly that they are more interested in the sound of adult voices than any other sound, including instrumental music.

When our son Graham was born, Danielle and I put this theory to the test. We talked to Graham as if he were going to respond, even when he was just a few weeks old. It often felt silly to carry on "conversation" with a pre-verbal infant, but we were rewarded when his eyes flashed, legs kicked, and his tiny mouth moved producing noises that would someday become speech. He loved it! And so did we.

It is no surprise that experts now consider infancy a crucial time for gaining the ability to use language effectively. Dr. William Fowler of the Center for Early Learning and Child Care in Cambridge, Massachusetts, a researcher of infant/parent interactions, concluded that parents who focus on speech early in the life of a child will enhance his chances of becoming a better communicator later in life. In fact, dozens of studies show that the mother's talk with her infant is the most significant factor in the later ability of the child to communicate.

How is this so? Dr. Carol Gibb Harding explains that mothers guess what the child's communication means and react in a certain way. Through this response, the infant becomes aware of the connection between its behavior and the mother's. As the infant starts to communicate, the mother "ups the ante," requiring ever more advanced communication. In this way, the mother demonstrates to the child the importance of communication. This phenomenon is called "motherese."

In order to begin putting this knowledge into practice, it might be helpful to know a little bit about your baby's stages of communication development.

**A mother's talk with her infant is the most significant factor in the later ability of the child to communicate.**

Children

*understand*

before they *act.*

Just as adults

can understand

more than they

can explain,

babies

understand

words before

their vocal

structures allow

them to

reproduce

those words.

## Getting to Know Your Baby

Even before they learn to speak, children communicate through gaze direction, eye contact, vocalizing, and reaching and pointing, whether or not they do this with the *intention* of communicating. Speech emerges through the course of time in a predictable pattern, though the *pace* will differ for each child. Understanding these patterns will help you become aware of normal development. It will also help you enjoy your child's growth more, since you will notice his passing from one stage to the next!

If your child is dramatically behind, you may wish to discuss the problem with your physician. Otherwise, just be sure you are creating a stimulating environment for your child, and be patient! A friend of mine did not speak, according to his mother, a single word until he was three years of age. Today he is a brilliant writer and gifted novelist.

Keep in mind that at every stage, children *understand* before they do. Just as adults can usually understand more than they can explain, babies understand words before their vocal structures allow them to reproduce those words. With that in mind, here are the major stages of infant speech development.

## Stage One: Vocalization

Vocalization starts immediately at birth. Cooing sounds, or "oohs and ahs," appear during the first and second months, and babbling ensues at about three months. Babbling usually is a consonant sound repeated over and over again such as "ba-ba-ba." Despite the hopes of many a proud father, the baby is not likely to say "pa-pa" with meaningful intent until much later!

## STAGE TWO: LALLING

Lalling is a sound that the child makes, likes and repeats. This stage usually begins at about six months of age. Somewhere between the babbling stage and the lalling stage you will notice your baby using his voice as he attempts to manipulate the objects he is playing with. The best explanation for this phenomenon is that your baby is "representing the objects" to himself, describing to himself what they are and what they mean. It is hard to say whether he is really thinking about them, or is just connecting the need to use his voice in response to the world around.

## STAGE THREE: ECHOLALIA

Echolalia comes from the word "echo" (to repeat) and "lalia" (speech), meaning "repeating what others say." Echolalia begins at about nine or ten months of age. At this point your child begins devising "fast maps," or rough meanings of words which serve as temporary definitions to use until he is sure of the meaning. You can expect your baby to *understand* certain words at this age (such as "no"). At about eleven months he may actually begin using words with meaning, although the words will be more clear to Mom and Dad or older siblings, who are able to make an immediate connection between the words used and what he wants.

## STAGE FOUR: JARGONING

At the jargoning stage, your child may look at you and rattle off a word or several words which you do not understand. Jargoning will occur sometime after echolalia, although the length of the time is different for each child. Children who are more physically active are less likely to speak, while those who do not express as much physical activity may develop more quickly in that area. Jargoning is sometimes called "prattling" or "baby talk." It actually has the rhythm of speech, although few words will make sense to adults.

The best way to make these words clearer is by trying to guess what your child is saying. Caution: this stage may require a great deal of patience as you gradually learn to interpret the words used. It is best not to scold or correct the child for the inaccurate use of a word. Instead, just keep saying the correct pronunciation. If the baby says "gamma," you say "grandma." Studies consistently demonstrate that your child will learn how to pronounce words from your use of correct pronunciation.

## STAGE FIVE: SENTENCES

The final stage is the use of *sentences*. Most children begin using simple sentences at about 18 months of age. At first, these sentences are for the purpose of requesting information or objects, such as "What that?" or "Give ball." Eventually, the child begins making statements about the world such as "That dog," or "Ball on chair." His language system will become more sophisticated, yet growth may come rapidly at times and very slowly at others. Language learning is like a volcano; just because there is no smoke does not mean it is extinct! It may brew and stew and steam and build up pressure for quite a while before erupting! Often children go for days or weeks without any visible signs of speech development, and then "boom"—your ears hardly have time for a rest.

Understanding these five stages will help you track the development of your child. Next we will apply all of this theory and make it eminently practical through fourteen powerful, practical ideas.

## FOURTEEN POWERFUL IDEAS
## YOU CAN USE RIGHT NOW

Recent studies have shown, noted one reporter, that babies are, in fact, human! As awkward as it seems to talk to a child who cannot respond, you must make a conscious effort to be verbal around your baby. Mem Fox explains that children "learn to read by reading. They learn to write by writing. And they learn to talk by talking." Here are some helpful suggestions:

## ONE: TALK TO YOUR BABY!

Remember, you're the best teacher your child will ever have. You can talk about anything. Even talking aloud about whatever is on your mind will give your baby a model of speech. When putting away the dishes, talk about where the dishes go. When reading the sports page, talk about how your favorite team is doing and why. It is your voice, rather than the words you say, that matter most at this age.

To model this, we talk with our children about everything: what we were wearing, how to get dressed, our plans for the day, etc., and marvel at how intensely they seem to listen. Your voice is music to your child's ears!

Keep in mind that babies can pick up on emotional states, so be careful what you say and how you say it! Set a good example by not using baby talk. Your baby will appreciate a pleasant adult voice much more.

Another way to share talk with your baby is to whisper lightly in his ear or right next to his ear. He will listen intently to this very personal form of communication.

Once again, strive for a healthy balance. Don't try to keep up a constant chatter. *Share conversation* with your baby, treating everything he says as if it were actual speech.

**Always respond**

**to whatever**

**your child looks**

**at or feels by**

**making it a**

**"teachable**

**moment."**

## Two: Practice Turn-Taking

As you talk to your baby, pretend that you are having a conversation. If he gurgles or coos, act as if it represents a question or an answer to *your* question. To the observer, it seems quite strange, but by doing so, you encourage your baby to interact, thus drawing communication out of him. How do you do it? Make eye contact and just *talk*. If he grabs his foot, say "Yes, here's your foot." As Barbara Beckwith suggests, "Always respond to whatever your child looks at or feels by making it a 'teachable moment.'" At this level, the fact that you are taking turns is more important than *what* you say. For example:

Baby: "Ehh."

You: "Yes! I did notice that it is a beautiful day outside. What are you planning to do on such a beautiful day?"

Baby: "Ba, ba, ba, ba."

You: "Well! Such big plans for such a little tyke! I suppose we had better get you dressed and ready then, hmmm?"

Baby: "Ehh."

Be creative! Your baby is hearing your voice and recognizing that his vocalizations are meaningful to you. Maybe you could use this time to practice making up stories for when your baby reaches toddler age!

## Three: Talk with Other Children

Include your baby in conversation with others, especially with his siblings or other children. This provides "competition" in which the infant vies for attention. Human beings use communication to establish themselves in relationship to each other. Including an infant in conversation helps him learn to communicate in a real-world context.

## FOUR: ASK LOTS OF QUESTIONS!

Asking lots of questions of your baby actually demonstrates to him that you are interested in conversation. According to Dr. Catherine Snow, one of the top experts in the world on infant communication development, such conversation with your child, even when he can't respond, helps him develop a sense of the "structure" of communication for later years when he can respond.

Here are some examples of how to ask questions of your baby:

- It's really a pretty day outside, hmm?

- That's a pretty color, isn't it?

- Oh, can you tell me more about your opinions on that issue?

- Oh my, we're feeling a little fussy, are we?

Any question that "passes the turn" to your baby, even though you know full well he cannot respond, is a great way to develop a strong foundation for future communication skill.

"Wh" questions, those which ask *what* and *where*, are also excellent:

- What is that? Can you say bird?

- Where did the ball go?

## FIVE: SCHEDULE TIME WITH OTHER SIBLINGS

Teach your baby's older siblings, if he has any, how to communicate around him. Babies learn a great deal from older siblings about how to communicate effectively. Studies between older and younger children showed that older siblings who spent time with the baby, and were not physically aggressive with him, were more likely to be imitated by the baby and to be received by him in a friendly way.

Here are some things that older siblings can do to develop this kind of relationship with the baby:

- Imitate him when he makes sounds or kicks or moves his body.

- Start games with the baby, such as peek-a-boo.

- Help wash the baby.

- Feed the baby.

- Brush the baby's hair.

- Show toys to the baby.

## SIX: IMITATE YOUR BABY

Strangely, babies pay special attention to mothers when mothers imitate an act they have just performed. Somehow, babies recognize that their movements and gurglings and smiles communicate. Even if it seems silly, when the baby throws his arms and legs in the air and makes exclamatory noises, imitate him by throwing your arms in the air and repeating the sound.

## SEVEN: REPEAT YOURSELF

According to Professors Jones and Adamson, babies learn words when they hear them used over and over in a variety of contexts, so do not be afraid of repeating yourself in talking to your baby. For example: "Oh, Keisha! My little Keisha! Would you like to take a bath right now? Bath? How about a bath to wash you all up?"

## EIGHT: READ TO YOUR BABY

Read aloud when your baby is in the room. Read the Bible, a children's book, or anything in which you are interested. Reading will help your baby adjust to the rhythm of speech.

## NINE: LEAD IN COMMUNICATION

Draw your child into communication by encouraging him to be verbal about what he wants. If he gestures and grunts for a bite of applesauce, ask, "What do you want? *Applesauce?* Tell me, so I can give it to you." Ask "Yes?" while nodding your head or "No?" while shaking it. Sometimes he will be able to do so, sometimes not. With patience, you will elicit clearer responses from your child.

## TEN: SHARE INITIATION OF CONVERSATION

In addition to asking questions, some experts suggest that you gradually begin to ignore grunts, and require some sort of verbalization before you respond to your baby's needs. One study reported by Dr. Harding showed that the most communicatively advanced infants were those whose mothers initiated less *than half* of the interactions. The most advanced infants learned to initiate "conversation." This means that you don't have to be the first to start conversation with your

One way to spur your child's communicative development is to gradually begin ignoring grunts, and to require some sort of verbalization before you respond to your baby's needs.

baby. Every once in a while let *him* make conversational noises or attempt to initiate conversation with *you*.

### ELEVEN: TAKE NAMING WALKS

Carry your baby around the home, pointing out objects. As you name them, put action into the sentence such as "Shari likes to touch the pillow." Name the objects consistently; don't say "dog" one day and "pet" the next. Add complexity by noting the size and shape of the object. As she gets older, add more descriptive adjectives.

### TWELVE: PLAY SIMPLE GAMES

Simple games that include conversation are always enjoyed by babies. "This little piggy went to market" or "Peek-a-boo," spoken in a playful, sing-song voice, will entertain your baby again and again. This kind of game can be repeated as long as your baby is responsive. Games do not have to be complex to be entertaining. You might simply hide an object such as a pacifier in your hand, and ask, "Where is the pacifier?" Let your baby pull your hand away, and then acknowledge the object. Dr. Jerome Bruner maintains that games such as these are like miniature conversations, reinforcing the structure of conversation.

### THIRTEEN: USE RHYTHM AND MUSIC

Rhymes and soothing music have a rhythm that have an effect on the level of spontaneous activity in the brain. According to Dr. Frank E. X. Dance, an expert on the origin of speech, the spontaneous activity promoted by rhymes and music helps organize the brain, preparing it for the rhythm of speech. Take advantage of this fact by playing music regularly, reading rhyming books and dancing to music while holding your baby.

## FOURTEEN: MAINTAIN EYE CONTACT

It has been said that the eye is the gateway to the soul. Make eye contact with your baby and respond to eye contact which he initiates, even when it isn't accompanied by vocal sounds. Ignore the old wives' tale that babies go cross-eyed if you put your face or objects too close. Get close to your baby, smile at him, and allow him to get to know more about being human from the one person who can best teach him—you.

## WHERE TO GET MORE INFORMATION

These fourteen ideas will help you get started on a higher level of communication with your baby. However, they are just a start. I suggest scouring used bookstores for children's books and audio tapes which would be appropriate for your baby. Many libraries have resources on infant care which you might find helpful. Many shopping centers I have visited lately also have children's learning stores with educational toys and games. Make use of these resources. Few parents think twice about buying stimulating toys and games for toddlers and older children. Don't wait until then! Start now, while your child is still an infant. It may make a dramatic difference in his life.

As we will see in the next chapter, communication development can be accelerated as your child develops more complex language skills in what is commonly referred to as the toddler stage.

● ● ● ● ●

# CHAPTER THIRTEEN

# TODDLER COMMUNICATION

## THE EXCITING NEW WORLD OF TODDLERHOOD

A toddler is like a human sponge; he is constantly soaking up information through his five senses. He wants to see, hear, taste, smell and touch everything—especially touch. Who can blame him? Each experience is a world-class event to those for whom it is utterly new.

Most adults remember their own toddlerhood dimly, if at all. As I prepared to write this chapter, I struggled with how to *describe* something in the way a toddler might experience it, as a means of conveying the intensity of this period of life. Some of my memories from toddlerhood are especially vivid, so I'll describe one of my own. It was at a carnival. If I close my eyes, the wonder of it returns: the smell of caramel corn and greasy fried cakes...diesel engines chugging and the squeak of the carousel as it grinds to a halt and delivers an endless stream of beaming adults and children...screams of delight whirling around...music soliciting me from five different places at once clashing in a cacophony of sound that makes me hold a little more tightly onto my father's chest...and the comforting squeeze that lets me know I am safe...the vendors barking out challenges to anyone who will listen...baseballs whapping against a canvas net as burly men heave

**Even when it**

**seems that**

**your toddler**

**is not**

**absorbing**

**and learning,**

**you can bet**

**he is.**

them at bowling pins with all their might…a million lights flashing…the thrill and terror of embarking on a ride…the cotton candy lady rapidly stirring her concoction, and the skip of my heart as she hands us a wonderful pink cloud…and how it tickles my nose when I try to take a bite, and melts in my mouth so quickly that it startles me…feeling my heart drop into my stomach as the Ferris wheel whisks us high above the din into the cool night air…looking around at the wonderful view from above…and then my heart dropping again as we plummet earthward once more….

Being a toddler is like that first carnival, a state of perpetual sensory overload. Experiences come rapidly and are absorbed, categorized, analyzed, compared, written into the permanent memory and employed again in the mind of a toddler faster than in any computer known to man. Even when it seems that your toddler is not absorbing and learning, you can bet he is.

It is within this context that we must discuss building communication skills in toddlers. In this chapter, I will present research demonstrating why this age is so crucial for communication development, review the stages of development you can expect your child to pass through, and list several specific activities you can arrange in your home to maximize your child's learning in this important period of life.

## WHY IS COMMUNICATION TRAINING VITAL TO TODDLERS?

Child psychologists have now come to recognize that all of the functions of the intellect are defined and matured at a very early age. Children master spoken language between the ages of one and five, and then spend the rest of their lives smoothing it out and adding to the framework that already exists. Some researchers maintain that the critical years for developing communication competence are all prior to age three! The age at which children increase most rapidly in their vocabulary is probably around the age of learning to walk. Apparently, the advent of a new motor skill is a significant plateau in language development as well. Toddlers learn an average of nine words a day.

## WHAT ARE THE STAGES OF SPEECH DEVELOPMENT IN TODDLERS?

The toddler period, while a popular notion, is not a very accurate category for scientific study. I define "toddlerhood" as the period between 18 months and three years of age. Researchers actually divide this age into two segments, the *presyntactic* and *syntactic* periods. *Syntax* is "the orderly arrangement of words," so the presyntactic stage means "before the orderly arrangement of words," generally from 12 to 24 months of age. During this period, the main communication of a child is through gestures and crying, relying on the ability of the parents to interpret and understand. However, the normal child begins saying recognizable words between nine and fourteen months. These first words are usually nouns which the child uses to describe objects in the surrounding environment. Nouns such as bottle, milk, ball and dog occur at about 12 months.

As discussed in the last chapter, children are capable of putting together two and three word sentences at about 1-1/2 to 2 years of age. According to Dr. Roger Brown, a researcher who studied the language development of hundreds of children, these early sentences usually lack connecting words (a, the, and), and fit into six categories:

**Some researchers maintain that the critical years for developing communication competence are all prior to age three!**

| | Category | Example |
|---|---|---|
| **You can** | Reference | "See baby." |
| **expect your** | | |
| **toddler to** | Nonexistence | "Mommy all gone." |
| | Recurrence | "More milk!" |
| **experience** | | |
| **dramatic** | Location | "Dog couch." |
| | Possession | "Daddy chair." |
| **spurts in** | | |
| | Attribution | "Big ball." |
| **language use,** | | |

**but be patient;**

**every child**

**has his**

**own time**

**schedule.**

Interestingly, in any given language, word order comes naturally to a child. The ability to put sentences together properly is built into the structure of the brain. According to Dr. Roger Brown, for example, a child will always say "dog couch" to mean that the dog is on the couch, rather than "couch dog."

You can expect your toddler to experience dramatic spurts in language use. He may amaze you with the way he puts words together into sentences. In preparing for this chapter, I asked my own mother about *my* early sentences. She told me that until 20 months of age, I rarely spoke, but just played quietly (those who know me now find this hard to believe). My first sentence, apparently, was, "I wanna pickle." Complete sentences came suddenly—and continued. My second sentence, incidentally, was uttered as our family drove past a local fast food restaurant: "I smell like french fries." These answers proved my wife's longheld belief that I must have been a strange child!

Your toddler will probably have a short attention span, may enjoy playing alone, and seem often restless. On the other hand, according to Alice Chapin in *Building Your Child's Faith*, toddlers also love pictures, being read to, sung to and rocked. Although "teaching" of language is not advised, there are four ways to stimulate language learning in your toddler: emphasize talking, give experiences which stimulate the child, require communication, and last but not least, read aloud!

### EMPHASIZE TALKING!

Since children learn to talk by talking, the best stimulation is to have "live" talk directed toward your child. Decades of research show that families in which talk is directed toward the child have more communicative, intelligent children.

Here are four things to keep in mind when talking with your child:

1. **The child need not respond in order to learn new language skills.** He benefits by paying attention to how others communicate well.

2. **Be sensitive when he wants to communicate with you.** Provide pauses in the conversation so he can respond.

3. **Gradually cut down on answering his questions through non-verbal communication.** This includes shrugging your shoulders, raising your eyebrows, or making dramatic facial gestures. Responding with words forces your toddler to pay more attention to your words and to the environment itself rather than your response to it.

Give your child

opportunities to

experience the

world with all

five senses:

touching,

tasting,

smelling,

looking at, and

hearing. Once

the stuff of his

environment

has emotional

content for him,

you can bet

your toddler

will begin

commenting

on it.

4. **Let common sense be your guide.** No matter how hard they study, researchers haven't come up with any techniques better than mother's intuition! Researchers use the term "motherese" to describe the unique communication style that mothers use with their children. When mothers are with their children they emphasize the present, tailor their vocabulary to the level of the child, paraphrase complicated ideas, use simple yet well-formed sentences, deliberately slow their rate of speech, and use lots of repetition.

## PROVIDE STIMULATING EXERIENCES

Children initiate communication about things which interest them. The more fascinating the child's environment, the better. Lots of books, pictures, posters, and toys on shelves will visually stimulate your child's young mind. Give your child opportunities to experience the world with all five senses: touching, tasting, smelling, looking at, and hearing. Once the stuff of his environment has emotional content, you can bet your toddler will begin commenting on it. According to Dr. Mabel Rice, these "comments" will generally express desires, commands, requests and threats, all highly emotional. Exclamations such as "da-da!" or "mama!" or "ball!" or "pret[ty]" just burst right out!

Here are three suggestions for providing stimulating experiences for your toddler:

1. **Emphasize nouns.** Dr. Rice points out that children who first develop a large vocabulary of nouns and then later expand the number of verbs have been found to master grammar more easily. Emphasize nouns by commenting on objects which are of immediate interest to the toddler. For example, if the child seems interested in a wooden spoon, give it to him and comment:

"Spoon. That is a spoon. Do you like spoons? Mommy uses spoons to make something for you to eat. Yes, spoon!"

2. **Answer questions.** Toddlers often ask questions (even if the question is "unh?", meaning "what is that?") simply to hear your voice. As much as possible, give satisfactory answers to your toddler's questions. This will encourage him to ask more questions, often a mixed blessing, but one which will dramatically expand his opportunity to learn language.

3. **Make comparisons.** Help your child understand his environment better by having him analyze it. If your toddler "helps" you in the kitchen by getting all of the pots and pans out, have him make comparisons: which one is bigger, which ones are the same color, which one is red, which one is like the one you are using, or which one is heavy? Enlist your toddler's assistance by having him put spoons, knives and forks in their proper place or arranging storage container lids by size. Simple instructions, accompanied by hardy praise, will turn an everyday event into an opportunity to organize your child's mind.

### REQUIRE COMMUNICATION

Perhaps the best way to stimulate your toddler's perception of the environment is to require him to *communicate* verbally to get what he wants. Professor Carol Gibb Harding explains that, "As mothers require certain communicative behaviors before they respond, they are not only encouraging those specific behaviors but also 'teaching' the infant that a mutual means of communication exists." Once the child knows how to use words like "drink," family members should be instructed not to respond to the child's pointing grunts until the child attempts to use the words he knows.

**"As mothers require certain communicative behaviors before they respond, they are not only encouraging those specific behaviors but also 'teaching' the infant that a mutual means of communication exists."**

Professors Ostrosky and Kaiser, in an essay on "Teaching Exceptional Children," suggest several activities which you can use to require communication in your toddler:

1. **Choice making.** Give your toddler a choice between two toys. Say, "Tell me which one you want" or ask him to name each toy. As he begins to verbalize these responses, teach him alternative ways of asking, such as "Yellow truck, please." At the very least, most children can say "please" and something that sounds like "thank you."

2. **Out of reach.** Place your toddler's favorite toys and books just out of reach, so that he must ask for assistance in getting them.

3. **Assistance.** Show your toddler attractive materials which he will need help in opening or operating. Examples: a drinking bottle, a closed box, or a swing.

4. **Silly situations.** Violate your toddler's expectations. At snack time, for instance, put a ball on his plate rather than a cracker. Attempt to put his shoes on your own feet and see if he comments (either verbally or non-verbally). Put a silly picture on the mirror and see if he notices.

5. **Sabotage.** Require communication by not providing all the materials needed to complete a task. For example, provide a coloring book but no crayons (not the other way around unless you want the furniture redecorated!). If your toddler expresses confusion, encourage him to communicate his need.

6. **Inadequate portions.** At meal or snack time, serve an inadequate portion of food, such as a small piece of a cookie rather than the whole thing. If you are blowing

bubbles, blow just one or two and wait for the child to ask for more. If he is playing with blocks, give him just one block at a time until he asks for what he needs.

NOTE: These episodes should be brief, and should conclude well before they become frustrating to the child! The rule of thumb for educators is that children have a one-minute attention span for each year in age. However, communication play greatly lengthens the attention span, so you may find your child willing to cooperate for longer periods of time.

### READ! READ! READ!

Reading aloud serves two functions. First, it broadens your toddler's experiences. Second, it begins to construct the bridge to later reading and writing.

Here are three ideas to enhance reading with your toddler:

1. **Nursery rhymes.** According to Emma Grant Meader, one of the first researchers to apply what is known of communication development to child education, children naturally enjoy rhythm and learn speech best when they can learn it rhythmically.

2. **Sing-song.** Pick up on the words your toddler uses and repeat them in a sing-song voice. When you wish to change the activity, add words or change the words you are "sing-songing." Notice how television programs for children often create simple sing-song phrases to encourage children to be kind, or clean the house. Children pick up on this quickly.

3. **Animated reading.** Make the noise or demonstrate the motion of each character; say, for instance, "A

rabbit goes 'hop, hop, hop,'" and bounce your child slightly. Or ask, "Where is the mouse? Can you put your finger on the mouse?" while helping him do so.

## PATIENCE MAKES PERFECT

As in every pursuit, patience produces rewards. You may be surprised at how simple communication, simple games and simple praise advance your toddler's communication skill. If progress is slow, keep in mind that children grow internally first before the results show themselves to the world. You *will* see a difference eventually.

As your child grows in age, his communication needs become more complex. The next chapter focuses on children ages three to seven. In order to describe each activity in more detail, I have provided "project pages" which describe the reason behind each project, the instructions, and variations which give you a virtually infinite set of communication-building projects.

# CHAPTER FOURTEEN

# AGES THREE TO SEVEN

## HOW TO CREATE A DESIRE FOR COMMUNICATION

As with infants and toddlers, many things happen between ages three and seven which make it a vital time for developing communication skills. In this chapter you will discover how to use storytelling, drama, games and other communication development tools to give your child a communication "head start." You will learn how to use your child's desire for communication to teach practical skills such as learning your telephone number.

Before we get started, however, a few pages of introduction will help orient you to the stages of communication development through which your child will progress from ages three to seven. First, we'll discuss what sort of communication skills children are developing during this age range, and then we will overview the six skill areas on which the "project pages" in this chapter will focus.

Incidentally, because of the trial and error nature of communication building in young children, it may be counterproductive to "drill" children in new communication skills. By age eight, children should be ready for the "speech-making" part of communication development. During the three-to-seven years, focus on creating an environment in which your child can explore and direct at least

**Focus on**

**creating an**

**environment**

**in which**

**your child**

**can explore**

**and direct at**

**least some**

**of his**

**education**

**himself.**

**Upgrading the**

**quality of your**

**child's play**

**means**

**providing the**

**opportunity for**

**make-believe**

**and exploration.**

some of his education himself. Imagination, enjoyment and flexibility are the guiding words. If your child begins to think of communication as fun, the foundation you are laying will be that much easier to build on.

## How to Use Play to Develop Communication Skills

The most important thing you can do for your child is upgrade his quality of play. Most of his play should be interacting with books, props, self-created toys, and communicating with you and others. It is far better for the child to play "grocery store" or "house" than to watch television or play video games. According to Professors Huckleberry and Strother, constructive, interactive activities allow the child to relive his observations and create vivid impressions about the world.

As a teenager, my parents let me buy a 35-year-old pickup truck at an auction. My youngest brother and sister got as much use out of the truck as I did. Parked in the back yard, they loved using it as a springboard to imaginative adventures: one day it would be a fire truck (complete with garden hoses), the next a farm truck, (with our two dogs playing their assigned roles as cows or sheep), or whatever. No toy could have provided such creative play opportunities, and both children grew into creative and talented young people.

Upgrading the quality of your child's play means providing the opportunity for make-believe and exploration. Yet keep in mind that creativity does not occur in a vacuum: a musician must master the fundamentals of music in order to exercise "creativity." As professors Huckleberry and Strother remind us, "Creativity needs social judgement so that it may be examined and refined."

## COMMUNICATION DEVELOPMENT BETWEEN AGES THREE AND SEVEN

We'll discuss what sort of fundamentals you can work on with your child in just a minute. First, let's take a bird's eye view of the sort of changes you'll notice in your increasingly communicative child.

### BECOMING MORE ARTICULATE

By age five, children should have fully intelligible speech, although some lack of articulation is normal. Children this age will use complex sentences and clauses. If your child is having a problem with these, arrange a checkup with a speech therapist.

Starting toward the beginning of this age range, your child should gradually be weaned from gesture language. Experts believe that gradually refusing to understand and respond to the child's tendency to "point and grunt" is a major step in bringing about true speech. Experiment: Use pantomime and gesture to draw communication out of your child. Say, "Now *you* try to guess what I am pointing to." Grunt a few times until he becomes frustrated with his inability to decipher your communication. It won't be long before these teachable moments move your child in the direction of clearer communication.

In addition, begin expanding your use of conversation with your child. Drs. Dance and Larson have theorized that talk which helps your child "displace" from the immediate situation is very helpful in expanding the usefulness of language for him. This means asking your child questions about the past ("Do you remember where we went in the car yesterday?") or the future ("What do you think we will see when we go to the zoo tomorrow?").

Although it will be difficult, experts believe that gradually refusing to understand and respond to the child's tendency to "point and grunt" is a major step in bringing about true speech.

**Keep in mind**

**that during the**

**three-to-seven**

**stage, children**

**understand far**

**more words**

**than they**

**actually use.**

## DEVELOPING A LARGER VOCABULARY

Children develop so rapidly from three to seven that at first glance; it seems futile to even highlight such a range for this book. However, while development is rapid, it is more an expansion of existing skills rather than development of new ones. Vocabulary, for example, will grow rapidly, usually tripling between the second and third year, and doubling again by age five with as many as 1,800 words in correct use. Your child might even make up some words of his own. One of our family favorites is "Sprickles," which are the rays of the sun. Enjoy this time of creativity!

Also by age three children begin to correctly use pronouns, make comparisons (big vs. little), and recognize and point out colors. "Baby talk" should begin to diminish, as you stop using it and gradually and gently quit reinforcing it in your child.

You can enhance your child's vocabulary development by playing naming games. Ask questions such as, "Can you see three things that are white?" and "Whar can you see out the window?" Show your child a picture of an object such as a car, and ask, "What are all the words you can think of to describe that car?" Simple questions such as these will help your child learn to recall and use words he knows, an important vocabulary building activity.

Keep in mind that during the three-to-seven stage, children understand far more words than they actually use. By age six, for example, your child may have an expressive vocabulary of about 2,500 words, but understand up to 15,000 words. The wider the range of experiences your child has, the higher this so-called "receptive" vocabulary will be.

## DEVELOPING A BETTER UNDERSTANDING OF EMOTIONS

As they emerge from the toddler stage, children deepen in their recognition of emotions in others. Professor Baltaxe reviewed studies showing that at age five, boys perceive emotions more accurately than girls, but these results are reversed in children ages six to twelve. Children who have weathered emotional trauma during the toddler stage may experience more difficulty in recognizing emotion in the voice and facial expressions of adults. All of this means that your child will be sensitive to your moods, and may actually react to them. This is all a natural part of learning to communicate with others.

Here is a simple way to reinforce your child's recognition of emotions: using cheap paper plates, draw eyes and a mouth to reflect different emotions. Here are five examples:

To create other variations, use pieces of yarn to create different eye and mouth shapes. Mimic what your child creates and have him mimic what you create. Your child will immediately begin to observe the facial expressions of others and even think more carefully about his own expressions. A good spiritual lesson here, incidentally, is to teach your child what sort of expressions indicate that someone is angry. Read the Proverbs that tell us about angry people, such as, "An angry man stirs up dissension, and a hot-tempered one commits many sins" Proverbs 29:22 (NIV).

Mimic what your child creates and have him mimic what you create. Your child will immediately begin to observe the facial expressions of others and even think more carefully about his own expressions.

## SIX AREAS OF VITAL COMMUNICATION DEVELOPMENT BETWEEN AGES THREE AND SEVEN

The projects in this section work on six different areas of communication development in a fun and creative way. Whether you use them in an educational or recreational fashion, being aware of the six specific skills will allow you as a parent to sense the areas of greatest importance for your child.

1. **Smoothness.** Elise Hahn's classic study of six-year-olds demonstrated that at least 50 percent of children need to overcome broken or choppy rhythm, and more than one out of three demonstrate a very narrow range of inflection. One out of four speak too softly, and over a third fail to articulate and pronounce words properly. Working on these skills might involve:

   • **Rhythm.** Assist your child in overcoming false starts, repetition of words and phrases, and purposeless hesitations.

      *Idea:* "Let's pretend the world is in slow motion, so we must talk more slowly."

      *Point:* "Sometimes our mouths get ahead of our brains!"

   • **Volume.** Demonstrate and practice soft or loud volume as the particular occasion demands.

      *Idea:* "Let's practice soft and loud voices. Why don't you say your Bible verse very, very softly, and then move farther away and get louder, and then close again."

*Point:* "We must be careful to use the right loudness depending on how close or far away we are." When answering the telephone, for example, don't yell for the requested person into the ear of the caller!

- **Pitch.** Engage in activities which broaden your child's range of inflection while teaching him to control emotion in his voice.

  *Idea:* "Let's practice what different animals might sound like if they could talk: high, low, soft, and loud. What would a robot sound like?" You can even have singsongy repetitions, such as a beginning children's piano lesson I once heard:

  "Hel $_{lo}$ Bar $_{ney}$ $^{my}$ name's ———."

  This teaches voice inflection, reinforced by high and low keys on the piano.

  *Point:* "If we want others to listen, we must not talk like robots. We must use our voices in an interesting way."

- **Timing.** Work to smooth awkward hesitations, breathlessness, and slowness.

  *Idea:* (Getting down on the child's eye level) "Don't worry, I'm listening! I would like for you to slow down, collect your thoughts, and then tell me what you need to say."

  *Point:* "People sometimes lose track of what you are saying, so be careful to speak smoothly without stopping a lot."

Keep these points in mind as you work through the activities in this section.

2. **Discernment.** Learn color, shapes, size, rhythm, good vs. evil, and loud vs. soft. You can enhance your child's motor skills through marching, clapping, tapping, judging space, size, color, and judging of emotional states.

- **Colors.** Announce a special day to celebrate a particular color. On "Green Day" have your child wear green clothes, look for green in the great outdoors, put lettuce on his sandwich, and use food coloring to make green frosting for his graham crackers. Play a game, "I see green." Give hints to your child until he guesses what you are seeing.

- **Shapes.** Announce a "round day," for instance. Cut sandwiches into circles, make round cookies, and look for round things in the neighborhood.

  Think of other activities which reinforce the discernment between various things. Discernment is the key to observation, which is the foundation of many of the most significant communication skills.

3. **Clarity.** Speech is not truly communication until others understand what the child is trying to say. For example, say, "I am trying to understand what you are saying. Help me. Say it again for me. Again, slowly. Point to something to help me understand you." With patience, you will develop a system of reinforcement that also builds your relationship. Once again, use gentle coaching rather than "drills."

4. **Appropriate language.** Appropriate language focuses on the effectiveness of communication in various speaking situations. Children between ages three and seven are old enough to begin learning how to communicate in a socially acceptable way. Most people believe that it is improper etiquette for a young child

to treat adults like children, or to communicate a lack of respect for authority. Practicing appropriate language helps children understand what constitutes proper behavior in social situations. Social graces, much like those taught by Professor Higgins to Eliza in "My Fair Lady," are learned through practice and repetition. Teach each skill to your child, reinforce it, praise him for his improvement, and practice it again.

5. **Quick, effective thinking.** Children can enjoy learning to think quickly, connecting names with objects, comparing one thing to another, processing information out loud without boring the listener, and becoming more observant.

6. **Courteous and critical listening.** Children will practice hearing, understanding, remembering, discerning and judging as they learn to interact more effectively with the world around them. As a child, I balked at attending family reunions. "It's just a bunch of old people," I complained. Then my mother arranged for "story circles," in which family members sat and visited about their childhood experiences. Fascinated and impressed, I saw these elderly relatives in a new light, interacting with them differently from that point forward.

## How to Use the "Project Pages"

Now that we have discussed the six skill areas on which the projects in this chapter will focus, you are ready to begin. I suggest first skimming all of the projects to get an idea of an order in which you would like to try them. Also, keep in mind that simple completion of a project does not guarantee mastery of it. Rather, each project should be used repeatedly, as opportunities arise, to create a wealth of communication *experiences* for your child.

# NOTES

# STORYTELLING

## PROJECT SKETCH

Storytelling is perhaps the best way to invigorate communication skills in small children. Stories infused with emotion will enhance both their memory and imagination. When children listen to a well-told story and repeat it, they are able to develop strong memories and use them imaginatively. As Mary Jo Puckett-Cliatt and Jean Shaw explain, as children retell the story, they move from being passive listeners to active participants in the story-making process. This storytelling project is followed by several related projects, giving you a wealth of ideas for this important approach to communication development!

## HOW-TO

Simply create a story from scratch or relate one from a children's book. Tell the story slowly, using facial expression and voice inflection. Take on the role of the characters, using their "voices" and emotions. You might even make the story memorable through costumes or sound effects.

When you finish, ask your child questions about it. He should be able to remember the central point, characters' names, the pictures, the emotional state of the characters, choose which of the events happened first, etc. You can also ask about what the story means, what the author wanted him to learn, and how he might respond if he were in a similar situation.

Ask your child to retell the story as best as he can remember. Encourage him with warm, positive feedback, such as "Yes! *Then* what happened?" Clap when he finishes. The purpose of this activity is to capture the essential components and the emotion with which the story can be told. Over time, require greater detail, such as correct order of events and dialogue. Encourage your child to tell the story to friends and relatives for additional reinforcement.

Elements to focus on: conveying the story with clarity (so that other adults could understand), placing the elements of the story in the correct order, using different voices to represent different characters and their emotional states, and gesturing. As you repeat this activity on a regular basis, your child should be able to listen for the central point, recognize what kind of voice is needed to convey emotion and characterization, and develop smoother mannerisms, a sense of rhythm, and the ability to invent dialogue.

## TIMELY TIP

Children especially like stories which incorporate *them* as characters or which tell of your own childhood. My mother, for instance, enrolled in a writing class and was assigned the task of recalling and recording childhood stories. These stories became the joy of the whole family!

## FUTURE ADVENTURE

Create check points in stories. Stop at crucial points and ask the child what happens next or what should happen next, "sabotage" the story by using voices which don't match the characters (such as a high, squeaky voice for the giant) and get your child to "correct you."

## MAKE IT MEMORABLE!

If you have a piano, allow your child to compose an accompaniment while you read, or allow him to use pots and pans and other household items to reinforce the rhythmical, musical nature of stories. Sound effects are simple to create; tapping shoes on a large piece of cardboard with sand on top gives the effect of footsteps. Banging two dried coconut halves together simulates the sound of horses' hooves. Crinkling tin foil sounds like firecrackers. Use your imagination!

# NOTES

# MAGNETIC STORIES

## PROJECT SKETCH

This activity allows you to focus on placing characters in the past and present, developing a theme, and teaching your child to recognize and repeat a sequence of events in the proper order. It also gives your child "props" to ease his transition into storytelling.

## HOW-TO

Cut out pictures from magazines, paste them onto a poster board or "chip" board backing, and cut to size. Magnetic strips with adhesive backing are available from most discount stores. Place the magnets on the backs of the pictures, and ask your child to create a story by arranging pictures in sequence on a cookie sheet.

## TIMELY TIP

If your child needs encouragement, begin by telling a story yourself, asking him to place the cut-outs on a cookie sheet for you. When finished, take the pictures down and ask the child to verbally reconstruct the story as he places them back on the cookie sheet.

## FUTURE ADVENTURE

Flannel Graph Stories. Create a story board approximately 3' by 3' from reinforced cardboard and cover with flannel material purchased at a discount store. Bible story characters and many other items may be purchased from any large Christian educational supplier. Cut out the characters and place them on the board as the story progresses. Flannel graph stories provide a visually exciting story option.

## MAKE IT MEMORABLE!

The refrigerator is often a central message center in a home. Stick magnetic cut-outs on the refrigerator so your child can make up stories or practice old ones while you are busy in the kitchen.

# SEQUENCE STORIES

## PROJECT SKETCH

Stories enhance thinking skills largely by teaching that what happens later in the story is affected by what happens first. Actions have consequences, and decisions made by characters will influence the outcome of the story. Learning to think sequentially is a valuable lesson in life as well as an important exercise in developing logical thinking and speaking skills.

## HOW-TO

Clothesline stories. To focus on the sequence of events in a story, tie a clothesline in the room and have your child clip pictures to it based on the action found in the story. After you tell your sequential story several times, let your child try it.

Map stories. To help your child focus on the sequence of events, as well as to teach map skills and perspective, draw a large map of the area where your story might take place. For example, draw a map of the battlefield where David met Goliath. Along the path, glue "pop-ups" of the characters or scenery one might encounter. Place pop-ups face down so your child can stand them up as the story progresses.

## TIMELY TIP

You may need to explain what a map is and why we use them. Once your child grasps the concept, encourage him to put events that occur in the story in the correct order. Focus on the "gist" of the story, not the details.

## FUTURE ADVENTURE

Use map stories to follow up your child's experiences with the popular media. After viewing a movie, have him draw a map of where the action might have taken place and create characters. This reinforces the idea of sequence in the "real world" and allows a simple learning tool to enhance outside entertainment.

## MAKE IT MEMORABLE!

Tie stories into real life! Use real maps and a globe to help your child gain a sense of place (i.e., where he lives, where the story takes place or where the author lived). If the story takes place in another country, try to convey how far away it is and how the culture might have influenced the author to write as he did.

# CARTOON STORIES

## PROJECT SKETCH

Much of effective communication involves organizing one's thoughts and relaying information in a sequential manner. The purpose of this activity is to create an awareness of how a plot unfolds and creates action in a story.

## HOW-TO

Show your child several cartoon strips from the newspaper, reading the words and explaining the action. Then work with your child to create your own cartoons! Begin by drawing pictures detailing a sequence of actions. This might include: the number of objects in the picture increasing, the size of something expanding (as someone inflates a balloon), or someone with food on the plate, eating and then having eaten something. Ask your child to describe the action involved, and speculate on what the characters might say. As he begins to grasp the idea that things happen in a time-space sequence, you can encourage your child to actually tell the story represented by the cartoon. This activity may be repeated over and over again, even spontaneously in the car or while waiting at the doctor's office.

## TIMELY TIP

Do not worry if your drawings seem elementary. Unless you're headed for syndication, just focus on making sure the content is sequential! Also, encourage your child to sign his name in the corner and date each cartoon, placing them in a scrapbook. He will enjoy looking at them over and over.

## FUTURE ADVENTURE

Using liquid correction fluid, white out the words in newspaper cartoons and ask your child to come up with his own. Paste them into a notebook to keep. You can even make several pages of cartoons at once to keep your child occupied in a creative activity.

## MAKE IT MEMORABLE!

Allow your child to create his own cartoons. With a ruler, draw a sequence of 12 boxes (four each in three lines) on a sheet of white paper, and make several photocopies (make the boxes larger for younger children). Draw pictures inside these boxes. Once the pictures are drawn, try to guess what is happening, or have the child describe the situation. Record the dialogue in the space below the picture. Explain to your child the idea of "blocking," that television advertisements, cartoons and movies are made by first drawing a one-frame picture of each scene. You can use these sheets for "blocking" later puppet shows and drama productions. Who knows! You may have a budding screenwriter in the family!

# SITUATION CARDS

## PROJECT SKETCH

The purpose of this activity is to create "ready-made" dramatic situations from which your child can create a story. This allows him to become creative with what he is given, merging it with his own efforts. It will also give your child the opportunity to think about interesting character traits: what makes a person good or bad, and how to change one's own life to have stronger character.

## HOW-TO

Write down several simple descriptions of situations or objects and put them in a box. You can also have your child contribute situations. Examples of situations include:

1. *You walk out into the back yard and discover an old shed with a rusty lock.*

2. *You wake up in the morning and find that instead of being in your bed, you are in a cave, and a friendly dinosaur is sniffing at you.*

3. *You are in the Old West riding on a wagon train.*

4. *You suddenly wake up and find yourself in a beautiful castle. A servant comes in and asks "What would you like to do today, O' Queen? (or King)?"*

5. *You hear a knock on the door. When you open it, there is a box with a small puppy in it.*

Ask the child to draw from the box and create a story based on the situation.

An off-shoot of this project is to have your child choose from among three or four sacks, closed, with objects inside. Upon opening the sack, they can make up a story about the item inside. Your child can make whole stories out of items such as a tea bag, a treasure map, a pneumatic drill, an unusual flower, or bubble gum! For variations, allow your child to draw a card from which *you* make up a story. Incorporate elements of effective communication and set a good example!

## TIMELY TIP

If your child has difficulty, ask questions which draw out his own creativity, such as "what do you suppose would be inside the shed?", "What kind of things are usually inside a shed?", "What would surprise you if you found it in there?" Questions are better than actual suggestions. In addition, save the cards, since there is an infinite number of stories which may be created from each!

## FUTURE ADVENTURES

1. **Make several boxes:** one for characters (including animals) and one for situations in which characters might find themselves. For older children, include one for items to include in the story, one for the physical descriptions of characters, and even one for moods. Each story should include one situation, at least two characters with physical descriptions and moods, and three items which must be included in the story.

2. **Use an old apron with pockets instead of boxes.** The storyteller, whether adult or child, gets to wear the apron and draw cards out of the pockets. You can even cut out pictures, paste them on cardboard, and fasten them to the apron as the story progresses.

3. **Fish for a story.** Decorate a large cardboard box with an ocean theme. Paste magnet strips (available at all discount stores) to the back of magazine cutouts mounted on cardboard. Make a fishing rod with a dowel and string, with another magnet on the end of the string. The child fishes out elements and tells a story about each.

## MAKE IT MEMORABLE

Allow your child to decorate the storyteller's box with tin foil, construction paper, and cut-outs. Make it special!

# NOTES

# HALF-TOLD STORY

## PROJECT SKETCH

Another way to make storytelling interesting and exciting to your child is the half-told story. The half-told story will teach your child to listen carefully to the details of the story, and then insert himself into the plot and answer the "what-if" questions that arise. Most important, this storytelling technique will teach your child how to resolve a plot and create a definite ending to a story. He will learn to initiate and complete thoughts in a precise, imaginative manner.

## HOW-TO

There are two ways to create the story. First, create it as you go, with you and your child taking turns adding lines. Here's a sample:

Adult: *Johnnie Jensen went into the garage and got his fishing pole and a shovel.*

Child: *Then he dug some big fat worms from the garden and went fishing.*

Adult: *Well, he started to go fishing, but first he decided he would like a friend to go with him, so…*

Child: *He asked Allen to go with him.*

Adult: *Allen said, "I cannot go because I have to stay home to practice my piano." So Johnnie thought, "What shall I do?" He went to Brad's house and knocked and knocked on the door.*

Notice how the adult keeps the story going and adds complex processes, action, sound effects, characters and dialogue.

The second way to develop a story is to share the first half of a new story with your child, leaving off at a crucial point in the action: a dangerous predicament, a difficult decision, or a moral dilemma. Leave enough cues to ensure a development of action.

When the child finishes, compare your ending with his. Ask questions which encourage him to discern the dilemmas which arise about good vs. evil, and what good and bad characters act like.

Focus on helping your child create dialogue, remembering enough details from your half of the story to incorporate them into his half. If your child starts to stray from the descriptions of characters as given, or inadvertently changes or forgets something, ask questions to lead him back to it. The purpose is to construct a faithful ending to an already existing story.

Use an old three-ring binder or portfolio to hold the half-created stories, both yours and your child's. Allow your child to decorate the binder with magic markers. If you wish, use paper report folders or snap-lock binders, one for each story. Leave enough room on each page for drawings which accompany the story line. Have the child "read" or tell the story to younger siblings, neighborhood children, relatives or guests in your home. His pride in his work will make it easier for him to communicate with others, which is, of course, the whole point of this project!

## TIMELY TIP

Encourage creativity and vivid detail. Instead of simply a "giant," the child could tell of an "enormous, loud man, eighteen feet high with size 96 shoes and beady eyes, who hadn't shaved in probably forty-two years."

## FUTURE ADVENTURES

1. Have your child construct the story, and *you* finish it.

2. Have your child take on the persona of one of the characters and finish the story from their perspective.

3. Tell the story to a tape recorder for later editing and transfer to paper.

## MAKE IT MEMORABLE

Write down each ending created and "publish" it as a completed story, with you and your child as the authors! Nice binders with occasional color pictures make your child's investment of time seem more worthwhile.

# NOTES

# STORY-ROUND-THE-FAMILY

## PROJECT SKETCH

The purpose of this activity is to enhance your child's ability to think quickly and imaginatively. It is also great for family time, being particularly suitable for car trips, dinner-time conversation, or time around the campfire. It teaches your child how to create and build suspense. Because suspense creates curiosity in the audience, it is one of the communicator's most useful tools.

## HOW-TO

Begin a story which you tell for a minute or so and then leave at a point of interest. Each participant continues the story and also leaves it at a point of interest. This technique may be used with as many as six people without losing its focus, or it can be traded back and forth between adult and child.

Each story should contain an economy of incidents, usually three. You can control this by thinking of three objects that should play into the story: a bear, an old red flannel shirt, and a blender, for example. The more unexpected, the better. Of course, both children and adults will require a great deal of practice! Once you try it just a few times, you will find it easy to create an interesting, creative story.

Again, create as many details as possible: years, background situations, specific amounts, and specific times. Make the characters interesting as well. Reward specific descriptions with praise: "Wow, that is really specific!" or "I can almost see the giant as you describe him!" or "That's a very creative way to describe someone." If details are hard to elicit, ask questions which lead your child in that direction: "What do you suppose the giant would look like? Hairy or bald? Skinny or fat? *How* skinny or fat? So skinny that when he turns sideways, he nearly disappears? So fat that it takes 16 minutes for the grease from his fried chicken to dribble all the way down his 16 chins?"

## TIMELY TIPS

1. **Work in a lesson on character.** Debrief stories by asking "what if" questions, determining whether the characters were heroes or villains and what made them that way.

2. **Play an adjective game.** If your child is finding it difficult to describe a character or situation in detail, stop the story and have the entire family brainstorm about possible descriptions.

## FUTURE ADVENTURE

Give your child the opportunity to pick an incident, item, character, or setting for the story.

# PUPPETS

## PROJECT SKETCH

A puppet show can either be a planned or spontaneous activity, and can be accomplished even by children who are pre-verbal. There are many benefits to using puppets to build communication skills: 1) they demonstrate the connection between body movements, emotional expression, and words, 2) they provide an example of a story line and plot progression, and 3) they give an opportunity to perform without the pressure of standing in front of an audience.

## HOW-TO

Make a puppet stage by simply spreading a sheet over two chairs. A custom stage may be made with a cardboard "cutting board" used for sewing. Find one that folds up in an accordion fashion, and cover it with wrapping paper. You could also use shipping boxes from appliances or home office equipment, cutting them to size. Adding windows or special features makes a puppet stage even more fun.

Puppets can be made from paper dolls or flannel graph figures glued to old socks. Or you could decorate socks with magic markers and cloth scraps cut into costumes and facial features. If your budget allows, purchase some t-shirt paint from a craft store and paint white socks with it. Children especially enjoy paint which puffs when ironed. Be creative! Any old household items can serve as puppets or props.

Use puppets to: 1) carry out any storytelling activity, 2) demonstrate a concept or task, 3) occupy your child as you or one of your older children tell a story, 4) help your child act out a story as you read it, and 5) allow your child to create a puppet play based on a story he has written.

Encourage experimentation! Your child may want to play with the stage, create his own puppet characters and conduct plays on his own time. This is the kind of play that builds communication skills!

### TIMELY TIPS

1. **Have your child watch as well as perform, so he can see what his puppet movements might look like.** Videotape him for playback if you have equipment available.

2. **Use puppets to help your child refine his perception of emotions.** While you work the puppet, have him guess which emotion is being expressed: happiness (whistling), anger (yelling), sadness (crying or moaning), surprise (wide open mouth with a quick air intake), etc. Exaggerate at first, and become more subtle as the child grows older.

### FUTURE ADVENTURES

1. **Bible stories.** Alice Chapin suggests that you can use drama to reinforce scripture lessons by making puppets represent biblical characters, and using the stage to act out stories as you read. For example, an animal puppet could tell an animal story (Noah's ark, Balaam's donkey, or Daniel in the lions' den).

2. **Life-size cutouts.** As an interesting alternative to puppets, use large pieces of cardboard to make "life-size" cutouts of the characters in the story.

### MAKE IT MEMORABLE!

You can help your child improve communicatively by getting him to interact with puppets. Encourage your child to ask questions of the puppet, such as "What is your job?" or "What makes you happy or sad?" A friendly puppet can help small children overcome shyness. If your child doesn't speak loudly enough for others to hear, a "hard of hearing" puppet can prompt him to speak loudly and slowly. Or if your child is restricted in using gestures, this same puppet may "benefit" from having things acted out in pantomime.

One last hint: keep the puppets special by boxing them up as you would a game, rather than throwing them in a toy box. Also, try to "keep them" from biting the fingers of the audience and other such playing. Puppets will be more useful for story-telling and related play if they maintain a higher status than mere toys.

# Notes

# DRAMA

## PROJECT SKETCH

The ability to demonstrate dramatic behavior (as opposed to melodramatic behavior) will greatly enhance your child's ability to express himself effectively. Drama helps children develop clear, audible speech while allowing them to express personality, a sense of humor, and flexibility. Drama draws from and reinforces drawing, writing and storytelling skills, since children often use body language and oral language to communicate meaning.

## HOW-TO

Use your imagination and encourage your child to use his in creating props and dramatic circumstances. The goal of the present activity is *expressiveness*. Professors Huckleberry and Strother suggest you begin with simple exercises such as, "Show me how a lazy man walks," "Show me how a burglar walks," or "Show me how a little girl chases a butterfly." Or you can ask questions about stories you have read together: for example, "What does Snow White say and do when she wakes from her long sleep?" Be sure to applaud and teach your child to say "thank you" by bowing.

Another simple way to start is for your child to act out stories as you read to him. During Christmas time, he can act out Mary and Joseph journeying to Bethlehem. Reinforce his acting with questions: What does the donkey do? How does it eat and drink? What do the angels and shepherds do? Each activity should reinforce drama skills, getting your child to use his body to be expressive.

## TIMELY TIP

1. **Focus on dialogue.** One of the benefits of a dramatic activity is that it can reinforce the role of dialogue in increasing excitement.

2. **Use the situation cards discussed in this chapter.** This is especially fun if there is more than one child, because they can play off of each other in impromptu acting. One example suggested by Diana Morgan is two children sit on a bench, one feels for his watch and it is gone, so he accuses the other of taking it, etc.

3. **Define your expectations.** Decide how much educational value you want the activity to include. Children enjoy creating their own dramas, but also need to be challenged to add structure, plot and well-developed characters to their efforts.

4. **Encourage creative set design.** There is an important, yet somewhat intangible benefit for children learning how to use lighting, design costumes, and create props. You can probably find a wealth of creative and hilarious props at second-hand stores and garage sales.

## FUTURE ADVENTURES

1. **Reinforce the reading skills of your older children by asking them to read while the younger children act.** Make fun "rules" for this time, such as the more vividly the story is read, the more dramatic the action must be.

2. **Play charades.** Silent acting forces dramatic behavior, since the child cannot use his voice to emphasize his acting.

## MAKE IT MEMORABLE!

Gather an audience. Just like adults, children need to learn to derive satisfaction from an activity planned and executed. Allow your child to "sell" tickets to family members for the performance. As he gets better, maybe he could conduct a neighborhood "drama club" during the summer!

# NOTES

# RECITATION

## PROJECT SKETCH

In ancient Hebrew culture children began memorization at a very early age. Bible passages which formed acrostics helped Hebrew children memorize the alphabet. Proverbs and sayings committed to memory using rhyming poetic forms helped children remember important information. Psalms set to music and dancing sealed biblical principles into the mind. Even today, difficult information memorized in a rhyming form or using mnemonic techniques is much easier to recall than mere lists. Memorizing and reciting short Bible verses and poems are an exciting way for young children to begin working on verbal skills. Poems and rhyming verse, especially when accompanied by physical activity, may actually strengthen the cognitive foundation for future learning.

## HOW-TO

Children as young as 20 months can "fill in the blanks" in a simple story that you recite. Four-and five-year-olds love memorizing simple poems and rhymes. Finding good materials may be your most difficult task. First, check your local library for books with nursery rhymes and poems for children. You may opt to purchase some books at a Christian bookstore. Used bookstores often offer a large children's section.

Poems may be memorized while riding in the car or just lying down looking at the sky. I still remember a poem I learned in kindergarten:

If I had a spoon as tall as the sky,
    I'd dish up some clouds as they go slip-sliding by
I'd take them inside and give them a cook
    and see if they taste as good as they look.

## TIMELY TIPS

As Professors Huckleberry and Strother indicate, young children enjoy the "short and sweetness" of poems, so don't try to introduce difficult concepts yet. Select poems that might be accompanied by physical activity such as jumping, skipping or dancing ("I'm a little teapot" is a good example). For young children, exercising motor skills helps both memorization and oral delivery.

## FUTURE ADVENTURE

"Fill-in-the-blank" stories. Obviously, a child who can barely speak will face some limitations at memorizing poems and scripture verses. But as soon as he masters a few words, you can teach him fill-in-the-blank stories. I recently observed a mother and 20-month-old child who had studied the story of Jonah. It went something like this: "Jonah was a man who *disobeyed* God. He *ran (making running motions)* away and got on a *boat.* The waves came up *(wavy motions with arms)* and the men threw Jonah into the water *(splashing sound).* A big *fish* came and swallowed Jonah *(gulping sound).* Then Jonah prayed *(with praying motions)* and the fish *spit (with spitting sound)* Jonah onto the *beach.* After that, Jonah *obeyed.*"

## MAKE IT MEMORABLE!

Memorize Bible verses. Young children can understand the basic truths found in Scripture. Even very young children can memorize Bible verses that are paraphrased simply, such as in the Living Bible. At a Christian book store, ask for a Bible memory program for children which allows them to memorize a verse for each letter of the alphabet, and contains a poem accompanying each verse. Otherwise, select a verse for your child and develop your own program. Your child can transfer the verse and poems to a scrapbook which he decorates with crayons, markers, or glitter glue.

# DRAWING

## PROJECT SKETCH

According to Lee Karnowski in an essay on how young writers communicate, speech can be a pre-writing strategy when it is used to explore a topic and decide on the content of a story or discourse. While adults communicate primarily through words, and resort to graphs and pictures for further explanation, children use art, music and drama to make sense of the writing process. For younger children who do not yet know how to "write," try drawing. Your child can draw a picture and communicate the story behind it, or simply describe what he has drawn. Many children will communicate orally as they draw, or they may hum or sing. While this activity may seem simple, it is also profoundly meaningful. It allows the child to focus on oral communication skills as a part of everyday life.

## HOW-TO

Give your child drawing material and ask him to make a picture. Encourage him to tell you out loud what he is going to draw and ask questions as he does it. When he finishes, sit with him and listen to the story behind the picture. if he simply describes its elements, encourage him to make up a story to go with it.

## TIMELY TIP

Remember that the purpose of this activity is oral communication, which means that you should be present! Some families have created a play room or craft room with the noble intention of hiding their child's sometimes messy activities. However, your adult presence and oral interaction will make a qualitative difference in everyday play.

## FUTURE ADVENTURES

1. **Play a music tape while the child draws.** Music soothes the soul and enhances creativity. According to Mr. Karnowski, children actually use the sounds of music to make meaning. You can also play a story tape and ask your child to draw the action and characters, or simply whatever comes to mind.

2. **Use crafts other than drawing.** Walk through a large craft store sometime just to see what is available: they have everything from colored glue to plastic beads which melt together to form colorful place mats. Money invested in craft materials is almost always a wiser investment than the toys advertised on Saturday morning television!

## MAKE IT MEMORABLE!

Encourage drawing or coloring when you read together as a family. Every member of the family will enjoy drawing, coloring, stitching or assembling models while listening. On an 11" by 17" piece of paper, use a black magic marker to draw an outline of a picture and a short saying or scripture that reinforces the lesson. Make photocopies for the family, and allow them to color as you read. Occasionally, take these masterpieces back to the copy store and have them laminated. My parents have a whole drawer of such "place mats" in which their children took great pride!

# JOURNALING

## PROJECT SKETCH

Journaling provides an excellent opportunity to refine and communicate thoughts and feelings. It also helps the child learn to reflect on his experiences and to begin focusing on the world outside. A journal might include commentary on a family vacation or field trip, letters to oneself, observations of the world, and reflections on pleasures and disappointments.

## HOW-TO

Children ages three to seven are almost exclusively in a pre-writing stage. This means that any journaling must be dictated to you. Just as you help him write down stories and "publish" them, help your child record his thoughts, feelings and perceptions.

## TIMELY TIPS

1. **If you are writing the journal on behalf of your child, resist the temptation to "fill in" details which the child does not give.** Writing down his observations as closely as you can to what he offers will provide a means of evaluating his improvement over a period of time.

2. **Ask questions instead of making suggestions.** The journal should be the child's creation, and he may have a clear preference for what sorts of things he would like to have in it. If he is stumped or seems at a loss for words, ask questions which draw out his thoughts.

## FUTURE ADVENTURES

1. **Note-taking.** Take time on a trip or outing to help your child record his observations. Note-taking can be as simple as writing down what colors he sees, how many trucks, windmills, and barns. It can also include sense-impressions: What do you see? How does it make you feel? What do you expect to see when we get there? How do the buildings, homes and people look different here than at home? What smells are here? Have you heard any new sounds?

2. **Have the child help with writing.** If you are writing letters to relatives or friends, ask your child to dictate to you some things he would like to tell that person. If old enough to write, he can do it himself. If not, maybe he can sign his name or draw a simple picture. Either way, it gets him to see firsthand the value of communication!

### MAKE IT MEMORABLE!

**Make lists.** Children like to make lists. Encourage this! Your child can use lists to become more organized, understand the sequence of events for the day, or make a list of tasks to be accomplished. For younger children, lists may be as simple as recording desired Christmas or birthday gifts or listing toys in a certain order (by group, kind, preference, etc.).

**Take pictures.** Photograph events and order double copies. Give one set to your child to paste in his own scrapbook. As he tells the "cut line" that goes with each picture, write it underneath. Include the dates and names of the people and places in the pictures. Encourage your child to share his scrapbook with guests in your home, or to take it along when you go visiting.

# COPYING

### PROJECT SKETCH

Speech, as in all child behaviors, emerges in part through children copying adult behavior. Therefore, the more opportunities a child has to copy, and in the greater number of contexts, the deeper the learning experience. Copying enhances a child's powers of observation, a foundational ability which feeds into communication skill.

### HOW-TO

Show your child how to copy pictures, and encourage him to copy anything he finds interesting: the words to an appealing song, poems, Bible verses or quotations from books. Allow him to decorate and post them on the wall. If your child is unable to write, suggest that he allow you to help him.

### TIMELY TIP

Once again, involvement is more important than perfection. The complexity of that which is being copied and the art involved should match the child's skill level. Don't be concerned if the copied version bears no resemblance to the original! At this point in life, the child's perceptions of objects or situations may be far different from your own, and his motor skills are not as refined as yours. Resist the temptation to get him drawing "within the lines" at too early an age.

### FUTURE ADVENTURE

Give your child poems, quotations and Bible verses of enduring value to copy. Those which promote positive character traits will have timeless value in the life of the child. In church, children can benefit from copying hymn titles and page numbers and still manage to catch some of the sermon!

## MAKE IT MEMORABLE

Encourage your child to copy *occasions* as well as objects. Your child might "preach" behind a pulpit, design a "movie set," host a "talk show," or produce his own radio and television advertisements. [Note: this is one occasion in which the child's imagination might be exercised more if you are *not* there to observe. Let him take chances by himself first. He will let you know when he is ready to perform!] A piano bench with a tinker toy microphone makes a wonderful pulpit from which to preach. A card table can serve as the desk for a talk show host. A movie camera can be crafted from an empty cereal box with a cardboard tube or two sticking out the end. Chances are you can create more fun toys with household items than could be purchased at the store at an exorbitant cost!

# TAPE RECORDER GAMES

## PROJECT SKETCH

Children find tape recorders fascinating. They love listening to sounds and guessing what they are. They like to record their own voices, and develop sound effects. Since tape recorders are fun, children effortlessly develop listening and observation skills which help form the foundation for later communication development.

## HOW-TO

Here are two ways to use a tape recorder to develop communication skills:

1. **Listening and sound identification.** When your child is not present, take the tape recorder around the house and record the sounds of everyday events. Be creative! The blender, microwave oven timer, door shutting, toilet flushing, doorbell ringing, bird singing, or car starting. Take the tape recorder on errands, recording sirens, cash registers, and sounds at a construction site. Record as many sounds as you can, and make a game of identifying them. Help your child recognize emotion in the voice without the benefit of seeing facial expressions. Record happy voices, sad voices, and angry voices. Record friends, family, and television programs, making a game of helping your child identify them.

2. **Recording your child's voice.** Record your child performing one of the other activities in this section, and play it back for him. He will begin to reflect on and adjust his speech behavior as he becomes accustomed to the sound of his own voice. Develop some

structured activities as well; maybe your child can listen to some radio advertisements and develop some of his own.

Encourage your child to "just play" with the tape recorder to enhance creativity.

### TIMELY TIP

Use the recordings of voices to discuss *emotions* heard in your child's world. When in public, point out emotional displays such as a crying child at the grocery store and speculate with your child on why the person feels that way.

### FUTURE ADVENTURE

For a child who is old enough to operate the tape recorder for himself, switch the "sound identification" game around. Allow *him* to record sounds for *you* to identify. Encourage him to "create" voices with different emotions which you then attempt to identify.

### MAKE IT MEMORABLE!

Sound effects are a loud, crazy, creative, and fun way to improve your child's powers of observation. As mentioned previously, crinkling a piece of tin foil sounds like fireworks and banging two dried coconut halves together sounds like horses' hooves. Once he gets the hang of it, challenge your child to try recreating a wide variety of sounds.

# CHAPTER FIFTEEN

# AGES EIGHT TO TWELVE

Joe's parents just can't figure him out. He alternates between being loud and energetic, and quiet, almost melancholy. As he becomes more sensitive to the reactions of those around him, he sometimes seems more uncomfortable with close physical contact from his parents. His mother wonders what is going on inside, but Joe isn't really able, or willing, to tell her. What is happening?

The time between ages eight and twelve may be an awkward growing time for your child. The good news is that communication activities serve as a fantastic antidote to some of the complications that pre-adolescents face. Let's assume that we know Joe well enough to diagnose what is happening in his life (these struggles are actually quite common for children this age):

- Joe's incredible growth spurt leaves him feeling gangly and awkward.

- As Joe tries to identify his place in the world, he is highly impressionable.

- Joe has a hard time describing what is going on inside.

- Joe feels uncomfortable in social situations.

- Joe feels somewhat bored by his circumstances.

**Communication activities serve as a fantastic antidote to some of the complications that pre-adolescents face.**

The activities in this chapter might help Joe to:

• Become more confident in his social skills.

• Develop the ability to discern good or bad influences from the world around him.

• Learn to express his feelings and thoughts more effectively.

• Find greater comfort in social situations.

• Develop more enthusiasm for life.

The building of communication skills at this age is more direct than at the three-to-seven age range. Because your child is better able to understand the commands and suggestions you give him, learning to improve is more a matter of *patience* and *practice* than of play and participation. In order to equip yourself to work with your child in this age range, consider the following overview of his likely characteristics.

## WHAT WILL HE BE LIKE?

Children ages eight to twelve usually retain the terrific imagination from their younger years, but may begin turning it toward research, discovery and learning of new things. Whereas before he may have needed some help in being kept busy, your child may now be more interested in doing things with others, working with groups, and spending time with peers.

## NOW YOU'RE THINKING!

L. S. Vygotsky, the Russian researcher, demonstrated that during this time period, children gain the ability to think abstractly. A phrase such as "a stitch in time saves nine" may, when explained, remind them of the virtue of prevention rather than just the skill of sewing! When you ask your child to "set the table," this will mean something other than "sit at the table." He will gradually begin to understand the abstract concepts behind the Bible stories and books you read to him, so it is a good time to focus on the character traits that heroes and role models possess.

## I KNOW HOW YOU FEEL!

Although children at this age should become more sensitive to the needs of those around them, according to David Elkind, they will be most concerned about issues which have immediate impact on their lives. Politics, for example, may become more meaningful to your child as he grows older, but he is likely to reflect your political beliefs without much question. He will probably be far more concerned about his performance and the outcome of his team's performance in a baseball game. He often needs an empathetic ear, but he also needs to understand the source of his feelings and thoughts.

Moreover, your child will not yet understand the shortcomings and flaws of those he respects. He is likely to imitate adult behavior without considering whether it is appropriate or wise to do so. At the same time, your child will become more proficient at distinguishing the emotions expressed by others, not only in what people say but by the tone they use. He may express concern or joy in response to the emotional reactions of others. His questions may turn from the nature of what people are like to what they believe, and what his own purpose in life entails.

## HOW WELL CAN I COMMUNICATE?

Professors Allen and Brown, among the foremost experts on child speech, concluded that the following

**Although children ages 8 to 12 should become more sensitive to the needs of those around them, they will likely be concerned about issues which have immediate impact on their lives.**

communication characteristics will most likely define children in the eight-to-twelve age group:

- they know how to use evidence to support their claims,

- they can present persuasive arguments to support their actions,

- they can take into account another person's point-of-view if asked to do so,

- they can present and understand information that relates to objects that are not immediately visible, and

- they can understand the feedback that others give them, and can give feedback themselves.

As you begin working with your child using the activities in this chapter, you will notice improvements in his ability to:

- evaluate the messages of others and make comments about them,

- take the role of another person without being pushed to do so,

- present concepts from his own thoughts as well as those of others,

- use messages that refer to situations or ideas that are not part of his present situation, and

- adapt his messages to the needs of those who are listening.

## HELPING YOUR CHILD UNDERSTAND HIS BEHAVIOR

Commenting on and reviewing situations and interactions will help your child understand his behavior. You can help your child identify what worked and what didn't in the way he spoke to and listened to another person. Professor Friedman of the University of Kansas suggests you teach him to ask, "How did that interaction turn out?" "What was the effect of that person's behavior on me?" "What was the effect of my behavior on that person?" Help your child evaluate how he feels after interacting with someone: excited or bored, secure or threatened, comfortable or uncomfortable. Ask *why* he felt that way, and enable him to understand how the unspoken behavior of the person, the circumstances, and his own expectations play a role in how he relates to others.

## WHAT KIND OF ACTIVITIES WILL BE HELPFUL?

The projects in this section take advantage of the fact that your child is becoming more sensitive to his actions and how he relates to others. While the level of energy and increasing competitiveness of some children may mask their feelings, be assured that your efforts to help your child become more aware of the world around him will eventually pay off.

A word of warning: children at this age take put-downs and sarcastic language personally. Be very careful that your mood around them is controlled, and be sure your child knows that *your* emotional state is not *his* fault. In fact, if you are upset with something that does not involve the child, carefully explain the situation to him. And as always, take responsibility for your feelings: instead of saying, "That person makes me mad," emphasize that, "I do not hate that person, but I feel very frustrated when they do that."

The activities in this chapter will begin the process of giving your child the opportunity to stand and speak, although for very short periods of time and in front of limited audiences. This breaking-in period is essential for him to be comfortable in front of larger audiences and in more intense person-to-person relationships in the future.

# OBSERVATION SKILLS

## PROJECT SKETCH

Observation skills are the life blood of communication. We use our eyes and ears to deepen the well of experience from which we draw the life-giving waters of communication. In short, our fuel for descriptive talk comes from sharp powers of observation.

## HOW-TO

You can help your child develop sharp powers of observation through a few simple activities, consistently repeated. Here is a small sampling:

1. **"If I were in your shoes."** Brainstorm a list of characteristics such as "homeless," "single mom," "angry driver," and "bully." Have your child draw a characteristic from a box and brainstorm a list of thoughts, feelings and attitudes that such a person might have, as well as some impressions of what that person might be going through. Ask, "What would Jesus do if he met that person?" If possible, engage your child in a ministry activity around this project. After a while, he will think about himself less and thus become a blessing to others.

2. **"What are they thinking?"** This game allows your child to speculate about the feelings, motives and thoughts of others. Use television and movie characters, book characters, people in news articles, and public figures. Ask questions such as, "Why do you suppose they did that?" and "What led them to act that way?"

## FUTURE ADVENTURES

1. **Observation Game.** Play a game where you and your child take turns glancing at a scene (along the road or

in a picture book) for ten seconds, and then closing your eyes and listing as many things as you can that you observed.

2. **Question asking.** With the "If I were in their shoes" and "What are they thinking" games, have your child speculate on what *he* would do in that situation. This skill is important to interpersonal communication throughout life.

## TIMELY TIP

Every moment is not a teachable moment! In the car, your child may prefer to play cards in the back seat or read a book than observe the world around. This is often irritating to parents, who want each trip to be "memorable." Since you cannot force him to appreciate the scenery as much as you do, be content with small doses of participation!

## MAKE IT MEMORABLE!

Every family does, or should, go on lots of field trips. Where possible, invest in the trip by conducting some research in advance. For example, before visiting a sheep ranch, study sheep in the Bible, examine how shepherds live, and learn how wool is processed. Have your child call the market for the price on virgin wool, or to inquire about the cost of raising sheep. If you are planning a nature hike, help your child memorize the names and identities of a couple of trees, flowers, birds and animals you might see. On a more extensive adventure, use pre-planning as a way to generate enthusiasm. Before visiting a Civil War battlefield, for instance, read biographical stories about the Civil War and its major players or draw out a battle map. Consider checking out a wholesome movie drama or documentary about the place you are visiting.

# NAMING GAMES

## PROJECT SKETCH

This exercise emphasizes higher-order observation skills. Its purpose is to teach your child to use his observation skills as a springboard to imaginative description. The greatest communicators in the world are successful because of their ability to create vivid and memorable images in the minds of an audience, even getting an audience to feel personally affected by and responsible for those images.

A good case in point is Winston Churchill. Acknowledged by many as one of the greatest speakers in history, Churchill was a master of vivid description. Churchill's biographers take great pleasure in pointing out his imagination in even the most ordinary circumstances. For instance, a bulldozer Churchill once rented for landscaping his estate became stuck in the mud, and he described the plan to extricate the machine in a letter to his wife: "The animal is very strong with his hands but feeble with his caterpillar legs, and as the fields are sopping, they had the greatest difficulty in taking him away. They will have to lay down sleepers all the way from the lake to the gate over which he will waddle on Monday." Note the effort used to describe such a simple process. By investing the machine with animal-like qualities and giving it a personality, he enlivened an otherwise drab description.

## How-To

The purpose of this project is to sharpen your child's ability to use his eyes to *observe* rather than just to *see*. Here are two exercises to help accomplish this goal.

1. **Encourage imaginative description.** Cut pictures out of newspapers and colorful magazines such as National

Geographic. Start with pictures of people or things with which the child is not familiar.

- People. What might this person's life have been like? Make up a story about where they grew up. List as many words as you can to describe this person.

- Objects. What is its function? What animal does it look like? How do you make it work? What would you do with it if you had one?

2. **Describe without naming.** Put the cutouts into a box, and ask the child to draw and describe one. Try to guess what is being described.

## FUTURE ADVENTURE

**Observe people in public.** Go for a soft drink at a busy restaurant and observe people. Observe how they greet others, how they walk, and the expressions and posture they exhibit.

## TIMELY TIPS

Imaginative description takes a long time to develop. Don't rush the process, but reward your child for being more coherent and fluent than he was before. You will notice an increase in descriptive ability over time.

## MAKE IT MEMORABLE!

Good literature is fertile soil for growing imaginative minds. Reading to your child and encouraging him to read will help hone this skill. Classic literature is far better for this purpose than modern children's books. Standards such as *Treasure Island*, *The Three Musketeers*, and *Robinson Crusoe* are outstanding, not only because they have an imaginative thesis, but because they contain lessons of moral value.

# VOCABULARY BUILDING

## PROJECT SKETCH

Good communication skill requires words that accurately describe what you wish to convey. As language becomes more vivid, you can actually become more powerful in your speech. A healthy vocabulary also builds the foundation for the greater use of natural intelligence.

## HOW-TO

### 1. Pictures and objects.

- Find an object or picture that looks interesting and discuss it.

- Tell me a story about this object.

- List as many words as you can think of to describe this object.

- What are some other things like this? *How* are they like it?

- What is its purpose? How would you use it?

- What else can we use in the same way?

For variety, make a contest out of describing the object. Choose an object that is unfamiliar to your child, such as a piece of machinery. Praise him for thinking of the funniest, most creative use. For example, the speaker cover of a transistor radio could be seen as "a computer keypad for woodpeckers," "a place to plant very small seeds," etc.

2. **Use crossword puzzles and word games.** Extend your investment in activity books beyond coloring! Choose inexpensive books at your child's age and skill level to keep him busy during "down times" at home or on trips. "Mad-Libs," for example, asks the child to create a list of descriptive words such as an action verb, emotion, color, or thing. The more descriptive the words, the funnier the resulting fill-in-the-blank story.

3. **Flash cards.** This is a time-proven means of learning new words—all the way to adulthood! When you encounter a new word, encourage your child to look it up and write the word on one side of an index card and the definition on the other. These cards can be used in a variety of ways:

- Lay the flash cards with the words face-up. Give your child clues about each definition until he guesses all of the words correctly. Then, reverse the cards, give him the definition and ask for the correct word.

- Time trials. Show the definition or the word, asking your child to guess it as quickly as he can. Work toward the most correct answers in the shortest time.

## FUTURE ADVENTURE

Try object flash cards. Create several dozen flash cards with objects and characteristics such as "barn," "green," "happy," "fun," "car," etc. The object of the game is for the "reader" to describe the object or characteristic to the "guesser" without using the word on the card. For a more difficult game, list several *other* words which may not be used in the description.

## TIMELY TIP

A child must encounter a word three times, on average, before he knows it. Point out words as they come up. By the way, the old adage "look it up for yourself" really works!

## MAKE IT MEMORABLE!

Encourage your child to brainstorm pictures for each new word. We learn words most effectively when they are used colorfully, with vivid descriptions and mnemonic devices. Remember the word "distraught," for example, by picturing a lost person panicked because they are a *"distance"* from where they *"ought"* to be. It takes practice, but it really works!

## NOTES

# MEMORY

## PROJECT SKETCH

Memory skills are integrally related to communication. A sharp memory will help your child become a clearer thinker and a more interesting conversationalist. It will prepare him for the memorized outlines which are essential to a good speech, and if he memorizes material with solid moral content, he will have a much deeper message to communicate.

## HOW-TO

In this exercise, we will focus on two unique ways to heighten your child's skills of memorization.

1. **Enhance Bible memory options.** Alice Chapin, in her book *Building Your Child's Faith*, suggests the following activities:

A. **Use a quiz.** "I am thinking of a verse in _____ referring to a _____." Give your child hints while he looks it up in the Bible. You might even try sketching clues in the form of pictures, or play Bible verse "Pictionary" in which one family member draws clues and the others try to guess what verse is being described.

For instance, "The wages of sin is death, but the gift of God is eternal life in Jesus Christ our Lord" (Romans 6:23), might look like this:

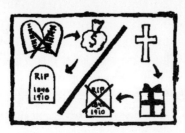

B. **Verse puzzle.** Put the verse on a card, cut into pieces with one word per piece. Put the pieces in an envelope and use the timer to see how quickly your child can assemble them correctly. For a more challenging version, put several verses together in the same envelope!

C. **Memory walk.** Write one word or a phrase on "foot prints" cut out of construction paper. The child steps from one to the other, reading as he goes. You can place verses on the floor from his room to the bathroom, from the living room to the kitchen, up and down stairs, or wherever you or your child wish to put them.

2. **Sequence and substance game.** Make up two identical sets of cards, about 50 in all. Draw a simple picture on each with a magic marker. Place one set in another room, and keep one set with you. Show your child a certain number of cards in a certain order for about 10 seconds. Have him go to the other room and pick out those same cards and place them in the same order.

Continue the competition to see how many cards he can correctly identify and place in the correct order. If he finds the task too difficult, start with just getting the right cards, working on sequence when he becomes proficient at the initial task. You can also use actual objects, giving instructions of what to do with them, in which order to put them, or how to organize them. For example, put a sack, a rubber band, a potato, and some dried beans in another room. Instruct your child to "Go to the other room, pick up the potato, put the rubber band around it, put it in the sack and add five beans. Close the sack at the top and bring it back, being sure to close the door when you return." Give praise liberally for successfully completed tasks, and make them more complex with each success.

## FUTURE ADVENTURE

To help your child prepare for future speech lessons, assign poems, sayings, and quotes for him to memorize. Use them to create short speeches on several topics. A good speech makes liberal use of such tools.

## TIMELY TIP

Employ memory techniques. Two commonly overlooked techniques are 1) bizarre images and 2) sequence. If you are memorizing a list, for instance, think of a bizarre representation of the objects, fitting them together in an action-oriented way. Let's say you wish to pick up four items from the grocery store: lettuce, cereal, shaving cream, and bananas. Imagine pouring cereal on a bowl of lettuce and topping it with bananas and a flourish of shaving cream.

## MAKE IT MEMORABLE!

Host a friendly family competition. Alice Chapin suggests making a contract with your family for memorizing a certain number of Bible verses. If the kids win, the adults will _____. If the adults win, the kids will _____. Beware of a child's power of memory!

NOTES

# LISTENING

## PROJECT SKETCH

Children who become better listeners will become better learners. Studies show that better listening leads to a better vocabulary, increased comprehension and greater retention. The benefits are practical as well. Most careers require refined listening skills. This makes sense—listening is the most common form of communication. There are no tricky techniques to learning listening skills. If you as a parent are merely aware of the need, you can begin to structure your activities to emphasize listening.

## HOW-TO

Here are a couple of simple ideas:

1. **Listening retention.** Read a quote, paragraph or even a whole selection from a book or magazine and ask questions about the selection. Do the same with a radio or television program.

2. **Active listening.** This involves listening carefully to what another person says to be sure you understand what they mean. You can try this by making a statement or claim and having your child ask one of two types of questions:

Questions to Restate:

"From what I hear you saying…"

"Are you saying that…"

"So from your point of view…"

"Let me restate what you are saying to make sure I understand. Are you saying that..."

"Did I understand you to say..."

"So what you're saying is..."

Questions to Reflect:

"How did that make you feel?"

"What do you think about it now?"

"How did that affect you?"

"Tell me more about it."

"I'd like to know more.

## FUTURE ADVENTURES

1. **Allow your child to ask questions of you, or if you have more than one child, have your children ask questions of one another.**

2. **Play detective games.** Think of a random object (or person) and instruct your child to ask "yes" or "no" questions to guess what it is. Become increasingly obscure in the objects you choose. The goal of the game is to get your child to really listen to the clues you give and if others play, to the questions *they* ask. Through asking methodical questions, it is possible to guess virtually anything.

## TIMELY TIP

Children are most likely to listen when the stimulus is varied, so alternate study periods with play periods and don't dwell on any one topic for too long.

## MAKE IT MEMORABLE!

By age twelve your child should have the ability to take simple notes from a speech, a sermon, or a television or radio program. Show him a basic outline format, explain how to take down a few key words or ideas, and allow him to practice. It is a fact that most people listen much better and retain more when they take notes.

## NOTES

# TELL ME HOW

## PROJECT SKETCH

Being able to verbally describe what we see is a key to precision as well as imagination in speech. "Tell Me How" teaches your child to give and receive directions for copying an object without being able to see the object he is copying. This exercise builds on the skills of observation and description. It emphasizes listening, and reinforces the interactive nature of communication. Through practice, your child will learn how to quickly process information and develop "common sense" about following directions. He will learn how to give directions as well, turning his observations into coherent speech.

## HOW-TO

Erect a screen between you and your child (a sheet on a clothesline will do) or seat yourself and your child around the corner from one another. Build a structure out of blocks, and describe to the child what you are building, so he can build an identical structure based on your description. For additional difficulty, set rules such as, "I will only give the direction once" and "Only one question about each direction." At the end, debrief and point out how small mistakes dramatically change the outcome. You will discover that your own communication may lack precision (thus a side benefit of this exercise is the opportunity to improve communication with your child).

## FUTURE ADVENTURES

1. **Have your *child* build the structure and describe it to *you*.** Also, try using paper and pencil, or crayons instead of blocks.

2. **Try a "Where Do I Go?" game.** Blindfold your child and help him negotiate an obstacle course through verbal instructions (two small steps to the left, three steps straight, etc.).

## TIMELY TIPS

1. **Purposefully give incomplete instructions on occasion.** Teach your child how to recognize that he doesn't have enough information and how to ask for more by stating, "I don't understand. Can you give me more information?" He can ask more specific questions as well.

2. **Overcoming frustration.** Explain that when we feel frustrated, it is best to stay calm and practice being patient. When we are calm, the instructions seem less confusing and our attitude helps the other person be more clear. This activity, along with many of the others in this section, provides good opportunities to teach the character trait of patience.

## MAKE IT MEMORABLE!

"Make a Peanut Butter Sandwich" game. This is an old, hilarious game which emphasizes the need for precise communication in giving instructions. Tell your child you want him to give you precise instructions on how to make a peanut butter sandwich. Take all of his instructions *literally*. For instance, if his first instruction is, "Put the peanut butter on the bread," take the jar of peanut butter and set it on top of the loaf. And so on.

# EXPRESSIVENESS

## PROJECT SKETCH

It is said that the eye is the gateway to the soul, but it would be more accurate to say that the *whole face* is the gateway to the soul. Children *at birth* have the ability to distinguish between positive and negative emotional expressions by looking at a face. The goal of this exercise is to encourage children to more accurately distinguish the emotions of others while refining their own expressiveness.

## HOW-TO

Make a list of the 26 letters of the alphabet and assign one emotion and corresponding facial/body expression for each. You don't need to do *every* letter, but just enough to make the formation of several words possible. Here are some suggestions:

A = Angry, aggressive, anxious, arrogant

B = Boisterous, bashful, blissful, bored

C = Content, confident, curious

D = Disgusted, determined, disappointed, disapproving

E = Excited, enraged, envious, exasperated

F = Frightened, frustrated, fretful

G = Goody-goody, grieving, goofy

H = Happy, horrified, hurt

I = Impatient, indifferent, idiotic, innocent, interested

J = Jubilant, jealous, joyful

K = Kidding

L = Loving, lonely

M = Mean, meditative, miserable

N = Nervous

O = Obstinate, optimistic

P = Paranoid, perplexed, prudish, puzzled, proud

Q = Quiet, quizzical, quirky

R = Regretful, relieved

S = Sad, satisfied, shocked, sheepish, smug, surprised, suspicious, sympathetic

T = Thoughtful, transfixed

U = Undecided, uppity

W = Withdrawn

Make expressions yourself, and see if your child can decode them. Then let him try it!

## FUTURE ADVENTURE

Try the same thing with body postures! For example, C = Confident, L = Lazy.

## TIMELY TIPS

1. **Begin observing the facial expressions other people use.** When you are in public, get feedback from your child on what sorts of expressions he has noticed.

2. **Help your child think through the expressions himself.** Do not be too quick to provide an easy answer.

## MAKE IT MEMORABLE!

Teach your family members to apply this exercise by becoming more sensitive to the emotional state of other family members. Instead of encouraging them to continually point out expressions to each other, impress on them the need to think about what that expression means, how the person feels, and how to respond accordingly.

# NOTES

# DISCUSSION

## PROJECT SKETCH

Children should recognize that we get new ideas and make friends through sincere, courteous and active discussion. Through discussion we learn to understand how other people think and feel about important issues. Discussions perform the "linking" function of communication. Being able to explore ideas, listen critically and keep one's cool in a discussion will allow your child to excel in a variety of social situations.

A discussion is free-form, yet directed enough to ensure that each individual's concerns have been fully discussed, and to maintain an atmosphere of respect and courtesy.

## HOW-TO

Begin with an informal and loosely-structured atmosphere. It is best to have at least three people involved. According to Professors Huckleberry and Strother, there are five basic kinds of discussion questions:

1. **Content.** "How did Moses get across the Red Sea?"

2. **Similar Experience.** "Have you ever had bad feelings toward someone?"

3. **Comparison.** "We have read another story like the one we just finished. What was the name of it?"

4. **Judgement.** "What was wrong with Adam and Eve taking and eating the fruit?"

5. **If-You-Were-There.** "If you had been on the boat with the disciples when the storm came up, what would you have done?"

## FUTURE ADVENTURES

1. **Draw topics out a of a box.** Each person in the discussion can insert topics.

2. **Use puppets.** With younger children, use puppets to discuss things. Assume the identity of the puppet and express its "feelings" and "thoughts." Older children can help teach, using puppets to develop discussion skills in younger children.

3. **Tennis ball game.** Toss a ball to someone and ask him to make a statement or ask a question and then toss it to someone else. See how long you can go.

## TIMELY TIP

Especially in a family environment, it is important for each member to show respect for the other members by taking turns, restating, and reflecting what the other person has just said before he can speak. Find opportunities in family meetings, family night or even during arguments to practice.

## MAKE IT MEMORABLE!

Here is a technique to use during family meetings to make sure everyone s voice is heard! The speaker holds an object (a prized family souvenir or just a kitchen utensil) while he is speaking. During the time he has the object, others are not allowed to interrupt. For the sake of practice, have the other participants raise up their hands when they wish to say something. When the first speaker is finished, he can hand the object to the next speaker. This helps the discussion proceed in an orderly manner, requiring all participants to show respect for the others.

# QUESTION-ASKING

## PROJECT SKETCH

Children who know how to ask questions of others provide more enjoyable company and are better able to learn and absorb information. Moreover, the ability to ask good questions is seen by many as a sign of intelligence. According to Josh McDowell, scholars during Bible times demonstrated their understanding of a subject through "Rabbinical riddles," which meant answering a question with an equally well-phrased and ponderous question. Teaching your child to ask good questions is not an overnight assignment; it takes years of practice. However, here are some tips which can set your child in the right direction.

## HOW-TO

Who, what, when, where and why questions may be easily taught. Set up situations, such as field trips or visits with friends, in which your child can ask them.

Here are four ways, suggested by Professors Mackay and Watson, to use questions:

1. **Recall or repeat a question asked by you.**

2. **Select an idea from a bank** (a list of questions you devise).

3. **Apply a pre-learned question in a new situation.** For example, on a field trip to a local business, ask, "What subjects did you study in school that might help you in this job?"

4. **Ask your child to think up his own ideas, and ask questions based on them.**

## FUTURE ADVENTURES

1. **Interviews.** Ask a business person for some sample questions they use in employee interviews. Have your child take the lead in asking these or similar questions of family members. He most likely will need to plan questions in advance, and may need assistance in anticipating responses.

2. **Video or audio tape a mock interview situation.** By viewing or listening to himself, your child can discover areas in which he might improve. This will help make the lessons more concrete. Check the quality of questions asked (clarity and relevance) and delivery (volume and articulation).

## TIMELY TIPS

1. **Prepare in advance.** If you know something about the person with whom you will be visiting, relay some details to your child that he might find interesting, or that will make the person seem less intimidating. Praise your child for a job well done!

2. **Give your child an idea of the kind of topics people like to discuss:** family, hobbies, something exciting that happened to them, a dream vacation, where they grew up, childhood memories, and the most important lesson they have learned.

3. **The best questions are open-ended, requiring more than a "yes" or "no" answer:**

   CLOSED: "Do you like the Colorado Rockies baseball team?"

   OPEN: "What sports do you enjoy watching or playing?"

## MAKE IT MEMORABLE!

Teach your child to ask questions that refer to ideas, thoughts and feelings rather than just the immediate situation. This will help him grasp deeper concepts and build a more powerful vocabulary. Ultimately, your child will learn best from your example! When you express genuine interest in another person by asking substantive questions, you will set an enormously powerful example for your child.

# NOTES

# TELEPHONE SKILLS

## PROJECT SKETCH

Every time you answer the telephone, you have an opportunity to make a good first impression. If the caller's impression is a good one, you have the opportunity to develop a relationship with that person. If not, your negative impression may last in their mind for years.

There are many reasons to teach telephone etiquette to your child. First, you will become more comfortable with him answering the telephone and even taking messages. Second, your child reflects you and your family in everything he does. If he is polite and communicative in telephone etiquette, one of the primary forms of communication in our culture, he will be an example of a well-taught child.

The benefit to your child is also great. He will learn to speak clearly and enthusiastically, endearing him to others throughout life.

## HOW-TO

The key to telephone etiquette is devising an appropriate way to answer, and then practicing a variety of situations. The following is a standard, polite telephone greeting:

"Good morning, _____ residence, this is
_____. How may I help you?"

Other rules:

- Before transferring a call to the intended recipient, always ask, "Who may I say is calling?"

- If the person being requested is not able to take the call, just say "_____ is not able to come to the phone right now. May I take a message?" Don't explain where they are. If the caller asks "Where are they?" ask in return, "Why do you ask?"

- Always take a complete message, noting the person s name with correct spelling, what the call is regarding, telephone number, date and time.

- Never tell strangers anything until they identify themselves. Even then, divulge information cautiously.

- When you are alone, never tell a stranger that your parents are not home. There is no need to lie; a simple, "He or she cannot come to the phone right now, may I take a message?" will do.

## TIMELY TIPS

1. **Practice exact wording and tone of voice, and create various situations to which your child can learn to respond.** Practice what to do if callers do not want to identify themselves, what to do when you are not home, etc.

2. **Use telephone etiquette as a prerequisite to telephone privileges.** Insist that your child learn to answer the telephone properly and take messages responsibly before being allowed to call friends. It might be a good idea to establish rules for telephone use as well (i.e., time limits, number of calls per day, who may call him, etc.). Do not take for granted that your child understands things such as "no long distance calls without permission," or "no taking calls during designated family time or homework time."

## MAKE IT MEMORABLE!

Be a little sneaky and use random reinforcement! Ask your friends to call and test your child at random intervals and report the results to you. Offer some sort of small prize or privilege for success.

# NOTES

# "DESCRIBE A PROCESS" SPEECH

## PROJECT SKETCH

This project will familiarize your child with the sequential structure of a speech. Structure (a sense of before, during and after) is what makes the speech experience possible. Even though your child's experience with the world is still limited, he can learn to construct meaning from events, and use this as the basis for conveying thoughts in an orderly manner.

## HOW-TO

This speech is like an oral report used to debrief activities. After you visit a factory, for instance, ask your child to rehearse the process through which the product is made. He may need some assistance in discerning the most important features of the process. After visiting a logging mill, for example, he can give a speech about how trees are turned into lumber. This is done by dividing the process into three or four identifiable, easy-to-remember steps.

Have your child organize the speech by giving an overview, explaining the main points and then concluding with a review. As the old speech coach advised, "Tell them what you are going to tell them, tell them, and then tell them what you told them." At this age, you can begin requiring increasingly rigorous standards of delivery and organizational skill. This means, for starters, that the introduction of the speech should capture the attention of the audience. For the logging speech, it might be:

*Imagine yourself on a construction site. You hear the pounding of hammers, the buzz of a saw, and the voice of the foreman shouting instructions to the crew. All of a sudden, a large truck pulls up with an enormous load of freshly cut lumber. The smell is sweet, almost like being in a forest. We see construction projects all the time but rarely stop to consider how we get construction lumber from trees. I recently visited a saw mill and observed the process. Basically, there are three steps...*

Good speeches also have an appropriate conclusion, which might be something like this:

*So the next time you sit on a wooden deck, or go to a lumber yard and smell the fresh smells, or pound a nail, think of all of the steps in the process from the tree to me.*

## FUTURE ADVENTURE

Try an "impressions speech." Have your child describe his *impressions* of a process he has observed. What was particularly memorable and why? Praise him for accuracy and colorful descriptions.

## TIMELY TIPS

1. **Help your child focus on the *process* rather than on the specific details.** If your child has watched a movie and is describing it to someone else, the most important thing is not the funny scenes which stand out in his mind, but what the story was *about*.

2. **Ask lots of "why" questions, such as, "Why did the men in the lumber mill wear hard hats?"**

3. **If your child is having difficulty getting the steps in the right order, jot them down.** This will help him see the correct order in a more objective way, so that if the details are out of order, the main point is still clear. This is actually the first step in learning to take outline notes.

## Make It Memorable!

Allow your child to help establish the plans for a family outing. Then ask him to brief the family on the plans for the day in three or four identifiable steps. Take turns as family members.

## NOTES

# DEMONSTRATION SPEECH

## PROJECT SKETCH

The age range from eight to twelve is a good time for your child to move from just relating experiences to doing so in a disciplined manner. As Professors Huckleberry and Strother note, speaking formally will help him refine his thoughts and feelings and reconstruct them in the light of previous failures. A demonstration speech is a good place to start, because your child can rely on props as the center of attention. Demonstration speeches focus on process, identifying the steps necessary to complete a task. This skill is vital to any future success in speech making or story telling.

## HOW-TO

Begin with giving a speech about a process in which the child has recently engaged. For instance, if he has learned how to make ice cream in a churn, have him demonstrate the process in identifiable steps. Make sure the speech is complete with an introduction:

I. Introduction.

*"I scream, you scream, we all scream for ice cream! Eating ice cream is such a popular thing to do in America that it could probably be called a 'great American pastime.' The problem, however, is that buying ice cream in the store is so expensive. How would you like to learn a way of making ice cream that only costs about 25 cents a serving, is more tasty, and far more healthy than store-bought ice cream? It is as simple as following these three steps."*

II. Point 1: Assemble materials.

III. Point 2: Mix ingredients.

IV. Point 3: Stir them in an ice cream churn.

V. Conclusion.

## FUTURE ADVENTURES

Try other speeches with a similar structure such as the "three reasons" speech. "Three reasons why I would like to go camping this weekend," or "Three reasons why I am upset with Joe."

## TIMELY TIPS

1. **Be persistent!** Giving speeches in the home may seem awkward, but the only way to learn is to practice. All successful speakers rehearse at home and in their hotel room before each important speech.

2. **Focus on careful speech.** Have your child concentrate on speaking slowly and carefully. There is no rush to finish, and speaking somewhat deliberately is a sign of mature speech.

3. **Focus on posture.** Formal and informal speech is often distinguished by posture. Have your child stand straight—with his shoulders back, although not unnaturally so. The important thing about posture is that the your child should stand in such a way as to express confidence. He can also begin improving his hand gestures and facial expressions.

## MAKE IT MEMORABLE!

Use speeches to create a positive atmosphere in your home. Reminisce about shared memories and anticipate future family experiences. You can do this through the "three things I like" speech. For example, "Three things I like about Grandpa," or "Three things I am looking forward to at the fair."

# NOTES

# MYSTERY PROJECTS

## PROJECT SKETCH

This project shows you how to increase your child's interest in speech through suspense, enthusiasm, and curiosity. It is not as much a specific speech activity as an exciting way for your child to learn communication skills without thinking about it. These activities reinforce the need for creating curiosity, building it, sustaining it and fulfilling it.

## HOW-TO

1. **Mystery letter.** Write and send your child an "anonymous" letter with strange characteristics such as misspelled words, smeared with something that forms a clue. Include a clue or promise a reward if he performs a certain task, such as memorizing a certain Bible verse or poem, putting it on tape and burying it in a designated spot. You can continue the project or add creative variations as you wish.

2. **Treasure hunt.** Have a "pirate" hide a treasure with a clue hidden on a piece of map paper in the chapter of a book your child is assigned to read. You could reward his work with pieces of a map so that after the completion of a set number of tasks he can find the treasure.

## FUTURE ADVENTURES

1. **Use video or audio tape to record the messenger's voice and the child's response.** Be expressive, and encourage your child's expressiveness.

2. **Ask your friends to help.** You probably have some friends who are good enough sports to dress up in

costumes for a mystery project. Even a slight disguise will throw your child off their scent.

### TIMELY TIP

Make *learning* a requirement for solving the mystery. At the same time, do not make the tasks so difficult as to discourage the child from trying. Also, use creative mystery sparingly. Otherwise you will run yourself ragged trying to conceive new ideas, and your child may become bored. These projects are best used to "spice up" a topic during a learning dry spell.

### MAKE IT MEMORABLE!

Invite special guests. If you know people who are knowledgeable about the subjects your child is studying, invite them to visit. For instance, during a study of a war, find a war veteran who will come visit, preferably someone your child will know. They can send an old picture or photocopy of a newspaper article, anonymously, saying "I was there at the battle of _____. To find out more about it, read the encyclopedia." All the clues come together when the person arrives to give a presentation and answer questions.

# CHAPTER SIXTEEN

# AGES THIRTEEN AND UP

By age thirteen, the seeds you have planted over a life-time will begin to bear fruit in your child's life. To many parents, this is a highly discouraging prospect! Don't despair. The teen years are often marked by an awkward transition into adulthood. While steady, fast improvement in communication ability is certainly not the norm in teenagers, you can expect that activities such as those in this section will help your child emerge as an articulate, graceful young adult.

During the period starting at about age thirteen, your child will reach the most advanced level of communication. Thus, this chapter will focus on all kinds of skills required of an excellent communicator, from critical thinking to the ability to "think on your feet." In order to give you an idea of why the activities in this section have been chosen as they have, let's take an inventory of what a socially adept adolescent should be able to do communicatively.

## TRAITS OF A SOCIALLY-ADEPT ADOLESCENT

I know what you're thinking: "What if my teen doesn't measure up?" Don't worry. First, these traits are goals to strive for, not measures of intelligence. Second, the very fact that you and your teen are focusing on these skills will put him ahead of others his age. Incidentally, if your teen is experiencing great difficulty in any of these areas, review

**Ironically,**

**during the very**

**time of their**

**lives when**

**teens are**

**yearning for**

**independence,**

**parental**

**influence and**

**involvement is**

**increasingly**

**vital.**

the related projects in the section on eight-to-twelve-year-olds to strengthen his foundation.

Here are some expectations that the projects in this section are designed to meet:

- **Interpersonal skills.** A socially-adept teenager should know how to greet others and have a conversation with them. He should be able to recognize the feelings and emotions of others, and express accurate emotions himself. He should also know how to communicate *acceptance* to other people.

- **Ability to research and organize information.** Your teen will need to know his way around a library, become proficient at using a set of encyclopedias, and discover how to look up information in periodicals, on CD-Rom, and on the Internet. I have included an exercise in library research in this section as a means of bringing attention to this vital skill.

- **How to phrase thoughts.** As an adolescent, it will be important for your child to know how to organize and express his thoughts. He needs to be able to answer a question with "This is what I think and here's why" type answers.

- **Critique information.** According to the National Assessment of Educational Progress, nearly 40 percent of 13-year-olds lack the ability to locate information or make generalizations based on what they read. It is even more important that your child, as he enters the teen years, be able to recognize the good and bad elements of information he is exposed to. Critical inquiry takes advantage of a teen's natural inquisitiveness and argumentativeness. As Douglas Wilson states in *Recovering the Lost Tools of Learning,* "If you encourage disagreement for disagreement's sake, then you will get disagreeable children. But if you teach them that it is good to question (provided the questioning is intellectually rigorous and honest), then you are *educating*."

- **Exercise well-developed delivery skills.** During the teen years, you will begin expecting your child to act like an adult. Being able to demonstrate eye contact, energetic body language and vocal enthusiasm will be important for your teen to interact in an adult world, especially in speaking situations.

- **Understand persuasion.** In order to critically evaluate the world around them, as well as to make an effective speech, your child will need to know what makes a message persuasive and how to create persuasive messages himself.

## WHAT IS MY ROLE AS A PARENT?

Frankly, the question most parents ask about teens is not, "How do I teach my teen to communicate," but, "How do I communicate with my teen?" Ironically, during the very time of teen's lives when they are yearning for independence, parental influence and involvement is increasingly vital. Do not make the erroneous assumption that because your child is growing up, he does not need as much love, understanding and acceptance. In fact, he may need more.

What is a parent's role in the life of a teenager as it regards communication skill development?

1. **Continue to challenge your teen.** As a parent, you have the opportunity to give your teen a broad base of experience during his teen years. You can continue to provide him with a challenging environment, help him develop new goals, and encourage him to improve his communication skills.

2. **Help your teen discover his purpose in life.** I am told that the number one fear of adolescents is that they will not discover their purpose in life. As a parent, you can continue to encourage your teen in this pursuit, allowing him to explore various trades, hobbies and interests. According to Dr. Ross Campbell in *Kids Who Follow, Kids Who Don't,* having one or two well-defined areas of interest will help a teen avoid the boredom that often leads to a disastrous teen experience.

3. **Listen to your teen.** It will take work to understand the messages your teen is giving and the feelings he is experiencing. It is almost impossible for us to remember our teen years well enough to identify with our own teenage children. Dr. Kathryn Koch suggests that interacting with your teens requires a lot of "active listening." To that end, she offers "clarifying comments" that create communication with teens. Here are some sample clarifying comments:

- "So what you're saying is _____. Right?"

- "You feel I'm being unfair because none of your friends have the same rule."

- "You sound like you find that assignment boring."

- "You seem to feel left out and lonely because it is hard to make friends at the new church."

- "How do you feel about what happened?"

- "What is your reason for saying (or doing) this?"

- "Can you give me an example of what you mean?"

- "What else can you tell me that will help me understand?"

- "What's the most important part of what you're telling me?"

  It is important to note that listening in this way does not obligate you to believe and give your assent to everything your teen says and does. However, it does give you a way to make sure he knows you are *really listening*. He recognizes that he is important to you, that you trust him, and that he can continue to communicate with you.

4. **Communicate acceptance.** It is all too easy, in your effort to challenge your child, to give him the impression that you will not accept him unless he conforms to your expectations. This is potentially disastrous, especially if your expectations are not clear. As a high school student, Justin Swets surveyed his classmates and discovered that there are five messages that every teen desperately wants to hear. These five messages are recorded by his father, Paul Swets, in *How to Talk so Your Teenager Will Listen*. These should come through loud and clear on a regular basis:

- "I'm proud of you." This encourages your teen to set high goals and creates a strong desire to reach them. It communicates that you are on his side, win or lose.

- "You can always come to me with anything and I will listen and try to understand." Your communication with your teenager will be his lifeline through difficult times. In order to earn the right to hear him, work on giving him your undivided attention, use clarifying comments, do not ridicule him, and do your best to understand.

- "I want to understand you." This will motivate your teen to keep trying to communicate with you even if it is a struggle.

- "I trust you." The teen years are the perfect time to establish an "elevator" of trust and responsibility, a system where your teen earns freedoms when he can demonstrate a mature ability to take responsibility. Communicate to your child that there are clear ways to gain additional trust. Outline the system you choose for him so he can set goals based on it.

- "I love you." Dr. Ross Campbell notes with sadness that the very time when children need an increasing amount of love and acceptance is usually the very time where we begin to deny it to them. It never hurts to say, "I love you." Your love may be the anchor which holds your teen firm in a restless sea of ungodly philosophies and temptations.

## TAKE ADVANTAGE OF REAL WORLD OPPORTUNITIES

There are a multitude of opportunities for teenagers to develop communication skills. The organizations listed here will give your teen practice, assistance, and most important, an audience.

1. **4-H Clubs.** If you live in rural America, 4-H Clubs offer an excellent opportunity for the development of communication and leadership skills. Your child will be able to participate in and run meetings by a strict parliamentary system and give demonstration speeches at contests; he will learn to try out new things and develop talents in new areas. Contact the county extension office in your county (or parish).

2. **Toastmasters, Jr.** Toastmasters is a "civic organization," their stated goal being to help members of the community improve their speech skills. Many Toastmasters clubs have now established a junior club, so high school students can learn the same skills. Look in the Yellow Pages under "community organizations" to see if a chapter has been formed in your community.

3. **Contests sponsored by civic organizations.** Civic organizations are a part of nearly every community. Many of them take the responsibility for encouraging leadership development in young people, especially in the area of speech. The Optimist Club International sponsors speech contests, judged by club members, in which any student age 12 to 16 may participate. The topic usually calls for a four-minute motivational speech (ie., "Destiny: Choice or Chance?"). Another organization to contact is the American Legion, whose speech contests offer college scholarships and the opportunity to advance to a national tournament. Again, check the Yellow Pages for "Civic Organizations" or "Community Organizations."

4. **Bible clubs.** Child Evangelism Fellowship hosts *Christian Youth in Action* programs in nearly every state. These programs train teens during a ten-week seminar to run "Five-day Clubs," summer Bible clubs for neighborhood children. For additional information, contact C. E. F. in Warrenton, Missouri.

5. **Church school, Sunday school or children's youth clubs (such as AWANA).** Nearly every church is looking for teenagers to assist in teaching younger children. Your teen will have the opportunity to give lessons, conduct puppet shows, and generally be a positive influence in the life of a younger child.

6. **Speeches at Civic Organizations.** Many civic organizations are willing to listen to speeches by young people at their meetings. These organizations include the Optimist Club, Rotary Club, Lions Club, Jaycees, Kiwanis, Sertoma, Disabled American Veterans, Serenity Club, Christian Businessmen's Committee, Women Aglow, American Legion, Veterans of Foreign Wars, International Association of Business Communicators, military club gatherings, political party meetings, and senior citizens clubs. Your teen should contact them when he has a speech already developed, and offer to come speak whenever they cannot find a speaker or have a last-minute cancellation. One national leader I know started his career in leadership by impressing community leaders through speaking to these associations. Check the Yellow Pages for organizations in your area, and have your teen write them a letter describing his speech topic and asking for the opportunity to present it. You never know what might happen!

Speeches for these organizations should focus on a teenager's perspective on an issue, stories about people who have overcome great difficulties, or book reviews (reading and then drawing out important lessons for those who might not have time to read).

7. **Mission trips.** Many missionary organizations offer short-term missions which give young people the opportunity to travel, teach, evangelize and participate in building projects. Some of these organizations encourage young people to learn drama and mime as a way of communicating across language barriers. What an excellent way to accomplish several of your goals for your child, while building strong communication skills in the process!

The teenage years are a fantastic time to build communication skills. The ability to communicate fluently and in a socially appropriate way will smooth the transition to adulthood for your teen. Perseverance on your part, even through the rough times, will be rewarded by the emergence of a confident communicator.

# NOTES

# GETTING TO KNOW THE LIBRARY

## PROJECT SKETCH

It has often been said that, "If you want to be a leader, you've got to be a reader." Leaders are masters of great ideas, and great ideas come largely from reading. This exercise is only indirectly related to communication skills, but it reinforces critical thinking skills and sets your teen on the path to discovering something worthwhile on which to speak!

It is wise to have a personal collection of good books, as well as subscriptions to newspapers, newsletters and magazines. It is also important to visit a library for about two hours each week. One hour should be spent culling through periodicals from that week and month; the other should be spent on a research project. Assist your teen in brainstorming a topic that interests him and then assign research goals.

## HOW-TO

1. **Make an appointment with the librarian for a tour.** You will discover resources you didn't know existed! Most libraries carry microfilm and microfiche records of newspapers a hundred years old, pictures of your town, historical records, and computer access programs which connect the library's computer to larger research facilities. Be sure to spend time playing with the computer access terminals if available, or perusing the card catalog or *Readers Guide to Periodical Literature*.

2. **Invent research games which will require your teen to be creative in his search for information.** Have the librarian help you discover an obscure fact (see

the example below) as well as clues as to how it might be discovered by your teen. Like a trivia game, each clue should be successively easier, the goal being to discover the information with as few clues as possible. Devise a point system to reward his perceptiveness. Here is an example taken from *Can You Find It?*, a clever book full of library scavenger hunts.

*"Knowing I lov'd my books, he furnish'd me, from mine own library with volumes that I prize above my duke-dom."* This quotation is taken from what famous play?

*Clue 1. What you need is a violent brainstorm — a sort of tempest of the temporal lobes, as it were.*

*Clue 2. Shakespeare and Bartlett's...what a pear.*

*Answer: Shakespeare's play "The Tempest," the quote found in* Bartlett's Familiar Quotations.

## FUTURE ADVENTURE

Research something in-depth, such as the history of your town. Examine historical records, old newspapers, and interviews with old-timers. Choose a project which requires you and your teen to use a wide variety of resource materials. When in high school, I researched the history of the railroad in our town, read old newspapers on microfilm, interviewed a retired railroad employee, and took slides of local landmarks. This project will make an excellent presentation to community organizations, and it can also be a great parent/child or family activity.

## TIMELY TIPS

Make use of many different kinds of resources: newspapers, magazines, microfilm, books, and reference tools.

Remember: in research, it's not what you know but how much access you have to what is known by others!

## MAKE IT MEMORABLE!

Try a library scavenger hunt. Scavenger hunts are a common party theme, but you can throw your party-goers a curve by making a bit of library research part of yours. Find some obscure piece of trivia which forms the clue to something else. Be careful to reinforce the library's rules (maybe subtract points for those who run or are loud in the library). It is an off-beat idea—will teens go for it? They might! It just depends on how badly they want to solve the puzzle and win the competition!

# NOTES

# CRITICAL INQUIRY

## PROJECT SKETCH

The purpose of this project is to 1) give your teen four key questions he can use to critically analyze difficult and complex issues, and 2) introduce the idea of analyzing the media. This project is not intended to make your teen argumentative, but to teach him how to get to the heart of a matter. A polite persistent argument can be a good educational experience.

## HOW-TO

### 1. Teach your teen the key questions to critical inquiry:

- *"What do you mean by _____?"* Always ask for a definition of the key terms. Socrates said, "If you wish to debate with me, you must first of all define your terms."

- *"How do you know that to be true?"* Always question how a particular fact is known. Most people blindly miss this step, and assume that because a statement is made in a factual way, it must be true.

- *"Where do you get your information?"* What is the source of the fact in question, and can it be verified? Much of what the media calls factual is based on dubious "studies," or shallow analysis of issues. The key to the ultimate success of this question is intensive library research.

- *"What happens if you are wrong?"* Most people don't like to think that they might be wrong, but you must ask what is at stake in holding the position they do.

2. **Analyze the news.** Begin with editorials or letters to the editor which are hostile to your family's beliefs. Your teen can use the above four questions as tools of analysis to uncover flaws in reasoning. If he has difficulty, reveal some of the red flags a particular piece raises for you. Ask the following questions: Which sides are presented? Who are the sources and how are they characterized? What is the tone of the report? What underlying assumptions does the news story hold? How is an action described? What statistics are used? What is *left out* of the news story? What words, negative or positive, are used to describe the incident, people involved, position taken, or emotions expressed?

### FUTURE ADVENTURE

Rewrite the headlines and news articles. For example, Ruth Beechick suggests you select a headline about your town's sports team to rewrite as the headline might have appeared in the town of the other team.

### TIMELY TIP

Analyze the differences between news articles and editorials. Clip out articles and editorials on the same topic. What is the difference between the two? Outline the arguments used by the editorial writer, and compare them to the article. Is the article completely neutral?

### MAKE IT MEMORABLE!

Advance your family's skills of critical inquiry by finding a book at the library on logical fallacies. A logical fallacy is an argument that appears to be logical but is actually illogical. Consider, for example, the fallacy of "ad hominem," meaning "to the man." This is an argument which tries to stop the discussion through a personal attack, such as when a secular humanist dismisses Christians as "extreme right-wing fundamentalists." There are dozens of logical fallacies which may be studied and even posted in your home to help you analyze the flaws in newspaper articles, editorials, editorial cartoons, and television news reports.

# NOTES

# ADVANCED LISTENING SKILLS

## PROJECT SKETCH

The ability to listen to others is a sign of maturity. This project introduces advanced listening skills which your teen can exercise in observing the world around him.

## HOW-TO

The goal of this exercise is to practice listening skills in two contexts: during a speech and during a one-on-one conversation.

1. **Listening to a speech.** We indicate our listening skill by our ability to recall what was said. Humans can absorb information three to ten times faster than a speaker can present it, so our minds tend to wander during speeches unless we exercise self-discipline. The best way to teach your teen to listen to a speaker is to have him take notes. Encourage him to write down the main thrust of the speech, the main points used to support it, one or two words which remind him of the supporting evidence used, and comments about the mannerisms and speaking style exhibited by the speaker, good and bad. Take notes yourself, and review with your teen after the speech.

2. **Listening in conversation.** There are at least six definable steps to being a good listener in a conversation: Be attentive, Show interest, Reflect back, Clarify, Re-state everything, and Summarize. To examine these steps in detail, refer to the chapter earlier in this book on helping your child relate to others. This process takes a long time, and is rarely carried through to completion. However, it will help

your teen understand the process more clearly if you deliberately go through the steps, practicing a response even if it seems silly.

For purposes of feedback, review the listening rules with your teen before going into a conversational setting. Check each other's listening behavior and offer feedback.

## FUTURE ADVENTURE

Look for opportunities for you and your teen to practice listening skills. Volunteer to provide child care at a public event (younger children love to talk, but just need someone to listen), participate as a counselor at an evangelistic crusade, learn peer counseling skills, volunteer at a crisis pregnancy center or crisis hotline, or sign up for the visitation team at your church.

## TIMELY TIP

Listening may require your family to set new priorities. Even if it takes a great deal of self-control to listen actively, resolve to always *listen* to people rather than brushing them aside. Resolve in advance that you will listen patiently. The resulting patience will develop deeper character in both parent and teen.

## MAKE IT MEMORABLE!

Present listening to your family as a key to gaining wisdom. Proverbs 1:5 says, "Let the wise listen and add to their learning." We can learn something from everyone, no matter how irrelevant it seems at the time. Create a climate in your family where you are known by others as good listeners, and reinforce the process by thinking about the wisdom gained in listening.

# INTERVIEW

## PROJECT SKETCH

Interviewing is a highly useful way to gain information. It involves telephone and/or face-to-face encounters with those who might be informed about an issue, or with those who can give a sampling of public opinion. You can give your teen some basic interviewing skills in a short period of time, and in so doing, give him opportunities to gain courage and astuteness.

Refer, if necessary, to the "Question-Asking" project in the section for children ages eight to twelve, in which we discussed how to formulate questions to ask in a conversational setting. Below, I have suggested two specific projects which you might use or modify to give your teen the opportunity to gain interviewing experience.

## HOW-TO

1. **Interview an elected official.** Call the office of an elected official and arrange to have an interview. Express to the official or to the assistant what kinds of questions you would like to ask (i.e., that you are studying how government operates and want to know more about what they do). Prepare the questions in advance.

2. **Surveys.** Any time you are studying a particular issue, conduct a survey of the public. For example, if you are studying the history of communism, put together a survey which asks people, "Is communism dead?" as well as other related questions. Your teen can conduct the surveys anywhere: the public park, city hall, or a local mall (most malls are privately owned, so check with the management office first). The value of this

exercise is that you get a clearer idea of what people are thinking about the issue. Moreover, your teen learns to be bold in approaching total strangers and communicating with them, and he also gets interesting material for a speech. You might need to help your teen write questions objectively. For example, if he is assembling a survey on abortion, your teen should ask, "Are you for or against abortion?" rather than "Are you for or against killing babies?"

### FUTURE ADVENTURE

For an extra assignment, your teen can call the local newspaper and talk them into letting him write a "special editorial" from a teen perspective on the elected official he will be interviewing. When the official discovers that your teen has been "commissioned" by the newspaper, an interview will almost certainly be granted! Note: While representing the newspaper is an exciting option for this project, keep in mind that it will change the dynamic of the interview, and the elected official may be more cautious and hard to get to know personally.

### TIMELY TIPS

1. **Be willing to do whatever you ask your teen to do!** Accompany him on the interviews and surveys—at least at first. He should learn to do it by himself eventually.

2. **Interviews are a good time to practice active listening.** Review some of the listening principles before you go.

3. **Watch television news reporters conducting interviews, and critique them.** What did they do right or wrong.

## MAKE IT MEMORABLE!

Use interviews to reinforce your teen's sense of purpose in life. The following variation on the public opinion poll was suggested by Beverly Norsworthy, a teacher from New Zealand. She assigns students the topic of "How God has been good to me." They interview their parents and grandparents, and assemble in the process a clearer understanding of how God has worked through history to affect each of their lives.

## NOTES

# BEING ASSERTIVE

## PROJECT SKETCH

As your child enters his teen years, it is vital that he learn to communicative assertively, especially in saying *no* when enticed to do something that is either wrong or would reflect wrong priorities. Assertiveness will help your teenager recognize when someone is trying to manipulate him, and know how to counter it.

## HOW-TO

You can teach your teen this skill through role plays, where you or another teen serve as the helper. Role plays should be conducted imagining that both people are equal, that one is not the authority figure.

1. Saying no. Create a situation in which the helper is trying to manipulate your teen into doing something wrong (i.e., underage drinking). The helper's pressure should become increasingly intense, and so should the answers by your teen. Here is an example (Asserter remarks are in italics):

1. Will you help me write my paper?
   *No, that would be cheating.*

2. Come on, please?
   *No.*

3. Just say yes. I need your help.
   *No.*

4. Why not?
   *I have said no three times, and I am getting irritated with your pressuring me. Will you please stop asking me?*

5. I asked you why not.
   *I gave you my reason; it would be cheating.*

6. Pretty please?
   *I said no. If that does not satisfy you, then I will end the conversation. Is that the only option you are leaving me with?*

7. Without your helping me, I'll fail. You don't want me to fail, do you?
   *Are you trying to make me feel guilty?*

8. No, I just thought we were friends.
   *Are you saying that unless I do what you want, I am not your friend?*

9. No. Oh well, just forget it.
   *Gladly. Let's change the subject.*

NOTE: The asserter is under no obligation to explain his answer beyond his initial reason unless he chooses to do so. The goal is to be consistent in the answer, and aggressive in not allowing the other person to manipulate.

### FUTURE ADVENTURE

Try other role plays such as refusing to take drugs or use alcohol, go to an inappropriate movie, help in a worthy, but time-consuming cause, skip work to do something fun, or neglect homework to goof around.

### TIMELY TIP

Persevere! Role plays are difficult because participants often feel giggly or uncomfortable at first. Keep going until you get some results.

## MAKE IT MEMORABLE!

Make this technique an integral part of teaching your children values and character. For each character quality, think of an opposing force that will try to destroy it (e.g., sexual purity vs. premarital sex). Help your teen recognize the forces at play and how to counter them.

## NOTES

# BEING PERSISTENT

## PROJECT SKETCH

Persistence is a vital character quality for a confident communicator. Your teen must know how to ask directly for what he wants, without manipulating, and stick with it until he gets a straight answer. This does not mean "nagging" someone or trying to trick or bribe them into doing what he wants. Instead, it encourages healthy ideas of persuasion.

### HOW-TO

In this role play, the helper tries to avoid saying yes to a request that is honest and direct. He sidetracks, gives very indirect "no's" and tries to change the subject. The asserter persists until he gets a direct response. Try role plays asking the person to participate in a church drama, working with him on a project, or doing an assignment that has been required of them both.

Here is an example of how it might work. (Asserter remarks are in italics):

1. *Will you participate in the church drama this year?*
   Well, I don't know.

2. *We could really use your help. What do you say?*
   Where is it going to be held?

3. *At the church. Will you help?*
   The acoustics in there are pretty bad.

4. *The acoustics won't affect what I am asking you to do. Will you help?*
   How much time will it take?

5. *About an hour and a half each day for a month. I would like to have your help.*
Speaking of dramas, did you see the new movie at the theater?

6. *I have asked you three times, and you haven't given me a direct answer yet. Will you give me a direct answer?*
Well, hmmm.

7. *Is that a yes or a no?*
I'm not sure. I'll have to think about it.

8. *Okay. May I check back tomorrow?*
Yes, that would be fine.

Notice that the asserter didn't demand a "yes," but he *did* insist on a direct answer. The asserter should not pressure or plead, or act in any way as if he expects a "yes" answer.

## TIMELY TIP

Practice non-verbal communication. Your teen and the helper should sit forward rather than slouch, and maintain eye contact.

## FUTURE ADVENTURE

Write out several situations to try as a family or with a group of teens. Put them in a box to draw from. Each person should take a turn as the asserter and as the helper.

## MAKE IT MEMORABLE!

Learn how to recognize manipulation. Manipulation is attempting to get someone to do what *you* want by making them feel guilty. It is one of the most unhealthy forms of communication because it is almost always selfish, having no concern for the interests or feelings of the other person. Manipulative people are usually afraid of being rejected or have found manipulation to be an effective means of getting what they want. As "teachable moments" arise, show your child how communication can be manipulative. For instance, role play what to do if a friend of your child says, "If you're my friend, you'll do it." or "What are you, a chicken?" Your child should be able to respond with, "I am your friend, but I will not do what you ask." or "I think you are calling me a chicken because you can't think of another way to get me to do something that I don't want to do."

# NOTES

# COMMONPLACES

### PROJECT SKETCH

"Commonplaces" are the secret behind the incredible memory and speech powers of ancient Greek and Roman orators. A commonplace is a means of organizing and remembering a speech by picturing in one's mind the segments of the speech as the "commonplaces" in a house. Through time the term "commonplaces" has evolved to refer to short "mini-speeches" which are pieced together in various combinations to form longer speeches. Cicero is said to have used this technique to memorize three-hour-long speeches word-for-word!

### HOW-TO

Use the "commonplaces" technique to help your teen speak more confidently and to give him something to contribute on a variety of topics. Follow these steps:

**1. Format.**

   I. Introduction. A short statement about the topic at hand. *"One of the most important traits of a leader is that he has the courage to say what needs to be said and do what needs to be done."*

   II. Quotation. A memorable comment by a memorable character. *"We need leaders like Winston Churchill. He refused to give in, even when it looked as if Germany would certainly win. He said, 'We shall go on to the end. We shall never surrender.' His courage motivated the people to press on."* An alternative is to tell a story or give an illustration.

   III. Bible verse. *"Many times in the Bible, God encouraged his chosen leaders to have courage. He told Joshua four* times to 'Be strong and courageous for the Lord thy God is with thee.'"

IV. Concluding remark. "*Next time you face a difficult situation, remember that God will give you the courage you need to do the right thing.*"

2. **Choose character-building topics for commonplaces:** courage, honesty, trust, kindness, mercy, integrity, vision, perseverance, responsibility, and others.

3. **Use books of quotations and a Bible concordance to find quotes to memorize.**

4. **Your teen should be able to develop at least one new commonplace each week and recite it when called on, even on the spur of the moment.** He should also be able to combine two or three related commonplaces to make a short speech.

## FUTURE ADVENTURE

Use commonplaces to stimulate conversation. Much of this book focuses on conversational communication skills. When having a conversation with someone, you and your teen can use your quotes or Bible verses to encourage them.

## TIMELY TIP

Don't be afraid to use humorous quotations or even a humorous approach to the ideas at hand. This will be good practice when it comes time for your teen to start giving speeches in public. Humor is greatly appreciated by an audience, and the ability of a speaker to use it confidently will depend on how familiar they are with his material.

FOR THE RECORD: "Humor" which makes fun of who people are (i.e., their nationality, race, physical infirmity, or mental deficiency) is not funny. To get laughs at the expense of the way God created someone is to mock God. Instead, good humor should be based on cleverness: laughing at yourself, telling a story with a cleverly constructed punch line, or surprising your audience with the unexpected.

## MAKE IT MEMORABLE!

Use the commonplaces technique to supplement Bible memory. Surround each verse memorized with a commonplace to put it in context and perhaps make memory easier. Each verse becomes a ready-made tool of encouragement!

NOTES

# IMPROMPTU SPEECHES

## PROJECT SKETCH

The word "impromptu" means "without preparation or advance thought." An impromptu speech is one given off-the-cuff. We have all, on occasion, been asked to stand up and give our ideas, or even been pushed to the podium with cries of, "Speech! Speech!" The impromptu speech project will give your teen excellent practice at thinking on his feet. He will learn to speak confidently and thoughtfully in public, whether or not the situation requires a speech.

## HOW-TO

1. **Format.** An impromptu speech for this exercise should be at least one minute but not more than three minutes in length, with an introduction, one or two points, and a conclusion. Your teen should be allowed no more than one minute to collect his thoughts and begin speaking.

2. **Topics.** Think of about 50 topics in advance and write them on slips of paper. Topics might include: "My most embarrassing moment," "Something exciting," "Mosquitoes," "My brother (or sister)," "What I would like to be," "My greatest dream," "If I could buy anything...," "The Presidency," "Climbing trees," and "Bubble gum." Let's look at a sample speech on bubble gum. This example may be more complex than your teen will attempt at first, but given practice, he'll improve.

> *Our topic today is bubble gum. When I think of bubble gum, I remember one horrible experience of chewing bubble gum in school where it was expressly forbidden. After about half an hour, my jaws started to hurt, so I*

*tried to dispose of the gum discreetly. I took it out of my mouth and just then, the teacher got up from her desk! In my haste to cover my misdeed, I dropped the gum. And wouldn't you know it, I dropped it right in the aisle. I learned my lesson that day—actually for about 30 minutes after school that day. Of course, with all of the problems in our schools today, I bet a lot of teachers would wish for the kind of problem I caused that day! In response to that I say, "Get rid of the guns and knives and bring back bubble gum!"*

## FUTURE ADVENTURE

After some practice, move on to "extemporaneous" speeches, in which the speaker has 30 minutes to prepare a speech and memorize it. These speeches should be on important issues of the day. With manila folders, devise a topical filing system to organize newspaper articles and editorials to use as resources for this kind of speech.

## TIMELY TIP

The secret to impromptu speaking is using the 60 seconds of preparation time to think of a couple of main points, and if there is time left, one quick, memorable example. Don't try to think about what words to use. As your teen becomes more proficient, make topics increasingly complex. Your teen should be able to move on to more difficult topics after about 20 speeches.

## MAKE IT MEMORABLE!

Try impromptu speaking yourself! This is a family exercise, so do not ask your teen to do what *you* are unwilling to do. Take turns drawing topics and giving speeches!

# ORGANIZING A SPEECH

Commonplaces and impromptu speeches are the building blocks of effective speaking. However, most speeches are more complex, and must be planned more carefully to have a full effect on the audience. This activity takes you through the steps necessary to devise a speech topic and gives your teen the opportunity to practice various elements of a speech.

## How-To

### 1. WHO IS IT I AM TRYING TO REACH?

**A. What is the audience like?** Are they business people? Stay-at-home moms? War veterans? Church members? As you reflect on the composition of the audience, perhaps it would be helpful to narrow down their various characteristics to one defining characteristic. Ask yourself, "What one thing, more than anything else, do the members of this audience have in common?"

- Think of possible audiences to whom your teenager might speak, and ask him to write down as many things as he can about the audience. Characteristics to consider include age, gender, race, national origin, economic status, spiritual maturity, and level of education.

**B. Why is this audience meeting?** What are the audience members' expectations? If you are giving a speech on "How to become involved in the community," you might "spin" your topic for different audiences. For example, if your audience is a Sunday school class, tie community involvement into the audience's sense of their spiritual responsibilities to those around them. If the audience is an Optimist Club, give its already active members ideas on how to persuade *others* to become involved. With a group of high school students, focus on convincing them that high school students can make a difference.

- Make a list of possible speech topics, hypothesizing several possible audiences for each topic. Give the list to your teenager and have him brainstorm ideas about reaching them.

C. **What are the needs of the audience?** Most audiences will unconsciously ask, "What can you do for me?" In other words, audiences may not listen simply because you have something to say. They will listen when they are convinced that they can benefit from the information you give. Your persuasive appeal carries considerably more weight if you understand what makes the audience tick.

- Ask your teenager to reflect on what *motivates* people. What are people really concerned about? Some possible motivations include *service* (doing the will of God or helping others), *status* (good standing in the eyes of others), *security* (self-preservation, financial well-being), *freedom from restraint* (freedom to do as they wish, such as to make beneficial economic and social choices), *attractiveness* (how they appear to others), and *sense of adventure* (how their life can be more exciting and rewarding).

## 2. WHAT WOULD I LIKE THE AUDIENCE TO DO OR BELIEVE?

There are many different organizational formats for speeches. For the purposes of this chapter, we will focus on speeches to *inform* and speeches to *persuade*.

A central element of these two basic formats is explaining clearly what you want the audience to do or believe. For some reason, audiences tend to miss the main point unless it is clearly and repeatedly stated. One study demonstrated that 70% of audience members, at the end of an average speech, could not describe the main point the speaker was trying to convey! Here are two ideas which combat that tendency:

A. **What do you wish to say?** What is the purpose of the speech? Write down as many ideas as you can, even if it takes several pages. From that list, highlight one point which seems to stick out, and no more than three points which logically explain that one point. Leave everything else for future speeches.

- Once your teen has written down his ideas, ask him to do two things:

  Complete the statement, "This speech is about _____." Use one to four words only.

  Write a topic sentence, such as, "The purpose of this speech is to _____ by _____." As professional speaker Ken Davis warns, "If you can't write the objective of your speech in a single sentence, then either you're trying to say too much or you don't know what you're talking about."

B. **Why is this important?** First, why do you wish to give this speech? Second, why is this topic important to the *audience?*

- Ask your teen to write down as many ideas as he can, based on a topic he chooses or the topics used above. This will help him clarify his thoughts, become convinced of the importance of the topic, and develop enthusiasm about it.

## 3. HOW CAN I MAKE SURE MY MESSAGE REACHES THE AUDIENCE?

**A. How do I get the audience's attention?** A speaker can win or lose the audience's attention within the first minute, so the speaker's first words should be carefully planned through an "attention device." Here are a few effective devices:

- **Rhetorical Question.** A rhetorical question is one which gets the audience thinking about your topic. It usually is not a question they can answer immediately, nor should it be. For instance, if you are giving a speech on behalf of a candidate for Congress, you might ask, "Did you realize that today you have the opportunity to make a simple decision which will change Congress forever?" Some popular rhetorical questions include "Did you know _____," "Have you ever _____," "What would happen if _____," or "Do you suppose…?"

- **Storytelling.** Dramatic stories which relate to the topic are highly effective in winning and maintaining the audience's attention. *Personal stories* are often the most effective, because they relate the speaker and his topic and emotionally involve the audience at the same time. Audiences like stories which communicate "shared values." That is, they want to hear about people who have dealt with the same kinds of issues they face. Stories should be short and to the point, contain plot and dialogue, and *clearly relate to the speech topic*.

- **Shocking Statement.** A shocking statement is simply a dramatic statement which focuses the attention of the audience. I once heard a speaker talk about getting the most out of life. He began his speech by boldly and loudly proclaiming, "There is one statistic of which all intellectuals, scientists and social scientists alike are absolutely certain: One out of every one person...*dies*." His shocking statement was funny and somewhat unexpected, thus it was highly effective in winning the audience and drawing them into his subject. When using this technique, remember to take into consideration the sensibilities of the audience. The point of a shocking statement is to get the audience's attention, not disgust them!

- **Dramatic Interpretation.** In my father's college speech course, one student inconspicuously began a speech by saying "Today, we will discuss the issue of self-defense. Why? Because you never know when..." Just then, the classroom door flew open, and in charged a rough-looking individual, shouting at the speaker: "There you are, you little twerp!" The speaker deftly blocked the attack, twisted the attacker around, knocked him to the floor, and sternly admonished, "Now get out of here, and don't come back!" As the attacker scrambled out of the room, the speaker turned to the audience said, "As I was saying, you never know when you will need to defend yourself!" He then demonstrated several simple self-defense maneuvers to his newly invigorated audience!

B. **How do I relate the topic to the audience?** To move the audience to do or believe what you are suggesting, you must point out the inconsistency between what audience members know they ought to be, and what they actually are. If you can show audience members that their actions are not consistent with their behavior, they are likely to stick around to hear how to become consistent again.

**C. How do I organize the speech for maximum impact?**
The way I listen to speeches changed forever with a sixteen-word piece of advice I heard when I was thirteen years old: *"Tell 'em what you're gonna tell 'em, then tell 'em, then tell 'em what you told 'em."* Effective speakers heed this advice by outlining the topic in the introduction, highlighting the main points in the body of the speech, and then reviewing the main points in the conclusion.

- How does one organize the individual *points* in a speech for maximum impact? One highly effective technique is the S. T. E. P. system taught by Dr. Lee Polk of Baylor University, one of the nation's foremost speech consultants. Here are the elements of the system, along with sample ideas for each point:

In order to describe the S. T. E. P. system, I have tied it into a sample speech on "Remembering Names."

## S = STATE

**Topic sentence**
*"The first way to improve your ability to remember people's names is called 'association.'"*

## T=TRANSLATE

**Definition**
*"To 'associate' something means tying it to something vivid and memorable."*

**Explanation**
*"As a memory technique, you would associate the name you want to remember with something that rhymes with it or something about that name that makes it stand out."*

### Analogy

"Associating the name you want to remember with something memorable is like attaching a permanent name tag to that person."

## E=EXEMPLIFY

### Example

"For example, let's say you meet someone named Fred Eaton. You notice that he is very skinny. You can remember 'Fred' by 'afraid' and 'Eaton,' with 'eating.' So whenever you see ol' skinny Fred Eaton you will remember his name by thinking that he is 'afraid of eating,' that's why he's so skinny."

### Personal Experience

"I once met a woman named Mary Friedlander. I discovered that she and her husband had recently moved to the country to begin farming. When I met her, she was wearing jeans and cowboy boots. I remembered her last name by thinking of being 'free in the land,' and her first name by thinking of her being 'merry' living in the country, thus remembering that Mary Friedlander was 'merry' being 'free in the land.'"

## P= PROVE

### Statistic

"I have discovered that I can remember 50% more names, and retain them for about twice as long using this method than just sheer memory power."

### Testimony

"Association really works. As Harry Lorayne and Jerry Lucas say in their book entitled The Memory Book, 'You can remember any new piece of information if it is associated to something you already know or remember.'"

Here's how to use the S. T. E. P. system with great effectiveness whether you are giving a speech, writing a paper or merely answering a question: devise an introduction, proceed through the S. T. E. P. system for each main point, and then devise a conclusion. With practice, someone who methodically applies the S. T. E. P. system will be much more organized, and thus sound intelligent. His ideas will be more acceptable to the audience. In addition, habitually organizing one's thoughts in this manner makes it much easier to "think on one's feet."

# INFORMATIVE SPEECH

## PROJECT SKETCH

The first of the two basic speech formats is the speech to inform. This speech will put your teen's powers of observation to work, allowing him to entertain an audience by imparting new information. In one sense, this kind of speech raises the self-confidence of a teenager because he is speaking on the one topic about which he knows more than anyone else in the audience (with the possible exception of the parent who coached him!).

The topics for such a speech are many and varied; among the fascinating topics I have heard are: how a paper mill works, why some people are left-handed, the history of the railroad in the community, what happens when you sneeze, the truth about brown recluse spiders, and how to improve your golf swing.

## HOW-TO

Once your teen has brainstormed and organized the material according to the main point and the needs of the audience, this outline may be used to mold the content into an informative speech format.

    I. Introduction (A story or shocking statement).

    II. Statement of purpose ("The purpose of this speech is to _____ by _____ .")

    III. Background. Give the relevant facts to understanding the subject. Assume the audience knows very little, and provide them with what they need to know to understand the topic.

IV. Initial summary ("In order to more fully explore
_____, I am going to take you through _____
steps.")

V. Main Points. Usually an audience can remember
three to four main points. *Organize each main point
using the S. T. E. P. system*, described in the project on
"Organizing a Speech."

> State
> Translate
>> Definition
>> Explanation
>> Analogy
> Exemplify
>> Example
>> Personal Experience
> Prove
>> Statistic
>> Testimony

VI. Focus. Tell the audience what you want them to
understand and remember from the presentation.

VII. Conclusion ("In conclusion, _____ .")

### FUTURE ADVENTURE

Combine the informative speech with a demonstration
speech. Your teen can fuse the two forms together to create a presentation in which to teach the audience a practical skill such as first aid, lifesaving, or map and compass
reading.

## Make It Memorable!

Teach your teen to teach. Show him how to use the informative speech format to explain how to do a particular job. Even if the presentation is not as detailed, and even if your teen is training only one person, it is still excellent experience in a practical life skill.

# NOTES

# PERSUASIVE SPEECH

## Project Sketch

The second of the two basic speech formats is the speech to persuade. The goal of such a speech is to persuade the audience to either 1) change their beliefs, attitudes or values, or 2) act on what you are telling them. Writing and practicing persuasive speeches is the most practical, helpful way to understand the nature of persuasion and how to become a more persuasive person.

## How-To

Review the "Organizing a Speech" project and ask your teen to organize the speech material into a persuasive format. Here is an outline of the most rudimentary persuasive speech, a speech to persuade the audience that a certain problem exists:

I. Introduction (a story or example).

II. Statement of need or problem ("My point today is that we face a serious problem, 'X.'").

III. Explanation of need or problem.

   A. Undesirable effects ("Some of the consequences of 'X' problem are 'A,' 'B,' and 'C.'").

   B. Extensiveness ("How far ranging is 'X' problem? According to _____, an expert on the subject, it is _____ .").

   C. Personal experience ("Perhaps my personal experience with 'X' problem will shed some light on it...").

IV. Conclusion ("As we close...").

## FUTURE ADVENTURE

When your teen is ready, he can move on to a more complex persuasive speech, one designed to persuade the audience to take action:

I. Introduction (a story or example).

II. Review of the problem/need ("You may be quite familiar with 'X' problem. But just to review...").

III. Statement of Solution/Plan ("I would like to present a plan that will remedy problem 'X.'").

    A. Explanation of the plan ("Here is how the plan operates...").

    B. An example of what would be different with this plan in effect ("How would this plan look in action? Let me give an example...").

    C. Proof that the plan will work ("A plan very similar to this one was tried in _____. The results demonstrated conclusively that the plan can do what it promises to do. Here are some of the benefits of that plan...").

IV Advantages of the plan ("Just so we're all clear, here are the specific advantages of the plan...").

V. Call to specific action ("Based on what I have presented, there is a specific action you can take...").

## TIMELY TIP

First, these formats are not intended to *confine* the speaker but to *guide* him in including the essential elements.

Within each main point refer back to the "S. T. E. P. system" proposed in the chapter on organizing a speech. Second, allow time for preparation. This kind of speech usually takes a couple of days to assemble. Assist your teen in finding a dramatic story and some quotes which can serve as evidence. Gradually, he should be able to do this on his own.

## MAKE IT MEMORABLE!

Find audiences. Your teen can give his completed speech to guests you have in your home, your co-workers, the family, and if possible the church. He must have the opportunity to give his speech as many times as possible. Practice is the key to speech success!

# NOTES

# BIOGRAPHICAL SPEECH PROJECT

## PROJECT SKETCH

A biographical speech is an informative or persuasive speech which highlights the character qualities of a hero from Christian history. The purpose of the biographical speech is to provide an exciting speech project with the side benefits of familiarizing your teen with the deep and wonderful heritage he enjoys as a Christian. It will help him recognize the admirable qualities of great men and women of the faith, using them as role models for his own life of leadership.

## HOW-TO

1. **Select a hero.** Use your best judgement in deciding which hero of the faith would be most appropriate. It is probably best to give your teen lots of choices and allow him to select one who sounds interesting. The speech should focus on the biblical character qualities held by that person. Consider choosing a hero who lived *after* Bible times and that you personally do not know. One purpose of this project is to learn about the influence of Christians on culture through the ages.

Here are just a few Christians who have been widely noted and are therefore easier to research: Abigail Adams, John Quincy Adams, Gladys Aylward, Johann Sebastian Bach, William Blackstone, Deitrich Bonhoeffer, William Booth, John Calvin, Amy Carmichael, George Washington Carver, Catherine of Vienna, Fanny Crosby, Elizabeth Fry, George Frederick Handel, C. S. Lewis, Martin Luther, Henrietta Mears, D. L. Moody, Mother Teresa, Florence Nightingale, Mary Slessor, Charles Spurgeon, Hudson Taylor, Corrie

Ten Boom, Harriet Tubman, Isaac Watts, Noah Webster, Susanna Wesley (John's mother) and William Wilberforce.

2. **Create a clear outline.**

I. Introduction

II. Background of the hero's life (what he or she did while young in preparation for influencing others, family influences, etc.)

III. The outstanding character quality the person possessed

    A. Definition of the quality and scripture verse about it

    B. Example of how the person displayed that quality

    C. How that quality affected the person's life

IV. A memorable quote from that person

V. Conclusion

### FUTURE ADVENTURE

1. **A campaign speech.** Your teen can pretend that the hero he has chosen is running for political office today. What kind of things could that person contribute based on their actions during their lifetime?

2. **A "This is Your Life" play.** Dress up as the character, or use a "reader's theater" format with a single light, stool, and dramatic script. Tell the story as if you are really that person. Several videos of this nature are available, and you can often find people portraying

historical characters in this way at historical gatherings and events. Done well, this type of activity is *extremely* popular and stands to win your teenager many speaking engagements!

## TIMELY TIP

How do you find heroes? Consult books such as *Foxe's Book of Martyrs*, *The Light and the Glory* by Peter Marshall, Jr. and David Manuel, *Men and Women We Call Heroes* by Ann Spangler, and *Lives of Famous Christians* by Tony Castle. There are also several series of biographies for children published by Bethany House Publishers and Mott Media. Also, examine the biographical history magazine *Christian History Today*.

## MAKE IT MEMORABLE!

Prepare a Sunday school lesson. Your teen can prepare a lesson about the character qualities of his hero in order to help others grow in character.

# NOTES

# VIDEO OR RADIO PLAYS

## PROJECT SKETCH

Media is so advanced today that a course in communication would not be complete without at least a short introduction to communication technology. You may find that your teen is interested in knowing more about radio or television, or you may conduct the project simply to give him a greater awareness of how it works. One way to create awareness is to actually write a script and conduct a video or radio play. Your teen will gain an understanding of persuasion, vocal enthusiasm, mood, sequence, and drama.

## HOW-TO

1. **Radio play.** A radio play is simply a story read out loud. The only equipment required is a tape recorder. Encourage your teen to plan the play so it can be recorded all at one time, like an old-fashioned "live" radio broadcast, including sound effects. Here are the necessary steps:

   A. **Conceive a story line, complete with a plot, action, suspense, and resolution.**

   B. **Write the story in the form of a play with each character's lines and directions.**

   C. **Choose actors or work on the voices of the various characters.**

   D. **Select sound effects and work on timing.**

   E. Select music.

2. **Video play.** Create a "television program" using a video camera. The steps mentioned above are the same, but additional work is required. Experiment with the camera to get a feel for lighting, zoom, etc. The "action" should be planned out on a story board, which is a page of squares representing television screens in which each scene is "blocked." Plan out as much as possible on paper first. Here are some things to consider: How is the lighting? Might I choose a better camera angle to get more detail or make the action more suspenseful? Are my actors using facial expressions that are pronounced enough to be seen on camera? Am I holding the camera steady and not zooming in and out too much?

## FUTURE ADVENTURES

1. **Mock news broadcast.** Use the material from your current events studies to put together a news program. Video or audio tape it and review. To see how this is done in the real world, tour a local television or radio station and obtain permission to watch quietly during a news broadcast.

2. **Create a video advertisement or documentary.** Use the video camera to assemble a mock promotional video or documentary of an interesting historical site or a business.

## TIMELY TIP

Examine a lot of samples. Your library probably owns a collection of video documentaries and audio tapes of old radio plays. Contact Moody Broadcasting in Chicago, Illinois, about their radio plays of great figures in Christian history. Also, children's radio plays are available from Children's Bible Hour in Grand Rapids, Michigan. Get as many tapes as you can to collect ideas. Using videotape equipment proficiently requires practice. Give your teen opportunities to practice by creatively videotaping events such as family reunions, picnics, and vacations. He can even think of a running dialogue to give while filming.

## MAKE IT MEMORABLE!

Allow your teen to create a video documentary of his hero of history from the biographical speech project. Using pictures and simulated scenes from their life, compose a five minute presentation.

# NOTES

# SLIDE SHOW

## PROJECT SKETCH

A slide show is a simpler, more controlled version of the radio and video play project. It is especially good for teens who are terrified of being in front of an audience. The goal of the project is to create a slide presentation of an interesting subject with "live" narration. The focus is on both visual and oral communication, and since the audience's attention is on the screen, a shy teenager can practice communication skills without the pressure of being "up front."

## HOW-TO

1. **Select a subject.** The topic may be the youth group missions trip, a historical narrative of a famous person who grew up in your town, a study of a historical monument or event, or even a made-up story.

2. **Take pictures.** Be sure to purchase lots of slide film. Plan for approximately 20 slides for each minute of presentation.

3. **Write a speech to go along with the show.** Plan out what to say just as with a speech. Devise an interesting introduction, several main points, and supporting evidence (stories, examples and quotes).

## FUTURE ADVENTURES

1. **Record the speech.** Write out a word-for-word script and read it on to the tape, along with music and other sound effects. Include interviews and color commentary.

2. Use slides as another means of conducting a demonstration speech or biographical speech.

### TIMELY TIPS

1. **Take a lot of pictures!** Your teen should take two or
three shots of everything he wants in the presentation, to make sure that at least one turns out. Try different angles, and make sure that the subject of the
slide is immediately obvious.

2. **Watch the time!** Slide shows always seem to be too
*short* to express the presenter's level of interest, but
too *long* for the audience's level of interest. Make the
presentation concise; it is always better to leave them
wanting than to have them wanting to leave.

### MAKE IT MEMORABLE!

Use this project as a spring board. A slide show is an
excellent communication activity for a shy child, but it
should not be the only project he does. Start with this,
move on to a puppet show, and eventually a Sunday school
lesson for younger children. Your goal as a parent is to take
your teen as far as you can in the development of his communication skills, so continue to love, instruct, praise,
encourage and challenge him!

# ADVERTISING CAMPAIGN

## PROJECT SKETCH

One fun and motivating project which will help your teen understand elements of persuasion is to assemble an advertising campaign. Many teens have actually decided to create and market a real product! Even a mock campaign, however, will give your teen an awareness of what advertising is and does, how advertising is persuasive, and how to be a better consumer.

## HOW-TO

Create a mock advertising scenario, ask your teen to create one, or have him create a campaign for something he actually wants to sell. Here are five steps to developing an advertising campaign:

1. **Outline a means of presenting the product.** Decide on a name and a campaign theme.

2. **Analyze the market, and write a short report.** This should include *who* the product will be sold to, *what* they are like, and *how much* they might be willing to spend. Interview some people in the target group. Would they buy a product like this and how much would they pay for it? Even if the product is not a real one, your teen should nevertheless ask people to choose from several possible prices.

3. **Choose media.** This is an information gathering stage. Every company that sells advertising prints a "media kit" which explains how many people you could reach if you buy their advertising space and what it costs. Collect media kits from radio stations,

television stations, newspapers, billboard companies, bus and taxi companies, printers, mailing companies and "premium" companies (those who sell logo key chains, pens, coffee mugs, etc.). Examine the materials, deciding how to reach the most people. Establish a budget that includes several different kinds of advertising.

4. **Write the campaign.** Prepare "mock up" advertisements:

A. **Magazine page.** Include copy and artwork.

B. **Script and story board for a 30-second television commercial.** Draw out the action with stick figures—one scene per box, writing the script underneath the appropriate square.

C. **Script for a 15- or 30-second radio commercial.** Record it onto tape with an enthusiastic voice, using music or sound effects as needed.

D. **Poster.** Design a "poster," to be used on a billboard, bus, or store display.

5. **Prepare a presentation.** As the "expert," prepare a presentation "selling" the advertising strategy, justify it and explain the benefits.

## FUTURE ADVENTURE

Offer to plan a real-world campaign for your church to promote the Sunday school program or Vacation Bible School. Volunteer for a political campaign and observe how they use their resources to influence as many people as possible.

## TIMELY TIPS

Review the exercise on "Interviewing" in this section to assist your teen in compiling a market survey.

## MAKE IT MEMORABLE!

Analyze "real-world" advertisements. Ask questions such as, "What makes it effective?" "What evidence supports their claim?", "How do we know the evidence is reliable?", "Is the proof they give the most convincing evidence they had?", "What appeals does the advertisement use?", "What audience are they targeting?" and "What might they have done *more* effectively?"

# MORE ABOUT JEFF MYERS' COMPANY:

Dr. Jeff Myers is President of the Myers Institute for Communication and Leadership. Through the Myers Institute, Dr. Myers offers seminars, video coaching systems, books and newsletters which help people unleash their gifts, find greater meaning and satifaction in life, and expend their influence. To find out about these resources, and to sign-up for Dr.Myers' free weekly e-mail coaching tips newsletter, visit the Myers Institute website www.inspiredleadership. com or call toll free 1-888-792-4445.

Here are three resources published by the Myers Institute which will help you and your family gain the skills you need to succeed. These may be ordered with a MasterCard or Visa by calling toll free 1-888-792-4445 or by visiting the website www.inspiredleadership.com.

Secrets of Great Communicators: Simple, Powerful Strategies for Reaching the Heart of Your Audience. The six-step video coaching system makes speaking to a crowd as simple and natural as singing in the shower! Many people think that public speaking is mysterious gift, but Dr.Myers demonstrates how anyone can master this vital skill and dramatically expand their confidence, poise and image. The video coaching lessons reveal the secrets of great communicators, and the 160 page study guide leads you step by step through overcoming your fear, organizing a presentation, tapping into power persuasion, and delivering your message to the heart of the audience.

Secrets of the World-Changers: How to Achieve Lasting Influence as a Leader. Looking for more joy, meaning, satisfaction and influence in life? This fast-paced video coaching system helps you achieve a strategic vision, break through the "noise" of culture to understand your unique mission in life, stay motivated through the tough times, and set goals that really work. Secrets of the World-Changers comes complete with an easy-to-use 75 page reproducible study guide. This coaching system has been used by more than 1,500 schools, athletic teams, study groups and homeschool co-ops to instill leadership skills in youth and adults alike.

Of Knights and Fair Maidens: A Radical New Way to Develop Old-Fashioned Relationships. Before their marriage, both Jeff and Danielle had been seaching for alternatives to the dating game. This book tells the funny, heart-winning story of how they got to know each other through old-fashioned courtship principles. Jeff and Danielle reveal the three keys to integrity in relationships to demonstrate how following God's Principles leads to joy, trust and romance.